Evangelicalism

Religion in America Series

Harry S. Stout, *General Editor*

EVANGELICALISM

Comparative Studies of Popular
Protestantism in North America, the British
Isles, and Beyond, 1700–1990

Edited By

Mark A. Noll
David W. Bebbington
George A. Rawlyk

New York   Oxford
OXFORD UNIVERSITY PRESS
1994

Oxford University Press

Oxford   New York   Toronto
Delhi   Bombay   Calcutta   Madras   Karachi
Kuala Lumpur   Singapore   Hong Kong   Tokyo
Nairobi   Dar es Salaam   Cape Town
Melbourne   Auckland   Madrid

and associated companies in
Berlin   Ibadan

Copyright © 1994 by Oxford University Press, Inc.

Published by Oxford University Press, Inc.
200 Madison Avenue, New York, New York 10016

Oxford is a registered trademark of Oxford University Press, Inc.

Library of Congress Cataloging-in-Publication Data
Evangelicalism : Comparative studies of popular Protestantism in
North America, the British Isles, and beyond, 1700–1990
edited by Mark A. Noll, David W. Bebbington, George A. Rawlyk.
p.   cm.
ISBN 0-19-508362-8
ISBN 0-19-508363-6 (pbk.)
1. Evangelicalism—North America—History—18th century.
2. Evangelicalism—Great Britain—History—18th century.
3. Evangelicalism—North America—History—19th century.
4. Evangelicalism—Great Britain—History—19th century.
5. North America—Church history.
6. Great Britain—Church history—18th century.
7. Great Britain—Church history—19th century.
I. Noll, Mark A., 1946–   .
II. Bebbington, D. W. (David William), 1949–   .
III. Rawlyk, George A.
BR1642.N7E83   1994
280□.4—dc20   92-46303

1 3 5 7 9   8 6 4 2

Printed in the United States of America
on acid-free paper

To Robert T. Handy

who helped to prepare the way

Acknowledgments

All but one of the chapters in this book were presented in earlier versions at a conference, "Evangelicalism in Trans-Atlantic Perspective," held on April 8–11, 1992, at Wheaton College, Illinois. The editors are grateful to the others who presented papers at this conference, to those who commented on them publicly or privately, and to all who, simply by attending, showed their concern for the subject of this book. The conference was sponsored by Wheaton's Institute for the Study of American Evangelicals; the Institute's staff—Darryl Hart, Edith Blumhofer, Katherine Tinlan-Vaughan, and especially Larry Eskridge—were diligent beyond expectation in managing the complex details of the meeting. The editors are also eager to thank the Pew Charitable Trusts, which provided the funding to make the conference possible, and its religion officer, Joel A. Carpenter, who combines wisdom and tact to an unusual degree. A special word of thanks is owed to Richard Carwardine, one of the pioneers in charting the transatlantic connections of British and North American evangelicals. Dr. Carwardine was not able to be present at the conference but graciously wrote a paper for this book.

The editors are deeply appreciative of the work done on behalf of the book by people associated with Oxford University Press, including Cynthia Read, Peter Ohlin, and Paul Schlotthauer for editorial guidance, Harry Stout for encouragement from the first, and Craig Noll for expert copyediting of a difficult manuscript. We would also like to thank an efficient crew of typists at Wheaton College: Beatrice Horne, Gina Lombardo, Mary Noll, Kristal Otto, and Lori Willemsen.

The book is dedicated to a scholar who, more than any other North American of his generation, has demonstrated how important it is to record the history of Christianity across national borders.

Contents

Contributors

David W. Bebbington is Reader in History at the University of Stirling in Scotland and is the author of *Evangelicalism in Modern Britain: A History from the 1730s to the 1980s* (London: Unwin Hyman, 1989; reprint, Grand Rapids: Baker, 1992) and *William Ewart Glandstone: Faith and Politics in Victorian Britain* (Grand Rapids: Eerdmans, 1993).

Edith Blumhofer is project director at the Institute for the Study of American Evangelicals, Wheaton College, Illinois. She has published widely in the history of pentecostalism, including *Restoring the Faith: The Assemblies of God, Pentecostalism, and American Culture* (Urbana: University of Illinois Press, 1993).

Richard Carwardine is Senior Lecturer in American History at the University of Sheffield in England. He is the author of *Transatlantic Revivalism: Popular Evangelicalism in Britain and America, 1790–1865* (Westport, CT: Greenwood Press, 1978) and *Evangelicals and Politics in Antebellum America* (New Haven: Yale University Press, 1993).

David A. Currie was introduced to the study of evangelicalism by Richard Lovelace at Gordon-Conwell Theological Seminary and is the minister of the Anchor Presbyterian Church, Penns Park, Pennsylvania. His dissertation, "The Growth of Evangelicalism in the Church of Scotland, 1793–1843," was recently completed at St. Andrews University, Scotland.

Michael Gauvreau has published *The Evangelical Century: College and Creed in English Canada from the Great Revival to the Great Depression* (Montreal and Kingston: McGill-Queen's University Press, 1991). He teaches in the History Department of McMaster University, Hamilton, Ontario.

David Hempton is Reader in Modern History, the Queen's University of Belfast. He is the author of *Methodism and Politics in British Society, 1750–1850* (London: Hutchinson; Stanford: Stanford University Press, 1984) and coauthor of *Evangelical Protestantism in Ulster Society, 1740–1890* (London: Routledge, 1992).

Samuel S. Hill is professor and the former chair of the department of religion at the University of Florida. He is editor of the *Encyclopedia of Religion in the South* (Macon, GA: Mercer University Press, 1984) and author of *The South and the North in American Religion* (Athens: University of Georgia Press, 1980).

Mark A. Noll is McManis Professor of Christian Thought at Wheaton College, Wheaton, Illinois, and is the author of *Princeton and the Republic, 1768–1822* (Princeton: Princeton University Press, 1989) and *A History of Christianity in the United States and Canada* (Grand Rapids: Eerdmans, 1992).

Susan O'Brien is head of history at Anglia Polytechnic University, Cambridge, England, and has published on evangelical communications networks in the *Journal of Ecclesiastical History* and the *American Historical Review*. She is now researching the lives of women Catholic religious in Britain.

Stuart Piggin is Master of Robert Menzies College, Macquarie University, New South Wales, and founder of the Centre for the Study of Australian Christianity. He has published books on the training of missionaries and the activities of women in Australian religious life and is currently at work on a history of evangelicalism in Australia.

George A. Rawlyk edits a series on religion for McGill-Queen's University Press, is coordinating a multiyear research project on evangelicalism in Canada, edited *The Canadian Protestant Experience* (Burlington, Ont.: Welch, 1990), and has authored several books on the revival tradition in Canada, including *Ravished by the Spirit* (Montreal and Kingston: McGill-Queens University Press, 1984). He is a professor of history at Queen's University, Kingston, Ontario.

Ian Rennie is the Dean of the Ontario Theological Seminary (Toronto) and helped spark the interest in comparative evangelical history with his University of Toronto dissertation, "Evangelicalism and English Public Life, 1823–1850."

Leigh Eric Schmidt is the author of *Holy Fairs: Scottish Communions and American Revivals in the Early Modern Period* (Princeton: Princeton University Press, 1989) as well as essays on holidays in American religious and commercial life. He has been a member of the Center of Theological Inquiry in Princeton and teaches in the Theological and Graduate Schools of Drew University, Madison, New Jersey.

Harry S. Stout is the Jonathan Edwards Professor of American Religious History and Master of Berkeley College at Yale University. He has written *The New England Soul: Preaching and Religious Culture in Colonial New England* (New York: Oxford University Press, 1986) and *The Divine Dramatist: George Whitefield and the Rise of Modern Evangelicalism* (Grand Rapids: Eerdmans, 1991).

Marguerite Van Die holds appointments in the Theological College and the History Department of the Queen's University, Kingston, Ontario. She has published *An Evangelical Mind: Nathanael Burwarsh and the Methodist Tradition in Canada, 1839–1918* (Montreal and Kingston: McGill-Queen's University Press, 1989).

Andrew Walls directs the Centre for the Study of Christianity in the Non-Western World at the University of Edinburgh. He has been Visiting Professor of World Christianity at Yale University. His many essays treat the expansion of Christianity in Sierra Leone, Nigeria, other parts of Africa, North America, and several other regions of the world.

J.D. Walsh is a Fellow of Jesus College, Oxford, where he has supervised many research students in topics related to evangelical history. His essays treat primarily the origins and early spread of Methodism.

David F. Wells is Andrew Mutch Professor of Theology at Gordon-Conwell Seminary in South Hamilton, Massachusetts. He has edited books on Reformed theology in America, has written on modern Catholicism, and is the author most recently of a theological assessment of evangelicals in modern culture, *No Place for Truth* (Grand Rapids: Eerdmans, 1993).

John Wolffe is Lecturer in Religious Studies at the Open University, Milton Keynes (UK). He is the author of *The Protestant Crusade in Great Britain, 1829–1860* (Oxford: Clarendon Press, 1991).

Evangelicalism

Introduction

During the first half of the eighteenth century, English-speaking Protestantism entered a new era. In London and English market towns, the Scottish Highlands and Lowlands, Wales and Ireland, and all three regions of the North American colonies, Protestantism was significantly renewed through a series of often intense religious "awakenings." The most visible human agents of these revivals were larger-than-life figures—the spellbinding preacher George Whitefield, the indefatigable evangelist John Wesley, and the brilliant theologian Jonathan Edwards. But if these three and a host of other leaders who were almost as well known in their day (men such as Howell Harris in Wales, John McLaurin in Scotland, or Gilbert Tennent in America) defined the revivals on a large canvas, experiences of countless ordinary men and women in the localities sustained the life of the evangelical awakening.

From the start, news about evangelical experiences in particular places was passed on with great excitement to other interested parties in the North Atlantic region. So it was that Protestants in Scotland, Wales, Ireland, and England read about the experiences of Abigail Hutchinson of Northampton, Massachusetts, who on a Monday morning in 1735 was turned from despair and alienation to God. As her minister explained the event, when "these words came to her mind, 'The blood of Christ cleanses from all sin' [they were] accompanied with a lively sense of the excellency of Christ, and his sufficiency to satisfy for the sins of the whole world. . . . By these things," Jonathan Edwards concluded, she "was led into such contemplations and views of Christ, as filled her exceeding full of joy."[1] Not long thereafter Protestants throughout the English-speaking world could read in the pub-

3

lished journal of John Wesley what had taken place at a society meeting on Aldersgate Street in London, on Wednesday, 24 May 1738, "where one was reading Luther's preface to the *Epistle to the Romans*. About a quarter before nine, while he was describing the change which God works in the heart through faith in Christ, I felt my heart strangely warmed. I felt I did trust in Christ, Christ alone for salvation; and an assurance was given me that He had taken away *my* sins, even *mine,* and saved *me* from the law of sin and death."[2] Many English-speaking Protestants followed just as closely the extraordinary work ("wark") at Cambuslang, near Glasgow in Scotland, which began in February 1742 and continued for several months, with results that are described in Harry Stout's chapter.

An evangelical pattern of intense religious experience was established very quickly. The British soldier Sampson Staniforth, who later became a Methodist preacher, left this record of what happened to him while on guard duty during a military campaign in Flanders. The year was 1744:

> As soon as I was alone, I kneeled down, and determined not to rise, but to continue crying and wrestling with God, till He had mercy on me. How long I was in that agony I cannot tell; but as I looked up to heaven I saw the clouds open exceedingly bright, and I saw Jesus hanging on the cross. At the same moment these words were applied to my heart, "Thy sins are forgiven thee." My chains fell off; my heart was free. All guilt was gone, and my soul was filled with unutterable peace. I loved God and all mankind, and the fear of death and hell was vanished away. I was filled with wonder and astonishment.[3]

Such experiences of intense, personal faith spread to others in the far-flung outpost of Britain's empire, like Henry Alline of Nova Scotia, who left this record of his experience on 26 March 1775:

> Being almost in an agony, I turned very suddenly round in my chair, and seeing part of an old bible laying in one of the chairs, I caught hold of it in great haste; and opening it without any premeditation, cast my eyes on the 38th Psalm, which was the first time I ever saw the word of God. It took hold of me with such power, that it seemed to go through my whole soul, and read therein every thought of my heart, and raised my whole soul with groans and earnest cries to God, so that it seemed as if God was praying in, with, and for me.[4]

Soon congregations and conventicles throughout the North Atlantic region were singing hymns describing such experiences—like the one Charles Wesley composed on 23 May 1738, the day before his brother's heart was strangely warmed:

> Where shall my wond'ring Soul begin?
> How shall I All to Heaven Aspire?
> A slave redeem'd from Death and Sin,
> A Brand pluk'd from Eternal Fire.[5]

Many other voices joined the refrain, including some that spoke first in a Celtic language, like William Williams (Pantycelyn), who translated his own hymn from Welsh into English:

> Guide me, O thou great Jehovah,
>   Pilgrim through this barren land;
> . . . .
> Strong Deliverer, Strong Deliverer,
>   Be thou still my strength and shield.[6]

Along with public preaching of repentance and free grace, institutions arising to perpetuate that message, and hymns memorializing its effects, experiences like those of Abigail Hutchinson, John Wesley, Sampson Staniforth, and Henry Alline constituted the evangelical movement. Such experiences were not unique to English-speaking Protestants, for a general turn to inwardness characterized European religion of the eighteenth century among Roman Catholics as well as Protestants, Jews as well as Christians.[7] Nor did these experiences constitute a new religion, for the individuals who were awakened in the evangelical revivals and the movements that grew out of these revivals sustained many of the convictions, ecclesiastical practices, and behavioral expectations of the British Protestantism that had existed since the sixteenth century, especially as that tradition had passed through seventeenth-century Puritanism.[8] If neither unique nor unprecedented, the eighteenth-century English-speaking evangelical awakening still created a distinct set of new emphases in the Christian world.

Since the mid-eighteenth century, evangelicals have played a significant role in the history of Christianity. They dominated the cultural life of several North Atlantic areas for much of the nineteenth century, provided the backbone of the English-speaking missionary movement, and survived through a variety of responses when shaken by economic expansion, intellectual secularization, and the modern revolution in communications. Today, groups descended from those eighteenth-century movements are probably more visible than they have been for several decades. In the established Church of England, a majority of those in full-time preparation for the ministry have, for some years, been trained in evangelical colleges.[9] In Canada, a majority of the Protestants in church on any given Sunday attend evangelical congregations.[10] In the United States, by one recent reckoning that used polling data from the University of Michigan's Center for Political Studies, evangelicals made up 33 percent of the American people, 38 percent of the United States's Protestants and Catholics, and 43 percent of the Christians who regularly attend church.[11] Throughout the world, pentecostal and charismatic movements, which trace their lineage to developments within Anglo-American evangelicalism early in the twentieth century, are far and away the fastest-growing segments of worldwide Christianity.[12]

This evangelicalism, which began in the English-speaking world during the eighteenth century and has blossomed in so many varieties over the centuries since, is the subject of this book. The Christian teachings of the movement and its "evangelism"—that is, the effort to propagate the gospel—are less the focus than the transnational contexts that have always conditioned evangelical convictions, behavior, patterns of organization, strategies of communication, responses to cultural change, and participation in ideological controversies. From the days of Whitefield, Wesley, and Edwards, to the present era of Billy Graham, InterVarsity Christian Fellowship, and John Stott, the interconnections among British, American, and Canadian evangelicals, as also their brothers and sisters in many other areas of the world, have been foundational to evangelicalism. To measure, interpret, and assess those connections is the purpose of the chapters that follow.

Definition

To understand how the terms "evangelical," "evangelicals," and "evangelicalism" are being used, however, we must pause for the delicate task of definition. Many Christian bodies have legitimately used the term to describe themselves, not least the Lutherans, who existed long before the groups featured in this book came into being. The contributors here do not claim exclusive use of the term. Rather, they assume that, whatever its other legitimate uses, "evangelical" is also the best word available to describe a fairly discrete network of Protestant Christian movements arising during the eighteenth century in Great Britain and its colonies. This historical sense of "evangelical" is complemented by a parallel use of the term designating a consistent pattern of convictions and attitudes. A recent history of evangelicalism in Britain has specified these as biblicism (a reliance on the Bible as ultimate religious authority), conversionism (a stress on the New Birth), activism (an energetic, individualistic approach to religious duties and social involvement), and crucicentrism (a focus on Christ's redeeming work as the heart of essential Christianity).[13] While other legitimate uses of the term are possible, and despite tensions between an idealized type defined by "evangelical" characteristics and a bewildering variety of actual "evangelical" movements, the "evangelicals" marked out by these two overlapping designations form a historically coherent subject.

The Need for Comparative Study

Serious study of evangelicalism has always featured nation-specific accounts, of which there have been many.[14] Over the last thirty years, as explained somewhat more fully in the Afterword, such studies have reached new levels of sophistication. Yet evangelicalism has never by any stretch of the imagination been a strictly national phenomenon. Important as transnational, and especially transatlantic, connections have always been for sustaining evangelicalism and explaining its development, however, relatively scant attention has been directed specifically to those connections. To be sure, works written in the 1960s and 1970s by Ian Rennie, Ernest Sandeen, Susan (Durden) O'Brien, George Marsden, and especially Richard Carwardine provided significant exceptions to that neglect.[15] These authors, by focusing on one problem or one era in evangelical history, intimated the rich fruit to be harvested if comparative study were ever broadened to take in the movement as a whole.

Gratifying historical results from more general comparative study have become strikingly evident since World War II, with exponential expansion during the last decade.[16] For writing focused on religion, in which evangelicals often figure prominently, several significant colloquia have brought together monographic treatments of individual regions or denominations.[17] A handful of evangelicals have exploited the transnational resources of the movement for purposes of edification.[18] A few integrated narratives on more general religious themes have either combined regions usually kept separate or incorporated substantial material from more than one area.[19] A few directly comparative works on religious subjects have been published.[20] And there is a growing body of scholarship exploring evangelical connections between English-speaking and broader ethnic regions.[21]

While none of this material contains, or amounts to, a full-blown comparative treatment of Anglo-American evangelicalism, all of it suggests in different ways how imperative such study now is. To paraphrase a dictum familiar from the teaching of foreign languages: who knows any region's particular form of evangelicalism who knows only that form of evangelicalism?

The Nature of This Book

The present volume offers a comparative picture of the English-speaking evangelicalism that emerged in the eighteenth century, that has played such a formative role in North Atlantic societies, and that has also become important in other parts of the world where British and American influence penetrated. Although most of the chapters here feature Britain, Canada, and the United States, the book also contains essays on Australia and Africa. The inclusion of these chapters is not meant to turn the book into a general history of evangelicalism but rather is designed to provide selective illustration of the worldwide character of the evangelicalism that originated in the North Atlantic region.

The book approaches its task by gathering case studies on specific aspects of evangelical history in the English-speaking world. The authors themselves are spread throughout that world, with seven located in the United States, four in Canada, seven in the United Kingdom (four England, two Scotland, one Northern Ireland), and one in Australia. Each chapter illuminates a specific subject, period, or relationship, but all are also intended to assess more generally the character, development, strengths, weaknesses, and future prospects of the evangelical impulse.

The volume is comparative history, not just in the general sense of containing essays on a wide variety of places and themes, but in the specific sense that each chapter attempts a comparative evaluation of themes, movements, controversies, or individuals common to more than one English-speaking region. The book thus puts actively to use the increasingly significant comparative scholarship on North Atlantic regions, while adding measurably to that scholarship itself. Where appropriate, comparisons *within* nations take their place alongside comparisons *between* nations.

The chapters are also distinguished by the effort to show connections between religious developments and surrounding political, economic, social, intellectual, or cultural conditions. Unlike older church histories that typically were relatively unconcerned about the general influence of environment, these chapters indicate how evangelical experiences were always part of larger social, intellectual, or cultural frameworks. But unlike some recent historians, who have described evangelical religion as merely a function, say, of personal or social psychology, these chapters treat evangelical convictions and behavior as irreducible realities in their own right. In other words, the authors practice connected but not reductionist history.[22]

Several general conclusions about evangelical history since the mid-eighteenth century arise from the various chapters that make up the book:

1. Evangelicalism is an extraordinarily complex phenomenon. Contributors show that since its origins in the mid-eighteenth century, evangelicalism has always been diverse, flexible, adaptable, and multiform. In particular, the chapters show how contextual settings have regularly colored the shape of evangelicalism (making, for example, some expressions very conservative politically and at least a few quite radical). But they also reveal ways in which evangelical movements have been shapers of culture (leading, for example, to certain general developments in Canada, the United States, Scotland, Ireland, England, and Australia that are explicable only with reference to the activity of evangelicals in these regions).

2. Evangelicalism has always been profoundly shaped by its popular character. Stimulated in no small measure by the path-breaking arguments of Nathan Hatch's *Democratization of American Christianity*,[23] as well as by older scholarship on the Methodists in Britain and America,[24] several authors examine in detail the character of English-speaking evangelicalism as a people's movement. At the same time, they are alert to ambiguities in this populism, such as, for example, where evangelicals bestow unusual authority on charismatic leaders or organizational geniuses who replace traditional autocracy with their own.

Many of the essays chart the way in which evangelicals have combined traditional aspects of Christianity (especially the doctrines of the Reformation) with innovative religious beliefs and behaviors. In fact, if evangelicalism can be characterized in terms of its religious form, it is best seen as a persistent mixing of innovation and tradition. The three tensions that Leigh Schmidt highlights at the end of his essay below (strict versus open-ended use of time, individual versus corporate construction of community, ascetic versus festive attitudes toward spectacle) go far in defining the essential puzzles that have marked evangelical history since the mid-eighteenth century.

3. Many evangelicals, though often rhetorically antitraditional, have been

expert builders of traditions. Controversies, alliances, and conundrums, often rooted in the eighteenth century, have continued to mark the movement. Charges of "enthusiasm" made against John Wesley, for example, are similar (in form, if nothing else) to charges made by more traditional Christians against the pentecostals and charismatics of the twentieth century. In another sphere, antitraditional exaltation of the Scriptures as the evangelicals' only creed has become, for at least some, a rock-ribbed tradition in which ways of reading the Bible, topics for preaching, and hermeneutical practices are just as predictable as the liturgies, devotional practices, and preaching styles of self-consciously traditional bodies. An irony of this situation is that, while evangelicals as a group usually prefer experience over tradition, many of the "new" procedures or controversies in evangelical history turn out to reflect similar phenomena from earlier generations. An advantage of this situation is that evangelicals possess a more connected, integrated history than they often realize.

4. Innovative networks of communication have sustained the transnational character of evangelicalism and given it much of its distinctive shape. Many of the chapters show how the critical agencies of transmission—voluntary associations (e.g., Bible societies), personalities (e.g., George Whitefield or Billy Graham), books (e.g., William Wilberforce's *Practical View of the Prevailing Religious System of Professed Christians* or Hal Lindsey's *Late Great Planet Earth*), magazines (e.g., *Christian History* of the 1740s or *Christianity Today* since the 1950s), hymns (e.g., by Charles Wesley or Fanny Crosby)—defined the specific character of evangelical expressions in the different regions of the North Atlantic and, eventually, around the world.

Limitations

The volume is not intended to be an exhaustive treatment of its subjects. Much more could have done, for example, to explore other regional expressions of evangelicalism (in Wales, for instance). Much more could have done with the ambiguous relationships between white evangelicals of British origin, on the one hand, and, on the other, African-American, Caribbean, and Hispanic Protestant churches (most of which are evangelical in a general sense of the term) as well as Protestant churches of European pietist background (such as the Mennonites, Moravians, free-church Lutherans, and Reformed). Contemporary gender concerns also could have been pursued more directly in order to chart specifically female and male dimensions of evangelical convictions and behavior. In addition, although we include Andrew Walls's essay on evangelicalism in Africa to indicate explicitly the worldwide character of modern evangelicalism, the book could have done much more with the burgeoning growth of evangelical Christianity in twentieth-century Africa, Asia, and South America.

To be sure, each of these issues appears somewhere in the book, but all of them deserve much fuller attention. We hope that the essays that are included will stimulate historians (including some of the contributors) to give such matters the attention they certainly deserve.

Arrangement of Chapters

We begin with five chapters on the founding era of evangelicalism. John Walsh's examination of the rise of Methodism shows how the movement associated with John Wesley was like, but also unlike, contemporary developments in the American colonies. Walsh's chapter also provides a paradigmatic overview for many of the religious themes that follow in the book. Susan O'Brien's study of early transatlantic networks of communication and Harry Stout's biographical account of George Whitefield also serve two purposes. Both chapters treat matters of considerable significance in the mid-eighteenth century; in addition, they draw attention to the great power that innovative communications and cults of personality have had in later evangelical history. By revealing differences in the interpretation of Whitefield's role, they also illustrate one of the many fruitful subjects for debate in the history of evangelicalism. The next two essays treat expressions of evangelical culture that bridge over from the eighteenth into the nineteenth century. David Currie's study of Cotton Mather's famous *Bonifacius,* a tract promoting evangelical activism, shows in miniature how emphases of an earlier Puritanism were transferred to, but also transformed by, the activistic evangelicals of the nineteenth century. Leigh Schmidt's sensitive account of evangelical structuring of hours, days, and years spotlights further continuities—back toward agelong patterns of Christian observance, forward toward newer coalitions of gospel and commerce.

The next three chapters discuss evangelicalism in the great age of revolution at the end of the eighteenth century and the start of the nineteenth. Mark Noll draws attention to a general pattern that saw evangelical social influence expand in the wake of political turmoil throughout the English-speaking world. George Rawlyk and David Hempton, by contrast, look at specific situations—Rawlyk at how revivalism in much of what is now Canada after the War for Independence may have been more democratically "American" than the parallel revivalism in the United States; Hempton at the reasons why English and Irish Methodists, who arose in similar circumstances and who shared much in every other way, developed contrasting attitudes toward national political goals.

The nineteenth century, which was the age of evangelical cultural dominance in the North Atlantic region, provides the chronological framework for the next four essays. In a sobering essay, John Wolffe draws attention to the way in which an often virulent anti-Catholicism was critical for evangelical self-definition in both the United States and England. Richard Carwardine expands upon his earlier pioneering work by looking at North-South divisions among American evangelicals in the era before the Civil War, but always through the lens of contemporary developments in England. By focusing on the Canadian "margin" in the Victorian era, Michael Gauvreau shows how forms of thought that prevailed widely among all sorts of evangelicals interacted variably with other cultural values in Scotland, Canada, and the United States. Marguerite Van Die also focuses on Canada, but with an eye toward explaining why the nineteenth-century "evangelical synthesis" survived for nearly a full generation in that country after it had begun to decline in Britain and the United States.

The next three essays break from the focus on British–North American comparisons. Samuel Hill studies more general differences between North and South in the nineteenth-century United States and so, with Richard Carwardine, shows that local cultures may have shaped the expression of evangelicalism even more than did national trends. Stuart Piggin's study of British and American contributions to Australian evangelicalism and Andrew Walls's account of the reception and diffusion of evangelical Christianity in Africa are additions to knowledge as well as implicit appeals. As contributions to scholarship, they outline the transfer of North Atlantic popular Protestantism to other regions of the world, and in particular the way that local conditions in those regions colored the deposit from Britain, Canada, and the United States. As appeals, they suggest the full range of research that is urgently needed to track the multivalent expansion of Protestant evangelical Christianity over the last century and a half *outside of* traditional English-speaking regions.

The book closes with four essays treating salient aspects of evangelical experience in the twentieth century. Ian Rennie examines the dense networks linking British, Canadian, and American conservative evangelicals in the early decades of the twentieth century, who, depending on where they lived, may or may not have been called fundamentalists. Edith Blumhofer opens a subject with immense importance for the future historiography, not to speak of the future history, of evangelicalism. Her study of how early pentecostal impulses leapt from Wales to California, and then with great rapidity to Canada and back to Scandinavia and England, reveals uncanny similarities to the personalities, periodicals, and processes described earlier in the book by John Walsh, Susan O'Brien, and Harry Stout for the age of Wesley and Whitefield. The last two essays are complementary in subject matter, but different in tone. David Bebbington regards the accommodation of evangelicals to modern cultural patterns as an opportunity as well as a peril. For David Wells that accommodation is more simply a threat. Bebbington's comparative account of some of the best-known evangelicals and evangelical institutions in Britain and the United States since World War II charts a number of significant similarities and differences but also goes on to the much more complicated task of explaining why the contrasts take the shape they do. Wells's essay on the fate of formal evangelical theology after World War II also performs two functions. Its account of three modes of evangelical theologizing summarizes important recent trends, but its barely hidden sense of alarm at what these trends portend is a reminder that, for those who care about it, evangelicalism is not just an interesting subject for historical inquiry but the essence of life itself.

Notes with the essays provide probably the fullest comparative bibliography ever assembled for the transnational features of evangelicalism since the eighteenth century. The notes to several of the chapters also examine traditions of historical interpretation. Finally, the editors have added an Afterword that briefly summarizes highlights of recent historiography, but it also indicates why future histories of international evangelicalism will almost certainly be different from the work presented on these pages.

Notes

1. *The Works of Jonathan Edwards*, vol. 4: *The Great Awakening*, ed. C. C. Goen (New Haven: Yale University Press, 1972), 193.

2. *The Journal of John Wesley*, ed. Nehemiah Curnock, 8 vols. (London: Epworth, 1938), 1:475–76.

3. John Telford, ed., *Wesley's Veterans* (London: Robert Culley, n.d.), 1:74–75.

4. "Alline's Journal," in *Henry Alline: Selected Writings*, ed. George A. Rawlyk (New York: Paulist, 1987), 85–86.

5. Frank Baker, ed., *Representative Verse of Charles Wesley* (New York: Abingdon, 1962), 3.

6. It says something about connections promoted by the eighteenth-century evangelical revival that the English translation of Williams's hymn was first published at the request of the Countess of Huntingdon for use in George Whitefield's orphanage in Georgia; see H. Elvert Lewis, *Sweet Singers of Wales: A Story of Welsh Hymns and Their Authors* (London: Religious Tract Society, [1889]), 35–36.

7. Ted Campbell, *The Religion of the Heart: A Study of European Religious Life in the Seventeenth and Eighteenth Centuries* (Columbia: University of South Carolina Press, 1991). W. R. Ward, *The Protestant Evangelical Awakening* (Cambridge: Cambridge University Press, 1992), shows that Continental precedents existed for many features of the early evangelical movement in English-speaking areas.

8. See, for example, Richard F. Lovelace, *The American Pietism of Cotton Mather: Origins of American Evangelicalism* (Grand Rapids: Eerdmans, 1979); and Gordon Rupp, *Religion in England, 1688–1791* (Oxford: Clarendon Press, 1986), 325–26.

9. Michael Saward, *The Anglican Church Today: Evangelicals on the Move* (London: Mowbray, 1987), 34.

10. John G. Stackhouse, "Preaching the Word: Canadian Evangelicalism since the First World War" (Ph.D. diss., University of Chicago, 1987), "Introduction."

11. Figures courtesy of Lyman Kellstedt, Department of Political Science, Wheaton College, Wheaton, Illinois.

12. David Barrett, "Annual Statistical Table on Global Mission: 1993," *International Bulletin of Missionary Research* 17 (1993); 22–23.

13. David W. Bebbington, *Evangelicalism in Modern Britain: A History from the 1730s to the 1980s* (London: Unwin Hyman, 1989), 2–17. Provocative discussion on how best to define "evangelical" is also found in Donald W. Dayton and Robert K. Johnston, eds., *The Variety of American Evangelicalism* (Knoxville: University of Tennessee Press, 1991).

14. Among older studies, see Robert Baird, *Religion in America; or, An Account of . . . the Evangelical Churches in the United States; with Notices of Unevangelical*

Denominations (New York: Harper and Bros., 1856); *The Evangelical Succession: A Course of Lectures Delivered at St. George's Free Church, Edinburgh, 1881–82* (Edinburgh: MacNiven and Wallace, 1882); J. Edwin Orr, *The Second Evangelical Awakening in Britain* (London: Marshall, Morgan and Scott, 1949); Marcus Loane, *Oxford: The Evangelical Succession* (London: Lutterworth, 1950); and idem, *Cambridge: The Evangelical Succession* (London: Lutterworth, 1952).

15. Ian Rennie, "Evangelicalism and English Public Life, 1823–1850" (Ph.D. diss., University of Toronto, 1962); Ernest R. Sandeen, *The Roots of Fundamentalism: British and American Millenarianism, 1800–1930* (Chicago, University of Chicago Press, 1970); Susan Durden, "A Study of the First Evangelical Magazines, 1740–1748," *Journal of Ecclesiastical History* 27 (July 1976): 255–75; idem, "Transatlantic Communications and Influence during the Great Awakening: A Comparative Study of British and American Revivalism, 1730–1760" (Ph. D. diss., University of Hull, 1978); George Marsden, "Fundamentalism as an American Phenomenon: A Comparison with English Evangelicalism," *Church History* 46 (June 1977): 215–32. The fullest and still most satisfying monograph remains Richard Carwardine, *Transatlantic Revivalism: Popular Evangelicalism in Britain and America, 1790–1865* (Westport, CT: Greenwood Press, 1978). Mention should also be made of an important study based on research done in the 1970s: Susan [Durden] O'Brien, "A Transatlantic Community of Saints: The Great Awakening and the First Evangelical Networks, 1735–1755," *American Historical Review* 91 (October 1986): 811–32.

16. Comparative themes were important in several notable studies of previous generations, especially Alexis de Tocqueville, *Democracy in America* (1835, 1840); Lord Bryce, *The American Commonwealth* (New York: Macmillan, 1888); idem, *Canada: An Actual Democracy* (Toronto: Macmillan, 1921); Andre Siegfried, *America Comes of Age* (New York: Harcourt, Brace, 1927); and idem, *Canada* (New York: Harcourt, Brace, 1937). Of the recent flood of works exploring North Atlantic connections, the following are some of the best historical studies most closely related to the themes of this book: Alison Gilbert Olson, *Anglo-American Politics, 1660–1775* (New York: Oxford University Press, 1973); Ned C. Landsman, *Scotland and Its First American Colony, 1683–1765* (Princeton: Princeton University Press, 1985); Jack P. Greene, *Peripheries and Center: Constitutional Development in the Extended Politics of the British Empire and the United States, 1607–1788* (Athens: University of Georgia Press, 1986); Edmund S. Morgan, *Inventing the People: The Rise of Popular Sovereignty in England and America* (New York: Norton, 1988); David Hackett Fischer, *Albion's Seed: Four British Folkways in America* (New York: Oxford University Press, 1989); Seymour Martin Lipset, *Continental Divide: The Values and Institutions of the United States and Canada* (New York: Routledge, 1990); Richard B. Sher and Jeffrey R. Smitten, eds., *Scotland and America in the Age of Enlightenment* (Princeton: Princeton University Press, 1990); Bernard Bailyn and Philip D. Morgan, eds., *Strangers within the Realm: Cultural Margins of the First British Empire* (Chapel Hill: University of North Carolina Press, 1991); Byron E. Shafer, ed., *Is America Different? A New Look at American Exceptionalism* (Oxford: Clarendon Press, 1991); and Ian Tyrrell, "American Exceptionalism in an Age of International History," *American Historical Review* 96 (1991): 1031–55.

17. See especially Keith Robbins, ed., *Protestant Evangelicalism: Britain, Ireland, Germany, and America, c. 1750–c. 1950: Essays in Honour of W. R. Ward* (Oxford: Blackwell, 1990); but also the important material on Protestant evangelicals in books such as Samuel S. Hill, ed., *Religion in the Southern States* (Macon, GA: Mercer University Press, 1983); and Ronald L. Numbers and Darrel W. Amundsen, eds.,

Caring and Curing: Health and Medicine in the Western Religious Traditions (New York: Macmillan, 1986).

18. For example, J. Edwin Orr, *The Eager Feet: Evangelical Awakenings, 1790–1830* (Chicago: Moody Press, 1975); Richard F. Lovelace, *Dynamics of Spiritual Life: An Evangelical Theology of Revival* (Downers Grove, IL: InterVarsity Press, 1979); William J. Abraham, *The Coming Great Revival* (San Francisco: Harper and Row, 1984).

19. For example, Robert T. Handy, *A History of the Churches in the United States and Canada* (New York: Oxford University Press, 1976); James Turner, *Without God, without Creed: The Origins of Unbelief in America* (Baltimore: Johns Hopkins University Press, 1985); and Keith Hunt and Gladys Hunt, *For Christ and the University: InterVarsity Christian Fellowship of the U.S.A., 1940–1990* (Downers Grove, IL: InterVarsity Press, 1991). The most remarkable flourishing of such works concerns developments in the seventeenth and eighteenth centuries and includes several major monographs—Marilyn J. Westerkamp, *Triumph of the Laity: Scots-Irish Piety and the Great Awakening, 1625–1760* (New York: Oxford University Press, 1988); Leigh Eric Schmidt, *Holy Fairs: Scottish Communions and American Revivals in the Early Modern Period* (Princeton: Princeton University Press, 1989); Michael J. Crawford, *Seasons of Grace: Colonial New England's Revival Tradition in Its British Context* (New York: Oxford University Press, 1991)—as well as a burgeoning quantity of exemplary essays, such as Ned C. Landsman, "Witherspoon and the Problem of Provincial Identity in Scottish Evangelical Culture," in *Scotland and America in the Age of the Enlightenment,* ed. Sher and Smitten; and Frank Lambert, "The Great Awakening as Artifact: George Whitefield and the Construction of Intercolonial Revival, 1739–1745," *Church History* 60 (June 1991): 223–46.

20. For example, Edward R. Norman, *The Conscience of the State in North America* (Cambridge University Press, 1968); Steve Bruce, *Firm in the Faith* (Brookfield, VT: Gower, 1984); a full-length symposium devoted to Canadian-American religious comparisons in the *Canadian Journal of Sociology/Cahiers canadiens de sociologie* 3 (Spring 1978): 147–286; Mark A. Noll, "Revival, Enlightenment, Civic Humanism, and the Development of Dogma: Scotland and America, 1735–1843," *Tyndale Bulletin* 40 (1989): 49–76; and Louis Billington, "British and American Methodisms Grow Apart," in *The End of Anglo-America: Historical Essays in the Study of Cultural Divergences,* ed. R. A. Burchell (Manchester: Manchester University Press, 1991).

21. For example, Frederick Hale, *Trans-Atlantic Conservative Protestantism in the Evangelical Free and Mission Covenant Traditions* (New York: Arno, 1979); Mark Ellingsen, *The Evangelical Movement* (Minneapolis: Augsburg, 1988); Ulrich Gäbler, *"Auferstehungszeit": Erweckungsprediger des 19. Jahrhunderts: Sechs Porträts* (Munich: C. H. Beck, 1991); and W. R. Ward, *Protestant Evangelical Awakening.* For at least the United States, there is also a lively literature examining commonalities and dissonances between Anglo-American evangelicals and Protestants from European ethnic stock; see for example, Milton L. Rudnick, *Fundamentalism and the Missouri Synod* (St. Louis: Concordia, 1966); C. Norman Kraus, ed., *Evangelicalism and Anabaptism* (Scottdale, PA: Herald Press, 1979); and James Bratt, *Dutch Calvinism in Modern America* (Grand Rapids: Eerdmans, 1984).

22. For noteworthy examples of more general history written from this perspective, see Randolph A. Roth, *The Democratic Dilemma: Religion, Reform, and the Social Order in the Connecticut River Valley of Vermont, 1791–1850* (New York: Cambridge University Press, 1987); Boyd Hilton, *The Age of Atonement: The Influence of Evangelicalism on Social and Economic Thought, 1785–1865* (Oxford: Clarendon

Press, 1988); William Westfall, *Two Worlds: The Protestant Culture of Nineteenth-Century Ontario* (Montreal and Kingston: McGill-Queen's University Press, 1989); and David G. Hackett, *The Rude Hand of Innovation: Religion and Social Order in Albany, New York, 1652–1836* (New York: Oxford University Press, 1991).

23. Nathan O. Hatch, *The Democratization of American Christianity* (New Haven: Yale University Press, 1989). See also Hatch, "Evangelicalism as a Democratic Movement," in *Evangelicalism and Modern America,* ed. George Marsden (Grand Rapids: Eerdmans, 1984).

24. Timothy L. Smith, *Revivalism and Social Reform: American Protestantism on the Eve of the Civil War* (New York: Abingdon, 1957); and a series of four books by R. F. Wearmouth: *Methodism and the Working-Class Movements of England, 1800–1850* (London: Epworth, 1937); *Methodism and the Common People of the Eighteenth Century* (London: Epworth, 1945); *Methodism and the Struggle of the Working Classes, 1850–1900* (Leicester: Edgar Backus, 1954); and *The Social and Political Influences of Methodism in the Twentieth Century* (London: Epworth, 1957).

ORIGINS

1

"Methodism" and the Origins of English-Speaking Evangelicalism

JOHN WALSH

Until very recently the evangelical awakenings of the 1730s and 1740s were treated as events in splendid isolation—as disparate movements, with their own principles of momentum, geographically contained by the bounds of a region or state. This has been the case with the history of the Great Awakening: it has been even more evident with that of the Evangelical Revival, for until recently the British have been a notoriously insular people. The unconscious chauvinism of a famous English newspaper headline might stand as an epitome for much English church history: FOG IN CHANNEL: CONTINENT ISOLATED. Isolationism has been often carried to extreme lengths in the history of the Evangelical Revival, which has been written for the most part not even in British terms but in English, as if Welsh, Scots, and Irish awakenings did not exist and Albion was safely insulated from its Celtic neighbours by Offa's Dyke, the Roman Wall, and the Irish Sea. Insularity has been compounded by denominational narrow-mindedness. We might have had a more synoptic vision of eighteenth-century revivals if Whitefield—the "wayfaring witness" and link man between many centers of revival in the Anglophone world— had, like John Wesley, created a huge and enduring denomination to celebrate his achievements.

The fragmentation of revival history would have surprised many early evangelicals, who, despite their controversies, were usually agreed that the outpourings of the Spirit witnessed by their age were generically the same. "Evidently one work with what we have here" was Wesley's comment on the American awakening.[1] On both sides of the Atlantic, the resemblance and the remarkable simultaneity of the revivals were noted and were interpreted as signs that the universal, millennial spread of the gospel might be imminent. The similarity of widely separated awakenings was sufficient to allow Whitefield to step easily from one center to another, from London to Boston, Lowland Scotland, South Wales, Philadelphia, or South Carolina, with little or no spiritual culture shock, feeling himself a fully passported citizen of a transatlantic revival community.

   In the last few years, historians writing from a secular perspective have begun to endorse the revivalists' perception of mid-eighteenth century awakenings as aspects of the same "work." Revivals are now being treated in terms of comparative history not merely as regional events but as constituent elements of an international and pan-Protestant phenomenon.

   The extent to which revivals were linked together by a highly effective communications network is now clear. In the early eighteenth century, Protestantism still possessed a sense of collective solidarity. Protestants, ironically, knew more about each other than they do today in the age of the fax machine and the satellite—and ecumenism. Religious news was transmitted from the Turkish border to New England by diplomats, émigrés, the exchange and translation of devotional works, newspaper coverage, and, above all, fraternal correspondence. From the pietist centre of Halle, a clearinghouse for Protestant intelligence, A. H. Francke, prophet of Protestant renewal, engaged some five thousand correspondents and maintained regular communication with some three or four hundred.[2] In the English-speaking world the old Calvinist international still survived: in a triangular exchange, English Dissenters, New England Puritans, and Scots Presbyterians kept up a flow of information about events in their churches.

   What gave this religious correspondence an edge of urgency was the sense of anxiety that suffused it. The morale of the Protestant world was at a low ebb in the half century before the awakenings of the 1730s and 1740s. Catholic expansion had shorn Continental Protestantism of much of its strength, a fact brought home to the Anglophone world by the successive waves of refugees who poured into it: the Huguenots, Palatines, Salzburgers, and Moravians. Behind such pressures lay not only religious intolerance but also the urge of the modern bureaucratic state to assimilate minorities and bring subordinate corporations under its will.[3] These migrations not only increased the efficiency of the Protestant intelligence system as expatriates reported back to their mother churches; they were also to have important effects in cross-fertilizing Anglo-Saxon Protestantism. What would the history of Methodism have been if John Wesley, High Church Anglican, had not met Peter Böhler, a Moravian?

   More alarming than the external threat from hostile governments was the sense of interior decay that afflicted much of Protestantism. "What a dead and barren time has it now been, for a great while, with all the churches of the Reformation," wrote William Cooper, in 1741. "The golden showers have been restrained; the influences of the Spirit suspended; and the consequence has been that the Gospel has not had any eminent success: conversions have been rare and dubious . . . and the hearts of Christians not so quickened, warmed and refreshed under the ordinances, as they might have been."[4] This was a Calvinist assessment of the situation, but its theme of declension from the faith of pious forefathers was common among ministers of most churches. A good deal of the intelligence that traveled along the networks of correspondence was concerned with the themes of present decay and future renewal. On either side of the Atlantic ministers felt similar anxieties. They fretted at the spiritual deadness of their people, the decay of clerical authority, the spread of rationalism, the prevalence of "luxury," and the frivolity and indifference of the young. In the decades leading up to the evangelical awakenings of the 1730s and 1740s, these themes inspired countless jeremiads.

They were also, as Michael Crawford has recently shown, the subject of continual debate along the triangle of correspondence between English, Scots, and American Calvinist divines.[5] Decades of failure had led to a reassessment of the best way to promote religious renewal. No longer did ministers repose much faith in reformation by state action or by voluntary societies such as those for the Reformation of Manners. In their disappointment they had arrived at the conclusion that only a direct outpouring of the Spirit could bring about the desired result. By the 1720s, Crawford suggests, a "transatlantic consensus" had been reached among renewal-minded Calvinist ministers on both sides of the Atlantic—English Nonconformists like Watts and Jennings; the Mathers, Danforth, and Stoddard in New England; Wodrow and the Erskine brothers in Scotland. All agreed that no reformation could be lasting until God poured out his Spirit on the people. Every effort must therefore be made to pray and preach down that Spirit. This could best be done by a less intellectualistic and a more deliberately affective homiletic style, which would present Christ's person and mediatorial role in a manner calculated to rouse the affections and bring conversions. Thus, by the 1730s, Crawford suggests, there was already a profound expectation of impending divine intervention. The tinder for a great awakening was in place; all that remained were the catalysts to ignite it. These were not long in coming, namely, the "surprizing work of God" in the Connecticut Valley revival of 1734–35, Wesley's famous conversion, and Whitefield's electrifying descent on the American colonies.

Once the revivals exploded, knowledge of them was immediately transmitted along the transatlantic network. Ministers seized eagerly on revival narratives, above all Jonathan Edwards's classic *Faithful Narrative* of the Northampton awakening, to arouse expectations in their own congregations. News of revivals at home and abroad was read out at Letter Days to inspirit congregations. Revival magazines in London, Boston, and Glasgow spread the news of worldwide conversions, giving the awakenings an international dimension as aspects of one vast outpouring of grace.[6] Whitefield, shuttling busily between one revival and another, helped knit them together by his charisma and a brilliant and innovative use of the techniques of publicity.

The swing of the historiographic pendulum toward a more unitary view of the early evangelical awakenings is salutary and long overdue. But it would be unwise to let it swing too far, to produce a new orthodoxy of a single homogenized transatlantic revival. There remain many contrasts, dissimilarities, and unresolvable problems. It would be dangerous to treat the outbreak of eighteenth-century revivals too teleologically as merely the inevitable result of careful preparation and efficient promotion. With hindsight, the revival outbreaks may have the semblance of inevitability as events long prepared for and expected, but we must note the astonishment with which they were greeted. (Not for nothing did Jonathan Edwards entitle his famous tract *A Faithful Narrative of the Surprizing Work of God.*) In this chapter I consider a few of these complexities as they appear in the context of early English Methodism.

Nowhere was the unpredictability of the English revival more evident than in its place of birth. As observers noted, when the revival arrived, it came, paradoxically, not among the Calvinist Dissenters, who had corresponded about it, published treatises about it, and prayed for it, but in an Arminian Church of England in which the old Puritan Calvinism was virtually extinct, and the prejudice against spirit-filled "enthusiasm" almost an obsession. The Nonconformist denominations that had preserved the Puritan "doctrines of grace" seemed at first less capable of propagating them than priests of the "apostate" Church of England, in which they had been largely forgotten. Though Whitefield became a convinced Calvinist some time after his conversion, the largest wing of the revival was led by the Arminian Wesley, who retained many of his old High Church principles and prejudices and held a doctrine of perfection that struck Calvinists as not only eccentric but downright popish. The first reproductive cells of the revival in the metropolitan centers of Bristol and London were not the Dissenting chapels but the religious societies, peopled with High Church Anglican youths.[7] In his 1737 preface to Edwards's *Narrative,* Isaac Watts had expressed the hope that such an outpouring of God's grace "gives us further encouragement to pray, and wait, and hope for the like display of his power in the midst of us," yet a year or two later he acknowledged the sensational success of Whitefield only grudgingly.[8] "My converse with him is not much, nor am I esteemed one of his admirers," he wrote coldly to Benjamin Colman of Boston in 1742.[9] He suspected Whitefield not only as a priest but as a rash, imprudent, and "enthusiastic" young man. Despite continual talk of the need for revival, it took decades for the Dissenting interest to profit fully from the example of the evangelical movement, and it continued to decline. Nonconformists were as yet unwilling to innovate; they were adverse to field preaching or itinerancy. God has "offered this work to the Dissenters, and they would not go out of their places," wrote the Welsh revivalist Howell Harris, severely.[10]

Why, then, did the revival begin in the Church of England, which had reneged spectacularly on much of the Reformed theology of its Thirty-Nine Articles? No simple, unitary explanation takes account of the complex of spiritual experiences and personal encounters visible in early evangelical biography. There were many tributaries. The spiritual odysseys of many early leaders and most converts are unrecorded. The revival has no one place or date of birth. Wesley's famous spiritual experience on May 24, 1738, was a momentous event, but one cannot view the revival as a chain reaction from Aldersgate Street, for several other leaders were already converted, including Howell Harris, Daniel Rowland, and George Whitefield in 1735. None of these men had been involved in transatlantic Calvinist networking or had been jolted into evangelicalism by reading revival narratives. The Welsh "Methodist" revival had its own local and independent sources of origin. A number of early evangelical clergy reached conversion in rural isolation, and many remained largely unconnected to the early Methodist movement.[11] Though early evangelicals met at the same central point—a vivid experience of New Birth—they came to it from very different points on the social and religious circumference.

The spiritual chemistry of the English revival in its first years shows a complex interaction of spiritual and intellectual influences in a highly volatile compound. The late 1730s and early 1740s were years of conflict and anxiety in English religion, and it is not surprising that this factor was reflected in the origins of the revival. In its inception evangelicalism was very much a *movement;* it was marked by mobility, excitement, restlessness, experimentation, fluidity, and controversy. "We see all about us in an amazing ferment," marveled Charles Wesley in January 1738.[12] Like some modern religious movements, early Methodism had the attributes of a *Jugendreligion;* many of its converts were young, and so too were many of their leaders—notably Whitefield, the "boy preacher." Emotions ran high. Feelings of pentecostal fraternity coincided with a combativeness that split Methodist from Moravian, and Arminian from Calvinist. There was movement to and fro, much spiritual wayfaring—a very rapid turnover of membership in the societies, as converts were not only won but lost. There were outbreaks of bizarre enthusiasm. There were false starts and some disasters—like Benjamin Ingham's early and flourishing connexion in the North Country, which disintegrated after wranglings over Sandemanianism.[13]

Though the first years of the revival were turbulent and confused, one can discern some common threads running through the biographies of its early leaders.[14] The English revival was at least broadly related to those elsewhere in that it emerged as a reaction to a perceived religious crisis. If a graph of clerical tension could be constructed along the lines of Rostow's famous social tension graph of early nineteenth-century Britain, the 1720s and 1730s would probably represent a high peak.[15] What made these decades particularly anxiety-inducing was the conjunction of several crises that could easily blend into one in the clerical mind.

The first factor was common to several revivals: the threat of a rationalism that, in both its Christian and "infidel" forms, was extending the frontiers of natural religion at the expense of revelation. This movement hit English churchmen more forcibly than American. The New England pastors had as yet been faced by only a mild epidemic of Arminianism; in old England rationalism came in more potent forms, often with the sanction of Establishment behind it. At Harvard College in 1740 to read the Anglican divines Samuel Clarke and John Tillotson was still regarded as shocking to some. At Oxford, by contrast, the deist Matthew Tindal was comfortably ensconced as a Fellow of All Souls College.[16] It can be no coincidence that the Evangelical Revival took off soon after the deist movement reached a high-water mark of popularity. In the 1730s the deist writings were fashionable reading in the salons, and freethinking ideas were beginning to filter down to the level of the coffeehouse and the inn. The alarm that deism engendered in English church leaders was extreme and out of all proportion to its popularity. In 1734 the High Churchman Richard Venn (father of the evangelical Henry) told Lord Egmont wildly that "infidelity had infected above half the nation and . . . the greater part of the nobility."[17] What made deism so alarming was not merely its apparent popularity but the difficulty of combating it. The state showed no signs of acting. Though "infidelity" was legally proscribed, it was tolerated and fashionable in aristocratic circles. There was little likelihood that Whig ministers, some of them well-known sceptics, would prosecute heretics. "There is no fear of being cast out of our synagogue for any tenets whatsoever," complained Samuel Wesley, Jr. "Did not Clarke die preferred? Were not Collins and Coward free from anathema?"[18]

Worse still, churchmen were unnerved by the difficulty of answering the deist case. Apologetic works such as Butler's *Analogy* had helped to counter "constructive" deism—the attempt to replace Christianity by an allegedly universal religion of nature—by showing that the cult of natural religion posed many of the same difficulties presented by revealed religion. But Christian writers found it altogether harder to meet "critical" deism (the pinprick attacks on the consistency, morality, and historicity of the biblical narratives). On the battlefield of history and exegesis it was hard to deliver a knockout blow to the carping infidel. A long succession of works defended the faith by appealing to the historical "evidences" of the miracles and the prophecies, but there must have been many who felt with William Law that laborious argumentation only compounded their unease. As he put it feelingly, "The more books there were written in this way of defending the Gospel, the more I was furnished with new objections to it."[19] Even though "infidel" propaganda often failed to convince, it still sowed doubts that were not easily erased. Early evangelical autobiographies suggest that many were shaken by deism. John Wesley himself appears to be one of them. At Oxford he had been not only shocked but "afflicted" by the deism of one of his friends; while in the trough of his spiritual crisis early in 1738, he had agonized whether the Bible was indeed "a cunningly devised fable."[20]

In clerical minds anxiety about deism merged with fears that the country was also passing through a deep moral crisis. There was nothing new about jeremiads on this theme; they were a conventional homiletic art form. Nonetheless, on the eve of the Evangelical Revival they seem to have acquired unusual force and frequency. Litanies of woe about the "dreadful degeneracy of the age" poured out from the pulpit and the press. Joseph Trapp, Oxford High Churchman, spoke for many of his generation when he wrote in 1734, "I presume it will be allowed by everybody that all manner of wickedness, both in principles and in practice, abounds among us to a degree unheard of since Christianity was in being. . . . I have lived in six reigns: but for about twenty years past, the English nation has been . . . so prodigiously debauched that I am almost a foreigner in my own country."[21] The idea that England was glissading like post-Antonine Rome into an abyss of profligacy and vice was commonplace; it was a theme developed in Pope's satires, Gay's *Beggar's Opera,* and Hogarth's prints. The Old Pretender, "James III," with his ear well attuned to the mentality of "country" Toryism, stressed in his declaration before the '45 Jacobite Rebellion that he would deal firmly with the "universal corruption and dissolution of manners."[22]

What particularly unnerved Anglican churchmen in the years immediately preceding the revival was the virulent attack on the clergy launched during the mid-1730s by Whig anticlericals in Parliament. The debates over the repeal of the Test Acts and the Quakers Tithes Bill revealed a bitter anticlericalism that has been considered to be unparalleled since the Reformation Parliament itself.[23] This is no place to discuss the accuracy of such lamentations, which may well have reflected dismay at social change as much as any deterioration in the mores of the nation. In the myth of declension highly disparate images of moral decay fused together: the fury of excluded Tories at Whig political "corruption"; disgust at the low moral standards of the court; "country" alarm at the spread of urban, commercial values; horror at the ravages of gin drinking among the urban poor; and fears aroused by a wave of violent crimes. It was much easier to bewail the prevalence of vice than to control it. What could be done? The forces of law and order in Hanoverian England were plainly inadequate. The church courts, which had formerly been an agency for the moral policing of society, had lost their powers. There had once been hopes that voluntary societies for the reformation of manners would fill the vacuum left by the church courts through private prosecutions of the vicious and immoral, but by the time of the revival they were weak, unpopular, and on their last legs—"almost worn out," complained one early Methodist.[24]

For decades, church leaders had been troubled by feelings of pastoral failure—this, as well as party politics, had lain behind the "Church in Danger" alarm of Anne's reign.[25] Since the Toleration Act of 1689 the Church of England had lost its powers to compel church attendance. Instead of coercing their parishioners, the clergy had to persuade them. The number of churchgoers had dwindled. Population growth and incipient industrialization brought unwelcome migrants to some parishes, forming new, disorderly settlements on their margins, not amenable to clerical control.[26] The collier colonies—like those at Kingswood, soon to be visited by Whitefield and Wesley—were regarded as spectacularly ignorant of things spiritual. Lord Egmont was astonished by the godlessness of the miners near Bristol in 1733. He was told that a local gentleman interrogating them about their absence from church had exclaimed, "Why . . . I believe you know nothing of the Commandments." To this "they all replied they knew such a family living in their parts, but they did not know them personally."[27]

Directly relevant to the birth of Methodism was the malaise that affected some areas of High Church spirituality. The "holy living" tradition of seventeenth-century Anglicanism, including the piety of Bishop Ken, the *Whole Duty of Man,* and, in its most rigoristic form, Law's *Serious Call,* still attracted many devout churchmen but proved too demanding for others, especially those who espoused it with intensity.[28] The call to perfection and the ascetic imitation of Christ still inspired some souls but set standards that were alarmingly high, as the familiar story of the Oxford Methodists proved. The "holy living" tradition could arouse aspirations that it did not satisfy.[29] There was a certain joylessness in the call to a regime of unrelenting worship, closet devotion, introspection, and asceticism; it conveyed an anxiety-inducing severity. It is not surprising that some High Churchmen were beginning to buckle under the psychic strain. William Law himself swerved off to find relief in the mystical religion of Böhme.[30]

For each of these problems evangelical religion offered a solution and so eased the transition of some receptive Christians to a new mode of religious thinking and experience. A revulsion from deism and reductionist latitudinarianism drove many seekers along the track toward conversion. There were many who could have said with John Newton, "I was weary of cold contemplative truths which cannot warm nor amend the heart."[31] To some of those perplexed by doubts about the authority of the Bible, the interior evidence of personal acceptance by Christ offered the relief that learned argument about Christian "evidences" did not give. Apologists who concentrated their attention on the external evidences of the faith, argued Joseph Milner, were like military commanders who defended the outworks of the fortress while allowing the enemy to seize the citadel. Rational arguments by themselves did not engage the inner man. The best argument against the infidel was "the evidence of internal experience: I feel myself . . . lost and miserable: I experience such a healthful change in my whole moral system. . . . [T]hat is the true cure for scepticism."[32] "Experience," wrote Henry Venn, "is a living proof, stronger than a thousand arguments."[33] Many early evangelicals appear to have traveled along such paths. John Newton, who had been converted to free thought by a naval captain in his seafaring days, considered that, although his case was "in some respects uncommon, something like it is known by one and another every day, and I have conversed with many who . . . after years spent in defending Deistical principles . . . have been like me brought to glory in the Cross of Christ and to live by that faith which they had before slighted and opposed."[34] The spectacle of so many striking conversions proved that God was not the impersonal *Dues absconditus* of the deists, remote from a world governed by impersonal natural law, but the living God of the Bible. The direct evidence of God's Spirit possessed a compelling power that transcended barriers of class and culture. It could be appreciated by all—by the simple and ignorant, who could not follow learned treatises on Christian "evidences," as well as by the sophisticated and literate. "One thing I know: I was blind, but now I see"—this, wrote Wesley, was "an argument so plain that a peasant, a woman, a child may feel all its force."[35]

So too with the moral crisis. The early sermons of the Wesleys and Whitefield suggest that they regarded moral reformation as one of the highest priorities of the revival. One of the Wesley brothers' declared objectives in setting out on their mission was to effect "a reformation not of opinions . . . but of men's tempers and lives; of vice in every kind."[36] John Wesley assured the assembled dons of Oxford University in June 1738 that nothing but salvation by faith could "give a check to that immorality which hath overspread the land as a flood."[37] The impact of Methodism on outlandish groups such as the colliers of Kingswood suggested that the gospel achieved results where the magistrates could not. By conversion, moral norms were internalized. "That reformation which is brought about by a coercive power, will be only outward and superficial; but that which is done by the force of God's Word, will be inward and lasting," Whitefield observed in 1739.[38] By transforming the heart and the will, the gospel would achieve results far beyond the remedial capacity of a formal religion of "mere morality." "We have seen the inefficacy of mere moral doctrines for several years," exclaimed Robert Seagrave, an early clerical admirer of Whitefield. "What have they done? What have they brought forth, comparatively to the despised labours of a poor, travelling evangelist?"[39] The claims of the early Methodists to have effected rapid and dramatic moral reformation were often extravagant, but they helped to attract converts. In Newcastle in 1742, Charles Wesley was welcomed with the words "he is a good man and is come to reform the land."[40] Among the reasons listed by an early clerical convert, Walter Sellon, for his adherence to Methodism was admiration for Wesley's resolute campaign to "stem the tide of wickedness" when local magistrates shrank from the task.[41]

The story of the meeting of High Churchmen and Moravians in 1738–39 is too familiar to need retelling. The Brethren were uniquely fitted for their historic role of grafting experiential pietism onto the stock of Anglican High Churchmanship. By their claim to the historic episcopate, by the quasi-apostolic simplicity of their lives, and by their strong communitarian sense they seemed to embody the elusive spirit of the primitive church, which so many High Anglicans had sought to recapture. The effect of their message— that grace was not only free but immediately accessible, and that an assurance of saving faith could be instantly enjoyed—had electric effect on hearers and provided what for many was a missing ingredient in their spirituality. The effect of this news on the religious societies of London and Bristol, in which hundreds of devout young men, the cream of Anglican lay piety, were collected, was depicted by James Hutton, who had been reared in a strict nonjuring family. "It was not to be described with what joy and wonder we then grasped the doctrines of the Saviour, His merits and suffering and justification by faith in Him, and thereby freedom from the power and guilt of sin. This was to us all something so new, unexpected, joyful, penetrating: for the most of us had sorely striven and fought against sin without profit or result."[42] The reintroduction of the Reformation doctrine of justification by faith alone, not merely as a credal proposition but as an experiential reality, set the revival in motion.

But what turned the conversions of a handful of Anglican clergymen into a missionary movement? It was perfectly possible for a converted parish priest to pass through a conversion experience and yet hide his light under a bushel in an obscure parish. It was the crucial determination of Wesley and Whitefield to launch into itinerancy, making the world their parish and not the parish their world, that turned Methodism from a small awakening to a full-scale revival.

The leadership of the revival by Anglican priests was essential to its initial success in England and Wales. Wesley immediately saw that the Church of England, the national church "by law established," had such overwhelming hegemonic ascendancy that no ambitious reform movement could succeed unless it was at least nominally under the canopy of its authority. If converts had been hived off into separatist churches in 1739, the movement could not have tapped the massive institutional loyalty that accrued to the national church. Nonconformity, which could claim only a tiny proportion of the population, could hardly have provided the leadership.[43] The Moravians, though vital as a catalyst, were hampered by the eccentricity of Count Zinzendorf. They were also averse to field preaching, and their self-professed role as *ecclesiolae in ecclesia* (little churches within the church) made them extremely reluctant to accept converts from other churches into full membership. The Brethren were content to remain "the quiet in the land," focusing much of their energy into the community life of their settlements such as Fulneck, Ockbrook, and Lambshill.

If the Methodist leaders were Anglicans, they were no ordinary Anglicans, however. They exploited their clerical status, wearing gown and bands for outdoor preaching, but they were also prepared pragmatically to abandon Anglican precedents and break Anglican canons whenever it suited them. They swiftly picked up and developed evangelistic expedients that were often seen as hallmarks of nonconformity—extemporaneous prayer, hymn singing, small-group fellowship, even itinerancy. Though Wesley often spoke of his movement as Anglican, he also claimed that his societies were denominationally inclusive, open to all—whether Churchpeople, Dissenters, or Catholics—who desired to be saved from their sins. The Methodist societies were not to be tumors feeding on the tissues of other churches, but regenerate cells renewing the inner life of all communions. This calculated ambiguity was of great evangelistic utility. It enabled the early Methodist leaders to maximize their appeal, to play the field, to pick up converts from different points of the denominational compass. Whitefield was well aware that Anglicans were comforted by his praise of the liturgy and the Thirty-Nine Articles, while American Congregationalists and Scots Presbyterians were delighted by his status as a "Dissenter priest," a cheerful rebel, lambasting the "blind guides" of his own church, cocking an irreverent snook at the solemn Bishop Gibson and writing off the august Archbishop Tillotson as knowing no more of true religion than Mahomet.[44] His amphibious ability to move in and out of his clerical role when it pleased him was of great strategic use. James Hutton commented shrewdly in 1747 on the providentially varied appeal of the revivals. The Moravians, the quiet "small witness folk," drew in those who sought spiritual peace and retirement, while the Methodists appealed to the "great masses"; Wesley had been well fitted to gather in those emerging from High Church "Pelagianism"; Whitefield was well placed to attract the Calvinists.[45] One could continue the contrast: Whitefield, the publicist and orator of genius, "God's dramatist," who could make crowds either laugh or cry by the way he pronounced the word "Mesopotamia"; Wesley, the academic, the organizer, the master builder. Not all new movements are fortunate enough to possess a Boanerges as well as a Hezekiah.

The spread of early Methodism depended on its ability to integrate diverse constituent groups into the associational network of its societies. Not for nothing was Wesley's organization known as a "connexion," for it connected up and inspirited hundreds of scattered groups, many of them very small, threading them together like beads on a string. The motto "only connect," epigraph of E. M. Forster's most famous novel, could stand as a motto for the Methodist movement.

The early growth of the revival was due to its ability not only to win converts from the unchurched but to revitalize the faith of practicing Christians. The first converts, those in the religious societies, were important here, because they provided the early movement with disciplined and well-instructed cadres of members and leaders who helped to socialize the cruder converts won by outdoor evangelism. Other groups soon followed.

Though Wesley intended itinerant preaching as a means to convert "flagrant sinners," such preaching had the expected side effect of picking up Reformed saints.[46] As the itinerants crisscrossed the kingdom, they uncovered many scattered folk who were already well disposed to their message. "God had a faithful people in every age," wrote John Newton. "The preaching of the Gospel may be compared to a standard erected, to which they may repair, and thereby become known to each other, and more exposed to the notice and observation of the world."[47] In his journal, Whitefield noted how on his travels he found "some thousands of secret ones yet living amongst us who have not bowed the knee to Baal; and this public way of preaching brings them out."[48]

Many of these were Dissenters. It is here, in providing Methodist converts, that the old Nonconformity made its important input to the earliest years of the revival. The decline of Dissent helped the rise of Methodism. As the great wave of Puritanism receded, it left innumerable rock pools of piety behind it—little causes, especially in country places, whose numbers had shrunk to the point at which they could no longer afford a pastor but had to make do with family worship of a sort. For these, the connexional networks of Methodism provided the pastoral oversight they sought and lacked. There were also leaderless Nonconformists of a different kind, those (often the poorer members) who had clung to the old Reformation faith and separated from their chapels when their Presbyterian pastors slid into fashionable Arianism. Numbers of these too were gathered in by the Methodist itinerants.[49] There was much in the new movement to attract flagging Dissenters, particularly those who had found it difficult to reach the experience of regeneration that their Puritan culture expected of them. Evangelical preaching of an immediate, personal assurance came to some as a welcome surprise. Listening to Charles Wesley in 1742, Jonathan Simpson and his wife wrote that "we say that there was a privilege to be enjoyed which we had never experienced."[50] A London Dissenter explained candidly in a public letter to his pastor in 1743 that the new evangelical preaching was "more directly adapted to my present wants than any I can hear in town"; it offered an immediate deliverance from the power of sin, while the Calvinism of the Dissenters offered only a life of constant mourning over inward depravity, which was "like a general's commanding his soldiers to fight on towards taking . . . a city and at the same time telling them they must never expect to take it."[51] Wesley was well aware of the drawing power of the Methodist teaching on this score; he urged his preachers to avoid what he saw as the Puritanical overemphasis on divine wrath and to stress the joy of belief; they should hammer home the message that "a believer walking in the light is inexpressibly great and happy."[52]

There were other groups to be gathered up by the itinerant preaching. Soldiers herded together in the bleak life of barracks provided one constituency, especially in overseas postings such as Ireland and Gibraltar, or in the winter camps like those of Flanders in the summer of 1744, where John Haime attracted a thousand to his preaching and ruled over a society of three hundred members.[53] Immigrant groups, pastorless and deracinated, were another source of recruitment. Huguenot names such as Panou, Deschamps, and Lunell figure significantly in early Methodist lists. Among the early clergy we find Romaine, Perronet, Sellon, Rouquet, and de Coetlogon. In Ireland the preachers made contact with colonies of Palatine refugees, whose blond hair and German accents still startled Methodist preachers in the early nineteenth century. It was from this base, in the persons of Barbara Heck and Philip Embury, that Methodism was later exported to North America with momentous results.[54]

Early Methodism did more than regroup and revitalize existing pockets of piety. The revival was also a missionary movement, reaching out to the unchurched. There was frontal as well as lateral growth. The poor were always Wesley's primary target. "The rich, the honourable, the great we . . . leave to you," he told his fellow clergy; "only let us alone with the poor."[55] In the pursuit of the marginalized, the "outcasts of men," the "forlorn ones," itinerancy proved of the utmost value. The Methodist preachers moved quickly into some of the yawning gaps of the Anglican parochial system, treating them as a veritable *pays de mission*. Wesley had a sharp strategic eye for the new industrial settlements out of the sound of church bells and away from the old community life of the village and made detours to visit them.

Some of these isolated communities perhaps would have responded gratefully to almost any form of pastoral care, from whatever source it came. Nonetheless, early Methodism was well adapted to its early mission among the groups like the colliers of Newcastle or the tinners and fisherman of Cornwall. The demotic rhetoric of crude lay preachers and exhorters carried evangelical religion across the cultural divide that often hindered an educated parish priest from making contact with his wilder parishioners. The early evangelicals found that they possessed keys to evangelistic success among the poor in the resources of their own theology. The Pauline antinomies of law and the gospel had enormous dramatic potential when unfolded by a skillful preacher who used the homiletic shift from one to the other to full effect. A convert of Venn's described how "while he was unfolding the terrors of the law, he would put on a stern look that would make you tremble, then he'd turn to the offer of grace and go on entreating till his eyes filled with tears."[56] The doctrine of justification by faith alone—free grace—had unexpected resonance among poor people. Its implications were clear: acceptance by God was not dependent, as the poor had often been taught, on the performance of moral duties, on an antecedent life of "good works" to which in their mean- ness they could seldom attain. It was given to all who repented and believed. Furthermore, salvation by faith could be granted instantaneously; the process need not be long and drawn out; it could be offered and accepted now. Charles Wesley's hymns hammered home the message:

> This is the time: no more delay!
> This is the Lord's accepted day;
> Come in, this moment, at His call,
> And live, for Him who died for all![57]

How could the gift of grace be recognized? It could normally be felt by an immediate, self-authenticating assurance, impressed on the heart. The sub- jectivism of this close association of justification to assurance shocked many traditional Calvinists, but there was no doubt of its evangelistic value, for it brought the evidences of justification within range of the outcast and illiter- ate. The Methodists offered the poor a salvation that they felt to be within their reach, immediately attainable, and recognizable. This message was dra- matically represented by the attendance of Methodist preachers at public executions. Their presence at Tyburn represented, as in a *tableau vivant,* the accessibility of grace to the most despised and vulnerable of humankind. To the modern criminal, shivering on the scaffold, grace could still descend as freely and immediately as it had to the malefactor hanging beside Christ on the cross, to whom the promise had been given, "This day shalt thou be with me in Paradise." As the cart carried them to the scaffold, criminals mouthed the words of Charles Wesley's *Prayers for Condemned Malefactors:*

> Turn then, my Lord, my God unknown,
> Whom with my parting breath I own:
> In death the kind conviction dart,
> And cast a look and break my heart.[58]

It is here, perhaps, in its dedication to the ingathering of marginalized outsiders, that the English Evangelical Revival most differs from the Great Awakening, at least in its classic New England form. The revivals in New England and the much smaller Cambuslang "Wark" in Scotland were community-based revivals, led by parish ministers. They issued in excite- ments that affected whole parishes in their collectivity and spread conta- giously to others in such a way as to affect a region. Early Methodism was not like this, nor could it be. It did not spread like wildfire.[59] Its social and ecclesiastical situation was highly unpropitious for anything like a Great Awakening. In the aristocratic and tradition-bound society of old England, too many barriers existed to allow the swift diffusion of revivals that was often possible in more open and egalitarian societies like those of North America. All but a minute handful of the sixteen thousand clergy of the established Church of England held aloof from the new movement, conditioned as they were by traumatic fears of "enthusiasm."

In 1738–39 the Methodists claimed to be restoring the "old divinity" of the Reformation, but in the suspicious eyes of most clergymen it seemed more likely that they were reviving the illuminist fanaticism of the Civil War and Commonwealth, which had led to the killing of the king and the dismemberment of the Church of England. Any good they might do in the way of reformation was counterbalanced by the Dionysian forces of unruliness that they let loose. "I cannot but earnestly desire and pray for an effectual reformation of manners and propagation of the Gospel by all sober and Christian methods," wrote Bishop Lavington, "but this great work will never be accomplished by an enthusiastic and fanatical hand."[60] The same deep prejudice affected the landowning gentry, whose quasi-seigneurial control over many parishes was often highly effective in keeping out the new movement. Recent studies of English religious geography show how hard it was for popular evangelicalism to gain purchase in "estate parishes," where one or two landlords controlled the freeholds and could intimidate their tenants or prevent the sale of land for a chapel.[61] As a result, early Methodism was forced to operate on the fringes of social and religious life. This had its attendant blessings. It was largely because the Methodist clergy were denied Anglican pulpits in 1739 that they took to the open air and discovered a huge new mission field in the yawning gaps in the Anglican parish system. In isolated hamlets, proto-industrial settlements on moorland and wastes, colonies gathered round coal mines and iron forges. It was largely because they themselves were eccclesiastically marginalized that the early Methodists were driven to address those on the social margins. It was because so few clergy helped them that they were forced to use unlettered lay preachers and exhorters, and to make a direct and fruitful contact with the world of popular culture.[62] Wesley soon extrapolated from his own experience to advance the historical theory that all great religious revivals began on the edges of society among the poor and insignificant, rather than at the center, where power and prestige were located.[63]

There was a strong contrast between the social setting of the New England awakening, led by ministers of the Congregational establishment, who appealed to the consciences of well-instructed Calvinist flocks in their parish churches, and that of the societies of early Methodism, gathered promiscuously from a motley assortment of those seeking salvation. Spiritual outpourings like those in Edwards's Northampton or the great sacramental revivals in McCulloch's Cambuslang were community events, the collective penitential occasions of an assembled parish. Methodism rarely built on the parish community; on the contrary, it was bitterly condemned for splitting the parish in two and drawing people into a spiritual fraternity that competed with that of the parish church, the traditional focus for communal feeling. The difference of milieu is mirrored in the revival literature it produced. As Michael Crawford has noted, the characteristic narrative form in New England was that of Edwards's *Faithful Narrative,* which portrayed the awakening of a whole parish under its settled pastor. The English equivalent was Whitefield's or Wesley's *Journal*—the record of the itinerant evangelist, ranging the country, preaching to all who would listen.[64]

The differences between the Evangelical Revival and the Great Awakening were not lost on John Wesley. With a good deal of complacency he contrasted the slow growth of the English movement with the ephemeral success of the revivals in Scotland and New England. "What a glorious work of God was at Cambuslang and Kilsyth from 1740 to 1744. . . . But . . . when I diligently inquired a few years after, I could not find one that retained the life of God."[65] He compared the episodic nature of many North American revivals with the slow, steady extension of the work in England. "In the time of Dr. Jonathan Edwards," he wrote in 1786, "there were several gracious showers in New England, but there were large intermissions between one and another; whereas with us the work of God has been . . . continually increasing."[66] Though Wesley delighted in revivals, he became chary of expecting too much permanent growth from them, observing late in life that for the most part in an "extraordinary work of God . . . a swift increase is generally followed by a decrease equally swift."[67] He realized that his own movement owed more to careful institutionalization than to violent bursts of collective spiritual excitement. In old age, looking back on Methodism with a clinical eye, he observed that "showers" or "torrents" of grace often appeared at the beginning of the work in a particular place, especially in cities like London, Bristol, or Newcastle, but then subsided. Such descents of the Spirit might come thereafter, and should always be prayed for, but "in general," he concluded, it appeared that the kingdom of God would not "come with observation" but would "silently increase wherever it is set up, and spread from heart to heart, from house to house."[68]

In England the early extension of evangelicalism was accomplished by gradual, incremental growth rather than by the "big bang" of a Great Awakening. For decades the Evangelical Revival advanced by slow and somewhat fitful progression. It lacked the preaching strength to reach many parts of the country, let alone tend and nurture all the awakened. Not until the time of Wesley's death in the 1790s did evangelicalism, like the Industrial Revolution, with which it lived in such close symbiosis, "take off" properly into rapid and sustained growth. The work of the early Methodist preachers had much more in common with the patient work of evangelists in the undeveloped American back country than with the spectacular results of the New England ministers in the townships of the Great Awakening. Methodism was as much a missionary movement as a revival. It was sustained and refreshed by countless sudden, almost pentecostal moments of glory and transfiguration as the Spirit came down at a prayer meeting or a love feast. From time to time great collective spiritual outpourings energized the movement, especially in Wales. But the main cause of growth lay rather in patient, persistent evangelism in a myriad of dingy villages and seedy back streets. Much of the movement's success lay in quiet recruitment along networks of kinship and friendship, through little cottage meetings like those described in George Eliot's *Adam Bede,* through earnest discussions between people working side by side in the same workshop or farm, and through the reading of sermons and tracts.

Does the iconography of early Methodism perhaps mislead us here? Prints of early Methodism evoke images of mass evangelism, of vast crowds listening to Whitefield at Moorfields. Important as these occasions were, they were less significant in England than the patient leg work by itinerants in the "dark corners of the realm." It was Wesley's genius to recognize this difference, just as it was Whitefield's to recognize the importance of evangelism through the media of mass communication—a legacy that has come fully into its own in this century. Howell Harris noted shrewdly how Whitefield was most happy in front of large crowds, while Wesley went round systematically to the "little places."[69] Perhaps the most characteristic image of the English movement is, not that of John Wesley preaching to great crowds in the sunken outdoor amphitheater at Gwennap in Cornwall, but Wesley as he is described in John Barrit's diary, standing in a barn with a knot of shabby people around him, explaining the love of God in the process of regeneration. Would they recognize the presence of God's love? Yes, they would. For how did wives and husbands recognize the love they bore each other, or children know that they were loved by their parents? They *felt* it in their hearts. And so too it would be with God's grace.[70]

Notes

1. *The Works of John Wesley,* vol. 26: *Letters II, 1740–1755,* ed. Frank Baker (Oxford: Oxford University Press; Nashville: Abingdon, 1982), 128. To date, only the first two volumes of Wesley's letters have appeared in this edition, covering the period 1721–55. Henceforth these will be referred to as *Letters,* ed. Baker. For letters written after 1755, I have used the Telford edition (1931); see n. 35 below.

2. See W. Reginald Ward, *The Protestant Evangelical Awakening* (Cambridge: Cambridge University Press, 1992), 2.

3. Ibid., 31–36.

4. *The Works of Jonathan Edwards,* vol. 4: *The Great Awakening,* ed. C. C. Goen (New Haven: Yale University Press, 1972), 216–17, citing William Cooper's preface to Edwards's *Distinguishing Marks of a Work of the Spirit of God.*

5. Michael J. Crawford, *Seasons of Grace: Colonial New England's Revival Tradition in Its British Context* (New York: Oxford University Press, 1991), 1–86.

6. Susan O'Brien, "A Transatlantic Community of Saints: The Great Awakening and the First Evangelical Network, 1735–1755," *American Historical Review* 91 (1986): 811–32.

7. See J. D. Walsh, "Origins of the Evangelical Revival," in *Essays in Modern English Church History in Memory of Norman Sykes,* ed. Gareth V. Bennett and John D. Walsh (New York: Oxford University Press, 1966), 141–48.

8. Edwards, *Works* 4:132 (preface by Isaac Watts and John Guyse to 1st ed. of *A*

Faithful Narrative of the Surprizing Work of God in Northampton in New England [1737]).

9. *Massachusetts Historical Society Proceedings,* 2d. ser., 9 (1895): 402.

10. *Howell Harris, Reformer and Soldier,* ed. Tom Beynon (Caernarvon: Calvinistic Methodist Bookroom, 1958), 80.

11. See, for example, the Cornish group described by George C. B. Davies, *The Early Cornish Evangelicals, 1735–1760* (London: SPCK, 1951), 31; also Walsh, "Origins of the Evangelical Revival," 134–38.

12. Wesley, *Letters,* ed. Baker, 25:526.

13. See Luke Tyerman, *The Oxford Methodists* (London: Hodder and Stoughton, 1873), 140–52.

14. See Michael Crawford, "Origins of the Eighteenth Century Evangelical Revival: England and New England Compared," *Journal of British Studies* 26 (1987): 361–97, for a valuable historiographic survey.

15. Walt W. Rostow, *The British Economy of the Nineteenth Century* (Oxford: Clarendon Press, 1948), 124.

16. *George Whitefield's Journals* (London: Banner of Truth, 1960), 462. Deist works were also circulating in America. See, for example, ibid., 451, where Whitefield reports a Charlestonian who "burnt near forty pounds' worth of books written by such authors as Chubb and Foster." For Tindal, see Robert E. Sullivan, *John Toland and the Deist Controversy* (Cambridge, MA: Harvard Historical Series, 1982).

17. Historical Manuscripts Commission, Manuscripts of the Earls of Egmont, *Diary of the First Earl of Egmont,* vol. 2: *1734–1738* (London: His Majesty's Stationery Office, 1923), 39.

18. Wesley, *Letters,* ed. Baker, 25:681.

19. *The Works of the Rev. William Law,* 9 vols. (Canterbury: G. Moreton, 1893), 7:153.

20. *The Works of John Wesley,* vol. 18: *Journals and Diaries I, 1735–1738,* ed. W. Reginald Ward and Richard P. Heitzenrater (Nashville: Abingdon, 1988), 24, 211; Wesley, *Letters,* ed. Baker, 25:284. See also Vivian H. H. Green, *The Young Mr. Wesley* (Longon: Arnold, 1961), 147–48.

21. [Joseph Trapp], *Thoughts upon the Four Last Things: A Poem in Four Parts* (London, 1734), Advertisement to the Reader.

22. Eveline Cruickshanks, *Political Untouchables: The Tories and the '45* (London: Duckworth, 1979), 48.

23. See Stephen Taylor, "Sir Robert Walpole, the Church of England, and the Quakers Tithe Bill of 1736," *Historical Journal* 28 (1985): 51–77; Norman Sykes, *Edmund Gibson, Bishop of London, 1669–1748* (Oxford: Oxford University Press, 1926), 148–82.

24. *Christian's Amusement* (London) 18 (1741): 4.

25. See Gareth V. Bennett, *The Tory Crisis in Church and State, 1688–1730* (Oxford: Clarendon Press, 1975).

26. See Alan D. Gilbert, *Religion and Society in Industrial England* (London: Longmans, 1976). For an example of clerical anxiety about industrial settlements, see Leonard W. Cowie, *Henry Newman, an American in London* (London, SPCK, 1956), 74.

27. Egmont, *Diary* 1:400.

28. For the "holy living" tradition, see John Spurr, *The Restoration Church of England, 1646–1689* (New Haven: Yale University Press, 1991), chap. 6. For its development by the Oxford Methodists, see *Diary of an Oxford Methodist, Benjamin*

Ingham, 1733–1734, ed. Richard P. Heitzenrater (Durham: Duke University Press, 1985), 12–38.

29. See Spurr, *Restoration Church of England,* 309: "Far from demoting religion to the mere pursuit of virtue, 'holy living' required a rigorous pursuit of Christian perfection while asserting the impossibility of overcoming sin."

30. See Stephen Hobhouse, *William Law and Eighteenth Century Quakerism* (London: George Allen and Unwin, 1927).

31. *The Works of the Rev. John Newton,* 6 vols., 2d ed. (London, 1816), 1:85.

32. Joseph Milner, *Works,* 8 vols. (London, 1812), 8:87–88, 190.

33. Henry Venn, *Mistakes in Religion Exposed: In an Essay on the Prophecy of Zacharias* (London, 1774), 64.

34. Newton, *Works* 1:357.

35. Wesley, *Letters,* ed. John Telford, 8 vols. (London: Epworth Press, 1931), 2:384.

36. Ibid. 6:61.

37. *The Works of John Wesley,* vol. 1: *Sermons I,* ed. Albert C. Outler (Nashville: Abingdon, 1984), 129.

38. *Whitefield's Journals,* 241.

39. Robert Seagrave, *Remarks on the Bishop of London's Pastoral Letter: In Vindication of Mr. Whitefield,* 2d ed. (London, 1739), 12.

40. *The Lives of the Early Methodist Preachers,* ed. Thomas Jackson (London: Wesleyan Conference Office, 1865), 1:185.

41. *Arminian Magazine* (London) 1 (1778):327.

42. *Wesley Historical Society Proceedings* (Burnley) 15 (1925–26):208.

43. See Gilbert, *Religion and Society,* 16.

44. See William H. Kenney, "George Whitefield, Dissenter Priest of the Great Awakening, 1739–1741," *William and Mary Quarterly* 26 (1969): 75–93.

45. *Wesley Historical Society Proceedings* 15:211–12.

46. John Wesley, *The Principles of a Methodist Farther Explained* (1746), in *The Works of John Wesley,* 14 vols. (London: Wesleyan Conference Office, 1872), 8:476.

47. Newton, *Works* 4:313.

48. *Whitefield's Journals,* 275.

49. See John D. Walsh, "Elie Halévy and the Birth of Methodism," *Transactions of the Royal Historical Society,* 5th ser., 25 (1975):7.

50. *Arminian Magazine* 12 (1789): 470–71.

51. *A Letter from a Private Person to his Pastor concerning the People called Methodists* (London, 1743), 16.

52. *Minutes of the Methodist Conference* (London: Wesleyan Conference Office, 1862), 9.

53. Charles Atmore, *The Methodist Memorial* (Bristol, 1801), 173.

54. Charles H. Crookshank, *History of Methodism in Ireland,* 3 vols. (Belfast: R. S. Allen, 1885), 1:57, 96, 142.

55. *The Works of John Wesley,* vol. 11: *The Appeals to Men of Reason and Religion,* ed. Gerald R. Cragg (Oxford: Clarendon Press, 1975), 316.

56. John Venn, *The Life and a Selection from the Letters of the late Rev. Henry Venn,* ed. Henry Venn (London: Hatchard, 1834), 41.

57. *The Works of John Wesley,* vol. 7: *A Collection of Hymns for the Use of the People Called Methodists,* ed. Franz Hildebrandt and Oliver O. Beckerlegge (Nashville: Abingdon, 1983), 82.

58. *The Poetical Works of John and Charles Wesley,* ed. George Osborn, 11 vols. (London: Wesleyan Methodist Conference Office, 1868–71), 8:348.

59. See Geraint H. Jenkins, *The Foundations of Modern Wales, 1642–1780* (Oxford: Clarendon Press, 1987), 347.

60. George Lavington, *The Enthusiasm of Methodists and Papists Compar'd* (London, 1749), preface to pt. 1.

61. See Alan M. Everett, *The Pattern of Rural Dissent: The Nineteenth Century* (Leicester: Leicester University Press, 1972); and Golbert, *Religion and Society,* 98–99.

62. In 1789 Wesley commented: "God has wrought in Scotland and New England, at several times, for some weeks or months together; but among us He has wrought for near 18 years together, without any observable intermission. Above all, let it be remarked that a considerable number of the regular clergy were engaged in that great work in Scotland; and in New England above a hundred, perhaps as eminent as any in the whole province . . . whereas in England there were only two or three inconsiderable clergymen, with a few young, raw, unlettered men; and these opposed by well nigh all the clergy, as well as laity, in the nation" (Wesley, *Journal,* ed. Nehemiah Curnock, 8 vols. [London: Epworth Press, 1938], 4:122). Jon Butler has stressed the modern and patchy influence of the Great Awakening itself, in his "Enthusiasm Described and Decried: the Great Awakening as Interpretive Fiction," *Journal of American History* 69 (1982): 305–25.

63. Wesley, *Works, Sermons II,* 2:494.

64. Crawford, *Seasons of Grace,* 165.

65. Wesley, *Letters,* ed. Telford, 6:151.

66. Ibid. 7:352.

67. Ibid., 182.

68. Wesley, *Works, Sermons II,* 2:491–93.

69. *Howell Harris's Visits to London,* ed. Tom Beynon (Aberystwyth: Cambrian New Press, 1960), 251.

70. MS diary of John Barrit, Archives of the Methodist Church, John Rylands Library, Manchester University.

2

Eighteenth-Century Publishing Networks in the First Years of Transatlantic Evangelicalism

SUSAN O'BRIEN

In 1739 Nicholas Gilman, pastor of Durham in New Hampshire, was greatly stirred by news of the religious revivals in the Middle Colonies. One of his immediate reactions was to engage in an intensive program of reading that lasted about two years. Through a particular selection of texts this New Light minister was transported into a world where conversions and awakenings were not only imperative but frequent and widespread. Time and place were telescoped for Gilman as he studied classic conversion-centered Puritan literature, newly penned revival sermons, and contemporary revival narratives from America, England, and Scotland. In January 1740 alone he read George Whitefield's *Journal, Life, Nine Sermons, Answer to the Bishop of London's Pastoral Letter,* and *Account of the Rise of the Methodists at Oxford,* along with writings by earlier divines John Flavel and Matthew Henry and copies of the *Boston Gazette* containing reports of the New England revival.[1] All this reading served only to stimulate Gilman's appetite for more of the same, and on a visit to Boston at the end of January he spent a further 26*s.* 6*d.* on "small books" at Daniel Henchman's bookstore.[2] The small books were unspecified, but their type can be sensibly adduced from the detailed notes he kept. For the first time in his life Gilman read such Puritan classics as Joseph Alleine's *Alarme to the Unconverted* (1641) and Thomas Shepard's *Sincere Convert* (1641) and *Sound Believer* (1648), describing the last work as "an excellent performance which I don't know that I ever heard of till lately at Boston." Of the works of William Law, Richard Baxter, Solomon Stoddard, and James Jennings, he noted, "God in his Providence has deliver'd me to some excellent treatises."[3] He was eager to buy or borrow anything by the two leading contemporary revival preachers, Jonathan Edwards or George Whitefield, and as soon as the revivals began to produce their own newspaper and magazine literature, Gilman acquired these too. By October 1742 he was familiar with the narrative of conversions at Cambuslang in Scotland through the

Glasgow Weekly History, an evangelical newspaper, and in 1743 he obtained copies of revival magazines produced in Boston and Edinburgh.[4] He was thereby provided with detailed accounts of awakenings throughout the revival world.

The content of this literature traveled various routes out of Gilman's study to the people of Durham. At first it seems to have been simply filtered through his own preaching and conversation. But from November 1741 onward, people came in large numbers (not always invited) to frequent meetings at their pastor's house asking for public readings from revival literature. Readings from Edwards's sermons and his Northampton *Narrative* played a particularly important part in triggering mass revival in Durham in late November and early December 1741.[5] In addition Gilman turned his own collection into a public lending library for the seriously concerned, carefully recording, for example, that Sister Susannah borrowed *God's Gracious Dealings with Mrs. White* and "Mother Thing took home Edwards on Northampton."[6]

Not all ministers were in a position to afford the extensive library developed by Gilman over such a short period, and perhaps not all would have been so generous with its contents. Yet Durham's experience is only an intensified version of what occurred in many places on both sides of the Atlantic. Rev. Henry Davidson of Galashiels, Scotland, for example, labeled himself an "omne-gatherum of pamphlets." In *Letters to Christian Friends* he described how he kept himself and others in touch with the latest events in America and England as well as Scotland, despite the fact that he was impoverished and isolated.[7] He cultivated fruitful correspondences with Thomas Davidson, minister of the Scots congregation at Braintree in Essex, England, and with William Hogg, a wealthy Edinburgh merchant committed to the revival. Hogg in turn had contacts with Whitefield's London Tabernacle and received American letters coming into London, as well as those arriving in Scotland. One of Henry Davidson's greatest sources of comfort was news of revivals "in the West."[8]

Gilman and Henry Davidson were representative of people who lived on the periphery of the eighteenth-century British Empire yet could still think and act within an Atlantic world. During the headiest years of the revival—1740 to 1745—ministers, revival activists, and the converted could all place themselves within an international movement by reading, writing, listening, and talking. Indeed, as the revival progressed, the flow of news and accounts made it difficult for readers to see what was periphery and what was center. Some places, such as Northampton, Massachusetts, and Cambuslang, Scotland, did occupy a special place in the topography of revivalism, but there was also a lively sense, as Jonathan Edwards wrote to one of his Scottish correspondents, that "the Church of God, in all Parts of the World, is but one. The distant members are closely united in one Glorious Head. This Union is very much her Beauty."[9] This sense of union was created by a number of forces, partly ideological, partly personnal, and partly commercial. It could not have worked without a shared theology of conversion; nor would it would have existed to anything like the same degree without the itinerancy of George

Whitefield. But it was made effective and given reality by the development of advertising, publishing, and distribution networks that crisscrossed the Atlantic Ocean and reached thousands of people.

I

Until recently historians of the Great Awakening, the Cambuslang "Wark," and the Calvinist Methodist revival in England and Wales paid scant attention to the processes that lay behind the exchanges of books and pamphlets across the Atlantic, or the meanings they may have had. A large gap opened up in the historiography between the earliest historians of the revival, who were participant-observers and keen to emphasize the widespread "stirring of dry bones,"[10] and many later professional historians, who became increasingly immersed in national, denominational, or local histories.[11] Those who attempted to bridge the gap tended to be either evangelical historians writing in the spirit of the earlier tradition, but without detail or fresh interpretation, or biographers of George Whitefield who could hardly avoid a transatlantic setting but did not necessarily do very much with it.[12] Exceptionally, as in Clarence Goen's contribution to the Yale collected works of Jonathan Edwards, the sinews of the transatlantic revival were laid bare.[13]

So negligible was the influence of the wider perspective that Jack Bumsted, in a 1969 survey of recent literature on the revival, concluded that the Great Awakening "has typically been reviewed as part of a religious readjustment in splendid isolation on this continent."[14] For Bumsted, the trend toward increasingly specialist local studies was fragmenting the larger, comparative picture he believed more likely to yield insights and less likely to mislead colonial scholars into exclusively American explanations. In fact, the localism of revival studies simply matched the overall thrust of colonial history from the 1950s to 1970s, which was seeking "to recover the the context and texture of colonial life" through concentration "upon smaller and smaller units."[15] Apart from those studying royal government and administration, the imperial focus was lost. In a more recent reflection on this postwar historiography, Timothy Breen selected Richard Hofstadter's *America at 1750* (1971) as representative. According to Breen, Hofstadter "provided a thorough analysis of demographic and religious trends in eighteenth-century America, but nowhere in this valuable little book can the reader find a sustained discussion of the links that bound the colonies to the mother country, indeed of what it meant to them to be members of a transatlantic empire."[16] For the record, one should note that there was little discussion of what membership of a transatlantic empire meant to those living in the mother country. The revival there was most often seen through the lenses of competing denominational interests or as a chapter in the emergence of an English working class with an increasingly contested meaning.[17] A further stumbling block to a broader revival history has been the Englishness of much "British" history. While the "thorough analyses" of social structure, demographic trends, and the like have been invaluable to our understanding of the forms and variations of the revival on both sides of the Atlantic, a new look at Anglo-American relations in the eighteenth century was due.

The historiographic contexts for this refocussing are twofold. One lies in the interpretation of rituals, symbols, and mental worlds and makes use of the insights of anthropologists and ethnographers. It has promoted recognition of continuities between Old and New World cultures.[18] The other, which is more directly relevant to the discussion here, is the vigorous research into material culture, including print culture—books and pamphlets as well as pots and nails—and the emphasis on a consumer revolution in the eighteenth century. Between the 1740s and 1770s England and her colonies were bound together in an "empire of goods," in Timothy Breen's phrase.[19] These twin emphases on symbols and "things," and the relationships between them, are leading to a revisionist imperial history. If it develops as Breen recommends, it will concentrate "on common folk rather than on colonial administrators, on processes rather than institutions, on aspects of daily life that one would not regard as narrowly political." The new imperial story, he suggests, "will be an integrated story, neither American nor English but an investigation of the many links that connected men and women living on both sides of the Atlantic Ocean."[20] Recent work on eighteenth-century evangelicalism both belongs to and is helping shape the new imperial history and our understanding of an emerging consumer society.

II

In an earlier study, prior to the most recent developments outlined above, I attempted to demonstrate that "through an exchange of ideas and materials Calvinist revivalists in the eighteenth century built a 'community of saints' that cut across physical barriers."[21] Once the structure and operation of the community was established, it was possible to see how it was used. At the most basic level the movement's internationalism was a source of inspiration and millennialist speculation. Additionally, it was an instrument in the development and comunication of revival techniques and strategies. The significance of this analysis was to reduce the distance between so-called spontaneous eighteenth-century transatlantic revivals and those of the nineteenth, generally seen as becomingly increasingly "managed" and commercial.

This work attempted to show how a transatlantic revival was created from a web of personal correspondence that was rapidly transformed into a large-scale media through the establishment of evangelical magazines and newspapers, whose main diet was reprinted letters and revival narratives.[22] In addition, the role of printed sermons, theological discussions, and polemical essays, particularly those written by or about Jonathan Edwards or George Whitefield, was seen as highly significant in the creation of a community.[23] But even though it showed the existence of a transatlantic revival through networks and shared literature and suggested that "ministers and those in the book trade developed methods of large scale distribution which were novel for the middle-eighteenth century,"[24] this research did not integrate its findings into any larger explanation of mid-eighteenth-century society and culture.

More recently Frank Lambert and Harry Stout have reexamined the workings of the revival in the context of a burgeoning Anglo-American consumer society.[25] The results have been enlightening, both about transatlantic evangelicalism and about the diffusion of a new commercialism. Religion and commerce are shown to have been partners in the creation of a transatlantic revival, and the revival was an early instance of the narrowing gap between colonies and mother country taking place between the 1730s and 1760s. Ironically, at least for one who attempted to demonstrate that the transatlantic revival was about more than George Whitefield, these two studies mark a reemphasis on the activities of the evangelist. But this time it is a Whitefield described and analyzed as a "pedlar in divinity," adept at promotion and advertising "puffs," successfully marketing himself and all his works—oratorical and written. The revised Whitefield is, among other things, an entrepreneur who uses the language of commerce and can strike the right kind of bargain with newspaper editors and publishers. Whitefield broke with convention by taking religion to the marketplace and offering it to a mass audience. In their turn, the converted and the unregenerate can be seen as consumers who come to the marketplace. Here they had choices put before them and out of their choices could create their own identity—in this case, a spiritual one. Not only was there no conflict of interest for Whitefield between religion and commerce, but he embraced the opportunity offered by the marketplace and market forces to break with old hierarchies, monopolies, and identities.[26] This new perspective is essential to an understanding of the transatlantic revival, but I would like to suggest three refinements, all of which are concerned to restate the importance of ideology and residual cultures.

First, Whitefield's itinerancy, ceaseless attention to publicity, and shrewd business decisions explained the growth of communications out from the existing Dissenting network and its ability to reach a mass audience. Yet by themselves they cannot explain why the strongest bonds in the transatlantic revival were not with England, Whitefield's native land, or Georgia, his adopted home, but between Scotland and New England. To understand this connection we need to give due weight to the theological discourse and culture of Calvinism. The language of the transatlantic revival was the language of covenant, conversion, and New Birth, and the attempt to build a community worked best where this language could be employed and understood.[27]

Second, to identify a relationship between revival events and the development of mass marketing allows us to appreciate better the innovations within evangelicalism in this period, such as the penny magazines and the theatricality of field preaching. But it is also essential to evaluate the significance of evangelical Calvinist theology and culture in this relationship. According to historians of print culture, the 1740s was the key transitional decade between an older informal face-to-face publishing world and a more integrated market with new trade strategies.[28] In such a transitional period attention should be paid to the part played by evangelical traditions and predispositions. Not every religious tradition was so well adapted to the possibilities and demands of large-scale print culture, for example. And not all traditions placed such weight on the value of networking or exploited its possibilities so assiduously. Some religious groups were more likely to maximize the new opportunities presented by mass communication than others.

Finally, enthusiasm for the discovery of what is new may lead to an under-valuing of continuities, particularly in terms of the distribution of print culture of a religious type. The Anglo-American book trade was indeed being trans-formed into an "impersonal and ideologically neutral mode of transaction" in the eighteenth century,[29] but to what extent was this really true of the distribu-tion of religious literature in the 1740s? It seems premature to push the changes in the book trade back to the 1740s, and we must therefore look for other distribution methods. I would suggest that we find them within the evangelical subculture itself.

III

With all this in mind, we can return to Nicholas Gilman's library to explore how such a collection might have been put together and what might be learned from it about transatlantic publishing and the revival. Though Gilman was an unusual bibliophile, his reading is a window into the literature of the transatlantic revival and was fully representative of the range and authorship of print material available. Its contents fall into three main types: works from the past in the Reformed and Puritan traditions, sermons and discursive writ-ing generated as part of the current revival, and revival news. How did the revival generate these particular types of literature, in terms of both their mental and material production? What value did each have to the revival? How transatlantic was the production and consumption of each type?

An early step for many "seekers" and newly awakened was to familiarize themselves with the literature of the Reformed and Puritan traditions, or at least with works emphasizing personal experience and conversion. As a result, works first printed in the seventeenth century, which had continued to be, as David Hall has shown, the steady sellers of the late seventeenth- and early eighteenth-century Anglo-American book trade, became highly important once again.[30]

This is not to argue that pastors and people turned to this literature simply because there were insufficient alternatives. On the contrary, they continued to buy them in increased numbers, even when there were newer revival works available. In 1743, for example, William McCrea, a shopkeeper in White Clay Creek, ordered from his supplier "30 copies of Bunyan on Two Covenants, 2 dozen 'Sincere Converts,' 11 Alarme's, 8 Baxter's Call," and many other seventeenth-century works as well as contemporary works by Edwards, the Erskines, John Willison, and Charles Chauncy.[31] Ordinary people as well as pastors confirmed that earlier piety suited their state of mind and met their emotional needs, and a number of titles were referred to so consistently by

44   *Origins*

revivalists in Britain and America that they composed what might be called a common or shared pool of reading.[32]

Ministers played a large part in creating this consensus through repeated direct reference and through their influence on printers. Whitefield took it on himself to compile a list of basic reading for "seekers" that advertised in the London evangelical magazine and in the *Charleston Gazette*.[33] But consumers were part of the equation too and influenced printers and booksellers through their purchasing power. The results were striking. In the experience of Daniel Rogers, a tutor at Harvard, "There is a new face upon Things. Stoddard and Shephard [*sic*] are the Books now; little did I think this when you recommended them."[34] According to Samuel Davies in Virginia, "Such were awakened, as they told me, either by their own serious reflections . . . or on reading some authors of the last century, such as Boston, Baxter, Flavel, Bunyan etc, and they often wondered if there were such doctrines taught anywhere in the world at present as they found in the writings of these good men."[35] On both sides of the Atlantic, readers greeted with enthusiasm works of piety such as *The Experiences of God's Gracious Dealings with Mrs. Elizabeth White as they were written down in her Own Hand* . . . (1699) and praised them for the comfort they gave.[36]

The relevance of Puritan literature, coupled with recommendations from ministers, created a thriving reprinting industry. To some extent this operated on a transatlantic basis, with London imprints being exported to the colonies. Given the nature of the mid-eighteenth-century book trade, this commerce was inevitable.[37] But from the point of view of the transatlantic revival, it is probably more important to emphasize the idea of a common fund of reading that spanned the Atlantic and led to the reprinting and reading of the same works on both sides. As Welsh itinerant preacher Howell Harris wrote to a Scottish correspondent, "We all agree with the Good old orthodox reformers and puritans."[38] Thomas Prince, Jr., of Boston noted in his revival account (reprinted in Scotland) that "the People seemed to have a renewed Taste for those old Pious and Experimental writers: Mr. Hooker, Mr. Shepard, Guthrie, Alleine . . . The evangelical writings of these deceased Authors, as well as of others alive, both in England, Scotland, and New England, [are] now read with singular Pleasure: some of them reprinted and in great numbers quickly bought and studied."[39] Alleine's *Alarme to the Unconverted,* the single most influential work, was reprinted in large print runs in Boston, Philadelphia, London, and Glasgow.[40] In 1742 Boston bookseller and printer Daniel Henchman recorded that he paid a bill with Green, Bushell and Allen, another firm of Boston printers, by printing two thousand copies of Shepard's *Sound Believer.* In 1743 he did the same by reprinting two thousand copies of Hooker's *Doctrine of Christ* and an equal number of the *Marrow of Modern Divinity,* while William Bradford of Philadelphia printed a thousand copies of a Flavel sermon for Samuel Hazard, a local merchant.[41] Further evidence of the popularity of these works can be found in auction catalogs and booksellers' records. Both Henchman and Philadelphia printer William Bradford sold Puritan works that do not seem to have been reprinted in the colonial printshops. Many would have been imported from Britain, but possibly some were old stock or had been bought secondhand. There was certainly a thriving secondhand book trade, which the increased demand for older texts may have stimulated.

IV

As the revival got into its stride, the reprinting of older material began to be matched and then surpassed by newly written literature. Both supporters and detractors of the revival took to their pens. "The presses are ever teeming with books and the women with bastards," complained Timothy Cutler, Anglican minister for the Society of the Propagation of the Gospel in Boston, to a friend in London.[42] In Cutler's eyes the awakening had encouraged an outpouring of uncontrolled passions—hence his inference that it had resulted in an excess of babies as well as printed material, both equally unwanted and squalling. There was widespread agreement among contemporaries that the revival has produced a deluge of literature. Even prorevivalists expressed alarm about the distracting effects so much print might have on ordinary people. In the opinion of the dean of Edinburgh's Chapel Royal, for example, "These trifling pamphlets fill the heads and mouths of too many."[43] What the views of such social conservatives show, whether opposers or supporters of the revival, was an understanding of the mass basis of revival printing and book buying. There was an implicit assumption in their fears that ordinary people could afford to buy some of this literature and were sufficiently literate to read it, an assumption amply borne out by all studies of revival participants.[44]

Historians have also confirmed the impressions of contemporaries that the presses were indeed teeming with new revival literature.[45] Almost all these publications found their way across the Atlantic through evangelical networks. In 1743 James Robe in Edinburgh counted the number of separate publications sent from America to Scotland and found thirty supporting the revival and only six against. By the same year at least one copy of all Scottish revival publications had been sent by John Erskine in Edinburgh to William Cooper in Boston,[46] and it seems likely that Jonathan Edwards and Thomas Prince, Sr., also had comprehensive collections. A core of ten ministers—Edwards, Colman, and Prince, Sr., in New England; McCulloch, Robe, Gillies and McLaurin in Scotland; and Watts, Whitefield, and Doddridge—had created a complex interlocking web of correspondence. Other ministers, financial supporters, lay exhorters, booksellers, and printers could tap into this entire network if they had only one correspondent who was linked to it, and in this way literature was made available for private circulation and reprinting either whole or in part.

The new revival literature can be divided into the two types already mentioned: sermons and essays on the one hand, and revival news on the other. The former might be represented by Samuel Finley's *Christ Triumphant* or Jonathan Edwards's *Religious Affections,* and the latter by Edwards's *Faithful Narrative of the Surprizing Work of God . . . in Northampton,* George Whitefield's *Journals,* and the evangelical magazines edited from London, Boston, Glasgow, and Edinburgh. It is tempting to characterize the two types as *savante* and *populaire,* highbrow and lowbrow. Most authors published writing in both categories, however, and many readers and listeners consumed both. Certainly *everyone* read or heard the news. The two categories are useful in indicating the differing purposes behind different kinds of writing. These differences in turn can be linked to the scale of sales and to the degree of internationalism achieved.

Few exegetical sermons, other than those by Whitefield and Edwards, enjoyed more than a regional market, although individual copies were frequently circulated through the correspondence networks.[47] There were occasional exceptions, such as Samuel Finley's *Christ Triumphant* and Benjamin Colman's *Souls Flying to Jesus Christ,* which were originally delivered to important meetings convened in Boston in 1741 and promptly reprinted by Methodist publisher Samuel Mason in London. Mason in turn circulated fifty copies of each to his Edinburgh bookseller, who wrote that he had disposed of them and could sell more if they were to arrive before Whitefield left Scotland.[48] Sermons by Scottish ministers Ebenezer Erskine and John Willison were widely available in the colonies, but in general new sermons did not travel well and were either privately printed or printed by subscription.[49] Only the attraction of a big name could sell sermons on a large scale to a transatlantic market, and it is this factor that gives George Whitefield such primacy in any measurement of the role of sermons in the transatlantic revival.[50]

Polemical works, some originally delivered as sermons, many written as open letters, fared much better in a transatlantic context. The exchanges between Whitefield and Tillotson, the Archbishop of London, were distributed widely, as were the hard-hitting debates between pro and antirevivalists in New England. James Robe noted that three colonial antirevival publications had been reprinted in Scotland.[51] According to John Erskine, these had been "reprinted with a View to expose the Work carried on in New England and to prejudice the people against that in the West of Scotland."[52] Several other pieces were sent from New England by disaffected or critical Congregational ministers, usually to members of the Scottish Associate Presbytery, whose opposition was well known, and to moderates within the church. Rev. Charles Chauncy, New England's most effective critic of the revival, sent literature over to his correspondents in Scotland, with the result, as James Robe informed Jonathan Edwards, that "the most unseasonable accounts from America, the most scurrilous and bitter pamphlets, and representations from mistaking brethren, were much and zealously propagated."[53]

Charles Chauncy, who wrote his first critique in the form of an open letter to a friend in Edinburgh, thought it vital to disillusion those who had been misled into glorifying events in New England.[54] His letter took for granted British familiarity with New England affairs and aimed to counterbalance the positive picture given by the revivalists with a description of the awakening as chaotic and ungodly, its leaders as ignorant and hysterical men of "very narrow minds and great Bigotry."[55] He hoped to "correct the same follies and superstitions, which are getting too much Footing amongst us, by representing many Inconveniences and Disorders which ensued upon like Methods of teaching abroad."[56] The letter showed an intimate knowledge of what had been circulating in Britain concerning New England and focused its attack precisely on what was familiar and known to British readers. Altogether it was a powerful piece, and the speed with which George Whitefield and John McLaurin responded indicated how seriously they took the attack.[57] But the best defense, the Scots agreed, came from Jonathan Edwards. New England was locked in serious conflict for the soul of Scotland, and it seems reasonable to conclude that ministers, at least, were versed in the literature of argument produced on both sides of the Atlantic and that a wider circle read debates conducted in the form of open letters.[58]

The most widely read and disseminated new literature of the transatlantic revival was not the sermon or the polemical or theological treatise but reportage. Revival news-telling came in a variety of forms: individual testimony, revival narrative, mission journals, printed correspondence, and evangelical magazines. Some, such as the personal testimony of a pious individual, had established Puritan credentials. Others, including revival narratives and personal journals written for publication, were developed in the 1730s and 1740s from an existing genre. In the case of the evangelical magazine the form was pioneered during the revival and was one of the most striking innovations of eighteenth-century evangelicalism. What they all had in common was immediacy, a firm basis in personal or collective experience, engagement with the material details of everyday life, and action. Revival news made transatlantic evangelicalism an exciting reality for ordinary men and women and emphasized the significance of their own participation in an international movement.

Much of the credit for these developments in eighteenth-century evangelical publishing has gone to George Whitefield because of his ability to write in a range of journalistic voices for a mass audience and with a journalist's sensitivity to timing and speed. Perhaps the best example of these qualities is to be found in the seven *Journals* brought out between 1738 and 1741 as a record of his missionary travels to and around the colonies and throughout Britain. Although the first journal had not been written for publication and was originally printed without Whitefield's knowledge, he was quick to learn from its widespread success on both sides of the Atlantic. In the *Journals* and parallel *Accounts* of his early life, Whitefield combined elements of the Puritan conversion story and revival narrative with several eighteenth-century genres, including the travelogue and the adventure story told in the first person singular. Together these elements created a literature that was popular and accessible and that brought evangelical writing into the most contemporary of modes.

The same can be said for the establishment of revival magazines in London, Glasgow, Boston, and Edinburgh in the period 1740 to 1748. To a later society the religious periodical press seemed both inevitable and necessary. As the preface to the first edition of the British *Evangelical Magazine* said in 1793, "Thousands read a Magazine who have neither money to purchase, nor leisure to puruse, large volumes. It is therefore a powerful engine in the moral world."[59] By the middle nineteenth century the number of distinct religious magazines on both sides of the Atlantic was vast. But it was a pioneering venture when mid-eighteenth-century evangelicals launched magazines to carry revival news and articles for serious Christians. These short-lived experiments were at one and the same time a significant development in the history of evangelicalism and an integral part of the transatlantic revival.

The idea for a Christian and evangelical magazine originated with printer John Lewis, a Welshman who had moved to London and set up a printshop. By 1740 he was attending the Methodist tabernacle and the society at Fetter Lane, aligning himself with the Calvinist tendency and against the Arminian and Moravian groupings in the English revival community. As a printer, bookseller, and publisher as well as a committed evangelical, Lewis brought his professional expertise to bear on the religious publishing scene, and he became enthusiastic about the possibilities of a Christian magazine, although he received little encouragement and a good deal of opposition from other Methodists.[60] In September 1740 he launched the *Christian's Amusement,* a four-page weekly penny paper.[61] Its title reflects Lewis's intention to provide a new kind of reading matter for the "children of God," something that was spelled out in more detail by one of his correspondents: "Shall the polite world have their Spectators, Tatlers, Guardians and comedies? Shall the curious have his daily and weekly news, his Advertiser, Gazeteer, Miscellany? and shall the children of God also have their weekly amusement, the Divine Miscellany and historical account of the progress of their Lord's Kingdom?"[62] His second aim, as the full title suggests, was to follow "the Progress of the Gospel both at Home and Abroad" by means of printing letters and accounts from preachers, including correspondence from Whitefield, who was in the colonies.

The *Christian's Amusement* continued in print for six months before it was suspended in order to be adopted and relaunched by George Whitefield directly on his return from the colonies. The paper had experienced a number of problems, chief of which were an insufficient supply of news and an inadequate distribution network. But it had also shown the way forward for an evangelical periodical press. The periodical format, the setting of the price low enough to reach a lower-class readership, and the method of obtaining news through letters and society accounts provided models for future ventures. The problems that had dogged Lewis presented no difficulties for Whitefield, who recognized the potential of the *Christian's Amusement* and was ideally situated to develop and reshape it. Lewis continued to print the new paper and to act as nominal editor, but its real focus was clearly indicated in the new title—*The Weekly History; or, An Account of the Most Remarkable Particulars Relating to the Present Progress of the Gospel. By the Encouragement of the Rev. Mr. Whitefield.* The editor promised "not to put in things of my own head, but to submit (as a Professor ought) to my Spiritual Directors," and readers were informed that every week the paper would contain fresh news supplied by Whitefield.[63]

In fact, many early issues were full of news and letters from the American colonies, dating from Whitefield's tour in the winter of 1740. Such items were not recent but were new to the readers and served Whitefield's purpose in drawing attention to the breadth of the revival. Up-to-date American correspondence was included, as were advertisements for American books.[64] Occasionally in the first months of publication the *Weekly History* was wholly given over to American news. But by the summer of 1742 the news from Scotland was the most dramatic and exciting in the revival world, and letters poured in. Since the state of religion in the colonies was also referred to in American correspondence, and vice versa, the paper began to reflect the complex corresponding network as it developed. A third, steady, and increasingly important source of information, encouraged by John Lewis, came in the reports from circuit preachers in England and Wales and helped to secure the paper's identity as the public mouthpiece of the Calvinist Methodist movement.[65]

The London papers were circulated among revival ministers in America and Scotland, where they were also recognized as valuable, both for the part they could play in furthering the revivals, and as a way of communicating joint ventures and sharing news. If imitation is the hallmark of a successful product, then the advent of two Scottish revival magazines and an American one is an indication of the value attached to the format. With these additions transatlantic revivalism and publishing reached a peak in 1742 and 1743. Copy for each paper consisted of a mixture of fresh material and reprints from one of the other papers, with the balance being largely determined by the pace of the revival and the precise aims of the editor. The first six months of the *Glasgow Weekly History,* for example, reprinted selections from the London paper. Its editor, William McCulloch, had added a subtitle to the paper signaling that it was "a Collection of Letters partly reprinted from the London-Weekly-History." Because he was working from a backlog of papers, McCulloch was able to rearrange and consolidate the revival story to create a narrative of some considerable length.[66] From May 1742 onward, he was able to print firsthand news of the Scottish revival and so dropped the word "reprinted" from the masthead.[67]

Letters made up about 80 percent of the total content of twelve months' publication, with the reprinting of ten conversion narratives from Kilsyth also making a major contribution to the paper's composition. Beyond his interests in the most recent news and in conversion-centered writings, McCulloch showed a particular concern to stress the general and widespread nature of the revival. There was information about the awakenings in Holland and in some of the German pietist churches, which came through correspondence between Scottish ministers and the Reverend Hugh Kennedy of the Scottish Church in Rotterdam. McCulloch reprinted Kennedy's preface to a Dutch translation of the *Kilsyth Narrative* in which Kennedy emphasized the internationalism of the revival.[68] Over 20 percent of the items came from America, while many others seem to have been selected for the references they made to revivalism in the colonies. Given the strength of networking between New England and Scotland, McCulloch had ample firsthand news to select from.

A weekly paper was a considerable project for a minister such as

McCulloch to add to his duties. Cambuslang was no sleepy rural parish, and McCulloch had an exacting summer in the Communion season of 1742. When he decided to discontinue the paper in December of that year, he told his printer that it had become difficult to find sufficient materials now that the Scottish and American awakenings had passed their peak. Perhaps McCulloch believed that the paper had served its purpose, which, so far as he was concerned, was to reflect the widespread nature of the awakening and to emphasize the themes of millennialism and conversion in order to encourage and promote more of the same. Although McCulloch's precise reasoning is unknown, it is worth noting that by the start of 1743 the London paper had become more of an institutional organ of English Calvinist Methodism, and the two papers that were begun in 1743 in Boston and Edinburgh were periodicals rather than newspapers.[69]

The editors of the Boston and Edinburgh magazines were more self-consciously editors than Lewis or McCulloch and styled themselves historians of the revival. The Reverend Thomas Prince, Sr. (the real editor of the *Christian History* behind his son the Reverend Thomas Prince, Jr.), and Rev. James Robe, editor of the Edinburgh *Christian Monthly History,* were situated differently from Lewis and McCulloch in several respects. Both were established and accomplished writers; they were able to stand back and judge the earliest papers, and they were conscious that the revival had moved into a different phase by 1743. The awakening was now seen as less problematic and more in need of defense. Above all, however, because they could sense that the moment was passing, Prince and Robe wished their magazines to capture it and provide a record. Robe, who described himself as "a faithful Historian,"[70] had a trio of aims: to leave a record to posterity, to maintain the community of sincere Christians in present times, and to encourage further conversions and sustain those already converted.[71] Thomas Prince had expressed very similar aims six months earlier when the first edition of his *Christian History* had appeared and Robe had received copies of it.

These were magazines—weekly in one case and monthly in the other—written with a view to permanence. It was hoped that purchasers would collect them and have them bound together to form an accurate history of events. Because of their goals the content was sifted, sorted, and presented thematically. Correspondents were informed about the importance of providing accurate and attested information. Dates, numbers, places, and names were to be verifiable.[72] Both papers lived up to their advertised intention to give "Accounts of the Revival and Propogation of Religion in Great Britain and America." Whereas only one-fifth of the total letters printed in the Edinburgh paper were Scottish and fifteen issues were given over to American material, almost one-third of Prince's Boston paper was taken up with news and articles from Scotland, including twenty-two issues devoted to the Scottish revival.

The editors of all these papers clearly relied on the exchange of personal letters, books, and pamphlets between all parts of the revival world. Since letters so often became publications, and printed works were often reprinted whole or in parts, this entire exchange became a public duty undertaken by correspondents for the sake of the revival. Thomas Prince contacted John Lewis in the summer of 1743 to ask for a correspondence with him, mainly in order to arrange an exchange of literature, including their respective magazines. A regular and purposeful correspondence existed between the editors. When a packet from Prince to McCulloch went astray, he replaced it immediately and was concerned to sort out the error. In the missing parcel he had sent "*The Christian History* Nos 1–15; *Advice of the County of Hampshire Churches: Declaration concerning Mr. Davenport; a letter from Scotland printed here in Octo; a Testimony to our Little Convention; Mr. Moorhead's Poetical Address to Mr. Davenport;* Mr. Dickenson's *Display;* Mr. Edwards' Book; the *Boston Evening Post* of May 16."[73] It was his intention, he told McCulloch, to send him "a constant supply of our *Christian History*," including any back copies he had missed. In return he was grateful for the copies of the Glasgow *Weekly History* McCulloch had sent him.

Records afford only glimpses of the circulation and distribution of the magazines, but they are sufficient to affirm the widespread transference of news and information between preachers and leaders, and through them to ordinary men and women. Lewis had distributed his original paper through hawkers, but it seems that the revival's own networks proved to be more effective than commercial ones. The London paper, for example, was distributed via the Methodist societies. In 1747 the London Tabernacle leaders agreed to take 400 copies of the paper from John Lewis at "bookseller's price." Then 150 were to be sent to a Mr. Kennedy at Exeter, 60 to Plymouth, 80 to Alderman Harris at Gloucester, 50 to Mr. Pearsal in Birmingham, 40 to Portsmouth, and the remainder to go to the London Tabernacle for distribution in the Home Counties.[74] Howell Harris acted as distributor for the *Weekly History* in Wales and built up an impressive list of subscribers.[75] Robe needed 400 subscribers for the *Christian Monthly History* before he would proceed, but the paper was also sold by agents, usually ministers, in Glasgow, Aberdeen, Dundee, Dumfries, Biggar, Perth, and Stirling.[76] Although these magazines had all ceased publication by 1748, they were to great significance to the transatlantic revival.

V

This survey of literature and publishing in the Evangelical Revival of the middle eighteenth century has sought to show what kind of print culture was produced by the transatlantic revival and how it was shared between Calvinist evangelicals in the English-speaking world and even beyond. I have argued implicitly and explicitly that the traditions and subculture of evangelicalism were vital for such a transfer of literature. Advertising and publicity were of increasing importance, but ministers were still the crucial reference point for the printer and consumer. The marketplace was where most revival literature was bought and sold, but there continued to be a place for noncommercial transactions such as the charitable interventions by evangelical sponsors who paid for literature to be given away or the creation of lending libraries by ministers. Some publishing ventures, such as Lewis's *Christian Amusement,* were acts of faith, not business, and lost money for a period. Publishing was too much a part of evangelism to be left simply to commerce. In the crucial matter of distribution, where so much was changing in the eighteenth century, the subculture of evangelicalism played a vital role alongside the growing capabilities of the commercial empire. Fellowship, fraternal correspondence, and the concept of the community of saints were of particular importance in sustaining a publishing network. It is in this context that the links between Scotland and New England, the strongest of the transatlantic revival, can be explained.

This religious publishing network in turn benefited from the application of new commercial techniques such as advertising and from new types of publishing such as magazine and newspaper literature. The lowered costs of much of the literature combined with the greater spending power enjoyed by many people put this literature within the realm of the possible for many of the converted. As a result, knowledge of a widespread revival could be gained directly either through personal reading or by listening to readings or indirectly through the sermons and conversation of revival leaders.

All of this is not to say that there was complete understanding within the revival world. Colonists, for example, continued to be mystified by the opposition of the Erskine brothers, whose hymns were widely sung by the pious in America, even when it had been explained to them by Scots revival ministers. Nor were the finer (or tougher) points of disagreement among New England Congregationalists really appreciated in Britain. It was easier to caricature a Charles Chauncy than to understand his principled and closely argued opposition. Nor were the complex details of division and disagreement within early English evangelicalism of much interest to outsiders, no matter how vital they were to insiders. Leaders in the Calvinist evangelical community were aware of all these differences, because they were fought out through the written word. But what they most wanted from the publishing network was a sense of the shared. Because the idea of a widespread work of God mattered greatly in itself, the transatlantic publishing network served the community best when it acted as a magnifying glass. For a short period this glass reflected an image of a united evangelical community and a special providence of God operating on a large scale.

Notes

1. Nicholas Gilman MS diary, New Hampshire Historical Society. See also W. Kidder, "Nicholas Gilman, Radical New Light" (M.A. thesis, University of New Hampshire, 1972).
   2. Gilman diary, 28 January 1740.
   3. Ibid., 17 November 1741.
   4. Ibid, 19 October 1742.

5. Gilman received a copy of *Sinners in the Hands of an Angry God* on 13 November 1741. At that stage there had been no general awakening in Durham. He began to read aloud from Edwards: "In the Evening tho' Dark and Dirty a throng of people assembled at my House to hear Mr. Edwards' *Narrative* of Conversions at Northampton" (20 November 1741). By 6 December he was writing of "great out-crying and anguish," and by 10 December that "numbers awakened daily."

6. For a list of the books borrowed by Gilman, and by whom, see Susan Durden [O'Brien], "Transatlantic Communications and Influence during the Great Awakening: A Comparative Study of British and American Revivalism, 1730–1760" (Ph.D. diss., University of Hull, 1978), Appendix 4.

7. Henry Davidson, *Letters to Christian Friends* (Edinburgh, 1811), 43 and elsewhere.

8. Ibid., 58.

9. James Robe, ed., *Christian Monthly History* (Edinburgh, 1745), vol. 2, no. 8, p. 235.

10. For example, Thomas Prince and James Robe, whose contributions are discussed below, and John Gillies, *Historical Collections relating to remarkable periods of the success of the Gospel, and eminent Instruments employed in promoting it,* 2 vols. (Glasgow, 1754). In addition to the *Historical Collections,* Gillies edited *Appendix to the Historical Collections . . .* (Glasgow, 1761) and *A Supplement to the Historical Collections . . .* (Glasgow, 1796).

11. For a discussion of the historical literature in the context of the transatlantic revival, see Susan [Durden] O'Brien, "A Transatlantic Community of Saints: The Great Awakening and the First Evangelical Network, 1735–1755," *American Historical Review* 91 (1986): 811–15.

12. For example, Arnold Dallimore, *George Whitefield: The Life and Times of the Great Evangelist of the 18th Century Revival,* 2 vols. (London: Banner of Truth, 1970), 1:14—"Whitefield's ministry was the one human factor which bound their work together in the lands it reached."

13. Clarence C. Goen, ed., *The Works of Jonathan Edwards,* vol. 4: *The Great Awakening* (New Haven: Yale University Press, 1972).

14. J. M. Bumsted, " 'What must I do to be saved?' A Consideration of Recent Writings on the Great Awakening in Colonial America," *Canadian Association for American Studies Bulletin* 4 (1969): 50.

15. Jack P. Greene and Jack Pole, eds., *Colonial British America: Essays in the New History of the Early Modern Era* (Baltimore: Johns Hopkins University Press, 1984), 7.

16. Timothy H. Breen, "An Empire of Goods: The Anglicization of Colonial America, 1690–1776," *Journal of British Studies* 25 (1986): 471.

17. For an excellent discussion of this literature, and the way out, see David Hempton, *Methodism and Politics in British Society, 1750–1850* (London: Hutchinson, 1984).

18. For example, Leigh E. Schmidt, *Holy Fairs: Scottish Communions and American Revivals in the Early Modern Period* (Princeton: Princeton University Press, 1989). An essay on the similarities of the two societies can be found in W. A. Speck, *British America, 1607–1776* (London: British Association for American Studies Pamphlet, 1985).

19. Breen, "Empire of Goods," 467–99.

20. Ibid., 473.

21. O'Brien, "Transatlantic Community of Saints," 813.

22. Susan Durden [O'Brien] "A Study of the First Evangelical Magazines, 1740–1748," *Journal of Ecclesiastical History* 27 (1976): 255–75.

23. See Durden, "Transatlantic Communications and Influence," chaps. 5 and 6.

24. Ibid., 88.

25. Frank Lambert, "Pedlar in Divinity: George Whitefield and the Great Awakening, 1737–1745," *Journal of American History* 77 (1990): 812–37; and Harry S. Stout, *The Divine Dramatist: George Whitefield and the Rise of Modern Evangelicalism* (Grand Rapids: Eerdmans, 1991).

26. This section draws heavily on the work of Lambert and Stout.

27. Stout makes many insightful comments about the special nature of the link between New England and Scotland, and about their position in relation to England.

28. Stephen Botein, "The Anglo-American Book Trade before 1776: Personnel and Stragies," in *Printing and Society in Early America,* ed. William L. Joyce and David D. Hall (Worcester, MA: American Antiquarian Society, 1983).

29. Ibid., 56.

30. David Hall, "The Uses of Literacy in New England, 1600–1850," in *Printing and Society in Early America,* ed. Joyce and Hall, 29.

31. MS account book of Colonel William Bradford of Philadelphia, 1742–60, Historical Society of Pennsylvania.

32. The most commonly cited prerevival works were Joseph Alleine, *An Alarme to the Unconverted* (1672); Richard Baxter, *Saints Everlasting Rest* (1650), *Call to the Unconverted* (1657), and *Divine Life* (1664); Thomas Boston, *Fourfold Estate* (1720); John Bunyan, *Pilgrim's Progress* (1678) and *Grace Abounding* (1666); John Flavel, *Works,* particularly *A Saint Indeed* (1673); William Law, *Serious Call to a Devout and Holy Life* (1728); Henry Scougal, *The Life of God in the Soul of Man* (1677); Thomas Shepard, *The Sincere Convert* (1641) and *The Sound Believer* (1648). Other commonly cited authors were Halyburton, Matthew Henry, and Hooker. This list has been compiled from the journals of Whitefield; the journals of Howell Harris; *Living Christianity delineated in the Diaries and Letters of . . . Hugh Bryan and Mrs. Mary Hutton* [preface by J. Condor and T. Gibbons] (1760); MS letters of Benjamin Colman, Massachusetts Historical Society; MS diary and notes of Nicholas Gilman, New Hampshire Historical Society; MS diary of David Hall, Massachusetts Historical Society; "The Diary of Ebenezer Parkman," ed. E. G. Wallett, *Proceedings of the American Antiquarian Society* 72, 73 (1962, 1963); *Diary of Rev. Daniel Wadsworth* (Hartford, CT, 1894); "Letters of Dr. Watts," *Proceedings of the Massachusetts Historical Society* (February 1895); A. S. Pratt, *Isaac Watts and His Gifts of Books to Yale College* (New Haven: Yale University Library, 1938); B. Fawcett, ed., *Extracts from the Diary, Meditations, and Letters of Mr. Joseph Williams of Kidderminster* (Shrewsbury, 1779).

33. *The Weekly History; or, An Account of the Most Remarkable Particulars Relating to the Present Progress of the Gospel. By the Encouragement of the Rev. Mr. Whitefield* (London, 1741–42), no. 13; and *Charleston Gazette,* 6 September 1740.

34. *Weekly History,* no. 16.

35. *Letters from the Rev. Samuel Davies, and Others shewing the State of Religion in Virginia, South Carolina, etc., particularly Among the Negroes* (London, 1761), 4.

36. For example, one of the converts at Cambuslang noted that *The Experiences of God's Gracious Dealings with Mrs. Elizabeth White* (1699) was very comforting because "it described her state and resulted in assurance" (Cambuslang MSS 1:305, New College, Edinburgh).

37. Hall, "Uses of Literacy"; and Botein, "The Anglo-American Book Trade."

38. Gomer M. Roberts, *Selected Trevecka Letters,* 166; Harris to James Erskine, 19 February 1745.

39. Thomas Prince, ed., *Account of the late Revival of Religion in Boston 1741–2–3* (Boston, 1744), 19, reprinted in Robe, *Christian Monthly History,* vol. 2, no. 6, p. 162.

40. It was also reprinted in Scotland. In 1742 Andrew Taite, minister of Carmunnock, left £100 in his will so that copies of the *Alarme* could be bought and distributed free (Hew Scott, ed., *Fasti Ecclesiae Scoticanae* 3:379, cited in Archibald Fawcett, *The Cambuslang Revival: The Scottish Evangelical Revival of the Eighteenth Century* [London: Banner of Truth, 1971]).

41. MS David Henchman ledger (DH10), Hancock Collection, Harvard Business School; and MS account book of Colonel William Bradford, 1742–60, Historical Society of Pennsylvania. See also Daniel Henchman Wast Book 1741 (DH5), Daybook 1741–50 (DH6), Hancock Collection, Harvard Business School; and G. S. Eddy, *Account Books Kept by Benjamin Franklin, Ledger "G"* (New York: Columbia University Press, 1929), original in American Philosophical Society, Philadelphia.

42. MS letter of T. Cutler to Z. Grey, 24 September 1743, Boston Public Library. He went on to say that "people were [n]ever so busy in reading."

43. To W. McCulloch, 4 April 1743, in the *Edinburgh Christian Instructor* for September 1839.

44. According to Schmidt, "Reading skills among the saints at Cambuslang were nearly universal. Literacy made the devotionals viable, and conversely the devotionals . . . provided major incentives to acquire reading skills" (*Holy Fairs,* 253 n. 59). See also T. C. Smout, "Born Again at Cambuslang: New Evidence on Popular Religion and Literacy in Eighteenth-Century Scotland," *Past and Present* 97 (1982): 114–27. The awakening in New England had its greatest impact on churchgoers, and literacy rates were high among this group; see, for example, R. Hofstadter, *America at 1750: A Social Portrait* (New York: Knopf, 1973), 218. For a discussion of literacy, literature, and the laity, see Durden, "Transatlantic Communication and Influence," chap. 6. More generally on the increase in literacy in England, see R. A. Houston, "The Development of Literacy: Northern England, 1640–1750," *Economic History Review,* 2d ser., 35 (1982): 199–216.

45. See Lambert, "Pedlar in Divinity,"

46. Erskine to Cooper, 8 January 1743, Erskine Papers, 8–14, Massachusetts Historical Society. See also Robe, *Christian Monthly History,* Preface, vol. 4, no. 30, and vol. 1, no. 2, p. 3.

47. For a classic example of such a correspondence, see that between Isaac Watts and various American ministers ("Letters of Dr. Watts," *Massachusetts Historical Society* [February 1895]). Watts gave away so many books and pamphlets to New England ministers that he was forced to write on one occasion, "I have made my cupboards thin" (ibid., 377).

48. W. McCulloch, ed., *Glasgow Weekly History,* vol. 5, no. 4.

49. For example, William Bradford's accounts show how popular Gilbert Tennent's works were in the region served by Bradford (New Jersey and Pennsylvania), whereas these works were not much referred to elsewhere. For the role of subscription, see Hall, "Uses of Literacy," 9.

50. See Lambert, "Pedlar in Divinity," 817–24.

51. Two of these were sermons: John Barnard, *A Zeal for Good Works Excited and Directed* (Boston, 1742; reprint, Glasgow, 1742); and John Caldwell, *An Impartial*

Trial of the Spirit operating in this Part of the World; by comparing the Nature, Effects and Evidence of the supposed Conversion with the Word of God (Boston, 1742; reprint, Glasgow, 1742).

52. John Erskine, *The Signs of the Times Consider'd ; or, A high Probability that the present Appearances in New England, and the West of Scotland are a prelude of the Glorious Things promised to the Church in the Latter Ages* (Edinburgh, 1742), 24.

53. Sereno E. Dwight, ed., *The Life of President Edwards,* 10 vols. (New York, 1830), vol. 1, p. 200, Robe to Edwards, 16 August 1743.

54. Charles Chauncy, *The State of Religion in New-England since the Rev. Mr. Whitefield's Arrival there in a Letter from a Gentleman in New-England to his friend in Glasgow, to which is subjoin'd an Appendix containing Alterations of the principle Facts in the Letter, by the Revs. Mr. Chauncy, Mr. John Caldwell, Mr. John Barnard, Mr. Turell, Mr. John Parsons, Dr. B. Colman* (Glasgow, 1742).

55. Ibid., 3.

56. Ibid. (2d ed.), Editor's Preface, i. The second edition was printed in Glasgow and was advertised as being sold in Edinburgh and London. It had an Appendix, "to which is prefixed a reply to Mr Whitefield's Remarks on the first edition."

57. G. Whitefield, *Some Remarks On a Late Pamphlet Intitled, The State of Religion in New-England, since the Rev. Mr. George Whitefield's Arrival there* (Glasgow, 1742); reprinted as *A Vindication and Confirmation of the Remarkable Work of God in New-England* (London, 1742; reprint, Boston, 1743). John McLaurin's defense was printed in the *Glasgow Weekly History.*

58. J. Edwards, *Distinguishing Marks of a Work of the Spirit of God,* first printed in Boston in 1741, was reprinted in London and Glasgow in 1742 with prefaces by Isaac Watts and John Guyse, and John Willison respectively. The arguments were developed by Edwards and published as *Some Thoughts concerning the Present Revival,* which was printed in Edinburgh in 1743 and forcefully promoted by revival ministers as the best answer to criticisms of the revival. For a further example of this dialogue between Scotland and New England, see *The Testimony of a Number of New England Ministers met at Boston Sept. 25 1745 professing the ancient Faith of these Churches . . . Reciting and Recommending An excellent Act concerning Preaching lately made by the General Assembly of the Church of Scotland* (Boston, 1745).

59. *Evangelical Magazine* (London, 1793–1812), preface.

60. See William Seward's MS journal, University College of North Wales, Bangor: "Received a letter from my Dear friend Bro. Mason—informing me that ye Methodist Journal was disapproved by our friends and desiring me to dissuade ye Author from going on. I Answered that I dare not hinder it because I could do nothing against ye Truth but for ye Truth—that however mean ye Instrument was if ye Lord will work who shall hinder" (20 August 1740, when Seward was in the colonies with Whitefield; I am grateful to John Walsh for this reference).

61. John Lewis, ed., *The Christian's Amusement Concerning the Progress of the Gospel both at Home and Abroad* (London, 1740), printed by John Lewis, September 1740–March 1741, 4 pp., price 1*d*. Then it became *The Weekly History; or, An Account of the Most Remarkable Particulars Relating to the Present Progress of the Gospel. By the Encouragement of the Rev. Mr. Whitefield* (London, 1741, printed by John Lewis, 11 April–13 November 1742), 4 pp., price 1*d*. For its further development and name changes, see Durden, "First Evangelical Magazines."

62. *Weekly History,* no. 13.

63. Ibid., no. 4.

64. Ibid., nos. 23, 27, 53.

65. The paper began to reflect the organization of the Calvinist Methodist movement in its use of societies, bands, tickets, circuits, and eventually association meetings for ministers and exhorters. See ibid., no. 89.

66. For example, in issues 6 to 60 with John Cennick's reports from Wiltshire during his tour from June to September 1741.

67. The full title was originally *The Glasgow-Weekly-History Relating to the Late Progress of the Gospel and Home and Abroad; Being a Collection of Letters partly reprinted from the London-Weekly-History* (Glasgow 1742, printed by William Duncan, December 1741–December 1742), 8 pp., price 1*d.*

68. For a detailed analysis of the religious connections between Britain and the Continent, see W. R. Ward, *The Protestant Evangelical Awakening* (Cambridge: Cambridge University Press, 1992).

69. Thomas Prince, Jr., ed., *The Christian History, Containing Accounts of the Revival and Propagation of Religion in Great Britain and America . . . 1743 and 1744,* 2 vols. (Boston, printed by S. Kneeland and T. Green, 5 March 1743–23 February 1745), 8 pp., bound with indexes. See also James Robe, ed., *The Christian Monthly History, or, An Account of the Revival and Progress of Religion Abroad and at Home,* 2 vols. (Edinburgh, 1743, printed by R. Fleming and A. Alison, November 1743–January 1746).

70. Robe, *Christian Monthly History,* vol. 1, no. 6, p. 61.

71. Ibid., Preface, vol. 1, no. 4, p. 49.

72. Ibid, Preface 15: "The General Principle upon which our Belief of Facts upon the Testimony of others is founded, is this, that when Matters of Fact are attested by Witnesses who have sufficient Means of Knowledge of Information . . . then an Assent to Testimony is well founded." Also, Thomas Prince, Sr., to W. McCulloch: "We are particularly obliged to you for your *Weekly History* out of which my son intends to take what has a name subscribed and insert in his *Christian Weekly History* it being a rule He would keep as close to as possible to forbear inserting anything of fact of History without some name or other to give it credit" (13 December 1743, New York Public Library, Misc. MSS Print; taken from J. H. Benton sale, American Art Association, 1920 catalog, 3d session).

73. Ibid., Prince to McCulloch, 13 December 1743.

74. Edwin Welch, *Two Calvinist Methodist Chapels, 1743–1811: The London Tabernacle and Spa Fields Chapel* (London: London Record Society, 1975), 13.

75. Printed in the *Journal of the Calvinist Methodist Historical Society* 25, no. 3 (1940): 159.

76. Printed at the front of vol 1. of the *Christian Monthly History.*

3

George Whitefield in Three Countries

HARRY S. STOUT

How does the career of George Whitefield help us to understand evangelicalism in a transatlantic perspective? That question framed a biography of
Whitefield that I recently completed. I concluded that the story of his ministry and the rise of modern evangelicalism are inseparable; such was his
importance that he single-handedly made a difference in forging a new
Anglo-American evangelical paradigm that was revival-driven, nondenominational, and international in scope. In the following chapter I will summarize aspects of Whitefield's revivals in England, Scotland, and the North
American colonies, noting both what was common to all three countries and
what was unique to each.[1]

I

We start in England, and more particularly London, for there, beginning in
the summer of 1736, the young methodist convert honed the skills and pol-
ished the techniques that would soon make him an international phenomenon. In a series of preaching experiments that culminated in the urban
"fields" of Kennington Common, Moorfields, and Hyde Park, Whitefield
rewrote the book on revivals and mass preaching. He combined itinerant
ministry, outdoor preaching, weekday sermons, and extemporaneous speech
to produce religious audiences and a level of religious enthusiasm without
precedent in the English-speaking ministry.[2]

Whitefield's revival preaching was novel both for his shameless pathos and
for his equally shameless self-promotion through the press and word-of-
mouth. As he experimented with his delivery and with advertising, mass
revival assumed ever-greater scope. In London during the late 1730s, Whitefield discovered how revival could become, in effect, a consumer product that
could be marketed alongside of, and in competition with, the rising swirl of
goods and services feeding into an incipient "consumer revolution."[3] His

product—the New Birth—he would market, not primarily in the churches and meetinghouses, but in the public square of the marketplace.

Although Whitefield would never enjoy the unrivaled success in London that he did in Scotland or North America, it was essential that he begin there and move outward. In eighteenth-century Anglo-America, London was the only city from which to launch an international event of any sort. Perhaps at no other time in its long and noble history had London represented a more ideal site to stage a preaching revolution. It was Europe's largest city, leaving Amsterdam and Paris far behind. Within the city limits lived one in seven English men and women. Contained in its widely diverse population were the heights of aristocratic privilege and the depths of urban poverty.

Equally important for Whitefield's revivals, London was the center of commerce and the exporter of culture throughout the British Empire. As the center of an eighteenth-century consumer revolution, London represented, in historian Neil McKendrick's apt phrase, "the shopwindow for the whole country."[4] As never before, culture had become a product marketed from London to the provinces as far away as Scotland and America. Its marketplace increasingly defined social reality and dictated the terms by which society and various subcultures came together in new associations outside traditional institutions and centers of power such as church, state, military, or nobility. The market became both a social fact and a shaping metaphor for a new social order dominated by impersonal rules of supply and demand. As politics moved ever closer to an ideology of popular sovereignty, so society and economics moved ever closer to a parallel and accompanying ideology of consumer sovereignty in which market forces governed social order.

As with so many cultural transformations, religion was originally left out, or, more accurately, left behind in the rush to compete for market shares. While a "shared language of consumption" threatened to overtake social discourse, it did not, at first, include religion. Religion was confined to the tradition of the old churches and Dissenting meetinghouses, or to the privacy of family devotions. The public square was naked; there was no sacred vocabulary or ritual to fill its stalls of goods and services.

George Whitefield's greatness lay in integrating religious discourse into this emerging language of consumption. In the fields of London he discovered, in effect, how to ply a religious trade in the open air of the marketplace. By making religion dramatic and entertaining, and by promoting it in outdoor spaces alongside competing secular diversions, he led the way in showing how religion could be made *popular,* hence marketable to a dawning age of religious "consumers."

How did Whitefield make religion popular and entertaining? In a word, he made it dramatic, transforming the pulpit into a form of sacred theater. More than any of his peers (or successors), Whitefield spoke to the passions of his hearers. Other revivalists—Stoddard, the Wesleys, Edwards—would speak to the "affections," but none did so in as powerful and viceral a way as Whitefield. Unlike many evangelical leaders who grew up in ministerial homes, Whitefield grew up in a tavern and "suffered" through an early love affair with the English stage and acting. Following his conversion at Oxford, he repudiated the theater entirely, while at the same time borrowing its secrets for the pulpit. After Whitefield it would never again be entirely clear what was stage and what was church.[5]

What about the stage distinguishes acting from so much of preaching prior to Whitefield? Most important is the stage's emphasis on passions and feeling rather than abstract thought and understanding. Where other revivalists appealed to the heart only after informing the head, Whitefield went right to the heart. In his classic treatise *To the Actor,* Michael Chekhov observed: "It is well known that the realm of art is primarily the realm of feelings. A good and true definition would be that the atmosphere of every piece of art is its heart, its feeling soul. Consequently it is also the soul, the heart, of each and every performance on the stage."[6] Great art, in the form of drama or opera, may have simplistic plots and superficial content, but that does not matter; it is the passions that count, and it is the passions to which the audience responds in shared experience.

In directing his message to the heart and the experience of the New Birth, Whitefield preached with everything he possessed, body as well as soul. Also his use of the body was more in the nature of the stage than the pulpit. Any passion-based art like theater or opera depends chiefly on body and voice. The body, in Chekhov's terms, becomes the "instrument for expressing creative ideas on the stage."[7] Where most intellectually oriented disciplines such as preaching and lecturing express their creativity through the content of their thought, actors exhibit their creativity through their bodies; they become the window into the soul. The effect of all of Whitefield's innovations was to free his body for performance, erasing all intermediaries between him and his audience. Outdoor settings and extemporaneous speech freed and animated his body to move vigorously—a characteristic trait noted in virtually every description of his preaching. Oftentimes it was the *audience* who left emotionally drained and exhausted after a Whitefield revival. In Whitefield's preaching, the words were the scaffolding over which the body climbed, stomped, cavorted, and kneeled, all in an attempt—as much intuitive as contrived—to startle and completely overtake his listeners. The more he experimented in London, the bolder he became. Everywhere he went, the response was electric as he conveyed to his audiences a kind of revelation they had never seen before.

The movement out-of-doors was important not only for freeing the actor-preacher within but also for situating religion in a different context. Central to Whitefield's evangelical revivals was less the creation of a new denomination than an international movement centered on the revival. This revival-centered world, Michael Crawford observes, "set evangelicals apart from nonevangelicals."[8] Before Whitefield, revivals were local, or at most regional, and episodic in nature. All of that changed with Whitefield and his single-minded determination to market revivals internationally, across two continents. London was only the start of a transatlantic evangelistic campaign.

II

Before even leaving England, virtually all of the characteristics of Whitefield's ministry were set. The time was ripe for a preaching mission to America. Once before Whitefield had visited the colonies briefly to establish an orphanhouse in Georgia, but on his return visit in 1739, his central focus was not the Georgia orphanhouse but the northern urban centers of Philadelphia, New York, and Boston. Just as he had adapted the marketplace to religious ends in England, so he would adapt new international linkages of transportation, trade, and communications to a self-conscious, intercolonial "Calvinist Connection" built around the revival.[9] Similar to the integrating power of Georgian politics, the East India Company, or Wedgewood pottery, Whitefield's revivals could break down ethnic and denominational differences and forge a new, potentially powerful religious market around the key trading centers of Philadelphia, New York, Boston, Edinburgh, Glasgow, London, and Bristol. And from there the revivals could move inland.

In internationalizing his product—the revival—Whitefield would add a wrinkle of his own to the emerging Anglo-American web of consumption and integration. Economic and political integration—what historians term Anglicization—originated in London and migrated exclusively one way. London was the core, and all else the dependent periphery.[10] Whitefield's revivals, in contrast, while originating in London, could in time reverse the cultural exchange. Scotland and America could become centers of religious piety that would reverse the direction of Anglicization. This was a heady enterprise that Scottish and American Calvinists were prepared to embrace, and one that would endear Whitefield to his "periphery" audiences. It would reinstitute America's "Puritan errand" to a wayward Europe in the modern guise of mass revival and transdenominational, open-air appeal. To be sure, not all of this strategy was fully clear to Whitefield in 1739. But the outline was fixed and the plan set in motion from the moment he stepped on American soil.

Between 1739 and 1740, Whitefield proceeded to write a new chapter in American religion as he had done earlier in London. His highly publicized revivals would take the Middle Colonies and New England by storm, reviving in the process an entire population. If England marked the birth of new, mass-produced revivals, America represented its triumph. Before his whirlwind tours of the colonies were complete, virtually every man, woman, and child had heard the "Grand Itinerant" at least once. And where English audiences were primarily poor and working class, Whitefield reached all levels of American society from slaves to governors, convicting all and persuading many to accept the New Birth.[11]

So pervasive was Whitefield's impact in America that he can justly be styled America's first culture hero, the first in a long line of celebrities who through the sheer force of personality compelled the attention—and adoration—of an emerging nation.[12] For their part, Americans experienced through Whitefield their first international and intercolonial cultural movement. Before Whitefield there was no such unifying person or event. Indeed, before Whitefield, it is doubtful whether any name other than royalty was known equally from Boston to Charleston. Whatever opposition he faced in America was minor in contrast to enemies in England. And what opposition there was among Old Light clergy and Anglican priests gradually melted away. By 1750 virtually every American loved and admired Whitefield and saw him as their champion.

Why was Whitefield so popular in America? Part of the reason was his Calvinism. Though never deeply versed in Reformed theology (Whitefield once confessed to never having read Calvin), Calvinism was a cause he unceasingly championed; in a Calvinist America, it was a note certain to win friends. For Americans to hear an Anglican priest extolling total depravity, predestination, and strict morality was, in Whitefield's words, like "putting fire to tinder."[13]

Even more important than Whitefield's Calvinism, however, was his dramatic delivery. If Whitefield's dramatic proclamations were the rave in London, where theater was well known and widely frequented, they were even more powerful in the colonies, where many Americans were seeing a form of theater for the first time.

In fact, Whitefield's personality and evangelical, nondenominational ministry fit perfectly with New World circumstances. In Whitefield, American colonists found a speaker who embodied their own uncertain and highly ambitious status as English provincials. In time Whitefield and his audience would discover many commonalities. Both coveted English praise and legitimacy even as they chafed against hereditary and arbitrary powers; both were at their righteous best when challenging authority in the name of the popular audience; both craved recognition from the very authorities they loved to challenge; and, most important, both leaned toward creative, extrainstitutional solutions to entrenched problems of liberty and order—solutions that bypassed traditional authority and sought new principles of association, exchange, and order.[14]

As an American culture hero, Whitefield's influence went well beyond religion to encompass society, politics, and even war. His legendary success in helping to raise troops for the Louisbourg expedition of 1745 marked the start of a long-standing infatuation between Whitefield and the American Soldiery. In preparation for the military expedition against Louisbourg, a French-built fortress on Cape Breton Island, the New England commander, William Pepperrell, asked Whitefield to preach an enlistment sermon. Pepperrell persuaded his close friend Whitefield, urging that "if I did not encourage it, many of the serious people would not inlist." Never one to act half-heartedly, Whitefield threw himself into the task of recruitment and by February 1745 could point with pride to the role he had played in raising the largest expeditionary force ever assembled up to that point in North America. On the eve of embarkation, he supplied the somewhat apprehensive troops with their motto, *Nil desperandum Christo duce* (If Christ leads, never fear), and preached a sermon promising that, if Christ was truly King, "we should receive good news from Cape Breton."[15]

Good news for the Americans did come with unexpected surrender of the French fortress, and with that triumph Whitefield became a virtual military icon. Through subsequent wars with France and England, he was associated with American military success. Soldiers through the Revolution would take his motto to heart, believing also that if *Whitefield* was for them, they need never fear. Not until George Washington would Americans discover a new culture hero to enlist at the head of their sacred cause.[16]

III

As important as America was to Whitefield's plans, it was only the second leg of three. Left remaining was the great province of Scotland. In many ways, America and Scotland were kindred spirits in the eighteenth century. Both perceived themselves to be on the margins of British culture and civilization.[17] Like Americans, the Scots chafed at British superiority even as they claimed its pretensions for their own. Scotland's principal city, Edinburgh, dwarfed Philadelphia and Boston, yet remained tiny in contrast to London. The modern proximity of London and Edinburgh should not obscure the distance (both geographic and symbolic) separating the two in the eighteenth century. In modern equivalencies, Edinburgh may as well have been 2,400 miles from London; in cultural distance, it was closer to America than London was.

In religious terms the two were also similar in ways that fit well with Whitefield's Calvinist evangelicalism. Like America, Scotland emerged from the English Reformation with a strong dislike of episcopal government, Anglican ritual, and Arminian theology. Doctrinally the Scots continued to adhere to the strict Calvinism of the Westminster Confession. Institutionally they organized themselves into a national Scottish Kirk that, though state supported like the Church of England, followed the Presbyterian blueprint of John Knox. As with American Puritans, so with Scottish Presbyterians— Calvin's Geneva had established forms of faith that created a perfect environment for Whitefield's novel presentation.

The Scottish Kirk permeated all levels of society, creating a people who were highly literate and theologically sophisticated. Though respectful of a learned and settled ministry, they could and did do battle with the ministers on the clergy's own terms. Surviving lay confessions and testimonies confirm a literate population that regularly read the Bible and devotional manuals. In fact, Scottish lay religiosity was probably more informed and systemic than even that in New England. While American Puritans paid lip service to the Westminster Confession, they never accorded it the centrality in their culture that it enjoyed in Scotland.[18] Scottish Presbyterians internalized the larger catechism and could quote entire passages by memory. Total depravity, imputation, original sin, predestination, and effectual calling were common tokens of their everyday discourse and the terms they used for self-examination and understanding in private spiritual exercises and prayer.

Throughout the seventeenth and eighteenth centuries, revivals struck the Scottish Kirk with a cyclic regularity not unlike that of the New England town. Most of these were local and communal affairs that reinforced local authority and the church. They differed from those in England or pre-Whitefield America, however, in that some were led by "stranger preachers" or itinerant "field" preachers who toured the "mountains and valleys" sowing the seeds for local revival. Where American revivals, operating in an environment where church membership was voluntary, were most dramatically registered in suddenly expanded church membership rates, Scottish revivals, operating within the context of a national church, were most immediately registered at "holy faires" in which multiple "action sermons" would bring long lines of newly awakened to the Communion table—and subsequently into active participation in the life of the church.[19]

Before Whitefield's arrival in Scotland, the Scots already knew of his triumphs in London and North America thanks to his own religious magazine and the Edinburgh press. And from Jonathan Edwards's best-selling *Narrative of Surprising Conversions,* they also knew how to interpret them as a great work of God presaging yet greater gospel triumphs.[20] Now it was their turn.

Whitefield first arrived in Scotland in August 1741. In all, he made fourteen trips to Scotland and grew steadily in popularity. Although never a political or military hero in the American sense, he enjoyed unparalleled popularity as the greatest revivalist of his age. As in America, Whitefield's Scottish audiences resonated to the Calvinism of his preaching and flocked in huge numbers to hear him preach. And, as in America, his audiences transcended class and encompassed all levels of society. A letter in Whitefield's periodical, the *Weekly History,* included an extract from a "gentleman of Edinburgh" who described "a most excellent sermon" by Whitefield in Edinburgh's orphan park that attracted "People of the first Rank."[21]

So Calvinist was Scotland that, for the first time in his career, Whitefield encountered strong criticism from the Calvinist rather than the Anglican or Wesleyan camp. There a contingent of hyper-Calvinist "Seceders" censured Whitefield for refusing to renounce his Anglican orders and condemn all churches but the Scottish Seceders.[22] Their demands forced Whitefield to make a hard choice between degrees of Calvinism—one that would extend to America, where he had earlier flirted with hyper-Calvinist separatists such as Andrew Croswell and James Davenport. In a fateful decision Whitefield repudiated the separatists, both in Scotland and America, and thereafter identified with the more established, moderate Presbyterians and Congregationalists. Although counterfactual speculations are always risky, it is interesting to hypothesize what might have happened had Whitefield allied with the radical separates in America and Scotland as he initially seemed to do. The fact that he did not may help to account for the survival of Calvinism in its socially moderate guise for another generation.

Of all the Scottish revivals in which Whitefield participated, the most dramatic came on his second visit to Scotland. Throughout the spring of 1742, Whitefield received strange and exciting news from the small village of Cambuslang, outside of Glasgow. There, under the local ministry of William McCulloch, large numbers of "inquirers" were "awakened" to the gospel and turned to Christ. From all accounts, it sounded like another Northampton in the making.

Throughout the spring of 1742, news of "The Cam'slang Wark" spread throughout southern Scotland, attracting people from other towns and villages. On 4 March, Whitefield heard of a "great awakening" in progress and wrote McCulloch a letter of encouragement, urging him to continue daily preaching. By April the awakening showed no sign for abating, and McCulloch wrote Whitefield that "in less than three Months past, about 300 Souls have been awakened . . . Some have computed the Hearers, these two last Lord's-days, to have been Nine or Ten-thousand." He closed the letter by saying, "I long much to see you here. Let me know by the first opportunity when you think to be with us."[23]

Words like these had the desired effect. Whitefield arrived in Scotland on 3 June, just in time to catch the revivals at their peak. En route to Cambuslang, he stopped at Glasgow and preached to an expectant audience estimated at twenty thousand. Many of his listeners had been dividing their time between Glasgow and Cambuslang, and now they carried the exciting news of Whitefield's arrival to McCulloch. Whitefield proved to be less the creator than a powerful catalyst and symbol of success, bringing a sense of international significance and culmination to the local work.[24]

By 6 June, Whitefield was at Cambuslang. He began immediately to preach that morning and evening. His evening service attracted thousands and continued until 2:00 A.M. The excitement was unforgettable. "There were scenes of uncontrollable distress, like a field of battle. . . . All night in the fields, might be heard the voice of prayer and praise." Such was the excitement that he concluded, "It far out-did all that I ever saw in America." Once begun, enthusiasm steadily gained in momentum. On Saturday, Whitefield, in concert with area pastors, preached to an estimated twenty thousand people in services that stretched well into the night. On Sunday, at a special Communion service celebrated in the fields, over 1,700 communicants streamed alongside long Communion tables set up in preaching tents. Following the sacrament, Whitefield preached again in the evening on Isaiah 54:5, a sermon entitled "Thy Maker Is Thy Husband." By many accounts, this was the most powerful sermon of the revival. Later he recalled that wherever he walked, "you might have heard persons praying to, and praising God. The children of God came from all quarters."[25]

Printed accounts of the Cambuslang awakening quickly appeared in journals, magazines, and newspapers. Other more elaborate accounts were prepared by clerical friends of this and surrounding revivals who sought to confirm their lasting impact. In style, their accounts were all modeled directly on Edwards's *Narrative of Surprising Conversions.*[26] First the writers provided a physi-

cal description of the town and a general summary of manners and morals
before the revivals. These they followed with accounts of the revivals and
descriptions of lasting changes in piety and morals. Ecstatic behavior alone,
they knew, could not legitimate Cambuslang as a work of God. As in Northampton, it had to be followed with a reformation of manners and morals.

The moderate Presbyterian minister Alexander Webster confessed his initial skepticism about the revivals but reported that after having visited the
meetings at Cambuslang he had changed his mind:

> A solemn profound Reverence o'erspreads every Countenance;—They hear
> as Creatures made for Eternity, who don't know but next Moment they must
> account to their great Judge. Thousands are melted down into Tears;—
> Many cry out in the Bitterness of their Soul. . . . Talk of a precious Christ,
> ALL seem to breathe after him.—Describe his Glory, how ravished do
> *many* appear!—How captivate with his Loveliness!—Open the Wonders of
> his Grace, and the *silent* Tears drop almost from *every* eye. . . . These, *Dear
> Sir,* are the visible Effects of this *extraordinary* Work.[27]

Webster conceded that some conversions might be transient. But in the main,
he believed, the converts were sincere, and their feelings were no mere "passing conviction." Rather, there ensued a permanent alteration in character that
confirmed the event as a work of God.

The Scottish revivals of 1742 were indeed a great awakening that exceeded
their American counterparts in numbers and intensity. James Robe, pastor at
Kilsyth, wrote *Faithful Narrative of the Extraordinary Work of the Spirit of
God at Kilsyth,* in which readers learned how an entire town had been transformed almost overnight. They read of audience enthusiasm that bordered on
uncontrollable passion: "The Bodies of some of the Awakened are seized with
Trembling, Fainting, Histerisms in some few Women, and with Convulsive-
Motions in some others." They learned as well that all of these manifestations
had already been seen "in our *American* colonies . . . that hath occasioned
the Rev. and Judicious Mr. Edwards . . . to preach and publish a sermon upon
the distinguishing Marks of a Work of the Spirit of God."[28]

Robe's parallel to Northampton and the American revivals is striking. Yet
there were also important differences that become apparent from the descriptions of the converted in Scotland and America. Most notable here is the
extreme bodily emotions manifested in Scotland. Heightened passions appeared in the colonies to be sure and assumed unforgettable proportions in
the infamous New London bonfire. But in the main, there appeared to have
been much less of the "convulsions," "histerisms," and, above all, visions in
America than appeared in Scotland.[29]

In Cambuslang itself, Pastor William McCulloch also prepared a remarkable handwritten collection of conversion narratives that are so rich in detail
and dialogue that they have been featured in five outstanding new histories
treating the revivals in Scotland.[30] The document, preserved in manuscript
form in Edinburgh's New College, is massive, filling two volumes and over
1,300 pages of closely written manuscript. In all, it included the accounts of

106 converts, mostly young, between the ages of sixteen and twenty-five. Females outnumbered males by a ratio of two to one, a figure that matches general church membership rates in America, but not the much greater representation of converted males during America's Great Awakening.[31]

It is not clear whether the predominance of women in the accounts represented a comparable predominance of women in the audiences. What is clear is the extreme level of enthusiasm manifested at Cambuslang and surrounding towns. One Cambuslang convert, a woman "about 30 years of age," recalled how Whitefield said, "Ye wonder what makes these people cry so: but if the Lord would be pleased to open your Eyes, as he has done theirs, ye would see your hearts all crawling with Toads of Corruptions, and surrounded with Legions of Devils."[32] This image, she continued, "did not affect me much at the time, yet when I came home I took on a Strong apprehension that it was so, and imagined that I felt them within me crawling up my Throat to my mouth, and turned away my eyes that I might not see them coming out of my mouth."

Although small in numbers, male converts were equally prone to the supposedly "female" extremes of visions and faintings. One forty-year-old man confessed how, while hearing Whitefield at Cambuslang,

> I fell under great Terror, and thought I would certainly perish for ever: and while I was hearing in this condition, with my hand over my Eyes, Hell was represented to my mind, as a Pit at the foot of a Hill, and a great drove of people marching into it, and I along with them, and when I was got very near it, I thought I looked over my shoulder, and saw a very beautiful man, who smiled on me and made a motion to me with his hand to come back at which I was very glad.

Whitefield's preaching in Scotland encouraged powerful out-of-body visions to a far greater extent than it had in America. Following one of Whitefield's evening sermons on the preaching brae, a young man recalled,

> I fell into a swoon, (tho I did not cry any) a horror of great darkness coming over me. . . . And in the middle of this Swoon, my bodily eyes being shut, I thought I saw a clear light all at once shining about me as when the Sun shines bright at Noon, and apprehended that I was in a very large room. There was represented to my mind a very large scroll of papers, let down as from the roof above filling the breadth of the room . . . and it appeared to be all printed over in large distinct lines and letters. But when I thought I essayed to read I found I could not read. . . . Only it was impressed on my mind that was a scroll containing all my Sins that were all marked and recorded before God. And after a little the Scroll was drawn up again, and I recovered out of my swoon.

How do we understand this greater proclivity to visions in Scotland? Although an explanation of the spiritual and psychological dynamics of visions in religious experience is not possible, we can at least identify environmental dimensions of the revivals in Scotland that might encourage more swooning, visions, and sleep. First is the higher incidence of late-night meetings in Scottish revivals. Late-night revivals were discouraged in the colonies but accepted in Scotland—often into the late hours. Related to time was duration. Scottish revivals could last hours and even days as groups of ministers, including Whitefield, would preach seriatim. Although linked to the holy fairs and Communion tables of Scottish custom, the protracted intensity more closely approximated nineteenth-century American camp revivals than the more localized, town revivals of the eighteenth century.[33] As in the nineteenth-century camp meetings, the bodily and emotional extremes were conspicuous in all accounts.

IV

In summary, Whitefield's itinerant career furnishes compelling testimony to the importance of one individual on the subsequent shape of religion in Anglo-America. In recent historiography, biography has fallen out of favor in deference to broader social or economic studies concerned with large numbers of people and impersonal forces. One casualty of this "New" history is a diminished sense of the importance of individuals in the process of historical change. Rightfully fearful of mythologizing "great men" at the expense of ordinary men and women, and wary of naive claims to fame that discount the times in which people have lived, we have overcompensated to the extent that we lose sight of biography altogether; with that loss, we lose sight of the important truth that individuals *can* make a difference. Whitefield was such an individual.

Whitefield's successes in three countries carried broad significance in many ways. First, they marked a revival for Calvinism and for theological moderates. Although never profound, Whitefield's Calvinism was, like the gospel he proclaimed, sincerely felt and honestly communicated with great power. Whitefield was neither Arminian nor a social radical, and the revivals he promoted embodied the man. The imminent eclipse of Calvinism was stayed a generation, as least in part through the triumphs of his transatlantic "Calvinist Connection."

If Calvinism was essential to Whitefield's personal faith and ministry, it was not central to his revivals. There his significance was much broader and more portable. The process of commercialization, begun in London, necessarily transformed concepts of religion and religious experience generally in more individualistic and subjective terms. "Experience," "taste," and "attraction" became sufficient criteria for purchase. Relatedly, "religion" came to mean the New Birth and dramatic encounter on an intensely personal basis as much as staid teaching and doctrinal instruction. Religion as personal experience was both cause and effect for a dawning religious culture created by self-selected consumers.

Ultimately, Whitefield pioneered a new, evangelical conception of religious association that could accommodate many different theological traditions and orientations. His revivals were themselves a new religious form, neither "church" nor "sect." His revivals were not really a church, nor were they connected to local communities and congregations. The appearance of Whitefield's audiences as religious congregations defied the traditional sense of the term "congregation." They changed with every meeting and were routinely enjoined to support their local congregations and parishes, even as they were assured of bigger things afoot. In effect they were the first "parachurch," the first in a long line of extrainstitutional religious associations designed to compete outside of normal confessional and denominational lines and forge new religious associations premised on revival. Central to that revival was the experience of the New Birth.

Whitefield's itinerant ministry taught him the invaluable lesson that rival churches with visions of national hegemony could be a thing of the past: they were old history—the history of a traditional, aristocratic, and hierarchical culture. A new religious history, fit for a new consumer age, would have to be voluntary, and this meant popular and entertaining. Whitefield's revivals were just that. In them, existing churches were not supplanted so much as they were sidestepped in the interest of creating larger, translocal associations. Whitefield's mode of revivalism—theatrical, passion based, nondenominational, international, experience centered, and self-consciously promoted through media and word of mouth—would outlive his Calvinism and prove as receptive to Arminian prophets as to Calvinist. It would transcend media and embrace television and characterize evangelicalism into the twentieth century.

Finally, a word about culture and ideology. Except when protecting his friends from persecution or libel, Whitefield was largely nonpolitical and not especially well versed in the radical "neo-Whig" ideology surrounding him in England and, by the 1760s, in the American colonies. Yet, his anti-institutional and extrainstitutional rhetoric appealed especially to popular experience and had powerful social and political consequences in a society where no overarching culture or charistmatic leadership existed. In profound ways, America was a cultural vacuum during the period of Whitefield's greatest triumphs. It was a society-in-creation badly in need of common cultural values and leaders. If Whitefield's religious significance was common to England, Scotland, and America, his cultural significance as symbol for an age was uniquely American. He came to America as one in a long line of religious outsiders, but he died an evangelical American insider. No leader before him, religious or political, was able to transcend his section in the manner of Whitefield. His American evangelicalism represented an integrating cultural system—the first such—that predated and in important ways previsioned the ideology of republicanism that was gathering force at the times of his death in 1770.

In this essay we have seen how, in social, ideological, and, above all, religious terms, Whitefield helped to shape an age. The man and his times were of a piece and together produced a religious movement that was modern and "evangelical." Such was the enduring legacy of Whitefield in three countries.

Notes

1. See Harry S. Stout, *The Divine Dramatist: George Whitefield and the Rise of Modern Evangelicalism* (Grand Rapids: Eerdmans, 1991) Four recent, and extremely useful, comparative studies of revivalism in a transatlantic setting are Richard Carwardine, *Transatlantic Revivalism* (Westport, CT: Greenwood Press, 1978); Leigh Eric Schmidt, *Holy Fairs: Scottish Communions and American Revivals in the Early Modern Period* (Princeton: Princeton University Press, 1989); Marilyn J. Westerkamp, *Triumph of the Laity: Scots-Irish Piety and the Great Awakening, 1625–1760* (New York: Oxford University Press, 1988); and Michael J. Crawford, *Seasons of Grace: Colonial New England's Revival Tradition in its British Context* (New York: Oxford University Press, 1991).

2. Whitefield's early career is traced in Stuart Henry, *George Whitefield: Wayfaring Witness* (Nashville: Abingdon, 1957); and Arnold A. Dallimore, *George Whitefield: The Life and Times of the Great Evangelist of the Eighteenth-Century Revival*, vol. 1 (Westchester, IL: Crossways, 1970).

3. A recent spate of literature traces the origins of a modern, transatlantic "consumer revolution" to the middle and late decades of the eighteenth century. See especially T. H. Breen, " 'Baubles of Britain': The American and Consumer Revolutions of the Eighteenth Century," *Past and Present* 119 (1988): 73–104; and idem, "An Empire of Goods: The Anglicization of Colonial America, 1690–1776," *Journal of British Studies* 25 (1986): 467–99. See also Christine L. Heyrman, *Commerce and Culture: The Maritime Communities of Colonial Massachusetts, 1690–1750* (New York: Norton, 1984); Ned Landsman, *Scotland and Its First American Colony, 1683–1765* (Princeton: Princeton University Press, 1985); Peter Burke and Roy Porter, eds., *The Social History of Language* (Cambridge: Cambridge University Press, 1987); Ronald Paulson, *Popular and Polite Art in the Age of Hogarth and Fielding* (Notre Dame, IN: University of Notre Dame Press, 1979); Jean-Christophe Agnew, *Worlds Apart: The Market and the Theater in Anglo-American Thought, 1550–1750* (New York: Cambridge University Press, 1986); and Bernard Bailyn and Philip D. Morgan, eds., *Strangers within the Realm: Cultural Margins of the First British Empire* (Chapel Hill: University of North Carolina Press, 1991).

4. London's central importance to the emerging Anglo-American "empire of goods" is traced in Neil McKendrick, John Brewer, and J. H. Plumb, eds., *The Birth of a Consumer Society: The Commercialization of Eighteenth-Century England* (Bloomington: Indiana University Press, 1982); and E. A. Wrigley, "A Simple Model of London's Importance in Changing English Society and Economy, 1650–1750," *Past and Present* 37 (1967): 44–70.

5. This theme is traced more extensively throughout Stout, *Divine Dramatist*.

6. Michael Chekhov, *To the Actor: On the Technique of Acting* (New York: Harper, 1953), 53.

7. Ibid., 1. On body and passion, see also Constantin Stanislavski, "When Acting Is an Art," in *An Actor Prepares* (New York: Theatre Arts, 1948), 12–30. In many ways, Whitefield's actor-preacher style anticipated the sort of contemporary "method acting" described in Lee Strasberg's *Dream of Passion: The Development of the Method* (Boston: Little, Brown, 1987). In this sense he was actually ahead of his eighteenth-century contemporaries on the English stage. I am indebted to Nina Moore for this insight.

8. Crawford, *Seasons of Grace*, 127. Elsewhere, Crawford observes that, by

1743, the term "revival" had become "so common that, without ambiguity, authors could write simply of 'the revival,' dropping the explanatory 'of religion' " (180).

9. George Whitefield's American career is admirably summarized in Frank Lambert, "George Whitefield and the Great Awakening," *Journal of American History* 77 (1990): 812–37.

10. See Roy Porter, *English Society in the Eighteenth Century* (Harmondsworth: Penguin, 1982); John Brewer, *The Sinews of Power: War, Money, and the English State, 1688–1783* (London: Hutchinson, 1989); and Keith Robbins, "Core and Periphery in Modern British History," British Academy, *Proceedings* 70 (1984): 275–97.

11. On Whitefield's universal American appeal, see Edwin S. Gaustad, *The Great Awakening in New England* (New York: Harper and Row, 1957); and Stout, *Divine Dramatist,* 249–68.

12. I borrow the term "culture hero" from cultural anthropology as it is used to describe individuals—both mythic and historical—who personify and embody the collective self-awareness and corporate identity of their people. For one such example see Anthony F. C. Wallace's masterful description of the Iroquois prophet Handsome Lake in *The Death and Rebirth of the Seneca* (New York: Vintage, 1969).

13. See William H. Kenney, "George Whitefield, Dissenter Priest of the Great Awakening," *William and Mary Quarterly* 26 (1969): 75–93.

14. The best description of American extrainstitutional ideology is Pauline Maier's *From Resistance to Revolution: Colonial Radicals and the Development of American Opposition to Britain, 1765–1776* (New York: Knopf, 1972).

15. George Whitefield, *Journals* (London: Banner of Truth, 1960), 551.

16. As different as George Whitefield and George Washington were as personalities, they both enjoyed a parallel process of mythologization in the American setting. Compare, for example, Frank Lambert, "The Great Awakening as Artifact: George Whitefield and the Construction of Intercolonial Revival, 1739–1745," *Church History* 60 (1991): 223–46, with Paul K. Longmore, *The Invention of George Washington* (Berkeley: University of California Press, 1988).

17. See John Clive and Bernard Bailyn, "England's Cultural Provinces: Scotland and America," *William and Mary Quarterly* 11 (1954): 200–213; Eric Richards, "Scotland and the Uses of the Atlantic Empire," in *Strangers within the Realm,* ed. Bailyn and Morgan, 67–114; and Bruce Lenman, *Integration, Enlightenment, and Industrialization: Scotland, 1746–1832* (London: Arnold, 1981).

18. Westerkamp, *Triumph of the Laity,* 31.

19. For complete descriptions of Scottish Communions, see Schmidt, *Holy Fairs.*

20. For an expertly edited text of Edwards's *Narrative of Surprising Conversions,* along with some indication of its overseas influence, see C. C. Goen, ed., *The Works of Jonathan Edwards,* Vol 4: *The Great Awakening* (New Haven: Yale University Press, 1972).

21. On the popularity of Edwards's revival treatises in Scotland, see Crawford, *Seasons of Grace,* 127, 151.

22. For descriptions and analyses of the Seceders, see Andrew Dummond and James Bulloch, *The Scottish Church, 1688–1843: The Age of the Moderates* (Edinburgh: Saint Andrew, 1973), 51–53; and Landsman, *Scotland and Its First American Colony,* 240.

23. The most thorough description of Cambuslang is Arthur Fawcett, *The Cambuslang Revival: The Scottish Evangelical Revival of the Eighteenth Century* (London: Banner of Truth, 1971). An excellent documentary of Cambuslang is D. MacFarlan,

The Revivals of the Eighteenth Century, Particularly at Cambuslang With Three Ser-mons by the Reverend George Whitefield, Taken in Shorthand (Edinburgh, 1847; re-print, Wheaton, IL: Richard Owen Roberts, 1980). I am grateful to Richard B. Steele for calling this source to my attention.

24. On Whitefield's powerful, but auxiliary, role in the Scottish revivals, see Westerkamp, *Triumph of the Laity,* 187.

25. For a fuller discussion, see Stout *Divine Dramatist,* 133–55.

26. See especially James Robe, *A Faithful Narrative of the Extraordinary Work of the Spirit of God at Kilsyth, and Other Congregations in the Neighbourhood* (Glasgow, 1742).

27. Alexander Webster, *Divine Influence the True Spring of the Extraordinary Work at Cambuslang and Other Places in the West of Scotland* (Edinburgh, 1742), 3.

28. Robe, *Faithful Narrative,* vii.

29. Ned Landsman discusses differences between Scotland and America in *Scotland and Its First American Colony,* 185.

30. See the works cited above by Ned Landsman, Marilyn Westerkamp, Leigh Schmidt, Michael Crawford, and Arthur Fawcett.

31. Michael J. Crawford analyzes the Cambuslang narrators in *Seasons of Grace,* 251–54.

32. All quotations from the Cambuslang narratives are taken from the manuscript deposited at New College, Edinburgh.

33. The preaching of the Nova Scotian revivalist Henry Alline bears striking simi-larity to that of the Scottish revivalists. For descriptions, see G. A. Rawlyk, *Ravished by the Spirit: Religious Revivals, Baptists, and Henry Alline* (Montreal and Kingston: McGill-Queen's University Press, 1984).

4

Cotton Mather's *Bonifacius* in Britain and America

DAVID A. CURRIE

Historians of early America and New England Puritanism long have recognized *Bonifacius*—or, as it became better known, *Essays to Do Good*—as certainly Cotton Mather's most popular and possibly his most important work. Benjamin Franklin claimed that *Bonifacius* was a significant influence upon the development of his own thought and practice. This connection has led some to view this work as a signpost pointing American Puritanism away from orthodox Calvinism and toward moralism and pragmatism.[1]

Such analysis, however, overlooks the character and commitments of those who maintained the popularity of *Bonifacius* by republishing it. Despite his admiration for this work and being a printer himself, Franklin never brought out an edition. Almost a century after Mather's original imprint, *Bonifacius* first reappeared in 1807 under the title *Essays to Do Good,* not in the United States, but in England. Its editor was George Burder, a Calvinist Congregational minister, secretary of the London Missionary Society, and the editor of the *Evangelical Magazine.* Sixteen additional editions quickly followed on both sides of the Atlantic during the first half of the nineteenth century, largely due to the efforts of others sharing the perspective of Burder's magazine. Interestingly, most of the American versions were simply reprints of Burder's "improved" London edition, which sought to update Mather's language, rather than the Boston original.

The surprising editorial history of *Bonifacius* helps to illumine the emergence of evangelicalism out of Puritanism and pietism in the early eighteenth century and, for nineteenth-century evangelicals in Britain and America, suggests several lines of continuity both with their predecessors and among themselves. Their continued interest in this book, not as an antiquarian curiosity, but as a work that spoke directly to their contemporary situation, highlights the centrality of activism as a distinctive characteristic of transatlantic evangelicalism.[2] In part, this emphasis simply carried on a basic tenet of Reformed piety; namely, true faith produces good works. Nonetheless, the strongly voluntary and institutional approach to doing good in *Bonifacius* and among those who republished it also reflects Enlightenment influences upon both Cotton Mather and later evangelicals.

The similarities among those who admired this work represent a general picture of nineteenth-century evangelicals, or at least Calvinist evangelicals, regardless of their location. They were Christians who combined a concern both for encouraging experiential piety within the church and for promoting evangelism and social morality outside it with participation in a variety of institutions designed to further that concern.

Although his death in 1728 antedates by a couple of years the commonly designated starting point for evangelism as a discernible movement, Cotton Mather's enduring influence through *Bonifacius* makes him one of its fathers. His transitional role in Puritanism and this work's transitional role in his own life marks Mather as a proto-evangelical and reveals the movement's diverse origins in Puritan and Enlightenment thought and practice.

Bonifacius emerged out of a change in Mather's own approach to religion. Around 1709 he shifted in his diary from recording the details of his inner spiritual struggles to describing his weekly cycle of "Good Devices." The growth of this more outward, activist perspective roughly coincided with the commencement of his correspondence with August Hermann Francke, suggesting that German pietism's organized approach to benevolence was a catalyst upon Mather's thinking. This new Continental model reinforced activist tendencies within his own family and in Puritanism in general, as well as providing more systematic and institutional means for their expression.[3]

Moreover, New England Puritanism seemed in need of a fresh strategy at this time. Traditional theocratic attempts to produce godliness in society were appearing largely ineffective, and with the appointment of the Anglican-sympathizing Joseph Dudley as governor of the colony in 1702, the government's support of Puritan aims became increasingly doubtful. *Bonifacius* sketched out a more voluntary approach that, while allowing for the Christian magistrate's participation in efforts to reform and convert society,[4] did not make legal coercion a cornerstone of its plan as preceding generations of Puritans had done. Instead, Mather emphasized individual Christians' pursuing their particular vocations in a godly manner and united together in voluntary associations devoted to encouraging piety, evangelizing, aiding the poor, and suppressing disorder.

In addition to balancing earlier Puritans' strongly introspective spirituality and supplanting their theocratic strategy, Mather's activism in *Bonifacius* also fostered a more ecumenical attitude toward other Christians than that held by his forebears. Rather than speculating on which other groups were elect or reprobate, Mather urged Puritans to unite with pious Protestants around the world in pursuing a common agenda of doing good.[5]

Mather's international and ecumenical intentions for *Bonifacius* were reflected in its preface. He dedicated the book to Sir William Ashurst, a prominent London politician and businessman who was also the governor of the New England Company, a voluntary society founded in 1649 to promote missionary work among Native Americans. In November 1710 Mather sent over to Ashurst a copy of his work, the first transatlantic crossing for *Bonifacius*.[6] The following April Mather recorded his desire to extend the work's influence elsewhere in England by sending it to one of his relatives who was a tutor at the college of Saybrook.[7]

Mather seems to have had high hopes that *Bonifacius* would be particularly well received in Scotland. In the preface he boasted:

> There will be found a set of excellent men in that Reformed and Renowned Church of *Scotland,* with whom the most refined and extensive essays to *do good* will become so natural that the whole world will fare better for them. To these, this Book is humbly presented, by a great admirer of the *good things* daily doing among them; as knowing if nowhere else, yet among *them,* it will find some reception; they will *not be forgetful to entertain such a stranger*![8]

While this may have been no more than a thinly veiled expression of his gratitude to the University of Glasgow for awarding him a doctor of divinity that year, his diary suggests that he was sincere. In February 1711 he noted that he sent some copies of *Bonifacius* and a couple of other works to Scotland, "unto those Hands thro' whom they may, if God please, do good unto many others," perhaps alluding to a Scottish bookseller or one of the many ministers in the Church of Scotland with whom he corresponded.[9]

In addition to Puritanism and pietism, Mather also drew a bit of his inspiration, and more of his practical application, in *Bonifacius* from nascent Enlightenment ideas. As in Puritan history, he was a transitional figure in the development of modern thought, combining belief in the reality of witchcraft and angels with such a strong interest in science that he was elected a Fellow of the Royal Society. In *Bonifacius* Mather applied the scientific method to doing good, developing an organized system of benevolence for human society broadly parallel to efforts such as that of Linnaeus to systematize the natural world.

Contemporary economic thinking and practice also shaped the work's program. Mather argued that it was shameful for Christians to develop "devices" to do business but not for doing good.[10] He sought to remedy this problem by suggesting that Christians organize groups for nurturing their own piety, establishing schools, distributing Bibles and religious books, sending out missionaries, and restraining public vice, at a time when their contemporaries increasingly were organizing commercial ventures for transatlantic trade and rudimentary industrial production.

Mather's long-range vision may reflect his acceptance of, or at least kinship with, the Enlightenment ideal of progress.[11] Doing good was never an end in itself for Mather, however, but simply a means "to Answer the Great END of *Life*," as he expressed it on the title page of *Bonifacius*. This description suggests that the Puritan ideal of glorifying God and enjoying him forever was Mather's primary motivation for benevolence.

Much to his disappointment, Mather's comprehensive dream in *Bonifacius* largely went unrealized during his lifetime. While his own life abounded in individual "Good Devices," such as collecting firewood and clothing for the poor in winter and giving away thousands of "books of piety" every year (and writing many himself), he seems to have had less success in attracting wide-spread imitation. Moreover, the societies he organized in Boston for the religious improvement of young men, the suppression of disorder, and the promotion of charity schools met with limited success, largely dissolving before his death.[12]

This lack of concrete fulfillment of *Bonifacius*'s proposals partly stemmed from their sheer number and variety and from Mather's typically Calvinist vision for the Christianization of all of society. Contemporary tensions within New England society, particularly the decreasing influence of Puritans upon the government and the decline of piety, also contributed. Greater fulfillment awaited a time when the church in New England and elsewhere had greater social, economic, and spiritual resources to pursue these visionary endeavors.

Such a time arose soon after Mather's death in 1728, as spiritual renewal began to break out and spread throughout America, Britain, and the Continent during the next half of the eighteenth century. During this period a number of *Bonifacius*'s recommendations were put into practice in various places. Perhaps the most obvious continuity was between its "private meetings of religious people for the exercises of religion" and the Wesleys' class meetings.[13] Another similarity was Mather's emphasis upon the power of the printed word to encourage conversion and piety and the subsequent growth of evangelical publishing networks.[14]

Both of these developments, however, reflected general emphases expressed outside of *Bonifacius,* so it is difficult to determine precisely what direct influence Mather's work had. I have uncovered no record of any prominent early evangelical leaders citing it, and Thomas Holmes lists no eighteenth-century editions in his extensive bibliography of Mather's works.

Ironically, the clearest case of *Bonifacius*'s influencing someone during this period involved a deist, Benjamin Franklin, rather than an evangelical. He alluded to its impact in his *Autobiography* in 1771[15] and as follows in a 1784 letter to Cotton Mather's son: "When I was a boy, I met with . . . *Essays to Do Good.* . . . It had been so little regarded by its former possessor, that several leaves of it were torn out, but the remainder gave me such a turn of thinking, as to have an influence upon my conduct through life; for I have always set a greater value on the character of a doer of good than any other kind of reputation."[16]

Even if Franklin had not made these specific references, the influence of *Bonifacius* upon him would be evident. The language and emphasis in the 1728 rules for his "Junto Club" for mutual self-improvement were similar to Mather's "Young Men's Associations," albeit without their religious dimension.[17] Conceptually, *Bonifacius* and Franklin shared three overall principles: the belief that good people lead to a good society, a desire to systematize and institutionalize benevolence, and an emphasis upon the importance of cooperative action.[18]

These similarities have led some to charge that *Bonifacius* reads "like a slightly more pious version of *Poor Richard's Almanac*" and that it contains the seeds of moralism and utilitarianism.[19] Some elements in Mather's work tend to support these charges. He frequently commended pagan examples of virtue and occasionally appealed to pragmatic motivations for doing good.[20]

Considered as a whole, however, *Bonifacius* cannot be reduced to mere moralism without doing violence to some of its overriding themes or taking elements out of context. On his title page, Mather attempted to define his rationale for doing good and to designate his intended audience. Although Franklin, and almost everyone after him, referred to *Bonifacius* as *Essays to Do Good,* Mather's original subtitle was "An ESSAY Upon the GOOD, that is to be DEVISED and DESIGNED, BY THOSE Who Desire to Answer the Great END of Life." This description reflects a concern for sanctifying all of life before God, not moralism. This emphasis continued on the title page, where he offered the book, not to everyone, but specifically "unto all CHRISTIANS."

Mather spent much of the first section of *Bonifacius* attempting to make it clear that his recommendations were indeed intended for Christians alone. He denied that anyone could do anything truly good apart from the grace of Christ and urged non-Christian readers to close the book, repent, and turn to God before they read any further.[21] All of his exhortations to diligence and his practical suggestions that follow rested upon this theological foundation of justification by faith alone and regeneration. While these theological emphases may sometimes be obscured by the multiplicity of practical suggestions later on in the book, overall *Bonifacius* maintains a consistently religious orientation.

The comprehensive Christian perspective of *Bonifacius*'s program of benevolence contrasted greatly with Franklin's. Much of what this work outlined as "doing good" concerned evangelism, missions, the promotion of piety, and other essentially religious activities. Even when addressing seemingly secular issues, Mather kept spiritual issues close at hand, uring doctors to inquire about their patients' spiritual health and encouraging reforming societies to hold an annual day of prayer.[22]

Franklin passed over these kinds of recommendations in his own program. Richard French observes that even when they addressed the same issues, "themes which are subdominant in the work of Cotton Mather become dominant in the ideology of Benjamin Franklin."[23] We could say that Franklin majored in *Bonifacius*'s minors.

Yet, if *Bonifacius* was essentially Christian and not a watered-down moralistic treatise, why did Franklin claim that it had such a significant effect upon him? In part, it may have been because the pages torn out of his copy included the important introductory theological section, revealing how greatly the work's approach differed from Franklin's. But even if he had read those particular pages, his eclectic mind probably had sifted through them to find practical suggestions. Franklin was as little bothered by whether a Christian source conflicted with his deism if it appeared to say something useful as

Mather was when a classical pagan source conflicted with his theology. As Mather "spoiled the Egyptians" for practical ideas and sayings, Franklin "plundered the Israelites," even when Mather was the Israelite.

Besides their shared eclecticism, another reason that *Bonifacius* may have been particularly appealing to Franklin was Mather's attempt, as Richard Lovelace expresses it, "to meet the moralists on their own ground and wrestle them over to Christian foundations."[24] Perhaps at times Mather gave up too much ground in this attempt, making it easier for Franklin to strip his suggestions from their theological underpinnings. However, Mather should not be judged too severely for his failure in print to win Franklin over to Christianity. Even as formidable and persuasive an evangelical "wrestler" as George Whitefield was unable to do so in person.

Franklin's relationship to *Bonifacius* has several important implications for understanding the development of the movement Whitefield helped bring to fruition. It suggests that part of evangelicalism's appeal may have lain in its benevolent orientation. It offered a practical program to produce a more moral and caring society grounded upon traditional concepts of conversion and sanctification, yet reflecting some current Enlightenment ideas. This up-to-date religious approach grew increasingly attractive toward the end of the eighteenth century as the excesses following the French Revolution discredited rationalistic efforts to improve conditions from a purely secular basis. Inherent in this appeal, however, was the danger that those attracted to evangelicalism as a method of social improvement would embrace its activist organizational structure more fully than its spiritual foundation. To put it in *Bonifacian* terminology, "Good Devices," and a fascination with devising ever more ingenious ways of producing them, might overshadow "the Great END of *Life*," thereby producing evangelicals with a form of moralism similar to Franklin's.

The attractiveness of evangelicalism's social program was reflected in the remarkable proliferation of new editions of *Bonifacius* during the first half of the nineteenth century. While this increase may be due in part to advances in printing technology that made it easier and cheaper to print books, none of Mather's other works were reproduced in anything like the same quantity,[25] suggesting that the popularity of *Bonifacius* was due to more significant reasons.

Its resurgence roughly paralleled the development in Britain and America of an extensive network of interconnecting religious voluntary societies promoting missions, the distribution of Bibles and tracts, religious education, and moral and social reformation. This "Benevolent Empire" was remarkably similar to Mather's organizational suggestions in *Bonifacius*. The work's emphasis upon individual Christians' expressing their faith in their daily occupations echoed contemporary evangelical leaders such as William Wilberforce in his *Practical View of Christianity*.

These similarities do not necessarily imply that *Bonifacius* single-handedly stimulated these developments, which reflected broader trends such as the overall growth of commerical and industrial organization during the first half of the nineteenth century and the traditional Reformed doctrine of vocation.

Nonetheless they do suggest that *Bonifacius* became popular with nineteenth-century evangelicals because it concisely expressed and reinforced their general approach to the Christian life and because it provided a multitude of specific practical ways of working out this general approach individually and corporately.

Mather's personal stature as both an orthodox Calvinist and a respected scientist and intellectual made him a helpful ally to evangelicals responding to diverse criticisms of their program, particularly as voluntary societies first emerged in force. On the one hand, *Bonifacius* provided a historical precedent for the society approach from someone with impeccable Puritan credentials to counter the kind of hyper-Calvinist suspicions of novelty that greeted William Carey's initial efforts in organizing the Baptist Missionary Society. On the other hand, the work's Enlightenment elements helped evangelicalism to seem intellectuallly respectable and up-to-date, turning the tables on rationalist Christians such as those in the Moderate party of the Church of Scotland who voted down an evangelical motion to support missionary societies with accusations that this scheme was "highly preposterous."

The editorial history of *Bonifacius* during the nineteenth century reveals an evangelical social consensus spanning a variety of geographic, denominational, and, to a lesser degree, theological backgrounds. The work was not reprinted in America alone, but also in England and Scotland, and was distributed in Ireland. In America it appeared in New York, Philadelphia, and even near the edge of the frontier as well as in Boston and New England. The introductions to and recommendations for these editions indicate that *Bonifacius* was viewed not as some sort of an antiquarian curiosity but, as Perry Miller puts it, as an "engine of piety."[26] An examination of the lives of the editors and recommenders also demonstrates its contemporary relevance, as they were almost all exemplary *bonifacii,* putting many of the work's teachings into practice to a remarkable degree.

In light of much current historical interpretation that cites *Bonifacius* as exemplifying a characteristic American penchant for activism, it is ironic that it was revived not in America, Mather's homeland, but in England. *Bonifacius,* under the new title *Essays to Do Good,* was first reprinted in 1807 in London. At this time the social program of the Second Awakening was gathering full steam in England. The 1790s and early 1800s had produced missionary, tract, and Bible societies, and Parliament abolished the slave trade in the year of its publication. George Burder, the man responsible for reprinting it, was both a product and a leader in this spiritual movement. His involvement in this project and his life in general demonstrate the similarity between the teachings of *Bonifacius* and the evangelical program of the first half of the nineteenth century.

Burder's life spanned the First and Second awakenings and illustrates the continuity of the spiritual influences behind them. He underwent a classic Calvinist conversion experience under the direction of his parents. His mother had been converted under Whitefield, and later Burder himself heard the great evangelist preach, which stimulated his own interest in ministry.[27]

From this time on, Burder's life sounds like it was taken from the pages of
Bonifacius. At the age of twenty-four he helped to organize the Evangelical
Society to encourage piety and evangelism among his peers, a group similar to
Mather's Young Men's Associations.[28] About a decade later he was the initia-
tor of Sunday schools at Coventry, exemplifying not only the strong educational emphasis of *Bonifacius* but also its ecumenical hopes by setting up a
joint committee of Anglicans and Dissenters to oversee them.[29] Combining
elements of a ministers' association with a missionary society,[30] Burder was
involved in the formation of the "Warwickshire Association of Ministers for
the spread of the Gospel both at home and abroad" in 1792.[31] He was also
influential in the formation of the London Missionary Society in 1795, the
Religious Tract Society in 1799, and the British and Foreign Bible Society in
1804.[32]

In addition to *Bonifacius*'s teachings concerning voluntary societies,
Burder also exemplified its many exhortations to produce and distribute pious
literature. He published sermons oriented for weavers and sailors, in keeping
with Mather's advice to enrich "the Tradesman's Library."[33] Most of Burder's
literary endeavors, however, were as an editor, both of a contemporary London religious periodical founded in 1793, the *Evangelical Magazine,* and of
numerous older books. In addition to *Bonifacius,* he edited and republished
several other Puritan works, including those of John Bunyan and John Owen.

Burder's interest in these Puritan works was not primarily historical, but
practical, in keeping with his biographer's comment: "In all his publications,
his one exclusive aim was usefulness."[34] Burder felt that these older divines
spoke to his current situation, and he took extensive editorial liberties with
their original texts to ensure that they were understood. In his preface to
Essays to Do Good, he explained that he only wanted to try to make the work
a more effective instrument to promote good among his contemporaries by
updating its language, or, as he put it, substituting for "quaint and obsolete
words and phrases . . . others more intelligible and pleasant."[35]

Although he considered some of *Bonifacius*'s language to be obsolete,
Burder, in the remainder if his preface, indicates that he viewed its content as
eminently contemporary and applicable to his readers' lives. The work's main
appeal to Burder was that it was an expression of Mather's own life, "not the
idle speculations of an ingenious theorist."[36] Not only did it offer a concise
compilation of new ways to do good, but it also reinforced those that recently
had been put into practice. Burder drew attention to contemporary fulfill-
ments of the work's specific suggestions in several footnotes to the text,
deleting Mather's section concerning slaves, since "the subject happily has no
connection with our country," and putting in a plug for the Religious Tract
Society after the recommendation that pastors should distribute good books
during their visits to homes.[37]

The similarities between Burder's life and *Bonifacius* suggest that he
clearly viewed Mather as a kindred spirit and believed that many of his fellow
evangelicals would do so as well. Ironically, Burder formed this opinion even
before he had read the work himself. In 1801 after alluding to Benjamin

Franklin's favorable comments to Mather's son about *Bonifacius,* Burder remarked: "The writer of this article has often heard of this book, but could never obtain it. Would it not be a public benefit to re-print it? The times require every exertion of this kind, and the public mind seems disposed to beneficence."[38]

Burder's remarks proved to be self-fulfilling prophecy. Pent-up demand from others who knew *Bonifacius* by reputation but had no access to the original 1710 edition exhausted the first impression of his new edition within six months, perhaps aided by advance publicity and a highly favorable review in his own *Evangelical Magazine.*[39] This review suggests that part of the work's attractiveness stemmed from its affinity with the Enlightenment. In addition to favorably quoting Franklin's letter to Mather's son from the preface to the new edition, the reviewer called Mather a Francis Bacon of "Christian benevolence," "discovering and pointing out the unexplored regions of human knowledge."[40]

Burder came out with a second London edition in 1808, and the quick succession of reprints of this version in other places during the next few decades testifies to its popularity, serving as both a stimulus to and an organizational manual for doing good, as well as reinforcing the legitimacy of many newly formed efforts. As Burder's situation prior to 1801 attests, *Bonifacius* did not necessarily directly produce the benevolent activities it commends. Broader social, intellectual, and spiritual trends produced similar results among succeeding generations of evangelicals from a variety of backgrounds. *Bonifacius* was like a double mirror in which Burder and his contemporaries saw not only Mather's life reflected but their own as well. Gazing into this mirror confirmed the authenticity of their lives and went on to spur them to bring what were merely vague outlines in Mather's time into sharp, clear reality in their own.

About a century after its first voyage, *Bonifacius* recrossed the Atlantic in the form of Burder's "new improved" edition, an exact reprint of which was issued in Boston in 1808.[41] While it may seem odd that Mather's hometown borrowed from abroad rather than producing its own copy, several circumstances may explain this development. Boston probably contained more copies surviving from the original 1710 imprint than did London, lessening the demand for another printing. In general, American voluntary society development lagged about a decade behind Britain, with the American Board of Commissioners for Foreign Missionaries forming in 1810, the American Bible Society in 1816, and the American Tract Society in 1825, making the need for a book reinforcing the society system seem less urgent. The updated language of Burder's edition also may have made it more appealing than Mather's original.

As evangelicalism developed in America, however, *Bonifacius* appeared in new places. By 1815 the Boston reprint of Burder's edition had extended beyond the confines of New England, when it was itself reprinted in Johnstown, New York, near Albany.[42] The publishers made two additions that distinguish this book from the Boston edition. They printed three short articles after the main text, one by Jonathan Edwards; an excerpt on the religious education of children from the *Christian Observer,* the mouthpiece of Anglican evangelicals; and another by Sir Matthew Hale. The addition of these "useful" articles imitated Mather's own penchant in *Bonifacius* for bringing diverse sources together in one place, and the British origin of two of them suggests that practical eclecticism was a hallmark of transatlantic evangelicalism.

The second addition was the inclusion of recommendations written by local pastors. These recommendations reveal that they viewed this work as directly applicable to their contemporary situation, providing both impetus for benevolence through its theological argument and practical direction to this impulse through its concise compilation of suggestions. As did Burder's, the lives of these men exemplify many of the same ideals and programs that are set forth in *Bonifacius,* thus sharing a common evangelical heritage in the Second Awakening.

The author of the first recommendation, Elisha Yale, pastor of the Congregational Church in Kingsborough, New York, seems to have been converted in one of the revivals around the turn of the century occurring under the ministry of a disciple of Jonathan Edwards.[43] Yale emphasized the timeliness of the publication, noting that it was "adapted to be useful in this part of the country, at the present time."[44]

The pastor of the Reformed Dutch Church of Albany, John M. Bradford, who wrote the second recommendation, was known for preaching "in perhaps more than an ordinary degree, evangelical truth."[45] He was particularly concerned about education, a strong emphasis throughout *Bonifacius,* and helped to establish Albany Academy and New Brunswick Theological Seminary. He also supported the Albany Bible Society.[46]

William Neill, pastor of the Firsty Presbyterian Church in Albany, wrote the final recommendation, emphasizing Mather's "living exemplification of what he proposes to others" and highlighting the evangelical spiritual impulse behind the work's exhortations to be involved in practical affairs, namely "to be imitators of the Divine Exempler *'who went about doing good.'* "[47] Like Bradford, Neill also was particularly concerned about education, though his varied career involved him in several ministries and organizations proposed in *Bonifacius.* While in Albany he formed one of the first Bible classes in America, later helping to organize similar classes in Philadelphia. He was a founding director of Princeton Theological Seminary and served as president of Dickinson College from 1824 to 1829. From 1829 to 1831 he performed laborious pioneer work as secretary of the Board of Education of the Presbyterian Church. Late in life he was a volunteer city missionary in Philadelphia, ministering to the Widows Asylum, a Magdalen Asylum, and other charitable institutions. He also helped to organize the American Bible Society.[48]

A nearby Presbyterian colleague of Neill's, Samuel Blatchford, added his concurrence with these recommendations. He was another exemplary *bonifacius* and child of the awakenings, with a transatlantic evangelical background. Born in England in 1767 and raised by parents who had been converted by John Wesley, Blatchford studied for the ministry at Homerton College. Following his ordination in 1791, he opened four Sunday schools in England before accepting a Presbyterian charge near Albany in 1804. Blatchford brought his zeal for voluntary societies to America, becoming an early supporter of home missions and the American Bible Society.[49]

These recommendations by pastors from different local churches illustrate the ecumenical influence of *Bonifacius*. While Congregational, Dutch Reformed, and Presbyterian churches do not represent a wide range of denominational diversity, they did cater to different ethnic backgrounds as well as have slightly different theological and ecclesiological emphases. They could put aside these and any local differences and unite behind *Bonifacius*'s overall purpose and specific plans for doing good, as Mather himself hoped would happen. This unifying effect may be one reason for the work's increasing popularity during the first half of the nineteenth century. Almost all Christians agreed that they needed to do good. *Bonifacius* provided a concise compilation of proposals that most could identify with and work together to put into practice.

After this Johnstown, New York, edition in 1815, *Bonifacius* continued to spread geographically. In the same year a copy of this edition apparently made its way down the Hudson to New York City, where it was reprinted and sold in several other towns, including Troy, New York; New Haven, Connecticut; and Philadelphia. *Bonifacius* also remained popular in Britain as new issues of Burder's editions appeared in 1816, 1824, and 1826.[50]

In the 1820s new reprints appeared throughout the United States. In 1822 one was issued in Wilmington, Delaware, "for the Benefit of missions," a purpose in keeping with *Bonifacius*'s spirit and specific proposals.[51] In that same year a printer in Lexington, Kentucky, at that time near the edge of the frontier, came out with an edition. While it may seem surprising that a London revision of work by a New England Puritan divine should have been chosen to be reprinted so far west and south, it turned out to be fairly popular, attracting 730 subscribers. The subscribers' list also suggests something about the nature of *Bonifacius*'s popularity. Although a few of the names are preceded by the title "Rev.," the majority are not, which implies that laypeople composed the bulk of those reading the work, precisely the audience that Mather originally hoped to address.[52] Perhaps the periodic frontier revivals around this time motivated lay interest in benevolence, and thus in a concise, practical handbook for doing good like *Bonifacius*. Its popularity seems to have exceeded the number of these original subscribers, and even the expectations of the publisher, since he put out a second edition in 1823.[53] Nor did interest in *Bonifacius* wane in New England during this time either, with reprints emerging from New Hampshire—from Portsmouth in 1824 and Dover in 1826.[54]

Mather's expression in his preface of confidence that *Bonifacius* would be well received by "a set of excellent men, in that Reformed and Renowned Church of *Scotland*," proved justified for their descendants as well. Familiarity with the original 1710 version seems to have continued until the beginning of the nineteenth century, and Burder's new edition met with a positive reception from Church of Scotland evangelicals, both individually and in the *Religious Monitor,* their main religious periodical.[55] Some of those commending *Bonifacius* were John Erskine, the venerable leader of Scottish evangelicals and correspondent with Jonathan Edwards; Walter Buchanan, the editor of the *Religious Monitor;* and William H. Burns, in whose parish revival broke out in 1839. All three of these ministers were actively involved in developing various Scottish religious voluntary societies.

Although a reprint of Burder's edition was published in Glasgow in 1821, a distinctively Scottish version also based upon Mather's original appeared in 1825 as the twenty-fourth publication in a popular series called Select Christian Authors. This series contained a predominant number of Puritan works, with *Bonifacius* serving as one of the few American representatives, and seems to have been partly in response to contemporary concerns that evangelicals neglected good works, as reflected in the introduction to another work in this series: "[The author], however was very far from being a mere *Evangelical,* in the sense imposed upon that term by the flippancy of modern sarcasm. It is true he considered the sovereignty of grace, and the entire moral inability of man, as doctrines absolutely fundamental . . .; but, like all who are enlightenedly evangelical, he was also a Christian moralist of the very highest order."[56]

Bonifacius provided an excellent model for evangelicals of balancing orthodox Calvinism and "enlightened" morality, a model reflected in the life of its Scottish editor, Andrew Thomson, minister of St. George's Parish in Edinburgh's fashionable New Town. Thomson supported numerous religious voluntary societies and was the founding editor of the most influential Scottish periodical of its day, the *Edinburgh Christian Instructor.*[57] He was a particularly prominent advocate of educational reform and of the abolition of slavery.

As the only evangelical involved in republishing *Bonifacius* who came from an established church, Thomson may have found it particularly well suited to his situation, which paralleled Mather's. Both faced the problem of seeking to Christianize society apart from increasingly unworkable and ineffective coercive theocratic methods. Thomson found attractive supplements to the traditional establishment approach both in *Bonifacius*'s organized voluntary system and in its emphasis upon Christian professionals' working out their callings in their daily lives, the latter being particularly well suited to his largely upper-middle-class congregation.

Thomson used his introduction to *Bonifacius* to address a number of problems with contemporary approaches to doing good, exceeding the number of pages originally allotted for this section in his enthusiasm for commending the work's applicability to his peers. His basic assumption was that "we endeavour to do good to others when we aim at securing their final introduction into heaven," arguing that even efforts to improve the temporal condition of the poor must include a religious dimension.[58] Nonetheless, he denied that benevolence should be narrowly pietistic. For example, broadly based education played a key role in this process, since it generally enlarged students' capacities to act morally and to understand spiritual truth. Thomson's own educational experiments in the mid-1820s reflected this perspective, which he found echoed the suggestions of *Bonifacius*.[59]

Thomson went on to try to turn the tables on contemporary rational moralists by asserting that a focus on the eternal issues of conversion was the most effective means to eliminate temporal social problems, since other approaches lacked its internal incentive to do good.[60] This argument imitated Mather's own attempts to wrestle moralists over to Christian foundations and reflected Thomson's general efforts to woo intellectuals to evangelicalism, often expressing orthodox spirituality through Enlightenment styles and thought forms.[61] *Bonifacius* contained a sufficiently enlightened approach to the "economy of benevolence" to appeal to Thomson's peers, the intellectual descendants of Adam Smith, and he emphasized that the work of religious charity made it "quite necessary that we bring our reason more into play."[62]

Thomson found *Bonifacius*'s combination of Puritan piety and Enlightenment efficiency a helpful counterbalance to various evangelical errors in doing good. Following its foundational belief that true benevolence must flow out of a regenerate heart desiring to please God, he rejected both a passive approach to morality that sought merely to avoid evil and an overly activist perspective that held that the end of doing good justified any means. Thomson adapted this argument to refute those who claimed that contributions to voluntary societies reduced giving to the poor and to warn those who participated in these groups simply because they had become fashionable.[63]

Perhaps as a result of Thomson's new version of *Bonifacius*, the work seems to have become well known in Scotland in the late 1820s, especially in missionary circles. John Wilson, an evangelical Church of Scotland missionary to India, came under its influence while still a theological student.[64] In the closing remarks of his farewell address to the Edinburgh University Missionary Association, he quotes Mather's reference to the Church of Scotland in the preface, seeming to assume that his audience will recognize his allusion without specifically identifying its source.[65]

Those associated with American voluntary societies also acknowledged *Bonifacius*'s usefulness. Around 1838 the American Tract Society published an abridged version of Burder's edition for general distribution.[66] This group, a realization of the work's proposals, in effect acknowledged its influence upon the organization's own existence by republishing it. In 1845 the Massachusetts Sabbath School Society, another group reflecting the spirit of *Bonifacius,* went even further to acknowledge the work's influence by reprinting the text of Mather's original edition.[67] While this action may reflect a more antiquarian view of this work than that held earlier in the century, the overall impression it gave me was that *Bonifacius* would continue to be relevant and influential among their contemporaries.

This 1845 edition, however, marked the last time *Bonifacius* was reprinted in the nineteenth century. The work's popularity seems to have declined during the latter half of that century for a number of reasons. As the so-called Benevolent Empire began to wane and many people began to resent seem-

ingly intrusive evangelical attempts at further social reform such as temperance, *Bonifacius*'s emphasis upon voluntary societies increasingly appeared to
be an outdated throwback that could best be done without. As industrialization and urbanization intensified during this period, the cultural distance
between Mather and his readers increased, and thus many of his individual
proposals seemed irrelevant. The bifurcation of orthodoxy and social action
culminating in the fundamentalist-modernist controversy may also have contributed to *Bonifacius*'s decline, since its synthesis of regeneration through
justification by faith alone and a rigorous, systematic approach to benevolence would alienate both groups.

Bonfacius's decline, however, should overshadow neither its remarkable
achievement of remaining highly relevant for almost a century and a half nor
its illuminating role in the development of transatlantic evangelicalism. While
this work's appeal lay partly in moralistic tendencies evident in its original text
and amplified in many of the nineteenth-century editions,[68] *Bonifacius* went
beyond moralism, even as Mather's life and the the lives of the evangelicals
involved in reprinting it went beyond moralism.

These evangelicals recognized a theological rationale, a spiritual impulse,
and a practical plan for benevolence in the pages of *Bonifacius* that were
similar to their own. It balanced inner piety and outer activism, combining a
concern for conversion and social renewal with participation in institutions
designed to further this concern. People such as Burder, Yale, Bradford,
Neill, Blatchford, and Thomson directly identified with Mather as his life was
reflected in *Bonifacius,* and hence indirectly identified with one another,
despite their temporal, geographic, theological, and denominational distance.
They recognized a common bond in their similar Puritan-based spiritual motivation and Enlightenment-inspired practical organization and activity.

These evangelicals viewed the work's flexible application to their contemporary situation as its primary strength, reinforcing their own social program
and spurring it on to greater realization by suggesting a diversity of specific
ways of working it out. *Bonifacius* was a concise compilation of a multitude of
useful ideas that others around them, especially laypeople, could put immediately into practice. Therefore, they continued to reprint it, transforming
Burder's edition into a kind of nineteenth-century "*Reader's Digest* Con-
densed Handbook for Doing Good."

The spiritual dynamism of transatlantic evangelicalism following the First
and Second awakenings partly explains why Mather's successors were more
successful in seeing *Bonifacius*'s suggestions implemented in their society than
he was in his. In this work Mather distilled the wisdom of his predecessors and
his own experience of doing good into an overall structure, like a master sailor
developing an elaborate set of riggings and sails. Yet, no matter how sophisticated this setup might be, it would have little impact in a becalmed sea. When
others, however, drawing upon Mather's design, developed a similar set of
riggings, the awakenings filled their sails and propelled their ships at record
speeds, leaving a trail of benevolent activity in their wakes reaching both sides
of the Atlantic.

Notes

1. James W. Jones, *The Shattered Synthesis: New England Puritanism before the Great Awakening* (New Haven: Yale University Press, 1973), 83–86; and to a lesser extent, Perry Miller, *The New England Mind: From Colony to Province* (Cambridge: Harvard University Press, 1953), 410–16.

2. David Bebbington cites activism as one of the four primary characterisitcs of evangelicalism in Britain, especially in the nineteenth century (*Evangelicalism in Modern Britain: A History from the 1730s to the 1980s* [London: Unwin Hyman, 1989], 10–12, 105–50).

3. Richard Lovelace, *The American Pietism of Cotton Mather: The Origins of American Evangelicalism* (Grand Rapids: Christian University Press, 1979), 32–35, 162–63; Josephine Piercy, "Introduction," in *Bonifacius: An Essay . . . to Do Good,* by Cotton Mather (Gainesville, FL: Scholars' Facsimiles and Reprints, 1967), viii.

4. Cotton Mather, *Bonifacius, an Essay upon the Good,* ed. David Levin (Cambridge: Harvard University Press, 1966), 135 (unless otherwise noted, all further references to *Bonifacius* refer to this edition).

5. *Bonifacius,* 5. See also Joyce Olson Ransome, "Cotton Mather and the Catholic Spirit" (Ph.D. diss., University of California at Berkeley, 1966), 96, 245.

6. Kenneth Silverman, ed., *Selected Letters of Cotton Mather* (Baton Rouge: Louisiana University Press, 1971), 90–91, 95.

7. W. C. Ford, ed., *Diary of Cotton Mather* (1911–12 ed. reprinted by New York: Frederick Ungar, 1957), 2:60.

8. *Bonifacius,* 58–60.

9. Ford, *Diary* 2:42.

10. *Bonifacius,* 23–24.

11. Kenneth Silverman, *The Life and Times of Cotton Mather* (New York: Harper and Row, 1984), 233–34.

12. Lovelace, *American Pietism of Cotton Mather,* 216, 221, 223; Ransome, "Cotton Mather," 84–85, 97–99.

13. *Bonifacius,* 63–67; Lovelace, *American Pietism of Cotton Mather,* 215–18.

14. See Susan O'Brien, "Eighteenth-Century Publishing Networks in the First Years of Transatlantic Evangelicalism," chap. 2 above.

15. Levin, "Introduction," in *Bonifacius,* ix.

16. Chester Jorgenson and Frank Mott, eds., *Benjamin Franklin, Representative Selections,* rev. ed., American Century Series (New York: Hill and Wang, 1962), 471.

17. Richard E. French, "Cotton Mather and the Development of American Values" (Th.D. diss., Harvard University, 1978), 174–76.

18. Philip Campbell, "Cotton Mather" (Ph.D. diss., Brown University, 1955), 187–88.

19. Jones, *Shattered Synthesis,* 84.

20. For example, arguing for applying business approaches to benevolence because of their productivity (*Bonifacius,* 23).

21. *Bonifacius,* 27–28.

22. *Bonifacius,* 104, 135. Note the religious character of almost every one of the suggestions listed in the closing "CATALOG OF DESIRABLES, waiting for the *zeal of good men* to prosecute them" (138–42).

23. French, "Cotton Mather," 105. The complex relationship between Mather and Franklin has received extensive scholarly attention. See David Levin, "Edwards, Franklin, and Cotton Mather: A Meditation on Character and Reputation," in *Jona-*

than Edwards and the American Experience, ed. Harry Stout and Nathan Hatch (New York: Oxford University Press, 1988); Mitchell Robert Breitwieser, *Cotton Mather and Benjamin Franklin: The Price of Representative Personality* (New York: Cambridge University Press, 1984); G. D. McEwan, " 'A turn of thinking': Benjamin Franklin, Cotton Mather, and Daniel Defoe on 'doing good,' " in *The Dress of Words: Essays on Restoration and Eighteenth Century Literature in Honor of Richmond P. Bond,* ed. Robert B. White, Jr. (Lawrence: University of Kansas Press, 1978); and Phyllis Franklin, *Show Thyself a Man: A Comparison of Benjamin Franklin and Cotton Mather* (The Hague: Mouton, 1969).

24. Lovelace, *American Pietism of Cotton Mather,* 164.

25. Thomas Holmes, *Cotton Mather: A Bibliography of His Works* (Cambridge: Harvard University Press, 1940), 1:90.

26. Miller, *New England Mind,* 410.

27. Henry Forster Burder, *Memoir of the Rev. George Burder* (New York: Jonathan Leavitt; Boston: Crocker and Brewster, 1833), 8–9, 15.

28. Ibid., 20.

29. A. Gordon, "George Burder," *Dictionary of National Biography* 7:294–95.

30. See *Bonifacius,* 80, 89–90, for models of both groups.

31. Burder, *Memoir of George Burder,* 133.

32. Gordon, "George Burder," 294–95; Burder, *Memoir of George Burder,* 193–96.

33. *Bonifacius,* 140.

34. Burder, *Memoir of George Burder,* 318.

35. George Burder, "Preface," in *Essays to Do Good,* by Cotton Mather (London: J. Dennett, 1807), v.

36. Ibid., x.

37. Ibid., 58, 86.

38. *Evangelical Magazine* 9 (February 1801): 72.

39. Ibid., 15 (April 1807): 182; (May 1807): 232; (July 1807): 323–24.

40. Ibid., 15 (July 1807): 323.

41. Holmes, *Mather* 1:327.

42. Ibid., 229.

43. William Sprague, *Annals of the American Pulpit* (New York: Robert Carter and Brothers, 1857), 2:364, 366.

44. Elisha Yale, letter dated 1 March 1815, in *Essays to Do Good,* by Cotton Mather, ed. George Burder (Johnstown, NY: Child and Clap, 1815), iii.

45. Sprague, *Annals* 9:151.

46. Ibid., 150, 152.

47. *Essays to Do Good,* iv.

48. P. P. Faris, "William Neill," *Dictionary of American Biography* 13:411.

49. Sprague, *Annals* 4:159.

50. Holmes, *Mather* 1:330–31.

51. Ibid., 332.

52. *Essays to Do Good,* by Cotton Mather, ed. George Burder (Lexington, KY: Thomas T. Skillman, 1822), 243–56. Holmes does not mention these pages in his bibliography, but they are present in the copy in Houghton Library at Harvard University.

53. Holmes, *Mather* 1:333.

54. Ibid., 334, 336.

55. *Religious Monitor* 3 (March 1805): 105–6; 14 (June 1816): 215; Islay Burns, *The Pastor of Kilsyth* (London: T. Nelson and Sons, 1860), 69.

56. David Young, "Introduction," in *The Saint Indeed and the Touchstone of Sincerity,* by John Flavel (Glasgow: Collins, 1830), vii.

57. For a list of the groups in which Thomson participated, see David Currie, "The Growth of Evangelicalism in the Church of Scotland," (Ph.D. diss., University of St. Andrews, 1990), 478–79.

58. Andrew Thomson, "Introduction," in *Essays to Do Good,* by Cotton Mather (Glasgow: Chalmers and Collins, 1825), x–xviii.

59. Ibid., xix–xx, lxxxv–lxxxvi.

60. Ibid., xvii–xxx.

61. Thomson adapted elements of Moderate preaching style to communicate evangelical content to his largely educated parishioners and elements of the *Edinburgh Review*'s periodical style to communicate this same message in the *Edinburgh Christian Instructor.* See Currie, "Evangelicalism in the Church of Scotland," 60–72.

62. Thomson, "Introduction," lxviii–lxxx.

63. Ibid., xl–lxii. Scottish evangelicals debated many of these same issues in the pages of Thomson's *Edinburgh Christian Instructor* and other religious periodicals (Currie "Evangelicalism in the Church of Scotland," 216–20).

64. George Smith, *The Life of John Wilson* (London: John Murray, 1878), 28.

65. Edinburgh University Missionary Association Minutes, 1 March 1828, New College Library.

66. Holmes, *Mather* 1:337.

67. Ibid., 89.

68. For example, Burder reduced Mather's full title to *Essays to Do Good,* omitting any reference to answering the great end of life, and substituted a rather bland verse, "To do good and to communicate, forget not" (Heb. 13:16) for the more divinely oriented original, "Knowing that whatsoever good thing any man does, the same shall he receive of the Lord" (Eph. 6:8). Nonetheless, Burder still viewed doing good primarily as a means of glorifying God: "May the God of all goodness smile on every attempt to promote his glory, by promoting the happiness of his creatures!" ("Preface," *Essays to Do Good* [London: 1807], xii).

5

Time, Celebration, and the Christian Year in Eighteenth-Century Evangelicalism

LEIGH E. SCHMIDT

Cotton Mather, like his father, Increase, and other Puritans, had little but disdain for the observance of Christmas. "Can you in your *Conscience* think, that our *Holy Saviour* is honoured, by *Mad Mirth*, by long *Eating*, by hard *Drinking*, by lewd *Gaming*, by rude *Revelling;* by a *Mass* fit for none but a *Saturn*, or a *Bacchus*, or the Night of a *Mahometan Ramadam*?" Mather queried rhetorically in a sermon in 1712. Though the preservation of Sabbatarian simplicity in worship—the plain and unsullied religion of the Lord's Day—was invariably a hard charge to keep, Mather took solace that the Puritan churches of New England were in good company in their efforts. In resisting Christmas, Mather assured his congregation that they "harmoniz'd with their *United Brethren* in *Scotland*" in "their not having a *Yule* observed among them."[1] To be sure, Congregationalists in New England and Presbyterians in Scotland long prided themselves on their rejection of Christmas and their utter abandonment of the traditional Christian year. Many eighteenth-century evangelicals on both sides of the Atlantic inherited these deep-seated suspicions and animosities toward the red-letter Christian feasts that stretched from Advent and Christmas through Lent, Easter, Pentecost, and Trinity Sunday. Even John Wesley, liturgically conservative by Puritan standards, concluded in his *Sunday Service of the Methodists in North America* (1784) that "most of the holy-days (so called)" were "at present answering no valuable end"—a conclusion that seemed to invite his followers to lay aside many of those festivals that he himself had observed.[2]

In a modern world ever on the alert for Scrooges and Grinches, the spurning of Christmas and other feast days has garnered considerable notoriety for the Sabbatarian rigors of Puritans, Presbyterians, and evangelicals. But evangelical views of celebration, festival, and the Christian year offer a far richer story than simply one of opposition and iconoclastic leveling. Puritans bequeathed a calendar punctuated not only by the Sabbath but also by fast and thanksgiving days and other civil religious solemnities. Scottish Presbyterians added to this Puritan cycle a complex tradition of eucharistic festivity and renewal, focused on elaborate annual celebrations of the Lord's Supper. General Baptists and a number of other groups, such as the Glasites or Sandemanians, enriched the liturgical traditions of North Atlantic evangelicals with foot-washing ceremonies and love feasts. For their part, Methodists preserved at least the outline of the traditional Christian year, while adding a whole panoply of rituals such as watch nights, covenant services, and love feasts. Clearly eighteenth-century evangelicals did not simply find themselves, in the words of a popular gospel hymn, "tossed and driven on the restless sea of time."[3] Like other Christians, they had various ways of bringing order to the year and redeeming time.

Sociologists and anthropologists regularly remind us that the ordering of time and the calendar is one of the most fundamental cultural constructs that guides a community or a people. Eviatar Zerubavel, who has focused his scholarly work on developing a sociology of time, emphasizes the importance of discerning the "temporal map" that shapes the understanding and experience of time in a given society. What patterns, rules, structures, conventions, and cycles make up this map? How are social or religious identities forged and maintained through distinctive calendrical observances, through different constructions and construals of time? How are sacred times differentiated from the profane? How do private experiences of temporality relate to public versions of timekeeping? Of recurrent importance in the sociology and anthropology of religion, such "sociotemporal" questions have also drawn examination from historians. For example, in *Albion's Seed* David Hackett Fischer calls attention to the "time ways" of the regional folk cultures of Britain and North America. In a suggestive if overly schematized way, he highlights Puritan efforts at "improving the time," Quaker visions of "redeeming the time," Cavalier notions of "killing the time," and backcountry ideas of "passing the time." Fischer's work points to the importance of exploring how time and celebration were variously patterned in the North Atlantic world.[4]

Charting the time ways or temporal maps of eighteenth-century evangelicalism in Scotland, England, and North America is a large task. A welter of local, regional, and denominational constructions of time and celebration were evident; even within the same "time zone" of one tradition or one region, tension and debate were often as prevalent as consensus. Also various layers and levels of timekeeping were apparent. Liturgiologist James F. White has spoken of the "four main cycles of liturgical time: daily, weekly, yearly, and lifetime."[5] In both their public and private lives, eighteenth-century evangelicals clearly manifested a wide range of daily, weekly, seasonal, and calendrical rhythms—liturgical and otherwise. Sundry, too, were the rituals and sacraments that marked out passages or transitions in the life cycles or pilgrimages of evangelical Protestants. As David Hall has said of Samuel Sewall and the Puritans, so too for eighteenth-century evangelicals: They "lived amid several modes of time."[6] This essay can scrutinze only some of these modalities, only certain patches in what is a mottled quilt. It begins with an exploration of the evangelical inheritance of Reformation and Puritan debates about the calendar, celebration, and the Christian year. The essay then examines the Scottish Presbyterian configuring of celebration and festi-

val around the Lord's Supper and the influence of that tradition on evangelical revivalism. The essay proceeds from there to the Methodist movement and
its evangelical via media, its openness both to the traditional Christian year
and to new evangelical solemnities. In a final section, points of convergence
are underscored, and three long-term tensions or trajectories in the evangelical accounting of time are explored.

I

Reforming the Roman Catholic calendar was a major part of the Protestant
agenda from the first years of the Reformation, but how far these reforms
should go and what form they should take were questions that elicited a wide
spectrum of answers. In addition to Sunday the Catholic year revolved around
three interrelated sets of holy days: those dedicated to Christ, those devoted
to the Virgin Mary, and those in honor of the saints. Which of these solemnities to keep, if any, exercised early modern Protestants in ongoing debate.
Most critical of the sanctoral and Marian cycles, the reformers were often far
warmer toward the christological feasts. The Second Helvetic Confession
(1566), one of the foundational texts for the Continental Reformed churches,
codified a moderate Protestant perspective. "Although religion be not tied
unto time," the confession concluded, "yet [it cannot] be planted and exercised without a due dividing and allotting-out of time." This Reformed allot-
ment of time meant, first and foremost, keeping the Lord's Day, but also
religiously celebrating the Lord's nativity, circumcision, passion, resurrection,
ascension, as well as the pentecostal outpouring of the Holy Spirit. While
rejecting Lent and saints' days, it embraced public fast days and "the remembrance of the saints" as "holy examples."[7]
    If in the sixteenth century there was already a diversity of Protestant
calendars, this fragmentation became still more apparent in the seventeeth
century, and nowhere more so than in England. At one end of the spectrum
was the calendar of the Anglican establishment. It largely preserved the
rhythms of the Roman Catholic year, while streamlining the Marian and
sanctoral feasts and adding a number of civil religious days devoted to the
English monarchy and state. Puritans of various stripes saw the Anglican
calendar as one of the sure signs that the English church remained only half-
way reformed, an abominable hybrid that blurred the boundaries between
Protestant and Catholic conceptions of time. English Puritans and Scottish
Presbyterians responded with a calendrical purge that far outstripped the
prevailing Reformed and Lutheran traditions on the Continent (with the
prominent exception of Calvin's Geneva). They urged the complete elimination of the christological feasts along with the Marian and sanctoral cycles.
Radicals such as the Quakers gave this Puritan predilection its extreme formulation in arguing that worship should be limited by neither place or time, that
it should be guided only by the "secret inspirations" of the Spirit, and that all

set times and liturgies were "but superstitions, will-worship, and abominable idolatry in the sight of God."[8] By this radical line of argument, even the Sabbath itself tended to be leveled or spiritualized; it was considered of no greater sanctity than any other day. North Atlantic evangelical conceptions of time and celebration emerged out of this crucible of calendrical strife in early modern England and Scotland.[9]

In these Reformation and Puritan debates over the patterning of the church year, a number of underlying principles were at issue. Foremost, the debates hinged on different valuations of Scripture and tradition, on weighing the relative authority of each in the formation of Christian worship. What constituted the devotional cycles of primitive Christianity as revealed in the Bible? How did those patterns stand in relationship to the ancient traditions of the church? Controversy also pivoted on what Christian liberty meant, on the degree to which Christians were to be free of ceremonies and forms. Were the fasts of Lent (or, conversely, the rigors of the Puritan Sabbath) legalistic encumbrances upon the faithful, inimical to Christian freedom? Disputes revolved as well around whether feast days were edifying and served a useful end or whether they were a diversion from genuine faith, communicating the shadow and not the substance of the gospel. Arguments also centered on whether such ceremonies and customs, if not contrary to Scripture, could be seen as counting among the things indifferent, adiaphora that churches were free to celebrate, rearrange, or emphasize as they saw fit or found useful.[10]

Finally, and less theologically, debates over the church year revealed conflicting attitudes toward popular culture and the celebratory repertories that characterized popular festivals. Did folk customs—such as the topsy-turvy revelry at Christmas, Shrove Tuesday, and Easter Monday—condemn the celebrations as a whole, or should Christians continue to observe these occasions, harshly attempting to purge them of abuse or perhaps jovially accepting such activities as innocent tomfoolery? Such questions interlocked with issues of how a Christian's time was best improved. Were holy days inherently idle days, times of dissipation in tension with disciplined labor and industry?[11] Debates over all these issues echoed time and again in Protestant discussions of worship and constituted a major legacy of the Reformation and Puritan eras in the formation of evangelical discourse on time and celebration.

A Christmas Day sermon in 1758 by Presbyterian Samuel Davies, an acknowledged leader of the revival movement in the colonies, gives some specific sense of how these questions about the observance of holy days recurred in evangelical thought and how one figure, on the Puritan side of the spectrum, answered them. Faced with the continued popularity of Christmas, Davies had finally decided "once for all" to "declare my sentiments more fully upon this head." Noticeably defensive about even acknowledging Christmas from the pulpit, Davies saw little hope in trying to convert a day of "superstition" and "extravagant mirth" into a time of "rational and scriptural devotion." Indeed, he prefaced his reluctant observance of Christmas with a dismissal:

> I do not set apart this day for public worship, as though it had any peculiar
> sanctity, or we were under any obligations to keep it religiously. I know no
> human authority, that has power to make one day more holy than another,
> or that can bind the conscience in such cases. And as for divine authority, to
> which alone the sanctifying of days and things belongs, it has thought it
> sufficient to consecrate one day in seven to a religious use, for the commemo-
> ration both of the birth of this world, and the resurrection of its great
> Author, or of the works of creation and redemption. This I would religiously
> observe; and inculcate the religious observance of it upon all.

The Lord's Day is what mattered, not an "endless list" of Catholic and Anglican holy days, of which Christmas was but the exemplar.[12]

Davies had a clear sense of his principles of worship. The primacy of
Scripture was the foundation; recapturing "the old, plain, simple religion of
the Bible" was for him the basis of evangelical liturgics. The pure, scriptural
worship of primitive Christianity was set against "the corrupt medium of
human tradition," which he accorded virtually no authority. Davies also saw
such humanly imposed feasts in commemoration of Christ, the saints, and the
Virgin Mary as legalistic impositions—infringements upon Christian liberty.
Such ceremonies were viewed as being but the shadow, not the substance of
the gospel; they drew people away from Christ into an absorption with outward forms. He also found that, despite the ostensibly "pious design" of
Christmas, it was hopelessly corrupt in its popular observance—"a season of
sinning, sensuality, luxury, and various forms of extravagance." In this respect, Yuletide was but symptomatic of the larger lassitude and license at the
heart of all holidays. "Thus the people are taught to be idle," Davies concluded, and to slight "the ordinary labours of life." If for his part he would do
away with Christmas and "all other holy-days instituted by men," he was
nonetheless willing to grant that such feast days were among the things indifferent, "the extra-essentials of religion," and he did not want "to widen the
differences subsisting among Christians" or "to awaken dormant controversies" over "these little differences." He could imagine the utility of Christmas
for the edification of the faithful and allowed that "many are offering up
acceptable devotion to God on this day." His very willingness to mark Christmas with a special sermon on the Incarnation suggested a certain moderation
and flexibility reflective of the larger Protestant understanding of adiaphora.[13]

Davies's sermon was not exceptional, but it was typical in its suppositions.
It reflected the evangelical engagement in the core liturgical concerns of the
Reformation and Puritan epochs: biblicism, primitivism, Sabbatarianism,
anti-Catholicism, the reevaluation of the uses and role of tradition, Christian
liberty, issues of adiaphora, and the reform of popular calendrical customs
and the folk mores reflected in them. The liturgical issues that engaged evangelicals from place to place and from period to period were strikingly similar,
but the liturgical results at which they arrived were multiple. Out of long
debate and experience, diverse patterns of evangelical celebration and worship emerged. This pluralism was to be expected and was often accepted
without perturbation. As the Methodist Articles of Religion declared in 1784,

following a similar statement in the Anglican confession, "It is not necessary that rites and ceremonies should in all places be the same, or exactly alike; for they have been always different, and may be changed according to the diversity of countries, times, and men's manners."[14]

II

The Reformed calendar in Scotland was among the most stringent in its focus on the Lord's Day and in its attack on the Roman Catholic calendar. Under the first heading in the first *Book of Discipline* (1560), John Knox and his compatriots forswear the "keeping of holy days . . . such as be all those that the Papists have invented, as the Feasts (as they term them) of Apostles, Martyrs, Virgins, of Christmas, Circumcision, Epiphany, Purification, and other fond feasts of our Lady." Seeing no warrant in the Bible for these festivals, the Scottish reformers urged that they be "utterly . . . abolished from this Realm."[15] In the place of "festivall and superstitious dayes," the reformers envisioned a new ideal of keeping "perpetuall and spiritual festivities with Christ and his saints."[16] The devout were to mold their religious lives out of such day-to-day devotions as prayer and meditation—practices of piety that revolved around preparation for the Lord's Day, not around great festivals like Easter or Whitsunday.

By the 1620s and 1630s a growing group of Presbyterians in Scotland was fortifying this cleansed Reformed calendar with an emergent festival of their own improvisation and devising, centered on outdoor preaching and the Lord's Supper. In the ongoing battle with episcopal opponents, the Presbyterians had come to stake much of their religious identity on the liturgical purity of their sacraments and their calendar. When this purity seemed threatened by new monarchical and episcopal designs to enforce kneeling at communion and to reinstitute the christological feast days, Presbyterians increasingly revolted and took to the fields and churchyards for preaching and the Eucharist. Soon their resistance to Episcopalian forms had issued in a Presbyterian awakening—the most famous instance of which was the "solemn Communion" at the kirk of Shotts in 1630, a four- or five-day meeting led by the itinerating preacher John Livingston. Nearly five hundred people were said to have had experiences of conversion or confirmation on that occasion.[17] Lengthy and crowded communions, like that at the kirk of Shotts, emerged as the prevailing model of Presbyterian renewal. By the turn of the eighteenth century, summer and early fall sacraments were clearly established in the popular Presbyterian callendar as the high days of the year, times of pilgrimage and sustained devotion, times of conversion and eucharistic solemnity.[18]

Sacramental occasions continued to underpin Scottish patterns of renewal and piety amid the eighteenth-century Evangelical Revival. This was most dramatically revealed in the famed revivals at Cambuslang and Kilsyth. One wide-eyed account by a young layman captured the excitement and bustle of the Cambuslang Communions in 1742:

There were two sacramental occasions at Cambuslang s[ai]d year[.] [T]he
last was about the first of A[u]gust where was many ministers from distant
parts and such a multitude of folk from distant parts as far as Edinburgh,
Stirling, Air, Pasley, & the agasant country in this nighbourhood that I never
expect to see such a multitude again in one place in this world[.] [T]here was
three tents up that day two for sermon & one for dispensing the sacrament
and as many at each tent as could hear besids grate numbers seated in the
fields & goeing from one place to another. The work began at 8. o'clock &
the sun was set before the tables were finished.[19]

At Kilsyth the Communion was similarly spectacular and enlivening; sacrament and revival, eucharistic ritual and tent preaching, blended there as
elsewhere in the familiar Scottish mode.

These sacramental occasions deeply affected the rhythms of people's piety.
Looked to as long-awaited seasons of renewal, the Communions were the
peaks in the topography of this Reformed spirituality. Faced recurrently with
disconsolation or doubt, the saints craved the revivification and assurance the
sacrament often brought. As one evangelical at Cambuslang related, "For a
considerable time I fell under damps & long'd for a Sacrament Occasion to get
a revival." Similarly, another saint involved in the awakening, having found
renewal at a sacrament, "went home with much love & joy longing for another Communion occasion."[20] Stretching over several days and often with
thousands of people in attendance from over a wide area, the sacramental
occasions of summer and early fall were the consummate celebrations or
festivals among evangelical Presbyterians. Prepared for through the whole
range of Reformed spiritual disciplines—secret prayer, meditation on the
sufferings of Christ, personal covenanting, fasting, self-examination, and
study of the Bible and sacramental manuals—the Communion stood out as
the devotional high point in the year. Such intensive, anxiety-ridden prepara-
tions for a worthy approach to the Lord's Table often issued in dramatic
experiences of spiritual resolution, including ecstatic moments of vision, fainting, tears, and trembling as souls were drawn into loving union with the
Bridegroom.[21]

This Scottish Prebyterian patterning of the year around festal Communions contained various implications for the course of evangelical worship in
the North Atlantic world. Two particularly seem worth highlighting. First,
the Scottish model of renewal served as a paradigm for conceiving revivals as
annual events woven into the very fabric of church life. In the United States
the Scottish example helped inspire the organization of camp meetings;
James McGready's gatherings in Kentucky, often hailed as the prototypical
camp meetings, were developed seamlessly out of Old World Presbyterian
sacramental occasions. The camp meetings, like the Communion seasons,
institutionalized revival and renewal as part of the annual circuit of denominational and congregational life. The yearly revival meeting, which became a
staple of nineteenth-century evangelicalism, had its echo and antecedent in
seventeenth- and eighteenth-century Presbyterian Communions.

Second, the Scottish sacramental occasions serve as a reminder of the centrality of the Eucharist in much of the eighteenth-century evangelical move-ment. Perhaps because of the images of later revivalists from Charles Grandi-son Finney to Billy Sunday and the meetings they led, it has sometimes been easy to forget the focal importance of sacramentalism in the eighteenth-century revivals. Besides this being the case for Presbyterians in Scotland, Ulster, and North America, it was also true in the Welsh and Methodist revivals. Howell Harris's account of the coincidence of the Lord's Supper and revival in Wales sounds, as Ted Campbell has recently observed, very similar to narratives from the Scottish tradition.[22] Likewise the Wesleys' eucharistic piety was infused with the mystery and presence of Christ—a piety most strikingly revealed in their sacramental hymns.[23] Though this intense eucharis-tic spirituality among eighteenth-century evangelicals could lead to discord—for example, over the frequency of Communion or the validity of visions—there was widespread agreement about the devotional centrality of the Lord's Supper. The Scottish sacramental occasions were the hallmark of much wider traditions in which Eucharist and awakening converged.

III

In contrast to the thorough purging of Roman Catholic and Anglican holy days among Scottish Presbyterians, the Christian year among early English Methodists looked more traditional and compromising. Unlike Knox and his compeers, John and Charles Wesley, as evangelical Anglicans, worked within the framework of the established Christian year, even as they encouraged new solemnities, like watch nights and love feasts, that often eclipsed in popularity the historic feasts. In order to examine the two sides of the early Methodist calendar—its retention of the church festivals and its invention of new evan-gelical gatherings—an illustration from each side is helpful. On the one hand, the hymns of Charles Wesley are an inlet into the traditionalism of the year in the early Methodist movement; on the other, watch night services, especially as they developed into an evangelical alternative to the folk customs of New Year's Eve, are an illuminating example of the popular dimensions of the Methodist calendar.[24]

Charles Wesley's prodigious productivity as a hymnist is legendary. Frank Baker puts the number of hymns and poems that Charles Wesley composed at nine thousand; his verses address just about everything from simple domestic scenes to the glories of heaven.[25] With such thoroughness did he versify upon the Christian life that one can reconstruct out of his poems and hymns a remark-ably full picture of the day-to-day, even hour-to-hour, piety of eighteenth-century English evangelicalism. There are hymns for morning and evening, hymns upon waking and going to bed, hymns for before and after meals, hymns for work and home, hymns for before, during, and after school, and hymns for midnight and sleep. He had such an eye for the domestic dailiness of the Christian life that he even composed hymns with titles such as "For a Child on His Birthday" and "For a Child Cutting His Teeth."[26]

Amid this impressive corpus were several hymn collections dedicated to the feast days of the church. His first collection, *Hymns and Sacred Poems,* published jointly with his brother John in 1739, includes hymns for Christmas, Epiphany, Easter, Ascension, and Whitsunday. The "HYMN for CHRISTMASS-DAY" opened with the stanza:

> Hark how all the Welkin rings
> "Glory to the King of Kings,
> "Peace on Earth, and Mercy mild,
> "GOD and Sinners reconcil'd![27]

(Interestingly, it is George Whitefield who emended the first two lines to the more familiar "Hark, the herald angels sing / Glory to the new-born King" for inclusion in his *Collection of Hymns for Social Worship* in 1753.)[28] Wesley's hymn combined traditional recognition of Christmas as the holy day of the Incarnation with evangelical themes of new birth:

> Veil'd in Flesh, the Godhead see,
> Hail th'Incarnate Deity!
> Pleas'd as Man with Men t'appear
> JESUS, our *Immanuel* here!
>
> Mild He lays his Glory by,
> Born—that Man no more may die,
> Born—to raise the Sons of Earth,
> Born—to give them Second Birth.

Like his Easter hymn "Christ, the Lord, Is Risen Today" and his Ascension hymn "Hail the Day That Sees Him Rise"—both of which also appeared in this 1739 collection—Wesley's Christmas hymn left an enduring imprint on evangelical piety.[29] As Bernard Manning observed, such hymns came to stand as the functional equivalent to formal liturgies for evangelical Protestants at Christmas and Easter.[30]

The hymn for Whitsunday in the 1739 collection, though less well known, also combined the traditional liturgical themes of the holy day with evangelical motifs. Pentecost inherently held peculiar potential for inspiring evangelical worship, and Wesley made the most of these possibilities:

> Come, Divine and peaceful Guest,
> Enter our devoted Breast;
> HOLY GHOST, our Hearts inspire,
> Kindle there the Gospel-Fire.
>
> Now descend and shake the Earth,
> Wake us into Second Birth;
> Now thy quick'ning Influence give,
> Blow—and these dry Bones shall live![31]

In Wesley's hymns there was an interfusion of the historic Christian year and the new evangelical revival.

The 1739 collection was only Wesley's initial foray into composing hymns for the Christian year. In the 1740s there followed a number of discrete compilations of hymns for the high holy days. *Hymns for the Nativity of Our Lord* appeared in 1744; *Hymns for Our Lord's Resurrection* followed in 1746, as did *Hymns for Ascension-Day* and *Hymns of Petition and Thanksgiving for the Father.* An overarching collection for the church year, *Hymns on the Great Festivals, and Other Occasions,* also appeared for the first time in 1746. As it did for John Keble in the next century, the Christian year provided Charles Wesley with a framework for his recapitulation of the whole of Christian piety in verse and song. In *Hymns on the Great Festivals,* he moved through the nativity, crucifixion, resurrection, ascension, the sending of the Holy Spirit, and the Trinity. He followed these compositions with a selection of hymns for other occasions—one, for example, that serves as an invitation both to the Lord's Table and to repentance, and three others that deal with the last things of death and heaven.[32] As in his other collections on the Christian year, the work represented a synthesis of Anglican time and evangelical time—the new wine of Methodist piety in the old wineskins of the Christian year.

Also included among Charles Wesley's verses for specific times and celebrations were his *Hymns for New-Year's-Day* and his *Hymns for the Watch-Night.* These collections are indicative of how an openness to liturgical innovation coexisted with traditionalism in the Wesleys. New patterns of worship, which were clearly one of the distinguishing marks of the Methodist movement, included corporate covenant services extrapolated by John Wesley from Puritan models of personal covenanting;[33] love feasts of bread and water based on Moravian example and including ample time for song, prayer, and testimonials;[34] class and band meetings for mutual edification, discipline, and devotion;[35] and outdoor revivals, epitomized in field preaching, quarterly conferences, and camp meetings.[36] To this popular Methodist calendar was also added the watch night. Begun near Bristol among Kingswood Methodists in the early 1740s as one more improvised gathering of the faithful for extended "prayer and praise and thanksgiving," watch night services were initially held at various times throughout the year, especially timed to full moons for purposes of lighting people's way to and from these midnight vigils. Seeing great spiritual results in what he tellingly termed "the novelty of this *ancient* custom" of vigils, John Wesley quickly endorsed these meetings and encouraged their "more general use" among the Methodist societies.[37]

The preeminent occasion for the watch night soon emerged as New Year's Eve, and in this choice the Methodists attempted to set up, as Henry Rack has recently observed, "a spiritualized counter-attraction to that pagan folk-festival."[38] In their watch nights these evangelicals renounced the entrenched festivities of popular culture; they found new self-definition as well as community identity through their opposition to the familiar celebrations of the New Year. Charles Wesley aptly captured this spirit in the opening stanza of his first watch night hymn:

> OFT have we pass'd the guilty night,
> In revellings and frantic mirth:

> The creature was our sole delight,
> Our happiness the things of earth;
> But O! suffice the season past,
> We choose the better part at last.[39]

Itinerant Joseph Pilmore expressed similar themes in his journal covering his ministry in the colonies from 1769 to 1774. Participating in meetings for Christmas Eve, Christmas Day, and New Year's Eve in New York in 1770, he was struck by "how widely" these services diverged "from the feasting and entertainments of the wicked." For New Year's Eve, he observed specifically: "We had our Watch-Night. The Mob had threatened great things, but the terrors of the Lord made them afraid, and we continued till after midnight, that we might end the *old,* and begin the *New Year,* in the service of God." With the advent of Methodist watch nights, New Year's Eve became a kind of cultural battleground. The boisterous noise of drunken and violent celebrants in the streets was set against the joyful shouts of evangelicals in side-street chapels.[40]

For Methodists, the cultural battleground at New Year's extended beyond the open conflict with "the slaves of excess" and "the drunkards" who, "in a circle of riot," threatened to break up their meetings. It also took in "the civiller crowd" with their masques, balls, visits, entertainments, and other pleasures and luxuries.[41] Far more than Christmas, New Year's was in the late eighteenth century the bellwether of consumer-oriented holidays—an occasion of sumptuous gifts and pompous display, especially among the nobility and the privileged. In 1770 a New York merchant, James Rivington, ran an advertisement for New Year's gifts in the *New-York Journal* that read like a catalog of the eighteenth-century consumer revolution: necklaces, lockets, snuff boxes, toothpick cases, watch chains, silver-plated tea urns, dress swords, silk stockings, backgammon tables, among other goods, were all offered to "Ladies and Gentlemen" as "proper Presents."[42] Puritans had long objected to the pagan frivolity of New Year's gifts, and George Whitefield in typical evangelical fashion centered a New Year's sermon on the need for immediate repentance; his sermon identified "the best *New Year's Gift* as "a Penitent Heart." Likewise the solemnity, plainness, and otherworldliness of the Methodist watch nights (as well as their covenant services, which also were often timed to the New Year) stood in stark contrast with the New Year's rituals of the well born and the well heeled.[43]

The power of the watch night service at New Year's was built not only on its oppositional qualities but also on its constructive possibilities. Core evangelical beliefs found embodiment and expression in watch nights hymns, exhortations, prayers, and testimonials. The end of another year added urgency to the evangelical call to repentance, to turn to Christ before it was too late, to confirm one's commitment while there was yet time. The close of the year heightened reflection on the hurtling of the soul toward death and eternity, and one of the refrains of the watch night was to redeem the time. Being vigilant until late into the night also placed these services in the eschatological framework of being ready for Christ's second coming. Included in the watch

night was a kind of Advent piety in which the evangelicals envisioned themselves as watchmen in the night for the long-expected Jesus. This sense is
captured in another of Charles Wesley's watch night verses:

> Then let us wait to hear
> The trumpet's welcome sound;
> To see our Lord appear,
> Watching let us be found;
> When Jesus doth the heavens bow,
> Be found—as Lord, thou finds us now.

Like the wise virgins with the oil in their lamps, the faithful were ready for
"the midnight cry" of the Bridegroom.[44]

The early Methodist movement sought to transform the popular festivities
of Christmas and New Year's into evangelical observances. Rather than trying
vainly to obliterate their observance, the early Methodists recognized the
power of such folk celebrations and wanted to remold them into their own
image. The sentiments of the Wesleys' sometimes estranged coworker George
Whitefield were revealing in this regard. In a sermon entitled "The True Way
of Keeping Christmas," Whitefield sharply contrasted the sinful and pious
ways of observing that holy season. Those who ate and drank to excess, those
who played at cards and dice, those who neglected their worldly callings,
those who indulged in luxury and extravagance misspent the holiday, but
these abuses did not mean that the devout should spurn Christmas. Instead
redeeming and reclaiming Christmas, turning it to evangelical ends, was
Whitefield's call. And he was not beyond singling out his own devotional
fervor at Christmas as an exemplar of how Christians should redeem the
season. In *Christmas Well Kept, and the Twelve Days Well Spent,* Whitefield
used his journal to model a new evangelical Christmas of tireless evangelism,
unflagging prayer, and unstinted worship—a pattern so commendable indeed
that even a New England writer remarked, "Would to GOD that *Christmas,* if it
must be observed, were kept something after *this Manner* thro' all *Christendom!*"[45] Like singing hymns to the tunes of popular ballads, the early Methodists sought to take the festivities of popular culture and give them new ritual
form and content. As itinerant Freeborn Garrettson commented in his journal
on Christmas Day in 1824, "We must avail ourselves of this festival," not slight
it like those "in the Presbyterian way."[46]

To take the deep-seated patterns of cultural celebration and transform
them into Christian observances may have been a familiar proposition in the
history of the church, but it was never an easy one to fulfill. Preaching at a
Christmas service in South Carolina in 1805, Francis Asbury moaned that
"*Christmas day* is the worst in the whole year on which to preach Christ; at
least to me." Of another Christmas Day some years earlier in Virginia, Asbury noted, "I felt warm in speaking; but there was an offensive smell of rum
among the people."[47] The early Methodists and those who shared their perspective of remolding Christmas, rather than rejecting it outright, may have
won a victory in the end. The cozy, domestic shape of the Victorian Christmas

and its popularity with evangelical Protestants in the home, church, and Sunday schools suggest how reform sentiments eventually carried the day.[48] But the victory was always partial. Popular evangelical shibboleths today, like "Jesus Is the Reason for the Season" or "Jesus is the ♥ of Christmas," harken back to eighteenth-century struggles to redeem the time.

IV

In the diversity of evangelical worship and calendrical observances, there were various points of convergence. Common issues and concerns often overarched disparate patterns of evangelical celebration. On some heads, there was admittedly considerable disagreement: for example, the observance of the christological feasts—especially Christmas, Good Friday, Easter, and Pentecost; the frequency of Communion (for example, John Wesley's emphasis on the duty of constant Communion versus the infrequent, intensely preparationist model among Presbyterians); and the baptism of infants versus believers only. But there was much in matters of liturgy upon which eighteenth-century evangelicals largely agreed, including the centrality of the Lord's Day and the Lord's Supper; the elimination of the Marian and sanctoral cycles; the introduction of revivalistic, conversion-centered forms of worship and preaching; the calling of fast and thanksgiving days; the focal emphasis on primitivism and biblicism (of course, with *sola Scriptura* in common, one might ask, who needs differences?); the reform of popular festivals like Christmas or May Day; and the application of the concept of adiaphora to rites and ceremonies (what matters most is inward belief and spirituality, not the outward forms that give faith embodiment). No doubt various other sources of difference or agreement could be added to these lists, but here, by way of conclusion, I want to move away from these more familiar theological and liturgical issues and instead highlight three underlying tensions or trajectories in the eighteenth-century evangelical accounting of time.

For one thing, a sharp and growing tension existed between the rigorous redeeming of time and the exuberant, open-ended, and lengthy patterns of devotion that so often characterized evangelical worship. Like Puritans and Quakers, evangelicals were almost invariably great redeemers and improvers of time, who worried regularly about idleness and excessive sleep and who sought constantly to instill industry and self-discipline. Evangelical worship, however, tended to abrade these ideals. People came together and lost track of time; love feasts, watch nights, or prayer meetings went on late into the evening as testimonies, hymns, and exhortations followed one upon another. Sacramental occasions and camp meetings went on for days and nights on end, often with little regard for people's worldly callings.

Such evangelical patterns of celebration and worship were in tension not only with their own ideals of improving time but also with more modern sensibilities of time reckoning. The Protestant attack on Catholic holy days as conducive to dissipation was increasingly turned on the celebrations of evangelicals. In Scotland enlightened critics attacked sacramental occasions as "idle days," for which far too much economic productivity was sacrificed. "The people lose many laboring days by them," one critic said, "and the country is deprived of the fruit of their industry."[49] Similarly, in the United States antagonists of the camp meetings took aim at the same issues. As one critic groused in 1822, "If '*time* is money,' and '*labor* is the wealth of the community,' as is granted by all, it must be admitted that camp meetings, . . . [are] one of the most expensive measures to the community where they prevail, that could be devised."[50] Evangelicals were pressured, both from within and from without, to harmonize their forms of worship with modern timekeepers. To shorten worship services, to streamline and standardize them, to run worship by the clock—these were modern trends that all Christians increasingly faced. This rationalization of time was a cross-cultural concern in the North Atlantic world, a pervasive aspect of modernity that brought with it significant consequences for liturgy and worship.[51]

A second underlying tension in evangelical devotion was that between corporate and individual allotments of time. Evangelicalism is often seen as having various affinities with modern forms of individualism, and one can at some level see this privatizing thrust played out in evangelical markings of time. In some sense, the real high days for an evangelical are those in which God has acted upon the individual soul; private devotion, to some degree, centers on the remembrance and recapturing of those precious times of conversion, renewal, or blessing. This singular emphasis on personal regeneration is aptly suggested in the original heading in 1740 for Charles Wesley's famous hymn "O for a Thousand Tongues to Sing," which read "For the Anniversary Day of One's Conversion." Written in commemoration of his own rebirth, the hymn dwelled on this private experience as the day of days:

> On this glad Day the glorious Sun
> Of Righteousness arose,
> On my benighted Soul he shone,
> And fill'd it with Repose.[52]

Like the devotion of personal covenanting, evangelical celebration hinged on the private experiences of individuals—experiences that might be largely disconnected from the corporate tracking of time.

But these tensions between the corporate and the individual in eighteenth-century evangelicalism were minimal by later standards. Wesley's hymn on conversion made this private anniversary day a matter of corporate worship, and testimonials always made individual experiences an aspect of community building. In eighteenth-century evangelicalism, notions of the privatization of religion or the privatization of time have only limited bearing. The Romantic sacramentalism of the self in isolation, evidenced in Longfellow's poem "Holidays," has but a remote echo in eighteenth-century evangelicalism: "The holiest of all holidays are those / Kept by ourselves in silence and apart; / The secret anniversaries of the heart."[53] One sees in eighteenth-century evangelicalism only a faint augury of "Sheilaism," in which religion is defined in terms of the individual, and only a mild foreboding of a privatized and atomistic time, in which there are "as many clocks as we like."[54] For all their emphasis on personal experience, North Atlantic evangelicals envisioned patterns of worship and celebration that would knit together communities with a shared, even universal, sense of time and eternity. As the Wesleys had insisted in their first collection of hymns, the gospel is not about "Solitary Religion," but "Social Holiness."[55]

Third and finally, eighteenth-century evangelicals, like their late nine-teenth-century descendants who became engrossed in the art of church deco-ration at Christmas and Easter, demonstrated a deep ambivalence toward the grandeur of festival. Presbyterians were both drawn to the spectacle of their own sacramental occasions and repulsed by the festal ritualism of Epis-copalians. Methodists saw their camp meetings as the antitype of the festi-vals of the Old Testament, while continuing to excoriate the ceremonies and celebrations of Roman Catholicism. This ambivalence is nicely revealed in an odd episode in George Whitefield's wayfaring ministry. When Whitefield found himself in one of his tours laying over in Lisbon during Lent and Holy Week, he was predictably inflamed with prophetic rage against the "Supersti-tions of the Church of Rome." But he was also transfixed by Catholic ritualism, drama, music, illuminations, and festivity. Of the various proces-sions and pageants, Whitefield remarked, "I was fond of attending as many of them as I could." Ever grateful for the purity and simplicity of worship in Britain, he found himself in Lisbon "running from Church to Church," so as not to miss a minute of the solemnities.[56] Although holding to the plainness of the Lord's Day was the Puritan and evangelical watchword, this simplicity never seemed quite enough. Rich forms of festival and worship emerged among evangelicals—sometimes in conjunction with the traditional Christian year, sometimes in competition with entrenched folk forms of celebration and merrymaking, and sometimes simply in moments of improvisation.

Notes

1. Cotton Mather, *Grace Defended: A Censure on the Ungodliness by which the Glorious Grace of God, Is Too Commonly Abused* (Boston: B. Green, 1712), 19–20. For his father's views, see Increase Mather, *A Testimony Against Several Prophane and Superstitious Customs, Now Practised by Some in New-England, The Evil Whereof Is Evinced from the Holy Scriptures, and from the Writings both of Ancient and Modern Divines* (London: n.p., 1687).

2. James F. White, ed., *John Wesley's Sunday Service of the Methodists in North America* (Nashville: United Methodist Publishing House, 1984), A1. See also pp. 17–18, 25–26 in the introduction.

3. These words are from the first stanza of the hymn "We'll Understand It Better By and By."

4. See Eviatar Zerubavel, *The Seven Day Circle: The History and Meaning of the Week* (Chicago: University of Chicago Press, 1985), 2; idem, *Hidden Rhythms: Sched-ules and Calendars in Social Life* (Berkeley: University of California Press, 1981);

David Hackett Fischer, *Albion's Seed: Four British Folkways in America* (New York: Oxford University Press, 1989), 8–11, 158–66, 368–73, 560–66, 743–47.

5. James F. White, *Protestant Worship: Traditions in Transition* (Louisville: Westminster/John Knox Press, 1989), 19.

6. David D. Hall, *Worlds of Wonder, Days of Judgment: Popular Religious Beliefs in Early New England* (New York: Alfred A. Knopf, 1989), 219.

7. "The Second Helvetic Confession," in *The Creeds of Christendom, with a History and Critical Notes,* ed. Philip Schaff, 3 vols. (New York, 1877; reprint, Grand Rapids: Baker, 1966), 3:899–901.

8. "The Confession of the Society of Friends, Commonly Called Quakers. A.D. 1675," in *Creeds,* ed. Schaff, 3:796.

9. The relevant work on Anglican-Puritan calendrical controversies is extensive. See David Cressy, *Bonfires and Bells: National Memory and the Protestant Calendar in Elizabethan and Stuart England* (Berkeley: University of California Press, 1989); Horton Davies, *Worship and Theology in England,* 5 vols. (Princeton: Princeton University Press, 1961–75), 2:215–52; idem, *The Worship of the American Puritans, 1629–1730* (New York: Peter Lang, 1990), 51–75; Leah S. Marcus, *The Politics of Mirth: Jonson, Herrick, Milton, Marvell, and the Defense of Old Holiday Pastimes* (Chicago: University of Chicago Press, 1986); James T. Dennison, Jr., *The Market Day of the Soul: The Puritan Doctrine of the Sabbath in England, 1532–1700* (Lanham, MD: University Press of America, 1983); William DeLoss Love, Jr., *The Fast and Thanksgiving Days of New England* (Boston: Houghton, Mifflin, 1895); Richard P. Gildrie, "The Ceremonial Puritan: Days of Humiliation and Thanksgiving," *New England Historical and Genealogical Register* 136 (1982): 3–16; Charles E. Hambrick-Stowe, *The Practice of Piety: Puritan Devotional Disciplines in Seventeenth-Century New England* (Chapel Hill: University of North Carolina Press, 1982), 96–103, 133–35; Kenneth L. Parker, *The English Sabbath: A Study of Doctrine and Discipline from the Reformation to the Civil War* (Cambridge: Cambridge University Press, 1988); John H. Primus, *Holy Time: Moderate Puritanism and the Sabbath* (Macon, GA: Mercer University Press, 1989); Winton U. Solberg, *Redeem the Time: The Puritan Sabbath in Early America* (Cambridge: Harvard University Press, 1977); James P. Walsh, "Holy Time and Sacred Space in Puritan New England," *American Quarterly* 32 (1980): 79–95; David H. Tripp, "The End of the Ages: Time in Christian Worship, in the Experience of the English Puritans," *Studia Liturgica* 14 (1982): 110–27.

10. The basic scriptural texts in the debate on whether or not to treat calendrical customs as adiaphora were Romans 14:5, Colossians 2:16–17, and Galatians 4:10–11.

11. The crucial text in this regard was Ephesians 5:15–16.

12. Samuel Davies, "A Christmas-Day Sermon," in *Sermons,* 3 vols. (Philadelphia: Presbyterian Board of Publication, 1864), 3:562–64, 570.

13. Ibid., 562–86.

14. "Methodist Articles of Religion," in *Creeds,* ed. Schaff, 3:812.

15. "The Book of Discipline," in *John Knox's History of the Reformation in Scotland,* ed. William Croft Dickinson, 2 vols. (London: Nelson and Sons, 1949), 2:281. On the fate of the Christian year in Scotland, see William McMillan, *The Worship of the Scottish Reformed Church, 1550–1638* (London: Clarke, [1931]), 299–329; A. Allan McArthur, *The Evolution of the Christian Year* (Greenwich, CT: Seabury Press, 1953), 157–66.

16. Archibald Simsone, *A True Record of the Life and Death of Master Patrick Simsone,* in *Select Biographies,* ed. W. K. Tweedie, 2 vols. (Edinburgh: Wodrow Society, 1845–47), 1:97.

17. The essential material on the Shotts Communion includes John Livingston, *A Brief Historical Relation of the Life of Mr. John Livingston, Minister of the Gospel* (n.p.: n.p., 1727), 8–9; William Cunningham, ed., *Sermons by the Rev. Robert Bruce, Minister of Edinburgh. Reprinted from the Original Edition of M.D.XC. and M.C.XCI. with Collections for his Life, by the Rev. Robert Wodrow, Minister in Eastwood* (Edinburgh: Wodrow Society, 1843), 140; Robert Fleming, *The Fulfilling of the Scripture* (Rotterdam, 1669; reprint, Boston: Rogers and Fowle, 1743), 394; Robert Wodrow, *Analecta; or, Materials for a History of Remarkable Providences; Mostly Relating to Scotch Ministers and Christians,* 4 vols. (Edinburgh: Maitland Club, 1842–43), 1:271; James Robe, *Narratives of the Extraordinary Work of the Spirit of God, at Cambuslang, Kilsyth, &c. Begun 1742* (Glasgow: Niven, 1790), 217–18.

18. On Scottish eucharistic and revival traditions, see George B. Burnet, *The Holy Communion in the Reformed Church of Scotland, 1560–1960* (Edinburgh: Oliver and Boyd, 1960); Henry Grey Graham, *The Social Life of Scotland in the Eighteenth Century* (London, 1899; reprint, London: Black, 1928), 302–14; John MacInnes, *The Evangelical Movement in the Highlands of Scotland, 1688 to 1800* (Aberdeen: The University Press, 1951); Arthur Fawcett, *The Cambuslang Revival: The Scottish Evangelical Revival of the Eighteenth Century* (London: Banner of Truth, 1971); Leigh Eric Schmidt, *Holy Fairs: Scottish Communions and American Revivals in the Early Modern Period* (Princeton: Princeton University Press, 1989); Marilyn J. Westerkamp, *Triumph of the Laity: Scots-Irish Piety and the Great Awakening, 1625–1760* (New York: Oxford University Press, 1988).

19. John Scot, "Memoir, 1729–1803," Strathclyde Regional Archives manuscripts, Mitchell Library, Glasgow, p. 4.

20. William McCulloch, "Examinations of Persons Under Spiritual Concern at Cambuslang During the Revival in 1741–42," 2 vols., Edinburgh University manuscripts, New College Library, 1:191–92, 200, 231.

21. I have analyzed this piety at some length in *Holy Fairs,* 115–68.

22. Ted A. Campbell, *The Religion of the Heart: A Study of European Religious Life in the Seventeenth and Eighteenth Centuries* (Columbia: University of South Carolina Press, 1991), 105–6.

23. See John C. Bowmer, *The Sacrament of the Lord's Supper in Early Methodism* (London: Dacre Press, 1951), esp. 187–205; J. Ernest Rattenbury, *The Eucharistic Hymns of John and Charles Wesley* (London: Epworth Press, 1948).

24. The literature on early Methodist worship is extensive. See, for example, Frank Baker, *Methodism and the Love-Feast* (London: Epworth Press, 1957); Horton Davies, *Worship and Theology in England from Watts and Wesley to Maurice, 1690–1850* (Princeton: Princeton University Press, 1961); Heather Murray Elkins, " 'On Borrowed Time': The Christian Year in American Methodism, 1784–1960" (Ph.D. diss., Drew University, 1991); John Bishop, *Methodist Worship in Relation to Free Church Worship* (London: Epworth Press, 1950), 78–111; William Nash Wade, "A History of Public Worship in the Methodist Episcopal Church and Methodist Episcopal Church, South, from 1784 to 1905" (Ph.D. diss., University of Notre Dame, 1981); A. Gregory Schneider, "The Ritual of Happy Dying among Early American Methodists," *Church History* 56 (1987): 348–63.

25. Frank Baker, *Charles Wesley's Verse: An Introduction,* 2d ed. (London: Epworth Press, 1988), 7. See also S T Kimbrough, Jr., and Oliver A. Beckerlegge, eds., *The Unpublished Poetry of Charles Wesley,* 3 vols. (Nashville: Kingswood Books, 1988–92), 1:11–12. The third volume in this collection includes a section on Wesley's manuscript hymns and poems on festivals.

26. George Osborn, ed., *The Poetical Works of John and Charles Wesley,* 13 vols. (London: Wesleyan-Methodist Conference Office, 1868–72), 7:89, 132; John R. Tyson, ed., *Charles Wesley: A Reader* (New York: Oxford University Press, 1989), 13, 345.

27. John Wesley and Charles Wesley, *Hymns and Sacred Poems* (London: W. Strahan, 1739), 206. For their joint works, sorting out which of the Wesley brothers composed which hymns and discerning the nature of their collaboration are issues that have vexed Wesley scholars for generations. Suffice it to say that Charles is credited with the vast majority of the hymns, and this is all the more the case with the hymns on the Christian year, especially the Christmas hymns. For a review of these issues, see Baker, *Charles Wesley's Verse,* 94–115.

28. See John Julian, *A Dictionary of Hymnology, Setting Forth the Origin and History of Christian Hymns of All Ages and Nations* (New York: Charles Scribner's Sons, 1892), 486–88. I am indebted to S T Kimbrough, Jr., for alerting me to the editorial history of this hymn.

29. Wesley and Wesley, *Hymns and Sacred Poems,* 207, 209–13.

30. Bernard L. Manning, *The Hymns of Wesley and Watts: Five Informal Papers* (London: Epworth Press, 1942), 135.

31. Wesley and Wesley, *Hymns and Sacred Poems,* 213–15.

32. See *Hymns on the Great Festivals, and Other Occasions,* 2d ed. (London: John Cox, 1753). For a compilation that accentuates Charles Wesley's calendrical traditionalism, see John Lawson, ed., *The Christian Year with Charles Wesley, Being a Devotional Companion to the Book of Common Prayer* (London: Epworth Press, 1966). See also J. Ernest Rattenbury, *The Evangelical Doctrines of Charles Wesley's Hymns* (London: Epworth Press, 1941), 165–79.

33. See David Tripp, *The Renewal of the Covenant in the Methodist Tradition* (London: Epworth Press, 1969); Marion A. Jackson, "An Analysis of the Source of John Wesley's 'Directions for Renewing Our Covenant with God,' " *Methodist History* 30 (April 1992): 176–84.

34. See Baker, *Methodism and the Love-Feast;* Clifford W. Towlson, *Moravian and Methodist: Relationships and Influences in the Eighteenth Century* (London: Epworth Press, 1957), 209–15.

35. See David L. Watson, *The Early Methodist Class Meeting* (Nashville: Discipleship Resources, 1985).

36. See, for example, Russell E. Richey, *Early American Methodism* (Bloomington: Indiana University Press, 1991), 21–32.

37. "A Plain Account of the People Called Methodists (1749)," in *The Works of John Wesley: The Methodist Societies History, Nature, and Design,* ed. Rupert E. Davies, vol. 9 (Nashville: Abingdon, 1989), 264. Of the new forms of Methodist worship, the watch night has been the least studied. It is arguably, however, the innovation of the widest and most lasting influence.

38. Henry D. Rack, *Reasonable Enthusiast: John Wesley and the Rise of Methodism* (London: Epworth Press, 1989), 412.

39. *Hymns of the Watch-Night* (London: The Conference-Office, 1803), 2.

40. Frederick E. Maser and Howard T. Maag, eds., *The Journal of Joseph Pilmore, Methodist Itinerant* (Philadelphia: Message Publishing, 1969), 70. See also the revealing account of conflicts centered on a watch night service in New York in 1777 in Samuel A. Seaman, *Annals of New York Methodism, Being a History of the Methodist Episcopal Church in the City of New York* (New York: Hunt and Eaton, 1892), 75–76.

41. These two different types of opponents are portrayed with bold strokes in the ninth hymn in *Hymns for the Watch-Night,* 9–11.

42. *New York; or, General Advertiser,* 27 December 1770, 235; 2 January 1771, 240. This kind of advertisement was admittedly rare in the colonies, but it reflected the customs of gift exchange among elites that were as yet little shared among plebeians. On New Year's gifts, see William Sandys, *Christmastide: Its History, Festivities, and Carols* (London, n.d.), 37–42, 59–60, 99–101, 110–11. On late eighteenth-century patterns of consumption and marketing, see especially Neil McKendrick, John Brewer, and J. H. Plumb, *The Birth of a Consumer Society: The Commercialization of Eighteenth-Century England* (Bloomington: Indiana University Press, 1982).

43. George Whitefield, "A Penitent Heart, the Best New Year's Gift," in *Works,* 6 vols. (London: Edward and Charles Dilly, 1771–72), 6:A2. For the Puritan objections to New Year's gifts, see Mather, *Testimony,* 36–37. See also Thomas Warmstry, *The Vindication of the Solemnity of the Nativity of Christ; Showing the Grounds upon which the Observation of that and Other Festivals Is Justified in the Church* (n.p.: n.p., 1648), 22–25.

44. *Hymns for the Watch-Night,* 11–12. For an excellent account of a watch night service that captures its central religious themes, see Miriam Fletcher, *The Methodist; or, Incidents and Characters from Life in the Baltimore Conference,* 2 vols. (New York: Derby and Jackson, 1859), 1:75–84.

45. Whitefield, "The Observation of the Birth of Christ, the Duty of all Christians; or the True Way of Keeping Christmas," in *Works,* 5:251–61. The New England writer's gloss on Whitefield's journal appears as a postscript in George Whitefield, *Christmas Well Kept, and the Twelve Days Well Spent* (Boston: S. Kneeland and T. Green, 1739), 11.

46. Robert Drew Simpson, ed., *American Methodist Pioneer: The Life and Journals of the Rev. Freeborn Garrettson, 1752–1827* (Rutland, VT: Academy Books, 1984), 364.

47. Elmer T. Clark, J. Manning Potts, and Jacob S. Payton, eds., *The Journal and Letters of Francis Asbury,* 3 vols. (London: Epworth Press, 1958), 1:584; 2:498.

48. Scotland was the exception. The renewed popularity of Christmas there ran well behind the Victorian embrace in England and the United States. See Gavin Weightman and Steve Humphries, *Christmas Past* (London: Sidgwick and Jackson, 1987), 18–19, 37.

49. *A Letter from a Blacksmith to the Ministers and Elders of the Church of Scotland in which the Manner of Public Worship in that Church is Considered; Its Inconveniences and Defects Pointed Out; and Methods for Removing of Them Humbly Proposed* (London, 1759; reprint, New Haven: Oliver Steele, 1814), 26–28.

50. "Camp-Meetings, and Agricultural Fairs," *Wesleyan Repository* 2 (August 1822): 140–42. See also Terry D. Bilhartz, *Urban Religion and the Second Great Awakening: Church and Society in Early National Baltimore* (Rutherford, NJ: Fairleigh Dickinson University Press, 1986), 87.

51. On this rationalization of time, see, for example, E. P. Thompson, "Time, Work-Discipline, and Industrial Capitalism," *Past and Present,* no. 38 (December 1967): 56–97; Gerard T. Moran, "Conceptions of Time in Early Modern France: An Approach to the History of Collective Mentalities," *Sixteenth Century Journal* 12 (1981): 3–19; Michael O'Malley, *Keeping Watch: A History of American Time* (New York: Viking Penguin, 1990).

52. John Wesley and Charles Wesley, *Hymns and Sacred Poems* (London: W. Strahan, 1740), 120.

53. Henry Wadsworth Longfellow, *The Poetical Works of Longfellow* (Boston: Houghton Mifflin, 1975), 322.

54. On the famed case of Sheila Larson, who described her faith as "Sheilaism" or "just my own little voice," see Robert N. Bellah, Richard Madsen, William M. Sullivan, Ann Swidler, and Steven M. Tipton, *Habits of the Heart: Individualism and Commitment in American Life* (New York: Harper and Row, 1986), 221. "As many clocks as we like" is a quotation from Einstein, cited in Stephen Kern, *The Culture of Time and Space, 1880–1918* (Cambridge: Harvard University Press, 1983), 19. Kern uses Einstein's phrase metaphorically as an inlet into the interiorization and privatization of time in turn-of-the-century literature, art, and psychology.

55. Wesley and Wesley, *Hymns and Sacred Poems* (1739), viii.

56. George Whitefield, *An Account of Some Lent and Other Extraordinary Processions and Ecclesiastical Entertainments, Seen at Lisbon* (London, 1755; reprint, London: J. and W. Oliver, 1768), 8, 10, 30. Harry Stout also notes Whitefield's fascination with and revulsion from the Lenten drama (*The Divine Dramatist: George Whitefield and the Rise of Modern Evangelicalism* [Grand Rapids: Eerdmans, 1991], 217).

THE REVOLUTIONARY ERA

6

Revolution and the Rise of Evangelical Social Influence in North Atlantic Societies

MARK A. NOLL

Study of evangelical movements in the North Atlantic region has reached unprecedented levels of sophistication.[1] As a result of painstaking work in archives and previously neglected printed sources, much more is now known than ever before about eighteenth- and nineteenth-century evangelical movements in England, Scotland, Wales, Northern Ireland, Canada, and the United States. For all of the remarkable insights on individual localities, however, the most noteworthy thing about this burgeoning scholarship may be what it discloses about the North Atlantic region considered as a whole. Of such matters, one of the most striking concerns the rise of evangelical influence. Evangelicalism, it appears, became a culture-shaping force in North Atlantic societies after revolution. This generalization holds, moreover, from the Scottish Highlands and the defeat of Bonnie Prince Charles in 1746 to the American South and the surrender of the Confederate armies in 1865. For the rise of evangelicalism to social influence, the key factor was not whether evangelicals were aligned with winning or losing sides, or whether they were politically active or passive. Rather, it was the presence of social crisis—compounded of political, intellectual, and often military upheaval—that created the circumstances in which evangelicalism rose to cultural influence. In the wake of revolutionary situations, evangelicalism provided what these societies wanted—for social elites, a flexible worldview to define and defend religious faith, but also to comprehend the moral, political, intellectual, and economic workings of society. For ordinary people as well as elites, evangelicalism also held out an energizing ideal of spirituality that offered inner security even as it mobilized groups for purposive action in the world.

Even a rapid survey of the major North Atlantic regions reveals the consistent relationship between revolution and the rise of evangelicalism as a social force. Such a survey is also valuable, however, because it advances our understanding of evangelicalism itself. Although evangelicals throughout the North Atlantic region shared a common capacity for improving revolutionary situations, they did so through a remarkably diverse range of social, political, and intellectual alliances. Precisely in this wide-ranging diversity of evangelical experience, however, it is possible to observe more clearly the essential character of Anglo-American evangelicalism as an experiential biblicism that, in both elite and populist expressions, in both established and dissenting forms, communicated a message uniquely suited to the turmoils of revolution or counterrevolution. Connections between revolutionary settings and evangelicalism must, however, be stated with care. To do so, it is useful to begin with a series of negations.

In the first instance, the connection between revolution and the creation of evangelical social influence was not instantaneous. Evangelicals became culturally powerful, even dominant, in nineteenth-century North Atlantic societies, but only over the course of one or two generations following revolutionary upheavals. The social influence exerted by evangelicals was also never thoroughly hegemonic. Each Anglo-American region always contained at least some subcultures that resisted or ignored the evangelicals. Among the most powerful of these alternatives were Roman Catholicism in Quebec and Ireland, Broad and High Church Anglicanism in all British regions and Canada, the cult of honor in the American South, and the values of the Democratic party, also in the United States.[2]

Political revolution was also never the only important factor in the rise of evangelical social influence. In particular, another pervasive change—the market revolution—advanced alongside evangelicalism at every stage in its North Atlantic history.[3] Neither is the contention that evangelicalism flourished in the wake of revolutionary situations an argument about the creation of revolutionary or counterrevolutionary attitudes. The question of how, or whether, evangelical impulses contributed to revolutionary or counterrevolutionary ideologies remains one of the liveliest (and most complex) questions for eighteenth-century English-language societies.[4] But for the question of how evangelicalism came to exert cultural influence, what happened after revolutions is more important than what occurred before they took place.

Finally, the argument of this chapter is not meant to address the contention of E. P. Thompson and others that revolution or counterrevolution *created* evangelicism.[5] Nor does it even address the remarkable number of cases in which leaders of eighteenth- and nineteenth-century evangelical movements—for example, Timothy Dwight, Elias Smith, and Barton W. Stone in the United States; Henry Alline and Egerton Ryerson in Canada; Dugald Buchanan, Robert Haldane, James Haldane, and Thomas Chalmers in Scotland; or Henry Cooke in Northern Ireland—were converted or had their destinies decisively altered directly in the midst of revolutionary turmoil.[6]

Rather, this essay treats specifically the uncanny similarity in the way that evangelical movements became socially influential in the wake of revolutionary or counterrevolutionary situations. In almost all North Atlantic regions, evangelicalism was already present as a religious impulse before the onset of political revolution. Perhaps with only one or two exceptions, however, evangelicalism did not exert a broad, culture-shaping influence in these societies until after the experience of revolution. A crude survey, as this one will be, of

North Atlantic regions can only suggest the consistent connection between revolution and the way evangelicals defined a general vocabulary for society and mobilized broad reaches of the population. Even a superficial catalog, however, will indicate how extraordinarily adaptable the evangelical impulse was in North Atlantic societies during an age of revolution. An understanding of evangelical adaptability, in turn, puts us in a position to grasp more clearly the historical character of evangelicalism itself. More than anything else, it was evangelicalism's singular combination of Protestant biblicism and experiential faith that enabled it to flourish in revolutionary settings, precisely because it was able to offer, when other props gave way, meaning for persons, order for society, and hope for the future.

Sketching the Connections

Six North Atlantic regions offer patent support for the connection between political revolution and the rise of evangelicalism. In these six a variable collection of other factors also shaped the history of evangelicals, especially changes in economic life and accompanying theories about political economy. For the timing of evangelicalism's rise to broad social influence, however, these others factors appear to be subordinate to the changes precipitated by political turmoil. In three other cases a clear-cut connection between political revolution and the rise of evangelical influence is more difficult to observe, but even in these instances, political revolution was clearly important as at least one of the factors explaining the significant social influence that evangelicals came to exert.

Scottish Highlands

The first and, in many ways, most direct connection between political revolution and the rise of evangelicalism as a culture-shaping force occurred in the Scottish Highlands. After the battle of Culloden in April 1746 and the collapse of the Jacobite Rebellion, Britian undertook a systematic dismantling of the clan system that had structured Highland life for centuries. Legislation banned the tartan and the bagpipe; the English, aided by Lowland Scots, constructed a new network of roads that linked the previously isolated regions of northern Scotland to the markets and ports of the South; the traditional land-tenure system was changed in such a way that cash and lease replaced the communal clan as the economic foundation of society; and the systematic "clearance," or agricultural rationalization, of the Highlands began that would fuel large-scale emigration for the next century. The result, as summarized by John MacInnes, was revolutionary: "The Highland small tenant, now a free and equal citizen in the eyes of the law, was . . . far more helpless than he had been under the old order."[7]

Into this disoriented social setting, Presbyterian evangelicalism entered with a force that was itself nearly revolutionary.[8] The ability of evangelicalism to reconstruct Highland society depended upon several factors—the general loyalty of Kirk ministers during the Jarobite Rebellion; the efforts of the Scottish Society for the Propagation of Christian Knowledge at establishing churches and schools; the earnest labors of "The Men," lay exhorters who provided public readings of the Scriptures in Gaelic and organized conventicles similar to Methodist cells; and the moving effect of a generation of Gaelic religious poets. The result was a dramatic transformation well summarized by the great contemporary historian T. C. Smout: "Few aspects of social change in the Highlands are more striking than the conversion of almost all the peasantry (except the Catholics) from a state verging on semi-paganism at the start of the eighteenth century to strict religious observance in the nineteenth century."[9]

This observance was marked by Calvinistic rigor, but it was also evangelical in being a religion of the heart. Following the outbreak of the French Revolution, evangelicalism took even deeper root in the Highlands, through both the exertions of the Kirk and efforts inspired by the voluntary agencies of Robert and James Haldane.[10] The evangelical character of Highland Protestantism would be indicated beyond doubt when, at the Disruption of the Church of Scotland in 1843, Highlanders moved almost en masse into the Free Church. A last element in Highland evangelicalism that enables us to locate it in comparison with other evangelical movements was its intense loyalism to the British crown. During the American Revolution, a substantial proportion of Highlanders who had migrated to North America resisted the move for independence, and some even migrated in protest to Canada. A few years later, the British troops that put down the Irish rebellion of 1798 included regiments from the Highlands.[11]

The two general matters of greatest importance for our purposes, however, are the nearly legendary extent of evangelical influence that came to prevail in the Highlands, and the timing of that social change. It was in reconstructing Highland society after the Jacobite Rebellion, and then providing security in response to the French Revolution, that evangelicalism became the great, and nearly unchallenged, arbiter of social values in this, the most northern of North Atlantic societies.

The United States

Roughly the same pattern, though with somewhat greater complexity, prevailed in the northern and middle sections of the new United States. In the South, the connection between revolution and the rise of evangelicalism may not be as clear, for reasons that are discussed below. The claim for a distinct connection between revolution and the rise of evangelical social influence in the United States depends on four interrelated observations—first, that evangelical religion was declining before and during the American War for Independence; second, that evangelicalism expanded rapidly in the wake of the war; third, that a bifurcated evangelicalism with contrasting elite and populist forms arose in the first decades of the new nation; and fourth, that the diverse forms of evangelicalism flourishing after the revolution established a predominant influence in the northern and middle states.[12]

A number of recent works have traced a declining religious situation in what would become the United States from about the middle of the eighteenth century into the 1780s or early 1790s.[13] The war itself was immensely disruptive for churches in several areas of the colonies. Religious publication declined dramatically in both absolute numbers and as a proportion of all publication from the mid-1770s on. Demographic evidence for the decline of religion is matched by the fate of Christianity in intellectual and political spheres. After the onset of the Revolutionary War, a far smaller proportion of the graduates from American colleges entered the ministry than had before the war.[14] The religious dispositions of the new country's most visible leaders were also anything but evangelical. A few Founding Fathers of the second rank were consistent evangelicals, but the ones who mattered most—Washington, Jefferson, Madison, Hamilton, Franklin, and John Adams—were not. While the faith of these founders did maintain certain aspects of traditional morality, their unitarian, deistic, moralistic, and anti-enthusiastic religion hardly anticipated an evangelical surge in the new nation. While both the Declaration of Independence from 1776 and the United States Constitution from 1789 echo traditional Christian attitudes, these crucial documents depended much more directly on secular sources than on religious ones.[15] In sum, as late as the early 1790s, no responsible observer of the new United States could have anticipated a surge in Protestant evangelicalism, and the notion that evangelicals would soon exert a pervasive influence in American society would have made no sense at all.

But immediately in the wake of the revolution, unprecedented evangelical expansion occurred. Jon Butler has recently depicted the period 1790 to 1840 as the great age of church expansion in the United States.[16] The best recent statistical estimate shows Methodists, the most consistently evangelical of denominations in the early United States, advancing from less than 3 percent of the churched population in 1776 to almost 35 percent in 1850, and that at a time of general church growth.[17]

Evangelical expansion in the United States after the American Revolution was ideological as well as demographic. On this score, however, it is imperative to recognize evangelicalism's bifurcated character in the early years of the new nation. In ways that paralleled, reflected, and perhaps even influenced the division between Federalists and Democratic-Republicans, American evangelicals possessed a two-party system of elitists and populists. At both levels, however, an ideological transformation was underway that joined selected principles of evangelical Protestantism with explicit themes of the revolution. At a popular level, as Nathan Hatch has demonstrated, "a cultural ferment over the meaning of freedom" became a powerful engine that Methodist, Baptist, African-American, and sectarian evangelicals drove in ever wider circles of evangelization and cultural influence.[18] In elite circles, more than a generation of evangelical minister-professors adroitly combined themes of republican politics, common-sense moral reasoning, and scientific Baconianism to provide "the first new nation" with a sophisticated Christian rationale for social order, political stability, and intellectual self-confidence.[19] Evangelical populists who promoted dissenting conceptions of freedom and evangelical establishmentarians who provided persuasive theories about the sources of order distrusted each other intensely, but together they created a social juggernaut.

The evangelicalism that emerged in the United States after the American Revolution became a juggernaut in large part because of the parlous state of other alternative institutions or ideologies in the new nation. After the War for Independence, the United States existed as an independent, republican, anti-authoritarian society. But it was also a nation beset by political, economic, social, religious, and especially regional fragmentation. To address this fragmentation, the largely secular founders offered the Constitution. Historians properly regard this document as a critical achievement for establishing political and social stability. At the same time, however, the United States was still, in John Murrin's telling phrase, "a roof without walls." As Murrin continues, "American national identity was . . . an unexpected, impromptu, artificial, and therefore extremely fragile creation of the Revolution. . . . The Constitution was to the nation a more successful version of what the Halfway Covenant had once been to the Puritans, a way of buying time."[20]

Into this vacuum stormed the evangelicals, representing not just the power of religion but also a successful fusion of faith and ideology. At first in antithetical elite and popular styles, but by the 1820s from elites becoming more democratic and populists re-creating the institutions of the elites, evangelicals filled the social vacuum that was the new United States. The expanding power of evangelical revivalism, combined with an exploding quantity of voluntary organizations, provided what Donald Mathews has called an effective "organizing process" for a thinly populated and widely fragmented society.[21] Evangelicals also demonstrated how individualism and communalism (which later historians find difficult to believe could coexist) were able to nourish each other in Methodist class meetings, Baptist congregations, and the more formal churches of Presbyterians and Congregationalists. Finally, by offering the United States a newer, nationalized form of convenant theology, evangelicals enhanced their own position as definers of the meaning of America. The belief that the United States was a chosen land designated by God for special, even millennial, purposes may not have been widely spread during the revolution itself, as Melvin Endy has recently argued. But as even Endy concedes, the notion did flourish in the decades after the war.[22] More than the strictly political principles promoted by the Constitution, this sense of elect nationhood, which was a peculiarly evangelical possession, constructed the national walls under the constitutional roof.

And the result? In 1789, Alexander Hamilton could quip that there was no reference to God in the Constitution simply because the framers forgot to put one in, but fifty years later political parties, like the Whigs, who embodied a general evangelical ethos, and the Anti-Masonic, Liberty, and American, who stood on specific planks from the general evangelical platform, were winning elections in New England, New York, and Pennsylvania.[23] A few more years and Abraham Lincoln was quoting Scripture—in a way unimaginable from the nation's earliest presidents—as a means of drawing the nation back together after the Civil War. During the American Revolution, comments from evangelicals on the patriot army mostly concerned the dissoluteness of the troops; during the Civil War evangelicals commented as much on revivals in the camps as on the evils of military life.

In sum, the American Revolution altered the course of religious history in the United States, not primarily because the revolution was brought about by evangelicals, but because evangelicals so successfully exploited the political, ideological, and social conditions it created.

Canadian Maritimes

The opposite political results, but the same connection between revolution and the rise of evangelicalism, followed the American Revolution in the Canadian Maritimes. Nova Scotia and surrounding areas were only lightly populated by the mid-eighteenth century. But because of the very thinness of the population itself, diversity among that population, and considerable uncertainty as to how political, ethnic, and religious loyalties would coexist, Maritime society was fractured, divided, and weak. The emergence of revolutionary agitation in nearby New England only exacerbated an already-fragile situation. Despite the disruption it caused, the American War for Independence not only created a stable Maritime identity but also brought evangelicalism to prominence as a culture-shaping force.

The conversion in March 1775 of Henry Alline, a talented but troubled native of Rhode Island who had resided in Nova Scotia since 1760, was the spark that ignited the evangelical fire. Alline's fervent preaching of the New Birth reminded listeners of George Whitefield, even though Alline's theology was as anti-Calvinistic as Whitefield's had been Calvinistic. In another contrast with Whitefield, who from the time of the Seven Years' War had regularly attacked tyranny, especially in French and Catholic guises, Alline's evangelical message was determinedly apolitical.

To Maritimers torn by doubts about their participation in the American Revolution and still insecure as recent immigrants in an outpost of empire, Alline's message was a tonic. Even after he died in 1784—on a trip into New England to "liberate" the newly independent states for Christ[24]—Alline's message continued to shape religion and society in the Maritimes. It also was a major factor in Nova Scotia's decision for political neutrality during the war. When Alline was offered a militia commission in 1775, he refused it with the reply that he had "a Commission from Heaven to go forth and enlist my fellow mortals to fight under the banner of King Jesus."[25] Following Alline, Protestants in the Maritimes turned their back on American patriotism. That action became, in effect, their own Declaration of Independence. The pursuit of "New Light," as defined by Alline and a powerful cadre of Methodists and Baptists, left citizens of the Atlantic provinces unwilling to join the American patriots. It also established them as the most influential cultural force in the region.

Even after the influx of Loyalists from the United States at the conclusion of the Revolutionary War and the quasi-establishment of the Church of England as Nova Scotia's state church, the evangelical influence in Maritime society remained extraordinarily powerful. The strong evangelical character of Nova Scotia, Prince Edward Island, and to a lesser extent New Brunswick (with its considerable Catholic population) survives to this day, as the Maritimes still maintain a more evangelical allegiance in belief and practice than elsewhere in Canada.[26] For our purposes, again, the key matter is that evangelical culture permeated the Maritimes in the crucible of political revolution.

Scotland and the French Revolution

If in North America the American Revolution sparked the emergence of evangelicalism as a powerful social force, in Britain it was massive reaction *against* the French Revolution. In this matter, however, as in many other historical circumstances, the story is considerably different in Britain's Celtic fringes than at its Anglo-Saxon center. Although reaction to the French Revolution contributed to the rise of evangelicalism in England, Northern Ireland, and Wales, the effects on evangelicalism as a culture-shaping force were most dramatic in Scotland. Even with the diversity among British regions and, especially, with the complexity in accounting for religious-cultural relationships in England, however, it is possible to summarize the general British situation in two propositions: The French Revolution was a key factor in the mobilization of evangelicals; it was also a key factor in opening British societies to evangelical influence. Nowhere are those propositions more evident than in Scotland.

Identifiably evangelical Presbyterianism had existed in Scotland from at least the early eighteenth century, as manifest in increasingly fervent "Communion seaons," the strife over piety and doctrine that led to the Seceder movement of the 1730s, and the local outbreaks of revival, of which the Cambuslang "Wark" of 1742 in conjunction with a Communion season was the most notable.[27] Yet the social influence of evangelicalism was not large throughout most of the century. Cambuslang was almost certainly more important than T. C. Smout's description of it as "a hysterical but ephemeral religious 'revival' in the west of Scotland."[28] As a thorough investigation of the Kirk's "Popular Party" has recently shown, however, even the ecclesiastical faction opposed to the rationalistic and moralistic Moderates was not pervasively or systematically evangelical. Rather, as John McIntosh has put the matter, a distinctly evangelical viewpoint, "which saw its mission in terms of its proclamation of the case for salvation through personal faith in Christ to a Scotland in which the majority of the people did not possess such a faith,"[29] only gradually emerged within the Popular Party in competition with the orthodox and Moderate viewpoints that could also be found among the opponents of patronage. Only with John Erskine's *Dissertation on the Nature of the Christian Faith* from 1765 does McIntosh perceive the beginning of a distinct evangelicalism at work in the Popular Party's understanding of conversion and assurance, and this definable evangelicalism was slow to develop within that party.[30] Outside the Established Church, some Seceders put more emphasis on the affective character of faith, but Seceder influence was restricted in a nation so thoroughly committed to the principle of a unifying state-church.

This situation changed dramatically in the context of Scottish reactions to the French Revolution, felt most keenly after the outbreak of war in 1793. This Frendh threat coincided with a remarkable, and sustained, outpouring of evangelical energy. In the established Kirk, as David Currie's dissertation has recently shown, the great initiatives of evangelism can be dated precisely from 1793.[31] Over the next half century, the fruits of this energy led to an outpouring of new publications, a plethora of new voluntary agencies for missions and reform, a concentrated effort to found new schools, and a diligent application to new forms of spirituality. Already by the first decade of the nineteenth century, the evangelical network in the Church of Scotland was beginning to exert new authority. By the 1820s, it was the dominant party in the Kirk.

Outside the Established Church, an equally vigorous mobilization of evangelical activity was evident, and from the same starting point in reaction to revolutionary events in France. Almost as soon as they turned to evangelical faith in the revolutionary year of 1793, Robert and James Haldane formed missionary societies for home and abroad and began to promote Sunday schools as a means of evangelizing and educating urban children. Soon they were also establishing new churches, setting up local seminaries to train men for the ministry, and exploring an ever-broader range of voluntary activities.[32] With the aid of like-minded Calvinist dissenters, the Haldanes sparked a veritable renaissance in evangelical piety and activity.

The differences among evangelicals in the North Atlantic region is revealed by the social and political conservatism that, in stark contrast to the United States, flourished in Scotland. Reacting to charges that he was promoting social anarchy by his activities outside the Kirk, Robert Haldane made a memorable response in 1800, *Address to the Public . . . concerning Political Opinions, and Plans Lately Adopted to Promote Religion in Scotland.* In it he disavowed radical intentions, proclaimed his conviction that "the Scriptures require the most conscientious and cheerful submission to the Government of the country, whatever it may be,"[33] and in general set his face against republicanism and democracy. The evangelicalism developing at the same time in the Kirk was, if anything, even more conservative in its political and social outlook.

If evangelicalism came to dominate the church life of Scotland in the generation after 1793, it also exerted an increasingly strong influence on the nation. Dissenters from the Kirk, who were gathered in Presbyterian, Baptist, and Congregational congregations, made dramatic gains in membership after the turn of the century, even as the Kirk itself launched ambitious plans for building churches in Scotland's expanding cities.[34] Leading Dissenters such as James Haldane (Robert had departed for the Continent in 1816) became influential voices beyond the churches. And the leading figures in the Kirk, especially the omnicompetent Thomas Chalmers, were heeded by general society to a degree difficult to imagine in the twentieth century. Chalmers was not only (in James McCosh's words) "the greatest preacher which Scotland has produced" and (as T. C. Smout put it) a person "acclaimed in a manner seldom accorded to any Scot in his own lifetime," but he was also a person (in Boyd Hilton's words) whose "influence was enormous—and not just in Scotland."[35] The reach of Chalmer's influence depended upon his ability to provide convincing explanations for the most pressing issues of the day—including the relation of revelation to science, the place of moral obligations in a rapidly industrializing society, and the points of contact between historic Scottish Calvinism and the romantic mood of the early nineteenth century.[36] Our concern is not so much with the content of Chalmer's thought but with the fact that his combination of moral paternalism and economic laissez-faire within a Christian framework was widely regarded as a momentous evangelical contribution to the world at large.

By the time of the Disruption in 1843, when Chalmers led out nearly half the ministers and more than half of the people in the Kirk to found the Free Church of Scotland, evangelical influence had permeated nearly the whole of Scottish society. Unlike the evangelicalism that had risen to great social influence in the northern and central United States over the same period, Scotlands's evangelicalism was antirepublican and mostly Calvinistic. Unlike the evangelicalism that had risen in the same period in the Canadian Maritimes, Scotland's evangelicalism was elitist. Yet like the evangelicalism in both the United States and the Maritimes, Scotland's evangelicalism gained its social influence in the wake of a revolution.

England and the French Revolution

In England the reaction to the French Revolution was just as intense as in Scotland, and that reaction also accompanied a substantial rise in the influence of evangelicals. Yet because of the character of English society, evangelicals never became as thoroughly influential as in Scotland, the United States, or the Canadian Maritimes. The structure of English society—with industrialization further advanced than elsewhere and London exerting more of a cultural influence than any other city in the North Atlantic region—made it difficult for any ideology, secular or religious, to gain total sway. Complicated interconnections of institutions and ideas also set England apart. While the Evangelical party in the Church of England grew steadily from the days of Whitefield and the Countess of Huntingdon, for instance, Anglicanism was never thoroughly captured by evangelical influence. From the other end of the ideological spectrum, radical political dissent could be aligned in some instances with evangelical Nonconformity, but the English radical tradition had a vigorous life of its own that as often competed as cooperated with evangelicalism.

Proper qualifications having been made, however, evangelicals still experienced dramatic increases on several fronts in the wake of popular reaction against the French Revolution. Within the Church of England, according to

Kenneth Hylson-Smith's recent summary, the number of evangelical incumbents expanded from roughly fifty in 1789 to five hundred in 1800 to perhaps as many as one-quarter of all Anglican clergy by 1835. In 1789 there had been no evangelical bishops, but by 1835 there were several, along with a full complement of evangelicals in other influential places in the hierarchy.[37] Over the same period a substantial evangelicalization as well as substantial expansion of Old Dissent was also under way. Deryck Lovegrove's monograph on the rejuvenation of Baptists, Presbyterians, and Congregationalists by itinerant preaching indicates that the takeoff point for renewed dissenter activity was the mid-1790s.[38] David Hempton has also recently charted the rapid expansion of Wesleyan Methodists in England from the 1790s through the 1820s.[39]

Unlike the situation in other North Atlantic regions, the surge of evangelicalism in reaction to the French Revolution did not create an evangelical hegemony, but it nonetheless gave evangelicalism unprecedented influence in English society. Until about 1820, as W. R. Ward has suggested, "it seemed possible that popular evangelicalism might sweep the board [in England] as it did in Wales, or as popular Catholicism did in Ireland."[40] But although the triumph of evangelicalism never became complete, its influence was substantial. An indication of that growing influence is provided by church membership statistics. The best estimate is that Anglicans outnumbered Nonconformists, most of whom would have been evangelical, by a ratio of approximately five to two in 1800, but by 1850 there were roughly ten Nonconformists for every nine Anglicans, and that in a period when a growing percentage of Anglicans were also evangelical.[41] In addition, if Boyd Hilton's recent argument can be sustained—that the first decades of the nineteenth century constituted in England "an Age of Atonement" in which moderate evangelicals such as Charles Simeon, J. B. Sumner, and especially Thomas Chalmers provided the conceptual categories with which elite England comprehended economic, scientific, and moral as well as religious realities—a new dimension is added to the significance of evangelical influence in England.[42]

Once again, the central point for our purposes is that evangelicals came to exert their considerable, if never overwhelming, influence in English society in the wake of agitation over the threat from France. For both England and Scotland, as well as for the other Protestant areas of the British Isles, John MacInnes's summary is apt: "In a measure, British Evangelicalism, as it permeated the life of the nation at the close of one century and the dawn of another, was at the same time a substitute for, and a reaction against, the French gospel of liberation and brotherhood."[43]

Northern Ireland

In Northern Ireland, the immediate impact of the French Revolution was ambiguous. While some among the large body of Presbyterians and the smaller numbers of Anglicans and Methodists recoiled at the notion of liberal change, still other Irish Protestants leaned toward liberal, or even radical, principles. The precipitate for widespread Protestant reaction against radical change, as well as the precipitate for rapid evangelical expansion, came in 1798, when a substantial number of Presbyterians, some of them evangelical, joined Catholic reformers and a few secular radicals in revolting against British rule.[44] In the event, the rebellion was speedily crushed, with more casualties than in the American Revolution. Following that failed revolution, dramatic changes took place in both Ulster religion and the place of religion in Ulster.[45]

In the first instance, reaction to radical revolution greatly strengthened the hand of evangelical Presbyterians, who, in the generation after 1798, succeeded in drastically reducing the influence of the rationalistic, Arian Calvinism that had enjoyed such a long history in Northern Ireland.[46] In addition, the Methodists, who were thoroughly evangelical, grew rapidly in the wake of the failed rebellion, in some rural areas doubling their membership in the years between 1799 and 1802.[47] And where once Irish Protestants had given at least some support to political liberalism and the push for Ireland's autonomy, the evangelical Methodists and Presbyterians who rose in the wake of the 1798 rebellion were determinedly unionist and antiliberal in their politics.

Once again the end product, to which much else contributed, was the rise of evangelicalism to a place of dominant social influence among Protestants in Northern Ireland, a dominance indicated both by the growing number of evangelicals in Presbyterian and Methodist churches but also by the growing influence of evangelical leaders, such as the Presbyterian minister Henry Cooke, who seems to have had something of the same influence among Ulster Prostestants—on political and economic issues as well as religion—that Thomas Chalmers enjoyed in Scotland.[48] That influence began to succeed once it was clear that the revolution of 1798 had failed.

In the Scottish Highlands, the northern and middle United States, the Canadian Maritimes, Scotland more generally, England, and Northern Ireland the revolutions came at different times, under different circumstances, and with different results. In the United States, evangelicalism flourished in the wake of a successful revolution. In the Scottish Highlands and Northern Ireland, revolutions that failed provided the context for a rising evangelicalism. In the Canadian Maritimes it was a rejected revolution, and in Scotland and England a counterrevolution. But in each of these regions, revolutionary agitation along with postrevolutionary crises of social and intellectual order gave evangelicals the opportunity to shape entire societies in their own image.

In three other regions—Wales, Upper Canada, and the American South—connections between revolution and the rise of evangelicalism are not as obvious. A brief examination of these three societies does show, however, that even when other circumstances exerted greater influence in shaping society and evangelicalism, revolutionary political change was never far from the surface in the creation of evangelical social influence.

Wales

Evangelicalism may have permeanted Wales as thoroughly as it did the Scottish Highlands, but the role of political revolution was not quite as obvious in the process by which evangelicalism, especially in the form of Welsh-speaking Nonconformity, came to dominate Welsh society. To be sure, the timing was just about right. Despite a vigorously sustained tradition of revival—powerfully begun by Howell Harris and Daniel Rowland, and zealously maintained by William Williams—evangelicalism inside and outside of the Established Church was politically suspect as well as socially subordinate to Anglican influence until after the French Revolution.[49] But after the general revulsion against French radicalism and specific reaction to the French attempt to land an army in Pembrokeshire in February 1797, Methodists within the Established Church as well as Dissenters outside both secured greater public acceptance by aligning themselves firmly against radical social change.[50] Furthermore, the rise of evangelical social influence followed the upsets of the French Revolution, which, in the words of E. D. Evans, "did more than anything to crystallize attitudes in this country."[51] The breakaway of the Welsh Methodists to form a distinct denomination in 1811, as well as rapid growth among Baptists and Independents, coincided with the increasing influence of Nonconformity in Welsh social and political life.[52] Without going further, therefore, it would seem that conditions brought on by the French Revolution might have held the same place in the social history of Welsh evangelicalism as in evangelical developments elsewhere in the English-speaking world.

The fact that evangelicalism in Wales was mostly *not* an English-speaking phenomenon, however, suggests why the pattern prevailing elsewhere was not quite as clear in Wales. Evangelicalism exerted its influence in Wales not just because evangelicals knew how to redeem revolutionary times but because revivalistic Protestantism had long been preached in Welsh. Although the various Nonconformist movements in Wales were doctrinally similar to their counterparts in England and Scotland, from its earliest days Nonconformity in Wales, as Thomas Rees put it, "took on a Welsh dress and found its expression through the medium of the Welsh language; it had a homespun quality which made it essentially Welsh in texture."[53] This link between evangelicalism and the Welsh language antedated the revolutionary situation of the 1790s; it also provided the foundation for expanding Nonconformist influence in nineteenth-century Wales. That influence, moreover, also had much to do with failures in the nineteenth-century Established Church to maintain an effective witness to Welsh speakers in rural and urban areas. It was concerned as well with the particular way in which industrialization changed the social landscape of Wales, with landowers and factory owners connected to the Established Church presided over by an English-speaking and often nonresident hierarchy—but with rural laborers, industrial workers, and the petite bourgeoisie connected to Nonconformist churches where a lively revivalistic evangelicalism was preached in Welsh. The result is, therefore, that while the reaction to revolution explains a good deal in the rise of evangelicalism to social prominence in Wales, it does not explain quite as much as the historic link between evangelicalism and the Welsh language or the particular configuration of linguistic, ecclesiastical, and economic arrangements of the nineteenth century.

Upper Canada

In Upper Canada, roughly equivalent to modern Ontario, something of the same situation prevailed as in Wales. While the rise of evangelicalism as a powerful force in Upper Canadian society followed revolutionary incidents, these revolutions do not seem quite as directly relevant to evangelical social expansion as do other parallel influences. Again, however, the chronology fits the general pattern. Evangelicalism—which in Upper Canada was initially a Methodist movement, but also supported by numerous Anglican and Presbyterian evangelicals as well as by most of the smaller number of Baptists—did grow in social influence in the aftermath of revolution. Upper Canadian culture possessed a distinctly counterrevolutionary character because of reactions against three menacing situations. As a result of the War of 1812, Upper Canadians not only rejected incorporation into the United States but also embraced a vigorous loyalism to Britain. The abortive rebellion of William Lyon Mackenize in 1837 warned off almost all leaders in church and state from democracy or republicanism. And the American Civil War strengthened the determination of Upper Canada's leaders to maintain a society of "peace, order, and good government," instead of one marked by violent ideological conflict.

The general path of evangelical growth in Upper Canada—as both demographic and intellectual expansion—can in fact be correlated with these three revolutionary situations. The Methodist proportion of the population increased steadily from 1812 onward, as did allegiance to the Presbyterians, especially with the creation, after the Disruption in Scotland, of a more distinctly evangelical Free Presbyterian Church.[54] In addition, as Michael Gauvreau, William Westfall, and Marguerite Van Die have shown in a remarkable trio of recent books, an evangelical synthesis of revolution, science, and history established a powerful intellectual and cultural vision that had more influence and lasted longer than probably any other comparable intellectual construct fashioned by evangelical in any other North Atlantic region during the nineteenth century.[55]

As in Wales, however, the impact of revolution seems to have worked indirectly more than directly in creating the evangelical ethos that became so strong in Upper Canada by the end of the nineteenth century. The War of 1812, for example, acted not so much to create an environment in which an already-existing evangelicalism could flourish but to change both the evangelical and political climate of the region together. While the war moved political convictions rapidly toward loyalism, it transformed evangelicalism from a frontier democracy to a much more restrained form of religion that soon began to value social order nearly as much as religious enthusiasm. Similarly, the significant accomplishment of Methodist and Presbyterian educators in creating a compelling evangelical worldview was not directly the result of political agitation in 1812 and 1837 so much as it was an effort to provide religious and moral ballast for a society eager to preserve its historic connections with Britain. Finally, the central place of Anglicanism in Upper Canada—at first as a quasi-established church and then as a center of influence with values at times opposing evangelicalism—meant that ongoing controversies over the Anglican establishment (such as the disposition of the Clergy Reserves) carried more force in Upper Canadian religious life than the episodic outbreak of revolution. In summarizing the fate of the "evangelical program" in mid-Victorian Ontario, John Webster Grant states well the differences with south of the border: "In the United States, it is generally agreed, the concentrated evangelical drive of the early nineteenth century was decisive in shaping the national ethos. . . . [In Ontario] it would be difficult to maintain that it was ever determinative of the provincial character to the same degree. Here and there its effects may be seen in purest form, but domination of provincial life has always—if sometimes only just—eluded it."[56] One of the reasons that evangelicalism never quite carried the culture in Upper Canada as it did in many regions of the United States may well have been that the revolutions experienced by Canadians were never quite as thorough as the revolution that began the United States.

The American South

The American South may indeed come closer to the more general picture of a direct connection between revolution and the rise of a socially influential evangelicalism. Excellent standard accounts by historians Samuel Hill, John Boles, and Donald Mathews, for example, have described the way in which white evangelicals became "powerful and dominant" in the South, achieved "cultural dominance," and "through creating their own institutions and networks of communication . . . achieved . . . the pinnacle of refinement and respectability," perhaps as early as the first decade of the nineteenth century or shortly thereafter in the wake of the revivals known as the Second Great Awakening.[57] This process certainly took place in the wake of the American Revolution, but whether it occurred precisely because it grew out of a revolutionary situation remains a question, as does also the issue of how deeply evangelical influence penetrated southern culture before the Civil War.

In the first instance, two other factors—the social crisis involved in civilizing the southern wilderness and the moral crisis engendered by maintaining the slave system—may have more influentially shaped the environment in which evangelicalism eventually flourished than did the revolution. In the second instance, recent work by T. H. Breen and Bertram Wyatt-Brown, among others, suggests that while evangelical culture exerted a strong and growing influence in antebellum southern society, evangelicalism was also always engaged in deepest competition with a culture of personal honor that contradicted evangelicalism in many particulars.[58] To the extent that such views are correct, evangelicalism may have been kept from exerting the same kind of dominant social influence in the American South that it did in the North.

If the suggestion is valid that evangelical social influence was in fact limited in the antebellum South because of competition from a culture of personal honor, it still may be the case that revolution was decisive in the creation of evangelical social influence. But if so, the revolution took place from 1861 to 1865, not from 1776 to 1783. Books by Charles Reagan Wilson and Ted Ownby, as well as reports of work in progress by other historians of southern religion, suggest the possibility that the thorough evangelization of southern culture did not occur until after the Civil War—until after, that is, the Union armies had smashed a southern way of life almost as decisively as the Duke of Cumberland's troops had smashed the Highland way of life at Culloden in 1746.[59] If in fact the South was only thoroughly evangelized in the revolutionary situation created by losing the Civil War, then the general thesis of this chapter is sustained much more directly than if evangelicalism came to social dominance in the South during the antebellum period.

To summarize, the situation in Wales, Upper Canada, and the American South is not as clear-cut as in the other North Atlantic regions. Even in these three regions, however, evangelical exploitation of revolutionary environments had at least something to do with the creation of evangelical social influence, even if the revolutions may not have been as directly related to the rise of evangelicalism as in the other North Atlantic regions. More generally, even though brief vignettes are hardly sufficient to demonstrate convincingly that revolutionary circumstance was the nursery for evangelical social influence, and even though a clear connection between revolution and the rise of evangelicalism is found in most, but not necessarily all, North Atlantic regions, still there seems ample reason for endorsing Michael Gauvreau's general claim that "in the context of the late 18th century, evangelicalism must be viewed as a movement of liberation, deriving its impetus from the same complex of cultural and social changes which produced the great revolutionary upheavals in Europe and America and the first great age of reform."[60] The connection between revolution and evangelicalism is obvious. It is also extraordinarily complex.

The Character of Evangelicalism

To observe the rise of evangelical social influence in the various North Atlantic regions is immediately to call into question simplisitic definitions of evangelicalism.[61] In the first instance, regional variations and nonreligious developments in host societies made a tremendous difference in molding the character of evangelicalism. A society able to absorb nearly limitless numbers of immigrants, such as the northern United States, provided a different scope for individual religion and the development of religious movements than one, like the Scottish Highlands, that, because it could not sustain its population, sent a steady stream of emigrants around the world. A society in which the definition of nationalism was primarily a question of language, as in Wales, colored religion differently than did a society in which nationalism evolved in a colonial context, as in Upper Canada, or than it did in a society where national self-definition was decided on the field of battle, as in the United States in both 1776 and 1861.

More important, however, even a rapid sketch of the evangelicalisms that flourished throughout the North Atlantic in the eighteenth and nineteenth centuries reveals the incredible diversity of these movements. On the question of salvation, for example, during this period English-speaking evangelicals in the Atlantic region embraced ardent Calvinism, equally ardent anti-Calvinism, and a bewildering variety of Moderate or moderating Calvinist positions that could be held as ardently as either of the polar positions. On the church, evangelicals could be both divine-right Anglicans or Presbyterians as well as rights-of-man "Christians" who forswore all traditional ecclesiastical structures. They supported republicanism over against monarchy, monarchy over against republicanism, and opted out of the political sphere all together. Evangelicals followed Wesley in pursuing Lockean notions of morality resting on freedom and Edwards in pursuing a nearly pantheistic sense of divine agency.[62] They were earnest intellectuals and captious anti-intellectuals. They defended both deferential hierarchy and democratic individualism as social patterns mandated by God. In a word, even a brief survey seems to call into question an identifiable evangelical character of any sort.

In fact, however, a historian, whose task in these exercises is quite different from a theologian's, finds it relatively easy to define an essential evangelicalism in the social settings of the eighteenth and early nineteenth centuries.[63] Differ as they certainly did in many particulars, still the individuals and groups that were recognized in their own settings as evangelical possessed a core of common characteristics. Two were most basic, and three others followed naturally. First, evangelicals throughout the North Atlantic were determined Protestants who took with particular earnestness the historic Protestant attachment to Scripture. They could differ wildly among themselves on the meaning of the Bible, but the Scriptures remained a bedrock of authority. Second, evangelicals shared a a conviction that true religion required the active experience of God.[64] Again, evangelicals prescribed myriad norms for that experience and even more ways for accommodating the experience of God with reason, traditions, and hierarchies. But that experience remained a sine qua non for the type of religion that many contemporaries and more historians have labeled evangelical.

The three characteristics flowing from the biblical experientialism of evangelicals were nearly as important, especially since they shaped the lived reality of this biblical experientialism. First was a bias—whether slight prejudice or massive rejection—against inherited institutions. Since no inherited institution could communicate the power of God's presence as adequately as Scrip-

ture and personal Christian experience, no inherited institution enjoyed the
respect accorded to experience and the Bible. Second, evangelicalism was, as
a matter of principle, though often inarticulate principle, extraordinarily flexible in relation to ideas concerning intellectual, political, social, and economic
life. Since such ideas possessed primarily instrumental value by comparison
with the ultimate realities found in Scripture and the experience of Christ,
they could be taken up, modified, discarded, or transformed as local circumstances dictated. Third, evangelicals practiced "discipline," to borrow a well-
considered phrase from Daniel Walker Howe. Their experiential biblicism
might lead along many different paths, and with contrasting conclusions, to
principles of conduct for self and others, but however derived, those principles embodied a common evangelical conviction that the gospel compelled a
search for social healing as well as personal holiness.[65]

If these five characteristics do in fact describe an evangelicalism that,
despite great local differences, yet existed as a common religion in the various
North Atlantic regions, it is almost immediately evident why evangelicalism
flourished in the wake of revolution. Successful revolutions, by their nature,
destroy traditions. Mobilization against revolution in defense of imperiled
traditions, by isolating the traditions from webs of unspoken assumption, can
have almost the same effect. It either case, revolutionary or counterrevolutionary, the past and its wisdom are set adrift. Both revolution and counterrevolution demand a search for anchors. Whether it *must* always happen is a
different question, but in the North Atlantic revolutionary situations of the
eighteenth and nineteenth centuries, a religion of biblical experientialism *did*
give meaning to persons and motivation for groups much more powerfully
than could a zealotry making all things new, a disillusionment of failed hopes,
or a panicked defense of old ways. In the turmoil of revolution, Scripture and
Christian experience held firm.

The evangelical recourse to Scripture and Christian experience also provided motivation and drive for the long haul. Evangelicalism was at its most
effective in revolutionary situations because, with unusual force, it communicated enduring personal stability in the face of disorder, long-lasting eagerness
for discipline, and a nearly inexhaustible hope that the personal dignity affirmed by the gospel could be communicated to the community as a whole.

Precisely because evangelicalism could be effective in these ways during
revolutionary situations, it could also appear in widely varying forms throughout the North Atlantic region. The relative weight accorded to inherited Protestant faith in relation to personal Christian experience varied immensely.
Thomas Chalmers, for example, incorporated an evangelical concern for affective faith into state-church Scottish Presbyterianism; by contrast, his contemporary the American Baptist populist John Leland had virtually no use for Protestant tradition.[66] Yet both Chalmers and Leland were active in creating new
institutions, the first as a supplement to traditional stuctures, the second as a
replacement for them; both eagerly attached themselves to powerful intellectual currents of the day as a way of expressing the social meaning of Christianity, though Chalmers favored Malthus while Leland advocated Jeffersonian-

ism; and both appealed to inner character as a means for developing the just society, which for Chalmers would have been Presbyterian and paternal, while for Leland radically disestablishmentarian and egalitarian. Chalmers, in short, was an Establishment evangelical, while Leland was a Dissenting evangelical, but in the commonality of their foundational convictions and the formal similarity of their social lives, Chalmers the moderate Scottish Calvinist and Leland the radical American Baptist shared as much in common as two such different individuals could hope to share.

In fact, all of the general convictions and characteristics marking evangelicals were present in both "establishment" and "dissenting" forms, with the result that combinations and permutations among evangelicals were multiplied almost beyond number. Since history-writing is usually an establishment rather than a dissenting exercise, it follows that the experience of Dissenting evangelicals has received less historical attention than that of establishment evangelicals—more good books on the Presbyterians than on the Methodists, for example, and much higher visibility in learned circles for evangelical Anglicans than for evangelicals who refused every name except simply "Christian."

Great internal variety and the skewing of historiography toward establishment evangelicals should nonetheless not obscure the main issue. It was evangelicalism, a religion tracing its roots back to the Protestant Reformation and beyond, but powerfully born again in the early-to-mid eighteenth century by the combined biblicism, experientialism, innovation, discipline, and adaptability of John and Charles Wesley, Jonathan Edwards, George Whitefield, Howell Harris, Daniel Rowland, Gilbert Tennent, Henry Alline, John Maclaurin, Dugald Buchanan, and other first-generation evangelicals—and then sustained with something like the original combination of commitments and capacities for more than a century—that put back together North Atlantic societies confused, disoriented, and fragmented by revolution.

A knotty interpretive question remains—how to picture the causal sequence relating revolution to the rise of evangelical social influence. Only a scheme informed by the most nuanced application of social psychology, the most careful understanding of economic and domestic institutions, and the most perceptive tracking of interchanges among political, economic, theological, and social conceptual languages will do the job. And even that construct will not suffice unless there is some understanding of why it is that "those who are well have no need of a physician, but those who are sick." The question of causation must await another day, but the direction to be followed has been well marked by scholars such as David Hempton, who, with characteristic comprehension, has summarized the rise of Methodism in Ireland at the end of the eighteenth century as follows: "A well established revivalistic tradition in south-west Ulster was given added urgency in the period 1799–1802 by the psychological impact of the '98 rebellion in an area of sectarian equilibrium. It was also a period of high food prices and serious scarcities."[67]

To explain the causes for the evangelical rise to social influence in the wake of revolution is infinitely more challenging than to note that it occurred. But it did occur.

Notes

1. For a discussion of the scholarship, see the Introduction and Afterword.

2. On competition between ideologies of honor and evangelicalism in the American South, see Bertram Wyatt-Brown, "Religion and the 'Civilizing Process' in the American South, 1600–1860," in *Religion and American Politics from the Colonial Period to the 1980s,* ed. Mark A. Noll (New York: Oxford University Press, 1990), 172–95; and on Democratic resistance to evangelicalism, Robert P. Swierenga, "Ethnoreligious Political Behavior in the Mid-Nineteenth Century: Voting, Values, Cultures," ibid., 146–71.

3. See the description of these connections in Harry S. Stout, *The Divine Dramatist: George Whitefield and the Rise of Modern Evangelicalism* (Grand Rapids: Eerdmans, 1991); and Danial Walker Howe, "The Decline of Calvinism: An Approach to Its Study," *Comparative Studies in Society and History* 14 (June 1972): 306–27.

4. See, for example, Alan Heimert, *Religion and the American Mind from the Great Awakening to the Revolution* (Cambridge: Harvard University Press 1966); Harry S. Stout, *The New England Soul: Preaching and Religious Culture in Colonial New England* (New York: Oxford University Press, 1986), 282–311; and David W. Miller, "Presbyterianism and 'Modernization' in Ulster," *Past and Present* 80 (1978): 76–84.

5. E. P. Thompson, *The Making of the English Working Class* (New York: Pantheon, 1963), 381, with critical reaction from David Hempton, *Methodism and Politics in British Society, 1750–1850* (London: Hutchinson, 1987), 74–75; idem, "Methodism in Irish Society, 1770–1830," *Transactions of the Royal Historical Society* 36 (1986): 133; and Steve Bruce, "Social Change and Collective Behaviour: The Revival in Eighteenth-Century Ross-shire," *British Journal of Sociology* 34 (1983): 561.

6. Charles E. Cunningham, *Timothy Dwight, 1752–1817* (New York: Macmillan, 1942), 49–51; Elias Smith, *The Life, Conversion, Preaching, Travels, and Sufferings of Elias Smith* (1816; reprint, New York: Arno, 1980), 24; *The Biography of Eld. Barton Warren Stone, Written by Himself* (1847; reprint, New York: Arno, 1972), 2–5; "Alline's Journal," in *Henry Alline: Selected Writings*, ed. George A. Rawlyk (New York: Paulist, 1987), 87; R. D. Gidney, "Egerton Ryerson," *Dictionary of Canadian Biography,* vol. 11:1881–1890 (Toronto: University of Toronto Press, 1982), 783; "The Confessions of Dugald Buchanan," in *Buchanan, the Sacred Bard of the Scottish Highlands,* ed. and trans. Lachlan MacBean (London: Simpkin, Marshall, Hamilton Kent, 1919), 194–98; James Alexander Haldane, *The Lives of Robert Haldane of Airthrey, and of his Brother, James Alexander Haldane* (London: Hamilton, Adams, 1852), 82; Stewart J. Brown, *Thomas Chalmers and the Godly Commonwealth in Scotland* (Oxford: Oxford University Press, 1982), 32; R. Finlay Holmes, *Henry Cooke* (Belfast: Christian Journals Limited, 1981), 4.

7. John MacInnes, *The Evangelical Movement in the Highlands of Scotland, 1688 to 1800* (Aberdeen: The University Press, 1951), 89.

8. MacInnes, *Evangelical Movement in the Highlands,* is outstanding on these developments. See also George Robb, "Popular Religion and the Christianization of the Scottish Highlands in the Eighteenth and Nineteenth Centuries," *Journal of Religious History* 16 (1990): 25, 30–34.

9. T. C. Smout, *A History of the Scottish People, 1560–1830* (London: Collins, 1969), 358.

10. MacInnes, *Evangelical Movement in the Highlands,* 128.

11. Ibid., 134, 129.

12. The following paragraphs abridge an argument from Mark A. Noll, "The American Revolution and Protestant Evangelicalism," *Journal of Interdisciplinary History* 23 (1993): 615–38.

13. Counts of church adherents differ markedly, but the best assessments concur that a decline had set in. See Patricia U. Bonomi and Peter R. Eisenstadt, "Church Adherence in the Eighteenth-Century British American Colonies," *William and Mary Quarterly* 39 (1982): 274; and Rodney Stark and Roger Finke, "American Religion in 1776: A Statistical Portrait," *Sociological Analysis* 49 (1988): 239–51.

14. John M. Murrin, "Introduction," in *Princetonians, 1784–1790: A Biographical Dictionary,* ed. Ruth L. Woodward and Wesley Frank Craven (Princeton: Princeton University Press, 1991), xxxiv–xxxvi.

15. See John M. Murrin, "Religion and Politics in America from the First Settlements to the Civil War," in *Religion and American Politics,* ed. Noll, 19–43.

16. Jon Butler, *Awash in a Sea of Faith: Christianizing the American People* (Cambridge: Harvard University Press, 1990), chap. 9, "Christian Power in the American Republic."

17. Roger Finke and Rodney Stark, "How the Upstart Sects Won America: 1776–1850," *Journal for the Scientific Study of Religion* 28 (March 1989: 27–44.

18. Nathan O. Hatch, *The Democratization of American Christianity* (New Haven: Yale University Press, 1989), 6.

19. D. H. Meyer, *The Instructed Conscience: The Shaping of the American National Ethic* (Philadelphia: University of Pennsylvania Press, 1972); Henry R. May, *The Enlightenment in America* (New York: Oxford University Press, 1976), 307–62; Mark A. Noll, *Princeton and the Republic, 1768–1822: The Search for a Christian Enlightenment in the Era of Samuel Stanhope Smith* (Princeton: Princeton University Press, 1989).

20. John M. Murrin, "A Roof without Walls: The Dilemma of American National Identity," in *Beyond Confederation: Origins of the Constitution and American National Identity,* ed. Richard Beeman, et al. (Chapel Hill: University of North Carolina Press, 1987), 344, 347.

21. Donald G. Mathews, "The Second Great Awakening as an Organizing Process," *American Quarterly* 21 (1969): 23–43.

22. Melvin B. Endy, "Just War, Holy War, and Millennialism in Revolutionary America," *William and Mary Quarterly* 42 (January 1985): 3–25.

23. See Daniel Walker Howe, *The Political Culture of the American Whigs* (Chicago: University of Chicago Press, 1979); and Richard Carwardine, *Evangelicals and Politics in Antebellum America* (New Haven: Yale University Press, 1993).

24. George A. Rawlyk, *Nova Scotia's Massachusetts* (Montreal and Kingston: McGill-Queen's University Press, 1973), 250.

25. Quoted in Maurice W. Armstrong, "Neutrality and Religion in Revolutionary Nova Scotia," *New England Quarterly* 9 (March 1946), as reprinted in G. A. Rawlyk, ed., *Historical Essays on the Altantic Provinces* (Toronto: McClelland and Stewart, 1967), 39. In addition to this essay, the following book by Armstrong is also crucial for my interpretation of Maritime history: *The Great Awakening in Nova Scotia, 1776–1809* (Hartford, CT: American Society of Church History, 1948).

26. Reginald W. Bibby, *Fragmented Gods: The Poverty and Potential of Religion in Canada* (Toronto: Irwin, 1987), 87–91.

27. Leigh Eric Schmidt, *Holy Fairs: Scottish Communions and American Revivals*

in the Early Modern Period (Princeton: Princeton University Press, 1989); Arthur Fawcett, *The Cambuslang Revival: The Scottish Evangelical Revival of the Eighteenth Century* (London: Banner of Truth, 1971).

28. Smout, *History of the Scottish People, 1560–1830,* 234

29. John R. McIntosh, "The Popular Party in the Church of Scotland, 1740–1800" (Ph.D. diss., University of Glasgow, 1989), 64.

30. Ibid., 464–65.

31. David Alan Currie, "The Growth of Evangelicalism in the Church of Scotland, 1793–1843" (Ph.,D. diss., University of St. Andrews, 1990).

32. Deryck W. Lovegrove, "Unity and Separation: Contrasting Elements in the Thought and Practice of Robert Alexander Haldane," in *Protestant Evangelicalism: Britain, Ireland, Germany, and America, c. 1750–1950,* ed. Keith Robbins (Oxford: Blackwell, 1990), 153–78.

33. Quoted in Haldane, *Lives of Robert Haldane and J. A. Haldane,* 276.

34. See Collum G. Brown, *The Social History of Religion in Scotland since 1730* (London: Methuen, 1987), 60–63.

35. James McCosh, *The Scottish Philosophy* (New York: Carter and Bros., 1875), 397; T. C. Smout, *A Century of the Scottish Peoples, 1830–1950* (New Haven: Yale University Press, 1986), 181; Boyd Hilton, *The Age of Atonement: The Influence of Evangelicalism and Economic Thought, 1785–1865* (Oxford: Oxford University Press, 1988), 55.

36. Along with Brown, *Thomas Chalmers;* and Hilton, *The Age of Atonement,* where Chalmers is a central figure, see also A. C. Cheyne, ed., *The Practicial and the Pious: Essays on Thomas Chalmers (1780–1847)* (Edinburgh: St. Andrews Press, 1985); and D. W. Bebbington, *Evangelicalism in Modern Britian: A History from the 1730s to the 1980s* (London: Unwin Hyman, 1989), 80–81.

37. Kenneth Hylson-Smith, *Evangelicals in the Church of England, 1734–1984* (Edinburgh: T. and T. Clark, 1988), 68.

38. Deryck W. Lovegrove, *Established Church, Sectarian People: Itinerancy and the Transformation of English Dissent, 1780–1830* (Cambridge: Cambridge University Press, 1988), 162.

39. Hempton, *Methodism and Politics in British Society,* 74–80. For a fuller sense of how remarkable this Methodist expansion was, see also Robert Currie, Alan Gilbert, and Lee Horsley, *Churches and Churchgoers: Patterns of Church Growth in the British Isles since 1700* (Oxford: Clarendon Press, 1977), 24–28.

40. W. R. Ward, *Religion and Society in England, 1790–1850* (New York: Schocken, 1972), 105.

41. Currie, Gilbert, and Horsley, *Churches and Churchgoers,* 25.

42. Hilton, *Age of Atonement.* But see the important concerns voiced by David Bebbington about Hilton's understanding of the religious character of evangelicalism, in "Religion and Society in the Nineteenth Century [a review article]," *Historical Journal* 32 (1989): 1003.

43. MacInnes, *Evangelical Movement in the Highlands,* 128. For another perspective stressing some of the same connections, see V. Kiernan, "Evangelicalism and the French Revolution," *Past and Present* 1 (1952): 44–56.

44. Thomas Pakenham, *The Year of Liberty: The Great Irish Rebellion of 1798* (Englewood Cliffs, NJ: Prentice-Hall, 1969).

45. For authoritative interpretation and full bibliography, see David Hempton and Myrtle Hill, *Evangelical Protestantism in Ulster Society, 1740–1890* (London: Routledge, 1992), 20–44.

46. Finlay Holmes, *Our Irish Presbyterian Heritage* (Belfast: Publications Committee of the Presbyterian Church in Ireland, 1985), 95–102.

47. Hempton and Hill, *Evangelical Protestantism in Ulster,* 30–35.

48. Holmes, *Henry Cooke,* 207.

49. Derec LLwyd Morgan, *The Great Awakening in Wales* (London: Epworth Press, 1988).

50. David Williams, *A History of Modern Wales* (London: John Murray, 1950), 172–75.

51. E. D. Evans, *A History of Wales, 1660–1815* (Cardiff: University of Wales Press, 1976), 94.

52 Ibid., 94–96; Williams, *History of Modern Wales,* 246–47.

53. Quoted in Michael Hechter, *Internal Colonialism: The Celtic Fringe in British National Development, 1536–1966* (Berkeley: University of California Press, 1975), 190. Also helpful on the significance of language is D. W. Bebbington, "Religion and National Feeling in Nineteenth-Century Wales and Scotland," in *Religion and National Identity,* ed. Stuart Mews (Oxford: Blackwell, 1982), 492–93.

54. Michael Gauvreau, "Protestantism Transformed: Personal Piety and the Evangelical Social Vision, 1815–1867," in *The Canadian Protestant Experience, 1760–1990,* ed. George A. Rawlyk (Burlington, Ont.: Welch, 1990), 48–97; Richard W. Vaudry, *The Free Church in Victorian Canada, 1844–1861* (Waterloo, Ont.: Wilfrid Laurier University Press, 1989).

55. Michael Gauvreau, *The Evangelical Century: College and Creed in English Canada from the Great Revival to the Great Depression* (Montreal: McGill-Queen's University Press, 1991); William Westfall, *Two Worlds: The Protestant Culture of Nineteenth-Century Ontario* (Montreal and Kingston: McGill-Queen's University Press, 1989); and Marguerite Van Die, *An Evangelical Mind: Nathaniel Burwash and the Methodist Tradition in Canada, 1839–1918* (Montreal and Kingston: McGill-Queen's University Press, 1989). An older study that anticipated some of the solid insights in these books in Goldwin French, "The Evangelical Creed in Canada," in *The Shield of Achilles,* ed. W. L. Morton (Toronto: McClelland and Stewart, 1968).

56. John Webster Grant, *A Profusion of Spires: Religion in Nineteenth-Century Ontario* (Toronto: University of Toronto Press, 1988), 112–13.

57. Samuel S. Hill, Jr., *The South and the North in American Religion* (Athens: University of Georgia Press, 1980), 31; John B. Boles, "Evangelical Protestantism in the Old South: From Religious Dissent to Cultural Dominance," in *Religion in the South,* ed. Charles Reagan Wilson (Jackson: University Press of Mississippi, 1985), 13–34; Donald G. Mathews, *Religion in the Old South* (Chicago: University of Chicago Press, 1977), xvii.

58. T. H. Breen, essays on the South in *Puritans and Adventurers: Change and Persistence in Early America* (New York: Oxford University Press, 1980); and Bertram Wyatt-Brown, *Southern Honor: Ethics and Behavior in the Old South* (New York: Oxford University Press, 1982).

59. Charles Reagan Wilson, *Baptized in Blood: The Religion of the Lost Cause, 1865–1920* (Athens: University of Georgia Press, 1980); Ted Ownby, *Subduing Satan: Religion, Recreation, and Manhood in the Rural South, 1865–1920* (Chapel Hill: University of North Carolina Press, 1990).

60. Michael Gauvreau, "Beyond the Half-Way House: Evangelicalism and the Shaping of English Canadian Culture," *Acadiensis* 21 (Spring 1991): 166.

61. Focusing on North Atlantic evangelicalism can also obscure the fact that the term "evangelical" has enjoyed longer currency in Lutheran, Roman Catholic, and

even Orthodox usages, which must not simply be read out of existence by the effort to explain recent developments among English-speaking "evangelicals."

62. Frederick Dreyer, "Evangelical Thought: John Wesley and Jonathan Edwards," *Albion* 19 (1987): 177–92.

63. In what follows I am building upon the best recent discussions of the term "Evangelicalism," namely, Bebbington, *Evangelicalism in Modern Britain,* 1–19; George M. Marsden, "Introduction: The Evangelical Denomination," in *Evangelicalism and Modern America,* ed. Marsden (Grand Rapids: Eerdmans, 1984), vii–xix; and Donald W. Dayton, "Some Doubts about the Usefulness of the Category 'Evangelical,' " and Robert K. Johnston, "American Evangelicalism: An Extended Family," both in *The Variety of American Evangelicalism,* ed. Dayton and Johnston (Nashville: University of Tennesse Press; Downers Grove, IL: Inter Varsity Press, 1991).

64. Especially helpful on this common feature of evangelicalism, with particular reference to the question of assurance, in Bebbington, *Evangelicalism in Modern Britain,* 42–50.

65. Danial Walker Howe, "The Evangelical Movement and Political Culture in the North during the Second Party System," *Journal of American History* 77 (March 1991): 1216–39. The relationship between internal religion and the push toward social holiness is a key theme in the work of Timothy L. Smith, for example, *Revivalism and Social Reform: American Protestantism on the Eve of the Civil War* (Nashville: Abingdon, 1957) and "Righteousness and Hope: Christian Holiness and the Millennial Vision in America, 1800–1900," *American Quarterly* 31 (1979): 22–45.

66. Brown, *Thomas Chalmers; The Writings of John Leland,* (1845; reprint, New York: Arno, 1969).

67. Hempton, "Methodism in Irish Society," 128.

7

"A Total Revolution in Religious and Civil Government": The Maritimes, New England, and the Evolving Evangelical Ethos, 1776–1812

GEORGE A. RAWLYK

In February 1805, the eastern extremity of what is now the Canadian province of New Brunswick witnessed the most violent and bloodiest manifestation of Maritime New Light antinomianism—one of the sometimes forgotten legacies of Henry Alline's charismatic ministry. In the spring of 1804, a religious revival had swept the region, a revival fueled largely by the memories of Alline's remarkable First Great Awakening, which had engulfed Maritime Canada a quarter of a century earlier. A few months after the revival fires had burned themselves out, a young woman named Sarah Babcock, encouraged by an itinerant New Light preacher, Jacob Peck, began to prophesy; among other things, she confidently proclaimed that the end of the world was imminent. And just before Jesus Christ returned, she, assisted by Peck, was to convert to her special version of Christianity all the local inhabitants, including the scores of French-speaking Acadian Roman Catholics.

Sarah's father, Amasa, was especially affected by her newfound spirituality; the evidence suggests that in fact her message plunged him into a form of insanity. On 13 February 1805, while grinding wheat in his handmill, Amasa took a handful of flour and sprinkled it over the kitchen floor, declaring boldly, "This is the bread of heaven." Then, further encouraged by his daughter, he took off his shoes and rushed outside into the deep snow, yelling wildly as he stumbled through the drifts, "The world is coming to an end, and the stars are falling!" On returning to his house, an exhausted yet ecstatic Amasa lined up his entire family—his wife and nine children, and his sister Mercy and brother Jonathan—and demanded that they silently wait while he honed his long "clasp knife." After the knife had been sharpened, Amasa walked towards Mercy and ordered her to take off all of her clothes and to fall on her knees and ready herself for immediate death and eternity. He then ordered his

137

brother Johathan to strip; like his sister, Jonathan eagerly obeyed his older brother.

Amasa glanced nervously out of the window a number of times, apparently expecting to see his Savior's face, and then clutching his knife, he screamed, "The cross of Christ!" and stabbed his sister fatally. As soon as Jonathan "saw the blood flow," he regained his senses and rushed out of the door, naked. Eventually, after hearing Jonathan's amazing story, a group of neighbours rushed to the Babcock house. On seeing them, Amasa cried out, "Gideon's men arise!"[1] Gideon's men, however, were not to be found. Amasa, after being quickly captured and securely bound, was taken away, obviously insane. Amasa was eventually tried for the murder of his sister and was hanged on 28 June 1805. The *Saint John* (New Brunswick) *Gazette* of 24 June reported concerning the trial that:

> It appeared in evidence that for some time before the trial, the prisoner with several of his neighbours had been in the habit of meeting under pretence of religious exercises at each other's houses at which one Jacob Peck, a well-known Baptist was a principal performer; That they were under strong delusions and conducted themselves in a very frantic, irregular and even impious manner, and that in consequence of some pretended prohecies by some of the company in some of their pretended religious phrenzies against the unfortunate deceased: the prisoner was probably induced to commit the horrid, barbarous and cruel murder of which he was convicted.

The "great . . . concourse of the people at the trial" must have realized that Sarah Babcock's crucial role in what came to be known as the Babcock Tragedy as well as the profound impact of "Alline antinomianism" had both not received the attention that they obviously deserved. Like so many early nineteenth-century women, Sarah had been unceremoniously removed from the religious environment that she had largely created. Moreover, as we must emphasize, Sarah was only one of many young Maritime women in the immediate post-Alline period who shaped the contours of radical New Light evangelicalism in the region—especially its antinomianism, or what contemporaries often referred to as its New Dispensationalist variant.[2]

There were other New Light prophetesses in Maritime Canada and many, many female preachers or exhorters. Perhaps the most widely known of the former was Sarah Bancroft, from the Granville area of Nova Scotia near present-day Annapolis Royal. In 1791, Bishop Charles Inglis, the first Anglican bishop of what is now Canada, was apparently obsessed with this woman and the threat that she posed to good Anglican order in Nova Scotia in particular and throughout the Maritime region in general. Inglis observed in his *Journal* in 24 August 1791: "Heard much of the prophetess Sarah Bencraft. . . . She lately told Mrs. Shaw and the family that it was a great honour to them to attend and wait upon her, *as she, the Prophetess, would be a pillar in Heaven.*" Despite a number of her prophesies that were not realized, "the prophetess retained much of her credit and influence" among her "enthusiastic Sect called New Lights."[3] Her followers were certain that God spoke directly to her, as he could to them, and that they were only subject to the New Dispensation—the Holy Spirit at work directly in their lives, and not to the Devil-encrusted regulations of the Old and New Testaments. They could not conceive of themselves as being merely "self renewed and revived" but rather as individuals whose contemporary inner selves had been "wholly eradicated and replaced" by the Almighty.[4]

The testimony of Inglis about the radicalism of New Light revivalism in the Maritimes is particularly important, since, in an earlier phase of his career, he witnessed firsthand the radicalism of the American Revolution. If, as Inglis implied, the religious radicalism of Nova Scotia was more extreme than the radicalism of the American Revolution, an illuminating contrast between evangelicalism in Canada and in the neighboring United States comes into focus. The burden of this chapter is to show that, although evangelicalism in the new United States was indeed shaped by its democratic and republican environment, Canadian evangelicalism—at least until the War of 1812—may have been even more radical, more egalitarian, and more democratic than its better-known variant to the south.

Even during his lifetime, many of Henry Alline's most gifted followers had spun out his powerful New Light gospel of Christian primitivism in the direction of antinomianism. Having experienced the "ravishing of the spirit" direcly and immediately, these women and men, with their profound experience of empowerment, could not imagine how they could ever lose their salvation. Their confidence in the permanency of their redemption, because of "the rapture of the New Birth," was such that some became increasingly indifferent to contemporary moral standards.

Alline himself, it should be observed, had carefully balanced his stress on the "perseverance of the saints" with what has been called a powerful "asceticism and bodily mortification worthy of the most austere monasticism."[5] In his *Two Mites,* for example, published originally in 1781, Alline maintained that "true redemption is raising the desires of life of the inner man out of this miserable, sinful, and bestial world, and turning it to Christ, from whence it is fallen."[6] And later, in *The Anti-Traditionalist,* first published in 1783, he contended that it was necessary for the Christian to "turn from all, Deny all: Leave all." He went on:

> I do not mean the outward and cirminal Acts of Idolatry and Debauchery only: but any and every Thing in the Creature that in the least Degree amuses the Mind or leads the Choice from God. For even the most simple Enjoyments and Pleasures of Life will keep the Choice in Action, and therefore the Creature amused from God, and consequently sinking deeper and deeper in its fallen and irrecoverable State. Nor will you ever return to the redeemed until every Idol, Joy, Hope, or Amusement so fails you that you are wholly starved out, and there is not only a Famine, but a mighty Famine in all created Good.[7]

Carefully blended, Alline's perseverance and asceticism produced "true zeal";[8] the former, without the latter, led to antinomianism. The balance apparently prevailed in the Chignecto Isthmus region of western Nova Scotia in 1782 and in nearby Shediac in the first decade of the nineteenth century.

And it was certainly the case in the Annapolis Valley region of Nova Scotia in 1791 and 1792.

Some contemporary observers, however, had firsthand opportunity to witness the imbalance. On first meeting Henry Alline in the spring of 1780, the Nova Scotia Methodist leader William Black described the remarkable New Light preacher as being "very zealous in the cause."[9] "He laboured freverntly, and his coming" to the Chignecto area, Black stressed, "was made a great blessing to many."[10] But by the time Black visited Falmouth, Alline's home, in June 1782, their earlier warm friendship had been replaced by a mutual feeling of bitter recrimination, hostility, and illwill. According to Black, Alline and his associates—men such as Thomas Handley Chipman and John Payzant, Alline's brother-in-law—had maintained that the Methodist preacher "was no minister of Jesus Christ, soon after, he was no christian; and in a little while, down-right minister of Antichrist."[11] Black was also very concerned with what he perceived to be the pernicious growth of Alline's antinomian, mystical, and primitivist gospel. In November 1782, an obviously distraught Black noted in his journal:

> I rode over to *Tantramar* [the present-day border between Nova Scotia and New Brunswick], where I was sorely grieved to find *Mysticism* and the foulest *Antinomianism,* spreading like fire; and its deadly fruits already growing up on every side. The people were informed publickly, *That they had nothing to do with God's law: that David was still a man after God's own heart; when wallowing in adultery, and murder: that his soul never sinned all that time, but only his body.* Mr. Alline himself told several persons one day that *a believer is like a nut, thrown into the mud, which may dirty the shell, but not the kernel.* That is, we may get drunk, or commit adultery, without the smallest defilement, etc. etc.[12]

Three years later, on 22 May 1785, Freeborn Garrettson, a Maryland Methodist preacher then itinerating in Nova Scotia, confronted in these areas of the colony which had been settled in the early 1760s by New Englanders, what he referred to as "a people . . . call'd Allinites."[13] "In general," he pointed out, with little concern for proper grammar, "they are as deluded a people as ever I saw." He went on to observe: "They are most all Speakers in Publick. I was conversing with one of their head Speakers. She told me she thought death would Slay more Sins for her than ever was before. And as for Sin, said she, it Can not hurt one. No Not Adultery, Murder, Swearing, drunkenness, nor no other Sin Can break yet Union between me and Christ. They have judged and passed sentence on me, as no Christian, Nor Call'd to Preach."[14] It is noteworthy that the shrewd and perceptive Garrettson underscored the key role played by the female "head Speaker" in the movement. Garrettson also pointed out that the "Allinites" believed that they could "tell whether a person is a Christian at first sight," and they were absolutely "sure of heaven as if they were already there, for sin cannot hurt them."[15]

Two Anglican ministers, the Reverend Jacob Bailey and Bishop Charles Inglis, also commented on what they regarded as the peculiar heretical views of some of Alline's disciples and of many New Lights. On 25 May 1789, the often-acerbic Bailey wrote from Annapolis Royal that the New Light itinerants were creating "great confusion among the lower people" and were "of inconceivable damage to a new country, by drawing multitudes almost every day in the week, at this busy season, to attend to their desultory and absurd vociferations." Bailey went on:

> These preachers, however, agree in rejecting the literal sense of the Holy Scriptures, and the Christian Ordinances. Their dependence is upon certain violent emotions, and they discourage industry, charity, and every social virtue, affirming that the most abandoned sinners are nearer to the Kingdom of heaven than people of a sober, honest and religious deportment, for such, they allege, are in danger of depending upon their own righteousness.[16]

Bishop Inglis, a lapsed Methodist, endorsed Bailey's description and embellished it significantly and in the process emphasized the considerable influence that Alline's theology was still exerting on the Maritime evangelical mind a decade after his death in 1784. The New Lights, as far as Inglis was concerned, were "rigid Predestinarians" who believed "that all mankind were present, and actually sinned with our primitive parents." He continued: "After conversion they are not answerable for any sins they commit, since it is the flesh and not the spirit which offends. . . . Many of them deny the resurrection, a future judgement, heaven and hell, though the Elect are to be happy and the Reprobates miserable after death. Their discipline is democratic. The right of ordination, dismission etc. lies entirely with the Brethren."[17]

A decade later, Joshua Marsden, a Methodist missionary in the border region betwen Nova Scotia and New Brunswick, noted that Alline's antinomian legacy was still being "industriously propagated . . . by some new-light preachers." These men and women stressed four points:

1. That a believer, though he sin ever so much, is still pure;—God sees no sin in Israel.
2. That the body of a believer only sins, and not the soul; as a nut thrown into the mud is only soiled in the shell, and not the kernel.
3. That the body of a believer may get intoxicated and commit whoredom, but not the soul; that being spiritual is not affected by such fleshy lusts.
4. That a sheep though he render himself filthy by going into the mud, and black, by rubbing against the stumps of burned trees, is a sheep still, as nobody ever heard of a sheep becoming a goat.[18]

For many Nova Scotians and New Brunswickers, the most significant and disconcerting example of eighteenth-century New Light antinomianism occurred in 1791, in the Allinite heartland of Cornwallis. At the core of the movement was to be found a Mrs. Lydia Randall, widely regarded as "their head Speaker" and leader who vociferously and eloquently denounced "all the orders of the church."[19] Randall was the Nova Scotian Anne Hutchinson—charismatic, intelligent, articulate, and obviously a social and religious revolutionary.[20] Lydia had married Green Randall in 1779 and with her husband became a member of the Cornwallis New Light Church. She may have been influenced by some Quaker beliefs as early as 1788, which may help to explain why she was so determined in May 1791 to restore radical New Light faith and practice. The Reverend John Payzant, who was her pastor, described her role in the radical religious movement that she virtually led:

> The Second Sabbath of May [1791] it was the turn to have the Church Meeting and Sacrament at Horton. Mrs. R[andall] rose against all the orders of the church and [said] that they were but outward forms and contrary to the Spirit of God. These novelties in the Church caused many to follow the same examples, which made troble in the Church. . . . She told me that she had seen by the Spirit of God, that Baptism and the Lord Supper, with all the Disciples, of the Church was contrary to the Spirit of God and his Gospel, and that Marriage was from the Divel. That she was determined to live sapate [separate] from her Husband, for it was as much sin for her to have children by him as by any other man and she saith that there were many that would follow her in it, that there were many young women that were converted, which she has as soon see them have children by any man; [than] to Marry.[21]

In reply, Payzant "told her that she was involving herself in an abstruse that she would find much defeculty to get out," and he "begged of her not to advance such sentiments for she had not well considered them for she would make herself an object of Redecule."[22] Mrs. Randall, who stressed over and over again that "she had seen" directly "the Spirit of God," quickly countered by contending that "her mind had gone farther on these things" than had Payzant's.[23] Lydia Randall, who frontally challenged marriage and male domination of any kind, was perceived by Payzant and his supporters as a pernicious and dangerous revolutionary.

By August of 1791, Payzant's church was badly split; everything was in a state of utter confusion, and support for what Payzant called these "fantastical notions[s]" quickly "spread from town to town and many adopted this new scheme." The church covenant and articles of faith were denounced as being "not[h]ing but forms and wholly contrary to Religion." The followers of Mrs. Randall even stopped Payzant from serving Communion. "They pretended," reported a distraught Payzant, "that they were taugh[t] by the Spirit of God to go beyond all order, that they had great discoveries beyond whatever was known before, eather by the premitive Christeans."[24] Absolutely convinced of the fact that they were specially selected conduits for the Holy Spirit, and that they were divinely inspired, the radical New Lights manifested an extraordinary zealousness and enthusiasm for their so-called New Dispensation, or their unique version of Christianity. They had obviously moved far beyond Alline's volatile mixture of Whitefieldian New Lights orthodoxy and his mystical heterodoxy.

In order to establish his authority, Payzant, sometime in 1792, decided to impose "Church Rules" on his disintegrating congregation. This move was vigorously opposed by James and Edward Manning, supporters of Randall who later became patriarchs of the Maritime Baptist denomination.

The Manning's "came to the Church meeting, and begun to dispute, and condemn the Church Rules, and say that all orders were done away, and that the Bible was a dead letter, and they would preach without it and such like things." It seemed clear to Payzant that Edward Manning, "in particular, was insinuating these Eronious Sentiments in young people minds." One of these young women named what Payzant called "this fantastical notion" the "new dispensation," and the movement continued its spread "from town to town and many adopted this new Sc[h]eme." Some began to "burlesque the Church" and contended that the New Dispensationalists "were the only lively Christeans." Lydia Randall evidently attacked "1st Marriages 2nd all order 31y the scriptures 41y Ministers proving their doctrine by the Scri[p]tures." She also, according to Payzant, maintained "that God had made the Elect; and the Divel had made the non Elect"; moreover, many "gave away to carnal desire, so that their new plan took a contrary effect, for instead of living So holy as they preted [pretended] to, they were light and carnal."[25] New Dispensationalism had become a Nova Scotia and New Brunswick version of antinomianism; as it lurched madly away from community behaviorial norms and from Alline's position, an understandable reaction set in.

Church meeting followed church meeting as the New Dispensationalists continued to attack their opponents. They maintained that they alone accurately interpreted the Scripture, since they alone "were lead by the Spirit of God and that their explanation of the Scriptures were all spiritual so that they were absolutely right."[26] There were endless discussions about the proper interpretation of certain key verses of Scripture, and the almost endless debate seemed to defuse the explosive issue. Although Payzant took exception to the new practices, he also continued to oppose the demand that the New Dispensationalist "Preachers" be summarily expelled. Payzant held to this middle ground, despite the fact that he realized his policy would lead to the permanent departure of many anti–New Dispensationalists from his church. Payzant hoped that "by gentle means" order and good sense and stability would return to his congregation.[27]

On 6 October 1792, the Cornwallis Church met, and it was finally decided that its members "would stand by the Church Rules, and that no person should have [the] liberty, to vote, to speak, in Church meetings but those that held to her Rules." At Falmouth, because of the strength of the New Dispensationalists and their continuing opposition to all "Rules," they "were merely denied . . . the ordinance." In response, some asserted "that all the world would be Saved."

> Some said, that there was no such man as Christ; and all the Christ that there was, was what we felt in ourselves; and therefore why should they hold to Baptism, and the Supper. . . . Others saith that the Divel made all Such as would be lost and that God made all them that would be saved. So that all that God made would go to him, and that all the Divel made would go to him, and these last sentiments they pretended to maintain from Serivture [Scripture].[28]

Much later, after he had become the general factotum of the Nova Scotia Baptists, an ardent Calvinist, and a vociferous critic of New Light enthusiasm, Edward Manning attempted to describe what he considered to be the heart of New Dispensationalism:

> Mr. Alline's lax observance of divine institutions fostered in the minds of his followers such ideas as these; that the ordinances are only circumstantial, outward matters, and mere non-essentials; that the scriptures are not the only rule of faith and practice; and that no person is under any obligation to perform any external duty until God immediately impressed the mind so to do. . . . Several began to question the propriety of having anything to do with external order or ordinances, and soon refused to commune with the church. . . . As they had no rule to go by but their fancies, which they called "the Spirit of God," great irregularities ensued.[29]

Manning, who for the remainder of his life would be embarrassed by his close association in the 1790–92 period with the New Dispensationalists, had deftly cut to the heart of the movement's ideology. Here was a man who had worked closely with Lydia Randall in coaxing the movement into existence and who had, moreover, significantly affected its evolution. If any single person understood New Dispensationalism and its appeal, Edward Manning certainly did. As far as he was concerned, it was Alline's "lax observance of divine institutions" and his emphasis on the "Spirit of Liberty" and "individual illumination" that persuaded many of his followers to break out of the radical evangelical and New Light framework to enjoy this "Quaker and Shaker" freedom. The radicals possessed a deep desire to experiment, to shatter existing religious values, to fundamentally reshape evangelical individualism, and to challenge community norms directly. With the Spirit of God within them, having experienced the profound intensity and the rapture of the New Birth, having been ravished by the Almighty, anything seemed possible and permissible. Their sin had been canceled out, once and for all, by the sacrifice of Christ; sinning, whether in the flesh or the spirit, could not distance them from their Savior. Instead of turning toward ascetic behavior, as Alline had preached and practiced, many New Dispensationalists, especially a number of young and gifted women, driven by the "Spirit of Liberty," and in order to test the viability of their New Birth and to flaunt their spiritual hubris at their neighbors, committed what Manning called "their extravagancies."[30] Their "great irregularities" obviously served a number of interrelated purposes. They were the means whereby one could both enjoy sin and appreciate salvation—no significant accomplishment in any age. "Antinomian excesses," moreover, enabled women in particular to express freely and creatively their innermost emotional and sexual drives at a time, and in an age, when such behavior was regarded as sinfully aberrant.

Edward Manning, his brother James, and other males, including Joseph Dimock, another future Nova Scotia Baptist patriarch, abandoned New Dispensationalism for two major reasons. First, wanting to be settled ministers of the gospel, they realized that antinomianism anarchy would undermine their leadership in the congregations. To assert their power and control they would espouse Calvinist order and Baptist closed membership. Second, the evidence suggests that by the middle of the 1790s a group a very gifted young male preachers—the Mannings, Joseph Dimock, and Thomas Handley Chipman, all of whom considered themselves disciples of Henry Alline—were becoming increasingly concerned about the growing influence of women such as Lydia Randall, Sarah Bancroft, and others such as the Blair sisters of Onslow and Charlotte Prescott of Chester and Betsy Parker of Nictaux.[31] In order to assert their male hegemony, the New Light men quickly marginalized their female competition, espeically in the Annapolis Valley region stretching from Falmouth to Annapolis. In other New Light regions of Nova Scotia and New Brunswick, however, this male offensive faced opposition until at least the third decade of the nineteenth century.

The conservative reaction by the Mannings and their Baptist colleagues only highlights the radical character of the religion they opposed. By taking seriously the testimony from both proponents and opponents of the radical New Light, we are in a position to begin a comparison with similar phenomena across the border in the new United States.

Concerning the decades immediately following the American Revolution, it has been effectively argued that in the new United States "traditional structures of authority crumbled under the momentum of the Revolution, and common people increasingly discovered that they no longer had to accept the old distinctions," which had marginalized them into a widely perceived subservient and vulnerable status.[32] Gordon Wood, among others, has shown that during these years popular evangelical Christianity seemed to be in a delicate state of spiritual tension "poised like a steel spring by the contradicting forces pulling within it."[33] There was a spiritual quality, but there was also a secular quality. There was a democratic bias but also an authoritarian bias, an emphasis on revelation but also an empirical tendency, both a growing concern with individualism and a continuing obsession with the collectivity.

In his award-winning and widely praised *Democratization of American Christianity* (1989), Nathan Hatch expands our understanding of these powerful, conflicting forces first delineated by Gordon Wood in 1980. Hatch underlines especially the importance of the democratic impulse that permeated evangelical Christianity and transformed it according to the dictates of a new, popular culture. This new evangelical culture, which fundamentally challenged elite orthodoxies and religious establishments, emphasized the vernacular in preaching and hymnody and encouraged popular participation in religious rituals such as the camp metting, the long Communion, and believer's baptism. Popular evangelicalism questioned and even denigrated the values of the educated elite by defining cultural authority in terms of dramatic presentation and emotional persuasion, the hallmarks of the untutored and Spirit-filled evangelical preacher. Ordinary folks were encouraged to place the emotional conversion experience on a much higher plane than either church membership or discipline. According to Hatch, "In this vast expanse of land"—the new United States—"there emerged an individualistic, democratic

American Christianity that was "audience centered, intellectually open to all, organizationally fragmented, and popularly led."[34]

Although British North America had rejected the American Revolution and all that American republicanism represented, a very good case can be made that in this even vaster "expanse of land"—present-day Canada—evangelicalism was more radical, more anarchistic, more democratic, and more popular than its American counterpart. Unlike the new American evangelicalism, Canadian evangelicalism did not have to carry the baggage of civic humanism, republicanism, and the covenant ideal. Without these encumbrances, and avoiding what Mark Noll has recently referred to as "the interaction of conceptual 'languages,' "[35] Canadian evangelicalism, a broad spectrum of belief connecting antinomian anarchists on one hand and Calvinist Baptist and British-oriented Methodists on the other, was able to cut itself free from secular concerns and obsessions. Religious concerns were the only concerns—all other matters were, as Henry Alline once simply put it, "mere non-essentials."[36] When confronted by the world of "Turnips, Cabbages, and Potatoes," is it surprising that the New Light followers of Alline's gospel instead embraced the cosmic reality of "the *One Eternal Now*"?[37] According to Alline and many of his disciples, those who experienced the New Birth had no sense of "Time, and Space, and Successive Periods." "Salvation and Damnation," it was emphasized over and over again,

> originate here at your own Door; for with God there never was any Thing, as before time began, and as many more, after Time is at a Period, being the same very instant; consider neither Time past nor Time to come, but one Eternal Now; consider that with God there is neither Succession nor Progress; but that with Him the Moment He said let us make Man, and the Sound of his last Triumph, is the very same instant, and your Death as much as your Birth . . . with God all things are NOW . . . as the Center of a Ring, which is as near the one side as the other.[38]

For many Canadian evangelicals in the immediate postrevolutionary period, regeneration was *the* central Christian experience—the only experience—the means whereby finite time and space were smashed by "the Eternity you once, were, and knew."[39]

It has been recently argued by Nancy Christie that "in both the Maritimes and the Canadas, popular evangelicalism was clearly dominant by 1812, with the New Lights, Baptists and Methodists clearly on the rise."[40] "Evangelical culture," according to Christie, "was re-creating a social world in which spiritual authority was vested no longer in the outward man-made institutions of church and government, but in the inner spirituality of the individual resulting from the personal encounter between the converted and God."[41] At the core of this evangelical culture, especially in Maritime Canada, was found what Anglican leaders such as Charles Inglis especially feared—"not that 'the Evangelicals' might immediately incite political revolt or mob rule, but that the democratic spiritualism of the evangelical ethos might unleash upon the embryonic society a host of newly assertive individuals."[42]

Throughout the 1790s Bishop Inglis of Nova Scotia was absolutely certain that the New Lights, whether Congregational, Methodist, or Baptist, were "engaged in the general plan of a *total revolution in religious and civil government.*"[43] "Ignorant men and women and even children under twelve years of age," he once reported, "were employed to pray and exhort, until the whole assembly groaned, and screamed, and finally ended with a falling down and rolling upon the floor of both sexes together." If this was not enough, "they added Dreams, Visions, Recitations, Prophecies and Trances."[44] Since his disconcerting tenure as a Loyalist Anglican priest in New York during the revolution, where he had seen the transformation of what he spitefully called "religious enthusiasts" into republican revolutionaries, Inglis was obsessed with the ways in which evangelical Christianity "dissolved" all forms of government and destroyed "all order and decorum."[45] The Inglis thesis, which underscored the truly radical nature of Maritime evangelicalism, was enthusiastically endorsed by the scores of Anglican ministers in the region who regularly reported to their bishop about the state of religion in their communities. Evangelical anarchy seemed to be the rule rather than the exception as Methodist, Baptist, and Congregational New Lights "undertook to prophesy, and to speak with new tongues, and to work miracles."[46] Various travelers deplored the "effects of fanaticism on the human mind" and the practice, especially along the St. John River in New Brunswick, of scores of ecstatic worshipers who would "bawl" and "roar" out praise to the Almighty as they "went crawling about like wild beasts with others riding on their backs."[47]

Anglican critics of the New Lights, whether proto-Baptists or Methodists or Congregationalists, even contrasted the "wild extravagances" they observed in Nova Scotia and New Brunswick and the Canadas with the relative decorum of religious worship in neighboring New England and New York. In drawing this sharp contrast, the Anglicans and other critics of Maritime and central Canadian evangelicalism found themselves enjoying the enthusiastic endorsement of their New Light enemies. At least three New Dispensationalist leaders, and later influential leaders of the Maritime Baptist Church, James and Edward Manning and Joseph Dimock, visited New England and New York in the 1790s. The Mannings were a disruptive force in northern Maine, attacking all the ministers they met as anti-Christian hirelings; they did everything they could to persuade their hundreds of listeners to abandon "lifeless" versions of Christianity for the Maritime version of New Light truth.[48] As far as the Mannings were concerned, Maine Christianity and American republicanism had merged to produce a pernicious antithesis of the pristine Christianity that they themselves preached and lived. The Mannings' critique of American evangelicalism and all that it represented was also expressed by Joseph Dimock. According to Dimock, American audiences found him "so Disagreeable . . . they can scarcely put up with it."[49] Confronting opposition because of his "incorrect" preaching,[50] and often lacking "the inlargedness of ideas and freedom of speech" that he always experienced in Nova Scotia, Dimock was eager to return to "the people of thy choice" in his native province.[51] Dimock had found "the same God" in the United States as he worshiped in Nova Scotia, but "still I find none that seem to have the life of God so pure in the soul as in Nova Scotia." "Much of the life and the power of religion here in the United States," he concluded, "seem to withdraw and forms are constituted in the room thereof."[52]

It is possible that the Mannings, Dimock, Bishop Inglis, and the others, including a myriad of present-day scholars, were, for a variety of reasons, exaggerating the uniqueness of Maritimes New Light evangelicalism. But how does one effectively explain away the words and actions of the influential American Methodist leader Francis Asbury? By the late 1790s, Asbury had become quite concerned about the questionable impact of the Maritime evangelical ethos on so many of his itinerants. He once observed that these young men returned to the United States "not so humble and serious as when they went."[53] And Asbury was determined to do something about the New Light cancer. He therefore decided not to send any more American Methodist itinerants to "Nova Scarcity," shifting the responsibility to Great Britain. This decision would mean, among other things, that the Maritime Methodists would be quickly replaced at the leading edge of Protestantism in the region by the Baptist disciples of Henry Alline.[54]

Asbury's critique of the Maritime evangelical ethos was also expressed in print and privately by four Massachusetts Baptist ministers who visited the region in the first decade of the nineteenth century. Isaac Case, Daniel Merrill, Henry Hale, and Amos Allen were all disturbed with the New Light excesses that they witnessed in New Brunswick and Nova Scotia.[55] They criticized openly and sometimes vociferously the religious anarchy that many Maritimers equated with "Spirit-filled worship." And they were determined to do everything in their power to impose on the religious revivals that accompanied their frequent visits a firm Calvinist Baptist organizational form—one they eagerly appropriated from Massachusetts. Despite their energetic efforts at organizational control, it was not until the late 1820s and 1830s that an effective Baptist denomination began to emerge in the region. The Maritime New Light legacy, in short, could not be contained in standard organizational forms.

This argument about Canadian New Light revivalism may still be critiqued for implicitly suggesting, as Tom Vincent has recently put it, that Henry Alline was *the* "mystical, larger-than-life, proto-Baptist who could leap tall Anglicans and Methodists at a single bound, a veritable Paul Bunyan of revival enthusiasm."[56] But even if Alline is pushed into the dark oblivion of late eighteenth-century Maritime historiography and even if his religious legacy is perceived as nothing more than Bay of Fundy fog, there is still more evidence to support the contention that the Maritime evangelical ethos was, in most respects, more radical, more democratic, and more individualistic than its New England counterpart. How else can one explain the remarkable career of the Reverend Jonathan Scott, Alline's most perceptive Nova Scotia critic? Ordained a Congregational minister in 1772, Scott remained in the Yarmouth region until 1794, when he moved to Maine, where he died in 1819. While in Nova Scotia, Scott was viewed as an Old Light—an ardent anti-Allinite. As soon as he started to preach in Maine, however, he was widely regarded as a

New Light—an evangelist who could even coax revivals into existence.[57] Scott did not change between 1793 and 1794. He merely changed environments, a point that is of crucial significance.

The essential question is how the two environments actually differed. Did the American environment of Massachusetts-Maine encourage a certain religious style while that of neighboring New Brunswick and Nova Scotia encourage a radically different one?

Fresh research, in fact, now makes it possible for the first time to compare the different ways in which northern Massachusetts and Nova Scotia developed generally in the period 1760 to 1820 and more specifically in the 1770s, 1780s, and 1790s. In her ground-breaking comparative history, Elizabeth Mancke contends that the two towns of Machias, Maine, and Liverpool, Nova Scotia, although both were settled by New Englanders in the early 1760s, were "through experiences in two political sysems, transformed into two distinct cultures."[58] Mancke shows that in Nova Scotia, unlike New England, towns as political entities actually ceased to exist. The Nova Scotia Yankees, who provided the core of the New Light movement, had to be satisfied with two political privileges—"they could elect a representative" for the Halifax Assembly, and "they could meet annually to levy a poor rate." "Beyond these privileges," she goes on, "a township's inhabitants had no political identity, as did their counterparts in New England, who elected town officers, levied taxes for town servies, and could meet to discuss local, colonial, state or national issues."[59] The absence of effective local government and a dependence on Halifax and London naturally stunted political and ideological development in Nova Scotia. But the absence of an effective form of town government was responsible for far more, especially in the realm of religion. As Mancke puts it, the "divergent patterns in the collapse of Calvinist Congregationalism in Liverpool and Machias, and Nova Scotia and Maine, were not caused by significant differences in the impact of the forces of dissolution but rather by differences in the forces for maintaining cohesion and containing dissent."[60]

In New England, both before and after the revolution, the churches were very much supported by town governments and by legislative assemblies and, at times, by the courts. In Nova Scotia, by contrast, the virtual elimination of town government had removed "a crucial source of local power for maintaining religious cohesion among Congregationalists and for channeling dissent into appropriate forms."[61] The differing political systems in the two regions "had the greatest impact on the course of the decline of Congregationalism, the social response to religious dissent, and the emergence of new sects."[62] For religious life at the local level in Yankee Nova Scotia, "difficulties were resolved by removing all group compulsion and allowing individuals complete freedom of choice." There was, in Nova Scotia, in other words, no "intermediate stage during which people could endow incorporated private religious societies with taxing rights buttressed by the government."[63] Ironically, in Nova Scotia greater individual rights characterized society, while in New England communalism still exerted a powerful influence. And this individualism, fostered by a powerful localism devoid of the societal cohesion provided by town government, democratized Christianity and largely depoliticized religion. In New England, the First Great Awakening may have prepared the way for the American Revolution and for American republicanism and democracy. In Nova Scotia and New Brunswick, the emerging evangelical ethos absorbed a powerful individualistic impulse and often stretched this well beyond the existing New England boundaries of even extreme religious behavior.

In what is now Canada, the postrevolutionary movement to democratize Christianity and to depoliticize evangelicalism was, in so many respects, merely a continuation of Maritime Canada's ideological response to the American Revolution. Most of the thousands of Yankees who had settled in what is now Nova Scotia and New Brunswick during the early 1760s did not share with their friends and relatives in New England what John Adams once referred to as "the radical change in the principles, opinions, sentiments and affections of the people."[64] For the Yankees and other residents of Nova Scotia, "resistance to revolution" showed that they viewed events and personalities through a pre-1760 ideological lens rather than through one from after 1765; through a basically religious lens rather than a secular one.[65] Nova Scotia Yankees did not conform to the general American pattern of ideological development because their form of government and the nature of their society, with its speical religious bias, precluded the development of what some contemporaries described as the "general enlightenment" and "eclairisement" of key sections of the population.[66]

Nova Scotia's unique response to the revolution was Nova Scotia's First Great Awakening. It was a purely religious response—an evangelical social movement connecting events in Nova Scotia in the 1770s and 1780s with the New England of the late 1730s and 1740s. Henry Alline, the charismatic leader of Nova Scotia's awakening, was able to perceive a special purpose for his fellow colonists in the midst of the confused revolutionary situation. But his message was completely devoid of republican content, though it was truly revolutionary in its implications. The religious revival that swept Nova Scotia during the American Revolution was not merely "a retreat from the grim realities of the world to the safety and pleasantly exciting warmth of the revival meeting," and "to profits and rewards of another character."[67] Nor was it basically a revolt of the outsettlements against Halifax, the capital, or an irrational outburst against all forms of traditionalism and authority. The First Great Awakening of Nova Scotia may be viewed as an attempt by many Yankee inhabitants to appropriate a new sense of identity and a renewed sense of purpose. Religious enthusiasm in this context, a social movement of profound consequence in the Nova Scotia situation, was symptomatic of a collective identity crisis as well as a searching for an acceptable and meaningful ideology. Resolution of the crisis came not only when the individuals were absorbed into what they felt was a dynamic fellowship of true believers but also when they accepted Alline's analysis of contemporary events and his conviction that their colony was the center of a crucial cosmic struggle.

In sermons preached as he crisscrossed the colony. Alline developed the theme that the Nova Scotia Yankees, in particular, had a speical predestined role to play in God's plan for the world. It must have required a special effort for Alline to convince Nova Scotians of their special world role. But Alline, drawing deeply on the Puritan New England tradition that viewed self-sacrifice and frugality as virtues, contended that the relative backwardness and isolation of the colony had removed the inhabitants from the prevailing corrupting influences of New England and Britain. As a result, Nova Scotia was in an ideal position to lead the world back to God.

The meaning of the unusual conjunction of events—of civil war in New England and an outpouring of the Holy Spirit in Nova Scotia—was obvious to Alline and the thousands who flocked to hear him. God was passing New England's historical mantle of Christian leadership to Nova Scotia (which then also included all of present-day New Brunswick). In the worldview of New Englanders fighting for the revolutionary cause, Old England was corrupt, and the Americans were engaged in a righteous and noble cause. There was therefore purpose to the hostilties. But to Alline, that "inhuman War" had no such meaning. Rather, along with all the other signs of the times, the Revolutionary War could indicate only one thing, that the entire Christian world, apart from Nova Scotia, was abandoning the way of God.

Alline's radical evangelicalism appealed to thousands of Nova Scotians and other Maritimers during and after the American Revolution. This radical evangelicalism had much more in common with the New England of the early 1740s than the New England of the 1780s and 1790s. It was a gospel that certainly energized religious individualism and denigrated political solutions, whether radical or reactionary. This New Light legacy would become the evangelical norm in much of postrevolutionary British North America. It would also be the norm for the hundreds of black Loyalist Nova Scotians, who, in the late 1780s and early 1790s, were also profoundly affected by what they knew as Allinite antinomianism.[68]

This is not to argue that some regions of Maine, in particular, did not also experience outbursts of antinomianism or "Christian primitivism" in the 1790s and the first decade of the nineteenth century.[69] But these outbursts may have owed a great deal, as Stephen Marini has suggested concerning the "New Light Stir" of the 1778–81 period, to events and personalities in New Brunswick and Nova Scotia.[70] Even so, the Maine version of New Light antinomianism was far more muted than the Maritime version; moreover, it was regarded by insiders and outsiders alike as being far more marginal. The Congregational Church as well as the Calvinist Baptists were far more successful in Maine than in the Maritimes in limiting the spread of Christian New Light primitivism. Moreover, much of radical evangelicalism in Maine was politicized and then channeled into what Allan Taylor has described as the "White Indians."[71] The influence of the "Liberty Men" and of their republican/evangelical strategy in Maine demonstrated graphically not only the pristine religiosity of Maritime Christian New Light primitivism but also a fundamental distinction between the two societies.

Only in Halifax was the Anglican and governmental elite able to stem the tide of the radical New Light evangelicalism in the 1780s and 1790s. Effective use of the urban mob and the British army and navy prevented preachers such as Henry Alline and the Methodist William Black from making significant inroads in the religious life of the community. In the Yankee outsettlements of the colony and even in much of Loyalist New Brunswick, however, the governing elite failed miserably in its infrequent and futile attempts to impose British and Anglican order on an increasingly individualistic and radical evangelicalism. There was a similar tendency in Upper Canada (present-day Ontario), where most of the rural Yankee inhabitants (some 60 percent of the population in 1810) had succeeded in pushing Anglican order and decorum into the narrow confines of present-day Toronto and the commercial and military center of Kingston. In an ironic twist of historical development, at the time when the War of 1812 broke out, British and Anglican "Peace, Order and Good Government" in present-day Ontario and the Maritime Provinces had been decisively defeated—not by American "Life, Liberty and the Pursuit of Happiness," but by the powerful forces unleashed by radical *and Canadian* evangelicalism. The War of 1812, along with the powerful forces of anti-Americanism and pro-British feelings it unleashed, significantly reshaped the contours of Canadian evangelicalism and significantly constricted the broad spectrum of permissible belief and practice. But these forces did not succeed in completely eradicating radical evangelicalism from the Canadian Protestant experience.

In August 1824, nineteen years after the Babcock Tragedy and thirty years after Lydia Randall's antinomian movement had peaked, a final wild outburst of New Dispensationalism took place not far from Henry Alline's home. A disconcerted Edward Manning described what suddenly happened at his regular Sunday morning service:

> No sooner was I seated than a young Woman whom I know not, screamed out (from the gallery) and a number below, all females, a melancholy sound to me, because I thought there was such an extravagancy of Voice, and such uncommon gesticulations, leaving their seats, running round the broad [a]isle, swinging their Arms, bowing their Heads to the Ground, Stretching their hands out right and left, then stretching them up as high as they could while the head was bowed to the floor almost. . . . The young woman up in the gallery came directly to me with an awfully dis-Figured face, screeching verry loud, indeed calling me brother, O my brother O my brother! until she was exhausted and then she turned away.[72]

This manifestation of what Manning referred to as Allinism must have compelled the leading Maritime Calvinist Baptist minister to remember ruefully his own enthusiastic involvement with the New Dispensationalism three decades before. So much had changed with him; so little had changed with the disruptive power of radical evangelicalism.

Notes

1. See my description of the "Babcock Tragedy" in *Ravished by The Spirit* (Montreal and Kingston: McGill-Queen's University Press, 1984) 100–101. See also D. G.

Bell, ed., *New Light Baptist Journals of James Manning and James Innis* (Hantsport, Nova Scotia: Lancelot Press, 1984), 331–54.

2. See my *New Light Letters and Spiritual Songs* (Hantsport, Nova Scotia: Lancelot Press, 1983), 38–75.

3. "Inglis Journal, 24 August 1791," Public Archives of Nova Scotia, Halifax.

4. K. W. F. Stavely, review of a variety of books about seventeenth-century New England, *William and Mary Quarterly* 49 (January 1992): 142.

5. M. W. Armstrong, *The Great Awakening in Nova Scotia, 1776–1809* (Hartford, CT: American Society of Church History, 1948), 101.

6. Henry Alline, *Two Mites* . . . (Halifax: Anthony Henry, 1781), 93.

7. Henry Alline, *The Anti-Traditionalist* (Halifax: Anthony Henry, 1783), 42.

8. See Henry Alline, *Life and Journal* (Boston: Gilbert and Dean, 1806), 174.

9. "Account of Mr. Black," *Arminian Magazine* (London, 1791), 178.

10. Ibid.

11. Ibid., 234.

12. Ibid., 298.

13. "Freeborn Garrettson Journal," United Church Archives, Toronto.

14. Ibid.

15. Quoted in N. Bangs, *The Life of the Rev. Freeborn Garrettson* (New York: Emory and Waugh, 1832), 167.

16. See J. Bailey to Samuel Peters, 29 April 1785, in W. S. Bartlet, ed., *The Frontier Missionary: A Memoir of the Life of the Rev. Jacob Bailey* (Boston: Ide and Dutton, 1853), 222–23.

17. Quoted in Armstrong, *Great Awakening in Nova Scotia,* 124.

18. J. Marsden, *A Narrative of a Mission* (Plymouth-Dock: J. Johns, 1816), 49.

19. See "Freeborn Garrettson Journal" and B. G. Cuthbertson, ed., *The Journal of John Payzant* (Hantsport, Nova Scotia: Lancelot Press, 1981), 43–48.

20. See Rawlyk, *Ravished by the Spirit,* 82–83.

21. Cuthbertson, *Journal of John Payzant,* 44.

22. Ibid.

23. Ibid.

24. Ibid., 45–47.

25. Ibid., 47.

26. Ibid., 49.

27. Ibid., 52.

28. Ibid., 55.

29. Quoted in J. M. Cramp, "History of the Maritime Baptists," 24, Acadia University Archives.

30. Ibid. See also "The Manning Journal," Arcadia University Archives, for a detailed description of the New Dispensation movement from the inside.

31. See my *New Light Letters and Songs.*

32. See Gordon Wood, "Evangelical America and Early Mormonism," *New York History* 61 (October 1980): 366.

33. See ibid., 360–73.

34. Nathan Hatch, *The Democratization of American Christianity* (New Haven: Yale University Press, 1989), 209.

35. M. Noll, "The American Revolution and Protestant Evangelicalism," *Journal of Interdisciplinary History* 23 (1993): 615–38.

36. Alline, *Journal,* 84.

37. Alline, *Two Mites,* 20.

38. Ibid., 20–21.
39. Alline, *Anti-Traditionalist,* 65.
40. N. Christie, "In These Times of Democratic Rage and Delusion: Popular Religion and the Challenge to the Established Order, 1760–1815," in *The Canadian Protestant Experience, 1760–1990,* ed G. A. Rawlyk (Burlington, Ont.: Welch, 1990), 21.
41. Ibid., 34.
42. Ibid., 37.
43. Quoted in I. E. Bill, *Fifty Years with the Baptist Ministers and Churches of the Maritime Provinces of Canada* (St. John, N.B.: Barnes, 1880), 191.
44. Quoted in Armstrong, *Great Awakening in Nova Scotia,* 130.
45. Quoted in Bill, *Fifty Years,* 190.
46. See P. Campbell, *Travels in the Interior Inhabited Parts of North America in the Years 1791 and 1792,* ed. H. H. Langton and W. F. Ganong (Toronto: Champlain Society, 1937), 255–56.
47. See Armstrong, *Great Awakening in Nova Scotia,* 129.
48. See the disjointed Manning correspondence from the 1790s in the Arcadia University Archivies.
49. G. E. Levy, ed., *The Diary and Related Writings of the Reverend Joseph Dimock (1768–1846),* (Hantsport, Nova Scotia: Lancelot Press, 1979), 43.
50. Ibid., 52.
51. Ibid., 67.
52. Ibid., 29.
53. Quoted in G. French, *Parsons and Politics* (Toronto: Ryerson Press, 1962), 34.
54. This theme is developed at greater length in my *Wrapped Up in God* (Burlington, Ont.: Welch, 1988), 63–64.75.
55. See their correspondence in the *Massachusetts Baptist Missionary Magazine* for the year 1808 in particular. Also see the Case Papers, located at Colby College, Waterville, Maine.
56. T. Vincent, "Henry Alline: Problems of Approach and Reading the *Hymns* as Poetry," in *They Planted Well; New England Planters in Maritime Canada,* ed. M. Conrad (Fredericton: Acadiensis Press, 1988), 203.
57. See H. E. Scott, ed., *The Journal of the Reverend Jonathan Scott* (Boston: New England Historic Geneological Society, 1980).
58. E. Mancke, "Two Patterns of New England Transformation: Machias, Maine, and Liverpool, Nova Scotia, 1760–1820" (Ph.D. diss., Johns Hopkins University, 1989), iii.
59. Ibid., 7.
60. Ibid.
61. Ibid., 284.
62. Ibid., 288–89.
63. Ibid., 330–31.
64. J. Adams to H. Stiles, 13 Febuary 1818, in C. F. Adams, ed., *The Works of John Adams,* vol 10 (Boston: Little, Brown, 1856), 282–83.
65. See Gordon Stewart and G. A. Rawlyk, *A People Highly Favoured of God: the Nova Scotia Yankees and the American Revolution* (Toronto: Macmillan, 1972).
66. Ibid., 61–62.
67. See M. W. Armstrong, "Neutrality and Religion in Revolutionary Nova Scotia," *New England Quarterly* 9 (March 1946): 50–62.

68. See Grant Gordon, *The Life of David George (1743–1810)* (Hantsport, Nova Scotia: Lancelot Press, 1992).

69. See, for example, A. Taylor, *Liberty Men and Great Proprietors: The Revolutionary Settlement on the Maine Frontier, 1760–1820* (Chapel Hill: University of North Carolina Press, 1990).

70. S. Marini, *Radical Sects in Revolutionary New England* (Cambridge: Harvard University Press, 1982).

71. Talyor, *Liberty Men,* 181–207.

72. "Manning Journal, 24 August 1821," Arcadia University Archives.

8

Evangelicalism in English and Irish Society, 1780–1840

DAVID HEMPTON

On at least a superficial level the comparisons between the growth and effect of evangelical religion in England and Ireland are striking. Both had their origins in the 1730s and 1740s as a result of Continental pietist influences, the evangelical enthusiasm of the Wesley brothers and George Whitefield, and the utilization of itinerant preaching and class meetings.[1] Both movements shared a similar theology and similar organizational characteristics. In both countries evangelical religion made some gains with the established churches as well as throwing up new forms of belief and practice. In both countries evangelicalism transcended the boundaries of social status and class by appealing to a wide constituency including landed aristocrats, urban manufacturers and merchants, and those in more humble stations in town and country. Both grew fast in the 1790s, when wider social, economic, and political changes ushered in a new era of religious excitment and structrual change. In both countries the older denominations experienced serious difficulties in accommodating new religious forms, and the rise of evangelicalism was inevitably associated with secessions and a greater degree of religious pluralism. Evangelicalism's conversionist and activist characteristics led to a remarkable growth of voluntary societies (including manifold Irish auxiliaries to the major English societies) and a corresponding growth of lay participation in new forms of relgious leadership. In England and Ireland evangelical religion offered new windows of opportunity for women in preaching, teaching, and philanthropy before the hardening of denominational structures reestablished more conventional gender relations in the second half of the nineteenth century.

Evangelicals in both countries engaged not only in evangelism but in a self-consciously civilizing mission to reclaim the disreputable in town and country. In England the urban working classes were the most common targets of evangelical zeal, whereas in Ireland the Roman Catholic poor were frequently singled out. In the war against irreligion and vice, evangelicals in both countries put their faith in elementary education, Sunday schools, Sabbatarianism, temperance, and family life, all of which added up to a shrewd and powerful

156

mixture of evangelical paternalism and self-improvement. In both countries there was an uneasy oscillation between pan-evangelicalism and denominational self-interest, depending on the issues at stake and on the respective balance of forces in towns and regions. Evangelicals in both countries shared a profound dislike of theological error, whether of the Roman Catholic, Tractarian, or Unitarian variety, and of class conflict, which threatened to undermine the biblical concept of an organic society.

Evangelical religion in England and Ireland was therefore self-evidently fruit of the same tree, even if one still needs to be sensitive to the different blossoming and ripening processes at work in the two countries. Despite these similarities, however, I want to suggest in this chapter that different social, political, and ecclesiastical conditions in the two countries gave rise to significant differences in the public expression of evangelical religion as it intersected with other interests. In England the fault lines of social and religious conflict, whether expressed in secessions or political and denominational competition, often exposed a delicate mixture of class and cultural divisions, whereas in Ireland the cracks were more often to be found in the bedrock of deep-seated religious, ethnic, and cultural loyalties, which evangelical competition inexorably widened. My aim, therefore, is to explore these differences by comparing the growth and social consequences of popular evangelicalism in both countries in the eighteenth and nineteenth centuries.

The Rise and Social Consequences of Popular Evangelicalism in England

Most of the many contested areas of Methodist historiography ultimately go back to rival explanations of its growth and decline; much else depends on positions taken on those fundamental issues. The facts themselves are not much in dispute, thanks to the convenience of class membership figures as a reasonable guide to Methodist strength, if not Methodist influence. The various Methodist connections grew faster than the population as a whole before 1840, held their own until the middle of the 1880s, and then declined relative to the total adult population until 1906, before declining in absolute terms thereafter.[2] Both the rapidity and the chronological and geographic unevenness of Methodist growth were clearly linked to wider changes in the English economy and society, but attempts to relate spurts of Methodist growth to economic depression on the one hand and the growth of political radicalism on the other have not proved entirely successful, despite the historical ingenuity devoted to it.[3] There are examples of Methodist growth in periods of economic depression, including Yorkshire in the 1790s[4] and Lancashire during the great cotton depression of the 1860s, but more generally the evidence is ambiguous. R. B. Walker is right to conclude that "no clear pattern of relationship between religious revivals and economic changes emerges" in nineteenth-century Methodism.[5] What does seem to be the case is that whereas short, sharp bursts of economic hardship or epidemics of contagious diseases could temporarily stimulate religious enthusiasm, longterm economic decline was a disaster for religious connections dependent upon voluntary subscriptions.[6] Similarly, the relationship between the growth of Methodism and political radicalism is more complicated than either Thompson's oscillation theory or Hobsbawm's concurrent expansion ideas would permit.[7] It is hard to resist the conclusion that religious attraction or repulsion is a transaction that is neither straightforwardly economic nor political.

A more constructive approach to understanding the expansion of Methodism, without in any way diminsihing the importance of its distinctive theology, organization, and evangelical zeal, is to see it as part of much wider structural changes in English society in the generation after the French Revolution. In this period a complex of social tensions caused by population growth, subsistence crises, and the commercialization of agriculture, and further exacerbated by prolonged warfare, sharpened class conflict and undermined the old denominational order.[8] As many Anglican parsons benefited from enclosure and tithe commutation, their influence among small freeholders and laborers steadily declined.[9] The rising social status of the upper clergy and their unprecedented representation on the bench of magistrates cemented the squire-and-parson alliance at the very time that establishment ideals were most under attack.[10] In such circumstances the Church of England was in no position to resist a dramatic upsurge in undenominational itinerant preaching and cottage-based religion, which even the various Methodist connections struggled to keep under control.[11] Methodism thus made its fastest gains in areas least amenable to paternalistic influence, including freehold parishes, industrial villages, mining communities, market towns, canal and sea ports, and other centers of migratory populations.[12] James Obelkevich's classic local study of South Lindsey is a vivid illustration of how the Church of England's attempt to reinforce an older paternalistic, hierarchical, and integrated society was vigorously challenged by more emotionally vibrant and populist forms of religion such as that offered by the Primitive Methodists.[13] The result was a mixture of class and cultural conflict that reflected the economic and social structure of the area and led to the growth of an agricultural trade unionism almost entirely under Methodist leadership.[14]

Methodism was not only the beneficiary of structural changes in English society; it was to some extent also a victim. The Wesleyan leadership, when confronted by rapid expansion in the years of high social tension between Wesley's death and The "Peterloo Massacre" of 1819, and pressed hard by successive governments to eliminate its radical underclass, tried to retain control by clamping down on religious revivalism, political radicalism, undenominational Sunday schools, and other popular causes. In the process, Methodism became more centralized, more bureaucratic, more clerical, and more respectable. These were the most commonly contested elements in Methodism's fissiparous history in the first half of the nineteenth century and could be brought into operation over a wide range of apparently minor issues, from the connectional interdict against the teaching of writing on Sundays to the introduction of an organ into a wealthy urban chapel, and from the founding of theological colleges to the metropolitan control of regional revivals and cottage prayer meetings.[15] Thus, in the period of Bunting's hegemony between 1820 and 1850,[16] when Methodism was convulsed by major secessions from which it never fully recovered, the divisive issues were not simply thrown up by problems of connectional government but had their roots in a more general hardening of denominational boundaries that made sectarian conflict, with overtones of social class and religious respectablity, one of the most characteristic features of English politics in the first half of the nineteenth century.[17]

The old dichotomy, therefore, between those who interpreted Methodist secessions as the sad but inevitable consequence of stresses within the religious community itself and those political and social historians who saw them as mere symptoms of external pressures affecting the whole of British and European society has been an unfortunate barrier to proper historical understanding. The manifold local studies of Methodist secessions have shown conclusively that superimposed on "religious" disagreements about the nature of the ministry, connectional management, and spiritual priorities there were undoubtedly class and cultural differences, conflicting political allegiances, and social tensions that were endemic in the wider society. The precise balance of forces varied from secession to secession and even from town to town, but they cannot be uncovered by either denominational or social reductionism.[18] Thus, what is striking about Methodism in the first half of the nineteenth century is the way in which its internal cleavages and structures of power acted as lightning conductors for the pervasive social and political tensions of the age. After mid-century, tensions declined, but so too did the importance of what was at stake within the Methodist community. After all, secession can be as much a product of intense religious commitment as unity can be a sign of comfortable acquiescence.

Perhaps the chief reason for the fragmentation of evangelical Nonconformity in the first half of the nineteenth century, however, was the way in which social tensions and class consciousness undermined the old denominational order and then posed insuperable problems of control for the leaders of new religious movements.[19] It is precisely in this area, of trying to assess the real significance of Methodism in the wider social history of England in the period of the Industrial Revolution, that most disagreement has occurred among historians. The most fertile conceptual frameworks, from Halévy to Thompson and from Hobsbawm to Semmel, though containing inspired insights, have not succeeded in doing justice to the complexity of relationships between religion and politics and belief and practice in English regions over the course of a century of bewildering change.[20] The main reason for this failure is that, despite their ideological claims to the contrary, many of the most influential theses about Methodism in English society have been imposed, sometimes on the basis of disconcertingly thin evidence, from above and without. More impressive for their intellectual coherence than for their capacity to explain the data, they have only recently had to come into contact with more sophisticated statistical approaches and with a cluster of impressively researched local and regional studies.

There is now widespread agreement that the remarkable growth of evangelical Nonconformity in the period 1790–1830 substantially undermined the Established Church, religious deference, and traditional systems of dependency that had been at the heart of the old order in church and state. Even Jonathan Clark, who is certainly no exponent of social and political determinism, has shown how English society, to a remarkable extent in such a short period of time, had moved beyond the pale of the Anglican parochial system and how the opposition to Sidmouth's Bill against itinerant preaching in 1811 showed that there had been a profound shift of allegiance in the country as a whole.[21] Parallel pressures from a more radical Irish Catholicism, the old anti-exclusionist wing of Protestant Dissent, urban popular radicalism, and new commercial interests did not make a constitutional revolution inevitable, but they did lay the foundations for alternative forms of politics in which religion was just as central as it had been in the ideological defense of the eighteenth-century constitution. Methodism could not, of course, avoid the social and political tensions that accompanied its own growth. In the quarter century after the French Revolution its leadership, both clerical and lay, struggled hard to maintain the connection's legal privileges while at the same time recruiting from sections of the population less interested in the chauvinistic traditions of the freeborn Englishman than in the political and economic causes of their appalling conditions.[22]

Ironically, the secretive committee of privileges that the Methodists had set up to guard their legal rights soon became an inquisitorial instrument in the expulsion of disaffected radicals in the years leading up to Peterloo.[23] This task was accomplished with such vigor, in the north of England in particular, that when the next great upsurge in urban popular radicalism occurred in the late 1830s, the Wesleyans were relatively untroubled and were able to devote most of their energy to the defense of their denominational corner against Catholics, Tractarians, and radical Nonconformists. In this way class control and denominational discipline were mutually reinforced, and class tensions were to some extent redirected into sectarian conflict.

It was in the first thirty years after Wesley's death, therefore, that Methodist growth most alarmed established interests, from bishops and parsons to landed and industrial magnates.[24] At the same time, Methodism's capacity to develop qualities of self-discipline, personal responsibility, and sobriety were appreciated by those able to set aside their prejudices against religious enthusiasm and who recognized in any case that the Established Church was in no position to reclaim the unchurched. This paradox, which has generated much heat but little illumination among historians, was there from the start and often depended on local circumstances for its resolution. In Belper, for example, which had grown from an insignificant village to the second largest town in Derbyshire, largely as a result of the entrepreneurial talents of the Strutt family, both Wesleyan and Primitive Methodism grew extraordinarily fast between 1790 and 1825. The Unitarian Strutts recognized the beneficial effects of Methodism among their work force with restrained paternalistic generosity, but they also saw fit to launch a fund for a hugely expensive Anglican church, which architecturally dwarfed its Dissenting rivals and was opened in 1824 amid much pomp and circumstances by the Duke of Devonshire, the county's greatest landowner. Here was no exercise in crude employer coercion; the Strutts merely paid symbolic tribute to a set of social arrangements that they had come to believe were instrumental in maintaining order and stability and that had consequently facilitated their own social advance. With so much at stake, a declaration of faith in a stable past offered more reassurance than a future clouded by unrestrained Ranterism or political radicalism. The imposing Anglican monument the Strutts helped pay for was thus not meant to eliminate religious deviance, but to show the limits within which it must be seen to operate.[25]

After 1820 the Wesleyans were not entirely immune from problems caused by urban radicals within their midst, as the celebrated case of Joseph Rayner Stephens showed, but increasingly it was the Primitive and secession Methodists who were most closely bound up with radical causes in both town and country.[26] Recent studies of the Chartist reforms in English localities, for example, have drawn attention to the importance of Methodist organizational models, the crusading zeal of local preachers, and, perhaps most important, the ideological fusion of biblical warnings against social injustice with Chartist denunciations of the rich and the powerful.[27] All over the North of England in the 1830s as the Anti-Poor Law, Ten Hours, and anti–State Church movements shaded off into Chartism, there was a sizable minority of non-Wesleyan Methodists, conspicuous for their leadership ability, who combined a radical critique of clericalism and the religious hypocrisy of the rich with a more general humanitarian mission to reform social and political abuses. Some were willing to make chapels available for Chartist meetings, and some chapels even severed their Methodist connections altogether, but there were also unresolved tensions between the two. As Chartists tried to create a mass movement of class solidarity, Methodist communities had alternative loyalties that caused them to repudiate Chartist bawdiness, tavern conviviality, and Sabbath breaking.

Although many Chartist leaders were aware of the potential of religion to offer ideological legitimation and crusading zeal to their movement, it soon became clear to Christian Chartists such as the Reverend William Hill, the editor of the *Northern Star,* that "in almost all the churches and chapels, appertaining to whatever sect, the principles of social benevolence and justice, of civil equality and of political right, though recognised by the Bible, are denounced by the priesthood."[28] Even the more radical Methodist sects, though closer in spirit to Chartist ideals than either Anglicanism or Wesleyanism, were sufficiently peripheral to mass Chartism to make large-scale theories about the relationship between Methodism and urban radicalism in these years seem rather forced. The same cannot be said, however, of those mining and agricultural communities of England where Methodism, especially the Primitive connection, became the dominant feature of both the religious and political landscape. The essential difference between Methodism's relationship with Chartism and its contribution to agricultural and mining trade unionism, however, is that within Chartism Methodism was only one strand among many influences, some of which were antithetical to Methodist piety or peripheral to Methodist interests, whereas in the other cases Methodist involvement in politics grew naturally out of its social setting and was widely approved as a legitimate expression of an essentially religious morality.[29]

Whatever may be said about the relationship between Methodism and popular radicalism, or religion and social class, the fact is that most nineteenth-century Methodists encountered the world of politics either as voters[30] or as participants in the great religiously inspired extraparliamentary pressure crusades, from Sidmouth's Bill at the beginning of the century to the preoccupations of the Nonconformist Conscience at the end.[31] No sense can be made of such politics through social and economic categories alone; rather, they show the profoundly religious basis—however narrow and sectarian—of much evangelical political behavior. At the heart of Methodist commitment to extraparliamentary pressure campaigns, despite the old Wesleyan no-politics rule, was a religious and evangelical worldview that sought to defend denominational interests against governmental and secularist encroachments; to wage war on the moral evils of slavery, sexual license, and intemperance; and to oppose the "heretical" advances of Roman Catholicism, Tractarianism, and Unitarianism. The peculiar twists and turns of such campaigns, their party political significance, and their intersection with the apparently inexhaustible church and chapel conflicts are some of the most important features of English politics and society in the nineteenth century.

Evangelicalism and Religious Toleration

Thus far I have suggested that the rise of popular evangelicalism in England, though not always hostile to the Established Church, helped erode the old order in church and state by dramatically expanding the number of non-Anglican churchgoers in the generation overshadowed by the French Revolution. A House of Lords report in 1811, for example, appeared to show that the Church of England was on the verge of becoming a minority religious establishment, and there was also a widespread recognition that itinerant preaching and the Methodist class system had driven a coach and horses through the existing laws dealing with religious toleration.[32] Accordingly, Lord Sidmouth brought forward a bill against itinerant preaching in 1811. Although this bill was defeated in Parliament, justices of the peace in the English localities behaved as if it had become law and refused to grant licences to Methodist preachers. What happened next reveals a great deal about the political consequences of the evangelical mission in both England and Ireland and is best followed through the prolific correspondence of Thomas Allan, the Methodist connectional solicitor and political adviser.[33]

In association with the traditional friends of religious toleration, the Dissenters and a section of the Whig aristocracy, Allan drafted and secured a new toleration act in 1812 that significantly extended the boundaries of religious toleration almost two decades before the more familiar changes of 1828 and 1829. The act established new principles as well as new practices. These were the inalienable right of every person to worship God according to conscience, the right of every person to hear and to teach Christian truths without restraint from the civil magistrates or the license of the crowd, and the recognition that no one had the right to disturb the peace under the pretense of teaching religion. In return for such favorable terms, the Methodists were expected to deliver on their own propaganda by quietening the disaffected multitudes in early industrial England, which the connectional leadership was only too willing to do.[34] Thus, despite pressure from Anglican bishops, the English state was prepared to accommodate the church's enemies in return for a more stable social order. Ironically, then, toleration was secured by political pragmatism, and liberalism was the unintended beneficiary of religious enthusiasm.

Allan's defense of religious toleration in England arose directly out of his evangelical desire to see the Methodist mission flourish without disabling restrictions. In the same year that he helped secure religious toleration in England, and with the same motive uppermost in his mind, Allan devoted his considerable energies to resisting Catholic Emancipation in Ireland. In January 1813 he became a founder member and chief publicist of the Protestant Union, which was chaired, ironically, by the most politically radical of all the Claphamite evangelicals, Granville Sharp. In his public utterances, Allan drew on his intimate knowledge of eighteenth-century constitutional lawyers and outlined a conventional distinction between the right to exercise religious freedom and the right to exercise political power.[35] The first, he argued, was a natural right, the second was not. In private correspondence Allan confessed to another motive. "One consequence [of Catholic Emancipation]," he told Joseph Butterworth, a Methodist M.P., "will be an end to Methodism in Ireland. Are not the Methodists in England to take care of this privilege of preaching the Gospel in Ireland?"[36]

For the next sixteen years the correspondence of Allan and Butterworth is riddled with material on the progress of Methodism and Church evangelicalism in Ireland, combined with draft resolutions on the subject of Catholic Emancipation.[37] The two subjects were indissolubly linked in his mind, and he never seems to have thought it odd that up to 1812 he worked in close association with the Whig peers to extend religious toleration in England and then spent the next two decades in close contact with Anglo-Irish landowners and ultra-Tory Protestant constitutionists in an attempt to resist Catholic claims in Ireland. On one level, of course, Allan's political and religious principles were entirely consistent in that they were based on a well-rehearsed and conventional distinction between the right to worship freely and the right to participate in civil government. But whereas in England Allan's principles put him on the side of religious pluralism and religious freedom—causes that would, over time, inevitably erode the old order in church and state—in Ireland his views aligned him with established interests and a stout defense of the Protestant constitution. With pardonable historical license one might suggest that this apparent paradox in the correspondence of Thomas Allan in

1812 is more widely applicable to the progress of evangelicalism on the two islands over the course of the nineteenth century.

Evangelicalism in Ireland

John Wesley's visit to Ireland in 1747, which came in the wake of earlier Moravian itinerant preaching, was the first installment of a forty-year commitment to the cause of Methodism in Ireland in which twenty-one visits were made, including his first to the province of Ulster in 1756.[38] Those who have followed the course of the Methodist revival in both England and Ireland in the eighteenth century have been struck by a remarkable difference of strategy and tactics employed by Wesley in the two countries. Whereas in England Wesley saw himself as having a special, but not exclusive, ministry to the poor, and frequently made barbed criticisms of the worldliness of the English church and its gentry patrons, "in Ireland his mission worked downward from the gentry class and outward from the garrison in a way that would have been unthinkable in England." The editors of the recently published and definitive edition of Wesley's *Journal* state that the total number of Wesley's contacts among the Irish gentry was "so great as to make it clear that Wesley's self-consciously asserted English mission to the poor was in Ireland refracted through the Protestant gentry class." Similarly, Wesley devoted a considerable amount of his preaching time to military garrisons, courthouses, and other places resonant of Ascendancy control, thereby guaranteeing that "he could reap no great Catholic harvest."[39] This fact helps explain why popular evangelicalism was unable to take more advantage of the ramshackle state of the Roman Catholic Church in the eighteenth century and why, unlike Wales in the nineteenth century, evangelicalism was never able to help the Irish express a mass-cultural identity outside the province of Ulster. Moreover, Wesley was also better received by the bishops and clergy of the Church of Ireland than by their equivalents in the Church of England and was consequently a good deal less critical of the Irish church, which in some respects he thought was superior to its English counterpart.[40] Hence Irish Methodism derived almost no benefit from the tide of anti-establishment sentiment that did so much to help English Methodism get established in the aftermath of the French Revolution.

The evidence suggests that Wesley's approach to Ireland was based not so much on a planned and considered strategy as on a set of religious and social assumptions that traveled with him from his Epworth and Oxford days. The first is that, contrary to a powerful but erroneous tradition of ecumenical scholarship since the Second World War, Wesley was not well disposed to Roman Catholicism in England or in Ireland.[41] In Ireland, however, Wesley thought he detected the baleful influence of Roman Catholicism in its most developed form. On his early visits to Ireland he devoured the standard Protestant accounts of Catholic atrocities in the seventeenth century, encountered what he deemed to be bloodthirsty papist mobs, had his congregations removed by Catholic priests, and wrote nervously about the potential disloy-

alty of Irish Catholics, should a suitable opportunity arise.[42] There was, therefore, "a gulf which it would be a mistake to regard as racial, but which went
very deep, separating Wesley from the Catholic Irish . . . Wesley found the
Irish indolent (which implied 'squalid') and 'fickle.' "[43]

It is scarcely surprising, therefore, that Wesley found himself most at home
among the unassimilated foreign Protestants—Huguenots and Palatines—
who had been forced to leave their homelands by the Catholic intolerance he
so much despised.[44] He equally enjoyed his encounters with those aspects of
English culture—building, landscape, dress, and mannerisms—that had been
successfully transplanted in Ireland. On his first visit to Ulster in 1756 Wesley
immediately noted the general superiority of the countryside. "No sooner did
we enter Ulster, than we observed the difference, the ground was cultivated
just as in England, and the cottages not only neat, but with doors, chimneys
and windows."[45] Wesley endorsed the Protestant ethic he thought he had
discovered, by exhorting the society in Derry "to avoid sloth, prodigality, and
sluttishness, and on the contrary to be patterns of diligence, frugality, and
cleanliness."[46] Wesley's admiration of Ulster Protestant thrift did not extend,
however, to its predominantly Presbyterian spirituality. Of Belfast he remarked that "between Seceders, old self-centred Presbyterians, New-Light
men, Moravians, Cameronians, and formal 'Churchmen,' it is a miracle if any
here bring forth fruit to perfection."[47] Wesley admired the English and European traditions of Christian pietism far more than Scottish or Irish Calvinism.

Methodism's early recruitment in Ireland was largely determined by the
geography of Wesley's missionary journeys and the characteristics that have
already been described. Most early growth took place in southern ports and
market towns, in military garrisons, and among European Protestant minorities.[48] By 1760 it was estimated that of the two thousand in Methodist societies, approximately half were located in the province of Leinster, and only a
tenth lived in Ulster. The following decade saw the beginning of a dramatic
and irreversible trend toward the concentration of Methodism in the north of
Ireland. By 1770, some 47 percent of Irish Methodists lived north of a line
drawn from Sligo to Dundalk, and by 1815 that had gone up to 68 percent.
Even in a religious movement that made its first impression in the south of
Ireland, the steadily increasing proportion of its members living in Ulster
from the late eighteenth century is a striking manifestation of a wider demo-
graphic trend of incalculable importance to the future history of the island.
Thus, the evangelical revival helped reinforce the peculiar concentration of
Protestantism in the north of the country and, if anything, sharpened its anti-
Catholic characteristics. But the anti-Catholicism of the Moravians, Palatines,
Huguenots, and Methodists was more than a crude expression of religious
bigotry; it was rooted in a folk memory of persecution within Continental
Protestantism and a settled conviction that Roman Catholicism was an enemy
of enlightened values, economic progress, and religious toleration. Irish Roman Catholics, for equally powerful reasons, had alternative and conflicting
explanations for their lack of social and political progress. The roots of a
lengthy confrontation had already been established.

After Wesley's death the 1790s proved to be as vital in the fortunes of Irish Methodism as in those of its English counterpart. Both connections grew vigorously in response to wider social and economic changes, but whereas in England Methodist expansion was regarded as a popular religious challenge to the established order in church and state, in Ireland Methodism grew strongest in old areas of English settlement and had a vested interest in separating itself both from Presbyterian radicalism and from Catholic grievances. Moreover, the smallness of Irish Methodism (only fourteen thousand by 1789), its close links with the Established Church, from which the majority did not separate until 1817 (1795 in England),[49] and its military connections made it an unlikely vehicle for radical opinions in Ireland. In the context of the rebellion of 1798, however, loyalty could no longer be merely assumed but needed to be demonstrated, and Methodist leaders were anxious to dissociate themselves from the disruptive elements operating in Irish society. Individual members who "swerved from their allegiance to lawful authority" were at once expelled, and Methodists swelled the ranks of the yeomanry that helped put down the rebellion.[50] Growing confidence in Methodist loyalty was reflected in the government decision to permit the 1798 conference of the society to go ahead, despite the disturbed state of the country and the prohibition of all meetings of more than five men. At the conclusion of the conference, letters were received from the government granting permission and protection to preachers setting out to their respective destinations.

Nonetheless, in an age of political innovation, debates on the nature of government, whether civil or ecclesiastical, were regarded as dangerous, and never more so than in 1798. Thus, a challenge to the Methodist constitution from thirty-two stewards and leaders in the Lisburn circuit prompted conference leaders to take firm and decisive action. The Lisburn protesters' demand "that the people shall have a voice in the formation of their own laws, in the choice of their own ministers, and in the distribution of their own property" left them open to charges of Jacobinism from both Dublin and London.[51] While it seems likely that these men were in fact earnest Methodists, wishing only for greater lay involvement in the leadership of the Methodist connection, the prevailing political situation determined the outcome of their requests. A conference anxious to exhibit its loyalty to both civil and religious establishments presented their "delinquent" views as "the result of the spirit of insubordination and lawlessness so prevalent." The protestors were expelled, and their subsequent appeal rejected. Although over two hundred members joined the dissidents in the formation of the Methodist New Connection, this was a much smaller secession than its Kilhamite equivalent in England and showed that Irish Methodism in the 1790s was much less troubled by appeals for lay democracy both within and outside its ranks than was its English counterpart.[52] That the leaders of the Dublin Conference went so far as to send a list of the protesters' names to the military authorities again shows the way in which political and religious ideas were thought to be interrelated and established Methodism's credibility as a champion of the established order. This status was given a sectarian dimension when stories of Methodist persecution and martyrdom at the hands of Catholic rebels in Wexford were widely circulated within the English connection.[53]

Evangelicalism in Ireland was undoubtedly given a boost by the manifold disturbances of the 1790s culminating in the so-called Rebellion of the United Irishmen. The Evangelical Society of Ulster was founded in 1798, the Irish-speaking Methodist mission was established in 1799, and there were remarkable outbreaks of rural revivalism in south and west Ulster at the turn of the century. Methodism was therefore a beneficiary of, and partly a contributor to, increased sectarian tensions in the last decade of the eighteenth century, when economic competition brought Protestant Orangemen and Catholic Defenders into vigorous conflict. It was in these years also that evangelical religion began to have a significant following within the ranks of the landed elite, a section of which was only too happy to welcome its newfound support from Protestant religious enthusiasts.

The first third of the nineteenth century saw an unprecedented attempt to convert Irish Catholics, not by the power of established churches or coercion by the state, but by the voluntary religious zeal of a host of evangelical societies.[54] These voluntary agencies, with their preachers, teachers, distributors, collectors, and visitors, bureaucratized evangelicalism and brought into being an army of subalterns beyond the immediate control of churches and their clergy. Committed to evangelical zeal and moral improvement, this army destabilized the old conventional boundaries between the Catholic and Protestant churches and introduced the arsenic of religious competition into Irish ecclesiastical life. It would be a serious misunderstanding of the religious mind to deny that the chief motivation for such activity was what evangelicals claimed it to be; that is, an earnest desire to see "vital religion" expand at the expense of Romish superstition and popular indifference. But the fact that many of the societies were either founded in England or had the support of Anglo-Irish landowners ensured that there was more at stake than conversion alone. The potential for controversy was there from the start because the most common evangelical methods—preaching, teaching, and the distribution of literature—carried with them overtones of religious proselytism and cultural imperialism. Whereas English evangelicals could get on with the task of converting the laboring poor safe in the knowledge that they had either the support or the silent acquiescence of most established interests in reining back atheism and infidelity (the midwives of radicalism and republicanism), in Ireland evangelicals were forced to make intricate distinctions between evangelism and proselytism that few outside their own camp could understand. Consider, for example, this response of the London Hibernian Society to the charge of proselytism in its schools:

> The committee would draw the distinction between instances of reported conversion, and cases of practical interference with the tenets of children in school. Cases of the description which are usually stated in the report are, facts of conversion wrought by the simple efficacy of divine truth, not by interference upon the part of the society with the religious peculiarities of the scholars; and however the policy of such statements may be questioned

by some, the statements themselves supply no proof of improper deviation from a strictly neutral practice in the schools.[55]

What is offered here is a painfully convoluted and disingenuous distinction between conversion and proselytism, but the inadequacy of the distinction is attributable not so much to crude hypocrisy and moral chicanery as to the fervent evangelical belief in the supremacy of Scripture and in the benefits that would accrue to the recipients from its version of "godliness and good learning."

Similar ambiguities arose over the so-called Second Reformation movement, especially when evangelical landowners were closely implicated. Lord Farnham, for example, inherited his 29,000-acre estate in County Cavan in 1823 and soon introduced a combined system of estate management and moral improvement that became a model for many other evangelical landowners. Farnham described the foundation of his system as the religion of the Bible, and his chief motivation as "the moral and religious character and improvement of the tenantry."[56] To facilitate its "moral management" the estate was divided into five districts. Each was overseen by a land and a moral agent under the "friendly supervision" of an inspectorate. The relation between landlord and tenant was understood to be one of mutual benefit, as each was dependent on the goodwill and cooperation of the other. The landlord would supply churches, day schools, Sunday schools, a lending library, and material aid for those who earned it. In return the tenant was expected to be responsive to such liberality. Punctual payment of rent, for example, was beneficial to both parties and rendered the employment of the much-hated "drivers" unnecessary.[57] The "moral agent,"[58] a new term in the tenurial system, was the mainspring of the plan, and the appointment of a worthy individual to the position was a particular concern of evangelical landlords preoccupied with the spiritual welfare of their tenantry.[59] Lord Farnham's moral agent between 1826 and 1838 was William Krause, a fervent evangelical, who interpreted his task as one of "trying to free Roman Catholics from bondage."[60] It was with the moral agent that tenants had the most frequent contact. Besides his practical duties of removing paupers and supervising schools and buildings, it was through him that all requests of the tenantry were passed. He in turn reported their conditions to the inspectors and land agent. On principle, he was kept apart from the business of rent collection and was expected to be "continually urging and exhorting the tenantry."

The system professed to heighten the individual responsibility of the tenants by cutting out middlemen and coercion. But the emphasis—indeed insistence—on high standards of personal and social morality meant that their lives were closely monitored and tightly controlled and that their choices were strictly limited. Children on the estate were expected to attend the schools sponsored by Farnham, which operated on the familiar but highly controversial evangelical pattern. They were remorselessly scriptural and opened and closed with the singing of a psalm or hymn, the reading of a Bible chapter, and a prayer. Some provision was made for more practical instruction in arithmetic and needlework. But while only Church of Ireland members were expected to learn their church catechism, the reading and memorizing of biblical passages was expected of all children, Protestant and Catholic. The giving of premiums, to which the Catholic Church was particularly opposed, was forbidden, but the children's progress was recorded in a Judgement Book. As Farnham was kept personally informed of the behavior of all his tenants—in and out of school—tenurial arrangements were clearly dependent on conformity to a moral and social code. The whole system seemed designed to erode traditional rural folk culture and replace it with an alternative set of values. The singing of bawdy ballads, for example, was discouraged, with psalmody taught in the schools in a direct attempt to replace them. Evangelical Protestantism and social and economic progress were therefore inextricably linked in the minds of its promoters in the same way as Irish Catholic culture was associated with backwardness and inefficiency.[61]

Farnham's whole system of estate management came under close scrutiny in 1826–1827, when a wave of conversions were recorded in Cavan that were investigated by a Roman Catholic deputation consisting of the primate and four bishops. They announced themselves unimpressed either by the nature of the conversions or by the character of the converts, stating that if "names and places be specified, . . . it will be found that many of the new converts are old Protestants, and that others are such as to make every decent Protestant blush for his new allies."[62]

Despite Farnham's insistence that none of the reported converts was an immediate tenant of his and that no rewards were given for recantation, the most common criticism leveled at evangelical estate management was that it was characterized by manipulation on the one side and a self-defensive pragmatism on the other. It was claimed that the evangelicals carried out systematic deception, using a combination of fraud and force to encourage the poor of the area to convert in exchange for clothing, food, or employment. "Misery acquaints us with strange bedfellows," wrote G. K. Ensor in a scathing attack on those attempting to "convert six million Roman Catholics to Protestant Parliamentary faith." "The converts were like birds, which visit milder climates at intervals—but their coming is proof of a great severity in their native country, and they return when the iron days are passed and the sun cheers them from home."[63] With Bible and missionary society agents, landlords and clergy joining forces in their campaign to dissuade the peasantry of their native faith, both Desmond Bowen and Irene Hehir depict the Catholic peasantry of Cavan as caught between Protestant enthusiasts on the one hand, and the Catholic clergy on the other, each battling for control of their souls.[64] George Ensor detected a hint of desperation in the "unholy alliance" of Protestants. "The Protestants had hitherto despised the Methodists and other interlopers on the episcopal domain—yet in this gossiping time of theology, this sacerdotal saturnalia, the lowest of tradesmen were employed to read the Bible to the unreading Catholics."[65]

This background of evangelical missionary enthusiasm and increased religious competition, quite apart from the more familiar trends in Irish politics and society in the 1820s, did not bode well for the successful settlement of the vexed issues of Catholic Emancipation, national elementary education, reform of the Irish Established Church, and the position of Ireland within the Union. The nub of the matter was this: Irish evangelicals of all denominations and social classes, supported by the majority of their English coreligionists, held a fundamentally religious view of Ireland's problems. These could not be solved by liberal concessions to Roman Catholicism because Roman Catholicism was itself the root of the problem. Hence there were many evangelicals in Ireland, including the remarkable Gideon Ouseley, who tried to keep up the old distinction between hatred of a religious system and love for its adherents.[66] This distinction, as with beauty, lay entirely in the eyes of the beholder.

While an influential minority of evangelicals in England and Ireland supported Catholic Emancipation in 1829 on ground of political consistency, governmental necessity, and missionary expediency, the great majority opposed it. Revealingly perhaps, the handful of Irish evangelical leaders who either supported or silently acquiesced in emancipation in 1829 as a final settlement of a much-agitated grievance came, in the 1830s, to regret their liberality, and they steadfastly set themselves against any further erosion of Protestant interests. The future of the Irish Established Church and national education, because they each raised issues of state funding, the nature of religious truth, and the future destiny of the nation, occasioned the most bitter religious disputes throughout the rest of the century. The same was true in England, but there the fault lines were primarily between the Established Church and Nonconformity on the one hand and between respectable religious values and the infidelity of the urban proletariat on the other. In Ireland the lines of division were between Protestantism and Roman Catholicism, and between the civilizing and modernizing values of evangelical pietism and the alleged superstitious and regressive values of the Catholic poor. Thus, in the second half of the nineteenth century evangelicalism in England came to have its most distinctive public representation in the free church liberalism of evangelical Nonconformity, while in Ireland it became most associated with the future of Protestantism and its associated cultural values, especially in the increasingly evangelical province of Ulster. Ironically these two traditions were brought face to face in the conflicts generated by Gladstone's first Home Rule bill in 1886. The events of 1886 had come as a shock to Irish evangelical Nonconformists, not only in the sense of having to come to terms with the possibility of Home Rule, but also in having to accept that English Nonconformist opinion was less reliable than they had supposed.[67]

On one level the questions facing English and Irish Protestantism in the nineteenth century were no different from those facing churches in other European societies. How established churches were to operate following the French Revolution and how popular religious movements should be controlled in the wider interests of political and social stability were issues that transcended national boundaries. In England and Ireland the issues were further complicated by a remarkable upsurge in evangelical religion that disturbed existing forms of organized religion and threw up some new ones. By the 1830s evangelicalism in Ireland, in addition to its Methodist and voluntarist forms, had made substantial headway within the Church of Ireland and within the self-regulating Presbyterian community of the north. Naturally the old poison of denominational conflict between Ireland's main Protestant churches had not been fully drawn, but the foundations had nevertheless been laid for a pan-evangelical and interdenominational resistance to renewed Catholic demands and to the prevailing "horrid spirit of concession." Reclaiming the Catholic poor and resisting the Catholic Church, which in the evangelical mind were contingent objectives, gave a unity of purpose to Irish evangelicals that their English counterparts could not match. They too could unite in campaigns to Christianize the urban masses through evangelism, temperance, Sabbatarianism, and moral reform, but on issues of public policy the old cleavage between Church and Dissent never lost its vigor.

Evangelicalism in England and Ireland set out with a shared theology, similar organizational structures, an overlapping leadership, and a common commitment to evangelism and the reformation of manners. What this chapter has sought to demonstrate is that whether one looks at patterns of growth or its political and social consequences, the relationship between evangelical religion and its surrounding culture was significantly different in the two countries. This in turn had a profound effect on the nature of evangelicalism itself, for although evangelicals were passionately concerned to change society, they were also influenced by its political conflicts and social tensions. Evangelicalism has more of a symbiotic relationship with its surrounding culture than either its stoutest defenders or severest critics are prepared to admit.

Notes

1. The standard history of the origins of Protestant revival movements of the eighteenth century is William R. Ward, *The Protestant Evangelical Awakening* (Cambridge: Cambridge University Press, 1992). Ward does not simply study eighteenth-century revivals in an Anglo-American context but pays more attention to a European perspective than others have done. For Britain and Ireland, see David W. Bebbington, *Evangelicalism in Modern Britain: A History from the 1730s to the 1980s* (London: Unwin Hyman, 1989); and David Hempton and Myrtle Hill, *Evangelical Protestantism in Ulster Society, 1740–1890* (London: Routledge, 1992).

2. Robert Currie, Alan Gilbert, and Lee Horsley, *Churches and Churchgoers: Patterns of Church Growth in the British Isles since 1700* (Oxford: Clarendon Press, 1977). For a more detailed analysis of the statistics, see Alan D. Gilbert, *Religion and Society in Industrial England, 1740–1914* (London: Longman, 1976).

3. I briefly survey this historiography, including the pioneering work of Edward Thompson and Eric Hobsbawn, in *Methodism and Politics in British Society, 1750–1850* (London: Hutchinson, 1984), 74–80. See also E. P. Stigant, "Wesleyan Methodism and Working-Class Radicalism in the North, 1792–1821," *Northern History* 6 (1971): 98–116; and Alan D. Gilbert, "Methodism, Dissent, and Political Stability in Early Industrial England," *Journal of Religious History* 10 (1978–79): 381–99. For a

recent, but limited, collection of essays on this subject, see Gerald W. Olsen, *Religion and Revolution in Early Industrial England: The Halévy Thesis and Its Critics* (Lanham, MD: University Press of America, 1990).

4. John Baxter, "The Great Yorkshire Revival, 1792–6: A Study of Mass Revival among the Methodists," *Sociological Yearbook of Religion in Britain* 7 (1974): 46–76.

5. R. B. Walker, "The Growth of Wesleyan Methodism in Victorian England and Wales," *Journal of Ecclesiastical History* 34 (1973): 267–84.

6. For interesting regional comparisons of this theme, see C. B. Turner, "Revivalism and Welsh Society in the Nineteenth Century," in *Disciplines of Faith*, ed. James Obelkevich, Lyndal Roper, and Raphael Samuel (London: Routledge and Kegan Paul, 1987), 311–23; and David Hempton, "Methodism in Irish Society, 1770–1830," *Transactions of the Royal Historical Society*, 5th ser., 36 (1986): 117–42. More extensive treatments of revivalism appear in Richard Carwardine, *Transatlantic Revivalism: Popular Evangelicalism in Britain and America, 1790–1865* (Westport, CT: Greenwood Press, 1978); and John H. S. Kent, *Holding the Fort: Studies in Victorian Revivalism* (London: Epworth Press, 1978).

7. E. S. Itzkin, "The Halévy Thesis—a Working Hypothesis?" *Church History* 44 (1975): 47–56.

8. William R. Ward, *Religion and Society in England, 1790–1850* (London: Batsford, 1972); and idem "The Religion of the People and the Problem of Control, 1790–1830," *Studies in Church History* 8 (1972): 237–57.

9. William R. Ward, "Church and Society in the First Half of the Nineteenth Century," in A *History of the Methodist Church in Great Britain,* 4 vols. ed. Rupert Davies et al. (London: Epworth Press, 1965–88), 2: 11–96; and idem, "The Tithe Question in England in the Early Nineteenth Century," *Journal of Ecclesiastical History* 16 (1965): 67–81.

10. David Hempton, "Religion in British Society, 1740–1790," in *British Politics and Society from Walpole in Pitt, 1742–1789,* ed. Jeremy Black (London: Macmillan, 1990), 201–21. See also Peter Virgin, *The Church in an Age of Negligence: Ecclesiastical Structure and the Problems of Church Reform, 1700–1840* (Cambridge: James Clark, 1989).

11. Deborah M. Valenze, *Prophetic Sons and Daughters: Female Preaching and Popular Religion in Industrial England* (Princeton: Princeton University Press, 1985).

12. Alan Everitt, *The Pattern of Rural Dissent: The Nineteenth Century* (Leicester: Leicester University Press, 1972); and John D. Gay, *The Geography of Religion in England* (London: Duckworth, 1971).

13. James Obelkevich, *Religion and Rural Society: South Lindsey, 1825–1875* (Oxford: Clarendon Press, 1976), 183–258.

14. Nigel A. D. Scotland, *Methodism and the Revolt of the Field: A Study of the Methodist Contribution to Agricultural Trade Unionism in East Anglia, 1872–96* (Gloucester: Alan Sutton, 1981); and Pamela Horn, *The Rural World* (London: Hutchinson, 1986).

15. David Hempton, *Methodism and Politics in British Society, 1750–1850* (London: Hutchinson, 1984), chaps. 4 and 7. See also John Kent, "The Wesleyan Methodists to 1849," in *History of the Methodist Church,* ed. Davies et al., 2:213–75; and idem, *The Age of Disunity* (London: Epworth Press, 1966).

16. Jabez Bunting (1779–1858) was Wesleyan Methodism's leading ecclesiastical statesman from 1820, when he became president of conference for the first time, until 1850, when the Wesleyan Reform secessions began. See T. P. Bunting, *The Life of Jabez Bunting,* 2 vols. (London, 1859–87); William R. Ward, *The Early Correspon-*

dence of Jabez Bunting, 1820–1829, Camden Fourth Series, 11 (London: Royal Historical Society, 1972); idem, *Early Victorian Methodism: The Correspondence of Jabez Bunting, 1830–1858* (London: Oxford University Press, 1976); and John H. S. Kent, *Jabez Bunting, the Last Wesleyan: A Study in the Methodist Ministry after the Death of John Wesley* (London: Epworth Press, 1955).

17. Ward, *Religion and Society in England,* 177–278.

18. D. A. Gowland, *Methodist Secessions: The Origins of Free Methodism in Three Lancashire Towns* (Manchester: Manchester University Press, 1979); John M. Turner, *Conflict and Reconciliation: Studies in Methodism and Ecumenism in England, 1740–1982* (London: Epworth Press, 1985).

19. William R. Ward, "Revival and Class Conflict in Early Nineteenth-Century Britain," in *Erweckung am Beginn des 19. Jahrhunderts,* ed. Ulrich Gäbler and Peter Schram (Amsterdam: Vrije Universiteit, 1986), 87–104.

20. Elie Halévy, *A History of the English People in the Nineteenth Century,* 4 vols. (London: Ernest Benn, 1949–51); Edward Thompson, *The Making of the English Working Class* (London: Gollancz, 1963); Eric J. Hobsbawm, "Methodism and the Threat of Revolution in Britain," *History Today* 7 (1957): 115–24; Bernard Semmel, *The Methodist Revolution* (New York: Heinneman, 1973).

21. Jonathan C. D. Clark, *English Society, 1688–1832* (Cambridge: Cambridge University Press, 1985).

22. David Hempton, "Methodism and the Law, 1740–1820," *Bulletin of the John Rylands University Library of Manchester* 70 (1988): 93–107.

23. MS minutes of the Committee of Privileges, 1803–22, Methodist Church Archives, John Rylands University Library of Manchester. I survey some of this material in *Methodism and Politics,* 104–10.

24. See, for example, the *Gentleman's Magazine* 70, pt. 1 (1800): 241, and pt. 2, p. 1077.

25. Valenze, *Prophetic Sons and Daughters,* 159–83; Eric Hopkins, "Religious Dissent in Black Country Industrial Villages in the First Half of the Nineteenth Century," *Journal of Ecclesiastical History* 34 (1983): 411–24.

26. Joseph Rayner Stephens (1805–79) was a Wesleyan preacher in the Ashton-under-Lyne Circuit (1833–34). He resigned under pressure for his commitment to the Church Separation Society, led a small connection in the Ashton area, and achieved national fame as an activist in the Ten Hours, Anti-Poor Law, and Chartist movements. See Dale A. Johnson, "Between Evangelicalism and a Social Gospel: The Case of Joseph Rayner Stephens," *Church History* 42 (1973): 229–42.

27. James Epstein, "Some Organisational and Cultural Aspects of the Chartist Movement in Nottingham," *The Chartist Experience,* ed. Epstein and D. Thompson (London: Macmillan, 1982), 221–68; T. M. Kemnitz and F. Jacques, "J. R. Stephens and the Chartist Movement," *International Review of Social History* 19 (1974): 211–27; Eileen Yeo, "Christianity in Chartist Struggle, 1838–42," *Past and Present,* no. 91 (1981): 109–39. Older, but still useful, accounts of the relationship between Chartism and Methodism include H. U. Faulkner, *Chartism and the Churches* (New York, 1916); R. F. Wearmouth, *Methodism and the Working-Class Movements of England, 1800–1850* (London: Epworth Press, 1937); and idem, *Some Working-Class Movements of the Nineteenth Century* (London: Epworth Press, 1948).

28. Yeo, "Christianity in Chartist Struggle," 139.

29. See Robert Colls, *The Collier's Rant* (London: Croom Helm, 1977); and Robert Moore, *Pit-Men, Preachers, and Politics: The Effects of Methodism in a Durham Mining Community* (Cambridge: Cambridge University Press, 1974).

30. Research on Methodist electoral behavior is still at an early stage, but see John R. Vincent, *Pollbooks: How Victorians Voted* (Cambridge: Cambridge University Press, 1967); T. J. Nossiter, *Influence, Opinion, and Political Idioms in Reformed England: Case Studies from the North-East, 1832–74* (Sussex: Harvester, 1975); Henry Pelling, *Social Geography of British Elections, 1885–1910* (London: Macmillan, 1967); J. P. D. Dunbabin, "British Elections in the Nineteenth and Twentieth Centuries, a Regional Approach," *English Historical Review* 95 (1980): 241–67; J. P. Parry, "The State of Victorian Political History," *Historical Journal* 26 (1983): 469–84; and D. W. Bebbington, "Nonconformity and Electoral Sociology, 1867–1918," *Historical Journal* 27 (1984): 633–56.

31. David W. Bebbington, *The Nonconformist Conscience* (London: Allen and Unwin, 1982); D. A. Hamer, *The Politics of Electoral Pressure: A Study in the History of Victorian Reform Agitations* (Sussex: Harvester Press, 1977); B. S. Turner and M. Hill, "Methodism and the Pietist Definition of Politics; Historical Development and Contemporary Evidence," *Sociological Yearbook of Religion in Britain* 8 (1975): 159–80.

32. *Returns of the Archbishops and Bishops of the Number of Churches and Chapels of the Church of England, in every Parish of 1000 Persons and upwards: also of the Number of other Places of Worship not of the Establishment* (London: House of Lords, 5 April 1811).

33. Allan MSS, Methodist Church Archives. Some of Allan's correspondence is cataloged, but there are some twenty-two boxes of material arranged under broad subject headings. See David N. Hempton, "Thomas Allan and Methodist Politics, 1800–1840," *History* 67 (1982): 13–31.

34. Resolutions of the Committee of Privileges, 12 November 1819, Methodist Church Archives. For more detailed treatment, see Hempton, *Methodism and Politics,* 98–110.

35. Thomas Allan, *Letters to a Protestant Dissenter Relative to the Claims of the Roman Catholics* (London, 1813). Allan's views are also to be found in the papers of the Protestant Union, for which he was an anonymous publicist.

36. Thomas Allan to Joseph Butterworth, 3 December 1812, Allan MSS.

37. See Hempton, "Thomas Allan and Methodist Politics," 22–26.

38. R. Haire, *Wesley's One-and-Twenty Visits to Ireland* (London: Epworth Press, 1947).

39. William R. Ward and Richard P. Heitzenrater, eds., *The Works of John Wesley,* vol. 18: *Journals and Diaries I (1735–1738)* (Nashville: Abingdon, 1988), 56, 76–77.

40. T. E. Warner, "The Impact of Wesley on Ireland" (PhD diss., University of London, 1954), 323–24.

41. Hempton, *Methodism and Politics,* 34–43.

42. Journal, 14 August 1747; 25 April and 3 June 1758; 24 June 1760; 3 and 10 April 1748; 25 June and 4 July 1756; 22 May 1760; 26 April 1778.

43. Ward and Heitzenrater, *Journals and Diaries,* 74.

44. David Hempton, "Religious Minorities," in *The People of Ireland,* ed. Pat Loughrey (Belfast: Appletree Press, 1988), 155–68.

45. Journal, 19 July 1756.

46. Ward and Heitzenrater, *Journals and Diaries,* 66.

47. Haire, *Wesley's Visits to Ireland,* 49.

48. Hempton, "Methodism in Irish Society," 117–42.

49. Even then, a sizable remnant remained within the Established Church. See R. A. Ker, "The Origins of Primitive Methodism in Ireland," *Proceedings of the Wesley Historical Society* 43, pt. 4 (May 1982): 77–85.

50. C. H. Crookshank, *History of Methodism in Ireland,* 3 vols. (London: T. Woolmer, 1885–88), 2:132.

51. *A Reply to Mr John Johnson's Remarks, on an Address Lately Published and Signed by 30 Men in Office amongst the Methodists: To which is Added an Affectionate Address to the People called Methodists Living in Ireland* (n.p., n.d.). See also J. R. Binns, "A History of Methodism in Ireland from Wesley's Death in 1791 to the Re-union of Primitives and Wesleyans in 1878" (Master's thesis, Queen's University, Belfast, 1960), 49.

52. E. Thomas, *Irish Methodist Reminiscences. Being mainly Memorials of the Life and Labours of the Rev. S. Nicholson* (London, 1889).

53. George Taylor, *A History of the Rise, Progress, and Suppression of the Rebellion in the County of Wexford in the year 1798* (Dublin, 1800), serialized in the *Methodist Magazine* (1804). See also *An Extract of a Letter from a Gentleman in Ireland to Mr William Thompson* (London, 1798), serialized in the *Methodist Magazine* (1799). Private letters also circulated among the leading men of the connection in England and Ireland. See Adam Averell to Joseph Benson, 7 June 1798, Irish Wesley Historical Society Archives.

54. For a fuller discussion, see Hempton and Hill, *Evangelical Protestantism,* 47–102; Desmond Bowen, *The Protestant Crusade in Ireland, 1800–1870* (Dublin: Gill and Macmillan, 1978); and I. M. Hehir, "New Lights and Old Enemies: The Second Reformation and the Catholics of Ireland, 1800–1835" (Master's thesis, University of Wisconsin, 1983).

55. Rev. M. C. Motherwell, *Memoir of Albert Blest* (Dublin, 1843), 230–31.

56. *A Statement of the Management of the Farnham Estates* (Dublin, 1830).

57. Drivers were the men paid to visit the tenantry in order to collect arrears. Their authority to impound livestock and other goods and their exploitation of the situation in their own interests (e.g., by charging extra fees for the release of stock) made them highly unpopular figures.

58. J. R. R. Wright, "An Evangelical Estate, c. 1800–1825: The influence on the Manchester Estate, County Armagh, with Particular References to the Moral Agencies of W. Loftie and H. Porter" (Ph.D. diss., N. I. Polytechnic, 1982). Wright points out that the term "moral agent" was new and finds no evidence of its use in England.

59. Advertisments for men of high moral character can be found in most contemporary newspapers. See also Moore to Porter, 4 March 1839, Correspondence of Lord Annesley, D1854/6/1, NIPRO (Northern Ireland Public Record Office).

60. C. S. Stanford, *Memoir of the Late Rev. W. H. Krause* (Dublin, 1854).

61. See, for example, Rev. C. White, *Sixty Years Experience as an Irish Landlord: Memoirs of John Hamilton* (London, n.d.); Report of the Commissioners appointed to Enquire into the Occupation of Land in Ireland, H.C. 19 (1845): 18–19.

62. G. Ensor, *Letters showing the Inutility and showing the Absurdity of what is rather fantastically termed "The New Reformation"* (Dublin, 1828).

63. Ibid., 14. For a flavor of the controversial literature thrown up by the Second Reformation, see "Fintona Farnhamites" in *Clogher Record,* 9 February 1827; *Correspondence between the Rev. Doctor Logan, Roman Catholic Bishop of Meath, and the Rev. Robert Winning, Superintendent of Irish Schools in the Kingscourt District with the Resolution of 125 teachers therein* (Dublin, 1827); *Specimens of the Conversions at Cavan by Bible Saints Submitted to the Common Sense of the People of England* (Dublin, 1827); Rev. T. Maguire, *False Weights and Measures of Protestant Curate of Cavan Examined and Exposed* (Dublin, 1833).

64. Bowen, *Protestant Crusade,* 95–96; Hehir, "New Lights and Old Enemies," 208.

65. Ensor, *New Reformation,* 17.

66. David Hempton, "Gideon Ouseley: Rural Revivalist, 1791–1839," *Studies in Church History* 25 (1989): 203–14.

67. For a fuller discussion of the evangelical response to Gladstone's Home Rule proposals, see Hempton and Hill, *Evangelical Protestantism,* 161–87. The various issues at stake may also be explored in the papers of the Nonconformist Unionist Association in the Northern Ireland Public Record Office, D2396.

NINETEENTH-CENTURY
EVANGELICAL CULTURES

9

Anti-Catholicism and Evangelical Identity in Britain and the United States, 1830–1860

JOHN WOLFFE

During the winter of 1836–1837, George Barrell Cheever, a rising New England Congregational minister, and his brother Nathaniel began their first visit to Europe.[1] In February 1837 Nathaniel wrote to their sister from Málaga in southern Spain, describing the atmosphere of the town on a Sunday.

> [T]here is but little *ever* here to show one that the Sabbath is at all observed as it should be. The influence of the Roman Catholic religion tends most inevitably to its most flagrant desecration—O that the time may soon come when this *soul*-ruining, degrading system of idolatry superstition and ignorance shall come to an end, here and throughout the world, and the Gospel with all its light and purity and elevating influence be established in its stead.[2]

This chapter is introduced with Nathaniel Cheever's reflections because they illustrate the close connections between anti-Catholicism and other characteristic evangelical concerns, notably Sabbath observance, eschatological expectation, and zeal for the spread of the gospel. It will be argued that, particularly during the middle third of the nineteenth century, anti-Catholicism was, on both sides of the Atlantic, very much of the essence of evangelicalism. Indeed, antagonism to "popery" served, in a positive as well as a negative sense, to help define evangelical identity. In order to develop this case the first part of the chapter will relate anti-Catholicism to a four-part model for characterizing evangelicalism recently set out by David Bebbington.[3] We shall then turn, secondly, to an examination of the social and institutional base of the organized anti-Catholic movements in Britain and the United States, which will serve to indicate, with certain exceptions that prove the general rule, that they were based on evangelical networks. Finally, there will be a reexamination, through the perspective given by anti-Catholicism, of those crucial years around 1850, which saw the formation and subsequent division of the Evangelical Alliance and the growing momentum of an anti-evangelical reaction, and division within the movement itself.[4]

The broad outlines of anti-Catholic activity in Britain and America in the mid-nineteenth century are well known.[5] There was an upsurge in militant Protestantism in both countries around the time of the passing of Catholic Emancipation in Britain in 1829. An initial peak was reached in the mid-1830s. The Ursuline Convent at Charlestown, Massachusetts, was burned in August 1834 against a background of widespread anti-Catholic preaching and publication in Boston, New York, and Baltimore. In Britain there was a campaign of large-scale public meetings between 1834 and 1836 in which the Roman Catholic Church was characterized as authoritarian and persecuting. In 1836 *The Awful Disclosures of Maria Monk* were published in New York, containing allegations that seduction, infanticide, and murder were routine activities at the Hôtel Dieu at Montreal. A second high-water mark of activity came in the mid-1840s with the savage riots in Philadelphia in 1844 and the organizing of the Native American party. In Britain in 1845 the campaign against Sir Robert Peel's measure to increase the state endowment to the Roman Catholic seminary at Maynooth was followed by sustained anti-Roman political activity. Meanwhile the Evangelical Alliance sought to unite Britain, continental Europe, and the United States in an international movement. In 1850 and 1851 there was an outcry in Britain against the formation of a Roman Catholic episcopal hierarchy, followed by further political campaigns against Maynooth and convents. A little later in the United States, controversy over Roman Catholic educational and political influence culminated in 1854 and 1855 in the extensive but short-lived triumphs of the Know-Nothings. In both countries there were also a variety of outbreaks of popular violence against Catholics associated with Irish immigration, as manifested in Britain in the Stockport riots of 1852.

The chronological parallels and resemblances between the pattern of events in the two countries provide at least prima facie grounds for considering that the exploration of comparisons and connections between them is likely to prove fruitful. I have argued elsewhere that evangelicalism was a central strand in a complex web of other factors that contributed to the force of mid-nineteenth-century anti-Catholicism.[6] These included ritualized traditional demonstrations—on 5 November (Guy Fawkes Day) in Britain, on 4 July (Independence Day) in the United States, and on 12 July (celebrating the Protestant victory over Catholics in Ireland, 1691) on both sides of the Atlantic. There was also a use of anti-Catholicism in political ideology and propaganda; a comparison of British and American material shows similar motifs being used in the services of widely divergent political traditions. A third element was the response to immigrants from Roman Catholic countries, of which the Irish were the most numerous.[7]

In the present context, however, there is no space to explore these aspects of anti-Catholicism in detail; the task, rather, is to indicate the distinctive nature of the evangelical contribution. Bebbington's model provides a fourfold characterization of evangelicalism in terms of conversionism, activism, biblicism, and crucicentrism. This should be regarded as a suggestive rather than conclusive means of identifying evangelicals, but the relationship of these four emphases to anti-Catholicism merits careful exploration. Subsequently, however, we must note some features of evangelical belief, not so explicit in Bebbington's categorization, which have a central relevance in connection with anti-Catholicism.

Bebbington's first characteristic, conversionism, relates to the central evangelical experience of a radical turning from sin, frequently associated with a sense of direct contract with God. This is clearly illustrated in a tract entitled *Remarks on the Progress of Popery* by Edward Bickersteth, a leading Church of England Evangelical, published in 1836. Bickersteth began with a statement of the "glorious gospel" and the conviction of assurance that the believer experienced in conversion: "In his very coming to Christ he knows that he is among the elect." Popery was a delusion that deprived its adherents of this crucial, life-changing encounter with God; it was a Christian duty to call on its adherents to make a clean spiritual break and come out from darkness into the light of true faith in Christ.[8]

One can compare the address given by Leonard Bacon to the meeting of the Christian Alliance in New York in 1845 in which Protestant missions in Italy were related to the wider enterprise of converting the world. God, Bacon said, "now commands all men everywhere to repent." The assumption that Roman Catholics were to be numbered among the unregenerate was axiomatic.[9] Anti-Catholic conversionist zeal was given a further cutting edge by links with revivalism. Although Charles Finney himself, for example, could see positive qualities in some Roman Catholics, some of his associates and sympathizers, notably the American Edward Norris Kirk and the leading English Congregationalist, John Angell James, associated zeal for the revival of religion with fierce antagonism to Rome.[10] There was also an eschatological expectation in which judgment was held to be imminent and the downfall of Babylon, equated readily with Rome, earnestly awaited. Thus in 1849 the Scottish preacher John Cumming concluded a lecture on the revolutions of the previous year, replete with eschatological and antipapal references, as follows: "And now, my dear friends, let me ask, How stands it with you? Be not satisfied with beholding the panorama which I have endeavoured to explain, or with hearing the voices and witnessing the lightnings to which I have alluded. Are your feet upon the Rock of Ages? Is your trust and confidence in the Lamb of God?"[11]

Second, anti-Catholicism stirred a vigorous activism. Numerous organizations were formed to advance the cause, some of the more important of which are listed in Table 9-1. There was a comparable delight in hard evangelistic endeavor to that noted by Bebbington for early Methodists. The American and Foreign Christian Union's 1852 annual report boasted that over a thousand sermons had been preached on behalf of the society; five million pages of literature distributed; and more than twenty thousand Roman Catholics visited. Nor was the galvanizing effect of antipopery limited to the specifically Protestant societies; it manifested itself strongly in the evangelistic efforts of

Table 9-1. Some Mid-Nineteenth-Century Anti-Catholic Societies

Date founded	Great Britain	United States
1819	Continental Society	
1827	British Society for Promoting the Religious Principles of the Reformation	
1831		New York Protestant Association
1835–36	Protestant Association	American Society to Promote the Principles of the Protestant Reformation
1839		Foreign Evangelical Society
1842		American Protestant Association
1843		Christian Alliance
1844		American Protestant Society
1845	National Club	
1845–46	Evangelical Alliance	Evangelical Alliance
1849		American and Foreign Christian Union
1850	Scottish Reformation Society	
1851	Protestant Alliance	

Note: For further details, see Billington, *Protestant Crusade;* and Wolffe, *Protestant Crusade,* 318–19. This list is not intended to be comprehensive, but merely to mention the more important organizations. It does not include British societies dedicated specifically to Irish purposes.

home mission organizations such as the London City Mission and in zeal for the promulgation of the gospel abroad in order to reduce or preempt Roman Catholic influence.[12]

Biblicism, the third of Bebbington's evangelical characteristics, is well illustrated by the claim of the Protestant agitator James Edward Gordon that scriptural education was "a master key to almost every religious and political intricacy of the present period."[13] He saw it as a cornerstone of efforts to secure the conversion and consequent social regeneration of Ireland. A similar conviction underlaid Hugh McNeile's campaign in Liverpool in the later 1830s against a nondenominational education system, and the American emphasis on the school question as a central focus of anti-Catholicism.[14] Certainly, particularly in the United States, reverence for the Bible was a wider Protestant cultural characteristic, not limited to evangelicals. Thus in Native American demonstrations, such as that in Philadelphia on 4 July 1844, the secular patriotic iconography of the parade included images of the Bible juxtaposed with schoolhouses or images of liberty. In 1856 Horace Galpin presented a revealing juxtaposition of ideals when he wrote of "Bible Republican independence." However, evangelical biblicism was, as Mark Noll puts it, experiential, characterized more by internal study and reflection than by the outward flaunting of symbols. Thus in 1843 George Barrell Cheever called on students at Amhurst College to ponder the Scriptures. If the church truly did this, he said, "then would that system of Antichrist, which has lived by the hiding, corruption, ignorance and inexperience of God's word, die. The *spirit* of Romanism would die also, whatever shape of formalism it may inhabit."[15]

The final component of this model is crucicentrism, the conviction that God was reconciled to humankind through the death of Christ on the cross, the spiritual benefits of which are appropriated to the believer through faith alone. The connection with anti-Catholicism was made explicit by Edward Bickersteth in 1836: "Popery is, to be looking to ourselves and our own doings for salvation. Real Protestantism is, to be looking simply to Jesus for every thing. . . . O it is hard and impossible to flesh and blood, to live by faith in Jesus: and to see, if we pray, it can only be by His Spirit freely given; if we love, it can only be as his Spirit first discloses to us God's amazing love to us rebels in the death of Jesus."[16]

Hence evangelical anti-Catholics had a strong hostility to all aspects of the Roman Church that seemed to them to imply that there were intermediaries between the believer and Christ, such as papal authority, the Mass, and veneration of saints. A speaker at a meeting of the American Protestant Association in 1843 gave an eloquently hostile account of religious ceremonies he had witnessed in Rome, culminating in the kissing of the pope's toe by the cardinals, "or if it was the cross on the toe, then how came that symbol of infinite love, the most endearing attribute of God, down there on the toe of a mortal."[17]

Evangelical anti-Catholicism thus relates well to Bebbington's model but points to the need for precision in its use, especially in relation to biblicism. Moreover, anti-Catholicism strongly reflected further aspects of evangelicalism, notably in underlying tension between an intensely individualistic response to God and a sense of the worldwide community of the saved. In Britain in the late 1820s and early 1830s the Reformation Society held a series of public debates with Roman Catholics, a central thrust of which was the rule of faith, as Protestants asserted their hostility to the claims of an authoritative church. The point was made equally forcefully in America, for example by Bacon: "For what is religious freedom? What is that doctrine, the assertion and universal reception of which, among a people works such changes? What is it? It is simply the development and application of that great principle which lies at the heart of the Gospel—the principle of the right, nay, let me say rather the duty, of private judgement. This is Protestantism—this is Christianity. There can be no Christianity without it."[18] Anne Norton fails to understand this point when, in a recent book on the antebellum period, she writes: "The understanding of political culture which emerged from the fear of Catholicism held that ideology was collective rather than individual, the product not of reason or of will but the historical experience of a commonly conditioned community."[19] Norton's stress on tradition and communal values in giving rise to anti-Catholicism may well represent a valid assessment of some of its political and popular manifestations, but in the context of evangelicalism such an assertion obscures a profound sense that at its roots ideology came not from a "commonly conditioned community" but from an individual's encounter with God, interpreting the Bible under the guidance of the Holy Spirit.

Norton accuses evangelicals of "rhetorical legerdemain" in portraying Catholic resistance to Protestant proselytizing as an assault on religious freedom, but the evangelical perception went far deeper than a mere reflex association of Protestantism with liberty and Catholicism with persecution. For evangelicals, Catholicism in its inherent nature was opposed to a personal freedom of spiritual response that was the essence of true religion. Hence we see that anti-Catholicism was closely linked with individualism, which has also been seen as a defining characteristic of evangelicalism.[20]

A counterbalance to this individualism was advocacy of Protestant interdenominational and international unity. Other chapters in this book provide ample illustrations of the range of transatlantic contacts, which went back to the Great Awakening. Important in sustaining these in the nineteenth century were the activities in Britain of American revivalists.[21] In a specifically anti-Catholic context too, consciousness of shared spiritual values was enhanced by visits of Americans to Britain and by publications. Even the writings of such staunch Anglicans as Edward Bickersteth and Charlotte Elizabeth Tonna were extensively reprinted in American editions; Americans seemed prepared to suffer a certain jarring of their sensibilities on questions of religious establishments in the cause of anti-Catholicism.[22] Moreover, a substantial proportion of the Protestant societies showed an international vision that spanned not only the Atlantic but the European continent as well, as represented by the Continental Society in Britain and, in America, by the Christian Alliance and the Foreign Evangelical Society.[23] From the early 1840s statements of transnational interdenominational evangelical unity became more explicit, as expressed by Bacon in a sermon for the Foreign Evangelical Society in 1845. He asserted that there was a vital and spiritual unity among evangelical believers. It existed in the face of superficial institutional and national divisions and had become particularly apparent in the recent past:

> The progress of Evangelical Christianity, amid all the diversities of language and government and nation, and all the conflicting influences arising from political alienations and wars and revolutions, . . . [is] one story, the story of a living unity. . . . whatever influence from above or from below moves on the common mind of Protestantism, there is a sympathy which carries that influence, slowly or swiftly, according to the presence and absence of obstructions, to any part of the vast body which, diffused and separated, is yet one and has one life.

Unity, however, was impeded by attempts at "popish" uniformity, links between the church and civil power, and failures to appreciate the essential truths of the gospel. Christians were called upon to propagate the faith at home and abroad and to cultivate extensive links with foreign believers.[24]

We thus can reach an intermediate conclusion that, in this period, anti-Catholicism was very deeply rooted in evangelical identity and ideology. It was not a mere negative prejudice but an impulse at the heart of the movement's spiritual aspirations and religious activity. Moreover, despite differences of emphasis, the fundamental processes of thought in Britain and America were strikingly similar. We now turn, in the second section of this chapter, to consider the nature of the support accorded to organized anti-Catholicism.

Table 9-2 indicates the character and geographic distribution of members

Table 9-2. Membership in the BRS and the APS during the Mid-Nineteenth Century

Membership	British Reformation Society[a] 1850		American Protestant Society[b] 1847	
	Number	Percentage	Number	Percentage
Clergy	171	20.9	525	81.1
Laymen	379	46.4	81	12.5
Laywomen	267	32.7	41	6.3
Total	817		647	

Sources: Wolffe, *Protestant Crusade,* 153, 164; *Fourth Annual Report of the American Protestant Society* (New York, 1847), 34–39.

[a]The most active branches of the BRS were those in Brighton, Cheltenham, Dover, Birkenhead, Edinburgh, Hull, Liverpool, Portsea, Reading, Sheffield, Leicester, London, Preston, and Southampton.

[b]The following figures show the total number of APS members in 1847 from each state and, in parentheses, the number of members per 10,000 in the respective state, according to the census of 1850: Connecticut, 34 (0.92); Maine, 7 (0.12); Massachusetts, 145 (1.46); New Hampshire, 32 (1.01); Rhode Island, 10 (0.68); Vermont, 17 (0.54); New Jersey, 49 (1.00); New York, 215 (0.69); and Pennsylvania, 54 (0.23). In addition, 34 members were from the South Atlantic states, 46 were from elsewhere in the country, and 4 lived abroad.

of two sample societies around the middle of the century. In terms of committed supporters, both were clearly relatively small, socially elite organizations. Full membership was expensive, costing a guinea a year for the British Reformation Society and $25 for life membership of the American Protestant Society.[25] There is little sign of an accumulation of the large numbers of small contributions that would indicate a significant body of support among the poorer classes. A partial exception to this limitation emerged in Britain in the late 1830s and 1840s when both the Protestant Association and the Reformation Society formed Operative Associations in London and other major cities, with a view to recruiting members among the working class. Also in 1845 the Islington Protestant Institute was formed in North London and acquired a considerable local cross-class membership. Such working-class involvement, however, was strictly controlled in a paternalistic framework.[26] In general, adherents of the more plebeian denominational groups—the Baptists and Methodists in America and the Primitive Methodists in Britain—were conspicuous only by their absence from the membership lists of all the societies. Among British radical Dissenters, hostility to Rome was likely to be subsumed in their antagonism to the Anglican and Presbyterian established churches; among their American counterparts, recently analyzed by Nathan Hatch, the elite Protestant clergy were quite as much the target of anticlericalism and charges of "priestcraft" as the Roman Catholics were.[27]

The geographic distribution of support for the BRS and the APS also points to the operation of middle-class (and, in Britain, aristocratic) evangelical networks rather than, primarily, popular reaction to the Irish Catholic presence. Certainly the societies were strong in some areas where Catholicism was growing, notably Massachussetts and Merseyside, but the relative proportions of membership of the APS in New Hampshire, New York, and Pennsylvania should provide a check to simplistic generalization of this kind. Likewise, the

British Reformation Society drew strong support from southern towns such as Brighton, Cheltenham, and Reading, where Roman Catholic numbers were relatively small, as well as from centers like Edinburgh, Preston, and London, where there were strong Catholic communities. Moreover, where one can discern a Protestant reaction to a Catholic presence, these were by no means exclusively to Irish Catholics. French Canadians in northern New England and German Catholics in the Midwest seem to have led to support for the APS in these regions, while in England the activity of the BRS in Brighton can be related to unusually early and vigorous activity by the Anglo-Catholics in the town.[28] Such factors indicate that hostility to Catholicism, as manifested in the Protestant societies, reflected genuine theological conviction rather than sublimated racialism and strengthens the case for viewing it as closely linked with evangelicalism.

The evidence summarized in table 9-2 also points to some significant differences between Britain and the United States. The presence of clergy in both countries was strong enough to confirm the religious motivation behind these organizations, but the contrast between the proportions among the membership is striking. Explanations have to be somewhat speculative but might include the supposition that there was a stronger tradition of involvement by laypeople in such activities in Britain and, at the same time, a caution among Anglican clergymen toward voluntary organizations of this kind, especially if they were fearful of censure from unsympathetic bishops. This latter supposition seems to be confirmed by the fact that in the Protestant Alliance, a British body that had substantially greater support from Nonconformists than did the British Reformation Society, the proportion of clergy in the membership was appreciably higher, at 38.4 percent.[29] The membership figures can be misleading, however, insofar as in both countries the leadership and organization of the anti-Catholic societies tended to be dominated by clergy, although in Britain, at least, male laity always managed to maintain a foothold in the committees. The differing levels of support from women are also striking, but this appears to have been as much a denominational as a national difference; in the Protestant Alliance in Britain only 7 percent of the membership was female.[30] Whether clerical or lay, male or female, membership furthermore overlapped with that of other reforming religious and philanthropic societies, in both countries with home and foreign missions and in the United States with the temperance movement and antislavery activity. In Britain the link between anti-Catholicism and temperance and teetotalism was rather less strong, but it did find a prominent representative in John Hope, an Edinburgh lawyer who explicitly declared his intention to teach children to "avoid the Mass House as the public house and popery as alcohol."[31]

Nevertheless it would be seriously misleading to infer from the strong links between evangelicalism and anti-Catholicism that all organized anti-Catholicism was necessarily evangelical in character. An important distinction was made between *religious* anti-Catholicism, which operated in a clearly evangelical framework, and *political* anti-Catholicism, which was generally supported only by rather isolated individual evangelicals who found themselves operating with nonevangelical associates. As might be anticipated from the tradition of separation of church and state, this distinction was particularly sharp in the United States. There was minimal overlap between the membership of evangelical societies such as the American Protestant Society and the American and Foreign Christian Union, and nativist political parties such as the American Republican party and the Know-Nothings.[32] The situation in Pennsylvania was particularly indicative. The strong anti-Catholicism that culminated in the Philadelphia riots in 1844 had little open support from the clergy, and there was a tacit division of roles, with the American Republican party assuming the political mantle and leaving theology to the American Protestant Association.[33] In fact, the 1847 figures for membership of the American Protestant Society in Pennsylvania fell well below the national average, in spite of, or perhaps even because of, the strong political nativism in the state. Granted that parts of the theology and propaganda of religious and political anti-Catholicism might appear similar, the orientations were different and, for most people, incompatible. The point is worth emphasizing, because it does suggest a need for a reevaluation of the blanket application of the "nativist" concept to American anti-Catholicism in this period.

In Britain, as one might expect, the distinction between religion and politics was not so sharply maintained, but it was still recognized and acted upon, an indication that the perceived distinction between these categories was a product of evangelicalism as well as of American constitutional culture. In 1835–1836 the Protestant Association was formed to pursue the political aspects of anti-Catholicism because the existing organization, the Reformation Society, held firmly to the view that its own task was specifically religious. The Protestant Association flourished in the mid-1830s when it drew on substantial nonevangelical support but subsequently declined when it was forced back on the resources provided by a circle of evangelicals who were showing themselves ambivalent toward political action. Other political anti-Catholic organizations in Britain, notably the Orange Order and the National Club, might gain the support of individual evangelicals, but their general character was formed as much by conservative High Church influences.[34]

There is no space here to consider more fully the nature of anti-Catholic politics, but the difficulties experienced by evangelicals in maintaining their integrity on this front is illustrative of a problem that sets the agenda for the final section of this chapter. Anti-Catholicism, as we have seen, was closely related to evangelical spiritual imperatives, but at the same time, in the hands of those of less elevated sentiments and calling, the message could readily become crude, negative, and the staple of demagogues. This possibility was appreciated by fellow evangelicals. In April 1841 Thomas Brainerd, a Presbyterian minister in Philadelphia, spoke of the danger of exaggerating the danger from Rome. Harsh words toward Roman Catholics would only harden them against Protestantism and serve to stir public sympathy for them. Brainerd concluded, however, with a distinctively evangelical call to concentrate energies on converting Catholics to Christ, but through kindness rather than denunciation.[35] In similar vein Lord Ashley in 1849 confided to his diary his reservations about the "violent, vituperative and declamatory" language of resolutions to be proposed at a meeting of the Irish Church Missions to Roman Catholics, but agreed that they "affirm no doubt what is true."[36]

Such differences among evangelicals do not remove the impression of an underlying, deeply held anti-Catholicism. To some extent, as in Ashley's case, disagreements were largely a reflection of differing tactical approaches to the question, but at a deeper level it can be surmised that they also at times stemmed from differing eschatological conceptions. Whereas postmillennialists, believing that an era of millennial peace would begin by peaceful change rather than violent cataclysm, could hold that Rome would gradually wither away, premillennialists expected an apocalyptic confrontation and accordingly were suspicious of any apparent compromise. Furthermore, at times there was a sense that the cruder forms of anti-Catholicism were not necessarily the most spiritually edifying; in January 1844 George Barrell Cheever advised his brother not to confuse "Protestant steam" with true enlightenment.[37]

Others less scrupulous than Brainerd, Ashley, and Cheever developed various mental mechanisms that permitted them to reconcile their belief in their own spiritual integrity with an awareness of the sometimes less-than-edifying dimensions of anti-Catholicism. Ironically one widespread approach was the kind of moral casuistry readily attributed to their Catholic opponents. Ends were used to justify means, theological dogmas such as the equation of Rome with evil or the identification of the pope as a personal antichrist were turned into absolutes and pivots of a whole worldview. A particular graphic illustration of this tendency to gullibility and blinkered moral vision was provided by the readiness in the mid-1830s of various prominent American evangelicals to give credence to the salacious allegations of Maria Monk against the Hôtel Dieu at Montreal. This "pert, brazen and rather pretty" young woman claimed to be an escaped nun from the convent, where, she maintained, the nuns had routinely performed sexual services for the priests. The resulting infants had been murdered and interred in a pit.[38] It transpired that there were inaccuracies and inconsistencies in her account of the nunnery, that she had never in reality been a nun at all, and that her story was a combination of delusion and outright fabrication produced in collusion with her lover, a traveling preacher by the name of Hoyte.[39] Nevertheless she was believed by men such as the Reverend W. C. Brownlee of New York, and for a time by the leading evangelical newspaper, the *New York Observer.* One evenhanded critic commented: "It would seem, indeed, as though these people had yielded themselves to this species of monomania, until from mere habit, they yield a willing credence to any story against the Roman Catholics, no matter what, or by whomsoever related, so that it be sufficiently horrible and revolting in the details of licentiousness and blood."[40]

Although Maria Monk's allegations were printed and circulated in Britain as well as the United States, they do not appear to have received the same degree of credence among evangelicals across the Atlantic.[41] However, there was an almost exactly contemporary parallel in the charges made by Robert M'Ghee and others against the Roman Catholic Church in Ireland on the basis of the evidence of persecution, sedition, and sexual immorality produced by a slanted reading of texts such as the *Theologia* of Peter Dens. Here, as in the Maria Monk affair, evangelicals projected onto Roman Catholics the antithesis of their own idealization of good order, domesticity, family life, and female purity. At a meeting in Liverpool in 1835, a speaker questioned how husbands and fathers could allow their womenfolk to undergo the ordeal of confession and attributed it to the manner in which all Roman Catholics allegedly had become familiarized with subjects, "the mention of which would usually excite feelings of abhorrence in the genuine professor of protestantism."[42]

A second consequence of the quest for integrity in the face of ambivalences of anti-Catholicism was the tendency to internal division, which was characteristic of the anti-Catholic societies on both sides of the Atlantic. Individualist activism prompted the proliferation of societies and publications, which provided their adherents with the opportunity to feel that, despite the corruptions evident elsewhere in the vineyard, their own portion of it was being satisfactorily tended. Here again anti-Catholicism, precisely because it lay close to the heart of the sense of identity of many evangelicals in these years, provided a good indication of the spiritual pathologies of the movement.

For others, drawn neither to casuistry nor to sectarianism, the disquieting dimensions of anti-Catholicism helped to crystallize reaction against evangelicalism. It is significant that when, in 1855, George Eliot published an article emphatically repudiating the evangelicalism of her youth, the means she chose was a devastating personal attack on a leading anti-Catholic, John Cumming. She drew much of her ammunition from Cumming's writings on Catholicism, which seemed to her to support her charges concerning unscrupulosity of assertion, perverted moral judgment, and absence of charity. She commented: "Dr Cumming is fond of showing up the teaching of Romanism, and accusing it of undermining true morality: it is time he should be told that there is a large body, both of thinkers and practical men, who hold precisely the same opinion of his own teaching—with this difference, that they do not regard it as the inspiration of Satan, but as the natural crop of a human mind where the soil is chiefly made up of egoistic passions and dogmatic beliefs."[43]

Eliot's case was an extreme one, but something of the same tendency can be discerned in the developing ideas of her friend Harriet Beecher Stowe, whose father, Lyman Beecher, had been prominent in anti-Catholic crusades in New England and the Midwest in the second quarter of the century. Unlike Eliot, Stowe remained essentially an orthodox Christian, but like Eliot, she became a trenchant critic of the embattled small-mindedness she perceived in the evangelicalism of the 1850s. More specifically, the introduction to an American edition of the works of Charlotte Elizabeth, written in 1844, already betrayed an embarrassment at "the unmingled bitterness with which she always speaks of the Catholic system."[44]

At the same time in the novels of Stowe and Eliot there was a more positive vision of evangelicalism, as a source of human dignity and self-fulfillment. For Eliot the implicit purpose was to point the way to her secular religion of humanity, but despite Dr. Cumming, she evidently felt that there was still much worth salvaging from evangelicalism.[45] For her, this approach entailed a playing down of the bigotry she perceived in Cumming, but for some in the evangelical ranks anti-Catholicism itself remained an energizing rather than a negative force. This paradoxical quality became strongly apparent in the movement for international solidarity and brotherhood that took at least fleeting shape in the formation of the Evangelical Alliance in 1846. The idea was founded on the sense of the universal unity of the saved. If Christians had a spiritual common ground in their experience of conversion and relationship to Christ, could this become a basis for a sustained identification of believers with each other as a check to compromise and distraction by nonessentials?

The Evangelical Alliance was established at a conference in London in August 1846 and drew support from Britain, the United States, and continental Europe. It represented the convergence of several different initiatives and movements. In a British context, the impact of the Scottish Disruption of 1843 was of considerable importance, but a more immediate stimulus was the response to the Maynooth Act of 1845, a measure passed by Sir Robert Peel's government, in the face of vigorous opposition from evangelicals, to enhance the state endowment of a Roman Catholic seminary in Ireland.[46] From the American perspective, Robert Baird stated in 1851 that the idea had originated with Leonard Bacon in 1843 and had also been discussed in 1844 with the leading Swiss Protestant, Merle D'Aubigné.[47] It accordingly seems unlikely that the idea had a single source, but rather it arose from a mood among evangelicals that transcended institutional and national boundaries. This climate was one in which hope and fear were inescapably mingled. On the one hand was an optimism and eschatological expectation stirred by recent revivals and the successful formation of the Free Church of Scotland; on the other, a consciousness that evangelicalism was becoming increasingly diffuse and lacked clear definition while being confronted by the forces of "infidelity" and "popery." Thus there was anxiety for a strong stand against Roman Catholicism, expressed most forcefully by Thomas Chalmers, leader of the Free Church of Scotland, but also a concern that this should not take "any mere *anti* form."[48]

The fervor and harmony that initially characterized the meetings of the Evangelical Alliance could not obscure the fact that the extent of its success in bringing evangelicals into any kind of visible unity was limited. From the outset particular individuals and groups were conspicuous by their absence, and although the movement enjoyed a modest institutional viability in Britain, the gulf between its ambitions and its achievements was a telling illustration of the continuing strength of individualism and denominationalism. The alliance's most dramatic and significant failure, however, was the split between the British and American participants at the founding conference in London in 1846.[49] On a superficial reading, the cause of the dispute, a call to exclude slaveholders from membership, was something far more likely to divide Americans from each other than to separate from the British. It was rather the manner in which the question was raised that caused the difficulty, as Baird explained:

> There was an appearance of foreign dictation. . . . And it came from the
> very last quarter,—I mean from England, from which, for obvious reasons,
> no thing of an unacceptable nature should come to us, if good is to be
> done. . . . Let British Christians pursue their great work of putting every
> thing right in their own vast dominion, and we shall do the same in our great
> country. . . . We believe that we understand this matter better than you
> do. . . . We shall get clear of slavery, but not at, or in consequence of your
> bidding, or to please you.

He went on to point out that revolution would be the inevitable consequence
of an uncompromising stand on slavery by the North, and to regret the
narrow-mindedness and ignorance of opponents of slavery who had no appreciation of the particular circumstances of individual slaveholders.[50]

The rock on which the alliance foundered was national pride. There was a
specific tension between British moral imperialism and the assertion of liberty
by the Americans in the face of outside interference. The Americans were
being frustrated in their own desire to use revivalism and anti-Catholicism as a
source of national cohesion in the face of the sectional force of slavery. The
wider perspective was one of evangelicals in both countries asserting a chosen-
nation status in the struggle against Rome and the call to spread the Christian
gospel. In 1829 Hugh McNeile, in a pamphlet on Catholic Emancipation (that
is, enfranchisement), had referred to Britain as "our modern Judah" in virtue
of its national adherence to Protestantism; in 1841 George Barrell Cheever in
God's Hand in America saw the nation as having a special place in divine
purposes now moving to their consummation. He believed that the United
States was to become a vehicle for the conversion of the world, in virtue,
among other things, of its freedom from the obscurantist and despotic influence of Roman Catholicism.[51] Although transatlantic contacts were maintained after 1846, the failure of the alliance was a body blow to aspirations to
an international evangelical coherence that went beyond idealistic professions
of spiritual community.

This development can be set in a wider framework. In terms of the internal
dynamics of evangelicalism, it showed the limits to which moves toward broad
unity could be pushed before the individualist side of the seesaw swung up
again. A formalized international structure, however loosely tied together,
was too redolent of the Roman Catholic Church itself for comfort.[52] The
intermediate communities implied by denominationalism and nationalism
proved to be more stable. The confirmation of the nationalistic tendencies of
evangelicalism at this particular historical juncture was especially significant
in the light of the development of continental European nationalist movements, more secular in orientation, but sharing their hostility to Roman Catholicism. In the early 1850s Alessandro Gavazzi, an itinerant former friar,
received a rapturous welcome from both British and American evangelicals
for his oratorical blend of Italian nationalism with militant anti-Catholicism.[53]
Lajos Kossuth, leader of the Hungarian Revolution of 1848, was enthusiastically received in America because of his perceived links with Protestantism,

and later in the decade, Italian nationalism again struck warm chords of sympathy in the North Atlantic evangelical world.[54]

In 1845 Bacon had compared the essential unity of "the great body of Protestant Christendom" with the United States, "that great expanding Union which spreads its protection over our freedom."[55] In light of the events of the next twenty years, the analogy seems unwittingly double-edged. Ernest Sandeen has pointed to the strength of denominationalism in both Britain and American in the mid-nineteenth century; it can be postulated that the parallel force of nationalism and sectionalism in the same period had some related roots in the fragmentation of evangelicalism. By 1856 the Republican party was successfully appealing to anti-Catholicism among a variety of evangelical emphases in its consolidation of the forces that were shortly to come into collision with the South. At the same time, the uncompromising zeal against slavery developed in the 1850s by Cheever and Stowe, among others, surely owed something to the mental processes derived from the evangelical anti-Catholicism of the previous two decades. Within the United Kingdom evangelicalism was closely associated with the development of Welsh and Scottish nationalism after the middle of the century; above all, it contributed power-fully to the cultural distinctiveness of Ulster Protestantism.[56] The nature of the processes involved require much closer investigation, but it may well be that here is to be found evidence of the most pervasive and enduring influence of mid-nineteenth-century evangelical anti-Catholicism.

The impact of anti-Catholicism on mid-century evangelicalism can be inter-preted in terms of two profound paradoxes. Firstly, hostility to Rome and zeal for the salvation of Roman Catholics were intimately bound up with deep spiritual vision, but they also generated moral ambivalences and provoked cultural reaction against evangelicalism. Second, parallel study of the move-ments in Britain and the United States shows considerable similarities in chronology, consciousness, and ideology but also suggests that these very similarities were of a kind that ultimately drove later nineteenth-century evan-gelicalism on to nationalist rather than internationalist paths of development.

In conclusion, we must address the question as to whether this kind of relationship between anti-Catholicism and evangelicalism was a constant char-acteristic of the movement throughout its history, or whether it rather arose from the particular conjunctions and conditions of the period under consider-ation in this chapter. To a considerable extent the issue is one that must be left to scholars of other periods. There were, however, particular facts in the mid-nineteenth century that contributed to the prominence of evangelical anti-Catholicism. These included notably the objective reality of a resurgent Roman Catholic Church and the arrival in both Britain and America of numerous Catholic immigrants. There was also the emergence of a premillennial eschatology—a symptom, it can be argued, of a wider crisis of confidence in a movement that was aware that it had reached or was even passing the pinnacle of its social and cultural influence. However, there were also aspects of anti-Catholicism, discussed in the early part of the chapter, that related in a more timeless ways to fundamentals of evangelical identity. Where conditions were different, as they generally had been in the early nineteenth century, specifically anti-Catholic ideology could remain beneath the surface, but in other periods it was to surface again, notably in the activities of the American Protective Association at the turn of the twentieth century, in the anti-Catholic campaigns waged in Scotland in the 1930s, and in the fervor of Ian Paisley's Free Presbyterian Church in present-day Northern Ireland. Such recurrences provide support for the generalization that evangelicalism assumed a particularly anti-Catholic form at times of crisis and conflict. This did not mean, however, that it was a transient reactive phenomenon. Rather, to use a geological analogy, it was like the granite that underlies the peat moors of Southwest England but breaks through in isolated places to form stark formations of weathered rock. Anti-Catholicism has been an inescapable part of the historical landscape of evangelicalism that can provide valuable viewpoints for understanding the geography of the whole.

Notes

1. The research for this chapter was made possible by a sabbatical leave from the University of York, and by fellowships from the American Antiquarian Society and the Newberry Library, assistance that is acknowledged with gratitude. I have also incurred numerous intellectual debts, particularly to David Bebbington, John Bossy, Christopher Clark, and Donald Lewis, and to my Special Subject students at York, whose ideas contributed substantially to my own thinking.

2. Nathaniel Cheever to Elizabeth Cheever, 6 February 1837, Cheever MS, American Antiquarian Society, Worcester, MA.

3. D. W. Bebbington, *Evangelicalism in Modern Britain: A History from the 1730s to the 1980s* (London: Unwin Hyman, 1989), 2–17.

4. The limitations of the present undertaking must be acknowledged. Material has been drawn primarily from England, Scotland, New England, New York, and Pennsylvania; in focusing on transatlantic comparison, regional variations within the United States and Great Britain cannot be explored in detail. Furthermore, for a full understanding of evangelical anti-Catholicism in the North Atlantic world there would also need to be ample consideration of the Irish and Canadian cases. This chapter represents an initial step toward this kind of wider synthesis.

5. The standard, if now somewhat dated, account of anti-Catholicism in the United States is R. A. Billington, *The Protestant Crusade* (New York: Macmillan, 1938). For more recent perspectives, see M. Feldberg, *The Philadelphia Riots of 1844* (Westport, CT: Greenwood, Press, 1975), 41–50. On Britain, see G. F. A. Best, "Popular Protestantism in Victorian England," in *Ideas and Institutions of Victorian Britain,* ed. R. Robson (London: G. Bell and Sons, 1967), 115–42; E. R. Norman, *Anti-Catholicism in Victorian England* (London: Allen and Unwin, 1968); W. L. Arnstein, *Protestant versus Catholic in Mid-Victorian England* (Columbia: University of Missouri Press, 1982); J. Wolffe, *The Protestant Crusade in Great Britain, 1829–1860* (Oxford: Clarendon Press, 1991).

6. Wolffe, *Protestant Crusade,* 312–17 and elsewhere.

7. For further information on the aspects of anti-Catholicism mentioned here, see the works cited in n. 5 above. Also, on popular culture and anti-Catholicism in Britain,

see R. D. Storch, "Please to Remember the Fifth of November," in *Popular Culture and Custom in Nineteenth-Century Britain,* ed. Storch (London: Croom Helm, 1982); and also D. G. Paz, *Popular Anti-Catholicism in Mid-Victorian England* (Stanford: Stanford University Press, 1992); on the United States, see John Higham, *Strangers in the Land* (New York: Atheneum, 1963). On politics, see Wolffe, *Protestant Crusade;* R. P. Formisano, *The Transformation of Political Culture: Massachusetts Parties, 1790s–1840s* (New York: Oxford University Press, 1983); D. W. Howe, *The Political Culture of the American Whigs* (Chicago: University of Chicago Press, 1979); and on the Irish, R. Swift and S. Gilly, eds., *The Irish in the Victorian City* (London: Croom Helm, 1985); Dale T. Knobel, *Paddy and the Republic: Ethnicity and Nationality in Antebellum America* (Middletown, CT: Wesleyan University Press, 1986); and Kerby A. Miller, *Emigrants and Exiles: Ireland and the Irish Exodus to North America* (New York: Oxford University Press, 1985).

8. E. Bickersteth, *Remarks on the Progress of Popery* (London: Seeley, 1836), 3–4, 26.

9. *Address [of the Rev. L. Bacon, D. D., and Rev. E. N. Kirk] at the Annual Meeting of the Christian Alliance [held in New York, May 6 1845, with the Address of the Society and the Bull of the Pope against it]* (New York, 1846), 16.

10. Kirk to Finney, 21 March 1831 and 27 June 1832, Finney MS, Oberlin College; Nathaniel Cheever to Elizabeth Cheever, 23 March 1841, Cheever MS; D. O. Mears, *Life of Edward Norris Kirk, D. D.* (Boston: Lockwood, Brooks, 1877); G. M. Rosell and R. A. G. Dupuis, eds., *The Memoirs of Charles G. Finney* (Grand Rapids: Zondervan, 1989), 443–44; R. Carwardine, *Transatlantic Revivalism: Popular Evangelicalism in Britain and America, 1790–1865* (Westport, CT: Greenwood Press, 1978).

11. J. Cumming, *Apocalyptic Sketches,* 9th ed. (London: Hall, 1849), 510.

12 *Third Annual Report of the American and Foreign Christian Union* (New York, 1852), 40; Wolffe, *Protestant Crusade,* 145–97.

13. Gordon to Liverpool, 22 December 1824, Additional MS 38299 (Liverpool papers), fols. 238–39, British Library, London.

14. G. B. Cheever, *Right of the Bible in our Public Schools* (New York: R. Carter and Bros., 1854); J. Murphy, *The Religious Problem in English Education* (Liverpool: Liverpool University Press, 1959).

15. G. B. Cheever, *The Religion of Experience and that of Imitation: An Address delivered before the Society of Inquiry on Missions in Amherst College, Augutst 1843* (New York: J. F. Trow, 1843), 7–9; J. H. Lee, *The Origin and Progress of the American Party in Politics* (Philadelphia: Elliot and Gihon, 1855), 136–63; A. E. Carroll, *Great American Battle; or, The contest between Christianity and Political Romanism* (New York: Miller, Orton and Mulligan, 1856), Introduction by Galpin, vii; Feldberg, *Philadelphia Riots,* 95.

16. T. R. Birks, *Memoirs of the Rev. Edward Bickersteth,* 2 vols., 2d ed. (London: Seeleys, 1852), 2:89.

17. *First Annual Report of the American Protestant Association together with a sketch of the Addresses at the First Anniversary, November 18, 1843* (Philadelphia, 1844), 12.

18. Bacon, *Addresses at the Annual Meeting of the Christian Alliance,* 13.

19. A. Norton, *Alternative Americas* (Chicago: University of Chicago Press, 1986), 90.

20. *Record,* 26 August and 14 October 1830 and elsewhere; *Addresses at the Annual Meeting of the Christian Alliance,* 13; Norton, *Alternative Americas,* 86. On evangelical individualism, see Richard J. Helmstadter, "The Nonconformist Conscience,"

in *Religion in Victorian Britain,* vol. 4: *Interpretations,* ed. Gerald Parsons (Manchester: Manchester University Press, 1988), 82.

21. Carwardine, *Transatlantic Revivalism.*

22. H. M. Baird, *The Life of the Rev. Robert Baird, D.D.* (New York: A. D. F. Randolph, 1866), 228, 232, 248, 255, 285; R. M. York, *George B. Cheever, Religious and Social Reformer, 1807–90* (Orono: University of Maine Press, 1955), 90–94, 177–81. There were competing New York editions of Charlotte Elizabeth's works; see *New York Observer,* 25 January 1845, advertisement by John S. Taylor; *The Works of Charlotte Elizabeth, with an Introduction by H. Stowe,* 2 vols., 8th ed. (New York: M. W. Dodd, 1850).

23. *Record,* 23 May 1828; *First Annual Report of the Foreign Evangelical Society* (New York, 1840).

24. L. Bacon, *Christian Unity. A Sermon Preached before the Foreign Evangelical Society in The Blicker Street Church, New York, May 4, 1845* (New Haven, 1845), 25 and elsewhere.

25. British Reformation Society minutes (in the custody of the present general secretary), 21 May 1827; *American Protestant Society, Circular* (New York, 1847), 15.

26. Wolffe, *Protestant Crusade,* 171–76; *British Reformation Society, Fifteenth Annual Report* (London 1842), 10–11; *Twelfth Annual Report of the Islington Protestant Institute* (London, 1859), 14–15.

27. Wolffe, *Protestant Crusade,* 57, 134–35; Nathan O. Hatch, *The Democratization of American Christianity* (New Haven: Yale University Press, 1989), esp. 162–89; *Priestcraft Unmasked* (n.p., 1830).

28. *Fifth Annual Report of the American Protestant Society* (New York, 1848), 6–7; Wolffe, *Protestant Crusade,* 286.

29. *Second Annual Report of the Protestant Alliance* (London, 1853), 18–35.

30. Ibid.

31. Hope to Cumming, 7 March 1848, Hope MSS, GD253/226/6, p. 669, Scottish Record Office, Edinburgh. The observation concerning the overlap with the membership of other organizations rests on extensive impressionistic evidence; systematic verification would require detailed comparison of membership lists.

32. This judgment is based on a comparison of the following lists: *Fourth Annual Report of the American Protestant Society* (New York, 1847), 34–39; *Proceedings of the Native American State Convention* (Newbury, VT, 1847), 2; *Native American State Convention, Harrisburg* (Philadelphia, 1847), 4–7; *Fifth Annual Report of the American and Foreign Christian Union* (New York, 1854), 69–89; Native American Party, MS membership list, American Antiquarian Society.

33. Feldberg, *Philadelphia Riots,* 59–60.

34. Wolffe, *Protestant Crusade,* 42–43, 74–76, 88–95, 215.

35. T. Brainerd, *Our Country Safe from Romanism. A Sermon Delivered at the Opening of the Third Presbytery of Philadelphia, at its Sessions in the Western Presbyterian Church, Philadelphia, April 1841* (Philadelphia: L. R. Bailey, 1843).

36. MS, SHA/PD/5, 19 May 1849, Department of Manuscripts, Southampton University Library, Southampton.

37. D. M. Lewis, *Lighten Their Darkness: The Evangelical Mission to Working-Class London, 1828–1860* (Westport, CT: Greenwood Press, 1986), 29–34, 100–103; George Barrell Cheever to Nathaniel Cheever, 22 January 1844, Cheever MS.

38. *Awful Disclosures by Maria Monk* (New York: Hoisington and Trow, 1836); William L. Stone, *Maria Monk and the Nunnery of the Hotel Dieu* (New York: Howe and Bates, 1836), 47.

39. *Awful Exposure of the Atrocious Plot formed by Certain Individuals against the clergy and nuns of Lower Canada, through the Intervention of Maria Monk* (New York, 1836).

40. *New York Observer,* 21 May 1836; Stone, *Maria Monk,* 53.

41. I have not noticed any reference to the affair in the *Record,* a leading Anglican Evangelical paper, during the period of 1836, when controversy was raging in the United States.

42. Mortimer O'Sullivan and Robert J. M'Ghee, *Romanism as it Rules in Ireland,* 2 vols. (London: Seeley and Burnside, 1840), 1:578; cf. Leonore Davidoff and Catherine Hall, *Family Fortunes: Men and Women of the English Middle Class* (London: Hutchinson, 1987).

43. T. Pinney, ed., *Essays of George Eliot* (New York: Columbia University Press, 1963), 186.

44. Charles Beecher, ed., *Autobiography, Correspondence, etc, of Lyman Beecher, D.D.* (New York: Harper and Brothers, 1864); Charles Edward Stowe, *Life of Harriet Beecher Stowe* (London: Sampson Low [and others], 1889); *Works of Charlotte Elizabeth,* Introduction.

45. Elizabeth Jay, *The Religion of the Heart: Anglican Evangelicalism and the Nineteenth Century Novel* (Oxford: Clarendon Press, 1979), 224–43.

46. J. Wolffe, "The Evangelical Alliance in the 1840s: An Attempt to Institutionalise Christian Unity," in *Voluntary Religion,* Studies in Church History 23, ed. W. J. Sheils and D. Wood (Oxford: Blackwell, 1986), 333–46. See also, R. Rouse, "Voluntary Movements and the Changing Ecumenical Climate," in *A History of the Ecumenical Movement, 1517–1948,* vol. 1, ed. R. Rouse and S. C. Neill (London: SPCK, 1967), 318–24; E. R. Sandeen, "The Distinctiveness of American Denominationalism: A Case Study of the 1846 Evangelical Alliance," *Church History* 45 (1976): 222–34; P. D. Jordan, *The Evangelical Alliance for the United States of America, 1847–1900: Ecumenism, Identity, and the Religion of the Republic* (New York: Edwin Mellen Press, 1983).

47. R. Baird, *The Progress and Prospects of Christianity in the United States of America* (London: Partridge and Oakey, 1851), 51; H. M. Baird, *Life of the Rev. Robert Baird,* 229–30.

48. Wolffe, "Evangelical Alliance," 340–41.

49. Sandeen, "Distinctiveness of American Denominationalism," 226–31; *Evangelical Alliance: Report of the Proceedings of the Conference held at Freemasons' Hall London, from August 19th to September 2nd . . . 1846* (London, 1847), 292–93, 405.

50. Baird, *Progress and Prospects,* 44–48, 56, 58.

51. H. McNeile, *England's Protest is England's Shield, for the Battle is the Lord's* (London, 1829), 16–17; G. B. Cheever, *God's Hand in America* (New York: W. M. Dodd, 1841); J. Wolffe, "Evangelicalism in Mid-Nineteenth-Century England," in *Patriotism: The Making and Unmaking of British National Identity,* ed. R. Samuel (London: Routledge, 1989), 1:188–200; E. L. Tuveson, *Redeemer Nation: The Idea of America's Millennial Role* (Chicago: University of Chicago Press, 1968).

52. *Record,* 7 September 1846.

53. George Cheever to Charlotte Cheever, 24 March 1853, Cheever MS; Billington, *Protestant Crusade,* 301–4; B. Hall, "Alessandro Gavazzi: A Barnebite Friar and the Risorgimento," in *Church, Society, and Politics,* Studies in Church History 12, ed. D. Baker (Oxford: Blackwell, 1975), 342–56.

54. York, *George B. Cheever,* 129–30; *Eighth Annual Report of the American and*

Foreign Christian Union, 90; C. T. McIntire, *England against the Papacy, 1858–1861* (Cambridge: Cambridge University Press, 1983), 29–39.

55. Bacon, *Christian Unity,* 27–28.

56. Sandeen, "Distinctiveness of American Denominationalism"; W. L. Gienapp, *The Origins of the Republican Party, 1852–1856* (New York: Oxford University Press, 1987), 444–47 and elsewhere; D. W. Bebbington, "Religion and National Identity in Nineteenth Century Wales and Scotland," in *Religion and National Identity,* Studies in Church History 18, ed. S. Mews (Oxford: Blackwell, 1982), 489–503; F. S. L. Lyons, *Culture and Anarchy in Ireland, 1890–1939* (Oxford: Oxford University Press, 1982), 113–45.

10

Evangelicals, Politics, and the Coming of the American Civil War: A Transatlantic Perspective

RICHARD CARWARDINE

The common experience of religious "awakening" in Britain and the United States in the first third of the nineteenth century produced an enlarged and invigorated evangelicalism on both sides of the Atlantic. One important result was to enhance the political influence of evangelical Protestantism at a time of dramatic changes in the countries' political systems. In the third and fourth decades of the century both America and Britain witnessed a widening of the franchise that in one case opened the door to discernibly modern mass democratic politics and in the other hastened the shift from the politics of influence to the politics of opinion.

"Christianity pervades the United States in vigorous action," wrote the English Methodist James Dixon, following a visit to American churches in 1848. "It touches and influences the entire social and political state. It is not meant by that that every individual is a pious Christian, but that the spirit of the evangelical system is in sufficient power to give to religious opinion and sentiment the complete ascendant in society."[1] Though evangelicals formed a minority of the population, and though a majority of them were disfranchised women and children, Dixon saw that they still exercised a huge cultural influence. Among them the largest denominational families (Methodists, Baptists, Presbyterians, and Congregationalists) boasted a membership in 1850 of nearly three million, some 13 percent of the total population. Even at a conservative estimate—adopting a ratio of church hearers to members of only 2:1—it seems that in the immediate antebellum years at least one American in three came under the direct influence of the major evangelical churches.[2] Though evangelicals were a numerically less potent force in British society, they were sufficiently well represented among the newly enfranchised middle classes, and among artisans, to exercise a political influence out of proportion to their numbers.[3]

As I have argued elsewhere, in a discussion of British religion and politics in the nineteenth century, there are enough parallels and linkages in the political experiences of British and American evangelicals in these years to question one of the implicit (and sometimes explicit) claims in much of the historiography: that American religiopolitical arrangements, constructed around the novelties of mass democracy and a free market in the religion, made the young republic historically unique and truly exceptional among contemporary nations.[4] In fact, there were, in contradiction to this view, certain common elements in the transatlantic experience. This contention may be developed by focusing principally on American and not British developments, and under three headings: evangelicals' perceptions of their proper political responsibilities; evangelicalism's contribution to the style, language, and substantive issues of the new political order; and the relationship between church affiliation and party political loyalty. This triple analysis will introduce a discussion of evangelicalism's role in the coming of the Civil War, and of the ways in which this too might be placed in a wider Atlantic context.

I

First, there was much that was similar in how evangelicals on both sides of the Atlantic perceived their role and duties as Christian citizens in a changing political cosmos. Through much of the American history there have been two Protestant approaches to political engagement, what George Marsden has labeled the pietist and the Calvinist responses.[5] The pietist (or quietist) tradition has sought to keep the worlds of politics and religion firmly separate. These conservative, nonpolitical evangelicals existed in all denominational families in America in the first half of the nineteenth century but were most likely to be found among southern Methodists and Baptists. They took a largely New Testament, experiential perspective and tended toward holiness or even premillennial revivalism. They pointed to Christ's instruction not to interfere with political institutions. A small minority even refused to vote. Millerite Adventists, for instance, regarded elections as supremely irrelevant during the last days before Christ's return.

Nonetheless, in antebellum America the vigorous Calvinist, or Reformed, tradition of political engagement (so influential during the revolution and the founding of the new nation) helped promote an assertive evangelical involvement in political life, even among Arminian Methodists, the largest single denominational family in the country. Calvinists believed that all Christians had a responsibility to sustain Christian behavior in public life, by using the vote to elect good men and by pressing for moral laws. Though they were hesitant about various aspects of the new political arrangements of Jacksonian America (which appeared to subordinate individual conscience to the demands of party and encouraged fierce, "unchristian" electoral competition), most evangelicals responded not by withdrawing from politics but by trying to reform politics. As the preeminent revivalist Charles Grandison Finney explained, "Politics are a part of religion in such a country as this." By mid-century most male evangelical Protestants (and quite a number of women, too, though they could not vote) were deeply involved in politics. They attended political rallies and subscribed to political papers. Many were party activists. Some stood for, and were elected to, public office. Some even called for the creation of a specifically Christian party.[6]

In Britain, too, the Reformed tradition gained at the expense of the quietist, so that by the mid-Victorian years it exercised a political influence unparalleled since the time of Cromwell. The "no politics" philosophy that had guided so many Nonconformists and Methodists at the turn of the century yielded to greater involvement, especially under the impact of the antislavery campaign of the 1830s and the movement for suffrage reform. Nonconformist ministers such as George Dawson and R. W. Dale encouraged their members to carry their religious energies and chapel morality into public affairs and to treat their votes as a sacred trust. They should scrutinize the moral pedigree of public men, to whom they looked for the development of a state that would actively promote the moral well-being of its people by eliminating sin. In sum, Nonconformists sought to match their enhanced social prestige with an equivalent political influence.[7]

A second common feature in the style and substance of politics in both countries during the mid-nineteenth century was profoundly influenced by evangelicals' language, religious sensibilities, and moral imperatives. The shapers of the American "second party system," which reached its mature form from 1840 to the early 1850s, both consciously and unthinkingly drew on the world of evangelical Protestantism, and in particular the revivalism of the Second Great Awakening. Seeking to create national political organizations in the face of local and regional loyalties, politicians drew on supportive elements in the wider culture. As Donald Mathews has observed, the awakening was itself an organizing process; national connections sustained itinerant revivalists and widely circulating newspapers, which gave recruits a sense of belonging to a community beyond the immediate locality. Politicians found in the culture of mass revivalism much they could build into their political practice. They had ministers open party conventions with prayers and addresses; they multiplied political meetings and rotated speakers, in direct imitation of protracted and camp meetings; their political songs incorporated the language and tunes of evangelical hymns; like religious revivalists, party activists sought to rally the faithful, draw in the undecided, and reclaim the backsliders. Political campaigners cultivated, as did revivalists, the sense of a world sharply divided between irreconcilable powers; the revivalists' antitheses of good and evil, heaven and hell, God and Devil found their way into politicians' appeals that presented voters with a choice, not between two sets of morally neutral policies, but between two moral orders, between political salvation and the victory of the Devil.[8]

In the Whigs' successful "log-cabin campaign" of 1840, for example, the party's propagandists sought to play on evangelicals' heightened anxiety that Protestant influence on public life was dwindling and that responsibility lay with the Democrats' twelve-year control of the executive branch. They pre-

sented their candidate, William Henry Harrison, as a man of religious outlook, humanity, and moral probity, wholly in tune with what Daniel Howe has
described as the party's concern for self-control, self-restraint, and the preservation of moral order through active government. Harrison emerged as a
good Christian, a Sabbatarian, and (despite being the candidate of hard cider
and the victor at Tippecanoe) the friend of temperance and the Indians. They
portrayed their opponents, the "Locofocos," as atheists and religious per-
verts, allied with Mormons, Catholics, and freethinkers; they cast the Democratic candidate, Martin Van Buren ("Patrick O'Buren") as a toady of the
pope and an appeaser of Irish and German voters.

Adopting a similar approach in 1844, Whigs tried to turn Henry Clay into
an upright, God-fearing, benevolent citizen, but now the strategy was less
appropriate. Clay was the son of a Baptist minister but was no moral paragon.
His record of dueling and gambling opened the way for Democrats to claim
that his life had been "one continued scene of vice and immorality from his
earliest manhood to decayed old age," and to sneer that the Whigs were "for
religion, but they want Clay first." Whigs sought to square the circle by
nominating for the vice-presidency Theodore J. Frelinghuysen, probably the
most illustrious lay evangelical in the country, one seen more frequently on
the religious platform than the political hustings. With Frelinghuysen "sanctifying the ticket," Whigs posed once more as the guardians of a Christian
polity under attack from a variety of quarters, especially Rome. At a time
when many evangelicals were fearful of what they saw as the Catholic threat
to Bible reading in common schools (fears that provoked bloody riots in
Philadelphia in the summer of 1844), who could better assert the Whigs'
pretensions to being the "Protestant party" than the stalwart of the American
Bible Society, Frelinghuysen himself?[9]

Party managers adopted political discourse of this kind because they recognized the electoral potential of evangelicals, who made it clear they expected
moral integrity among public men. Evangelicals' stress on individual moral
discipline and self-control had implications for social regulation and order.
Their emphasis on duty and conscience ensured that they treated political
issues less according to the measure of social utility than of moral propriety
and scriptural injunction. They brought their ethical perspectives to bear on
government economic policy. With even more energy they ensured that the
questions of education, Indian removal, Sabbath observance, war, drink, and,
above all, slavery were placed firmly on the political agenda, as part of the
Christian's obligation conscientiously to advance a moral republic. Without
political parties and professional political leadership, popular sentiments
would have tended to remain unchanneled. Party leaders, however, by no
means had a free hand in setting the terms of political debate.

In Britain, too, with the development of pressure politics after the Reform
Act of 1832, energetic religious groups and sympathetic political insiders together "moralized" politics. The Dissenters' campaign against slavery in the
1830s marked a new, evangelistic style of extraparliamentary effort. Other
crusades followed against the Corn Laws, Sabbath breaking, drink, sexual

license, and Roman Catholicism, to each of which reformers brought a biblicism, Manichaeanism, and suspicion of compromise that resembled the attitudes of their American counterparts. Their methods, including petitioning, "indignation meetings," questioning candidates, and lobbying political representatives, also paralleled those of American evangelicals. Through the 1840s and 1850s Nonconformists developed a coordinated electoral strategy, supporting or opposing the Liberal party according to its response to their demands, and reached the pinnacle of their influence as pressure politicians in the 1860s. Many Victorian politicians, and William Ewart Gladstone in particular, sought to harness the religious energies and political strength of evangelicals by appealing to their Protestant sensibilities. It was no accident that Victorian politics revolved around such issues as education, temperance, anti-Catholicism, and disestablishment.[10]

There is a third important common element that links Britain and the United States in this period. Since the appearance of Lee Benson's pioneering work on Jacksonian New York over thirty years ago, a generation of "ethnocultural" historians, including Ronald Formisano, Michael Holt, and Paul Kleppner, have argued that religious loyalties were a major, and often the main, determinant of party attachment among nineteenth-century American voters. Controversial as their work has been, and open as it remains to methodological criticism, it provides the basis for a number of important conclusions, namely, that evangelical support for the Whigs and Democrats, the two principal parties from the 1830s to the early 1850s, and later for the Republicans and Democrats of the "third party system," was not random; that interdenominational antagonisms and evangelicals' views of the proper relationship between church and state, of the role of government in regulating a moral society, and of what constituted a Christian republic all shaped party attachment; that though pious Protestants resided in both parties, certain denominational groupings demonstrated markedly stronger support for one over another; that "New Divinity" Calvinists, especially Congregationalists and New School Presbyterians, along with Quakers, were strongly Whig (and later Republican); that Democrats were especially strong among Catholics, Antimission Baptists, and "ritualist" Protestants; and that, though many Methodists, Baptists and Old School Democrats defected to Whiggery and Republicanism, vast numbers remained true to a Democratic party that under Jefferson had secured for their mothers and fathers some respite from the intolerance of the established or socially dominant Protestant churches.[11] Even in the South, where religious culture on the surface appeared much more homogeneous than in the North, denominational conflicts within Protestantism, reflecting antagonistic perspectives on the world, helped bind voters to particular parties. In some Appalachian communities, for instance, the most profound socioreligious divisions were those between Methodists (Whig) and Baptists (Democrat).[12]

In Britain, similarly, denominational and party loyalties were related. This was most evidently the case where Anglicanism and Dissent were in sharpest competition, notably in Wales and in most urban and industrial areas. While the American polarities were between Democratic "outgroups" and New England or Yankee-oriented Whiggish-Republicans, those in Britain were also based on tensions between Anglican "insiders" and Nonconformist and Roman Catholic "outsiders." At first, Old Dissent turned in its pursuit of religious liberty to the Whigs; then through the 1850s and 1860s politically active Dissenters moved increasingly to Liberalism, both as a negative reaction against Tory Anglicanism and more positively in response to the party's radical stance on free trade, class harmony, and international brotherhood. During the second half of the century most rising entrepreneurs, tradesmen, shopkeepers, and skilled workmen who composed voting Nonconformity were firmly Liberal. As "outsiders" seeking freedom and recognition, British Nonconformists played a role equivalent to that of evangelical Democrats in America. But their openness to state intervention in pursuit of temperance and Sabbatarian legislation, for example, and their optimistic faith in economic progress and social improvement made them more obviously and philosophically allies of postmillennialist and commercially oriented Whigs and Republicans.[13]

II

In some important respects, then, American political evangelicalism is best seen in a wider transatlantic context; it certainly cannot be treated as wholly exceptional. But what of evangelicals' role in the approach of what by definition was a uniquely American experience, the Civil War? The question prompts a number of inquiries about the consequences of evangelical thought and practice for social and political stability. What function did evangelicals play in creating and sustaining social order? How far did their cosmology and energies work to challenge and subvert the political status quo?

Such questions, thanks especially to the writings of Elie Halévy and subsequently E. P. Thompson, have long been on the agenda of British historians. The familiar argument that evangelicalism in general, and Methodism in particular, acted as a conservative instrument of embourgeoisement, as a diversionary bromide that saved Britain from social upheaval and revolution, needs no further rehearsal here.[14] Though there has been no dominating "Halévy thesis" among American historians, scholars of the early and middle periods of American history have spiritedly discussed the extent to which the religious radicalism generated by the eighteenth-century Great Awakening may have shaped the American Revolution,[15] and (paradoxically) how far the Second Great Awakening functioned to preserve social control and order in a rapidly changing world.[16]

But what of the breakdown of American national consensus in the 1840s and 1850s, and the coming of the Civil War? Though there is much perceptive scholarship on the public guises of evangelical Christianity in antebellum America, the precise part played by evangelicalism in promoting or retarding the greatest political upheaval in the Anglo-American world in the nineteenth century has, remarkably, attracted little systematic attention. Yet in the voluminous historiography of the causes of the war there are a number of indications of the relative importance of religious influences. It is clear that evangelical Protestants have played significant roles in two main polarities of interpretation, one based on the concept of the needless war, the other on that of an irrepressible conflict.

Early in the war itself, some contemporary observers claimed that hostilities were based on no fundamental differences between the two sections but were the product of abolitionists' and secessionists' emotional and extravagant reactions to artificial issues. David Ross Locke satirized the opinions of peace Democrats through the fictional character of Petroleum V. Nasby, who blamed the radical abolitionists of Finney's Oberlin College for beginning the war: "Oberlin wuz the prime cause uv all the trouble. . . . When I say Oberlin, understand it ez figgerative for the entire Ablishn party, wich Oberlin is the fountinhead." More solemnly, C. C. S. Farrar argued a similar case in 1864, particularly blaming northern Protestant ministers for promulgating abolitionism and doing more than all other groups together to bring about the crisis.[17] Many years later, during the 1930s and 1940s, when the "needless war" interpretation took on academic respectability through the writings of the so-called revisionist historians, the evangelically minded antislavery reformers of the North reappeared as "pious cranks" who, aided by "short-sighted politicians" and "overzealous editors," poisoned the minds of "well-meaning Americans" and conjured up distorted impressions of the other section.[18] Evangelicalism, or at least that part of it associated with radical abolitionism, emerges in this interpretation as a destructive force, feeding irrationality and fanaticism, forcing the South on the defensive and creating the climate in which southern fire-eating radicals could prepare the ground for secession.

That the conflict between the two sections was not artificial, but was based on deep-seated differences, was a perception current before the outbreak of war. In the 1850s both William Seward and Abraham Lincoln believed that the Union was facing what the senator from New York described as an "irrepressible conflict" rooted not simply in antagonistic labor systems but in deep differences of moral and religious outlook. James Ford Rhodes's influential, landmark history of the war also regarded the conflict as almost entirely about slavery, specifically about slavery as a moral question.[19] In the twentieth century some proponents of the "irrepressible conflict" interpretation have followed Charles and Mary Beard in minimizing slavery's role as a religious or ethical question, regarding the conflict as essentially a materialist clash between two economic systems. Most historians, however, have judged that economic differences alone need not have produced confrontation of the kind that split the Union, and that only divergent cultures, moralities, and values related to the conflicting systems of free and slave labor explain the country's political and social polarization.[20]

In this context many historians of antislavery and emergent abolitionism have adopted a more positive perspective on the "immediatists" than did the revisionists. If (as the cliometricians tell us) slavery was getting economically stronger in the antebellum period and not weaker, then it was not (despite the claims of Charles Ramsdell and other revisionists) an institution that could be left to die of its own accord.[21] Adopting a perspective prefigured in the 1930s by Gilbert Hobbs Barnes,[22] most modern scholarship on antislavery evangelicals backs away from treating them as irresponsible fanatics; rather, it has shown how a combination of millennialist optimism and a rationally based ethic of moral and social improvement drove many evangelicals toward antislavery reform.[23] In common with the revisionists, however, it sees them as moving spirits behind an agitation that contributed, through Liberty, Free-Soil, and Republican parties, to sectional breakdown.[24]

Although it is the minority of evangelicals who have appeared most prominently in the historiography of Civil War causation—as destabilizing abolitionists—the larger community of evangelicals, too, does intrude into the analysis, principally in the context of their experience of church division. The schisms in the major denominations (Baptist, Methodist, and Presbyterian) have been taken as at the very least emblematic of developing sectional chauvinism, and as in some ways contributory to the process of national breakdown. As Allan Nevins, one of the proponents of the "slavery and cultural conflict" interpretation, has written, by 1857 northerners and southerners "were rapidly becoming separate peoples," a process of alienation encouraged by the fracturing of the churches.[25] But only recently, in Clarence Goen's thoughtful extended essay, have the implications of church schism for the breakup of the Union been worked through in any detail.[26]

Paradoxically, the collective writings of the so-called ethnocultural or new political historians, which more than any others treat religion as a serious element in antebellum political life, have in some ways tended to work against incorporating religion into an analysis of the coming of war. Joel Silbey's influential essay "The Civil War Synthesis in American Political History" in particular, reinforced by some of the emphases in Holt's and Formisano's studies of Pittsburgh and Michigan, tends to present evangelical northerners as more interested in local religious questions (Bible reading in common schools, prohibition, Sabbath observance, restrictions on Roman Catholics) than in national debates on the slavery question.[27] There is an apparent dichotomy between "religious" issues in politics and "sectional" ones, the implication being that religion was a diversionary and somewhat irrational influence as far as the wider sectional conflict was concerned.[28] But as David Potter demonstrated some years ago, and as William Gienapp notes in his recent study of the origins of the Republican party, the relationship between ethnocultural issues and antislavery reform in northern Protestant thought and politics was complementary, not dichotomous. It is possible to hold on to the essence of the new political history, giving evangelicals a salient electoral role, and also to incorporate them as active agents in sectional breakdown.

III

Political historians, then, have by no means ignored evangelicalism in their analyses of the coming of the Civil War, which in the main have tended to emphasize religion's politically destabilizing and socially divisive impact. But despite their increasing attention to religion, even recent treatments of antebellum politics and sectional cultural antipathies continue to focus very largely on the secular dimensions of that crisis. We still lack a sustained explanation of how, and how far, evangelical religion shaped the political culture and sectional antagonisms of antebellum America.[29] But some generalizations may be essayed here.

The emergence of the Republican party, whose electoral victory in 1860 triggered the immediate crisis of the Union, was dependent on a particular understanding of politics, one that evangelicals had played a major role in shaping. That political ethic was rooted in the "Arminianized" Calvinist theology of the Second Great Awakening, marked by an optimistic postmillennialism and an urgent appeal to disinterested action. In the early decades of the century evangelicals' strenuous doctrines of duty and moral uplift led them to promote a variety of benevolent causes, including temperance, Sabbath observance, education, and Protestant nurture. At first they directed their efforts to cultivate a Christian republic through voluntary organizations outside politics. But as the nation moved from a more deferential form of republicanism toward a discernably modern mass democracy, evangelicals came to see that politics might be an agency for Christianizing the republic. The Sabbatarian and Anti-Masonic crusades demonstrated evangelicals' potential for mobilizing pious voters behind a program of political purification.[30] As we have seen, the significance of this lesson was not lost on the organizers of the amalgam of anti-Jacksonians that made up the Whig party. A doctrine of moral improvement gave that party its ideological glue, and this, along with Whiggery's emphasis on social and economic modernization, ensured that it attracted more than its fair share of postmillennialists.

Harsh reality, however, prevented Whigs from establishing themselves as the "Christian party" that would monopolize the evangelical Protestant vote. Evangelicals' perspectives and social aspirations were too varied for them to act as a political monolith. Furthermore, the more that northern Protestants fashioned an antislavery imperative and expected Whig politicians to obey the voice of conscience in dealing with that peculiar institution, the more difficult it became for those leaders, who needed southern votes, to respond as energetically as the "higher-law" people demanded. In fact, they survived the electoral inroads of the conscience-driven and strongly evangelical Liberty and Free-Soil movements. But when they also failed to meet evangelicals' expectations over Prohibition, the Bible in common schools, and other anti-Catholic strategies, the party's days as the vehicle for postmillennialist northerners were numbered.[31] For a brief period it seemed that the American, or Know-Nothing, party might provide a lasting basis for moral politics, but it too proved a flawed instrument.[32]

Northern political postmillennialism culminated in the Republican party. Republicans acquired their essential moral energy from evangelical Protestantism and drew on the public discourse of evangelicals as it had been elaborated over a quarter of a century. To some extent this was a discourse of paranoia.

Fears of Freemasons and Catholics as conspirators against the Christian republic had impelled many evangelicals into politics. Anti-Masonic and Know-Nothing parties certainly mobilized many new voters, and their concern over conspiracy carried over into the fear of the Slave Power that formed so potent an element of Free-Soil and Republican appeals. But evangelical discourse also brought to politics a less defensive emphasis on conscience, obedience to the higher law, Calvinistic duty, self-discipline, and social responsibility—a creed that reached its fullest expression in the triumphalist early years of the Republican movement. That movement's pious Protestant supporters went further than American evangelicals had ever done before in identifying the arrival of the kingdom of God with the success of a particular political party. When during the campaigns of 1856 and 1860 ministers officiated with equal enthusiasm at revival meetings and at Republican rallies, it was clear that religion and politics had fused more completely than ever before in the American republic.[33]

The religious meaning that Republican evangelicals attached to political action moved well beyond what most southern Christians could understand or tolerate. Evangelicals in the slave states were indeed not as apolitical as most of them insisted; while northern churchgoers fashioned an antislavery imperative, many southern Protestants simultaneously developed a justification for proslavery action. Nor were southern evangelicals unwilling to invest partisanship with moral meaning. They also shared northern evangelicals' dichotomized worldview, one reinforced by the honor code that still flourished in the South and to which they responded with some ambivalence. But most southern evangelicals resisted the explicit fusing of politics and religion and remained divided in their partisan allegiances. Most critical of all, they deplored Republican evangelicals' linking the inauguration of God's kingdom to the triumph of a party. When southern evangelicals protested that the North had breached the conventions surrounding the proper relationship between church and state, they identified a point of real distinction between the evangelicals of the two sections.[34]

The mutual alienation of northern and southern Protestants, which reached its climax in 1861, when two "Christian" sections faced one another in arms, was thus in part a product of their active molding of secular politics. As politically engaged citizens, evangelicals reached their own moral judgments on sectional issues, including the Fugitive Slave Law, the Kansas-Nebraska Act, the bleeding of Kansas Territory, the Dred Scott decision, and John Brown's raid at Harper's Ferry. What is poorly understood is that this sectional alienation also derived from events within as well as outside the churches, particularly the denominational schisms and the revival of 1857–1858. Both help us understand how evangelicals' generalized concern over slavery, abolitionism, and sectional aggression was given particular meaning by their experience as members of evangelical churches.

Each of the three schisms that rocked the national churches in the 1830s and 1840s was directly or indirectly related to the issue of slaveholding within the churches. Far from ending intersectional bitterness, as many predicted, the process of separation served only to generate new and persisting tensions. The split in the Methodist Episcopal Church provides the most dramatic and telling example. When the General Conference in New York in May 1844 voted to remove James O. Andrew of Georgia from the episcopacy for being married to a slaveowner, southerners moved down the road to schism. Under a Plan of Separation, resources were to be divided; the annual conferences in the slave states would establish an independent church. This they did at Louisville in May 1845, organizing the Methodist Episcopal Church, South. The border conflict that followed the setting up of the MECS and persisted through to the Civil War has rarely received its due in the historiography of developing sectionalism, no doubt because its Methodist label suggests a parochial collision of essentially ecclesiastical significance. (It curiously receives little or no attention in Goen's recent study.) But the events in this conflict were far-flung, dramatic, often ugly, and of great significance for the development of wider sectional antipathies.[35]

The Plan of Separation had sought to establish the basis for drawing a 1,200-mile line through those "border conferences" of the MEC that held jurisdiction over nonslaveholding territory but that also penetrated into the slave states of Maryland, Virginia, Kentucky, Arkansas, and Missouri. Here men and women of foreign and northern descent, and ordinary southern folk of antislavery pedigree, faced devoted members of the southern church. "Societies, stations, and conferences" along the slaveholding-nonslaveholding line could by majority vote decide their allegiance, and once that loyalty was established, the authorities of the other church would not attempt to form their own societies. MEC hardliners were unhappy about terms that seemed likely to leave most of the South to the operations of a "slavery church" and deprived thousands of MEC members of freedom of choice. The plan also left much unclear. In particular, if the dividing line between churches were redrawn as a result of a vote, was the society or station newly abutting the border also allowed to express its collective will? If so (as many southerners believed), what was to prevent a perpetual, unsettling campaign of recruitment?[36]

In practice, the plan gave rise to mounting aggravations, each side seeing the other as nullifiers and predators bent on violation of rights and invasion of territory. Throughout the border area split congregations and complaints of injustice were rife. In a setting where one Methodist's popular majority was another's dissatisfied minority, charges of manipulation and irregular voting proliferated. As sectional temperatures rose, the language of the warring parties grew in violence. The *Christian Advocate and Journal* and the *Western Christian Advocate,* the two most powerful newspapers in the church before the schism, were regularly burned by Virginia magistrates under an act of 1836 giving them power to suppress and destroy seditious materials.[37]

Anger and fear translated into physical intimidation. MEC preachers in Missouri were "threatened hard," seized, and told to go north. Armed southern sympathizers in Clarksburg, Maryland, camped out in the church to prevent MEC loyalists from holding services there. Nowhere was there more violent excitement than in Virginia—in the Kanawha Valley region and on the eastern shore, in Northampton and Accomac counties, where social prestige and judicial power united against the northern church. Here in July 1846 an MEC minister of the Philadelphia Conference was pulled out of the pulpit and dragged from the church. Later a mob at Guildford surrounded the church where another MEC minister was preaching, began shooting, throwing missiles, jeering, and shouting, and broke up the congregation. Thomas Bond concluded that the only rule operating on the eastern shore was mob law.[38]

The tussle for territory and church property led to legal action. The capital and income of the two book concerns, in New York and Cincinnati, proffered the biggest prize of all. Many northern Methodists thought "seceders" had no legitimate claim to a share. Southerners attacked the selfishness and illegality of those who sought to "swindle" them out of what they insisted was properly theirs. The MECS brought suits against the MEC in the United States circuit courts of New York and Ohio in the summer of 1849. The decision in the former suit held in favor of the MECS. The ruling on the Cincinnati Book Room went against the southern church, but on appeal the United States Supreme Court, under Chief Justice Roger Taney, reversed the judgment in April 1854. For thousands of northern Methodists the outcome exposed the proslavery coloring of Taney's court. Three years later antislavery forces exploited the Dred Scott ruling to show that the Slave Power controlled the highest judicial body in the land. But well before then a strategically placed body of opinion formers in northern Methodism had already taken that bitter lesson to heart.[39]

These suppurating intradenominational conflicts were to have a profound effect on evangelicals' political perspectives. Separation bequeathed a legacy of bitterness and sectional stereotyping that seriously corroded evangelicals' sense of belonging to a political and ecclesiastical Union based on common values. Southerners identified northern churchmen with fanatical, irreligious, antirepublican, revolutionary abolitionism and defended having taken the first open step toward national church breakup as a conservative stance against a "war of extermination" against the South. In the view from the South, northerners had sought to remove slaveholders from membership and had embarked on offensive, even conspiratorial, action to deprive the southern churches of their constitutional rights. They had not only betrayed the nation's unique religious mission; their attack on the South's civil institutions made them collaborators in a political scheme to deny southerners their rights under the federal Constitution. The battle being fought by an endangered South was not local but cosmic. The world, as South Carolinians James H. Thornwell and Whitefoord Smith saw it, was "the theatre of an extraordinary conflict of great principles" between true Christianity and social stability on the one side and false religion and "a spirit of insubordination and lawlessness" on the other.[40]

Northern evangelicals similarly attached political significance to the ecclesiastical traumas of the 1840s and 1850s. Schism itself was at bottom designed "to continue and protect slavery," not to defend doctrine or polity, and the emergent churches, seeking to conciliate not only Calhoun but all southern-rights politicians, took their place alongside the other agencies of the Slave Power. The MECS had become "a great politico-ecclesiastical party, for the defense and support of the peculiar political institution of the South." "Southern Aggression" had engineered the schisms. It was southerners who had "practically nullified" the terms of separation; denied freedom of speech, liberty of conscience, and religious toleration in the "border wars"; encouraged mobs and violence in a war of conquest against representatives of the northern churches; and linked up with southern-rights politicians and judges to advance the cause of slavery. Northern evangelicals were faced with a Slave Power and a battle against "rebels and secessionists" in their ecclesiastical operations at least as threatening as the challenge in the political arena.[41]

The depth of sectional alienation among evangelicals is also apparent in an event that at first sight seems to suggest a narrowing of the gap between North and South, namely, the revival of 1857–58. This extraordinary revival found its immediate origins in the midday interdenominational prayer meetings set up in the business district of New York City in September 1857 to call down God's mercy at a time of financial panic. By the end of the following year the main evangelical denominations had recruited several hundred thousand new members across the country.[42] Modern historians of antebellum America, though not entirely confident about the precise connection between this awakening and the momentous events that followed, sense a significant relationship between the two.[43]

In some ways the revival deserves to be seen as the expression of an evangelical impulse toward harmony and Christian reconciliation. The *New York Observer* rejoiced that it had created an "era of good feelings" between Christians who had forgotten "all past alienations and distractions." It also offered the hope of social harmony at a time when banking collapses and economic recession threatened the loss of jobs and financial ruin. Most significantly, many evangelicals celebrated its ultimate arrival as an antidote to destructive political excitement and worked diligently to "harmonize sectional differences." New York City prayer meetings carried notices forbidding the discussion of "controverted points," to ensure slavery remained off the agenda. Given the Unionism and southern commercial connections of those who provided the backbone of the revival in its earlier phase, the city's merchant class, the prohibition was especially comprehensible. Southern ministers, so often treated as pariahs in the North, found a welcome there.[44]

Ultimately, however, the revival did little to allay the sectional controversy, and as Leonard W. Bacon reflected in 1900, "it may have deepened and intensified it." The movement certainly reinforced ethical perspectives and conflicting sectional images that did nothing to further national harmony. In the North, the revival generated a highly charged sense of social responsibility in many of its converts, a passion to carry the message of life and love to others, including the slaveholder and the drunkard. Lyman Abbott was firmly convinced of the revival's invigorating contribution to antislavery and temperance movements. Northern evangelicals widely concluded that the Almighty had picked them out for special favor. The revival's origins in the northeastern cities, its spread into the small towns and villages of the free states, and its belated, imitative and seemingly ineffectual progress through the South indicated God's approval of the free states' social arrangements and confirmed their belief that slavery had corrupted the quality of southern religion. During the months of revival, antislavery evangelicals lamented that southern Christians' unyielding defense of slavery made it doubtful if the millennial day would ever arrive while "Christian slaveholding" flourished.[45]

Southerners, however, showed no sense of inferiority. They refused to fret about southern churches' relative exclusion from the religious excitement during the early months of 1858. Through spring and summer all the South's evangelical bodies sought to emulate northern churches; they were determined to *will* revival into existence. Their meetings in general had little of the drama and inventiveness of the arrangements in northern cities, but they still yielded enough conversions for celebration. Some believed the South uniquely blessed, convinced the revivals allowed her churches to look forward to the day when, as an Alabama Methodist predicted, "millennial glory shall fill the world." They saw the southern awakening as a vindication of slavery and missions to the blacks. At the same time southerners, having initially welcomed the revival in the free states as evidence of the North's enhanced religiosity, soon retreated to repeating their previous criticisms of deficient Yankee theology and morality. A southern Methodist visitor to New York in September 1858 lamented the Sabbath breaking, drunkenness, and other vices that, despite the recent revival, still scarred the city's face. New England's capacity for "appalling apostasy" from religious truth remained an issue. By 1860 hopes of a revival-inspired rapprochement between northern and southern evangelicals had withered, and the moral chasm separating them had grown wider than ever.[46]

The experience of America's evangelical Protestants argues for the existence of deep cultural and ideological fissures separating the North from the South in 1861.[47] Although the Civil War had to do with the defense of vested material interests, what engaged the passions of both sections was the moral meaning men and women gave to being northern and southern and to the systems of free and slave labor each had developed. Evangelicalism, more than any other element, provided the core of these divergent moral perceptions of the right social and economic direction of the Union. Henry Clay understood something of the power of ideology when he reflected with foreboding on the sundering of national denominations. As he told the editor of the *Presbyterian Herald,*

> If the Churches divide on the subject of slavery, there will be nothing left to bind our people together but trade and commerce. . . . [W]hen the people of these states become thoroughly alienated from each other, and get their passions aroused, they are not apt to stop and consider what is to their interest. . . . Men will fight if they consider their rights trampled upon, even if you show them that ruin to themselves and families will be the probable results.[48]

He did not live to see it, but by the later 1850s the prevalent fears on each side of the Mason-Dixon line were exacerbated by abrasive relations between sectional churches. In the crisis of 1860–1861, northern evangelicals widely hailed Lincoln's victory as God given; many southern evangelicals were prominent in taking a lead in commending the course of secession.[49] We have no means of knowing if without the evangelical element there would have been a war. What we can say is that the moral energies established by the Second Great Awakening were powerful enough to splinter national denominations and national parties; though conflicts of strictly material interest are often open to negotiation, they are rarely so when associated with a conviction of moral righteousness.[50]

IV

American evangelicals' optimistic postmillennialism, their Manichaean perception of the world as a battleground between good and evil, their moral absolutism, and their weak sense of institutional loyalty to political parties all acted to destabilize the American polity in the middle decades of the nineteenth century, at the very time that British evangelicals and their fellow citizens were entering an "age of equipoise," a period of mid-Victorian peace and good order for which evangelicals themselves have been given considerable credit. American evangelicals killed each other in a fight over slavery and the Union, while their British counterparts, deeply divided among themselves only over the more containable issue of disestablishment, sought as Christian soldiers to advance Christ's kingdom by less murderous means.[51]

This indeed is an oversimplified picture. In both countries evangelical doctrine and culture contained a variety of contradictory elements, some tending to sustain social conservatism, others political upheaval. Evangelicals' moral absolutism and perfectionism sat uncomfortably with acceptance of the social status quo; their desire for Christian harmony and the ingathering of converts implied a subordination of this-worldly conflicts and ambitions to more spiritual ones. On neither side of the Atlantic did evangelicalism push unequivocally in a single direction.

Therefore, if we are looking for the profound aberration, or fault line, in the Atlantic world, it was not to be found in the distinctiveness of United States' evangelicalism compared with the experience of Britain and the Old World; rather, it was the exceptionalism of theologically and socially conservative southern evangelicals as against the advancing, postmillennialist antislavery culture of ambitious British and Yankee reformers. Responses to *Uncle Tom's Cabin* indicated the cultural harmony of the humanitarians of the free states and Britain, and the isolation of a bitter and uncomprehending South.[52]

For its part, American evangelicalism was no more an uncomplicated force for instability than the British variety was for social order. It was not so much that some of the most sectionally chauvinist of American Protestants perceived themselves as social and political conservatives, defending their section against the radicalism, unchristian practices, and perverted doctrine of the other; such self-perceptions in fact worked to polarize and ultimately to destabilize the Union. Rather, it was that some of the staunchest defenders of the republic's unity through the testing antebellum decades were those conservative evangelicals who tried to protect American "brotherhood" from sacrifice "at the shrine of party Molochs."[53] Their faith in the Union as a divinely ordained instrument for extending Christ's gospel, religious freedom, and republican beauty to the benighted wider world underlay their fervent support for Clay's and Douglas's compromise proposals of 1850 and their angry condemnations of radicals and secessionists in the winter crisis of 1860–1861. They were to be found in all denominations, and their particular strength in the Old School Presbyterianism kept that church institutionally united until the very outbreak of war.[54]

That conflict may have been regarded by both Union and Confederacy as a holy war, but it was in no simple sense caused by evangelicals. We do not find the primary cause either of American disorder or of British domestic tranquility in the character of the two countries' evangelicalism, but in the whole complex of social and psychological reality of which it was a part. American evangelicals' role in the coming of the Civil War has to be placed in the context of the country's revolutionary and republican tradition, its racial order, its rapidly changing geographic boundaries, its mass immigration, its movement of population, its developing national market economy, and the flourishing of a staple-crop economy sustained by slave labor. At the same time, British political continuity and national cohesion (sustained in the presence of severe economic dislocation and much human misery) were a product of the interplay of many influences, including demography, climate, patterns of social deference, education, geographic insularity, the nation's imperial role, a tradition of political compromise, and the existence of a number of rival polarities that, because they cut across each other, actually made for social integration.[55] Nonetheless, the contrasting tendencies of each country's evangelical engagement in politics should be clear. Class, not slavery, was the genie as far as Britain's social and political stability was concerned, and there evangelicals' thought and ameliorative, nonviolent action worked to keep the bottle corked. British nineteenth-century observers would have had to leap back two centuries into their history, to their own Civil War, to find any equivalent to the religious war that so devastatingly divided the evangelical Christians of the northern and southern United States.

Notes

1. James Dixon, *Personal Narrative of a Tour Through a Part of the United States and Canada* (New York, 1849), 143.

2. Robert Baird, *Religion in the United States of America* (Glasgow, 1844), 600–603; idem, *Religion in America; or, An Account of the Origin, Relation to the State, and*

Present Condition of the Evangelical Churches in the United States (New York, 1856), 530–32.

3. D. W. Bebbington, *Evangelicalism in Modern Britain: A History from the 1730s to the 1980s* (London: Unwin Hyman, 1989), esp. 105–11, offers a balanced analysis of the purchase of evangelical religion on mid-nineteenth-century Britain.

4. Richard Carwardine, "Religion and Politics in Nineteenth-Century Britain: The Case against American Exceptionalism," in *Religion and American Politics: From the Colonial Period to the 1980s,* ed. Mark A. Noll (New York: Oxford University Press, 1990), 225–52.

5. George M. Marsden, *Fundamentalism and American Culture: The Shaping of Twentieth-Century Evangelicalism, 1870–1925* (New York: Oxford University Press, 1980), 85–93.

6. Donald G. Mathews, *Religion in the Old South* (Chicago: University of Chicago Press, 1977), 98, 197; Charles G. Finney, *Lectures on Revivals of Religion,* ed. William G. McLoughlin (Cambridge: Harvard University Press, 1960), 297; Mary P. Ryan, *Women in Public: Between Banners and Ballots, 1825–1880* (Baltimore: Johns Hopkins University Press, 1990), 132–41; Lori D. Ginzberg, *Women and the Work of Benevolence: Morality, Politics, and Class in the Nineteenth-Century United States* (New Haven: Yale Univeristy Press, 1990), 67–97.

7. Bebbington, *Evangelicalism in Modern Britain,* 72–74, 132–37; Carwardine, "Religion and Politics in Nineteenth-Century Britain," 229–32.

8. R. Laurence Moore, "The End of Religious Establishment and the Beginning of Religious Politics: Church and State in the United States," in *Belief in History: Innovative Approaches to European and American Religion,* ed. Thomas Kselman (Notre Dame, IN: University of Notre Dame Press, 1991), 237–64; Donald G. Mathews, "The Second Great Awakening as an Organizing Process 1780–1830: An Hypothesis," *American Quarterly* 21 (Spring 1969): 23–43.

9. Daniel W. Howe, *The Political Culture of the American Whigs* (Chicago: University of Chicago Press, 1980); Richard Carwardine, "Evangelicals, Whigs, and the Election of William Henry Harrison," *Journal of American Studies* 17 (April 1983): 47–76.

10. Carwardine, "Religion and Politics in Nineteenth-Century Britain," 232–38.

11. Lee Benson, *The Concept of Jacksonian Democracy: New York as a Test Case* (Princeton: Princeton University Press, 1961); Ronald P. Formisano, *The Birth of Mass Political Parties: Michigan, 1827–1861* (Princeton: Princeton University Press, 1971); Michael F. Holt, *Forging a Majority: The Formation of the Republican Party in Pittsburgh, 1848–1860* (New Haven: Yale University Press, 1969); Paul Kleppner, *The Third Electoral System, 1853–1892: Parties, Voters, and Political Cultures* (Chapel Hill: University of North Carolina Press, 1979). These works have helped inspire a more rounded approach to antebellum political culture. Of particular note are William R. Brock, *Parties and Political Conscience: American Dilemmas, 1840–1850* (New York: KTO, 1979); Howe, *Political Culture of the American Whigs;* and idem, "The Evangelical Movement and Political Culture in the North during the Second Party System," *Journal of American History* 77 (March 1991): 1216–39.

12. Frank Richardson, *From Sunrise to Sunset: Reminiscence* (Bristol, TN, 1910), 107–8. See William G. Shade, "Society and Politics in Antebellum Virginia's Southside," *Journal of Southern History* 53 (May 1987): 169–93; and Gary R. Freeze, "The Ethnocultural Thesis Goes South: Religio-Cultural Dimensions of Voting in North Carolina's Second Party System" (Paper delivered at the Southern Historical Association Convention, November 1988).

13. Carwardine, "Religion and Politics in Nineteenth-Century Britain," 238–44; D. W. Bebbington, "Nonconformity and Electoral Sociology, 1867–1918," *Historical Journal* 27 (1984): 634–39.

14. Elie Halévy, *A History of the English People in the Nineteenth Century,* vol. 1: *England in 1815,* trans. E. I. Watkin and D. A. Barker (London: Ernest Benn, 1961), 424–25. E. P. Thompson, *The Making of the English Working Class,* rev. ed. (London: Penguin, 1968), 419, sees the rapid growth of revivalistic Methodism in the early nineteenth century as "a component of the psychic processes of counter-revolution."

15. See, for example, Alan Heimert, *Religion and the American Mind from the Great Awakening to the Revolution* (Cambridge: Harvard University Press, 1966), and the many subsequent studies that have addressed Heimert's questions.

16. John R. Bodo, *The Protestant Clergy and the Public Issues, 1812–1848* (Princeton: Princeton University Press, 1954); Clifford S. Griffin, *Their Brothers' Keepers: Moral Stewardship in the United States, 1800–1865* (New Brunswick, NJ: Rutgers University Press, 1960); Lois W. Banner, "Religious Benevolence as Social Control: A Critique of an Interpretation," *Journal of American History* 60 (June 1973): 23–41; Nathan O. Hatch, *The Democratization of American Christianity* (New Haven: Yale University Press, 1989).

17. Thomas J. Pressly, *Americans Interpret Their Civil War* (Princeton: Princeton University Press, 1954; new ed., 1962), 135, 138.

18. Avery O. Craven, quoted in Kenneth M. Stampp, "The Irrepressible Conflict," in *The Imperiled Union: Essays on the Background to the Civil War* (New York: Oxford University Press, 1980), 191–245 (quotations 106–7).

19. James Ford Rhodes, *Lectures on the American Civil War* (1913; reprint, Freeport, NY: Books for Libraries, 1971), 84–85.

20. Stampp, "Irrepressible Conflict," 195–98. For a valuable discussion of how the study of religion, values, social structure, family life, and economic interest are linked and properly fuse together in the cultural interpretation of history; and for a linking of antebellum evangelicalism and the modernizing forces in American society, see Howe, "Evangelical Movement and Political Culture," 1222–39.

21. Charles W. Ramsdell, "The Natural Limits of Slavery Expansion," *Mississippi Valley Historical Review* 16 (September 1929): 151–71; Robert William Fogel and Stanley L. Engerman, *Time on the Cross: The Economics of American Negro Slavery* (Boston: Little, Brown, 1974).

22. Gilbert Hobbs Barnes, *The Antislavery Impulse, 1830–1844,* (1933; reprint, New York: Harcourt, Brace and World, 1964).

23. For a subtle attempt to fuse the revisionist critique of abolitionists as impatient moralists, and the more recent perception of them as shrewd and rational, see Lawrence J. Friedman, *Gregarious Saints: Self and Community in American Abolitionism, 1830–1870* (Cambridge: Cambridge University Press, 1982).

24. Richard H. Sewell, *Ballots for Freedom: Antislavery Politics in the United States, 1837–1860* (New York: Oxford University Press, 1976).

25. Allan Nevins, *Ordeal of the Union,* 2 vols. (New York: Scribners, 1947), 2:553.

26. C. C. Goen, *Broken Churches, Broken Nation: Denominational Schisms and the Coming of the Civil War* (Macon, GA: Mercer University Press, 1985). Also valuable on this theme are three works by Donald G. Mathews: *Slavery and Methodism: A Chapter in American Morality, 1780–1845* (Princeton: Princeton University Press, 1965); "The Methodist Schism of 1844 and the Popularization of Antislavery Sentiment," *Mid-America* 51 (January 1969): 3–23; and *Religion in the Old South,* 136–84. John R. McKivigan, *The War against Proslavery Religion: Abolitionism and the North-*

ern Churches, 1830–1865 (Ithaca: Cornell University Press, 1984), elucidates the relationship between abolitionist and nonabolitionist evangelicals in the free states. For southern evangelicals and sectional breakdown, see especially Anne C. Loveland, *Southern Evangelicals and the Social Order, 1800–1860* (Baton Rouge: Louisiana State University Press, 1980), 257–65; and James O. Farmer, *The Metaphysical Confederacy: James Henley Thornwell and the Synthesis of Southern Values* (Macon, GA: Mercer University Press, 1986).

27. Joel Silbey's essay (1964) is reprinted in his collection *The Partisan Imperative: The Dynamics of American Politics before the Civil War* (New York: Oxford University Press, 1985), 3–12.

28. Stampp, "Irrepressible Conflict," 209.

29. In *Evangelicals and Politics in Antebellum America* (New Haven: Yale University Press, 1993), I attempt to make good this deficiency.

30. Richard R. John, "Taking Sabbatarianism Seriously: The Postal System, the Sabbath, and the Transformation of American Political Culture," *Journal of the Early Republic* 10 (Winter 1990): 517–67; Paul Goodman, *Towards a Christian Republic: Antimasonry and the Great Tradition in New England, 1826–1836* (New York: Oxford University Press, 1988).

31. William E. Gienapp, *The Origins of the Republican Party, 1852–1856* (New York: Oxford University Press, 1987), convincingly demonstrates the role of temperance and anti-Catholicism in breaking down the "second party system" and creating the turmoil out of which a new political force arose.

32. Richard Carwardine, "The Know-Nothing Party, the Protestant Evangelical Community, and the American National Identity," in *Religion and National Identity,* Studies in Church History 18, ed. S. Mews (Oxford: Basil Blackwell, 1982), 449–63.

33. Victor B. Howard, *Conscience and Slavery: The Evangelistic, Calvinist Domestic Missions, 1837–1861* (Kent, Ohio: Kent State University Press, 1991), 142–55, 177–84; McKivigan, *War against Proslavery Religion,* 143–60.

34. Jack P. Maddex, "From Theocracy to Spirituality: The Southern Presbyterian Reversal on Church and State," *Journal of Presbyterian History* 54 (Winter 1976): 438–57; and James O. Farmer, "Southern Presbyterians and Southern Nationalism: A Study in Ambivalence," *Georgia Historical Quarterly* 75 (Summer 1991): 275–94, reflect on the degree of southern exceptionalism from a national norm of social and political engagement. Bertram Wyatt-Brown, *Yankee Saints and Southern Sinners* (Baton Rouge: Louisiana State University Press, 1982), considers the evangelical ethic and the South's code of honor.

35. Goen's *Broken Churches, Broken Nation* offers some valuable insights into the relationship between schism and civil war but gives little sense of political *process* and says little about the chronic infection of the border war.

36. William I. Fee, *Bringing the Sheaves: Gleanings from the Harvest Fields in Ohio, Kentucky, and West Virginia* (Cincinnati, 1896), 242–43; Lorenzo Waugh, *Autobiography of Lorenzo Waugh* (Oakland, CA, 1883), 156–58, 166–67; Henry B. Bascom et al., *Brief Appeal to Public Opinion, in a Series of Exceptions to the Course and Action of the Methodist Episcopal Church* (Louisville, 1848), 93–106, 127–34; *Christian Advocate and Journal* (New York), 12 January and 24 May 1848; Norman W. Spellman, "The Church Divides, 1844," in *The History of American Methodism,* 3 vols., ed. Emory S. Buckle et al. (Nashville: Abingdon, 1964), 2:62–63. Arthur E. Jones, "The Years of Disagreement, 1844–61," in ibid. 2:159–67, offers a lucid analysis of the plan's operations along the border before 1848.

37. John N. Norwood, *The Schism in the American Methodist Church, 1844: A Study in Slavery and Ecclesiastical Politics* (Alfred, NY: Alfred University, 1923), 138–40; Freeborn Garretson Hibbard, *Biography of Rev. Leonidas L. Hamline, D.D., Late One of the Bishops of the Methodist Episcopal Church* (Cincinnati, 1880), 192–93, 216; *Christian Advocate and Journal,* 3 November 1847 and 24 May 1848; *Western Christian Advocate,* 27 September and 25 October 1848, 9 October 1850; *Southern Christian Advocate,* 9 June 1848.

38. John Stewart, *Highways and Hedges; or, Fifty Years of Western Methodism* (Cincinnati, 1870), 245–60; Fee, *Bringing the Sheaves,* 213–14; Hibbard, *Hamline,* 211–15; T. J. Thompson to T. E. Bond, 30 October 1846; O. P. Twiford to T. E. Bond, 24 November 1846, T. E. Bond Papers, Dickinson College Library; *Christian Advocate and Journal,* 5, 12 October, 11, 18, 25 November 1846; 20, 27 January, 3, 10, 24 February 1847.

39. Bascom et al., *Brief Appeal,* 5; Hibbard, *Hamline,* 218–22; Edwin H. Myers, *The Disruption of the Methodist Episcopal Church, 1844–46: Comprising a Thirty Years' History of the Relations of the Two Methodisms* (Nashville, 1875), 151.

40. John B. Adger, *My Life and Times, 1810–1890* (Richmond, VA, [1899]), 179–80; Whitefoord Smith, *God the Refuge of His People* (Columbia, SC, 1850), 7.

41. Lorenzo Waugh, *A Candid Statement of the Course Pursued by the Preachers of the Methodist Episcopal Church South* (Cincinnati, 1848), 70; Waugh, *Autobiography,* 148–71; *Christian Advocate and Journal,* 5 January, 15 March, 24 May, 19 July 1848; 17 October 1850; Hibbard, *Hamline,* 205; *Southern Christian Advocate,* 6 June and 28 November 1851; Fee, *Bringing the Sheaves,* 239–40; *WCA,* 27 September 1848; Stewart, *Highways and Hedges,* 260; Edward Thomson, *Life of Edward Thomson, Late Bishop of the Methodist Episcopal Church* (Cincinnati, 1885), 87–88.

42. For the course of the revival and a discussion of its wider significance, see Timothy L. Smith, *Revivalism and Social Reform: American Protestantism on the Eve of the Civil War* (Nashville: Abingdon, 1957), 63–79 and elsewhere; Richard Carwardine, *Transatlantic Revivalism: Popular Evangelicalism in Britain and America, 1790–1865* (Westport, CT: Greenwood Press, 1978), 159–69.

43. See, for example, Roy F. Nichols, *The Disruption of the American Democracy* (New York: Macmillan, 1948), 135–36; Perry Miller, *The Life of the Mind in America: From the Revolution to the Civil War* (New York: Harcourt, Brace, and World, 1965), 88–95. For some shrewd thoughts on the revival both as a pursuit of harmony and as a source of social criticism and sectional divisiveness, see William G. McLoughlin, *Revivals, Awakenings, and Reform: An Essay on Religion and Social Change in America, 1607–1977* (Chicago: University of Chicago Press, 1978), 143; Kenneth M. Stampp, *America in 1857: A Nation on the Brink* (New York: Oxford University Press, 1990), 237–38; James H. Moorhead, *American Apocalypse: Yankee Protestants and the Civil War, 1860–69* (New Haven: Yale University Press, 1978), 21.

44. *New York Observer,* 5 August 1858; *Philadelphia Press,* 6 March 1858, quoted in Russell E. Francis, "The Religious Revival of 1858 in Philadelphia," *Pennsylvania Magazine of History* 70 (January 1946): 64; William C. Conant, *Narratives of Remarkable Conversions and Revival Incidents: Including . . . an Account of the Rise and Progress of the Great Awakening of 1857–8* (New York, 1858), 380–81; Talbot W. Chambers, *The Noon Prayer Meeting of the North Dutch Church, Fulton St., New York: Its Origin, Character, and Progress* (New York, 1858), 88–89, 130–33, 239–40.

45. Leonard W. Bacon, *A History of American Christianity* (New York, 1900), 345; Lyman Abbott, *Reminiscences* (Boston, 1915), 16–21, 117–40; Conant, *Narratives of*

Remarkable Conversions, 435; Garth M. Rosell and Richard A. G. Dupuis, eds., *The Memoirs of Charles G. Finney: The Complete Restored Text* (Grand Rapids: Zondervan, 1989), 565.

46. J. O. Lindsay, "The Religious Awakening of 1858," *Southern Presbyterian Review* 11 (July 1858): 252; *Southern Christian Advocate,* 27 May, 26 August, 16 September 1858; *North Carolina Presbyterian,* 11, 18 June, 23, 30 October 1858; 10 March 1860.

47. The divisive historiographic issue of how far the United States enjoyed a cultural unity, and how far the sectional conflict represented serious ideological divisions, is addressed, for example, in Edward Pessen, "How Different from Each Other Were the Antebellum North and South?" *American Historical Review* 85 (December 1980): 1119–49; and James M. McPherson, "Antebellum Southern Exceptionalism: A New Look at an Old Question," *Civil War History* 29 (September 1983): 230–44.

48. *Christian Advocate and Journal,* 16 August 1860.

49. There was no politically uniform evangelicalism in each of the two sections: northern sectarianism and cultural diversity kept many evangelicals resistant to the party of Lincoln, while the same forces ensured the complex reaction of southern Protestants to the events of 1860 and early in 1861. See William E. Gienapp, "Who Voted for Lincoln?" in *Abraham Lincoln and the American Political Tradition,* ed. John L. Thomas (Amherst: University of Massachusetts Press, 1986), 50–97.

50. Here I part company with Goen, *Broken Churches, Broken Nation,* whose final judgments (141–90) I find as historically unhelpful as they are morally admirable.

51. Bebbington, *Evangelicalism in Modern Britain,* 136–37. For the ways in which evangelical religion gave meaning to the war for both Confederates and Unionists, see especially Drew Gilpin Faust, "Christian Soldiers: The Meaning of Revivalism in the Confederate Army," *Journal of Southern History* 53 (February 1987): 63–90; and Moorhead, *American Apocalypse,* 42–172.

52. Betty Fladeland, *Men and Brothers: Anglo-American Antislavery Cooperation* (Urbana: University of Illinois Press, 1972). In Britain, Harriet Beecher Stowe's novel reached a million readers within eight months of its publication.

53. John Mason Duncan, *A Discourse Delivered on the Fast Day* (Baltimore, 1841), 21, 24–30.

54. See, for example, William T. Hutchinson, *Cyrus Hall McCormick,* 2 vols. (New York: Century, 1930–35), 2:37–47; Alexander T. Mcgill, *Sinful but Not Forsaken: A Sermon . . . on the Day of National Fasting, January 4, 1861* (New York, 1861), 15–16; Lewis G. Vander Velde, *The Presbyterian Churches and the Federal Union, 1861–1869* (London: Oxford University Press, 1932), 30–38.

55. Brian Harrison, *Peaceable Kingdom: Stability and Change in Modern Britain* (Oxford: Clarendon Press, 1982), 1–6, 123–56, and elsewhere. Eric Foner, "Politics, Ideology, and the Origins of the American Civil War," in *Politics and Ideology in the Age of the Civil War* (New York: Oxford University Press, 1980), 34–53, notes that for much of the period between the revolution and the 1850s American politicians were able to achieve a similar effect; they created and sustained coalitional parties that cut across class, religion, and section, thereby helping to relieve social tensions and integrate society. But from the 1830s "antagonistic value systems and ideologies grounded in the question of slavery" emerged in the North and South, putting the political system under a strain with which the normal processes of compromise could not cope. For a recent development of this theme, but with an attention to evangelical religion missing from Foner's work, see Bruce Levine, *Half Slave and Half Free: The Roots of Civil War* (New York: Hill and Wang, 1992).

11

The Empire of Evangelicalism: Varieties of Common Sense in Scotland, Canada, and the United States

MICHAEL GAUVREAU

It has by now become commonplace among historians to assert that between 1730 and 1850, the cultures, identities, and institutions of the English-speaking peoples in the North Atlantic world were decisively influenced by a wave of religious "awakenings." This movement, termed "evangelicalism," drew upon and shaped the political and social unrest attending the birth of the modern world, providing new models of human nature and society upon which a new social and cultural order could be constructed. The revolutionary, modern nature of evangelicalism[1] can best be understood by contrasting it to medieval or early modern forms of religious expression, whether Protestant or Catholic, which subsumed the individual in a web of divinely sanctioned, hierarchical relationships beginning with the family unit and culminating in a patriarchal king, who was accorded quasi-divine reverence as a lineal descendant of Christ's family tree. These social relationships were underwritten by elaborate political theologies, legal systems, and "ancient constitutions," interpreted and buttressed by established churches, which claimed either through sacraments or creeds, to mediate between the individual and God. By downplaying the importance of creeds, institutions, and sacraments in the all-important process of salvation, evangelicals effectively cut away the ideological underpinnings of so-called early modern culture. By placing the central emphasis upon the relationship of the individual and God, mediated through Christ's atoning act,[2] evangelicals relocated power away from visible hierarchies to the inner realm, in which the all-important question involved not status, rank, or obligation to one's superiors but the responsibility of the individual for cultivating the moral character and freedom of the conscience and will.

Despite the web of interconnections spun by a common religious language and rituals, constantly reinforced by traveling revivalists, a popular religious press, and the free movement of peoples in the nineteenth century,[3] evangelicalism was not transplanted in identical form to the various North Atlantic societies. Certainly in Britain, evangelicalism remained a minority influence in a Protestant culture and state in which early modern assumptions and institutions persisted in the form of allegiance to the monarchical constitution, the intellectual and social leadership of the Established Church, and a more deferential pattern of politics and social interaction.[4] By contrast, in the two North American societies, the United States and English Canada, evangelicalism had by 1850 achieved the status of cultural mainstream. In both societies, a majority of religious adherents belonged to "evangelical" denominations, and the privileges of religious establishments had been effectively abolished. More tellingly, evangelical groups in both the United States and English Canada had played a leading role in the democratization of politics and culture and had reshaped social relationships and institutions according to the tenets of voluntarism[5]—that is, organizations that in theory no longer operated according to hierarchical patterns of status and deference but were instead associations of individuals who freely chose to belong to them.

Evangelicals in English Canada and the United States contributed to a common North American culture defined by democracy and voluntarism, and yet they pursued different paths in the nineteenth and early twentieth centuries in at least two key respects. First, the shrill conflict between "modernists" and "antimodernists" that bedeviled several American denominations in the years after 1870 was largely absent from the English Canadian intellectual setting.[6] Although divergent emphases existed among Canadian evangelicals over the relationship of their creed to various forms of modern thought, the leadership of the major denominations succeeded in articulating a position that harmonized evangelicalism, biblical criticism, and evolutionary thought in such a way as to preserve the central imperatives of the evangelical impulse. Second, although American Protestantism has exhibited bitter conflict and polarization between rival theological parties, religion has consistently played a far more prominent and constructive role in politics and in the articulation of public values.[7] By contrast, Protestant religion in English Canada since 1930 has lost its vitality and has become an increasingly private matter, unable to interact creatively with or to influence the public realm.

It is possible to ascribe these divergent responses to the obvious social, cultural, and political differences that have historically existed between English Canada and the United States. Although such a broad subject cannot be addressed within the brief scope of the present chapter, any discussion of the subject would involve the way in which the evangelical impulse that emerged from the eighteenth-century age of revolutions intersected with the culture of each North American society. The religious differences that divided the Protestant cultures of the United States and English Canada can be traced to a fundamental divergence almost at the point of origin of the smaller North American society. It involved the way in which evangelicals in English Canada perceived, appropriated, and applied elements of the common stock of the transatlantic evangelical creed, in particular, the legacy of Scottish common sense and the related traditions of natural theology that governed the relationship of religion and science. The way in which English Canadian and American evangelicals used this eighteenth-century legacy in their encounter with aspects of modern thought had, in turn, wider implications for the eventual role occupied by religion in the public sphere in the early twentieth century in each North American society.

The Ambiguous Legacy of Scottish Common Sense

As it was defined in the context of social and cultural transformation in the eighteenth-century North Atlantic world, evangelicalism assumed shape as an interlocking series of beliefs concerning individuals, communities, and their relationship to God. The evangelical experience in English Canada and the United States was not, however, characterized by cultural uniformity. In order to assess the origin and implications of this discontinuity within the international culture of evangelicalism, the historian must first address two major issues. In recent years, students of American religion have directed our attention to the fact that the beginnings of the evangelical revival in the United States in the 1740s coincided with the height of the "Moderate Enlightenment."[8] Prominent evangelical leaders such as the Reverend John Witherspoon, the principal architect of Presbyterian higher learning in America, had close intellectual and cultural ties to the Scottish version of the Moderate Enlightenment represented by Francis Hutcheson, Adam Smith, Adam Ferguson, Hugh Blair, and William Robertson. These Scottish literati were all clergymen of the Church of Scotland who subscribed to the Westminster Confession but were willing to shift the emphasis of Calvinist doctrine away from predestination and election to the individual and social morality. Without surrendering the fundamental Christian ideal of salvation, they attempted to supplement this goal with ethical objectives designed to increase virtue and happiness. In their insistence upon the study of individuals in their social context, the Moderate clergy built upon an earlier Calvinist heritage that stressed that moral regeneration was not simply a matter of raising the level of personal or private virtue. Of equal importance was civic or public virtue, and they exhorted individuals to work for the welfare of the entire nation.[9] While Witherspoon, a leading spokesman of the "popular" party, clashed hotly with the Moderates over the issue of church patronage and subordination in secular politics, he accepted the broad outlines of their optimistic social and cultural program, which assumed the shape of a "moral Newtonianism" in its striving to discover and apply nature's secret laws to the human mind and social relationships.[10]

As president of the College of New Jersey (Princeton), Witherspoon introduced Hutcheson's philosophy of the "moral sense," which was premised upon a close analogy between the methods of natural philosophy and the empirical investigation of human mental and social phenomena. Although in both Scotland and America, moral philosophy retained close ties to religion, the Moderates believed that the providence of God in human affairs had become more general and was now interpreted through secondary causes that, these thinkers believed, could be investigated through the same empirical, Newtonian method so successfully applied to the physical world.[11] While remaining committed to a basically Calvinist theology, Witherspoon downplayed its distrust of human nature and lauded the achievements of science as triumphs of human ingenuity, rather than as testimony to God's glory.[12] The Moderate confidence in science's ability to interpret not only the moral laws that guided individual and social conduct but biblical revelation itself became even more pronounced in the hands of Witherspoon's successor, Samuel Stanhope Smith, who stood in an even closer relationship to the canons of the Enlightenment than did his mentor. Smith asserted the strictest analogy between natural science and moral philosophy in order to demonstrate how such rational evidence could demonstrate the truth of religion.[13]

In addition to the moral theory of the Moderate Enlightenment, American evangelicals such as Witherspoon were influenced by a second powerful intellectual current—the language of classical republicanism or civic humanism. Based upon the myth of a pure, ancient constitution, this ideology, like the Calvinism that many American evangelicals inherited, defined virtue in both public and private terms, by calling upon independent citizens to protect fragile civic virtue against the threat of corruption represented by unbridled executive power.[14] Although republican sentiment was muted in Scotland by the Moderate clergy's Whig-Presbyterian conservatism, which stressed allegiance to the constitutional settlement of 1688 and thus defined civic virtue as participation in the protection of the existing system of government,[15] men like Witherspoon were able to orient their denominations toward participation in the revolution by articulating a "Republican Christian Enlightenment" in which the study of rhetoric and moral philosophy composed the political arts necessary for the public citizen.[16] In the American context, the alliance of civic humanism and evangelicalism articulated a political theology based upon the language of citizenship, participation in the political community and, perhaps most important, justified a tradition of public opposition based upon the ideal values of the community, which constantly required vigilant defense against tyranny. American political leaders of the revolutionary age drew extensively upon the Scottish "faculty psychology" of Thomas Reid and, as moral Newtonians, were particularly inclined to draw close analogies between the physical world, the human mind, and the body politic.[17]

By contrast, evangelicalism in English Canada lacked deep exposure both to the Moderate Enlightenment and to the early modern political theology of classical republicanism, a phenomenon that I once described as a case of the "Missing Enlightenment."[18] During the formative decades of English Canadian society, culture, and ideology between 1780 and 1840, the easy accommodation between Newtonian science, Calvinist evangelical religion, and the moral sense philosophy characteristic of the Scottish and American eighteenth centuries had been shaken by the radical—some would say atheistic—implications of the French Revolution and by a liberal democratic impulse, buoyed by the commercial prosperity of the late eighteenth century, that threatened to dissolve the old bonds of status, hierarchy, and community in an anonymous marketplace of competitive, autonomous individuals in which all social relationships and ideas of virtue were contractual and relative.[19]

Given the coincidence in time between the rise of liberal market notions of humankind and society in the North Atlantic world and the foundation of British communities in Upper and Lower Canada, it is of more than passing interest that the dominant strand of Canadian historical writing on the late eighteenth and early nineteenth century has persisted in locating the source of fundamental "Canadian" values in a paternalistic, communitarian conservatism that rejected the "American" values of individualism and liberalism and supposedly fostered a greater reliance on the power of the state to protect the interests of the community. The roots of this interpretation can be traced to a strand of anti-Americanism fashionable in academic circles in the 1960s.[20] Against this interpretation, however, the study of evangelicalism as an international cultural movement serves to relocate English Canada within the context of North American and transatlantic intellectual changes. As Nancy Christie has recently argued, British North America, like the United States, developed a culture of liberal democratic expression during the years between the American Revolution and the War of 1812, a culture in which the transatlantic impulse of popular evangelicalism played a central role in asserting not only the independence of the individual from the social constraints of the old order but in positing a rival vision of community based upon the free association of equal, autonomous individuals.[21]

Although evangelicals participated in an international culture of democratic liberalism, they often displayed a profound ambivalence concerning the implications of an individualist, market-oriented society. Was there, they asked, any absolute standard of virtue if society was to be interpreted as a series of fluid, shifting, impersonal relationships? After all, the early modern social arrangements from which they had dissented were premised upon visible social hierarchies, theological creeds, ancient constitutions, and established churches that affirmed a divinely sanctioned place for the person in a social hierarchy and prescribed duties, privileges, and responsibilites based upon this status. By promoting a market-oriented, liberal model of society, the democratic impulse that drew upon evangelicalism had apparently liberated individuals only to mire them without any authoritative values in a morass of impersonal contracts and temporary social conventions in which human beings lacked both self-discipline and any precise personal or social identity.[22]

How, then, to discipline the individual, the locus of power and sovereignty in the early nineteenth-century world of democratic culture? It was precisely in the period between 1790 and 1840, the critical years in the process of defining the mind-set and values of liberal democracy and market capitalism, that evangelicalism encountered the Scottish philosophy of common sense. Although not part of the stock of basic theological convictions that formed the core of the evangelical creed, the Scottish philosophy of common sense was, in the words of Mark Noll, intimately related to "evangelical habits of thought and intellectual reflexes."²³ By 1860, it could be said without exaggeration that in both the United States and English Canada, the tenets of common sense directed much of evangelical thinking concerning human nature, the relationship of individuals to their society, and, perhaps the most important question of all, the role of reason in interpreting divine revelation.²⁴

At the outset, it is important to draw a subtle, but nonetheless vital, distinction between common sense and the earlier Moderate Enlightenment, which celebrated the affinities between Newtonian natural phlosophy and so-called moral science.²⁵ As defined by Thomas Reid, Adam Smith's successor in the moral philosophy chair at Glasgow and expounded and popularized by Reid's pupil, Dugald Stewart, professor of moral philosophy at Edinburgh between 1785 and 1810 (whose works such as *Elements of the Philosophy of the Human Mind* became the staples of the moral philosophy course at evangelical colleges in Scotland, Canada, and the United States by the 1830s),²⁶ common sense exhibited certain continuities with the earlier moral sense school of the Moderates but also displayed a number of significant shifts in emphasis. Where the earlier Moderate advocates of moral sense had blithely linked natural science and morality, Reid and Stewart were far less comfortable with such assertions. Indeed, Stewart argued against notions of a moral sense that Hutcheson and Smith believed was an emotion that functioned independently of the intellect or considerations of self-interest. Stewart recognized that his predecessors in the moral sense school defined morality in utilitarian terms and had come close to asserting, with Adam Smith, that morality was not transcendent but simply the study of human social history and that virtue meant simply adaptability to the values of an increasingly materialist world.²⁷ Such a definition of morals, he believed, opened the door to the scepticism and sensationalism of David Hume and the materialism and atheism of the French Revolution.

While adhering to the main outlines of the Newtonian spirit in his concern for fostering the empirical, inductive investigation of moral phenomena, Stewart's main concern was to define more precise limits than had his easygoing eighteenth-century predecessors in postulating analogies between the physical and moral realms. The Edinburgh philosopher was, in fact, deeply suspicious of the moral Newtonianism of the Moderates because it led to dangerous, revolutionary speculations and dogmatism in the sphere of political conduct.²⁸ Stewart opened his celebrated text *Elements of the Philosophy of the Human Mind* with the assertion that methods used in conducting physical and mathematical researches could not be literally applied to discussions of metaphysics, morals, and politics because of the imperfections of language, the difficulty of precisely defining the meaning of words, and, above all, the inability of many people to rise above the prejudices "which early impressions and associations create, to warp our opinions."²⁹ Appealing to the talismanic name of Francis Bacon, whom he identified as the progenitor of the inductive method, Stewart maintained that any attempt to draw analogies between the two spheres must rest upon experience, not unproven hypotheses.³⁰ In the sphere of human character and morals, Stewart declared, even greater circumspection was required than in the investigation of the phenomena of the natural world. While analogies were of great service in advancing the course of scientific discovery, "the science of mind" could be illuminated only through "hypotheses alone as are consonant to the analogy of its own laws. To assume as a fact the existence of analogies between these laws and those of matter, is to sanction that very prejudice which it is the great object of the inductive science of mind to eradicate."[31]

What Stewart hoped to show through his inductive study of the human mind was how the will controlled its very operations. He was thus able to anchor moral theory and a notion of virtue in the original constitution of the individual human mind, not in terms of the operation of society. For a generation that had experienced the excesses of the French Revolution and was struggling to define the nature of the individual in an age of unbridled market capitalism that dissolved the relationships and ideologies of early modern society, Stewart was able to show that the capacity for virtue did not rest upon the uncertain legacy of civic humanism, which defined virtue in dangerously social terms as public participation in the life of the body politic.[32] Rather, the source of virtue was redefined in radically individualist terms as a defense of the freedom of the will that would be assisted by a better understanding of the constitution of the mind.[33]

Having defined virtue in terms of the fine balance of freedom of the will and the moral discipline of conscience, Stewart was able to provide an absolute moral sanction for the new ideology of market liberalism. Unlike Adam Smith, Stewart was able to dispense completely with the old verities of civic humanism and the classical republican tradition, to say nothing of the even older political theology of patriarchalism that governed the British state. "Common sense" in the hands of Dugald Stewart involved a demystification of the political realm, for the source of political and social morality lay firmly anchored in the individual mind, which could be rationally understood and disciplined through the efforts of each human being. "A great part of the political order which we are apt to ascribe to legislative sagacity," explained Stewart, "is the natural result of the selfish pursuits of individuals."[34] Here was a view of government that did not rest upon the niceties of ancient constitutional origins, appeals to the legacy of quasi-mythical founders, balanced harmonies of orders and estates, or the need for vigilant virtue in resisting corruption of the body politic. For him, the essence of a sound and healthy political constitution was stated simply as the ongoing search for a "*vis medicatrix,* which is sufficient for the cure of painful disorders."[35] The perfection of political wisdom, he concluded, consists not in an "indiscriminate zeal against reformers, but in a gradual and prudent accommodation of established institutions to the varying opinions, manners, and circumstances of mankind."[36] It was a purely functional or administrative definition of the nature and tasks of a modern state, which lacked a political theology, for such a state rested upon the morality and self-discipline of individuals. There was, in fact, no ideal form of government or constitution that should be preserved uncorrupted. The worth of the state could be rationally measured through the extent to which it achieved the happiness of its members through "progress," defined in the materialist language of commercial prosperity.

The common sense of Thomas Reid and Dugald Stewart had several crucial points of contact with the central imperatives of the evangelical creed. First, and perhaps foremost, it posited a firm distinction between mind and matter, the self and the external world, and thus confirmed both the transcendent nature of God and the individualistic nature of the religious experience emphasized by evangelicalism. It was also democratic in its outlook, reaffirming the reliability of our common beliefs concerning the relationship of cause and effect, a view that had suffered a severe setback at the hands of David Hume. Thus, our perceptions, according to the advocates of common sense, revealed the world much as it is and were not merely ideas impressed upon the mind by sensations. In contrast to idealism, common sense asserted that the mind could know the world directly through the perceptions of the mind itself. Human beings required no special wisdom to unlock the laws by which the mind operated. Diligence and humility, those hallmarks of the evangelical personality, close attention to the phenomena of experience, and introspection would enable the student to discover and describe the powers and operations of the mind.[37]

The power of common sense, however, derived not only from its theory of knowledge but from its applicability to the realm of human conduct. The Scottish philosophers, with their "faculty psychology," posited an innate moral sense, or conscience, by which human beings know not only the basic realities of the physical world but also certain foundational principles of morality.[38] Such views were of great service to an evangelical culture that located the conscience as the arena of encounter between the soul and the word of God. Such a definition placed great stress on the responsibility of the individual for transgressions of a divinely revealed moral code and for the necessity of cultivating correct moral values. Indeed, nineteenth-century evangelicals asserted that the moral laws impressed upon the conscience were the same laws that the Bible revealed. This aspect was of particular importance in the convergence of evangelicalism and the emerging values of market liberal capitalism.

Finally, common sense also supplied a methodology by which evangelicals adjusted the respective claims of reason and revelation. Often termed Baconianism, this aspect of the Scottish legacy asserted that truths about consciousness, the world, or religion must be built by strict induction from irreducible facts of experience. Inspired by the achievements of Isaac Newton in the physical sciences, Reid and Stewart, despite their reservations concerning the application of physical analogies to the moral realm, still maintained that, in a general sense, Newton's legacy of empiricism could be made the model for studying human beings. Evangelicals were confident that if they applied this "scientific" common sense to Scripture and human experience more generally, they could derive a fixed, universally valid theology.[39]

Between 1790 and 1840, the convergence of evangelicalism, common sense, and ideologies of market liberalism in the North Atlantic world provided what was perhaps the central stock of concepts shaping new ideas of human nature and conduct, the organization of society along a voluntary-associational model, and a redefinition of the nature and role of the state in functional terms as the promoter and facilitator of economic prosperity. In Britain, however, these ideas that animated the "Age of Reform"[40] were appropriated and interpreted within a culture that retained a monarchical constitution and acknowledged the political guidance of a hereditary aristocracy and the intellectual leadership of an established church.[41] In the United States, both the spheres of private morality and public conduct were redefined along evangelical–common sense lines in the period 1800–1830 as that society experienced the social and cultural transfromations accompanying market capitalism. In the realm of politics and definitions of the nature of the state, however, evangelicalism and liberalism did not entirely displace the older tradition of civic humanism. Although American society operated along the lines of market individualism and voluntary associations, classical republicanism survived in the cultic, quasi-religious respect accorded to the Age of Revolution, the Constitution, and the mythical character of the founders, whose legacy provided an enduring source of political wisdom to which later generations could appeal. Even the values of commercial liberalism had to be accepted under the rubric of energized republicanism. In contrast to the "administrative" language of Stewart, the civic humanist legacy offered, in the United States, a continuing external, absolute sanction for the republican system of government.[42]

The old language of public virtue, of an earthly salvation to be sought for in the political realm through citizen participation in the ongoing struggle to keep the republican constitution free from corruption, was incorporated into the new liberal-evangelical ideology. Its promoters placed particular emphasis on reinterpreting republican ethics and upon the positive role of a Christian republic in the shaping of private morality.[43] But because a legitimate, opposition outlook lay at the heart of civic humanism, the existence of the republican tradition also allowed for the rise and institutionalization of a view of politics and the state that opposed the evangelical takeover of the public realm. As the stimulating work on antebellum American politics by Daniel Walker Howe has demonstrated, the attempt by northern evangelicals to secure the millennium by capturing the American state aroused considerable opposition from those who used the language of constitutionalism to protect private behavior from public intrusion. This division over the relationship of evangelical religion to the republican tradition contributed to intense party conflict between Whigs and Democrats.[44]

English Canada: The Reign of the "Middle Principles"

Between 1800 and 1860, the values of English Canada also came to be defined by a synthesis of evangelicalism, common sense, and market liberalism. Democratic politics in English Canada, however, exhibited certain dissimilarities from its American counterpart. Recent studies have described Canadian politics as characterized by extreme political stability, based upon a preponderance of power in the hands of the executive branch, or "Court." Although movements of political protest aimed at reducing executive power have been present in Canadian history, the central and Ontario provincial governments have usually been controlled by "moderate liberals" or "moderate conservatives" at both the federal and provincial levels. The relative absence of a "country" tradition of constitutional opposition or even of a language of "Whig" constitutionalism suggests the weakness of the older traditions of classical republicanism. And the English Canadian definition of politics lacks an absolutist quality—in other words, English Canada's definition of itself does not begin with a political theology that promises earthly salvation through millennial notions of an ideal republic or ideal monarchy. The form of the English Canadian state was defined in purely functional or administrative terms and was not seen as the repository of some inherent virtue. This conception explains why executive patronage played such an inordinate role both in securing political stability and as the raw material of political discussion and public debate.[45] Of all three transatlantic societies, only English Canada, however, defined its fundamental constitutional principle in the language of evangelicalism. "Responsible government" was the key notion for the way it linked the crown and the legislative branch and, of equal significance, reconciled responsibility for local affairs by the colonial state with control of foreign policy, defense, and the form of the constitution by the British imperial state.[46] The language of ministerial accountability to the legislature is personal, rather than communitarian, in its implications and is suggestive of the evangelical creed's emphasis upon the individual's responsibility for the private, inner state of conscience and soul. In its collective, or cabinet, sense its premise is the securing of a voluntary agreement or consensus among the various ministers, who must seek the "confidence" of their supporters on an ongoing basis. This imperative is derived from the evangelical view of the world as a constant arena of probation and moral trial by which human character is refined and led to God. The easiest way to manage this system is through the discipline of the political party, itself one of the nineteenth-century expressions of the voluntary-associational principle through which evangelicalism responded to and shaped the democratic impulse.

Fortunately, in attempting to link the culture of evangelicalism and the definition of the Canadian state, the historian is able to draw upon more than the similarities of language. Between 1820 and 1860, English Canadian evangelicals played a leading role in articulating a tradition of political and social reform that worked a compromise between what at first sight were mutually exclusive ideas—the principles of monarchy and the culture of liberal, democratic voluntarism.[47] It was no mere coincidence that Egerton Ryerson, who was so central to the articulation of the ideology of moderate reform and who created the system of common schools, perhaps the most vital link between state, individual, and society, was a Methodist.[48] Nor should it be regarded with any great astonishment that the achievement of "responsible government" in the 1840s occurred when both moderate conservatives and moderate reformers were led by William Henry Draper, Robert Baldwin, and Francis Hincks,[49] all Anglican or Presbyterian evangelicals. Indeed, Hincks, a staunch defender of the Free Church Presbyterians, always paired civil with religious liberty and envisioned religious voluntarism as a necessary bulwark in the larger struggle for responsible government.[50] All shared the belief that although Upper Canada was a "British" society and desired to affirm and strengthen the British connection, they rejected the political theology of divine-right monarchy and established church as the basis of private and public virtue. There was thus a fundamental difference between the colony, whose values were liberal, individualist, and North American, and the parent state. However, they also recoiled from the political theology of republicanism, which they regarded as the cause of social and political instability and, in 1837, of violent rebellion.

For these evangelical moderates, the fundamental question was how to elaborate a concept of virtue and a model of state and society that would assert colonial identity and local control while maintaining the beneficial connection to the parent state. In avoiding the identification of virtue with notions of loyalty to divine-right monarchy and established church, they had, at the same time, to avoid advocating the republican form of state and public virtue, which would separate Upper Canada from the British connection. Egerton Ryerson felt this difficulty particularly keenly, and he was always vocally insistent upon his undying loyalty to the monarchy, especially after the Rebellion of 1837, and to the importance of the royal prerogative in the colonial state structure, which tended to place him at odds with Baldwin and Hincks, the younger generation of reform.[51] As the son of a Tory Loyalist officeholder whose youthful reading on political themes was informed by such respectably monarchist works as William Paley's *Moral and Political Philosophy* and William Blackstone's *Commentaries on the Laws of England,* this loyalty was not surprising. Indeed, Ryerson would have emphatically agreed with his High Tory opponents, the Reverend John Strachan, the Anglican Archdeacon of York (Toronto), and John Beverley Robinson, Chief Justice of Upper Canada, that the origins of civil government lay not in a social contract but in patriarchy sanctioned by both the Bible and the structure of the family unit.[52] Significantly, however, Ryerson did not idealize the monarchy or endow it with divine status. It should be noted that according to his political theory only civil government enjoyed divine sanction, and this might well include a republican-presidential system so dreaded by Ryerson's Tory opponents. The form of civil government, as opposed to its existence, "may be said to emanate from the people." The continued existence of the British monarchy, in Ryerson's estimation, depended not upon a divine sanction but upon a voluntaristic one and was validated only by the "unanimous and cordial affections of the people."[53]

Ryerson's dissent from the precepts of eighteenth-century British constitutional theory drew from a number of sources, but he would have found the *Lectures on Rhetoric* of Hugh Blair, the Scottish Moderate man of letters, instructive in two important respects.[54] As Scottish conservatives who belonged to a society in which political power lay in London, Blair and his contemporaries were concerned to find a way to assert a distinctive identity for Scotland in the face of the close political link to the British state. Blair and his colleague William Robertson took the lead in explaining that the character of society was not defined by the political sphere, but rather, by manners, literature, culture, and religion. It was small wonder, then, that the Moderate literati devoted so much time to the foundation of clubs, associations, and societies and to the maintenance of the distinctive Presbyterian character of the Church of Scotland.[55] In an age of revolution and rapid social change, where both poiltics and the public sphere seemed to be the source of danger and immoral conduct, the Moderates reworked the public language of civic humanism in such a way as to emphasize the cultivation of virtue in the private sphere of the individual conscience, marriage, the family and small circles of friends, while avoiding participation in public controversies.[56] For a person like Ryerson, this reorientation of virtue from the canons of a public civic humanism to the private sphere dovetailed perfectly with his evangelical perspective, which naturally emphasized individual responsibility for sin and salvation. It was but a short step from Blair and the Moderates to the common sense philosophy of Dugald Stewart, which equated virtue with the conscience of the individual, and its pursuit not as allegiance to an external, political constitution but as the understanding of and cultivation of the internal constitution. Indeed, it was for this reason that in 1842, as the founding principal of Canadian Methodism's first institution of higher learning, Victoria College, Ryerson urged close attention to Stewart's *Elements of the Philosophy of the Human Mind*. As well, the writings of Blair and the Scottish Moderates accorded well with a rising British evangelical culture that placed great emphasis upon the domestic sphere as the source and ultimate repository of the values that must guide the public sphere, a view that set evangelicals emphatically at odds with the older "aristocratic" and "plebeian" cultures.[57]

Although Ryerson's political thought retained traces of the old British constitutionalist language of "royal prerogative" and "subject," and although he insisted on a high view of the powers of the executive branch of government, these concepts did not carry any inherent virtue.[58] Writing in 1824, Ryerson confided to his diary an emphatically private and internal definition of virtue. "The cool dictates of reason," he wrote,

> assisted by that inward monitor, conscience, placed within the breast of every individual, strongly condemns any deviation from propriety, justice, or morality. By mingling with society we learn human virtue, and the scenes of public resort afford us a field of useful observation, yet retirement is the place to acquire the most important knowledge—the knowledge of ourselves. What would it avail us to dive into the mysteries of science, or entertain the world with new discoveries, to acquaint ourselves with the principles of morality, or learn the whole catalogue of Christian doctrines, if we are unacquainted with our own hearts, and strangers to the business of self-government?[59]

In Ryerson's view, "self-government," or virtue, was a term used synonymously in later years with "responsible government." It did not flow from the civic humanist notion of allegiance to or defense of some idealized, external constitutional order. Instead, individual effort, humility, and diligence— attention to the importance of the human internal mental and spiritual constitution—epitomized the evangelical's quest for private virtue, which lay at the heart of the social order. Ryerson insisted on the individual's responsibility to concentrate all waking thoughts on God. By reading Scripture and attending to prayer and devotion, by being circumspect in conduct and conversation, and by diligent reading and self-examination, a person would be able to determine "wherein I have come short, or have kept God's precepts."[60]

Ryerson's theory of self-government for Upper Canada rested, in the final analysis, on his belief that in the colony, the source of virtue lay in the individual; in Britain, in contrast, the union of church and state gave divine sanction to the reciprocal obligations of ruler and ruled. In the 1820s, Ryerson imbibed the *Theological Institutes* of the British Wesleyan Richard Watson, who added conscience, defined as the right "which a man has to profess his own opinions on subjects of religion,"[61] to the discussion of the fundamental natural rights of life, liberty, and property. Ryerson skillfully deployed Watson's arguments in his polemics against the fledgling Anglican establishment, which he correctly identified as the fundamental prop of the political theology of the British state. While professing allegiance to the monarchy, he used the principle of individual liberty as a dividing line between the colony and the mother country. In his estimation, the basis of Upper Canada's charter was "to secure liberty of conscience and freedom of thought."[62] While prepared to acknowledge that a religious establishment might be part of the British Constitution (in Britain), Ryerson declared that it was no part of the constitution of the colonial empire.[63]

By defining the private sphere of individual self-government and liberty of conscience in religious matters as the basis of the constitution of the Upper Canadian state, Ryerson was able to articulate a public philosophy, or "loyalty," based upon a liberal, voluntaristic model of society. This loyalty, however, was not defined in terms of allegiance to external constitutional forms. For Ryerson, the public sphere was economic in nature, and its virtues were synonymous with the producer ethic of market capitalism and celebrated the values of work, thrift, and self-improvement through education, which would in turn contribute to the commercial progress and social stability of Upper Canada.[64] Power flowed outward from individuals who exercised "self-government" to voluntary associations such as leagues and parties that secured economic reform and responsible government.[65] In the manner of Dugald Stewart, Ryerson viewed the political state in strictly functional, demystified terms, referring to it as an engine or a machine of public utility.[66] Because Ryerson could separate the sphere of conscience, family, and culture, where ultimate virtue lay, from the political realm, he could define the role of the state in strictly materialist terms, for its role would be confined to the external realm of economic improvements and the removal of impediments to individual initiative.

While Ryerson's views might be dismissed as those of an ambitious Methodist desperately seeking respectability and recognition at the hands of the colonial elites, it is significant that Robert Baldwin, the scion of Anglican gentry and pupil of the High Tory John Strachan, emerged in the 1830s as the leader of the moderate reformers and architect of the Canadian constitutional principle of responsible government. He shared a similar view to Ryerson's, a circumstance that can be ascribed to the conjunction of evangelicalism and the late eighteenth-century Scottish moralists. Both believed that virtue rested in conscience and the private sphere, not in the political constitution or the public realm. Indeed, in his case, there is a direct link between responsible government and notions of the human "inner constitution." Baldwin's father, William Warren Baldwin, who in fact originated the idea of responsible government, studied medicine at the University of Edinburgh in the 1790s, when the influence of Dugald Stewart was at its apogee. More tellingly, the elder Baldwin was a member of the Speculative Society debating club, which included Stewart's brilliant pupils Francis Jeffrey, Henry Brougham, and FrancisHorner, the leading lights of the *Edinburgh Review,* who by propagating the new doctrines of economic liberalism, which denied the equation between commercial prosperity and corruption, were instrumental in undercutting the old civic humanism. While there, William Baldwin would have certainly encountered the ideas of Brougham, who viewed Britain's overseas colonies as a large economic empire, bound to the center by ties not of politics but of language and culture, which fostered investment and propserity.[67]

In addition to this direct link to the political legacy of Scottish common sense, the younger Baldwin discovered the link between private happiness and an evangelical conversion when in the same year he married his cousin Eliza Sullivan and experienced "the *thorough conviction* which after having been when a young man a sceptic—may God forgive me though I hope not wholly an unbeliever, I arrived at . . . the *absolute truth* of the Religion of the blessed Redeemer."[68] As his most recent biographers have noted, there was a close relationship between the privacy of Baldwin's family circle and the political realm. Indeed, Canadian political historians have unfairly scorned Baldwin's lack of interest in the practical details of political management and administration and have regarded his constantly expressed desire to withdraw to private life as a symptom of mental illness.[69] This desire, I would argue, was merely a more extreme version of the evangelical belief that the source of personal and social virtues was to be found in the private realm of conscience and domestic relations and that the public realm was not the repository of any inherent virtue. Indeed, it was Baldwin's private world of the family circle that gave him the strength to persevere despite political disappointment. Writing to his son in 1843, William Baldwin argued in terms of the inner religious language of evangelicalism that the struggle for responsible government was a matter of "heart & conscience," by which the individual was directed by God to enter into a providential struggle between "good Govt. and evil Govt."[70]

To assert the priority of the private sphere as the sole source of virtue, however, left unanswered the problem of how to channel the private sphere of conscience into the public realm, where it could discipline and Christianize the economic values of liberal capitalism. As Ryerson put it more succinctly, quoting Francis Bacon, English Canada's overriding cultural and political problem between 1820 and 1870 was how to ensure the reign of the "Middle Principles," which "alone are solid, orderly, and fruitful."[71] Where in Britain social harmony and political stability were ensured by the visible political institutions of the public sphere—monarchy and the Established Church—and in the United States by the checks and balances of a republican constitution and by the old civic humanist language of political virtue that mediated the impact of the rising culture of evangelical voluntarism, English Canada could not appropriate these early modern political and religious foundations. Ryerson believed that virtue and stability would be achieved in Upper Canada through the constant cultivation of the inner self-discipline of the individual and that the evangelical conquest of the private realm should reshape the institutional machinery of the state.

The centerpiece of responsible government was thus neither the old constitutional language nor the deference promoted by an established church. Rather, the new colonial state would be an institutional expression of the evangelical family's parental responsibility for encouraging the punctuality, thrift, diligence, cleanliness, obedience, and self-reliance of their children in the society at large. Paradoxically, while the political program of evangelical reform envisaged a much looser relationship with the imperial state, (regulated almost by treaty) and the dissociation of church and state, the achievement of colonial "self-government" involved an enormous centralization of power in the hands of colonial governmental machinery.[72] Because the very language of colonial self-government was so firmly linked to the moral virtues of evangelicalism, what was required was an institution that would incarnate the element of probation, discipline, and moral trial so vital to the individual search for salvation. Evangelicalism's intense emphasis on domesticity would be the model for a "a liberal system of common school education, free from the domination of every church," by which "we may rationally and confidently anticipate the arrival of a long-looked for era of civil government and civil liberty, social harmony, and public prosperity."[73] In turn, Ryerson and Baldwin firmly maintained that building the educational system as the centerpiece of a series of local institutions would foster a practical, ongoing training in self-government among the English-Canadian population,[74] thus resolving the problem of where to find virtue in the modern world of liberal capitalism.

From Science to History: An Evangelical Natural Theology

By 1870, the moderate reformers had succeeded in elaborating the new, demystified machinery of the liberal state as the visible expression of the private values of evangelicalism. The Baconian "Middle Principles," based upon Du-

gald Stewart's brand of common sense, however, not only underwrote the
political culture of moderate liberalism but represented an approach to the
relationship of Scripture, theology, and scientific and historical research that
stressed the necessity of accommodating a divine revelation perceived as authoritative with human knowledge. Although such a belief in the harmony of
revelation and human reason was common to the transatlantic evangelical
culture that had emerged by the mid-nineteenth century, George Marsden has
argued in his influential treatment of American fundamentalism that this
accommodating spirit was eroded in the United States in the years after 1870.
There, Baconianism and common sense served as the rallying points of an
increasingly militant coalition of antimodernists whose opposition to what
they termed modernism in theological and social thought eventually ruptured
major American churches and gave rise to a new evangelicalism that yet forms
a powerful social and political alternative culture in modern America.[75]

In the intellectual as in the political realm, English Canada diverged from
its neighbor. Between 1850 and 1890, the language of Baconianism and the
philosophy of common sense served as the means by which Canadian evangelical leaders made a cautious and selective appropriation of certain elements of
the new scientific and critical thought that preserved, in the face of considerable strain, the cultural supremacy of the evangelical creed into the first two
decades of the twentieth century.[76] In so doing, English Canadians were able
to exploit creatively a small but nonetheless significant gap that opened between Scottish philosophy as interpreted after 1800 and the older tradition of
Newtonian natural theology that had governed the relationship between science and Protestant Christianity in the eighteenth-century English-speaking
world. The Canadian evangelical adherence to the Middle Principles in the
cultural realm was powerfully reinforced by the continued mediating role of
nineteenth-century Scottish philosophy, which exercised nearly exclusive
domination over the church colleges until the 1880s,[77] and which preserved
the individualist emphasis of evangelicalism in face of the sociological tendencies of German idealism and French positivism.

Fundamental to the transatlantic language of both British constitutionalism and American republicanism was the elaboration of an intellectually
sophisticated relationship between nature, morality, and the political realm.
The British Whigs who emerged victorious from the turbulent events of 1640–
1688 constructed a "holy alliance" with the latitudinarian party of the Church
of England, based upon the scientific ideas of Isaac Newton. Fired by the
ambition to create a broad, comprehensive national church, the latitudinarian
clergy argued for a natural religion that would override fruitless doctrinal
disputes and would refute the theories of deists and freethinkers. Rational
argumentation, they argued, and not faith, was the final arbiter of Christian
belief and dogma; scientific knowledge and natural philosophy, and not Scripture, were the most reliable means of explaining creation, and these would
underwrite political and ecclesiastical moderation. Through the study of natural history, Newtonian science promised to discern the divine laws that made
for harmony and balance in the natural world, while the natural theology

based upon this science extended these laws to a moral philosophy that discerned the same natural laws governing individual conduct, social relations, and political institutions.[78]

This Newtonian natural theology reached its height in the works of William Paley, whose *Principles of Moral and Political Philosophy* (1785) and *Natural Theology* (1802) not only formed the staple of the Cambridge University curriculum but were widely used in American colleges before 1835.[79] Although Paley's views sought to buttress allegiance to the monarchical character of the British constitutional order through the sanction of natural law,[80] they neatly dovetailed with the Scottish moral sense philosophy of Hutcheson, Witherspoon, and Adam Smith, which formed the centerpiece of America's "Republican Christian Enlightenment." As with these moral Newtonians, whose moral philosophy was directed by analogy between the physical world and the human mind, and hence by the laws and procedures of natural philosophy,[81] Paley based his interpretation of nature and society upon a remarkable utilitarian optimism that sought to explain every item of the natural world as evidence of divine design. The fitness of organs to their purposes, the organization and symmetry apparent in nature, and the suitability of certain environments to the creatures that inhabit them all testified to the existence of a Designer. Indeed, the substance of Paley's method was to work from the laws of external nature to the moral realm and the character of God, where the same beneficial natural laws applied. Paley argued, in fact, that the proof of divine goodness rested upon the fact that the design of the contrivances exhibited in the natural world was generally of a beneficial character, and that the end purpose of creation appeared to be pleasure.[82]

Among both British and American evangelicals, Paley's influence went into a sharp decline in the first decades of the nineteenth century, particularly in the realm of moral philosophy. In the wake of the political upheavals of the revolutionary age and the social distress attendant upon the transformation of the old order under the dissolving influence of industrial revolution and market capitalism, a beneficent natural and moral order could no longer be automatically assumed. To put the matter briefly, early nineteenth-century evangelicals held that Paley's hedonism and easy conflation of the natural and moral worlds left no room for the ever-present facts of sin and suffering. More tellingly, evangelicals could not accept the essential premise of Newtonianism, namely, that science, and not revelation, provided the basis for the rational explanation of natural and human phenomena. In their estimation, Paley's emphasis on utility as the ultimate rule of human behavior substituted relative, earthly standards for absolute, divine ones and, by adopting the Newtonian view of God as operating through secondary causes, came close to limiting the independence of divine activity in the moral sphere.[83] Like the High Church opponents of Newton and his latitudinarian followers, evangelicals urged a renewed emphasis on revelation as the key to a proper ordering of individual and social life.[84]

In both England and the United States, however, elements of the old Newtonian holy alliance survived the evangelical challenge. After all, the idea that divine wisdom could be discerned in nature was attractive because it seemed to offer independent, rational proof of the Christian doctrines revealed in Scripture. In England it also served, as its latitudinarian promoters had intended, to offer a nondoctrinal basis of worship and thus stifle political and social conflict between different religious groups, a matter of no small moment at a time of intense stress upon the old constitutional order of church and state. Of equal importance was the fact that natural theology served to legitimate the scientific enterprise, by warding off religious criticisms of scientific activity. Its advocates argued that scientific endeavor could be interpreted as pious worship. This was all the more necessary, given the accelerating pace of scientific discovery in geology in the early nineteenth century, where scientific facts appeared to be at variance with the biblical chronology and accounts of natural and human origins.[85]

In the United States, what survived was not simply an arena called natural theology, where two increasingly divergent spheres of religion and science worked out an uneasy accommodation. American scientists and clergymen remained impressed with the Newtonian outlook, forged by the early Scottish moralists such as Hutcheson and Adam Smith, in which the same laws and procedures governed the natural and the moral worlds, the physical and the human sciences. After all, the republican tradition expressed in the American Revolution and constitutional settlement drew considerable intellectual authority from the moral Newtonianism of the Scottish Moderate Enlightenment.[86] Despite the evangelical questioning of the Newtonian outlook after 1800, nineteenth-century clergymen and scientists, influenced by a culture in which public virtue was anchored upon the direct correspondence between the physical and the moral realms, labored to preserve the direct connection between scientific discovery and the advance of Christianity.[87] According to George Marsden, nineteenth-century evangelicals maintained the two-tiered worldview that emerged from the Moderate Enlightenment, in which the laws of nature supported supernatural belief. There was a widespread assumption that the facts disclosed in the Bible would fit exactly with objective truths discovered in the natural and social sciences.[88] More tellingly, scientists and clergymen in the United States did not consider science and religion as separate departments of knowledge whose endeavors needed to be reconciled through natural theology. Rather, evangelicals believed that scientific activity was itself a form of religious teaching, or "doxology,"[89] an attitude that expressed an unbounded confidence in the coincidence in the aims and methods of theology and science. This spirit was best epitomized by Charles Hodge's massive *Systematic Theology* of 1873, which proclaimed theology a science, similar to the organization of knowledge and method in chemistry and "mechanical philosophy." "The Bible," he declared, "is to the theologian what nature is to the man of science. . . . In theology as in natural science, principles are derived from facts."[90]

The Newtonian outlook did not, however, retain its cultural authority in the smaller Atlantic societies of Scotland and English Canada. The common sense intuitionism of Thomas Reid and Dugald Stewart, which was formulated after

1780, was an explicit warning against the easy and premature postulating of analogies between the physical and moral realms upon which the moral Newtonianism of the Scottish Moderates had been premised. Indeed, as Nicholas Phillipson has persuasively argued, Dugald Stewart declared war on the budding sociological inquiry premised upon the close analogy between natural and moral law and put an end to the promising Enlightenment development of the "human sciences" in Scotland.[91] Although Stewart was careful to praise Newton as one of the great champions of the Baconian method, closer examination reveals that he worked from a rival tradition of natural theology, one that was adeptly exploited by his evangelical disciples such as Thomas Chalmers. Stewart's *Elements of the Philosophy of the Human Mind* contained numerous references to Bishop Joseph Butler, whose *Sermons* and *The Analogy of Religion Natural and Revealed to the Constitution and Course of Nature* were written in the 1730s, thus predating the better-known treatises of William Paley.[92] Unlike Paley, Butler argued that knowledge of God's character and activity did not begin from the adaptations and contrivances of external nature, but from the inner constitution of the human mind—the conscience, reason, will, and affections. It was only a short step to affirm the clear priority and supremacy of the laws of the moral sphere—the Christian doctrines of human sin and retribution, and redemption through Christ's atonement—over those of the natural world.[93] Butler's natural theology accounted not only for the paradox of sin in a world created by God but also for the sudden irruptions and infusions of grace that alone could transform the sinner's life. Natural theology was thus transferred from the physical to the mental world and applied to the relations between people.[94] This "natural theology of conscience" did not rest upon the uniformities of natural law, but upon the interaction of a personal God with the individual.

Among Scottish evangelicals, the alliance between Bishop Butler and Stewart's common sense was best epitomized by Thomas Chalmers, the founder of the Free Church. Although Chalmers praised natural theology in stimulating the human search for religious truth, he denied the Newtonian premise that there was a logical relationship between Christian truth and the light of nature. In his treatises on the relationships of science and religion, published in the 1830s, Chalmers posited a radical distinction between natural history, which dealt with description and arrangement, and natural philosophy, which classified the phenomena into uniform laws of matter and motion. Only natural history, Chalmers maintained, actually provided evidence for the being and attributes of God, while natural philosophy had to be interpreted through revelation. Thus, Chalmers was prepared to grant that the laws of *visible* nature displayed uniformity and regularity, but as the chain of causes led upward to the moral realm, they became inaccessible and mysterious, leading directly to God. Thus, God could intervene directly in the invisible realm of conscience without violating the uniformity of nature.[95] While both the physical and moral spheres could be studied inductively, Chalmers came very close to asserting that they in fact were separate, subject to very different modes of divine activity. In a further swipe at Newton, Chalmers stated that

Christianity must rest upon its own evidence in Scripture, not on an anteced- ent natural religion accessible through the physical sciences. The Newtonian worldview, which stressed harmonious design and beneficent adaptation, was useless at precisely the point of greatest importance for evangelicals—namely, how to explain the existence and nature of sin and to provide for the human need for redemption. These needs, Chalmers asserted, could be met only by the cross and the incarnation as revealed to the mind and conscience in the Bible and by the personal contact of the sinner and Christ.[96]

Thus, while Scottish evangelicals, like their American counterparts, might applaud the advance of the nineteenth-century scientific enterprise, they also moved in another direction. Unlike the Americans, their natural theology of conscience dictated that the laws governing the physical world and those governing human behavior were, in fact, quite different. Chalmers's succes- sors James McCosh, Robert Flint, and Henry Calderwood reinforced the alliance between evangelicalism and common sense in order to wage a run- ning battle against both German idealists and advocates of French positivism between 1850 and 1890.[97] Both of these latter tendencies, like the older Scot- tish moral Newtonians, assumed that human and social behavior corre- sponded exactly to the laws of nature, the latter interpreted increasingly in Darwinian, rather than Newtonian, terms.

Only one discipline, in their estimation, answered the evangelical need for inductive certainty and displayed the working of God in conscience and soci- ety while maintaining individual freedom from the determinism of uniform natural law. This, in the words of Robert Flint, the last of the heirs of Dugald Stewart, was history. Flint dedicated most of his life to formulating what he termed a natural theology, which he defined as the delineation of "the char- acter of God as disclosed by nature, mind, and history, and to show what light the truth thus ascertained casts upon man's duty and destiny." By far the best evidence for God's existence and character, Flint argued, was to be found in conscience and the history of human society.[98] Writing in 1894, he stated that while the mind could not regard nature and history as absolutely separate, in fact they were relatively distinct. The world apprehended as space was nature, and as time, history. While history was ruled by laws, and its proper study closely connected to the progress of other sciences, "the comprehension of history is not to be gained exclusively, or even mainly, by deduction from the laws of other sciences." History's ruling principles were, in fact, none other than the evangelical doctrines of human unity and human freedom,[99] through which the sacred history of the Scriptures could be related to the general record of the progress of human societies.

The Scottish evangelical rejection of Newtonian natural theology power- fully informed the emerging Protestant culture of English Canada in the decades 1820–70. Although Paley's *Natural Theology* continued to be read in Canadian colleges until the 1880s,[100] it was not used as religious apologetic but to promote a reverent attitude through contemplation of the natural world.[101] Firmly guided by professors such as Rev. George Paxton Young, who was personally trained by Thomas Chalmers at Edinburgh, several generations of Presbyterian students would have learned that although the universe bore testimony to its Author, there was "no logical connection" between nature and the divine existence. Natural theology, Young maintained, could be sustained only on the basis of thorough knowledge of the human mind and conscience, that is, what he termed Ethical Science rather than Natural Science.[102] Young's Dalhousie counterpart, Rev. William Lyall, broke decisively with the moral Newtonianism that posited a close analogy between the processes of the natural world and those of the human mind and society. "Revelation," Lyall declared in 1853, "supersedes moral investigation" and "supplies the only key by which the mysteries of the moral world can be solved."[103]

In the Methodist Church, whose membership composed 30 percent of the Protestant population of Ontario (Upper Canada) in 1871, the Newtonian natural theology had never enjoyed widespread support. Methodism drew upon a rich eighteenth-century popular culture that held that God was not some distant, heavenly mechanic operating behind impersonal laws but a being who often miraculously entered nature and the human soul.[104] John Wesley's own intellectual background was in High Tory Oxford, and the founder of Methodism was considerably influenced by the natural philosophy of John Hutchinson, which denied the possibility of a natural theology in the sense understood by Newton and his supporters. For Hutchinson, the only way in which knowledge of nature could be obtained was through the Scriptures, which, he believed, contained the true description of nature's processes. Newton's mistake, Hutchinson affirmed, was his rejection of the method of revelation and his total commitment to scientific reason for knowledge of nature.[105] Richard Watson, whose *Theological Institutes* were read by Canadian Methodist probationers from the 1820s to the 1870s, was a thoroughgoing Hutchinsonian who attacked the Newtonian natural theology as useless and irrelevant. "The true idea of the necessary existence of God is," Watson declared, "that he thus exists because it is his nature, as an independent and uncaused being, *to be,* his being is *necessary* because it is underived, not *underived* because it is necessary. The first is the sober sense of the word among our old divines; the latter is a theory of modern date, and leads to no practical result whatever." Inquiries concerning the divine nature, he concluded, must depend exclusively upon revelation.[106]

Although many Canadian Methodists of Egerton Ryerson's generation sought to distance themselves from old plebeian culture, they did not turn to the Newtonian natural theology as the model of divine activity in the natural and human worlds. Rather, they eagerly embraced the natural theology of conscience of Bishop Butler and Dugald Stewart, whose works formed the core of the moral philosophy curriculum at Methodist colleges until the 1870s.[107] Speaking at the opening of Victoria College in 1842, Egerton Ryerson included natural theology under the rubric "philosophy of mind," which

inquires into the nature of those spirits of which we have any certain knowledge, or which it concerns us to know—the Deity and the soul of man. The
former branch of the inquiry is termed Natural Theology; the latter has
sometimes been termed Psychology, or the philosophy of the human mind.
The latter prepares the way for the former. From the knowledge of ourselves
and our Creator arise our duty to both. This is the province of *Moral
Philosophy*—to explain our obligations and our duties to ourselves, to our
fellowmen, and to our Maker—to elucidate and apply the cardinal principles of the Scriptures to the various relations and circumstances of human
life.[108]

Following Butler and Stewart, Ryerson believed that natural theology must
start with the individual conscience; its proper role was to describe the relationship between God and the moral faculty, which did not rest upon the
mechanical analogies of Newtonian physics.

The "Ryersonian succession" of Samuel Nelles and Nathanael Burwash,
who between them guided the destinies of Victoria College from 1850 to 1913,
was heavily indebted to this approach to natural theology. Nelles, whose
lectures repeated James McCosh's view that Butler was "the greatest of all
ethical writers," praised the English bishop because he avoided the extremes
of the "selfish system" of Hobbes or the "excessive stress laid on benevolence" by Francis Hutcheson.[109] Butler and Stewart were held in particular
esteem because their moral inquiries were thoroughly Baconian and because
their intuitive, a priori notion of virtue reinforced the gospel view of an
absolute moral standard independent of the utilitarian calculus of pleasure so
favored by Paley and the moral Newtonians.[110] More tellingly, Burwash,
Nelle's student, who briefly served as professor of natural science before
assuming the chair of theology in 1870, articulated a doctrine of the separate
spheres of science and religion, based upon the common sense distinction
between mind and matter. Speaking in 1867, Burwash declared that it was
useless to attempt to harmonize science and the Bible in all its details. All
truth, he admitted, "is sacred & harmonious. That my Bible is true. That
science has in it much of glorious truth but Nature alone is absolutely true.
That I may hope one day to see face to face what now I see only through a
glass darkly. . . . I cannot harmonize science in all its teachings with the
general interpretations of Scripture. Nature is true. The Bible is true for both
are from the one perfect God."[111] Unlike many of their American evangelical
counterparts, whose mental culture had often been shaped by a Newtonian
natural theology, the rival natural theology posited by the Baconian common
sense approach of Dugald Stewart freed Canadian Methodists and Presbyterians from the need to affirm the detailed harmony of science and the Bible.
Moral philosophy rested, not on the correspondence of the laws of the human
mind with the laws of nature, but upon the internal relationship between
conscience and a personal God, whose principles could be studied over time,
in the record of human history. And history, according to both Scottish and
English Canadian evangelicals, displayed a progress that liberated people
from the deterministic laws of the natural world.

Divergent Trajectories in North America

After 1870, when the impact of Darwinism, Kantian idealism, and French positivism was experienced in the transatlantic Protestant culture, many American evangelicals were encumbered by the Newtonian legacy. Seeking to preserve the identity between natural and human worlds through some uniform notion of natural law, both emerging modernists, through the adoption of idealist and Darwinian modes of thought,[112] and fundamentalists, who remained tied to the Baconian-Newtonian model of the harmony of science and theology,[113] drew upon the older tradition of the happy identity between the laws of nature and the laws of God and human society. Where modernists eagerly participated in the introduction of new critical theories of the Bible and increasingly relied upon explanations of human behavior drawn from the new sciences of sociology and psychology, fundamentalists pessimistically viewed the challenge to Newtonianism as evidence of the decline of the American republic. It is this cultural rivalry between modernists and antimodernists for the guardianship of the republican tradition from which flows the lively discussion concerning the relationship between religion and politics in America.

In English Canada, by contrast, the natural theology of conscience allowed evangelicals to escape the division into rival camps because the legacy of Butler and Stewart ensured that there was no ground of dsipute over whether natural laws were in fact identical to moral laws. What emerged was a Protestant culture in which the middle principles of Baconian common sense ruled unchallenged until the 1890s, permitting a limited accommodation between evangelicalism and the new forms of critical thought. This intellectual climate sustained a social structure and political state that incarnated the evangelical principles of liberal individualism and voluntarism. Although the Canadian churches were challenged by the rise of industrial society and corporate capitalism after 1890, they failed to articulate an American-style Social Gospel founded upon idealist philosophy and the new social sciences.[114] The great paradox of twentieth-century English-Canadian culture is that the very power of the private values of evangelicalism to shape the liberal state between 1820 and 1870 ensured that the churches would be unable to offer any compelling critique or alternative vision of the relationship between the individual and society in the twentieth century and would have to retreat to the private sphere rather than engaging in constructive dialogue concerning the Canadian state and its future.

Notes

1. The "revolutionary" nature of evangelicalism has been insisted upon by David Bebbington, *Evangelicalism in Modern Britain* (London: Unwin Hyman, 1989). For the American context, see Nathan O. Hatch, *The Democratization of American Christianity* (New Haven: Yale University Press, 1989). For the relationship between evan-

gelicalism and the radical culture of the "age of revolution" in English Canada, see Nancy J. Christie, " 'In These Times of Democratic Rage and Delusion': Popular Religion and the Challenge to the Established Order, 1760–1815," in *The Canadian Protestant Experience, 1760–1990,* ed. G.A. Rawlyk (Burlington, Ont.: Welch, 1990), 9–47.

2. For the "political theology" of the old society, see the illuminating discussion in J. C. D. Clark, *English Society, 1688–1832* (Cambridge: Cambridge University Press, 1986). American historians have only recently begun to explore the "early modern" aspects of their own religious experience. See the illuminating discussion in Jon Butler, *Awash in a Sea of Faith* (Cambridge: Harvard University Press, 1990). For a splendid definition of the outlines and implications of the individualistic nature of evangelicalism, see Boyd Hilton, *The Age of Atonement* (Oxford: Oxford University Press, 1988). For a preliminary appraisal of the meaning of "evangelicalism" in English Canadian history, see Michael Gauvreau, "Protestantism Transformed: Personal Piety and the Evangelical Social Vision, 1815–1867," in *The Canadian Protestant Experience,* ed. Rawlyk, 48–97.

3. Many of these interconnections remain to be explored by historians. For a bold and effective examination of the problem of revivalism in Britain and America, see Richard Carwardine, *Transatlantic Revivalism: Popular Evangelicalism in Britain and America, 1790–1865* (Westport, CT: Greenwood Press, 1978).

4. See Owen Chadwick, *The Victorian Church,* 2 vols. (London: A. and C. Black, 1966–69); Bebbington, *Evangelicalism in Modern Britain;* A. D. Gilbert, *Religion and Society in Industrial England: Church, Chapel and Social Change, 1740–1914* (London: Longman, 1976).

5. For a suggestive discussion of this process in the American context, see Donald Mathews, "The Second Great Awakening as an Organizing Process, 1780–1830: A Hypothesis," *American Quarterly* 21 (1969): 23–44. See also Hatch, *Democratization of American Christianity,* and, for the Canadian context, William Westfall, *Two Worlds: The Protestant Culture of Nineteenth Century Ontario* (Montreal and Kingston: McGill-Queen's University Press, 1969); John Webster Grant, *A Profusion of Spires* (Toronto: University of Toronto Press, 1988); Christie, " 'In These Times of Democratic Rage and Delusion.' " See Gauvreau, "Personal Piety and the Evangelical Social Vision," for the census statistics of English Canadian religious affiliation for the period 1841–71.

6. For a discerning treatment of the origins of American antimodernist fundamentalism, see George Marsden, *Fundamentalism and American Culture: The Shaping of Twentieth-Century Evangelicalism, 1870–1925* (New York: Oxford University Press, 1980). William R. Hutchison, *The Modernist Impulse in American Protestantism* (Cambridge: Harvard University Press, 1976), provides an important study of the "modernist" theological tendency in the American context. William R. McLoughlin's *Revivals, Awakenings, and Reform: An Esaay on Religion and Social Change in America, 1607–1977* (Chicago: University of Chicago Press, 1978) has advanced the notion that a dialectical struggle between "new lights" and "old lights" is essential to understanding creative periods of cultural change in America. For the more harmonious English Canadian context, see the recent study by Michael Gauvreau, *The Evangelical Century: College and Creed in English Canada from the Great Revival to the Great Depression* (Montreal: and Kingston: McGill-Queen's University Press, 1991).

7. The literature on the intersection of American religion and politics is vast. See, however, Mark Noll, ed., *Religion and American Politics* (New York: Oxford University Press, 1990), an important statement of recent American scholarship. See also the

compelling discussion of the role of religion and politics in the United States in the 1980s by Garry Wills, *Under God: Religion and American Politics* (New York: Simon and Schuster, 1990). To date, English Canadian scholars have been most reluctant to approach this question, except for the debate launched by Richard Allen nearly two decades ago on the role of the early twentieth-century Social Gospel in forging Canada's minority tradition of democratic socialism.

8. For the division of the American Enlightenment into Moderate, Skeptical, Radical, and Didactic phases, see the influential work by Henry F. May, *The Enlightenment in America* (Oxford: Oxford University Press, 1976).

9. For the synthesis of Calvinism and the tenets of the Enlightenment in the thought of the Moderates, see Richard Sher, *Church and University in the Scottish Enlightenment: The Moderate Literati of Edinburgh* (Princeton: Princeton University Press, 1985), 35, 43–44, 57–59, 161, 167, for aspects of the Moderate emphasis in theology and social thought.

10. For the relationship between Witherspoon and his Moderate opponents, see ibid., 161, 167.

11. For the close links between the Newtonian natural philosophy and the "moral science" emphasis of eighteenth-century Scottish philosophy, see Roger L. Emerson, "Science and Moral Philosophy in the Scottish Enlightenment," in *Studies in the Philosophy of the Scottish Enlightenment*, ed. M. A. Stewart (Oxford: Clarendon Press, 1990), 32–36.

12. For Witherspoon's introduction of the culture of the Scottish Moderates to Princeton, see the new study by Mark Noll, *Princeton and the Republic, 1768–1822* (Princeton: Princeton University Press, 1989), 28–58.

13. For Smith's relationship to the Enlightenment, see ibid., 185–213.

14. See the important article by James Kloppenberg, "The Virtues of Liberalism: Christianity, Republicanism, and Ethics in Early American Political Discourse," *Journal of American History* 74 (1987): 9–33, who argues that in the late eighteenth century, Americans drew upon the traditions of Christianity, classical republicanism, and liberalism in order to define notions of public and private virtue. The basic statement of the importance of classical republicanism in Britain and America was made by J. G. A. Pocock, *The Machiavellian Moment: Florentine Political Thought and the Atlantic Republican Tradition* (Princeton: Princeton University Press, 1975).

15. For the Scottish Moderate use of the civic humanist language, see Sher, *Church and University in the Scottish Enlightenment*, 188, 198.

16. The alliance between republican ideology and evangelicalism during the American Revolution has been treated by Nathan O. Hatch, *The Sacred Cause of Liberty: Republican Thought and the Millennium in Revolutionary New England* (New Haven: Yale University Press, 1977). For the distinction between Witherspoon's civic humanism and that of Hugh Blair, one of the Scottish Moderate leaders, see Thomas P. Blair, "Witherspoon, Blair, and Civic Humanism," in *Scotland and America in the Age of Enlightenment*, ed. Richard B. Sher and Jeffrey R. Smitten (Princeton: Princeton University Press, 1990), 100–114. For the "Republican Christian Enlightenment" synthesis of Witherspoon and Smith at Princeton, see Noll, *Princeton and the Republic*, 185–213.

17. See the stimulating essay by Daniel Walker Howe, "The Language of Faculty Psychology in the Federalist Papers," in *Conceptual Change and the Constitution*, ed. Terence Ball and J. G. A. Pocock (Lawrence: University of Kansas Press, 1988), 107–36.

18. Gauvreau, *Evangelical Century*, 15–19.

19. For stimulating discussions of this process in the American context, see Joyce Appleby, *Capitalism and a New Social Order: The Republican Vision of the 1790's* (New York: New York University Press, 1984); Stephen Watts, *The Republic Reborn* (Baltimore: Johns Hopkins University Press, 1987). For the interaction of this rising liberal democratic culture and the evangelical impulse, see Hatch, *Democratization of American Christianity.*

20. The body of literature in this historiographic tradition is both substantial and monolithic. It takes its inspiration from the wave of anti-Americanism that dominated Canadian history faculties in the 1960s in the wake of George P. Grant's influential *Lament for a Nation: The Defeat of Canadian Nationalism* (Toronto: McClelland and Stewart, 1965). In terms of an interpretation of the early history of English Canada, it assailed the views of Louis Hartz, *The Liberal Tradition in America: An Interpretation of American Political Thought since the Revolution* (New York: Harcourt, Brace, 1955). For Hartz's principal Canadian critic, S. F. Wise, see Wise, "Sermon Literature and Canadian Intellectual History," in *Canadian History before Confederation,* ed. J. M. Bumsted (Georgetown, Ont.: Irwin-Dorsey, 1972); idem, "Upper Canada and the Conservative Tradition," in *Profiles of a Province: Studies in the History of Ontario,* ed. Edith G. Firth (Toronto: Ontario Historical Society, 1967); S. F. Wise and R. C. Brown, *Canada Views the United States* (Toronto: Macmillan, 1972); S. F. Wise, "Liberal Consensus or Ideological Battleground: Some Reflections on the Hartz Thesis," Canadian Historical Association, *Historical Papers,* 1975. More recently, Jane Errington, *The Lion, the Eagle, and Upper Canada: A Developing Colonial Ideology* (Montreal and Kingston: McGill-Queen's University Press, 1987), has refined the Wise thesis by positing a greater diversity within a general "conservative" paradigm among Upper Canadian political and commercial elites. Errington locates the source of some of these ideas, particularly before the War of 1812, in ideas derived from American Federalists. David Mills, *The Idea of Loyalty in Upper Canada* (Montreal and Kingston: McGill-Queen's University Press, 1988), has suggested the importance of conservative definitions of "loyalty" in defining the scope and limits of political debate in Upper Canada. A hidden but powerful influence on this hypothesis of a monolithic conservatism remains the prestige of Carl Berger's *Sense of Power* (Toronto: University of Toronto Press, 1970), a valuable study of late Victorian conservative ideology that does not claim that such sentiment existed prior to the 1880s. There is a temptation, however, to read this imperial sentiment back into the early nineteenth century.

21. Christie, " 'In these Times of Democratic Rage and Delusion.' " For a view that evangelicals promoted a different and democratic vision of community and social participation that rejected social rank, learning, and intelligence, see Donald Mathews, *Religion in the Old South* (Chicago: University of Chicago Press, 1977), 12.

22. For a particularly stimulating look at this crisis of identity and the consequent crisis of social authority in the United States, see Watts, *Republic Reborn.* Evangelical leaders also displayed a nostalgia for the old society, but this did not prevent them from articulating the ideology of liberal capitalism. The most prominent transatlantic example is Thomas Chalmers, who played a key role in fusing evangelical theology and the new political economy. However, he often looked to the parish structure of rural Scotland for inspiration in his attempts to relieve urban poverty. For Chalmers, see Stewart J. Brown, *Thomas Chalmers and the Godly Commonwealth in Scotland* (Oxford: Oxford University Press, 1982), chaps. 1 and 3. For the role of Chalmers and of British evangelicals in creating a "Christian Political Economy" based upon the evangelical doctrines of depravity, probation, moral trial, and the atonement, during the

early Industrial Revolution, see the brilliant analysis by Boyd Hilton, *The Age of Atonement: The Influence of Evangelicalism on Social and Economic Thought, 1795–1865* (Oxford: Clarendon Press, 1988).

23. See Mark Noll, "Common Sense Traditions and American Evangelical Thought," *American Quarterly* 37 (1985): 217.

24. For the role of common sense in the American religious setting in the nineteenth century, see Sydney Ahlstrom, "The Scottish Philosophy and American Theology," *Church History* 24 (1955): 257–72; Noll, "Common Sense Traditions," 216–38; George Marsden, *The Evangelical Mind and the New School Presbyterian Experience* (New Haven: Yale University Press, 1970); idem, *Fundamentalism and American Culture,* 55–62, 212–21; Theodore Dwight Bozeman, *Protestants in an Age of Science: The Baconian Ideal and Antebellum American Religious Thought* (Chapel Hill: University of North Carolina Press, 1977). For the role of common sense in defining the mind-set of Canadian evangelicals, see A. B. McKillop, *A Disciplined Intelligence: Critical Inquiry and Canadian Thought in the Victorian Era* (Montreal and Kingston: McGill-Queen's University Press, 1979), chap. 2; Gauvreau, *Evangelical Century,* chap. 1.

25. This distinction has been recently asserted by Richard Sher, whose final chapter of *Church and University in the Scottish Enlightenment* defines common sense as the product of the twilight of a Moderate Enlightenment already frightened by the implications of the American and French revolutions.

26. See Nicholas Phillipson, "The Pursuit of Virtue in Scottish University Education: Dugald Stewart and Scottish Moral Philosophy in the Enlightenment," in *Universities, Society, and the Future,* ed. N. Phillipson (Edinburgh: Edinburgh University Press, 1983), 82–83; Wilson Smith, *Professors and Public Ethics: Studies of Northern Moral Philosophers before the Civil War* (Ithaca: Cornell University Press, 1956); Gauvreau, *Evangelical Century,* chap. 1.

27. For Stewart's critique of the moral sense tradition and in particular of Adam Smith, see Dugald Stewart, *Elements of the Philosophy of the Human Mind,* (1792 and 1814; reprint, London: William Tegg, 1856), 538–39. For a stimulating reassessment of Stewart's place in the Scottish philosophical tradition, see Phillipson, "Pursuit of Virtue in Scottish University Education," 82–101.

28. Stewart, *Elements,* 516–25.

29. Ibid., 31–32.

30. Ibid., 500–501.

31. Ibid., 510–11.

32. Phillipson, "Pursuit of Virtue in Scottish University Education," 97–98.

33. Ibid., 97–98.

34. Stewart, *Elements,* 129.

35. Ibid., 128.

36. Ibid., 131.

37. This aspect is what Mark Noll defines as "epistemological common sense." See his "Common Sense Traditions," 220–21. For the distinction between common sense and the varieties of idealism, see J. David Hoeveler, Jr., *James McCosh and the Scottish Intellectual Tradition: From Glasgow to Princeton* (Princeton: Princeton University Press, 1981), 121.

38. Noll, "Common Sense Traditions," 223–24.

39. Ibid., 223. On the Baconian ideal, see Bozeman, *Protestants in an Age of Science.* Gauvreau, *Evangelical Century,* 38–45, discusses the application of Baconianism among Canadian Presbyterians before 1860.

40. See Hilton, *Age of Atonement,* esp. chap. 5, "The Mind of Economic Man,"

for the synthesis of evangelicalism, common sense, and the new liberal economics. For the influence of Stewart and his Edinburgh pupils on economic and political discussion in the first great age of reform, see Biancamaria Fontana, *Rethinking the Politics of Commercial Society: The Edinburgh Review, 1802–1832* (Cambridge: Cambridge University Press), 1985.

41. See the stimulating new interpretations by Peter Mandler, *Aristocratic Government in the Age of Reform: Whigs and Liberals, 1830–1852* (Oxford: Claredon Press, 1990); and Richard Brent, *Liberal Anglican Politics* (Oxford: Clarendon Press, 1987), which effectively challenge the myth of middle-class leadership in the process of early Victorian political and social reform and focus on the leading role of the Established Church and the aristocracy.

42. See Watts, *Republic Reborn*, 217–74; and Kloppenberg, "Virtues of Liberalism." A recent work by Ellis Sandoz, *A Government of Laws: Political Theory, Religion, and the American Founding* (Baton Rouge: Lousiana State University Press, 1990), has stressed the continued tension between classical Christian political concepts and the ideology of liberalism in the American Constitution.

43. See Smith, *Professors and Public Ethics.*

44. Daniel Walker Howe, "The Evangelical Movement and Political Culture in the North during the Second Party System," *Journal of American History* 77 (1991): 1216–39.

45. In recent years, historians of Canadian politics have finally made an attempt to address questions raised by the country's relationship to transatlantic ideas such as civic humanism. See Gordon T. Stewart, *The Origins of Canadian Politics: A Comparative Approach* (Vancouver: University of British Columbia Press, 1986); Paul Romney, "From the Rule of Law to Responsible Government: Ontario Political Culture and the Origins of Canadian Statism," Canadian Historical Association, *Historical Papers,* 1988, 86–119; S. J. R. Noel, *Patrons, Clients, Brokers: Ontario Society and Politics, 1791–1896* (Toronto: University of Toronto Press, 1990).

46. Canadian historical writing has suffered from an inability to address the meaning of "responsible government" and its implications in social and cultural terms. See, however, the ironic essay by Graeme Patterson, "An Enduring Canadian Myth: Responsible Government and the Family Compact," in *Historical Essays on Upper Canada: New Perspectives,* ed. J. K. Johnson and Bruce G. Wilson (Ottawa: Carleton University Press, 1989), 485–512, which suggests certain reasons for the "mythical" nature of the concept.

47. The literature on this important problem is exceedingly scanty, reflecting the unspoken Canadian convention that politics and religion should be kept in separate compartments. See, however, the older but still insightful study by Goldwin French, *Parsons and Politics: The Role of the Wesleyan Methodists in Upper Canada and the Maritimes from 1780 to 1855* (Toronto: Ryerson Press, 1962); and John S. Moir, *Church and State in Canada West: Three Studies in the Relation of Denominationalism and Nationalism, 1841–1867.* Westfall, *Two Worlds,* chap. 4, contains a stimulating reassessment of the breakdown of the alliance of church and state.

48. On Ryerson, see Goldwin French, "Egerton Ryerson and the Methodist Model for Upper Canada," in *Egerton Ryerson and His Times,* ed. N. McDonald and Alf Chaiton (Toronto: Macmillan, 1978), 45–58; and Alison Prentice, *The School Promoters* (Toronto: McClelland and Stewart, 1977).

49. Draper, the founder of the moderate conservative tradition, was the son of a Church of England clergyman and active in voluntary organizations in Toronto. For his life and career, see George Metcalf, "William Henry Draper," in *The Pre-Confeder-*

ation Premiers: Ontario Government Leaders, 1841–1867, ed. J. M. S. Careless (Toronto: University of Toronto Press, 1980). Robert Baldwin, who shares the honor with his father, William Warren Baldwin, as the progenitor of the idea of responsible government, was the son of Anglo-Irish gentry and was likewise a leader in the emerging "voluntaristic" culture. See J. M. S. Careless, "Robert Baldwin," in ibid.; Michael Cross and Robert L. Froser, "Rober Baldwin," *Dictionary of Canadian Biography,* vol. 8 (Toronto: University of Toronto Press, 1985), 45–59; Cross and Fraser, " 'The Waste that Lies Before Me': The Public and Private Worlds of Robert Baldwin," Canadian Historical Association, *Historical Papers,* 1983, 164–83. Francis Hincks, the son of an Irish Presbyterian clergyman, was Baldwin's successor as the leader of the moderate reformers and was likewise committed to the voluntary principle in church and state. For Hincks, see William Ormsby, "Sir Francis Hincks," in *The Pre-Confederation Premiers,* ed. Careless.

50. On Hinck's political and religious outlook, see *Pilot,* a Montreal newspaper that championed the reform in general and that in particular was founded to promote the Baldwinites' goal of responsible government.

51. Egerton Ryerson, *The Story of My Life,* ed. J. George Hodgins (Toronto: William Briggs, 1883), 26–29, 157.

52. Egerton Ryerson, *Civil Government—The Late Conspiracy,* A Discourse delivered in Kingston, U.C., 31 December 1837 (Toronto: Methodist Conference Office, 1838), 4. For the Anglican "political theology," which was premised on notions of the divine-right monarchy, see Clark, *English Society.* Clark argues that both evangelicals and Methodists in Britain held a similar concept of the origins of government (216–76).

53. Ryerson, *Civil Government,* 4–5.

54. Ryerson recorded that he read Hugh Blair's influential work in grammar school (*Story of My Life,* 25).

55. Sher, *Church and University in the Scottish Enlightenment,* 106.

56. Miller, "Witherspoon, Blair, and Civic Humanism," 110–12. See also John Dwyer, *Virtuous Discourse: Sensibility and Community in Late Eighteenth-Century Scotland* (Edinburgh: John Donald, 1987), esp. chap. 4, "The Symphony of Sympathy."

57. See, for the British context, Lenore Davidoff and Catherine Hall, *Family Fortunes; Men and Women of the English Middle Class, 1780–1850* (Chicago: University of Chicago Press, 1987), esp. pt. 1, "Religion and Ideology."

58. Ryerson, *Story of My Life,* 209–10, 168–69.

59. Ibid., 38.

60. Ibid., 6.

61. Richard Watson, *Theological Institutes* (1823; reprint, New York: Carlton and Porter, n.d.), 2:539.

62. Ryerson, *Story of My Life,* 81.

63. Ibid., 291.

64. David Mills, *The Idea of Loyalty in Upper Canada, 1784–1850.* The equation of the private virtues of the producer ethic with the fundamental values of the community has ensured their long persistence in Canadian history. See Allan Smith, "The Myth of the Self-Made Man in English Canada," *Canadian Historical Review* 59 (1978): 189–219.

65. Egerton Ryerson, *The New Canadian Dominion: Dangers and Duties of the People in Regard to their Government* (Toronto: Lovell and Gibson, 1867), 15.

66. Ibid., 27.

67. For William Baldwin's studies at Edinburgh and membership in the Speculative Society, see Careless, "Robert Baldwin," 93. On the Speculative Society itself and
the role of Stewart's pupils in it, see Fontana, *Rethinking the Politics of Commercial
Society,* 48, 59–69, 115. It has generally been assumed that the elder Baldwin's political
ideas were derived from the Irish Volunteers, who sought to reconcile the aspirations
for a measure of local independence with a continued British connection. It would be
interesting to sketch, however, the extent to which these Irish reformers were influenced by late eighteenth- and early nineteenth-century Scottish thinkers, who faced a
similar problem. As well, the prominent role of medical doctors, such as W. W.
Baldwin and John Rolph, in "reform" ranks awaits a historical assessment. With their
focus on the human "constitution," they articulated a different language from that of
the lawyers, who spoke of a more "external," political constitutional language.

68. Quoted in Cross and Fraser, " 'The Waste that Lies Before Me,' " 169.

69. For the most recent example of this bias, see Noel, *Patrons, Clients, Brokers,*
139–52, who credits Hincks with the construction of the "politics of accommodation"
that achieved responsible government. Cross and Fraser, in " 'The Waste that Lies
Before Me,' " present the argument that Baldwin was afflicted with an acute form of
mental depression and melancholia after the death of Eliza Baldwin in 1837. This took
the obsessive form of ritual celebrations of their wedding anniversary and the bizarre
clause in Baldwin's will which stipulated that upon his death, because Eliza had died
following the complications of a Caesarian section, his own corpse should be mutilated
with a similar incision. While not disagreeing with this analysis, I would argue here that
Baldwin's behavior expressed, in a more intense, obsessive form, the evangelical
desire to withdraw to the private sphere and the comforts of domesticity.

70. Ibid., 181.

71. Ryerson, *New Canadian Dominion,* opening epigraph. Ryerson also quoted
Lord Brougham, the apologist of commercial liberalism, and Francis Wayland, the
American Baptist promoter of the common sense philosophy.

72. See the recently published work by Bruce Curtis, *True Government by Choice
Men? Inspection, Education, and State Formation in Canada West* (Toronto: University
of Toronto Press, 1992), 25–27. For Baldwin's language of treaty, drawn from the
Scottish natural jurisprudence tradition of Adam Smith, see Romney, "From the Rule
of Law to Responsible Government." Romney's interpretation of this as "constitutionalism" is convoluted and is an ill-starred attempt to locate English Canadian reformers within the older Anglo-American culture of civic humanism. For the disestablishment of church and state in the wake of the great institutional reform of the English
Canadian state in the 1840s, see Westfall, *Two Worlds,* chap. 4.

73. Ryerson, *Story of My Life,* 301. Significantly, Alison Prentice's study of the
Ryersonian educational outlook and achievements, *The School Promoters: Education
and Social Class in Mid-Nineteenth Century* (Toronto: McClelland and Stewart, 1977),
contains a final chapter entitled "The Government as Parent." I would argue, however, that what Ryerson envisaged was not the extension of the state into the domestic
circle but the extension of the family values of evangelicalism into the state.

74. Curtis, *True Government by Choice Men?* 7.

75. For the link between Baconianism, common sense, and American antimodernist religious fundamentalism, see Marsden, *Fundamentalism and American
Culture.* For a recent study of late nineteenth-century divisions over biblical scholarship in American denominations, see Mark Noll, *Between Faith and Criticism: Evangelicals, Scholarship, and the Bible in America* (1986; rev. ed., Grand Rapids: Baker
Book House, 1991), chap. 2.

76. See Gauvreau, *Evangelical Century,* chap. 4. Aspects of this accommodation in the intellectual realm have been treated by Marguerite Van Die, *An Evangelical Mind: Nathanael Burwash and the Methodist Tradition in Canada, 1839–1918* (Montreal and Kingston: McGill-Queen's University Press, 1989).

77. For the continued hold of the "empire" of common sense in English Canada, see Gauvreau, *Evangelical Century,* chap. 4. With the notable exception of John Watson of Queen's University, a neo-Hegelian appointed in 1872, all professors of moral philosophy—including the Presbyterians William Lyall (Dalhousie), George Paxton Young (Toronto), and John Clark Murray (McGill), and the Methodists Samuel Nelles (Victoria) and Charles Stewart (Mount Allison)—followed some variant of the Scottish "mediating" tendency, which was heavily indebted to common sense. Among other church college professors, particularly among Presbyterians, there was a steady stream of emigrants from Scotland, or Canadians who returned to Edinburgh or Glasgow for theological training.

78. For the link between Newtonian science and Whig politics, see the fine study by Margaret C. Jacob, *The Newtonians and the English Revolution, 1689–1720* (Ithaca: Cornell University Press, 1976), 34–39. The term "holy alliance" was coined by John Gascoigne, whose *Cambridge in the Age of Enlightenment: Science, Religion, and Politics from the Restoration to the French Revolution* (Cambridge: Cambridge University Press, 1989), explores the institutional expression of the Newtonian "natural theology." For the close relationship between the study of natural history and that of natural theology, which began under the impact of Newton in the late seventeenth century, see Neal C. Gillespie, "Natural History, Natural Theology, and Social Order: John Ray and the 'Newtonian Ideology,' " *Journal of the History of Biology* 20 (Spring 1987): 1–49.

79. For Paley's influence at Cambridge, see Gascoigne, *Cambridge in the Age of Enlightenment,* 239; Martha McMackin Garland, *Cambridge before Darwin: The Ideal of a Liberal Education, 1800–1860* (Cambridge: Cambridge University Press, 1980), 53–54. For Paley's influence in America, see Wilson Smith, "William Palye's Theological Utilitarianism in America," *William and Mary Quarterly* 11 (1954): 402–24.

80. For Paley's role in articulating an Anglican political theology that defended patriarchal government from a utilitarian standpoint, see Clark, *English Society,* 50, 57.

81. For the "utilitarian" nature of the Scottish "moral sense" school, see Emerson, "Science and Moral Philosophy in the Scottish Enlightenment," 34–36. Likewise, Mark Noll in *Princeton and the Republic* has examined the Newtonian foundations of the brand of moral philosophy and republican ideology prevalent at Princeton between 1770 and 1800.

82. See William Paley, *Natural Theology* (1802; rev. ed., London: Ward, Lock, n.d.), 229, in which the argument moves from minute adaptations of animal bodies to infer general laws concerning morality and the character of the Deity. The assumption throughout is that the natural laws are, in fact, the same in the moral world. For Paley's hedonism or utilitarianism, see Garland, *Cambridge before Darwin,* 54–55.

83. Garland, *Cambridge before Darwin,* 56. For the decline of Paley in Britain, see Hilton, *Age of Atonement,* 170–71.

84. For the affinities between the High Church tradition and British evangelicalism, both of which rejected the Newtonian foundations of the "holy alliance," see Gascoigne, *Cambridge in the Age of Enlightenment,* 63–64, 263. See, more generally, Bebbington, *Evangelicalism in Modern Britain,* 34–35, which argues that evangelicals drew upon a number of pre-Enlightenment theological traditions, including the High Church of the seventeenth and early eighteenth centuries.

85. For a particularly illuminating discussion of the content and function of nineteenth-century English natural theology, see John Hedley Brooke, "The Fortunes and Functions of Natural Theology," in *Science and Religion: Some Historical Perspectives* (Cambridge: Cambridge University Press, 1991), 193–96. See also idem, "The Natural Theology of the Geologists: Some Theological Strata," in *Images of the Earth: Essays in the History of Environmental Sciences,* ed. L. J. Jordanova and Roy Porter, BSHS Monographs 1 (1979), 42.

86. See Garry Wills, *Inventing America* (New York: Alfred A. Knopf, 1977), for the influence of Francis Hutcheson and Scottish "moral sense" on Jefferson and the Declaration of Independence; and also Howe, "Faculty Psychology."

87. See George Daniels, *American Science in the Age of Jackson* (New York: Columbia University Press, 1968); Herbert Hovenkamp, *Science and Religion in America, 1800–1860* (Philadelphia: University of Pennsylvania Press, 1978).

88. George Marsden, "Evangelicals and the Scientific Culture: An Overview," in *Religion and Twentieth-Century American Intellectual Life,* ed. Michael J. Lacey (1989; rev. ed., Cambridge; Cambridge University Press, 1991), 30–32.

89. See Bozeman, *Protestants in an Age of Science,* 80–81.

90. Quoted in ibid., 155. Hodge, the leading figure of the Princeton theology in the nineteenth century, believed that theological statement is explicitly founded upon scientific analogy.

91. Phillipson, "Pursuit of Virtue in Scottish University Education," 99–100.

92. See Stewart, *Elements.* For the appropriation of Butler by the Scottish common sense advocates, see Stewart R. Sutherland, "The Presbyterian Inheritance of Hume and Reid," in *The Origins and Nature of the Scottish Enlightenment,* ed. R. H. Campbell and Andrew Skinner (Edinburgh: John Donald, 1982), 144–45; Hilton, *Age of Atonement,* 170.

93. Joseph Butler, *The Analogy of Religion, Natural and Revealed, to the Constitution and the Course of Nature* (1736; reprint, London: Routledge, 1884), 112–13. Indeed, it should be stressed that the popularity of common sense among evangelicals owed a great deal to its inclusion of Butler's natural theology.

94. Hilton, *Age of Atonement,* 186.

95. See the stimulating article by Crosbie Smith, "From Design to Dissolution: Thomas Chalmers' Debt to John Robison," *British Journal for the History of Science* 12 (1979): 59–70.

96. On Chalmers and natural theology, see Daniel F. Rice, "Natural Theology and the Scottish Philosophy in the Thought of Thomas Chalmers," *Scottish Journal of Theology* 24 (February 1971): 23–46.

97. For the common sense battle against French positivism, see the important new study by Charles Cashdollar, *The Transformation of Theology, 1830–1890: Positivism and Protestant Thought in Britain and America* (Princeton: Princeton University Press, 1989), 55, 329–31. For the battle between evangelicals and the Kantian approach of Sir William Hamilton in the 1850s, the classic study remains George Elder Davie, *The Democratic Intellect: Scotland and Her Universities in the Nineteenth Century* (Edinburgh: Edinburgh University Press, 1961). For a more recent treatment, see J. David Hoeveler, Jr., *James McCosh and the Scottish Intellectual Tradition* (Princeton: Princeton University Press, 1981).

98. Robert Flint, *Agnosticism* (Edinburgh: William Blackwood and Sons, 1903), 578; idem, *Theism: Being the Baird Lecture for 1876* (1877; reprint, Edinburgh: William Blackwood and Sons, 1883), 227–30.

99. Robert Flint, *Historical Philosophy in France and French Belgium and Switzerland* (New York: Charles Scribner's Sons, 1894), 6–7, 12, 16, 37, 105, 126.

100. See, for example, *Calendar of the University of Victoria College,* 1880 and 1884, where Paley was required reading for the junior year.

101. See Carl Berger, *Science, God, and Nature in Victorian Canada* (Toronto: University of Toronto Press, 1983), which suggests that the pious study of nature infused the evangelical culture of English Canada.

102. George Paxton Young, "Lecture on the Philosophical Principles of Natural Religion," *Home and Foreign Record of the Canadian Presbyterian Church,* 2, no. 2 (December 1862). For Young's background and teaching at Knox College and University College, Toronto, and the influence of Chalmers, see J. T. Stevenson and Thomas Mathien, "George Paxton Young: Sceptical Fideist," in *Religion and Science in Early Canada,* ed. J. D. Rabb (Kingston: Ronald P. Frye, 1988). Young's contemporaries Rev. William Lyall (Dalhousie) and Rev. James George (Queen's), who also taught moral philosophy, were also students of Chalmers.

103. William Lyall, *The Philosophy of Thought: A Lecture delivered at the Opening of the Free Church College, Halifax, Nova Scotia* (Halifax: James Barnes, 1853), 8–10.

104. For the contrast between Canadian Methodist and Anglican interpretations of God's presence and activity, see Westfall, *Two Worlds,* chap. 2, "Order and Experience." For the links between American Methodism and the "plebeian" culture of the eighteenth century, see Butler, *Awash in a Sea of Faith.*

105. For a description of Hutchinson's views, published in 1724 in *Moses' Principia,* see G. N. Cantor, "Revelation and the Cyclical Cosmos of John Hutchinson," in *Images of the Earth,* ed. Jordanova and Porter. See also C. B. Wilde, "Hutchinsonianism, Natural Philosophy, and Religious Controversy in Eighteenth Century Britain," *History of Science* 18 (1980): 1–24. John Wesley, whose Oxford education was significantly influenced by the High Church promoters of Hutchinson, made his works mandatory reading at the Kingswood Grammar School. See John Hedley Brooke, "Science and Religion in the Enlightenment," in *Science and Religion: Some Historical Perspectives,* 190–91; Robert E. Schofield, "John Wesley and Science in Eighteenth Century England," *Isis* 44 (1953): 331–40.

106. Watson, *Theological Institutes,* 1:334–35.

107. See *Calendar of the University of Victoria College, Cobourg,* 1870–71. For a fuller description of Methodist uses of Bishop Butler, see Michael Gauvreau, "The Golden Age of the Church College: Mount Allison's Encounter with Modern Thought, 1850–1890," in *Methodism in Atlantic Canada,* ed. C. H. H. Scobie (Montreal and Kingston: McGill-Queen's University Press, 1992).

108. Ryerson, *Inaugural Address,* 17. Ryerson's language acknowledges the obvious debt to Dugald Stewart. Ryerson also drew upon the leading American promoter of the Butlerian alternative to Paley, Rev. Francis Wayland, the Baptist president of Brown University, whose *Elements of Moral Science* (1835) was read with enthusiasm by Ryerson.

109. "Notebook of Lectures on Butler's *Sermons,*" October 1866, Samuel Nelles Papers, box 9, file 228, United Church Archives; "Lectures on Butler," October 1867, Nelles Papers, box 10, file 231.

110. "Notebook of Lectures on Butler's *Sermons*"; "Stewart's Discussion of God and a Future Life," 1872–73, Nelles Papers, box 10.

111. "Introductory Lecture on Natural History," Victoria College, August 1867," Nathanael Burwash Papers, box 16, file 444, United Church Archives.

112. For the modernist reliance upon Kantian idealism and its variants, see Hutchison, *Modernist Impulse in American Protestantism*. Idealism, like the Newtonian natural theology, rested upon the uniformity of natural law in both mental and physical realms.

113. George Marsden, in *Fundamentalism and American Culture*, 214–15, notes the different perception of scientific and biblical truth among fundamentalists, who adhered to a Newtonian view, and the so-called modernists, influenced by Kant.

114. For the social endeavors of the Canadian churches in this period, see Richard Allen, *The Social Passion* (Toronto: University of Toronto Press, 1973). Allen views the Canadian "social passion" as a replication of the American "social gospel." This view has been challenged in recent years. See Brian Fraser, *The Social Uplifters* (Waterloo: Wilfrid Laurier University Press, 1988), which argues that Presbyterian "progressives" worked out of the tenets of evangelical individualism; and Gauvreau, *Evangelical Century,* chap. 5, which also insists upon the persistence of the evangelical creed as the foundation of the social thought of prominent evangelicals. For a new interpretation of the Social Gospel in the United States, see William McGuire King, "An Enthusiasm for Humanity: The Social Emphasis in Religion and Its Accommodation in Protestant Theology," in *Religion in Twentieth-Century American Intellectual Life,* ed. Lacey, 49–77. A new study of the social sciences in English Canada, currently being undertaken by Nancy J. Christie, reveals that in the early twentieth century, social scientists were themselves constrained by the power of the "voluntary" model of social institutions and resisted relying on the state.

12

"The Double Vision": Evangelical Piety as Derivative and Indigenous in Victorian English Canada

MARGUERITE VAN DIE

Caught between a British cultural heritage that continued to shape them and a dynamic and equally influential American neighbor, it was not uncommon for nineteenth-century Canadian evangelicals to resolve the paradox of their situation by observing that in matters spiritual, theirs was a highly favored country. "In many respects Canada compares favourably with New York State; the people as a whole, are more religious and manifest more veneration for divine things," mused one Methodist preacher in 1877.[1] Comparisons to religious life in Great Britain were no less satisfying. The Reverend Morley Punshon, for example, during his sojourn in Canada from 1868 to 1873 as president of the Canada Conference of the British Wesleyan Church, noted with pleasure that in a number of Ontario's villages, Methodist places of worship greatly outranked in grandeur those of the Church of England. Elaborating for his countrymen the advantages of Methodism in Canada, he exclaimed with enthusiasm, "The freedom with which it works out here, with no shadow of an established Church to darken it, is amazing!"[2]

Freedom, however, was not without its dangers, and righteousness, even on new soil, can quickly tarnish. Canada's evangelical presses, therefore, also lost no opportunities to alert their readers not only to the benefits of freedom but also to its perils, most clearly exemplified in the experience of their republican neighbor. "Is there a civilized, not to say a Christian, country on the earth where divorces are so frequent as in the United States?" the Methodist *Christian Guardian* asked rhetorically, even as Canadian Presbyterians pondered the alarming statistical evidence that only one of every fifteen children who had attended the Sabbath school in the United States ultimately joined the church.[3]

In their favorable comparisons and in their concern to maintain evangelical continuity, these nineteenth-century commentators acknowledged that the experience of the gospel in Canada did not proceed in isolation but was set within a wider context. Part of the Anglo-American transatlantic world, Canada in the nineteenth century shared the dominance of the evangelical impulse and drew deeply on both American and British sources.[4] Nevertheless, while this dual heritage was profoundly influential, the form that evangelicalism came to assume in Canada significantly diverged from that of both the American and the British experience.

Nathan Hatch has convincingly demonstrated that in the United States for the period 1790 to 1830, the appeal of revivalism, which was such an integral component of evangelical Christianity, broke up traditional denominational allegiances and established an individualistic and populist expression of Christianity, fragmenting a coherent Christian culture into a religious pluralism.[5] Other historians such as George M. Thomas and Curtis Johnson, focusing more on the relationship between evangelicalism and market forces, have further underscored the mutable and often individualistic nature of American Protestantism in the nineteenth century.[6]

Although one cannot speak of a national Protestant presence until the 1870s, a very different picture emerges in Canada, or more specifically for the purposes of this study, in the province of Ontario. Though definitely not to be equated with English-speaking Canada, as her inhabitants sometimes appear to assume, Ontario in the nineteenth century was the heartland of a vocal and aggressive evangelicalism. Sharing the American experience of revivalism, what is now Ontario by 1854 had also rejected an official church establishment in favor of voluntarism. Yet here the impulse was not toward pluralism and individualism but, on the contrary, toward consensus and consolidation. Although there remained significant sectarian divisions within denominations, by 1861 four major groupings shared the Protestant spectrum: Anglicans, accounting for 22.3 percent of the population; Baptists, 4.4 percent; Methodists, 25.1 percent; and Presbyterians, 21.7 percent.[7] While in part this move toward consensus was fueled by a Protestant militancy directed at the province's Roman Catholic minority, who at mid-century represented a little under a fifth of the population, it was further encouraged by a series of internal unions in the 1870s and 1880s, bringing to an end differences that had been transported from the mother country.[8] Finally, in the early decades of the twentieth century, when elsewhere evangelicalism began to fragment under the impact of fundamentalist-modernist strife, three Canadian denominations—Methodists, Congregationalists, and two-thirds of the Presbyterians—drew on their common evangelical heritage to join forces and formed a United Church of Canada.[9]

While consolidation distinguished evangelicalism in Canada from the United States, its growing dominance would set it apart from Britain. There, as David Bebbington has pointed out, the evangelical movement by 1870 began to experience a noticeable decline in influence, taking on the form of an introverted subculture. In Ontario, by contrast, it commenced at this time to exercise a remarkable and enduring cultural hegemony.[10] The next decade, for example, would see a number of the province's major evangelical colleges enter into federation with the University of Toronto to form the country's most powerful institution of higher learning. Indicative of the prominence of the evangelical voice was the attendance of the prime minister, the premier of the province, the minister of education, and the chancellor and vice-chancellor of the University of Toronto at the 1886 Methodist Conference, which deliberated university federation.[11] In many ways an informal moral establishment, the influence of evangelicalism would extend well into the twentieth century, placing its stamp, to cite only two of many such influences, on the province's Sabbaths as well as on its drinking establishments.

Intellectually too, Canadian historian Michael Gauvreau has recently argued, the evangelical creed that was shared by the country's clergymen professors who dominated its colleges was able to withstand the ravages of both Darwinian science and the higher criticism of the Bible and retained its vitality well into the 1920s.[12] Most recently, Richard Allen, a historian of the Social Gospel movement in Canada and currently a cabinet member of Ontario's New Democratic Party, has contended that this same evangelical creed and tradition "fashioned a distinctive and accommodating English Canadian culture, a culture which, unlike the Americans, did not drive debate to extremes, but allowed the emergence of third party options, whether in academe or church or politics."[13] In their arguments for the longevity of the evangelical creed in Canada, both writers have stressed the correlation between its intellectual expression and its practical experiential piety. Yet, although this was not the first time this insight was offered, the nature of that piety still remains largely unexplored.[14] The purpose of this study is therefore to reconstruct central elements of evangelical piety in Ontario during the the formative period 1830 to 1875 and to suggest how this piety contributed to the endurance and vitality of evangelicalism in Canada in the last quarter of the century, when elsewhere it had begun to experience severe strain.

Evangelical piety, like its Puritan predecessor, as Jerald Brauer and others have effectively demonstrated, was a complex phenomenon with many interpenetrating dimensions.[15] Such complexity is only increased when, as in the case of Ontario's immigrant population, religious experience was derivative, drawing on both American and British sources. What follows will of necessity be an incomplete exploration, examining aspects of the piety of three denominations: Methodist, Baptist, and Presbyterian, all of which (though Presbyterians only marginally) laid claim to a dual heritage—first American, and then British.

While the larger configuration of Ontario's evangelical denominations included Congregationalists and Anglicans (among whom Low Church Irish figured prominently), these three denominations experienced the most rapid growth, with their combined forces increasing from 40.3 percent of the province's population in 1840 to 57.9 percent in 1881.[16] And it was these three, especially after the formation of the Free Presbyterian Church in 1844 and its successor the Canada Presbyterian Church in 1861 (joining Free and Secessionist Presbyterians), that most vocally and aggressively carried the evangelical banner in Ontario.[17] It may be argued that in spite of their very different traditions, these denominations were able to share an evangelical piety shaped by a "double vision" that was both derivative and indigenous in origin. Concerned to keep continuity with the past, this piety also sought to counteract the spiritual dangers of life in the New World—in particular, the individualism that appeared to be part of the North American experience.

This double vision, which drove many of Ontario's evangelicals to look to their British past and to face the challenges of a rapidly changing North American society, is of more than regional interest, for it throws into relief a tension between continuity and change that lay deep within nineteenth-century evangelicalism. Inherently conservative in their desire to maintain an organic understanding of life, evangelicals were progressive in their emphasis on moral transformation, first of the individual, but also, especially in countries untrammeled by an established church, of the nation.[18] Evangelicalism not only in Ontario but in all of Canada was able to maintain these two forces in balance and to retain its coherence and vitality longer than in Britain and the United States. While it too would ultimately undergo transformation, evangelicalism nevertheless left an enduring stamp on Canadian national life. Hence, to reconstruct the contours of evangelical piety in Ontario is to engage the wider historical discourse on the place of evangelicalism within the modernization and secularization of the transatlantic world.

I

In order to understand the Anglo-American nature of this double vision during the years 1830 to 1875, it is necessary first to examine briefly the earlier period. Before the War of 1812, the evangelical message had been carried into the province in a wave of revivalism from the United States, dominated by itinerant preachers from the Methodist Episcopal Church, with the lesser participation of Baptists and a few missionaries sent by the Dutch Reformed Church and the American Associate Presbytery.[19] After the war, however, this American and therefore (to the colonial authorities) suspect face of revivalism was recast by the influx of British immigrants, who began to pour into the province in increasing numbers especially after the 1830s. Between 1830 and 1880 some 1,444,851 people sailed from British ports to British North America, and though this number was considerably smaller than that of those who chose the United States as their destination (16 percent as opposed to 66 percent), their influence upon religious life in Canada was considerably greater.[20]

British Baptists, Wesleyans and smaller Methodist sects, Scottish Secessionists, Free Church Presbyterians, as well as significant numbers within the Church of Scotland (whose needs until the disruption of 1843 were primarily met by evangelical missionaries sent by the Glasgow Colonial Society) all began to give evangelicalism a distinctively British face. Revivalism continued to play an important role within all three denominations, lasting throughout the century, but its major impetus now came from Britain and, after the formation of the Evangelical Alliance and the YMCA in the 1840s, from the wider transatlantic evangelical world.

Among Presbyterians, revivalist practices originating in the Church of Scotland had been carried into the province as early as 1815 by a growing influx of Highland emigrants, many of whom had been influenced by the intense missionary efforts of Robert and James Haldane.[21] In areas of Highland settlement such as Glengarry County and Zorra Township, the annual long Communions with their Gaelic services, which continued well into the 1870s, frequently erupted into periods of revival and awakening, influencing an entire local population.[22] Recognizing that these Communions were part of a wider phenomenon of revival, whose strength lay to some extent in the dislocation experienced by immigrants in a new and unfamiliar world, one Presbyterian minister, Neil Mackinnon, many years later reminisced, "These seasons were a source of great spiritual comfort and uplift to these early settlers and much as they disapproved of Methodist revival services, they unconsciously were doing the same thing only in a different way."[23]

Often taking up settlement near their countrymen, significant numbers of Highland Baptists and somewhat smaller group of Congregationalists, whose origins also lay in the activities of itinerant preachers influenced by the Haldane brothers, further extended revivalism into the province.[24] In eastern Ontario in the Ottawa Valley, for example, a major revival among Baptists in 1834–1836 became the first in a series, as decade after decade the denominational press reported a new "outpouring of the Holy Spirit" upon the various congregations.[25] This first revival would be remembered not only for contributing a remarkable proportion of the denomination's future leaders but also for helping bring about rapprochement with church members in the West. These westerners had been influenced by earlier American revivalists to insist upon a closed communion; after revival Baptists allowed this form to become the general practice.[26]

The largest and most aggressively evangelical denomination, however, continued to be the Methodists. Reflecting the divisions of the old country, Methodists had by 1840 grown from one to six different bodies, but in 1847 the two largest—the British Wesleyans and a substantial part of the Methodist Episcopals—joined forces to form the Canadian Conference of the Wesleyan Methodist Church. Closely tied to the English conference, which until 1874 annually appointed one of its members as president, the Canadian conference shared in its conservative practices and theology, as well as receiving a considerable number of Irish and English clergy from among Wesleyan immigrants.[27] Revivalism remained central, however, to the self-definition of Ontario's Methodists, even though there was often criticism of some of its wilder manifestations. Associating these with its earlier American roots, Methodists were careful to align themselves with the more staid British expression. That they considered themselves to be successful in such a realignment may be surmised from the comments of the province's most influential Methodist, Egerton Ryerson, editor of the denominational *Christian Guardian*. After visiting a service in England in 1832, he told his home constituency that he found there "no more decorum in Canada, if as much."[28]

Although revivalism played a dramatic and central role in the piety of all three denominations, Ontario evangelicals significantly recast revivalism to counteract its inherent individualism. In the first place, although the province's evangelical ministers did not ignore the doctrinal differences between Arminianism and Calvinism, immersion and pedobaptism, there was a common agreement that the nature of theology was above all practical. The essentials of a true and saving faith lay in the biblical doctrines of sin, repentance, justification through acceptance of the atonement of Christ, and a sanctified life of service. Consider the succinct summary offered by a Free Presbyterian minister in 1871:

> For while we know what we do know as by a mirror and a riddle, *yet we know enough for all practical purposes. We know all that is needed for present action.* The way of salvation is plain and easy, so plain and easy that while it is often "hid from the wise and the prudent," it is "revealed unto babes." To trust and to follow Christ, that is the whole matter. "Believe in the Lord Jesus Christ, and thou shalt be saved."[29]

This emphasis on personal salvation through Christ alone was not, however, an endorsement of individualism in theology or religious practice. During the 1830s and 1840s, Ontario experienced its share of sectarian movements such as Disciples of Christ, the Christian Connection, Universalists, Millerites, Mormons, and Irvingites. The Methodists were especially vulnerable and lost some preachers and class leaders to these movements. As one historian has concluded, however, "The doctrinal stability and tight discipline of the province's most actively evangelistic denomination may have actually contributed to the failure of the new groups to secure followings as large as in many parts of the United States."[30]

The concern to maintain orthodoxy formed a constant theme in subsequent decades, for right belief and action were seen to be inextricably connected. "Take heed to your doctrine for your life will be affected by what you believe. . . . Atheism, Spiritualism, Mormonism, are the products of loose theology," warned the editor of the Methodist *Christian Guardian.*[31] By that date, in the early 1870s, the charge of loose theology was being primarily directed at the Plymouth Brethren, whose most zealous propagandist, Nelson Darby, regularly visited Ontario between 1862 and 1877, staging a sizable conference annually at the town of Guelph. The concern of the province's evangelical ministers, however, was not so much with the dispensationalism of the Brethren as with the seemingly antinomian implications of their teaching about a substitutionary atonement that did not call for sorrow for sin and the regenerating work of the Spirit.[32]

Here precisely in that intimate relationship between divine initiative and human response lay the focus that helped move all of the province's evangelical denominations to a common ground. While conversion remained central to evangelical piety, the individual freedom of the New Birth was tempered with an emphasis on moral responsibility and integration into the community of believers.

Such a close correlation between religious experience and its ethical expression inevitably led to a reevaluation of the place of the emotions in conversion, again helping to move the province's evangelical denominations closer toward a consensus. For evangelical immigrants in the early years, religious revivals were often emotional experiences and opened up the floodgates of memory. Describing their impact upon her Irish parents and their friends, one young Methodist later recalled, "Men and women sobbed together in a strange mingling of emotions. Men who would have borne any sorrow, any pain, any privation, without a murmur, melted to tears under the sound of the preacher's voice, heard last in the pretty homechapel on that green isle far away."[33] At the same time, however, Ontario's British Wesleyans were careful to take distance from the emotional manifestations associated with an earlier era of revivalism. In accounts of camp meetings, such as one held near Oshawa in 1858, the press paid special attention to "the absence of confusion, noise, excitement," noting that "all . . . gatherings were marked by reverence, solemnity, deep seriousness, and engagedness with God for the outpouring of His spirit in the conversion of sinners."[34]

Presbyterians, convinced that when it came to rousing the intellect and the conscience, "God's great instrument is the sermon," were generally apprehensive of emotional appeals for conversion.[35] Their position gradually modified, however, in part because they were also aware that there was sufficient circumstantial evidence that the warmth and sense of community that Methodist worship offered to people in a strange country was a strong inducement for some to change their denominational allegiance.[36]

More influenced than the Presbyterians by a dual American and British tradition of revival, the province's Baptists also tried to encourage a piety that balanced the intellect with the emotions. Accounts of revival in the mid-1850s, for example, in Breadalbane, a major settlement of Highland Baptists, emphasized that the experience of the converts was "remarkably clear; most of them pointing to some passage of Scripture that came to their minds and gave them relief."[37] In subsequent decades ministers never failed to warn against the dangers of "regarding emotional experiences instead of gospel declarations, invitations and promises, as the true warrant for religious belief."[38]

In the same way that the province's ministers attempted to maintain evangelical continuity by insisting on the practical implications of theology, they also defined the parameters of lay involvement. Although ordained clergy such as Wesley and Whitefield had directed the evangelical revival of the eighteenth century, the movement had been fueled by the participation and piety of laymen and laywomen. The practical need to sustain piety in the face of the disruptive experience of immigration and a scarcity of ministers enhanced the need for lay activity. In 1848, for example, in the annual pastoral address, Ontario's Wesleyans were encouraged to make contact with those immigrants who had been members or hearers "in the Wesleyan Church at home." "On their arrival here," they were exhorted, "we should kindly search them out, and affectionately invite them to the ordinances and privileges of our Church. They have suffered spiritual declension during the privations and exposures of a protracted voyage; they should therefore be carefully sought after and brought again to the means of grace."[39] Obituaries offered frequent appreciation of the work of lay leaders, who, "Abraham-like" or as a "Mother of Israel," had provided spiritual nurture and leadership as well as hospitality to new immigrants.[40] Such lay evangelism was a powerful means of ensuring continuity with the religious life as it had been practiced in the mother country.

Among Methodists in particular, the holiness preaching of two American revivalists, James Caughey and Phoebe Palmer, in major urban centers during the 1850s would be remembered as a source of new dedication among the laity. Although individual ministers with an interest in holiness or Christian perfection could be found as early as 1790, the preaching of Caughey and Palmer, as Richard Carwardine and others have demonstrated, was part of a general revival of interest within transatlantic Methodism.[41] Contemporary Canadian reports of services led by these revivalists placed a special emphasis on the careful prior preparation by ministers and laity, the lack of emotionalism that accompanied the revivals, and their appeal to the laity.[42] In later accounts describing the spiritual life of Methodists influenced by these revivals, their lasting impact and practical expression received prominent mention.[43]

While such lay consecration was essential for the continuity of evangelical piety, the future of religion nevertheless ultimately rested upon the next generation. Especially, therefore, in their common concern to "provide for the rising generation," the interests of laity and clergy intersected. The importance of family religion could not be sufficiently emphasized by all denominations; more than any other matter, it furthered the formation of an evangelical consensus.

Family religion was not a new concern, for evangelicals could look to a long tradition going back to Puritan times stressing the continuity of the devotional life in "the closet, the domestic hearth and the sanctuary."[44] The threat posed by immigration in disrupting this practice was recognized by laity as well as by clergy. In the 1840s and 1850s, for example, in south central Ontario, Presbyterian members of the newly formed Free Church sent a flurry of petitions to their presbytery pleading that a minister be sent and stressing in particular the need for catechetical instruction for the young in "townships being settled from eight to ten years (and scarcely as many sermons preached)."[45] During these years for those Presbyterians who were so fortunate as to have a minister, instruction in the catechism took place, following tradition, in private homes on Sunday evenings.[46]

The locale of such instruction underscored the importance of the family as the matrix of religious training. While all three evangelical denominations increasingly established their own Sunday schools and by the mid-1870s were prominently featuring the series of International Sunday School Lessons in their periodicals, they shared a concern to maintain the centrality of family devotions. Even Baptists, who did not mince words about their disagreement with other evangelicals on the matter of infant baptism, expressed an admiration for the religious training that pedobaptists offered their children and that, in the words of an 1871 editorial in the *Canadian Baptist,* "has proved the conversion of so many."[47]

At a time when in American circles the doctrine of infant depravity was giving way to a sentimental, Romantic view of childhood, Canadian evangelicals continued to emphasize that religious nurture without conversion could not ensure a child's eternal safety. "Let none presume that pious parentage will save them," William McLaren, minister of Knox Church, Ottawa, warned Canadian Presbyterians.[48] A statistical breakdown of obituaries in the *Canadian Baptist,* and the Methodist *Christian Guardian* for the early 1870s reveals that conversion was central to the piety of all age groups, young as well as old, and that adolescence was its favored period.[49]

While the communal bonds of religion were first expressed in the family, they also found expression in organized ecumenical activities that originated in Britain and the United States and helped integrate Canadians into the wider network of transatlantic evangelicalism. In 1854 a new publication entitled *The Gospel Tribune for Alliance and Intercommunion throughout Evangelical Christendom* began to draw the attention of the province's Protestants to such efforts at international ecumenical cooperation as the Evangelical Alliance and the YMCA.[50] Consistently promoted as progressive movements that were moving beyond an earlier denominationalism, such united efforts were intended especially to appeal to the young. They were further reinforced by an avid interest in the interdenominational nature of the 1857–58 Businessmen's Revival in New York and by two other concurrent events: a British proclamation in November 1857 appointing a day of "General Fast and Humiliation and of Prayer" to seek an end to war in India, and in January 1859 the beginning of the annual week of "World's Concert for Prayer," requested by the Evangelical Alliance. Such interaction also, incidentally, from time to time allowed Ontario's evangelicals to bask briefly in moral superiority. Thus the 1854 General Convention of the American YMCAS received a strongly worded rebuke from the Toronto delegation for excluding colored associations, while the Methodist press denounced Britain's mistreatment of the native population as the cause of the war in India and a flagrant denial of evangelical values.[51]

On the local level, although accounts in private journals reveal that union prayer meetings were not always successful in eradicating traditional denominational prejudices and stereotypes, these did provide an important forum for community cooperation and often lasted well beyond the appointed week.[52] With their yearly prayer agenda set by the Alliance, such gatherings also encouraged concentrated emphasis on key evangelical concerns. The 1861 diary entries, for example, of John Wells, a schoolteacher and recent English immigrant in the town of Ingersoll, attest both to their large attendance and to their evangelical agenda. That year townspeople were treated to nightly lectures entitled "The promotion of brotherly kindness among true Christians," "The attainment of a higher standard of holiness by the children of God," "A large increase of true conversions, especially in the families of believers,"

"Revivals," "A large outpouring of the Holy Spirit on bishops etc. etc.," and "The speedy overthrow of all false religions and the full accomplishment of the prayer, 'Thy Kingdom come.' "[53]

While not intended to supplant denominational loyalty (succinctly expressed in the words of the Methodist *Christian Guardian* as "Love all true churches of Christ, but love your own especially"), such cooperation was only part of a wider expression of voluntary association among evangelicals.[54] These included temperance and Prohibition meetings, Bible and tract societies, as well as, on a more social level, annual union Sunday school picnics. Though the agenda had refocused to food for the body rather than the spirit, such picnics vied with the January week of union prayer in popularity as community events. As described in the *Canadian Baptist,* the 1867 picnic in the town of Perth, for example, though marked by great hilarity, was also edified with closing addresses by the local Wesleyan and Presbyterian ministers, with both gentlemen "in their very best and happiest style, setting forth the pleasures and profits of true religion, and urging on all, especially the young, full and immediate consecration to God's service, as their *first duty,* and *highest interest* for both worlds."[55]

Such efforts to encourage evangelical continuity through practical piety, lay participation, family religion, union revivals, and voluntary associations were not unique to the Ontario experience. All of these were an expression of an understanding of reality that lay rooted in evangelical theology and that saw all of life as interconnected. Thus it was not out of place for clergymen, in even so bucolic a setting as a Sunday school picnic, to exhort evangelical youth to remember their duty in this world and the next, for evangelicals shared a view of life that stressed continuity between the old and the young, the living and the dead, private and public behavior. Studies examining a variety of expressions of piety in transatlantic evangelicalism have underscored this element of continuity and integration. Leigh Schmidt, for example, analyzing the symbolic significance of the Presbyterian long Communions in mid-nineteenth century America, has pointed out that in such rituals evangelicals became part of a larger community, thereby gaining "a sense of the continuity of the faith and the generations."[56] Similar observations on the organic nature of evangelical religion have been offered by Deborah Valenze in her skillful reconstruction of sectarian piety among the economically marginalized in pre-Victorian England and by Leonore Davidoff and Catherine Hall in their monumental work on the mores of middle-class English evangelicals in the first half of the nineteenth century.[57] While for Ontario's immigrant population such continuity acquired added significance, its roots lay within an evangelical ordering of reality.

As these and other studies of nineteenth-century evangelical piety have underscored, however, this assertion of the communal nature of religion must be understood within the wider context of socioeconomic change, for it was also directed specifically against the encroaching individualism and fragmentation of the nineteenth-century commercial and industrial revolutions.[58] Among England's rural laborers, for example, as Valenze has argued, evangelical religion played a central role in helping legitimate old ways, which were coming under assault in the early nineteenth century.[59] While Ontario's mainline evangelical denominations occupied a somewhat later time frame and were critical of some forms of sectarian behavior, there is nevertheless considerable evidence of anxiety in ministerial pronouncements about the destructive impact of socioeconomic change upon religious practice. Shared by all three denominations, and commonly referred to simply as worldliness, this concern formed the final link in the formation of an evangelical consensus in Ontario and should therefore be briefly examined, before proceeding to analyze reasons for its dominance and longevity in English Canada.

A many-headed monster, worldliness took on a variety of forms. In Presbyterian circles, for example, it found expression in "the intense pressure of business—the prospect of getting on in life, and reaching to something like a competence, if not to wealth," "the power of the world, long hours, weariness, especially on the Sabbath," and in the "haste to be rich, the love of money."[60] Baptists had begun to address the spiritual danger of life in the marketplace as early as 1837, when after a period of financial crisis, Newton Bosworth, a well-educated minister and recent emigrant from Cambridge, England, offered ethical and spiritual guidelines to evangelical businessmen in a published address, *The Aspect and Influence of Christianity upon the Commercial Character.*[61] Exhortations in a similar vein continued in the denominational presses, interspersed from time to time with positive models of godly laymen who were able to transform the lives of their associates and employees simply through their consistent piety.[62]

Though such examples were intended as a powerful reminder of the intimate connection between public and private behavior, their effective failure can be surmised from constant ministerial concern that male adherents appeared reluctant to assume the responsibilities of full church membership. Most explicitly addressed in Presbyterian circles, this observation had already led the Church of Scotland in 1842 to commission a tract, clearly directed at the denomination's men and unambiguously entitled, *An Address to those who have been baptized in infancy, and who have not yet joined themselves to the church by partaking of the sacramental supper.* "In a country in which so many are living without any profession of Christianity, the children of even pious parents are exposed to great danger," Presbyterian adherents were pointedly warned.[63] Thirty years later, when by even Presbyterian standards religious life in the country had significantly improved and it was conceded that "there is much outward respect paid to religion among all classes," the situation still appeared unchanged. By that date, lay preoccupation with worldly matters had infiltrated even the church elders, and in a desperate attempt to reassert the communal bonds of religion in the face of a recalcitrant lay male leadership, Kirk Synod was asked to consider enlisting in Sunday school work the services of "mothers and matronly women, whose deeper life and riper knowledge of divine things might be expected to exert a more salutary influence upon the youth committed to their care."[64]

Concerned to maintain evangelical continuity in a changing society whose demands were undermining male church involvement, these ministers were, not without grounds, alarmed. Feminist historians, such as Carroll Smith Rosenberg and Mary P. Ryan, who have examined the impact of the nineteenth-century commercial and industrial state upon women's lives, have drawn attention to the increased separation of private and public spheres of influence in the lives of men and women, with religious practice being more and more relegated to the private and hence female world.[65] Mark Carnes and other historians of masculinity have further drawn attention to the failure of American Protestantism to retain the allegiance of a growing number of men in the face of the pressures of the rapidly changing economic world of the second half of the nineteenth century.[66] The democratization and increased pluralism of American religion was therefore part of a larger pattern of fragmentation that broke up not only traditional denominational allegiances but also the ties of kinship and community that had bound society together in pre-industrial times. Seen against this backdrop, the efforts of Ontario's evangelicals to maintain continuity by asserting the communal nature of religion was motivated by more than the disruptive impact of immigration, and included the encroaching individualism and fragmentation that they saw to be part of North American life.

II

If the evangelical consensus that developed during the period 1830–1875 in Ontario was essentially conservative in its motivation to preserve and defend an integrated and religious view of reality, there remains the question why it did not become marginalized or fragmented, as was beginning to happen after 1870 in the United States and Britain. Why instead were evangelicals in Ontario, as elsewhere in English Canada, able to retain their cohesion and even increase their cultural influence?

Here the socioeconomic factors that contributed to a favorable climate for evangelicalism in Ontario must be briefly considered. Scholarship correlating economic status with religious belief in nineteenth-century Ontario is still in a beginning stage, but two analyses of local census returns and assessment rolls—one of Free Church Presbyterians in Guelph and in Perth for 1861, and the other of Methodists and Presbyterians in Belleville in 1884—point to a preponderance of evangelicals occupied as craftsmen, shopkeepers, skilled workers, and professionals.[67] This conclusion is further corroborated by the findings of a formidable survey correlating religion, ethnicity, and occupational structure in Canada in 1871, based on the census data of approximately ten thousand households. Although unfortunately not broken down by provinces, the results of this survey show further that approximately 59 percent of all evangelicals were employed as farmers and that their occupational profile and their British roots reflected that of the general population.[68]

While ministers obviously saw no grounds for complacency, fragmentary evidence drawn from journals and biographies does reveal that for some evangelical men at least, whether farmers, craftsmen, or entrepreneurs, religion had not been privatized and continued to absorb significant amounts of time and energy.[69] More generally, the socioeconomic and ethnic homogeneity of Ontario's evangelicals, coupled with their mainstream position in society, both sustained and reflected the ideals of community and continuity that figured so prominently in their piety.

Only after the 1890s did market forces, capital, new technologies, and waves of immigrants from the urban centers of Britain and from Europe begin to alter decisively this small-owner-operated and still largely rural economic pattern.[70] Compared with England and the eastern and midwestern United States, therefore, Ontario's economic development, as elsewhere in Canada, proceeded at a significantly slower pace, allowing the province's evangelicals a longer period to consolidate the position developed during the mid-century.

Thus, throughout the final decades of the century, evangelicalism was marked by continuity, even as its voice became increasingly dominant in culture and society and its attitude to change more liberal. Already in the 1870s, Canada's Presbyterians had begun to note with gratification the unusually large number of young men who were entering the ministry.[71] Further research has demonstrated a parallel development in Methodism, in both cases lasting for the remainder of the century, and has pointed to the growing prestige (and improved remuneration) of the ministry as a profession.[72] Raised in devout homes and immersed in an evangelical culture, these ministers were also increasingly college-educated. Thanks to the continued prestige of evangelical colleges and their clergymen professors, and the integrated approach of Scottish common sense and British idealism, they experienced little disjuncture between the faith in which they had been raised, their culture, and their intellectual understanding of reality.[73] Therefore, unlike British evangelicals, who, David Bebbington has noted, were forced increasingly to shift "the fulcrum of Christianity from the head to the heart," they were able to maintain the "rational piety" that had figured so prominently in the battle of an earlier generation of evangelical clergy against any privatization or sentimentalization of religion.[74] This continued success in mediating between the "religion of the heart" and scientific thought may help explain also why seepage into protofundamentalist sects such as the Brethren and holiness groups during the 1880s and 1890s was comparatively small.[75]

Continuity, especially within a dominant cultural group, does, however, exact a price, as William Hutchison has demonstrated in his study of the move toward a liberal theology on the part of a number of Americans raised in mid-nineteenth-century evangelical homes.[76] In Canada, while there is documentation for a shift toward theological liberaliam by isolated individuals, it was not until the 1920s that any serious rift occurred within denominations.[77] Thanks in part to the longevity of denominational leaders, evangelical piety, fueled by revivals, continued to be officially promoted until well into the first decade of the twentieth century and even became enshrined in the doctrinal statement of a new United Church.[78]

What distinguished and united evangelicals of all denominations during the final decades of the century was their activism and moral concern. Already gratefully observed by clergy in the 1870s, the scope for moral activity greatly increased when, in 1875, Presbyterians and, in 1883, Methodist entered into national unions, with a lesser union in 1888 of the two Baptist conventions of central Canada.[79]

During these years Ontario's evangelical consensus took on a national perspective and voice, aided by the move by some of its intellectuals to the West.[80]

Thus, when finally in the 1890s the stability of the old socioeconomic structures in the province came to an end, evangelicals were in a strong position to reaffirm the values that had been established in an earlier period. Their constituency had retained its homogeneity, becoming largely middle class in urban centers, where it was ineffective in attracting the membership either of the urban poor or, as a recent study of Presbyterian resistance to church union has argued, of the new economic elite of "self-made men."[81] As the dislocation caused by urbanization, immigration, and industrialization began to close in on many, the province's evangelicals would meet its challenge not by fracturing but by turning to the old consensus, updated and cast in a national mold, and revitalized by a postmillennial hope. Fashioned in an earlier age against an encroaching worldliness, its ideal of moral responsibility, continuity, and community continued to inform the actions and attitudes of a new generation's response to modernity, even after some could no longer share its piety.

Encapsuled both in church union and in the vision of a kingdom of God, theirs was not the last attempt within English Canada to challenge the disruptive forces of social and economic change with the reassertion of a moral understanding of community that kept faith with the ideals of the past, even as it tried to address the realities of the present. In subsequent years, from the time of the Great Depression in the 1930s to the present, with its economic dislocation and threat of political fragmentation, third-party options, representing both the left and the right, have emerged that have presented secular versions of the old evangelical concept of the integral nature of community and moral responsibility.[82]

Linking the agenda and ideals of such parties with the vision of an earlier generation of evangelicals is what Canada's influential literary critic, the late Northrop Frye, called a "myth of concern," a myth that, Frye argues, is anxious for continuity and intolerant of dissent.[83] While historians and literary critics have drawn attention to the significance of such a myth in fashioning an Anglo-Canadian sense of identity and have recognized its European and Judeo-Christian roots, the formative influence of evangelical piety has been quite overlooked.[84] And yet, by reconstructing that piety within its wider transatlantic context, it becomes clear that in a form that was neither British nor American but dependent on both, and developed in tension with the cultural forces that each represented, evangelicalism lies deeply embedded in the Canadian national consciousness.

Research for this chapter has received generous funding from a Queen's University Advisory Research committed award, and an American Theological Schools Research Grant during a sabbatical leave in 1991–1992.

Notes

1. Anson Green, *The Life and Times of the Rev. Anson Green, D.D.* (Toronto: Methodist Book Room, 1877), 31.

2. Quoted in F. W. Macdonald, *Life of Morley Punson* (London: Hodder and Stoughton, 1887), 316.

3. *Christian Guardian,* 2 January 1869; James George, *The Sabbath School of the Fireside & the Sabbath School of the Congregation as It Ought to Be* (Kingston: John Creighton, 1859), 120.

4. See, for example, John S. Moir, "American Influences on Canadian Churches before Confederation," *Church History* 36 (1967): 440–55; Frank Baker, "The Trans-Atlantic Triangle: Relations between British, Canadian, and American Methodism during Wesley's Lifetime," *Bulletin* (Committee on Archives of the United Church of Canada) 28 (1979): 5–21; W. Stanford Reid, ed., *The Scottish Tradition in Canada* (Toronto: McClelland and Stewart, 1976), 118–36.

5. Nathan O. Hatch, *The Democratization of Americna Christianity* (New Haven: Yale University Press, 1989).

6. Curtis D. Johnson, *Islands of Holiness: Rural Religion in Upstate New York, 1790–1860* (Ithaca: Cornell University Press, 1989); George M. Thomas, *Revivalism and Cultural Change: Christianity, Nation Building, and the Market in the Nineteenth-Century United States* (Chicago: University of Chicago Press, 1989).

7. George A. Rawlyk, ed., *The Canadian Protestant Experience, 1760–1990* (Burlington, Ont.: Welch, 1990), 96 and 103.

8. A brief analysis of the theological and social background of anti-Catholicism can be found in J. R. Miller, "Anti-Catholic Thought in Victorian Canada," *Canadian Historical Review* 66 (1985): 474–94. In 1875 the main Presbyterian denominations joined forces; Wesleyans in central Canada and the Maritimes united with the Methodist New Connexion in 1874 and in 1884 finalized union with the Primitive Methodists and the Methodist Episcopals.

9. The most comprehensive treatment of church union continues to be C. E. Silcox, *Church Union in Canada: Its Causes and Consequences* (New York: Institute of Social and Religious Research, 1933). Presbyterian resistance to union has been analyzed in N. Keith Clifford, *The Resistance to Church Union in Canada, 1904–1939* (Vancouver: University of British Columbia Press, 1985).

10. David Bebbington, *Evangelicalism in Modern Britain: A History from the 1730s to the 1980s* (London: Unwin Hyman, 1989), 141–46. For the impact of evangelicalism on Ontario, see, for example, William Westfall, *Two Worlds: The Protestant Culture of Nineteenth-Century Ontario* (Montreal and Kingston: McGill-Queen's University Press, 1989); John Webster Grant, *A Profusion of Spires: Religion in Nineteenth-Century Ontario* (Toronto: University of Toronto Press, 1988), esp. 170–203.

11. C. B. Sissons, *A History of Victoria University* (Toronto: University of Toronto Press, 1952), 180. The evangelical dimension to university federation has been explored in Marguerite Van Die, *An Evangelical Mind: Nathanael Burwash and the*

Methodist Tradition in Canada, 1839–1918 (Montreal and Kingston: McGill-Queen's University Press, 1989), 114–42.

12. Michael Gauvreau, *The Evangelical Century: College and Creed in English Canada from the Great Revival to the Great Depression* (Montreal and Kingston: McGill-Queen's University Press, 1991), 284–91.

13. Richard Allen, "Religion and Political Transformation in English Canada: The 1880s to the 1930s," Chancellor's Lectures 1991, Queen's Theological College, Kingston.

14. See the seminal essay by Goldwin French, "The Evangelical Creed in Canada," in *The Shield of Achilles: Aspects of Canada in the Victorian Age,* ed. W. L. Morton (Toronto: McClelland and Stewart, 1968), 15–35.

15. Jerald C. Brauer, "Types of Puritan Piety," *Church History* 56 (March 1987): 58. An excellent analysis of piety in the Reformed and the Wesleyan traditions can be found in Robin Maas and Gabriel O'Donnell, *Spiritual Traditions for the Contemporary Church* (Nashville: Abingdon, 1990), 202–21 and 303–19.

16. While Congregationalists initially probably outnumbered members of other denominations among American settlers, most were absorbed into other churches. Only in 1819 with the coming of English Congregationalists were they able to establish a permanent presence. See Grant, *Profusion of Spires,* 79. The dominance of the Irish in the Church of England in Ontario has been forcefully argued in Donald H. Akenson, *The Irish in Ontario: A Study in Rural History* (Montreal and Kingston: McGill-Queen's University Press, 1984), esp. 349.

17. In the early 1800s, missionaries representing these three denominations were the first to carry the thrust of evangelicalism into Ontario (Grant, *Profusion of Spires,* 57).

18. For themes touched on in this paragraph, see, for example, Bebbington, *Evangelicalism in Modern Britain,* esp. 1–17 and 34–42; Richard Helmstadter, "The Nonconformist Conscience," in *The Conscience of the Victorian State,* ed. Peter Marsh (Syracuse: Syracuse University Press, 1979), 135–73.

19. The best summary, though flawed by an uncritical reliance on the frontier thesis, is in S. D. Clark, *Church and Sect in Canada* (Toronto: University of Toronto Press, 1948), 90–172.

20. Marjory Harper, *Emigration from North-East Scotland,* vol. 1: *Willing Exiles* (Aberdeen: Aberdeen University Press, 1988), 25–26.

21. Donald Meek, "Evangelicalism and Emigration: Aspects of the Role of Dissenting Evangelicalism in Highland Emigration to Canada," in *Proceedings of the First North American Congress of Celtic Studies,* ed. Gordon W. MacLennan (Ottawa: University of Ottawa, Chair of Celtic Studies, 1988), 15–36.

22. John W. Grant, "Brands from Blazing Heather: Canadian Religious Revival in the Highland Tradition," *Canadian Society of Presbyterian History Papers* (1991), 59–74.

23. "A meagre record of the antecedants of Neil D. Mackinnon and a few incidents in his life," (MS in the possession of Margaret E. McLean, Kingston).

24. Meek, "Evangelicalism."

25. See, for example, *Upper Canada Missionary Magazine,* October 1836, 54; *Gospel Tribune* 2 (1855–56): 85.

26. For a detailed account of the Communion controversy and of the life of an influential Baptist converted in the 1834 revival, see Theo D. Gibson, *Robert Alexander Fyfe, His Contemporaries and His Influence* (Burlington, Ont.: Welch, 1988).

27. The conservative nature and British roots of Ontario's Wesleyan ministers are

noted in Goldwin French, *Parsons and Politics* (Toronto: Ryerson Press, 1962), 67–79; and in Clark, *Church and Sect,* 197–234.

28. Quoted in Grant, *Profusion of Spires,* 76.

29. Rev. J. M. Gibson, "Now and Then," in *The Canada Presbyterian Church Pulpit,* 1st ser. (Toronto: James Campbell, 1871), 178.

30. Grant, *Profusion of Spires,* 30.

31. *Christian Guardian,* 6 July 1870.

32. Phyllis D. Airhart, *Serving the Present Age: Revivalism, Progressivism, and the Methodist Tradition in Canada* (Montreal and Kingston: McGill-Queen's University Press, 1992), 44–45.

33. Camilla Sanderson, *John Sanderson the First* (Toronto: William Briggs, 1910), 18.

34. *Christian Guardian,* 31 March 1858.

35. *Home and Foreign Record of the Canada Presbyterian Church,* April 1968, 162–63.

36. *Home and Foreign Record,* May 1868, 195–97. Note also the criticism of "our everlasting preaching to the intellect, and making almost no provision for man's emotional nature," in *Acts and Proceedings of the Synod of the Presbyterian Church of Canada in Connection with the Church of Scotland* (1873), 128.

37. *Gospel Tribune* 2 (1855–56): 85.

38. A. H. Newman, *Memoir of Daniel Arthur McGregor, Late Principal of Toronto Baptist College* (Toronto: Dudley and Burns, 1891), 20.

39. Wesleyan Methodist Church in Canada, *Minutes . . . of Twelve Annual Conferences . . . from 1846 to 1857 Inclusive* (Toronto: Anson Green, 1863), 76.

40. See, for example, "The Late Mr. William Clarke," in *Home and Foreign Record,* April 1874, 159–63; and Nathanael Burwash, "Jane Clement Jones," *Methodist Magazine* 42 (July 1895): 45.

41. Richard Carwardine, *Transatlantic Revivalism: Popular Evangelicalism in Britain and America, 1790–1865* (Westport, CT: Greenwood Press, 1978). Carwardine contrasts Caughey's popularity in Canada and the United States with his critical reception by British Wesleyans (175). For Canada, see Peter George Bush, "James Caughey, Phoebe Palmer, and the Methodist Revival Experience in Canada West, 1850–1858" (Master's thesis, Queen's University, 1985).

42. Bush notes that emotional manifestations at Palmer's camp meetings in central Canada received greater emphasis in the American *Northern Christian Advocate* than in the Canadian *Christian Guardian* ("James Caughey," 113–14). A detailed account by Palmer on the formation of a "laity for the times" is in the *Christian Guardian,* 2 December 1857.

43. See, for example, W. H. Pearson, *Recollections and Records of Toronto of Old* (Toronto: William Briggs, 1914), 316–32; and "Autobiography/Biography, Chapter 7, 'Belleville,' " Nathanael Burwash Papers 28:628, United Church Archives, Toronto.

44. *Canadian Baptist,* 14 September 1871. Especially informative on Puritan and early evangelical family religion are Philip J. Greven, *The Protestant Temperament: Patterns of Child-Rearing, Religious Experience, and the Self in Early America* (New York: Alfred A. Knopf, 1977); and Peter Gregg Slater, *Children in the New England Mind* (Hamden, CT: Archon, 1977).

45. "To the reverend and honourable body of the Presbytery of Hamilton in connection with the Free Church, 9 April, 1854," McCollum Papers 4:1, Presbyterian Church Archives, Toronto.

46. *1845 . . . Our Kirk . . . 1945. A History of Knox Presbyterian Church, Acton,*

Ontario, 14; and Rev. John McMorine, *Address of the Synod of the Presbyterian Church of Canada in Connection with the Church of Scotland to the Members of that Church on Parental Responsibility* (n.p., 1850?).

47. *Canadian Baptist,* 11 January 1871.

48. Rev. William McLaren, "Come thou and all thy house into the ark," *Canada Presbyterian Church Pulpit,* 5 note 29.

49. In the *Christian Guardian* from 1870 to 1873, some 69 percent of obituaries noted the age of conversion of their subject to have been between twelve and twenty-nine; in the *Canadian Baptist* between 1867 and 1870, this was the case for 68 percent.

50. The *Gospel Tribune,* edited by the Baptist Rev. Robert Dick, terminated its existence in 1858. A strong voice for the YMCA, it expressed concern at the lack of support for the YMCA by Canadian evangelical ministers in contrast to the support it received in the United States (*Gospel Tribune* 1 [1854]: 23). For information on the Toronto YMCA, see Murray G. Ross, *The YMCA in Canada: The Chronicle of a Century* (Toronto: Ryerson, 1951), 37–52.

51. For further information on the stand against slavery, see Ross, *YMCA in Canada,* 44–46; and *Gospel Tribune* 1 (1854): 54. On criticism of the Indian War, see, for example, *Christian Guardian,* 13 August 1857.

52. See, for example, journal of Rev. John King, 148, Baptist Church Archives, Hamilton; diary of Rev. William McLaren, "11 January 1863," Archives of Ontario, Toronto.

53. Diary of John Wells, vol. 2, "7–24 January, 1861," Archives of Ontario. Wells was an evangelical Anglican.

54. *Christian Guardian,* 18 January 1865.

55. *Canadian Baptist,* 22 August 1867.

56. Leigh Eric Schmidt, *Holy Fairs: Scottish Communions and American Revivals in the Early Modern Period* (Princeton: Princeton University Press, 1989), 102.

57. Deborah M. Valenze, *Prophetic Sons and Daughers: Female Preaching and Popular Religion in Industrial England* (Princeton: Princeton University Press, 1985), 11 and 209; Leonore Davidoff and Catherine Hall, *Family Fortunes: Men and Women of the English Middle Class* (London: Hutchinson, 1987), 73 and 90.

58. In addition to Schmidt, *Holy Fairs,* for studies examining the role of popular piety in reasserting the bonds of community in the face of structural change, see Bruce D. Dickenson, *And They All Sang Hallelujah: Plain Folk Camp-Meeting Religion, 1800–1845* (Knoxville: University of Tennessee Press, 1974); and Gwen Kennedy Neville, *Kinship and Pilgrimage: Rituals of Reunion in American Protestant Culture* (New York: Oxford University Press, 1987).

59. Valenze, *Prophetic Sons and Daughters,* esp. 32.

60. "Report of the Committee on the Life and Work of the Church," *Acts and Proceedings* (1873), 128.

61. Newton Bosworth, *The Aspect and Influence of Christianity upon the Commercial Character: A Discourse, Delivered at Montreal, October 15, 1837* (Montreal: William Greig, 1837).

62. See, for example, the letter of a Baptist layman addressed to "heads of families," detailing his decision to resume daily family worship after receiving a letter from a former employee who attributed his conversion to the memory of his master's devotional exercises (*Canadian Baptist,* 11 January 1871).

63. Rev. James George, *An Address* . . . (Toronto: Hugh Scobie, 1841), 19.

64. *Acts and Proceedings* (1872), 148.

65. Carroll Smith-Rosenberg, *Disorderly Conduct: Visions of Gender in Victorian*

America (New York: Oxford Univesity Press, 1985), esp. 137–54; Mary P. Ryan, *Cradle of the Middle Class: The Family in Oneida County, New York, 1790–1863* (Cambridge: Cambridge University Press, 1981), 145–242. An example of a contemporary observation on the separation of spheres is, "We fear that careless husbands, who have pious wives, sometimes seek to free themselves from the thought of their responsiblity by the notion that a wife's earnestness and piety will prove in the domestic circle a counterpoise to a husband's indifference" (Rev. W. McLaren, *Canadian Presbyterian Church Pulpit,* 14), note 29.

66. Clyde Griffen, "Reconstructing Masculinity from the Evangelical Revival to the Waning of Progressivism: A Speculative Synthesis," in *Meanings for Manhood: Constructions of Masculinity in Victorian America* (Chicago: University of Chicago Press, 1990), 188–89; Mark C. Carnes, *Secret Ritual and Manhood in Victorian America* (New Haven: Yale University Press, 1989), 70–90. Curtis Johnson notes the negative impact of men of wealth upon revivalist piety in Cortland County, New York, at mid-century in *Islands of Holiness,* 31–32 and 160–69.

67. Richard W. Vaudry, *The Free Church in Victorian Canada, 1844–1861* (Waterloo: Wilfrid Laurier Press, 1989), 94; Doris Mary O'Dell, "The Class Character of Church Participants in Late Nineteenth-Century Belleville" (Ph.D. diss., Queen's University, 1990), 78.

68. A. Gordon Darroch and Michael D. Ornstein, "Ethnicity and Occupational Structure in Canada in 1871: The Vertical Mosaic in Historical Perspective," *Canadian Historical Review* 61, no. 3 (1980): 305–33.

69. See, for example, the diary of William Coates (1865), or diary of a Methodist Farmer and Cobbler, Near Picton, 11 August, 1869–10 November, 1877, both in the Archives of Ontario. The latter writer, whose entries are filled with references to lay preaching, the experience of holiness, and contacts with fellow believers, occupied a central role in community religious life, as was fairly common among cobblers in early nineteenth-century England (Valenze, *Prophetic Sons and Daughters,* 219–26).

70. Robert Craig Brown and Ramsay Cook, *Canada, 1896–1921: A Nation Transformed* (Toronto: McClelland and Stewart, 1974). The comparatively slow socioeconomic changes affecting women's lives are documented in Marjorie Griffin Cohen, *Women's Work, Markets, and Economic Development in Nineteenth-Century Ontario* (Toronto: University of Toronto Press, 1988).

71. " 'The State of Religion'. A Paper Read Before the Synod of Toronto by the Rev. J. M. King," *Home and Foreign Record,* May 1872, 131.

72. R. D. Gidney and W. P. J. Millar, "The Professions in Nineteenth-Century Ontario," manuscript in preparation for the Ontario Historical Studies Series for the Government of Ontario.

73. The role of Baconian thought in maintaining this continuity has been analyzed in Gauvreau, *Evangelical Century.* For an opposing, earlier view asserting declension and discontinuity in the final decades of the nineteenth century, see Ramsay Cook, *The Regenerators: Social Criticism in Late Victorian English Canada* (Toronto: University of Toronto Press, 1985).

74. Bebbington, *Evangelicalism in Modern Britain,* 171.

75. The comparatively small numbers attracted to protofundamentalism and holiness have been noted in Airhart, *Serving the Present Age,* 38–61.

76. William Hutchison, "Cultural Strain and Protestant Liberalism," *American Historical Review* 76 (April 1971): 386–411.

77. A partial shift away from a revivalist piety among Methodists in the period 1884–1925, as revealed in the *Christian Guardian* and the writings of a number of

younger leaders, forms the main theme in Airhart, *To Serve the Present Age.* See also Van Die, *Evangelical Mind,* 178–96, drawing attention to the inherent transforming nature of nineteenth-century evangelicalism in its efforts to be responsive to the needs of a changing culture. Baptists were the first to experience a large-scale modernist-fundamentalist division, but not until 1926. For Presbyterians, the period preceding union in 1925 had also been marked by controversy arising out of a complex series of issues, but unlike the United States, differing views on biblical inerrancy do not appear to be central. For the causes that led one-third of the Presbyterians to opt to stay out of union, see Clifford, *Resistance to Church Union in Canada.* A thoughtful analysis of issues involved in the Baptist controversy can be found in G. A. Rawlyk ed., *Canadian Baptists and Higher Education* (Montreal and Kingston: McGill-Queen's University Press, 1988), 31–62.

78. Van Die, *Evangelical Mind,* 143–77.

79. Grant, *Profusion of Spires,* 178–79.

80. For the role of transplanted easterners in the Social Gospel movement in the prairies, see, for example, Dennis L. Butcher, Catherine Macdonald, Margaret E. McPherson et al., eds., *Prairie Spirit: Perspectives on the Heritage of the United Church of Canada in the West* (Winnipeg: University of Manitoba Press, 1985), 100–121 and 216–32.

81. Demographic patterns in Toronto show that by 1899 Methodists in Ontario's major city had achieved largely middle-class status (Peter G. Goheen, *Victorian Toronto, 1850–1900* [Chicago: University of Chicago, Department of Geography, 1970], 188). For Presbyterians, see Douglas F. Campbell, "Presbyterians and the Canadian Church Union: A Study in Social Stratification," *Canadian Society of Presbyterian History Papers* (1991), 1–32.

82. The appeal of Canada as "God's Dominion" to both liberal and conservative Protestants in the 1920s and 1930s is noted in Rawlyk, *Canadian Protestant Tradition,* 151. The leader of Canada's most recent third party, the Reform Party of Canada, claims an evangelical heritage for his party, pointing to affinity with both the socialist Cooperative Commonwealth Federation and the conservative Social Credit in Alberta. See Preston Manning, *The New Canada* (Toronto: Macmillan, 1992), 94–95.

83. Northrop Frye, *The Critical Path: An Essay on the Social Context of Literary Criticism* (Bloomington: University of Indiana Press, 1973), 36–37. The "double vision" of a spiritual reality that transforms and expands the material world is the subject of Frye's last book and, with altered meaning, has provided the title for the present chapter (Northrop Frye, *The Double Vision: Language and Meaning in Religion* [Toronto: United Church Publishing House, 1991]).

84. See, for example, A. B. McKillop, *A Disciplined Intelligence: Critical Inquiry and Canadian Thought in the Victorian Era* (Montreal and Kingston: McGill-Queen's University Press, 1979), whose comments (pp. 1–5) have nonetheless been suggestive in shaping the themes of this chapter.

REGIONS

13

Northern and Southern Varieties of American Evangelicalism in the Nineteenth Century

SAMUEL S. HILL

While tramping about in search of the burial place of a great-great-grandfather of mine who lost his life as a Confederate soldier, my wife and I suddenly realized that for a time two nations inhabited the territory stretching from Mexico to Canada. (The repositories of the prevailing side, such as the National Park Service, do not keep records concerning the fortunes of the defeated fallen.) Two nations in one; it was not so for long. Indeed one can argue that it never was so, that the years 1861–1865 were a sham. What a grim way to register with some accuracy a tragic fact. Before the 1820s, the southern states and the northern states were distinguishable along geographic and geography-attendant lines. Regionalism escalated into sectionalism, a condition that hardened into acrimony, then conflict and official political disunion. For the rest of the nineteenth century, two regional cultures coughed and spluttered at each other—a situation relieved only recently by the adoption of full cultural union.

So far, all of my allusions to North and South have been political and military, with a hint of the cultural. We now know with historiographic approval what some of us knew for certain without it: religion was another salient aspect. Northern and southern varieties of American evangelicalism in the nineteenth century deserve to be studied because they are there and because they inform us about American and intra-American life in that epochal century.

An interpretive study ought to take into account what those varieties were as well as their sources and contexts; the principal received religious traditions of the two regions; the span or range of religious movements in each; which movements were region specific, which region straddling, which region interactive; what alternative or competitive movements lived alongside; what kinds of changes were taking place over that lengthy period; and so on.

At the start of the nineteenth century, the states north of what in 1784 became known as the Mason-Dixon line had just begun to know the impact of Methodists and Baptists—the former still fledgling, the latter lately come to size and respectability.[1] Yet it was clear that these groups would do well. Congregationalists and Presbyterians were losing ground, relatively, and they were less formidable for being more broadly distributed. Episcopal churches had been established in stable communities, but few new ones were being planted. On a smaller scale, the Lutheran story compares. Friends and Moravians and sectarian German Baptists appeared here and there, firm and notable but mostly living to themselves. Roman Catholicism was a tolerated, quite small minority. In general, one sees a picture of a mildly diverse Protestant population and culture. A Protestant population was more evident than a Protestant culture, however. While no legal obstacles to the construction of a Protestant culture appeared, the flow of cultural dynamics was more centrifugal than centripetal. As Lyman Beecher saw, to take only the most celebrated initiative, the culture was not yet formed and thus up for grabs. No rival claimants as actual religious bodies were on the scene, but indifference or Enlightenment secularism might be poised to stalk.[2]

What did exist was evangelical Protestantism in one or another form. This condition was reinforced by Methodism's incredible vigor and, later, Finney-style Presbyterianism/Congregationalism. The latter, remarkably, was to be a seedbed for all manner of evangelical impulses, abolition and prohibition in the public arena, and holiness and "modern revivalism" ecclesiastically.[3] As evangelicalism assumed those faces, a quasi-evangelicalism also made its appearance as Unitarianism. That is to say, even early-century Unitarianism was transparent to evangelical influence. William Ellery Channing was warm-hearted and christocentric enough to pass for an evangelical—almost, that is, unless one probed deeply enough to see how he was changing traditional Protestant doctrine.

Looking ahead briefly, let us remember what Timothy Smith revealed already in 1957 with *Revivalism and Social Reform*. The awakenings that roused northern urban society in the years just before the Civil War arose within those old-line denominations that were starting to spawn liberalizing ways of thinking as well. No glancing blows from sectarians or newcomer zealots generated those revivals; rather, it was the traditional supernaturalism of the long-entrenched bodies.[4] Bradley Longfield's study of the 1920s entitled *The Presbyterian Controversy* confirms the point. He writes: "One reason that [Robert] Speer and [Charles] Erdman so willingly supported a theologically broadening church in the 1900s was the church's overwhelmingly conservative, evangelical tenor."[5] Furthermore, we understand the ultraconservatism of Speer and Erdman's rival, J. Gresham Machen, when we recognize it as out of step with what Longfield calls the "northern evangelical tradition of evangelism and social reform."[6]

Below the Mason-Dixon line, conditions at the beginning of the nineteenth century were both like and unlike those in the North. Largely unchurched, uninstructed, and unconverted, the southern population too was absorbing

Methodist and Baptist impact—white and black together. The southern regional culture that was up for grabs, as yet inchoate, fit a different temporal scheme than the North's. After 1810 or so there was little fear of alien and seditious forces, only the potential for religious illiteracy and indifference. Transappalachia had already been invaded by evangelical Protestantism—in fact, its influence was being reciprocated eastward.[7] The South had a laggard period, but it had appeared earlier, antedating the formation of the American republic.

To note when the missionary plea was sounded, South and North, informs understanding of the two regional societies. The South's was early and weak—as seen in the work of the Anglican Society for the Propagation of the Gospel—and more spontaneous than planned, the Methodists and Baptists seemingly just came to life and found welcome audiences. The North's was later and formal and directed toward the conversion of "the West." Whether real or imagined, the call for claiming Ohio, Indiana, Illinois, Michigan, and the rest bespoke a rationalized strategy and an alertness to antireligious developments in Europe.

By contrast with the North's evangelicalism, which was more traditional—that is, rooted in a systematic, organic, and comprehensive frame of Christian meaning, expression, and experience—the South's was primarily experimental. Reformation and post-Reformation modes persisted in northeastern and midwestern Congregational and Presbyterian life. Methodism, a region-straddling community that was often region interactive as well, almost certainly perpetuated more of its formal Wesleyan theology in the North than in the South. In the South, Methodism may well have compartmentalized its constituent dimensions. Sometimes its people there did acknowledge theology, ethics, and social responsibility, but the crying need was to convert the lost, a passion Methodists shared with Baptists. There is some evidence that they were driven in part by competition with those Baptists for the larger share in the harvest of souls. At any rate, the South's evangelical fare differed. Dixie Christians did do more than preach to individuals for conversion; they built cultural and social institutions, and a kind of Christian civilization, as well. Yet, lacking an organic conception of the various Christian tasks, they tended to equate conversion with the conversion experience, a view that made the moment of entry into the Christian life an end in itself and sometimes the end of the church's responsibility.

Around 1800 in the South, then, there were newcomer Methodist and Baptist churches and a smaller number of older Presbyterian and Episcopal churches. The two largest denominations were definitely evangelical, the third somewhat evangelical, and the others not. Joining the Episcopalians in that last classification were scattered Lutherans, Friends, Mennonites, Moravians, Roman Catholics, and some others. What happened along the way through the nineteenth century is the body of our story in this chapter—and a major element in American social, cultural, and intellectual history.

The two regional evangelicalisms did differ somewhat in the early decades of the century, as we have noted. Perhaps it was their relationship to cultural surroundings that most distinguished them. Nevertheless, the patterns of personal evangelical experience looked remakably similar until 1825 or so.[8]

A glance at the early commonality and the later divergence reveals that both regions held a concern for Christian piety—a life punctuated and sustained by prayer and Bible study and shared with other righteous people in congregational worship and fellowship. Men and women "knew the Lord," speaking of him as friend and companion. He was as accessible as the next prayerful word or thought. His word was to be studied and treasured in the heart. Moreover, it was to be passed on to their children at the family table around the hearth.

Christ was indeed as near and close as breathing, a "very present help in trouble." But he was also Savior and Lord. One needed to trust him, bow before him, rely on him for forgiveness. Quite generally, women and men entered this presence with reverence, even a keen sense of their own unworthiness and guilt before the One who required as well as gave. Clearly, this is standard Christian piety with its emphasis on warm relationship, divine majesty, and personal shortcomings. Morphologically, northern Presbyterians and southern Baptists shared a great deal, as did Methodists from New York and Indiana to Virginia and Tennessee.

But patterns of divergence were appearing. Southern evangelical forms tended increasingly to take shape as whole pieces, separated bites, rather than an amalgam, a woven fabric, an easy flow, of the various elements of Christian reality. Relationship with God took on the form of notable events, less the air one breathes all day. Christian profession was a way of life, but it was also an inventory of particular moments, activities, and awarenesses. Guilt especially loomed large, emerging as the keenest awareness. A strong sense of one's obligation to God enveloped the soul, resulting in self-consciousness about one's standing before the Almighty. The religious life was coming to be seen more as what drives and limits one than as cause for celebration or occasion for public responsibility—or simply the essence of one's existence. A private introspectiveness that even the colonial Puritans had never known became the hallmark of southern righteousness.[9] Organizing the inner life, responding to inward convictions and compunctions, took over as the lineaments of faithfulness. Suggestibility of the Savior's love and, at the same time, to one's own failures and unworthiness sustained one on the ladder to heaven. This is less the religion of joy and hope than of sensitivity and inadequacy. This is not the spirituality that generated Phoebe Palmer's New York kind of Holiness, which was dotted by optimism and vigorous activity.

Beyond doubt, southern faith was expressed by the southern faithful in the public sphere. Southern evangelicals knew the sweetness of fellowship with others, they established schools and colleges, they organized reform societies, they gave leadership in the public domain, and they agonized over slavery, slaves, and their own connections with both institution and people.[10] But when southern evangelicals thought about or spoke of religion directly, they meant the inner life. Guilt and inadequacy, sensitivity, duty, and obligation—

these were the instinctual references. In this sense I speak of "whole pieces" and "separate bites." One is not infused with Christian reality; rather, one is visited by Christian realities. A system of gradations appears, some teachings and responsibilities clearly ranking ahead of others. Serial understanding, not systematic, is characteristic—not organic connections but episodic and piecemeal orderings.

Northern evangelicalism was moving in the other direction. While hardly less supernaturalist in orientation, it was less consumed by inward piety. Congregationalists and Baptists practiced prayer, affirmed the divine providence, honored the authority and veracity of Holy Scripture, and acknowledged the reality of heaven and hell. But they were at least as much given to organizing their outer lives as their inner lives. This is not to contend that they were ethical at the expense of being pious. Instead, piety underwrote and impelled practice in public. Guilty before God they knew themselves to be, guilt conscious they really were not. Perhaps the difference between them and their southern cofaithful was the limited role of introspection. Dwelling on the cleansing of the heart occupied a lower place on the scale of Christian responsibility. Getting on with believing in God in worship and service consumed their energies. Put another way, theirs was a piety placed in the service of service. Better acted upon than lingered on, expressed than dwelt upon.

We have been approaching the subject of revivalism. Nineteenth-century American evangelicalism introduced so-called modern revivalism.[11] The two luminaries of the century were major national figures: Charles Grandison Finney and Dwight L. Moody. Trailing them in celebrity were two men of the late century: Billy Sunday of Iowa and Illinois and Sam P. Jones of Georgia. With these revivalists, region meant a great deal. Where did the revivalists come from? Who responded to revivalism? What variations of revivalism existed? Was this an evolving phenomenon?

Finney was a son of Connecticut and New York whose evangelistic circuit lay largely in the northeastern states until he moved to Ohio in 1837, when the range of his influence enlarged to the Midwest.[12] He labored near the southern vineyard occasionally, but never in it, coming as close as Cincinnati and Philadelphia. Moody's habitation was Massachusetts and Illinois. He crossed the country numerous times, mostly in an arc from Boston and Philadelphia to Chicago and Minneapolis. He ventured south several times, to Atlanta and Augusta in Georgia, and Nashville and Memphis, for example.[13]

Billy Sunday made it to Baltimore, Tulsa, Atlanta, Tampa, Fort Worth, Richmond, and other cities (in the early twentieth century, actually).[14] Sam P. Jones, the "Moody of the South," was southern but did carry his message to northern cities, among them Boston, Chicago, and San Francisco. There were a few other itinerants, but that mode of evangelism attained prominence only after the automobile and radio became common.[15]

It is time to characterize "modern revivalism."[16] Taking Finney and Moody as principal models, it is possible to show the significance of revivalism for nineteenth-century evangelicalism, regionally considered. First, it flourished in the northern states during the antebellum period, at least in part because northern evangelicals had mastered organizational business practices and because the North had more centers of concentrated population. While hardly languid about aggressive approaches to growth and recruitment, the southern churches were far more localist. Revivals, that is to say, were matters for individual congregations to undertake with a view to reaching neighbors, people they knew or at least who lived near by. The southern churches were mirroring a regional penchant for localism in many phases of cultural life. Revivals there certainly were; Methodist and Baptist vitality geared directly to them. Often called protracted meetings, they were scheduled at seasons of the year suited to climate and the rhythms of agriculture. By the 1840s, camp meetings, which once had been so prominent, were all but extinct.[17] Camp meetings had drawn people from miles around; they were not functions of local congregational or community life. The revivals that replaced camp meetings were a function of the people in settled clusters.

The southern revivals accordingly were not big news on a large scale. They succeeded in drawing individuals into the fold and in solidifying families for church life. Or they may have sparked conversion experiences with no lasting effects, accomplishing what the preachers themselves seemed often to be saying: what is truly important is that one experience salvation so that the slate can be wiped clean of sins and the person can be assured of the rewards of heaven. Such a movement, however, did not permeate the community. It recruited individuals, changing the common life in that way. The North's revivals, increasingly urban, did permeate. They resulted in interest-group and sector meetings, involving businessmen, women, workers in an office or factory, or other community groups. Often they gave rise to reform efforts, such as Sabbatarianism, relief and welfare for the poor, improved prison conditions, and heightened business ethics. In sum, northern revivals revived society as much as they converted individuals.[18] Even in Finney's era, where personal regeneration was stock-in-trade, a kind of organic understanding prevailed. Not only were individuals converted, but the goal of personal perfection was promoted, righteous living in the public realm was urged, and communities and towns were affected. A variation on this network of themes was the abolitionism revivals of Theodore Weld and the Oberlin perfectionists.[19]

Accounting for causes and effects is complex. Did a localist framework of thought stimulate the South's more rural and small-town conditions (what Max Weber termed *Gemeinschaft*)? Was a permeative, all-impacting mentality predictable from the North's more urban and industrial form of society (Weber's *Gesellschaft*)? For purposes of our study, it makes no difference, for we do know that revivalism—one major evangelical expression in nineteenth-century America—differed significantly in the two regions. The setting, the immediate goals, and the resulting thrust of revivals were expressed quite distinguishably in the two regions. While we balk before the issue of cause and effect, we may be quite straightforward about conditions accompanying theological matters. The North's greater preference for comprehensiveness, system, and organicism marked its revivals, especially in the period 1830–1860. The southern Protestant proclivity for "whole pieces" and "separate bites" characterized the revivalism so popular there. No direct link existed in the South between the conversion experience and a systematic understanding of a social ethic.

Despite differences, a common supernaturalism did underlay revivalism in both regions. Secularist forces had not yet insinuated themselves into American thinking, certainly not appreciably in the theology of the Protestant churches, which were still consistently orthodox. On that score, the South and the North scarcely parted company. Yet, it is sobering to realize that virtually the same "correct opinions" can issue in notably distinct forms. The creative force, in sum, was the contrast between systematic and organic coordination, on the northern side, and serial thinking and arranging, on the southern.

This kind of analysis also enables us to approach another distinct evangelical group in the nineteenth century, namely, the indigenous company of Afro-American Protestants within the white Protestant churches that had introduced them to Christian faith and with whom they shared so much. Black and white evangelicals held the same beliefs, conducted—indeed, attended—the same revivals, and often belonged to the identical congregations. Evidence discloses little divergence between whites and blacks in belief and practice before emancipation, although cultural heritages clearly distinguished styles in music, preaching, and worship demeanor.[20]

Once on their own—which they were with startling alacrity once the Civil War ended—black Christians expressed evangelical faith with innovative flourishes.[21] For one thing, the minister acquired greater power. For another, the incentive for conversion shifted from consequences in the afterlife (which had been a basic, though not exclusive, motive for conversion in the South) to joy and celebration. Hell was deemphasized and lost the impelling qualities it once had. Indeed the distinction between church members and others dimmed. Life in the church as community took on central significance and was open to all at any time. But emphasis on enjoyment of God here and now was hardly the whole story. Mood and concern extended also to responsibility for the welfare of God's people here and now. Thus, in the new black churches the characteristic southern division between the personal relationship with God and the social responsibility for other people faded rapidly. The comprehensive and organic tones of northern evangelicalism came also to characterize the southern black church, in its own way, and growing out of its own unique history. Black preachers drove home the equality of the doctrines of the fatherhood of God and the brotherhood of man.[22]

In seeking to understand settings, received traditions, and emergent forms of evangelicalism before the Civil War, more is required than a narrow focus on religious matters. In addition, we are struck by changing contexts. Altered demography was most obvious. New peoples were coming to America, especially from Germany and Ireland. Lifelong Americans were also moving; thus, cities and towns expanded with newly arrived natives and immigrants. Economic conditions were changing with the development of the American system of government and industry. Naturally, evangelicals responded, or reacted, to such major shifts in national ways of living. At the end of the twentieth century we recognize readily the significance of these changes for American life. More easily overlooked are both the creativity and the restiveness within the larger Christian community. Internal and external surroundings were changing and having an impact. At one extreme, a new and quite heretical variation appeared: The Church of Jesus Christ of Latter-day Saints. Closer to the center, yet despised by traditional Protestants as deviants, were the Adventists and other millenarians and utopians. Then there were the Restorationists of the Stone-Campbell tradition. Perceived against the backdrop of America's rapidly changing societies, these various movements reflected yearnings for *more* (more purity, more authenticity, more authority), but also for *less* (less worldliness, less uncertainty, less reliance on old traditions).

Later scholars would debate which of these movements was and is evangelical, but that was hardly an issue in the 1840s. Adventism certainly shares some evangelical qualities; just as clearly the Stone-Campbell movements reflect others. But these "old new religions" swam outside the mainstream; all were at least idiosyncratic, some (by traditional standards) quite aberrant.

Unmistakably, the birth of the holiness movement further complicates the question of American varieties of evangelicalism. Far from original with America in the 1850s, a holiness strand ran deep within the Wesleyan tradition. But the movement associated with Phoebe Palmer, the 1858 urban revivals, Charles Finney, and Oberlin perfectionism imported a source of new life into old bodies. It lifted supernaturalism to a higher plane, both inward awareness of the divine Spirit and faithful service to humanity in need. Authority yielded primary place to empowerment; Scripture became a guide for the soul to a quite proximate God.[23] The distinction between holiness movements, on the one hand, and Methodists, Baptists, and Adventists, on the other, was only one of degree. But their single-minded devotion to the divine power who dwells within to purify toward perfection and to impel toward sacrificial service did set them off, adumbrating a major development late in the nineteenth century and early in the twentieth.

Two features of holiness, understood as an evangelical spirit outdoing older evangelicalism, demand attention. First, this was a middle-class movement; second, it made little or no mark in the South. It would not be necessary to notice that mid-nineteenth-century holiness broke out among the better classes in society within large and influential orthodox denominations if more notorious manifestations of the Holy Spirit had not taken place primarily among lower classes of people a half-century later. We do well to remember that there is nothing historically predictable about an alliance of spiritedness and underclasses of people.

Concerning the failure of the holiness movement to take root in the South, it is tempting to reach for an old chestnut: people who are already red-hot are not likely to warm up white-hot. The southern churches already knew about the Spirit, especially the explosion of the Spirit that converted the cool hearts of the unregenerate. And the southern faithful sought to walk in the Spirit day by day, turning to God in weal and woe, fully confident in forgiveness and of answer to prayer. Yet, disciplined approach to God of the sort that expected and awaited a continual taking over by the Spirit was largely missing. The Spirit's action in conversion was dramatic. The Spirit's daily guidance was simply folded into the daily walk. To suppose that the Spirit could act as forcefully on a continuing basis as he had in the beginning was for the South a foreign concept. "Disciplined," "expectant," and "vigorous" simply do not characterize nineteenth-century southern evangelical life.

In the 1870s and 1880s, however, the holiness emphasis did emerge in the South. Not surprisingly, the Methodist Episcopal Church, South, was the place. Two large personalities brought holiness to the region, both unmistakably sons of the South. Joseph H. King of northern Georgia, being gifted by and with the Spirit, began preaching holiness, then pentecostal power; with his charismatic influence, King gained a wide following. Later, he acquired an unofficial circuit of his own, itinerating extensively throughout the western Carolinas, eastern Tennessee, and northern Georgia, even into Ontario, New York, and into Ohio. But a combination of his forceful leadership and his heretical speaking in tongues made him persona non grata in the MECS. Hardly daunted, King became the founder of the southern pentecostal movement and of the group that became known in 1911 as the Pentecostal Holiness Church.[24]

Slightly farther west, the Spirit was conquering the heart and soul of John Lakin Brasher, a northern Alabama Methodist preacher and leader blessed with great vitality. His gifts were along perfectionist and holiness lines, not charismatic and pentecostal. Like King, Brasher ran afoul of Methodist jurisdiction, even though he belonged to the northern branch of the church. Bishops thought he went too far in claiming Spirit empowerment. Unlike King, however, Brasher desired to stay within the traditional body; he never even considered leaving the Methodist Episcopal Church. This affiliation, in fact, did not squelch his brand of piety or his ministry. What did happen was another instance of itineration. Brasher roamed far and wide, in the western and upper South and into the Midwest. He held services in Iowa and in Detroit and Cincinnati. In the process, he helped create a constituency for what became the Church of the Nazarene, but he adamantly remained Methodist and opposed sectarian proliferation. Indeed he was a delegate to the 1939 Uniting Convention that created The Methodist Church.[25]

In this brief recounting of the life of King and Brasher, we encounter a fascinating dimension of nineteenth-century evangelicalism, namely, its region-interactive quality. During the decades of Reconstruction, Jim Crow laws, Lost Cause mythmaking, and regional antagonism, two families of evangelicals refused to be bound by boundaries. The transcendent Spirit moved King and Brasher and hundreds of others in the devastated and aggrieved South to traverse the home territory, but also to do more in carrying the message to other states in the Union. Politics was not part of their baggage. In fact, they traveled light, the wind of the Spirit at their backs. As they itinerated, they linked hearts and hands with other men and women who had been won by the Spirit. In other words, holiness and pentecostal movements erupted here and there, from the 1850s (1880s especially), and in the black population as well as the white.

This brief survey cannot end without mention of the forces of pentecostal strength that arose on the western slopes of the southern Appalachian mountains, in the orbit of Cleveland, Tennessee. The bodies in the Tomlinson heritage that trace their origins to that time and place continue a vigorous existence, but for the greater part they have remained stateside, regional communions. They have also gained considerable strength overseas. Pentecostalism and holiness are profoundly general, but some denominations have always remained regional.[26]

Spirit-oriented movements were indeed a major element in American evangelical life in the nineteenth century. We may refer to them as soft. They concerned matters of the heart, inward personal experience, and the Almighty's indwelling to generate miraculous power. These groups naturally had their "hard" sides as well. That is, they stood for something; they held to strict doctrinal standards. Not only did they base their "soft" qualities on the solid rock of biblical teaching and sound doctrine, they insisted that the faithful acknowledge fundamental doctrines of the faith as true and as their testimony to the truth.

But the final criteria were "soft." They never equated faith with intellectual assent to propositions. Hardly liable to the accusation of being lenient on doctrinal requirements, they nevertheless were not given to defining faith in terms of doctrinal correctness. Some of their contemporaries, however, did just that. In the twentieth century they came to be called fundamentalists. Fundamentalists are "hard" evangelicals. In their hands, Christian reality becomes dominantly rational. They insist on assent to propositions. Not just doctrines are important, also the status of doctrines. Testifying, confessing, standing up for the Lord amounts mainly to definition, differentiation, and defense of the truth. Although fundamentalism is principally a twentieth-century phenomenon, its origins nonetheless lie in the nineteenth.[27]

It is usually inaccurate to describe social movements as reactionary, since most have a greater devotion to what they promote than aversion to what they oppose. Or if they come to birth to oppose, they grow into advocates, since most people do not thrive for long on resistance. By the teens and twenties of this century, fundamentalism had acquired its true dark colors. It lived off its enemies; it required concentration on the perverse to sustain its livelihood. The earlier expressions of fundamentalism late in the nineteenth century were less acrimonious for one basic reason. In the earlier period, churches were not as obviously interested or infected with secularizing trends of the broader American culture. The bogies that fundamentalist extremists railed against in the 1920s had actually sprung up some decades earlier. Science's new conventions that seemed to assault orthodoxy had been widely publicized by the 1870s. The application of literary methods and textual criticism in several forms to the study of the Bible had become a major enterprise well before the turn of the century. The corrosive effects of the new social sciences—in particular, sociology—were being noted at least by the 1880s.

What later fundamentalism attacked was the insinuation of these perspectives into the chuches. By the time Baptists (northern), Presbyterians (mostly northern), Methodists (similarly), and other once-evangelical denominations had adopted modernist views associated with the new intellectual conventions, the situation was greatly changed. It was time for traditionalists, the old orthodox, to build their fortresses and go on the attack. Thus, the focus of fundamentalist battles was within denominations that were once solidly and unambiguously evangelical. For our purposes, one point needs underscoring: sources of the trends against which fundamentalists reacted so forcefully were nineteenth-century phenomena. Only when the churches adapted to these trends did strident response arise from fundamentalists like William Jennings Bryan, John Roach Straton, J. Gresham Machen, William Bell Riley, J. Frank Norris, and others. Expunge these views of knowledge from the natural, textual, and social sciences, they could not; from the churches, however, they were determined to expel them root and branch.[28]

At the end of the nineteenth century, Dwight L. Moody and his contemporaries had plenty of enemies to contend with. But modernity was not yet firmly entrenched in the churches. What energized Moody and his peers was the urgency to reach newly moved and newly arrived people and to address conditions of personal and social uprootedness abundant in the late century. Their battles were over the souls of people who needed to hear and believe the gospel, now more than ever, a good deal less over the allegiance of the mind. Sam P. Jones was similarly driven to aid people in perilous social conditions as he moved in a society seeking to find a way in the aftermath of war and Reconstruction epitomized by thousands of people congregating in cities.

A continuing theme in this chapter has been contexts for the churches' life. In discussing the sources of fundamentalism and the new intellectual and demographic conditions that came to occupy center stage in the late nineteenth century, we gain another angle of insight into the North and the South. Above the Mason-Dixon line, evangelicalism was coming to be closely associated with large-scale, urban revivalism. In the North, this was also the era of new conservative denominations—the Free Methodists, the Christian and Missionary Alliance, the Church of God of Anderson, Indiana, Brethren Churches, and Scandinavian pietist bodies, among others. These newer denominations centralized government, gave heavy responsibility to laymen and laywomen, promoted worldwide missionary efforts, stressed personal piety and holiness, and began to question the increasingly wicked ways of the world. Much of that wickedness was associated with the new Roman Catholic and Jewish immigrants, as well as with the new urban ways. The leading edge of the North's evangelicalism late in the century thus was not occupied by the traditional denominations. Those bodies did not prove attractive to the newcomers to the United States or very effective in ministering to the growing cities and towns. Moreover, the older denominations were yielding, not always rapidly, to currents of thought that pushed them beyond orthodoxy. Evangelicalism was taking root for a long haul that extended beyond World War II in its visible revival crusades and small-size conservative bodies, where fundamentalist motifs played only a minor role.

Then there was the South. So much had happened and so little was changing. Yet a closer look does reveal changes, two of which we have mentioned.
First, in the months following the Civil War, black Protestants formed new
independent Baptist congregations, later denominations, and two African
Methodist bodies also came into existence. This development changed most
dramatically the social roles of the churches in the black community. Second,
at century's end, pentecostal and holiness movements were stirring among
lower classes of white people, and some black as well, in the western
piedmont of the seaboard states and just west of the southern Appalachian
Mountains.

These developments cannot be dismissed. Yet, to emphasize these changes
is to misunderstand southern culture taken as a whole. In the South during the
late nineteenth century, the real questions of interest still concerned what was
happening with the Baptists, Methodists, and Presbyterians. While those denominations in the North were feeling the impact of massive cultural change,
they remained the South's religious anchor. Their growth, especially the Baptists', was dramatic in the late century. Their cultural influence attained new
heights.[29]

They remained evangelical. But they too were undergoing some shifts.
Presbyterian numbers had stabilized and were dominated by people of Scottish lineage. Social ministries enlarged, especially in educational areas. At the
same time, the older doctrine of the spirituality of the church gained greater
support. This denomination continued to be doctrine minded and doctrinally
orthodox. It became a conservative preserve, strongest in the upper middle
classes and in selected locales. Outreach was hardly its hallmark, and it was
totally unaffected by Spirit-related movements. The revivalist impetus it once
sparked had disappeared.[30]

The Methodist Episcopal Church, South, was active and productive. The
many-sided nature of its heritage persisted. Thus, it spawned colleges, supported overseas missions, engaged in all manner of social reform, and took
the lead in Prohibition. The denomination grew more centralized, its judica-
tories more powerful. The doctrine of the Spirit was evident in Methodist
preaching (it could hardly have been otherwise), but when such themes became intense, they were suspected. The come-outer holiness impulses had
arisen in response to growth in the denomination's size and bureaucracy.
Evangelical it surely continued to be, but with less specificity and a diminished
spontaneity.[31]

The Southern Baptists constitute the big story of the late nineteenth century.[32] Aggressively they built churches and recruited new members. The impetus for expansion came from individuals and local congregations. Expansion
also arose from a self-conscious process of organization and centralization. As
that process went on, Southern Baptists began to shift away from the kind of
grass-roots ecumenism that had been so common in their communities. What
resulted was a denomination of great strength and pride, but one tending
toward isolationism. More than a few social ministries were conducted—in

education, for the poor and working classes, toward black people, in the Prohibitionist cause, and so on. But evangelism overshadowed all other activities. Saving the lost at home and abroad became the denomination's passion. Revival meetings acquired as much regularity as the Sunday school movement, which was also assuming a tighter structure.

The varieties of evangelicalism in the late nineteenth-century South were comparatively few in number. Slowly, new small bodies of explicitly evangelical Protestants (mostly holiness and pentecostal) were appearing. The southern Restorationists attained clear identity and grew in size.[33] In traditional ways, Presbyterians and Methodists perpetuated southern evangelicalism. Banner headlines went to the Southern Baptists, however. The future of the tradition lay largely in their hands.

Any discussion of nineteenth-century American religion leads to the conclusion that variety is not the only issue; rather, the applicability of the term "evangelical" also must be a concern. Southerners rarely use that term to describe themselves—nor has it ever been a standard self-description. Scholars need to investigate the extent of its use in the nineteenth century. My hypothesis is that "evangelical" is typically employed (anywhere) to register "alternativity," a position at some variance with conventional religious culture. In the South, the major denominations that might have been regarded as evangelical in fact *were* the center and strength of the religious culture.

More generally, a large-scale picture of evangelical Protestantism at the end of the nineteenth century shows that a movement that had once been dominant in the North was now diffused and beginning to evolve toward a division between private and public parties.[34] Rivals, foils, and severe challenges seemed to be everywhere in the North. In the South, by contrast, a popular movement that had become a virtual establishment by the 1830s persisted in strength and cultural dominance—indeed, became institutionalized and ever stronger.[35] Diversity was present, but within a narrow span, from historically moderate Protestantism (Presbyterian) to the new Spirit-based "sects." By contrast, in 1900 the span of religion in the North was enormous, with Catholicism a powerful force, Jews and untraditional Christians sizable, and Protestantism increasingly fragmented into liberal and orthodox groupings.

Understanding these developments sheds light on why, in the late twentieth century, visitors from the American North to the South, or vice versa, find the religious situation perplexing. Northerners coming south wish the locals would not be so explicit or aggressive and long for both the creativity that complexity affords and the particularity generated by alternatives. Southerners traveling north cannot seem to find Protestants, certainly not of the sort and style to which they are accustomed. The South's religion stifles, even suffocates, northern visitors. Looking about in the North, southerners repeat what their forebears were saying a century ago: the North has lost its faith, and we southerners are left as America's last godly society.

The drastic changes in nineteenth-century America are seen nowhere more clearly than in the transformations worked North and South in evangelicalism. For better and for worse, the northern monolith had fractured and declined; the southern embryo had grown into a juggernaut.

Notes

1. Russell E. Richey, *Early American Methodism* (Bloomington: Indiana University Press, 1991), xi–xii.

2. See Lyman Beecher, *A Plea for the West* (Cincinnati: Truman and Smith, 1835), 9–23.

3. The scope of Finney's concerns and involvements cannot be quickly grasped. One needs to canvas his remarkable career. See Garth M. Rosell and Richard A. G. Dupuis, eds., *The Memoirs of Charles G. Finney* (Grand Rapids: Zondervan, 1989).

4. Timothy L. Smith, *Revivalism and Social Reform: American Protestantism on the Eve of the Civil War* (1957; rev. ed., Baltimore: John Hopkins University Press, 1980), chap. 1.

5. Bradley J. Longfield, *The Presbyterian Controversy* (New York: Oxford University Press, 1991), 233.

6. Ibid., 229.

7. John B. Boles, *The Great Revival, 1787–1805* (Lexington: University of Kentucky Press, 1972), chap. 6.

8. Jon Alexander, "A Drift toward Disparity: The Religious Experience of Southerners and Northerners in the Antebellum period" (unpublished paper, used by permission).

9. C. C. Goen, *Revivalism and Separatism in New England, 1740–1800* (New Haven: Yale University Press, 1962), 44.

10. Donald G. Mathews, *Religion in the Old South* (Chicago: University of Chicago Press, 1977), chaps. 2, 3.

11. William G. McLoughlin, *Modern Revivalism* (New York: Ronald Press, 1959), esp. 3–64, 523–30.

12. Rosell and Dupuis, *Memoirs of Finney.*

13. James F. Findlay, Jr., *Dwight L. Moody: American Evangelist, 1837–1899* (Chicago: University of Chicago Press), chaps. 6, 9.

14. Lyle W. Dorsett, *Billy Sunday and the Redemption of Urban America* (Grand Rapids: Eerdmans, 1991), chaps. 5, 6.

15. Kathleen Minnix, "The Atlanta Revivals of Sam Jones," *Atlanta History* 33 (1989): 5–34. Minnix has prepared a full manuscript for publication, " 'Hammering the Brethren': The Life of Evangelist Sam Jones."

16. McLoughlin, *Modern Revivalism,* 217–81.

17. Dickson D. Bruse, Jr., *And They All Sang Hallelujah* (Knoxville: University of Tennessee Press, 1972), 56.

18. Smith, *Revivalism and Social Reform,* chaps., 2, 3.

19. Robert H. Abzug, *Passionate Liberator: Theodore Dwight Weld and the Dilemma of Reform* (New York: Oxford University Press, 1980), esp. chap. 7.

20. Albert J. Raboteau, *Slave Religion* (New York: Oxford University Press, 1978), chap. 3.

21. Katherine L. Dvorak, *An African-American Exodus* (Brooklyn, NY: Carlson Publishing, 1991), 69–79.

22. Edward L. Wheeler, *Uplifting the Race: The Black Minister in the New South, 1865–1902* (Lanham, MD: University Press of America, 1986), 44.

23. See Paul M. Bassett, "The Theological Identity of the North American Holiness Movement," in *The Variety of American Evangelicalism,* ed. Donald W. Dayton and Robert K. Johnston (Knoxville: University of Tennessee Press, 1991), 72–108.

24. For information about Joseph H. King, I am indebted to David A. Alexander of the Department of History, Southeastern College of the Assemblies of God.

25. J. Lawrence Brasher, *Between the Living and the Dead: The Ministry of John Lakin Brasher* (Urbana: University of Illinois Press, forthcoming).

26. Robert Mapes Anderson, *Vision of the Disinherited* (New York: Oxford University Press, 1979), 116–18, 289–90.

27. George M. Marsden, *Fundamentalism and American Culture* (New York: Oxford University Press, 1980), pt. 1.

28. For a biographical study of seven key fundamentalist leaders, see C. Allyn Russell, *Voices of American Fundamentalism* (Philadelphia: Westminister Press, 1976).

29. C. Vann Woodward, *Origins of the New South, 1877–1913* (Baton Rouge: Lousiana State University Press, 1951), 448–49.

30. Ernest Trice Thompson, *Presbyterians in the South,* vol. 3: *1890–1972* (Richmond, VA: John Knox Press, 1973), 36–44.

31. Hunter Dickinson Farish, *The Circuit Rider Dismounts* (Richmond, VA: Dietz Press, 1938), 362.

32. Kenneth K. Bailey, *Southern White Protestantism in the Twentieth Century* (New York: Harper and Row, 1964), chap. 1.

33. David Edwin Harrell, Jr., "Religious Pluralism: Catholics, Jews, and Sectarians," in *Religion in the South,* ed. Charles Reagan Wilson (Jackson: University Press of Mississippi, 1985), 68–80.

34. See Jean Miller Schmidt, *Souls or the Social Order: The Two-Party System in American Protestantism* (Brooklyn, NY: Carlson Publishing, 1991).

35. Gardiner M. Shattuck, *A Shield and Hiding Place: The Religious Life of the Civil War Armies* (Macon, GA: Mercer University Press, 1987), 133, 135, 136.

14

The American and British Contributions to Evangelicalism in Australia

STUART PIGGIN

Best known for hedonism and secularism, Australia is yet a major center of evangelicalism.[1] For about a century, Australia has been considered by the movement's overseas leaders to be an important bastion of evangelical Christianity. Recent attempts to assess the size of the evangelical movement in the world in general and Australia in particular[2] suggest that the evangelical movement in Australia may have a broad constituency[3] of about one in every six Australians, and this may have been a fairly constant figure throughout its two-hundred-year history.[4] The evangelical proportion of the population may be about the same as that of New Zealand, two-thirds that of the United States, and double that of the United Kingdom; those proportions may indicate the relative strength, and therefore influence, of the evangelical movement in each country. It suggests, for example, that the evangelical movement in Australia is sufficiently significant to challenge the neglect that the movement has suffered at the hands of most Australian historians.

In this chapter I attempt to answer specific questions related to the comparative themes of the book. My first and fundamental question is, How has Australian evangelicalism been shaped by American and British influences? My second question: Is evangelicalism a recognizably international movement, and of its branches, what is unique or distinctive about Australian evangelicalism? Finally I ask, What have been the patterns of interaction between evangelicalism and social and cultural forces in Australia, and how do they compare with the patterns of such interactions in Britain and America?

The question of how Australian evangelicalism has been shaped by American and British influences raises a number of important issues. Was Australian evangelicalism shaped primarily and definitively at the time of the origins of Australian settlement? Or have those exogenous factors continued to constitute the nature of Australian evangelicalism either by continuing to influence it as it grows or by repeatedly reintroducing varieties of it after other implants have died or grown too sickly to reproduce? The history of the Baptist churches in nineteenth-century Australia, for example, was probably not so much that of a single, continuous tradition but more of a series of implantations, some of which took root and grew.[5]

The question What is unique about Australian evangelicalism? prompts the observation that even the distinctive characteristics of Australian evangelicalism may still be the product of influences from Britain and America if those influences present themselves in a unique combination or in a unique environment. One thing distinctive about Australian evangelicalism, for example, is the hegemony of Anglican evangelicalism. Anglicanism has traditionally neglected the highly individualistic theology of the indwelling Spirit. Anglicanism in both its evangelical and Catholic expressions has opted for ordered and rational religious practices. This is a vital point for understanding the differences in the ambience of American and Australian spiritual life. American culture has always offered a religious as well as a secular legitimation for rebellion and change in its dissenting, non-episcopal protestant ethos. This is very different from Australia's more hierarchical, centralized, conforming Anglican/Roman Catholic ethos.[6]

Another characteristic of Australian Christianity in general is its apparent inability to foster new varieties of the old denominational structures. Not many Australian Christian denominations have managed to produce genuine homegrown or indigenous subcultures. The only religious subculture that has been generally recognized by historians as genuinely Australian, apart from Aboriginal religion, is larrikin (or boisterously rowdy) Irish Catholicism. I would argue that larrikin Sydney evangelical Anglicanism is another, and highly proper South Australian Methodism is a third.

The third major question—What have been the patterns of interaction between evangelicalism and social and cultural forces in Australia, and how do they compare with the patterns of such interactions in Britain and America?—does offer a very full agenda for profitable analysis. How has evangelicalism responded in Australia to working-class, including the convict, culture? How sectarian has it been?[7] How has it adjusted to secularization, especially to the separation of church and state? How has it coped with urbanization,[8] the growth of democracy,[9] the women's movement,[10] and aboriginal races?[11] What has been its contribution to the formation of the national ethos?[12] And how does it compare with the pattern of adjustment to these issues of evangelicalism in America and Britain?

Finally, keeping in mind Bebbington's four characteristics of evangelicalism—crucicentrism, biblicism, conversionism, and activism—how has Australian evangelicalism adjusted to religious issues considered important to evangelicals in other parts of the globe, such as missions, fundamentalism and inerrancy, piety, spirituality, and revival?[13]

Considering both social and religious areas together, in what ways has Australian evangelicalism legitimized leadership? What does this legitimation owe to American and British models and what to distinctively Australian conditions? Australians have a tendency to be anti–"tall poppy,"[14] anti-Pom,[15] and anticlerical. Many Australian evangelical leaders are infected with the same virus, thus making it harder for themselves, for debunkers draw fire on themselves. Two very successful evangelical Anglican leaders in Australia—Archbishop Mowll and C. H. Nash—being Poms, did not have the same psychological need to debunk others, which may help to explain their exceptional success.[16] The work on which the Evangelical History Association is currently engaged—namely, the compiling of an Australian Dictionary of Evangelical Biography—does reveal a large number of very commendable evangelical saints, but not a plethora of great ones. Our greatest Australian-born leaders tend to be rough diamonds; I refer here to Alf Stanway, Alf Dyer, and Phillip Jensen. The leadership of women may also have been critical to the growth of Australian evangelicalism.[17]

The major issues raised by all these questions can best be canvased through the analysis of some key events in Australian religious history, all of which may be paralleled in American history: the origins of settlement; the adjustment between church and state; the expansion of settlement and the gold rushes; Billy Graham crusades; and the ordination of women debate.

The Origins of White Settlement in Australia, ca. 1786

To begin to understand the extent and nature of the British and American evangelical influence on Australia, it is necessary to go behind the birth of the colony of New South Wales in 1788 to its conception in 1786, for the nature of the child is determined more by its conception than by its birth or its environment. The appointment of Reverend Richard Johnson as chaplain to Botany Bay was an outworking of the world vision of the eighteenth-century evangelicals of both Britain and America. Their world vision arose partly from revival and partly from the new voyages of discovery that in the eighteenth century opened up the Pacific world. In the revivals of the late 1730s and early 1740s, much was learned of the power of the gospel as an instrument for renovating whole societies and for converting those drawn from different races and cultures.[18]

In speculating on Isaiah 42:4, "And the isles shall wait for his law," Jonathan Edwards made an intriguing reference to Australia as early as 1724:

> What is peculiarly glorious in it, is the gospelizing the new and before unknown world, that which is so remote, so unknown, where the devil had reigned quietly from the beginning of the world, which is larger—taking in America, Terra Australis Incognita, Hollandia Nova, and all those yet undiscovered tracts of land—is far greater than the old world. I say, that this new world should all worship the God of Israel, whose worship was then confined to so narrow a land, is wonderful and glorious![19]

Before and at about the same time as the settlement of Australia, evangelicals were developing a strategy to cooperate with God to bring in the millennium and to extend the knowledge of the gospel over all the earth. This strategy was forged from the accumulating experience of overseas missions employing different methods, from the rising temperature of British evangelicalism as Anglicans, Wesleyans, and Dissenters spurred each other on to grander schemes for the conversion and betterment of humankind, and from the growing expertise and commitment of merchants to establish bases for evangelical outreach. These three converging developments are well illustrated by evangelical interest in India, Sierra Leone, and Australia, all of which reached a critical point in 1786.

In 1783 the Methodist, Thomas Coke sent a copy of his proposal for the evangelization of India to Charles Grant of the East India Company, soliciting support. In 1786 Grant and his friends put forward their own scheme for government-sponsored missionary activity in India.[20] Grant argued that Providence had given India to England for the advance of Christianity. If England did not do her duty, there would be divine retribution. This accorded well with William Wilberforce's well-known statement that the evangelization of India was "that greatest of all causes, for I really place it before abolition."[21]

Abolition, the other great cause of the evangelicals besides missions, prompted another major evangelical overseas endeavor. In 1786 Grandville Sharp, who in 1772 had been the chief instrument in securing the freeing of slaves in the British Isles, persuaded the government to resettle freed slaves in a settlement at Sierra Leone. It was settled in 1787, and a chaplain accompanied the 460 settlers. Effectively, the Clapham Sect, from 1791, was to take over this experiment through the establishment of the Sierra Leone Company, and one of their own, Zachary Macaulay, was to serve as governor. Granville Sharp was well aware of the proposed settlement at Botany Bay; among his papers is a copy of Sir George Young's 1785 proposal[22] for the settlement of New Holland.[23]

The simultaneous settlement of New South Wales and Sierra Leone and the evangelical link between them deserve closer attention than they have hitherto received from historians. The connection is personified in Lieutenant William Dawes,[24] who accompanied Phillip and Johnson to New South Wales as a marine officer on the First Fleet, subsequently became governor of Sierra Leone, where his strictness provoked the charge that he was invoking "convict methods," and, though a layman, was the first person appointed by the Church Missionary Society to train its prospective missionaries.[25] After he had returned from Sierra Leone, Dawes was recommended for appointment to the position of superintendent of schools in New South Wales by Wilberforce, who had developed an interest in the educational development of the colony through his correspondence with Richard Johnson, the first chaplain.[26]

The letter announcing that New South Wales was to be settled by convicts was signed by Home Secretary, Lord Sydney, on 21 August 1786 and back-dated to the eighteenth. The announcement was preceded by weeks, possibly months, of work, by the Cabinet and other members of Parliament. On 18 August 1786 Treasury was sent the "Heads of a Plan" for the settlement. This document[27] included the provision of a chaplain,[28] which appears to have come about through William Wilberforce's friendship with William Pitt the Younger, as is suggested by a letter from Pitt to Wilberforce, dated 23 September 1786: "The colony for Botany Bay will be much indebted to you for your assistance in providing a chaplain. The enclosed [probably the "Heads of a Plan"] will, however, show that its interests have not been neglected, as well as that you have a nearer connection with them than perhaps you were yourself aware of. Seriously speaking, if you can find such a clergyman as you mention we shall be very glad of it; but it must be soon."[29]

On the evening of that same day, the Reverend Richard Johnson received a visit from "a friend" who asked him if he had "the spirit of a missionary" or if he "wished to go abroad."[30] The friend may have been Wilberforce himself. Whether or not it was Wilberforce who dealt with Johnson personally on that evening, further evidence that Johnson's appointment was due to Wilberforce's close personal connection with Pitt is found in a letter, dated 15 November 1786, that John Newton wrote to Wilberforce: "To you, as the instrument, we owe the pleasing prospect of an opening for the propagation of the Gospel in the Southern Hemisphere. Who can tell what important consequences may depend on Mr. Johnson's going to New Holland? It may seem but a small event at present: so a foundation-stone, when laid, is small compared with the building to be erected upon it; but it is the beginning and the earnest of the whole."[31] Newton's description of Wilberforce as instrument suggests that the latter was implementing a stratagem already devised by more mature evangelical heads, and his advocacy of the Botany Bay chaplaincy appears to have been the first fruit of his calling to a life devoted to "the suppression of the slave trade and the reformation of manners."[32] Wilberforce had only months earlier arrived at settled evangelical convictions, after almost three years of agonizing soul-searching. Newton and Henry Venn now hoped that Wilberforce would do for the wealthy and powerful what Wesley had done for the poor and the multitudes and reach them with the evangelical gospel and employ their resources in grand designs and useful schemes.

Conceived by Newton, the converted slave trader; inspired by Cowper, the evangelical poet;[33] lent compulsion by Thornton, whose wealth was a "wedge of gold"; actualized by Wilberforce, Pitt's intimate; and accepted by Richard Johnson, curate of Henry Foster, foundation member of both the Eclectic Society and Church Missionary Society—that is the Botany Bay chaplaincy.[34] It was the result of the fellowship of some of the best-known members of a movement that was becoming a mass movement, touching the poor and the multitudes as well as the wealthy and the powerful. It was a movement energized by great preachers in the Puritan tradition to whom politicians and poets lent their support. They were conscious that in the gospel they had a powerful instrument of social and individual reform, and they had the zeal and the skill to use it effectively. So, while statesmen were provoked by the loss of America into rethinking their global strategy and were hatching schemes affecting Africa, India, China, and New Holland, evangelicals were hitching a ride for the gospel and dreaming of schemes of usefulness for Africa, India, and Australia. Australia's evangelical parentage, then, unlike that of most of the population, was very distinguished and bequeathed much of its character to its colonial offspring.

The Adjustment between Church and State in Australia, ca. 1830–1850

In the period 1788 to the end of Macquarie's governorship in 1822, New South Wales was a jail chaplaincy, "a command state." The way out of that status and the shape of its replacement was not plain for all to see in the early 1820s. Old England experimented with a landed aristocracy for a decade and a half. New South Wales was to be a squirearchy. Since every squire needs a parson, it was envisaged that the Church of England would, at last, be accorded the full-blown establishment status hitherto obscured in the mean jail chaplaincy. Then, from 1836 the direction of development—toward a capitalist, participatory democracy—became clearer.

The challenge, then, was to devise a system to educate and moralize an increasingly diffuse and (so it was feared) anarchic population. The accepted way of doing that was to increase the role of religion. Public opinion both in Britain and Australia was beginning to favor voluntary support for churches. In the infant colony, however, this would not have worked. The population was too scattered and convict ridden to support its own churches, and usually too small to support more than one school. The answer to this problem were the Church Acts of 1836, which, in an age of liberalism, gave precedence to no religious denomination but equitable government financial support to all who wanted it. Thus a situation developed quite different from that operating both in Britain, where there was no such open competition, or in America, where the competition was not state funded.

The act ended the Church of England's hopes of achieving establishment status and added fuel to the fires of sectarianism that continued to rage, instead of the fires of revival, for the next century. Americans labeled denominationalism "sanctified competition" or "holy emulation" and called it a good thing—so good that lots of new competitors were spawned as well. As a result, "Americans have always felt free to switch from one religious group to another with relative ease and impunity."[35] Australians labeled denominationalism "sectarianism" and called it a bad thing. There is another side. Evangelicalism prizes the unity of all true Christians, and in Australia the sparsity of the population encouraged evangelical Christians, especially those who were not edgy about liberalism, to experiment in "common Christianity." Hence, here, and even more in New Zealand, union churches came to dot the landscape. "Common Christianity" seems to have been strongest in South Australia, the paradise of dissent, until the Methodists realized that they could dominate the state without making any such concessions. Yet, of all Australian states, only in South Australia has anything like a community-wide evangelical consensus been achieved—again a marked contrast with the United States.

Another marked contrast with the United States has been the relative absence in the history of Australian evangelicalism of internecine warfare.

The Australian temperament is more phlegmatic than the American, and its evangelicalism more influenced by pietism, which produced an irenic approach to potential religious disputation. In Australia, furthermore, the Anglican Church has always had the support of a much larger percentage of the population than in America, and therefore ritualism and Anglo-Catholicism have been perceived in Australia as a much greater threat than in America. In Australia during the nineteenth century the evangelicals' enemy was Oxford and Rome, not other Protestant denominations. It is significant that the Church of England in Australia has not suffered anywhere near the clerical drain into Roman Catholicism as did the Church of England in England.[36]

An interesting case study of the impact of Britain and America on the relations between church and state is found in John Dunmore Lang, the fiery founder of clerical Presbyterianism in New South Wales, who visited the United States in 1840. Early in his career he was quite happy to accept state aid; theologically, however, Lang was mildly voluntarist. His chief biographer, Don Baker, suggests that among Lang's reasons for going to the United States was to observe and report back to Australia on the efficacy of a voluntary system of religion that would undermine the system of universal religious establishment then current in NSW.[37]

What he carried home was an evangelical ideal, the theological version of the American Revolution, where a nation of proud individualists stood alone before God, refusing all temptations to compromise with the world as represented by the state. Yet, on his return to New South Wales, he was not immediately prepared to suffer the persecution of leaving the church that paid his stipend out of state funds. As Baker points out, Lang also had to shake himself free of the establishment links of the church in which he had been brought up. The Westminster Confession was his guide, as evidenced by the fact that he had written it into the constitution of the Scots Church in Sydney. It presupposed, in such phrases as that which called on the civil magistrate "to give protection and support to Christ's Church," a tie between church and state. What was Christ's true church if not the Established Church?

The questions that Lang's experience in the United States raised took some time before circumstances provided a solution. It was only in 1842 that Lang was forced out of the Presbytery of Australia, and not over any theological differences about voluntarism but over his refusal to pay attention to the resolutions of the church courts, and for "slander, divisive action and contumacy." Out in the cold, Lang reverted to the idyllic American dream and preached voluntarism as the only way a church could retain its purity unsullied from the world. Just as young Australian clergy now come to the United States to see "what works," Lang took what was apparently working in the United States as a divine indicator of what was theologically correct. The American model, therefore, did not so much change Lang's evangelicalism as provide another mold into which it could flow when placed under other pressures. America was the great alternative, for political as well as theological rebels.

The Expansion of Settlement (ca. 1850–1920) and the Gold Rushes

The impact of the great outdoors on Australian Christianity has never been properly explored. It has just been assumed that the outback has had a different religious impact from the American frontier—a negative impact, of course. Whereas the American frontier fostered a speculative and emotionally exuberant religion, in Australia orthodoxy and restraint prevailed. Yet, from the days of the first fleet, when Johnson's main place of worship was under a Moreton Bay fig, the Church in Australia has been an open-air one. Chaplains itinerated long before churches were built. The tradition lives on in the Anglican Bush Brotherhoods, formed in 1897, and the evangelical Bush Church Aid Society, formed in 1919. The Bush Brotherhoods tended to be staffed by young English ordinands in search of adventure and self-sacrifice in the newly opened northern and western outbacks of Australia. But celibate Tractarians no more monopolized the Australian outback than they did the London slums. The Dissenters beat them to both places.

In fact a Bush Missionary Society had been formed as early as 1857. A missionary with that society reported in 1871 that Spurgeon's sermons were more popular in the bush than any others; they created most interest and seemed to do most good, perhaps because they were cast in an earthy style that would presumably appeal to bush folk. These sermons, printed in tracts and the newspaper *Sword and Trowel,* were read at house meetings in bush settlements every Lord's Day morning.[38] In C. H. Spence's novel *Gathered In,* the missionary, David Henderson, did not identify himself with any denomination but itinerated throughout the bush, content "to make a handful here and there in these neglected heathenish bush stations see some of the wondrous things of the gospel, the beautiful things of the world and the possible things in the three score years that we have here."[39]

Between 1863 and 1892 the majority of Baptist ministers who came to Australia from Britain trained at Spurgeon's College, far ahead of those trained by the Baptist Missionary Society or the Baptist Union. They were committed to evangelism, church expansion, and teetotalism (unlike their mentor, who smoked and drank). "Advance Australia" was their aim. Rough diamonds, Spurgeon's preachers labored with the Bush Missionary Society and championed what they understood as "General Evangelicalism." During the Downgrade controversy, when the British Baptists slid into liberalism, Spurgeon received greater support for his antiliberal stand in Australia than he did in Britain. Because of the impact of his manly sermons, it is not surprising that his many admirers should have supported him during the Downgrade, which was well publicized in Australia.

Another expression of outdoor Christianity was the tent mission. Introduced into England at the beginning of the nineteenth century from the American frontier, and outlawed in Wesleyan Methodism within a couple of decades, tent missions continued on in Australia, enabling most of the population to have some exposure to lay and revivalistic religion.[40] In that it was outdoors and anti-authority, it made an appeal to the Australian character and is reflected in the institution of the beach mission, which remains a major method of outreach to, and training of, the young in Australia. For the same reason, convention movements took deep root in Australian soil. George Grubb spoke at the first Australian Keswick convention in Geelong in 1891, which superseded an annual convention held in Melbourne by "The Bible and Prayer Union," a YMCA venture. At the Geelong convention, forty people offered themselves for missionary service, and at least two missionary societies were formed in response to Grubb's report on his Australian tour. Funded by moneyed laymen,[41] the conventions were characterized by the layman's contempt for theological precision. The speaker had to have fire and a personal gospel without political overtones.[42]

The evangelicalism of the American frontier and of the gold rushes was most conspicuously revivalistic in character.[43] The history of revival and revivalism in Australia is a good indicator of what happens to American religion in Australia. The revival experience of Australians was clearly far less intense than the American experience. There has been no burned-over district as experienced in western New York State during the Second Great Awakening. It is true that the time of greatest religious excitement in Autralia, say 1870–1910, coincided with its most creative time politically and socially. The conditions that produce the one, produce the other. But revival was not sufficiently full-blown in Australia to enable the Australian people to envisage a different world, as it did in prerevolutionary America when, according to Heimert,[44] the First Great Awakening also awakened people to the evils of monarchical and aristocratic government. American democracy had its roots in revival. In Australia, Protestant Christianity was only too conscious of its ideological rivals and left the political sphere to secular and Catholic forces. There was no Edwardsean or, indeed, Rauschenbuschean postmillennial optimism to reinforce the secular utopianism of the 1890s, and a great opportunity for creative nation-building and social engineering was lost. A republican world without the English was still inconceivable to the majority of Australians, and with the coming of the Boer War, they returned to the mother country generously of the fruit of their labor and of their loins.

Another reason why Australia has not been as revivalist as the United States is the Anglican hegemony of Australian evangelicalism. Nathaniel Jones, principal of Moore College from 1897, had a Plymouth Brethren rather than a Wesleyan view of justification and sanctification.[45] He stressed Reformation doctrine rather than the Wesleyan and Keswick systems, which stood for a second experience after conversion that seemed to be a hallmark of nineteenth-century revivalism.

Rather than express itself in collective revivalism or in politically won social justice, Australian evangelicalism was chiefly expressed in individualistic morality. Attempts to impose this on the rest of society however, earned evangelicals the label "wowser," a term coined in the 1890s by John Norton, editor of *Truth* magazine (which had a reputation for everything except its title). By "wowser," Norton meant a hypocrite—a Wesleyan. This fact may help explain why Methodism did not maintain its successful thrust in Australia; in some aspects it devolved into moralism, the very tendency that necessitated the Wesleyan Revolution in the first place.

The 1959 Billy Graham Crusades in Australia

Australia came closest to experiencing a national spiritual awakening in the Billy Graham crusades of 1959. During the three and a half months of the Southern Cross Crusade, which included New Zealand as well as Australia, nearly three and a quarter million people attended meetings—that is one-quarter of the entire population of Australia and New Zealand. Of these, 150,000 decided for Christ. In Australia 130,000, or 1.24 percent of the Australian population, responded to Billy's invitation. The Billy Graham Evangelistic Association, with their penchant for such things, reputed these to be the largest crowds to that date ever to hear the gospel, and the Southern Cross Crusade was adjudged to be the most successful evangelistic campaign in human history. What did it owe to the American influence, and what to the Australian?

In the 1950s Australians appeared uncritically disposed to things American, and America was beginning to displace Britain in the affections of Australians. Admittedly Australians were receptive to Sabrina and evangelist Canon Bryan Green but when Ava Gardner or Billy Graham came on the scene, they were voracious.[46] The interpenetration of American politics, public life, and religion meant that Billy sought and succeeded in obtaining the assistance of the secular arm for the Southern Cross Crusade. There was, predictably, the blessing of the president of the United States. At the last of the crusade meetings in Melbourne, Billy read a letter from President Eisenhower, which was applauded by appreciative Australians. More surprisingly, perhaps, is evidence of support at a diplomatic level by Richard Nixon.[47] It is difficult to avoid the conclusion that Billy was received so uncritically by the Australian press and people because he was a known anti-Communist, a well-connected ally in the Cold War. The crusades in Australia and New Zealand, preceded by a diplomatic letter from Nixon and accompanied by an open letter from Eisenhower, did look like the religious equivalent of ANZUS.[48]

Nor should we underestimate the impact on Australian evangelicalism of Billy's evangelicalism, which was ecumenical, pragmatic, and Arminian. Shortly before the Southern Cross Crusade, Billy's ecumenical spirit had escaped from the fires of fundamentalism. The Australian crusades marked the beginning of near-unanimous support for his crusades by the major Protestant organizations.[49] American evangelicalism, like most things American, is better organized than its Australian counterpart. Australian individualism may be no more rugged than American, but it does express itself in resistance to team activity in most areas except sport. The crusades were superbly organized and left Australian evangelical leaders convinced of the advantages of organization in the cause of the gospel. This lesson may explain the remarkable reorganization of the evangelical Diocese of Sydney during the episcopate of Hugh Gough (1958–1966).

The effectiveness of such crusades is probably dependent on the extent to which they harmonize with growth factors already present in the host country. The evangelical commitment of the majority of Anglican clergy in the Diocese of Sydney made Billy's task much easier, as did his personal friendship with Anglican clerical leaders Clive Kerle, Marcus Loane, Archie Morton, Leon Morris, Stuart Barton Babbage, and Archdeacon Arrowsmith. In an address at the Myer Music Bowl on the text from John 3, "Have You Been Born Again?" Billy said that Nicodemus was the sort of person who might be a bishop today. Then he added, "Perhaps not here in Australia, but in America."[50] At the last meeting of the Sydney crusade he waxed lyrical on the Sydney clergy: "I've been to many cities, but I've never been to a city where the caliber of the clergy has been so high, so devout, so spiritual, so evangelical as in the city of Sydney, and I seriously doubt if you quite realize what you have here."[51]

One growth factor that Billy did reinforce in Sydney was an expectation of revival, but it was revival with a difference. A desire for revival of sorts was nurtured in the 1950s by those, numerous at Moore Theological College, who embraced an otherworldly, premillennial eschatology[52] and who sought holiness within the second-blessing, entire-sanctification tradition.[53] Billy Graham did not do a lot to foster this understanding of revival. Billy's was an altogether more robust expression of the Christian faith. One could not fairly say of it as has been said of the holiness movement that it was "essentially neurotic, well-meaning, but emotionally damaging".[54] Billy's expectation of revival was centered neither in premillennial eschatology nor in sinless perfection but in human need and its remedy, the cross. A Billy Graham crusade is not a convention for the deepening of the spiritual life. I dare to assert that it is not revivalism. In turning his back on fundamentalism, Billy also turned his back on classic revivalism. With its addressing of current issues, albeit in a nonpolitical way, it is closer to the optimistic postmillennialism of Jonathan Edwards in the eighteenth century and Howard Mowll in the twentieth. It is addressed to the world, not some spitirual elite. The significance of Billy Graham to evangelical spirituality in Australia is that he dealt Keswick piety a fatal blow. He sought to replace it with an altogether healthier spirituality, but in the Australian environment he opened the way to a cerebral, Reformed formulation of the faith that valued scholastic and systematized Bible study more highly than prayer and spirituality.

Sydney Anglican evangelicalism was therefore greatly influenced by Billy Graham, but that influence, when combined with Australian cultural values, produced an evangelicalism unlike any to be found in other parts of the world. It fought some of the battles that all evangelicals fought with much less enthusiasm and some with far more. Sydney Anglican evangelicalism was much more resistant than American and British evangelicalism to takeover by the charismatic movement; it was far less excited about debates on the inerrancy of scripture, and far more intransigent over the ordination of women. It is with reference to the last that Australian conservative evangelicals were at their most confident and distinctive, using the arguments of British and American evangelicals only when they suited their own purposes.

The Ordination of Women Debate, ca. 1970–1992

In Australia, as in Britain and the United States, an ideology of separate spheres for men and women was a conspicuous cultural feature of the period 1850–1950. It is arguable that this ideology was more pronounced in Australia than in either Britain or America. Australia's early convict population was overwhelmingly male, as was its rural work force. The Australian creed of "mateship," embraced by working-class and nationalist settlers, elevated the male sphere. Concurrently, Australian feminism was inhibited[55] by the preponderance of women who adhered to Anglicanism and Catholicism,[56] which are more conservative, hierarchical, and patriarchal, than Methodism and Dissent, which so fed the feminist movement in America.[57]

Lake has suggested that two male types have competed for ideological dominance throughout Australian history: the Lone Hand (who read the *Bulletin* magazine, drank copiously, gambled energetically, and had an eye if not much opportunity for womanizing) and Domestic Man (who read the *Methodist,* supported temperance, family, and the church).[58] The relationship between them was not one of respect, and the Lone Hand branded the Domestic Man a wowser. But it has been recently argued persuasively that Domestic Man aspired to the qualities of the Lone Hand far more than the reverse, that even the competition between them was a very masculine thing, and that an ideology of masculinism was rampant in the church as much as in the realms of politics and business.[59]

With these complex social forces operating on the interpretation of gender relationships, it is not surprising that the debate over the ordination of women, which is being conducted all over the evangelical world, is particularly virulent and revealing in its Australian context. The movement for the ordination of women has been relatively slow in developing. The forces ranged against it have been uniquely tenacious. In 1973 the Commission on Doctrine of the Anglican Church of Australia unanimously reported that there were no theological objections to the ordination of women to the diaconate, and a majority reported that there were not theological objections to the ordination of women to the priesthood and the episcopate. The principal of Moore Theological College in Sydney, Broughton Knox, however, penned a minority report in which he declared that there were indeed fundamental theological objections. Then, to the astonishment of Sydney evangelicals, Leon Morris, principal of the evangelical Ridley College in Melbourne, let it be known that he was not convinced that the Bible was clearly opposed to the ordination of women.[60] Sydney and Melbourne evangelicalism were in disagreement.

In 1983 Patricia Brennan, who had worked as a missionary doctor in West Africa with the African Evangelical Mission, established the Movement for the Ordination of Women (MOW), modeled on the English group of the same name. MOW was joined by similarly tertiary educated and professional women from all denominations. But their greater intellectual strength was countered by Sydney's evangelical theologians, who kept the debate firmly on their own ground, declaring the issue to be one of biblical authority and hermeneutics. They were led by John Woodhouse and Robert Doyle, ably supported by Peter Jensen and David Peterson, all of Moore College.[61] For them the ordination issue became the platform from which to defend a high view of biblical inspiration.[62]

For international support in their defense of the true faith, the Sydney evangelicals turned increasingly to conservative American scholars,[63] thus buying into the equally emotionally charged issue of "biblical inerrancy." Moore College adopted as its set text on hermeneutics *Scripture and Truth,* edited by two conservative American evangelicals.[64] In Melbourne the evangelicalism of Ridley College was more akin to English Anglical evangelicalism. Unlike Moore College's theological orientation, which was toward the word of God, Ridley's was toward the cross and the blood of Christ. Its international links were strongest with St John's Nottingham and with the London Bible College.[65]

As Sydney's theological opposition to female ordination became increasingly refined, its power to carry the rest of the Anglican Church with it diminished. It reverted to law in an attempt to safeguard the apostolic witness and succeeded in bogging the movement down in the quicksands of the church's Apellate Tribunal. When the Bishop of Canberra and Goulburn, Owen Dowling, announced his determination to ordain women to the priesthood on 2 February 1992, a Sydney layman and two clergymen (not from Sydney) took out an injunction in the civil courts to stop the bishop. The injunction was upheld on appeal, and the emotions unleashed threatened not only the unity of the Anglican Church in Australia but also the residual unity of evangelicalism. An exasperated Bishop Dowling denounced "the outlook and attitudes of the controlling faction in the Diocese of Sydney, the most conservative diocese in the whole of the world-wide Anglican communion . . . who turn questionable tradition into immutable law."[66] Conservative evangelicalism, then, has done nothing to spoil the typical Australian male's appetite for a good fight.

Conclusion

Let us summarize some of our findings. Australian evangelicalism was shaped fairly decisively by its conception; it has always been conscious of the difficulty of its task and the resistance of most groups to its message, whether convicts, isolated rural settlers, impoverished urban workers, liberals, academics, or feminists. Yet Australian evangelicals have tended not to accept the marginalization that such groups have accorded them. Instead, they have claimed the right to influence values and to set standards through education, the media, and politics. They have been one of the most consistent movements for reform and improvement in Australian history.

Until recently, they have confined their sectarianism to anti-Catholicism, in both its Roman and Oxford varieties. They have promoted much cross-denominational religious and welfare activity and have not felt the need to create new denominations as in America or as Martyn Lloyd-Jones advocated in Britain.[67] They have adopted a characteristically British reserve toward American enthusiasms, and their informality and individualism have made them suspicious of both the uninhibited and the big-business expressions of American evangelicalism.

Australia has not proved as susceptible to revival as America, but it probably has been as significant a force in other expressions of evangelical life— missions and parachurch organizations may have attracted per capita the same support. For over a century Australia has been a major recruiting ground for evangelical missionaries.[68] Although Australian evangelicalism has been a picture painted in softer hues than in America, there are occasional splashes of bolder colors. It has been more Puritanical than in America, since it has been middle class and has rejected the strong drinking culture of the working class. It has had to respond to a more aggressively masculinist culture than American evangelicalism and to the fact that Australia's indigenous religious movements, such as mateship, tend not to be overtly Christian. At least in its Sydney Anglican guise, it has proved more resistant to the inroads of the charistmatic movement and of feminism and is more opposed to female ordination. And it has maintained these positions without the thoroughgoing fundamentalism of American evangelicalism, which has been consistently subdued in Australia along with other American exuberances, such as dispensational theology.

A consistent theme of this chapter has been the impact of Anglican evangelicalism on the movement as a whole in Australia. As an ecclesiastical party, evangelicalism achieved greater power in Australian Anglicanism than in Britain. It has proved more successful in generating at least one subculture, namely Sydney Anglicanism, which in turn has been more adept at politicizing the church.

From Britain and America, Australian evangelicalism developed its demonology—Catholics, liberals, and drink. But the tone of its opposition to such things, its individualism (but not dissent), pugnacity, and larrikinism, have been shaped in the crucible of Australian culture. The heady Australian brew consists of many more Irish evangelicals than is typical of British evangelicalism. Australian evangelicals love brawling, as do all Australians. But evangelicalism everywhere has always been combative,[69] and Australian evangelicals are perhaps no more inclined than the evangelicals of other countries to fight battles other than the good fight.

Notes

1. On the history of Australian evangelicalism, essential reading includes Stephen Judd and Kenneth Cable, *Sydney Anglicans* (Sydney: Anglican Information Office, 1987); Iain H. Murray, ed., *Australian Christian Life* (Edinburgh: Banner of Truth, 1988); David Parker, "Fundamentalism and Conservative Protestantism in Australia, 1920–1980" (Ph.D. diss., University of Queensland, 1982); J. Edwin Orr, *Evangelical Awakenings in the South Seas* (Minneapolis: Bethany, 1976); Stuart Piggin, "Towards a Bicentennial History of Australian Evangelicalism," *Journal of Religious History* 15 (June 1988): 20–37; and H. R. Jackson, *Churches and People in Australia and New Zealand, 1860–1930* (Wellington: Allen and Unwin, 1988). *Lucas: An Evangelical History Review* (journal of the Australian Evangelical History Association) contains many articles on Australian evangelicalism, as do the occasional papers of the Centre for the Study of Australian Christianity at Robert Menzies College, Macquarie University.

2. Admittedly, such attempts are too arbitrary and make too many assumptions to command the assent of the careful scholar. The committed partisans are not always impressed, either. Brian H. Edwards dismisses as "optimistic nonsense" the statistic that 7 percent of the population of the United Kingdom are evangelical Christians. See his *Revival: A People Saturated with God* (Darlington: Evangelical Press, 1990), 16.

3. Understood not as those who profess conversion or who take out formal membership in a church, but as those affiliated with evangelical congregations.

4. According to estimates compiled by Patrick Johnstone, director of research for WEC International, 17 percent of the Australian population is made up of evangelicals. It was about 18 percent in 1950, rose to about 19 percent in the mid-1960s, was 17 percent in 1985, and will probably be about 16 percent by 2000. New Zealand has about the same percentage of evangelicals (16.7 percent); the United Kingdom less at 7 percent, and the United States more at 23 percent. Johnstone defines evangelicals in this way: "The subdivision of Protestantism (including Anglicans and non-Western evangelical groups) which generally emphasize: 1. Commitment to a personal faith and emphasis on personal conversion or new birth. 2. A recognition of the inspired Word of God as the only basis for faith and Christian living. 3. Biblical preaching and evangelism." Johnstone calculates the number of evangelicals in a population by adding all those affiliated with a denomination that adopts the above theological position to the proportion of those from other Protestant denominations (though not wholly evangelical in theology) that holds evangelical views (Patrick Johnstone, *Operation World: A Day-to-Day Guide to Praying for the World* [Bromely, Eng.: WEC Publications, 1987], 496).

5. The small proportion of the population (1 percent) is a weakness that the Australian Baptists inherited from their English parents and would have avoided if they had earlier inherited some American genes.The rather sickly Baptist infant of mid-nineteenth-century New South Wales was further enfeebled by having to squabble with its equally feeble siblings and by its refusal to drink the milk provided by its putative foster mother, the state. For a small denomination in a vast land with a sparse population, the Baptists offered too many options: close membership and close Communion (the hypercalvinists), open membership and open Communion, close membership and open Communion. True to sibling rivalry, they were anti–each other. Interestingly, however, none of these sickly Baptist infants was professedly anti-evangelical, although the hypercalvinists (both Strict and Particular) in practice did oppose evangelicalism. See M. Petras, *Extension or Extinction: Baptist Growth in New South*

Wales, 1900–1939 (Eastwood: Baptist Historical Society of New South Wales, 1983), 19.

6. Ruth I. Sturmey, "Women and the Anglican Church in Australia: Theology and Social Change" (Ph.D. diss., University of Sydney, 1989), 265–66.

7. Sectarianism is probaby the most analyzed aspect of Australian religious history. See, for example, M. Hogan, *The Sectarian Strand* (Ringwood: Penguin, 1987). In Australia the mix of social classes was different from that in England. Hence there has been a stronger denominational pluralism than in England, which has resulted in the dampening of Anglican claims to hegemony and fueled a robust sectarianism in political and economic life. Historians have focused on this sectarianism, rather than the peace that more commonly has characterized relations between the denominations.

8. Urbanization as a factor in religious history may have operated differently in Australia than it did in Britain and America. By 1890 almost two-thirds of all Australians were living in cities. It was not until 1920 that America reached this proportion. Canada took until 1950. In both Europe and North America the development of urbanization was gradual, the product of a combination of factors, including changes in agriculture, industrialization, and sudden and sustained population growth. In Australia this process was in reverse. Urbanization preceded industrialization and rural development. The early urbanization of the Australian colonies was the result of geography (the inland could not sustain a large population), the deliberate siting of centers of population, the relatively small rural work force required, and the urban origins of most immigrants. Hence most of the denominations expanded more rapidly in the cities than in the country, especially the evangelical nonconformists and Methodists.

9. As in America, evangelicalism in Australia was associated with the growth of democracy. This is seen most clearly in its contrast with the thrust of High Church Anglicans influenced by the Tractarian movement. Bishops Broughton of Sydney and Short of Adelaide represented an antidemocratic propensity of identifying with the social elite, insisting on episcopal power and prerogatives, demanding state support for their church exclusively, disregarding the claims of the laity, and distancing themselves from any association with churches of other denominations. Broad Churchmen too probably did little to Australianize the church. Melbourne has been the only Anglican diocese in Australia to develop a strong Broad Church tradition. The evangelical wing of the Australian Anglican Church has been the least resistant to change of the three traditional wings of the Anglican Church. It is not surprising, therefore, that the principal of the evangelical Anglican theological college in Sydney should announce to the media during a recent visit of the queen that it is time Australia became a republic.

10. See the section below on the ordination of women.

11. John Harris, *One Blood: Two Hundred Years of Aboriginal Encounter with Christianity* (Sydney: Albatross, 1991).

12. The contribution of evangelicalism to the development of a distinctively Australian ethos deserves attention. Because all forms of Australian Christianity are apparently derivative of European and American models, it seems unlikely that it can have made a substantial contribution to the formation of Australian habits of the heart. The more fashionable Anglican congregations emulated the latest ecclesiastical trends in Britain with rare speed. The English as well as the Australian flags adorned the sanctuaries of Church of England churches in the twentieth century. Anglicans prayed for the monarch and supported Britain in her wars. Archbishops for the major metropolitan dioceses were imported from Britain until after the Second World War. Because of vast distances and weak links between dioceses, it has proved very difficult to

establish a national Anglican identity in Australia. It has been much easier to look to the crown and England as the focus of identity. See Barbara Darling, "Theological Education in Eastern Australia" (Preliminary master's thesis, University of Melbourne, Department of History, n.d.).

13. David W. Bebbinton, *Evangelicalism in Modern Britain; A History from the 1730s to the 1980s* (London: Unwin Hyman, 1989). See also Jackson, *Churches and People,* chap. 3, "Revivalism." Revival is a theme that helps us pinpoint the respective influences of American and British evangelicalism. It is normally said that Australia has never experienced a great awakening and that its "little revivings" (Ezra 9:8) have not been widespread and have reached only churchgoers. Whereas American Christianity is of British derivation transformed several times by great awakenings, Australian Christianity is also of British derivation but largely untransformed. This difference may help to explain why Australian Christianity appears to be so un-Australian and why a much lower percentage of Australians than Americans attend churches. The high American statistics for churchgoing and other indicators of religiosity probably reflect the fact that, due to their heritage of revivalism, Americans, when confronted with a survey or poll, feel obligated to claim Christian beliefs in excess of their actual belief. Perhaps because they feel guilty about their actual belief they hope that by stating what they should believe they will be moved closer to that ideal. Australians, unwashed by repeated waves of revivalism, are not so motivated by guilt in matters of religion. Apathy, the habit of the unrevived mind, is the prevailing Australian mood. American history is a succession of religious revivals and declensions with corresponding oscillations in the American sense of national identity and destiny. In Australia, popular religion has not been penetrated by revival. There have been great movements of revival in Australian history—more than have been hitherto documented—but these have not transformed the majority. In America, revival has been more than once a psychic earthquake. Australia, in religion as in geology, has experienced only a few tremors.

14. Among evangelical "tall poppies" might be included Samuel Marsden, John Dunmore Lang, Frederic Barker, Charles Perry, Dean Macartney and son, John Watsford, John MacNeil, "California" Taylor ("the Wesley of Australia"), Ebenezer Vickery, Cairo Bradley, R. B. S. Hammond, T. C. Hammond, G. H. Morling, C. J. Tinsley, C. H. Nash, H. P. Smith, Howard Mowll, Paul White, Stuart Barton Babbage, Marcus Loane, Leon Morris, and Alan Cole. Biographies have been written on most of these.

15. Australian slang for an Englishman.

16. It is interesting to speculate on why they do not appear to have been subject to anti-Pom sentiment. Each was opposed by a member of the Anglican establishment— Nash by Bishop Lowther Clark and Mowll by Archbishop Cosmo Lang, who was very adamant that Mowll should not have the Sydney job. So they personify the anti-Pom establishment.

17. See the section below on the ordination of women. See also Stuart Piggin, *Helpmeets and Heroines: Women and the History of Australian Evangelicalism* (Figtree: Mothers' Union, 1988); Florence S. H. Young, *Pearls from the Pacific* (London: Marshall Brothers, n.d.).

18. Strikingly, members of the lower orders were converted as well as those of the upper and middle classes; more striking still, in America "the poor negro" and the Indians, to whom David Brainerd and other missionaries ministered, experienced revival every bit as dramatic as whites. Demonstrably, the gospel was divinely designed to rescue all humankind. Furthermore, the large accession of converts into the

churches in the revivals fueled speculation that the millennium was just about to begin with its thousand years of unprecedented spiritual prosperity and that therefore the earth was about to be filled with the glory of God as the waters cover the sea.

19. Jonathan Edwards, *Apocalyptic Writings,* ed. Stephen J. Stein (New Haven: Yale University Press, 1977), 143.

20. Henry Morris, *Charles Grant, the Friend of William Wilberforce and Henry Thornton* (London: SPCK, 1904), 92–117.

21. Robert Wilberforce and Samuel Wilberforce, *The Life of William Wilberforce,* 5 vols. (London, 1838), 4:126.

22. *Historical Records of New South Wales,* Sydney, I.2, 11–13.

23. Information supplied by Graeme McKelvie of Melbourne.

24. See *Australian Dictionary of Biography,* vol. 1.

25. Stuart Piggin, *Making Evangelical Missionaries* (Abingdon, Eng.: Sutton Courtney Press, 1984), 189–90. See also Christopher Fyfe, *A History of Sierra Leone* (London: Oxford University Press, 1962), 48–49.

26. N. K. Macintosh, *Richard Johnson, Chaplain to the Colony of New South Wales: His Life and Times, 1755–1827* (Sydney: Library of Australian History, 1978), 89.

27. *Historical Records of New South Wales,* Sydney, I.2, 17–20.

28. "As many of the marines as possible should be artificers, such as carpenters, sawyers, smiths, potters (if possible), and some husbandmen. To have a chaplain on board, with a surgeon, and one mate at least; the former to remain at the settlement" (ibid., 18).

29. A. M. Wilberforce, ed., *Private Papers of William Wilberforce* (London, 1897), 1:15, cited in Macintosh, *Richard Johnson,* 25.

30. Richard Johnson's diary, Archbishop's Papers, Moore 22, Australian 1, Lambeth Palace Library, London. Also cited in Macintosh, *Richard Johnson,* 27.

31. R. I. Wilberforce and S. Wilberforce, *Correspondence of William Wilberforce* (London, 1840), 1:15.

32. *Journal,* 28 October 1787; Wilberforce and Wilberforce, *Life of Wilberforce* 1:149.

33. On the impact of Cowper on the evangelical middle class in Birmingham and East Anglia, see Leonore Davidoff and Catherine Hall, *Family Fortunes: Men and Women of the English Middle Class, 1780–1850* (Chicago: University of Chicago Press, 1987), 162–67. Cowper was characterized as "our favorite bard" in the evangelical *Christian Observer,* June 1818, 379. Cowper was also quoted extensively by the radical William Hone in *The Political House that Jack Built* (1819). Hone attempted there to extend Cowper's admittedly reformist critique of society to the plight of the urban poor. On the contrast between Cowper's evangelical reformism and Horne's radicalism, see Mark Clement, "True Religion: Christianity and the Making of Radical Ideology in England" (Master's thesis, Australian National University, 1990), 47–53.

34. For an interesting, but not entirely persuasive, refinement of this view, see N. Gunson, "The Contribution of the Calvinistic Methodist Movement in the Church History of Australia," *Church Heritage* 4 (March 1985): 28–59.

35. George Bedell et al., *Religion in America* (New York: Macmillan, 1982), 9.

36. K. J. Cable, *Australia and the Anglican Parson: Record of the Centenary Celebrations, Eleventh and Twelfth June, 1980* (Belair, South Australia: St. Barnabas' Theological College, 1980), 13.

37. D. W. A. Baker, *Days of Wrath: A Life of John Dunmore Lang* (Melbourne: Melbourne University Press, 1985), 161.

38. *The Christian,* 14 April 1871.

39. Spence, *Gathered In* (Sydney: Sydney University Press, 1977), 80.

40. Stuart Piggin, *Faith of Steel: A Histroy of Christian Churches in Illawarra, Australia* (Wollongong: University of Wollongong Press, 1984), 88–91.

41. The Katoomba Convention was started in 1899 by sugar plantation owner Ernest Young at his home, Khandala, named after the place in India where his father shot his first lion.

42. George Grubb's message was vintage Keswick: "If our church members were to receive clean hearts there would be a wonderful revival of true religion. It is defilement in our hearts that keep us from witnessing" (*The Katoomba Convention* [1912], 11).

43. See, for example, D. D. Bruce, *And They All Sang Hallelujah: Plain-Folk Camp-Meeting Religion, 1800–1845* (Knoxville: University of Tennessee Press, 1974).

44. Alan Heimert, *Religion and the American Mind: From the Great Awakening to the Revolution* (Cambridge: Harvard University Press, 1966).

45. W. J. Lawton, *The Better Time to Be: Utopian Attitudes to Society among Sydney Anglicans, 1885 to 1914* (Sydney: University of New South Wales Press, 1990).

46. K. S. Inglis, "Sydney, Meet Mr. Graham," *Nation,* 11 April 1959, 14.

47. See the letter from Vice-President Nixon to the American ambassador, William J. Sebald, in Australia, 3 April 1958: "I am sure you know Dr. Billy Graham is planning to come to Australia later this year for a series of meetings. When he was in my office recently, he informed me that Mr. Jerry Beavan, who heads his advance planning staff, will be coming to Australia this month to handle all the necessary arrangements for these meetings. I would greatly appreciate any assistance that the members of your staff may be able to provide Mr. Beavan in connection with his arrangements in Australia. I hope that you and Mrs. Sebald are enjoying your stay in Canberra. Certainly it would be most difficult to find people who were more friendly in their attitude toward the United States than the Australians" (Richard M. Nixon, Pre-presidential Papers, Federal Records Center, Laguna Niguel, CA).

48. The defense pact Between Australia, New Zealand, and the United States.

49. F. Butler, "Billy Graham and the End of Evangelical Unity" (Ph.D. diss., University of Florida, 1976). One evangelical group who elected not to support Billy Graham in 1959 was the Australian Fellowship of Independent Evangelical Churches. It had dropped the "Independent" out of its title to accommodate the small Australian Wesleyan Methodist churches that came to Australia after World War II. When Billy Graham came, however, the Wesleyan Methodists cooperated with the crusades, whereas the other churches stood by the fundamentalism of Carl McIntyre, rediscovered their independence, voted against cooperation with Billy, and took their leave from the Wesleyan Methodists. It was a tiny antipodaean flick from a large American tail. (James Ridgeway, interviewed by R. D. Linder, 26 August 1987).

50. Film 127, 28 February 1959, Billy Graham Archives, Wheaton College, Wheaton, IL.

51. Film CN 113, F153, 10 May 1959, Billy Graham Archives.

52. Bill Lawton, "The Winter of Our Days: The Anglican Diocese of Sydney, 1950–1960," *Lucas: An Evangelical History Review* 9 (July 1990): 1.

53. Bill Lawton, " 'That Woman Jezebel': Moore College after Twenty-Five Years" (Moore College Library Lecture, 1981), 14–17.

54. Ibid., 30.

55. The role of the churches in the lives of women in Australia has been neglected more than it ought, since most Australian feminists are themselves outside the

churches. There are three notable studies of the role of the churches: Jill Roe on Theosophy, *Beyond Belief* (Sydney: Angus and Robertson, 1985); Anthea Hyslop on the Women's Christian Temperance Union, "Temperance, Christianity, and Feminism: The Women's Christian Temperance Union of Victoria, 1887–97," *Historical Studies* 17 (1976–77): 66–69; and Sabine Willis, ed., on the Mothers' Union, *Women, Faith, and Fetes: Essays on the History of Women and the Church in Australia* (Melbourne: Dove and ACC, 1977).

56. Sturmey, "Women and the Anglican Church in Australia," 2.

57. Nancy Cott, *The Bonds of Womanhood: "Women's Sphere" in New England, 1780–1835* (New Haven: Yale University Press, 1977); Ann Douglas, *The Feminization of American Culture* (New York: Avon, 1977); Barbara Epstein, *The Politics of Domesticity: Women, Evangelism, and Temperance in Nineteenth Century America* (Middletown, CT: Wesleyan University Press, 1981).

58. Marilyn Lake, "The Politics of Respectability," *Historical Studies* 22 (April 1986): 86.

59. Anne O'Brien, " 'A Church full of Men': Masculinism and the Church in Australian History" (Unpublished paper, 1991).

60. John Gaden [and Leon Morris], eds., *A Woman's Place: Papers Prepared for the General Synod Doctrine Commission* (Sydney: Anglican Information Office, 1976).

61. B. G. Webb, *Personhood, Sexuality, and Christian Ministry,* Explorations 1 (Sydney: Lancer, 1987).

62. Sturmey, "Women and the Anglican Church in Australia," 212.

63. James Hurley, Westminster Theological Seminary, Philadelphia; Wayne Grudem, George W. Knight, and Don Carson of Trinity Evangelical Divinity School, Deerfield, IL; and J. L. Packer, Regent College, Vancouver.

64. D. A. Carson and J. D. Woodbridge, eds., *Scripture and Truth* (Leicester, Eng.: Inter-Varsity Press, 1983). See Sturmey, "Women and the Anglican Church in Australia," 213–14: "It would seem Moore College is moving away from its traditional English evangelical and Brethren alliances towards the theologically and socially conservative, Calvinist reformed, North American–based evangelical circuit, which includes Westminster Theological Seminary and Trinity Evangelical Divinity School. . . . Thus the training college for Sydney Anglicans was both aware of the debate and aligning itself with the heirs of American intellectual fundamentalism. This reflects Moore College's move since the sixties towards being a Calvinist reformed rather than an Anglican College."

65. And, it must be conceded, with Fuller Theological Seminary.

66. *Church Scene,* 7 February 1992, 2. The Bishop of Newcastle condemned events in the New South Wales Supreme Court when "the cold, clammy hand of legalism was placed on the heart of the church." The legalists were characterized as "a brood of vipers" who engage in "legalistic filibustering."

67. I. H. Murray, *David Martyn Lloyd-Jones: The Fight of Faith, 1939–1981* (Edinburgh; Banner of Truth, 1990), chap. 25.

68. C. W. Forman, *The Island Churches of the South Pacific* (Maryknoll, NY: Orbis, 1982), 14.

69. Like pietism, it has always been "oppositive." See the argument in F. E. Stoeffler, *The Rise of Evangelical Pietism* (Leiden: Brill, 1971).

15

The Evangelical Revival, The Missionary Movement, and Africa

ANDREW WALLS

Evangelicalism and the Missionary Movement

The modern missionary movement is a an autumnal child of the Evangelical Revival. Fifty years separate the great events of Northampton and Cambuslang from the formation of the earliest of the voluntary societies to promote Christian activity in the non-Christian world; yet, without the revival the societies would have been inconceivable. The revival clarified the rationale for such activity by transmitting the understanding that there was no difference between the spiritual state of a pleasure-seeking duchess (though baptized and adhering to the prevailing religious system of the higher and middle classes) and that of a South Sea Islander. That spiritual parity of the unregenerate of Christendom and the heathen abroad had important missionary consequences. Like the admonition to Lady Huntingdon's titled friend, who did not want to enter the kingdom of heaven in the same manner as her coachman, it took a hatchet to some axiomatic superiorities. A consistent view of human solidarity in depravity shielded the first missionary generation from some of the worst excesses of racism.

The revivial also supplied the logistic networks—interregional, international, interdenominational—that undergirded the movement. The chain that led to William Carey's pioneering missionary initiative of 1792 was forged by a gift from a Scottish Presbyterian to an English Baptist of a book by a New England Congregationalist.[1] Another New Englander, David Brainerd, became the principal model of early British missionary spirituality; his own work had been supported by the Society in Scotland for Promoting Christian Knowledge.[2] An unending stream of correspondence, crisscrossing the Atlantic, reveals just how important as a missionary factor were the African-Americans and Afro-West Indians.[3] The Church Missionary Society was hauled back from absurdity through the pastor of a German congregation in London who put them in contact with a seminary in Berlin.[4] Magazines on two continents gathered and disseminated "missionary intelligence" without regard to denomination or country of origin.[5]

Above all, the revival supplied missionaries. There had been various earlier schemes for missions, although none went further than paper because no one was likely to undertake them.[6] The first generation of the Protestant missionary enterprise was for practical purposes an evangelical undertaking. Jane Austen represents the bright society girl as saying to the earnest young clergyman: "When I hear of you next, it may be as a celebrated preacher in some great society of Methodists, or as a missionary into foreign parts."[7] Methodist preacher or foreign missionary—enthusiasm could go no further. By 1813 missions had some degree of official recognition implied by the charter (as renewed in revised form) of the East India Company, and by the 1830s serious Christians of every sort were ready to agree that missions were a good thing; well past the middle of the century, however, it was overwhelmingly evangelicals that staffed them. It may therefore be worth recalling some of the influences that shaped the early missionaries' own religion.

Evangelical Religion and Christendom

Historic evangelicalism is a religion of protest against a Christian society that is not Christian enough. It is eloquently expressed in Wesley's hymn about blind churchmen:

> O wouldst thou, Lord, reveal the sins,
>   And turn their joy to grief:
> The world, the CHRISTIAN world convince
>   Of damning unbelief.[8]

Evangelical preaching is primarily addressed to a world that is both Christian and unbelieving. Churchgoing, not always enthusiastic, is accepted within this world; to return to Jane Austen's *Mansfield Park,* even the smart set represented in the Crawfords are evidently regularly at church, and the reprobate Henry, who has "never thought on serious subjects," has nevertheless considered how certain passages of the liturgy should be read.[9] Regular, even intense, religious observance can also be found in this world, as is clear from the accounts of evangelical conversions, which regularly feature parental piety or describe a career that includes devout periods. Furthermore, despite bouts of rhetorical alarm, open rejection of Christian doctrine is generally muted. Wilberforce saw "sceptics and unitarians" as a fringe—though he feared a broadening fringe—of society.[10] The evangelical bugbears were less professed infidelity than professed Christianity without "the distinguishing doctrines of the gospel."

Evangelical Christianity, in a word, assumes Christendom, the territorial conception of the Christian faith that brought about the integration of throne and altar, that began with the conversion of the barbarians of the North and West. Perhaps we have not fully faced the extent to which all subsequent

Western Christianity was shaped by the circumstances under which the peoples of northern Europe came into the Christian faith—coming not as individuals, families, or groups but as whole societies, complete with their functioning political and social systems integrated around their ruler. *Individual* choice could hardly exist, even in concept. The ideal outcome could be pictured as the assembly of Christian princes and their peoples, all subjects to the King of Kings; it led inevitably to the idea of the Christian nation, where each member of the nation is within the sphere of the church. The tension between the principle of Christendom and its realization in practice is the history of Western Christianity. It may be noted that the vernacular movement in the northern parts of Christendom that we designate the Protestant Reformation left the territorial principle intact and the tension unresolved.

Mainstream evangelicalism in the period in which the missionary movement was born accepted the idea of a Christian nation. The idea is fundamental, for instance, to William Wilberforce's *Practical View* (1797). The book is not a spare-time avocation of a public man who happens to be an evangelical Christian; Wilberforce writes *because* he is a public man. Only a revival of religion, he argues, can rescue both the Christian nation and its most prominent symbol, the established church. "Unless there be reinfused into the mass of our society something of that principle which animated our ecclesiastical system in its earlier days, it is vain to hope that this establishment will very long continue. But in proportion as vital Christianity can be revived, in that same proportion, the church establishment is strengthened."[11]

The evangelical legislator is concerned to bring the nation in reality to what it is already in principle, and, as he believed, by history also. Hence Wilberforce's equal application of his energies to issues of national righteousness (the slave trade), social righteousness (dueling, and the Society for the Suppression of Vice), and personal holiness. "Real Christianity" can be expressed in and through a national church, whose baptism is the birthright of everyone born in the nation.

The full title of Wilberforce's book is *Practical View of the prevailing religious system of professed Christians in the higher and middle classes of this country contrasted with real Christianity.* The hallmark of evangelical religion is real Christianity over against its substitutes. Thus John Wesley arranges his 1780 hymnbook "according to the experience of *real* Christians" and includes in the section headed "Exhorting sinners to return to God" a subsection "Describing formal religion," lest the returning sinner get stranded in formal religion and proceed no further. A section "Describing inward religion" follows immediately. Evangelical faith is about inward religion as distinct from formal, real Christianity as distinct from nominal. In other words, the evangelicalism of the period takes its identity from protest, and in effect from nominal Christianity. Evangelical religion presupposes Christendom, Christian civil society.

That society is generally defective as regards "the distinguishing doctrines of the gospel," or, as Wilberforce calls them, "the peculiar doctrines of Christianity." He identifies three: original sin and consequent human depravity; the atonement of Christ; and the sanctifying power of the Spirit in the believer's life. The doctrines that distinguish evangelicals are anthropological and soteriological. They occur in a variety of wordings in the evangelical literature of the time.[12] They are reflected, for example, in Charles Simeon's summary of the aims of preaching: to humble the sinners, to exalt the Savior, and to promote holiness.[13]

The "prevailing religious system of professed Christians" does not understand the radical nature of sin. Consequently, it cannot understand the nature of the atonement that the church (and Prayer Book) confess; and it has no place for the life of holiness. By contrast, the evangelical paradigm of conversion begins with the personal knowledge of sin, moves to personal trust in Christ's finished work, and issues in godly personal life.

Evangelical religion stands in a long tradition of protest movements against superficial Christian profession, going back at least as far as the fourth century, when the desert fathers turned their backs on the attractive commodity then for the first time widely available—Christianity combined with self-indulgence. (If, as Khomiakov argued, the pope was the first Protestant, perhaps Saint Antony the Copt was the first evangelical.) But the Evangelical Revival is more than a protest movement; it represents a cultural development addressing the Christian message to its time and place as convincingly and appropriately as Antony ever did to his.

The Christendom concept as it had emerged over centuries was no longer adequate, and its practice was increasingly ambiguous. No longer was there a single Christian territory from Ireland to the Carpathians with a single sacred language accepting the rule of Christ as enunciated by a single church from a single apostolic see. Contrary to the first instincts of potentates and churchmen alike, states adopted compromises on religion and reluctantly recognized minorities. (Religious toleration is the offspring not of charity but of political realism.)

Religious pluralism was, however, only one factor pointing to the privatization of religion, its steady movement into the sphere of private judgment and personal decision. Intellectual and social developments pointed in the same direction. An increasing individualization of consciousness (where "I think, therefore I exist" can be an axiom), and an understanding of societies in terms of contracted mutual consent undermined the principle of territorial Christianity that had underlain Western Christianity (even in its Protestant form) since the time of the barbarian conversions.

Western Christianity therefore faced a cultural crisis—attrition of its basis in Western culture, with the weakening of the sanctions of the institutional church, the increasing efficiency of the centralized state, and the relegation of religion to the private sphere. The Evangelical Revival was perhaps the most successful of all the reformations of Christianity in the context of changing Western culture. Not, of course, that it arose de novo. Besides renewing the call to radical discipleship so often sounded in earlier Christian history, it retained the medieval concern (deep rooted in the European psyche) for propitiation. It also extended and clarified the Reformation idea (particularly as developed by the English Puritans) of a life of holy obedience in the secular world and in the family. Above all, it combined the traditional framework of the Christian nation and the established church (whether with or without a formal *principle* of establishment was really a matter of locality) with serious recognition of individual selfhood and personal decision. That reconciliation bridged a cultural chasm in Christian self-identity. It helped to make evangelical religion a critical force in Western culture, a version of Christianity thoroughly authentic and indigenous there. To use the appalling current missiological jargon, the Evangelical Revival contextualized the gospel for the northern Protestant world.

Beyond Christendom: The Crux of the Missionary Movement

There is, of course, a lurking peril in all successful indigenizations. The more the gospel is made a place to feel at home, the greater the danger that no one else will be able to live there. And the missionary movement required people whose personal religion had become effectively (though critically) aligned with Western culture to transmit the Christian message in non-Western settings where the assumptions that had shaped their religion did not apply. In early days, missionary regions contained no Christendom, no Christianized society. There was no nominal Christianity to act as the reference group—indeed as the target group—of preaching. And in many, perhaps most, newly reached societies, the audience had no capacity to make individual choices without regard to the networks of kinship. Indeed, the encouragements or successes of early missions may have been more baffling to the understanding of evangelical missionaries and their supporters than the more frequent episodes of failure, heartbreak, and disaster. There were events that missionaries could ascribe only to the hand of God. How else could one interpret a whole island people rejecting their traditional worship and acknowledging Christ? And yet this could take place without any sign of the long-established patterns of evangelical conversion. When the missionaries on Tahiti—Congregationalists at that— ceased to record the names of converts on the ground of "the profession becoming national,"[14] it was a sign of the extension of the meaning of the word "conversion." It might now denote a wholehearted recognition of a change of religious allegiance; conviction of sin and longing for holiness might follow later. Time after time missionaries noted apparently sincere professions of faith that lacked these features. "I have came to the conclusion," said an American missionary by way of explanation, "that deep and pungent convictions are not to be looked for in the heathen when they first become converts to Christianity. 'By the law is knowledge of sin'; but this is imperfectly understood. It has not had time to work down into the heart."[15]

Nevertheless, taking it as a whole, in its Catholic as well as its Protestant aspect, the missionary movement has changed the face of Christianity. It has transformed the demographic and cultural composition of the church, with consequences not yet measurable for its future life and leadership and theology and worship. The most remarkable feature of this transformation has been in the African continent, minimal in Christian profession when the missionary movement began, but now, when so much of the West is in the post-Christian period, moving to the position where it may have more professing Christians than any other continent.[16]

The instances that follow illustrate the encounter of evangelical Christianity with Africa; every incident bears a historical relationship to evangelical missionary endeavor. What makes them different comes from the interaction of the evangelical themes with factors at work in Africa.

Christianity and African Initiatives

The sheer size of its professing Christian community must be one reason for taking seriously the significance of Africa. But Christian mission is not simply about the multiplication of the church; it is about the discipling of the nations. It is about the penetration of cultures and ways of thought by the word about Christ. It is about translation—one might almost say the translation of the word into the flesh, since its starting point is the incarnation, which brought the Divine Son to live in the very culture-specific situation of Jewish Palestine.[17] It is about the translation of Scripture into thought and action, as the word about Christ is brought to bear on the points of reference within each culture, the things by which people know themselves and recognize where they belong. Our attempted assessment of significance must thus take some account of the processes of translation as well as of multiplication; if the argument so far is correct, the Evangelical Revival is itself an example of such translation.

Modern African Christianity is not only the result of movements among Africans, but it has been principally sustained by Africans and is to a surprising extent the result of African initiatives. Even the missionary factor must be put into perspective.

There is something symbolic in the fact that the first church in tropical Africa in modern times was not a missionary creation at all. It arrived ready made, a body of people of African birth or descent who had come to faith in Christ as plantation slaves or as soldiers in the British army during the American War of Independence, or as farmers or squatters in Nova Scotia after it.[18] They were eleven hundred in number, arriving in 1792 in Sierra Leone, in the strip of land purchased by the Clapham philanthropists as a Province of Freedom. They marched ashore (it is said) singing a hymn of Isaac Watts— "Awake, and sing the song of Moses and the Lamb." Their choice of hymnody was significant. They had left the house of bondage, they had crossed the Red Sea, they were now entering the promised land. They brought their own preachers with them, and their churches had been functioning for nearly twenty years in Sierra Leone when the first missionary arrived. (Indeed, they ejected their second missionary as "too proud for a Methodist preacher," or, as he thought, because of their "American Republic spirit.")[19]

Sierra Leone—a tiny country in the nineteenth century, not to be identified with the borders of the present republic—supplied African missionaries in quantities for the rest of West Africa and could even spare one or two to work elsewhere. (Sierra Leone missionaries were appointed to Kenya in the 1880s.)[20] Over a sixty-year period Sierra Leone produced a hundred ordained men for the Church Missionary Society alone, in addition to countless cate-chists, teachers, and other mission workers—all from a population of perhaps fifty thousand.[21]

On the other side of the continent, Louise Pirouet has drawn attention to the process of Christian expansion in the area that now forms the state of Uganda. It was Ganda evangelists who carried out the work, often operating far from home in areas quite different from their own in language, tradition, and food, as much "foreign missionaries" as any European.[22] It is a reminder of the vital importance of the evangelist and the catechist in African Christian history—a person usually without much formal education in the Western sense; not fluent, perhaps not literate, in English; but the terminal connection through which the Christian faith passes into African village society. But even the evangelist-catechist is only part of the story. I recall a survey of how the numerous congregations within one densely populated area of Nigeria had come into being. Time after time the seminal figure was a new court clerk who was a Christian, or a worker on the new railway, or a tailor, carrying his sewing machine on his head, or some other trader. Some such stranger, or group of strangers, had arrived and had started family prayers, stopped work on Sunday, and sang hymns instead, and some local people got interested. Or perhaps the initial impetus came from people from that village who had gone elsewhere—to school, to work, to trade, in more than one case to jail—and on return home sought the things they had found in their travels. The survey yielded no instance of a congregation founded by a missionary, and hardly one founded by any official agent of the church at all. In most cases the role of the mission had been to respond—sometimes, through straitened resources, belat-edly and minimally—to an initiative within the community.

Another factor in Christian expansion in Africa has been the emergence of dynamic figures who owed little in any direct way to church mission, and nothing to any commission from one. Such figures are especially important in West Africa between the First World War and the end of the Great Depres-sion. The most celebrated of these figures, and by far the most important figure in Ivory Coast Christian history, is the Liberian prophet William Wadé Harris. In an important study, D. A. Shank calls Harris a prophet of modern times.[23] Certainly Harris was convinced of his prophetic call, and he mediated deeply on Scripture, which, as Shank shows, he read in a way quite different from that of the missionaries but one quite intelligible within his own frame of reference. He called people to repentance; he persuaded thousands to aban-don traditional African religious practices; he pointed them to the God of the Scriptures, which as yet they could not read, sometimes leaving King James Bibles as a sign of the source of the teaching to follow; he baptized with water and, by prayer and exorcism, triumphed over the spirits. Mission representatives, however much they might regret omissions in his teaching or deplore some features of it, still strove to get Harris's approval to be his successors in the work; yet he had set out on that work in response to what he believed the call of God, with no seal from any mission body.

The Methodist Church in Ashanti, Ghana, owes much to the preaching of a charismatic jailbird called Sampson Oppong.[24] Oppong always claimed that he had little knowledge of Christianity at all before his call as a preacher. The dramatic events that led up to his entry on his vocation included a prophetic dream and its fulfillment the next day, an attempt to poison a Christian that failed because the intended victim vomited the substance after saying grace, and an alcoholic stupor during which Oppong was punitively kicked by a sheep he had stolen. The Methodist mission estimated that as a result of this man's preaching, twenty thousand people came under their pastoral care within five or six years. In Nigeria two major religious bodies, the Apostolic Church and the Christ Apostolic Church, derive eventually from the work of Joseph Babalola, a streamroller driver who found the divine imperative in the breakdown of his engine and because the key figure in a mass movement that stirred Yorubaland in the depression years.[25] Nor were such phenomena confined to West Africa. In Lesotho, for instance, at much the same time, the Paris Mission was recognizing that multitudes came into the church following the preaching of a young layman called Walter Mattita, who not long before had been at most a wayward and negligent church attender.[26]

None of these figures easily fitted into the structures of ministry and leadership of any of the mission churches, yet those same churches recognized their effectiveness. Each claimed a direct commission from God imparted by dream or vision and confirmed by sign following. The work of each led to a massive expansion of churches (and in all but Babalola's case, mission-led churches) that were already in existence. We might take another set of figures on the lowly rungs of the mission's ladder who instituted comparable Christian movements outside the missionary sphere altogether. There is Garrick Braide, otherwise known as Elijah II, Anglican catechist in the Niger delta, founder of the healing church, the Christ Army.[27] Most spectacular of all is the legacy of the Baptist catechist Simon Kimbangu, arrested for subversion by the Belgian authorities in Congo in 1917, after a few short months of preaching and healing. He spent the rest of his life in prison. The movement he began was proscribed, went underground, gave a Christian expression to the independence movement, and, as colonial rule collapsed, emerged under the leadership of a son of Kimbangu as L'Eglise du Jesus-Christ sur la terre par le Prophète Simon Kimbangu, claiming a membership over five million.[28]

Conversion in Context

The African reasons why Africans became Christians are manifold. In current historiography it is common to assert that the reasons were secular and ulterior—a means of access to the power possessed by Europeans or of acquir-

ing desirable things dispensed from that source. A recent work by C. C.
Okorocha argues that in the context of Igboland, where there was a particularly
rapid response to Christianity, it is wrong to call such reasons secular.[29] Religion
was always in Igboland directed to the acquisition of power; the gods were
followed inasfar as they provided it. So the combination of military defeat by
the British, the desirable goods and capabilities in the power of the whites, and
the association of all this with the power of the book now on offer to them
declared the inferiority of the traditional religious channels. There was every
religious reason to abandon them. To abandon them, however, did not require a
complete redrawing of the map of the spiritual world. The Igbo had always
recognized a Supreme Being—Chukwu or Chineke. Christian preaching
seemed to offer direct access to Chukwu/Chineke; what it enjoined was a
redirection of religion away from the now-discredited lesser divinities. This
was, Okorocha argues, a genuinely religious response, a reordering of the
relationship with the transcendent. It involved an act of decision, a break with
part of the past, a new pattern of worship that was enthusiastically followed,
and a code of dos and don'ts close enough to the traditional one to be recognizable (except perhaps for men important enough to have more than one wife). It
provided immediate access to the book and the power it conveyed.

Okorocha's account of the Igbo story is, in fact, curiously reminiscent of
the account given by Bede of the conversion of the English Kingdom of
Northumbria. Edwin, the king, well disposed to Christianity himself, called a
council to test the consensus. The first speaker was a priest of the old gods
who put in his vote for Christianity. His argument ran thus: No one has served
the gods more faithfully than I, yet I see many who enjoy much more of the
royal favor than I do. I conclude, therefore, that there is nothing to be gained
from their service. After the vote was taken, the priest was the first to defile
the shrine of the gods who so let down their faithful worshiper.[30] In work not
fully incorporated into his book, Okorocha detects a dual movement in Igbo
Christianity. The first abandonment of the old divinities was marked by vigorous adhesion to Christian worship and what one might call a Deuteronomic
theology: honor God, and he will honor you. A later generation knows the
lurking feeling that there may be something in the old ways, but its Christianity includes a new emphasis on the cross and on taking up the cross. And
Okorocha raises the question of the part played in this itinerary by the area's
dreadful sufferings during the Nigerian Civil War.[31]

In Igboland and Northumbria alike, Christianity was first accepted in
terms of a traditional worldview and in relation to traditional goals. It is
impossible for any of us to take in a new idea except in terms of an idea we
already have. But in Igboland and Northumbria alike the new element
adopted into the belief system had a dynamic of its own that entered deep into
the traditional system and interacted with it.

The impact on Africa of alien influences from the Western world produced
an array of reasons within the traditional framework of thinking to seek for
radical religious adjustment and change. The religious effects of a river dam,
of a concrete building constructed over the abode of the water spirit, of an
exodus of young men to work for cash, of a virus caught from incomers for

which the local society has no immunity—these things are potentially more shattering religiously than years of preaching to a stable and satisfied society. In stable primal societies the tradition of the elders—a body of knowledge, wisdom, and interpretation built up over centuries—provides the means of coping with every conceivable situation. But when situations arise for which the tradition has no answers, the society may be in danger of disintegration unless it can find either a means of containing the invading elements or a new rule of life to act as an alternative or supplementary tradition. Without such a key to conduct, the relationships, the hierarchies, and the values of the society are alike disturbed. People are left in confusion—they face conflicting obligations, and ambiguities strew the path of proper conduct. Frequently in Africa the adoption of Christianity has been a means of adapting to burdensome and potentially dangerous situations. The search for a new key to life, a yearning to be able to make assured choices with a good conscience, is surely a thoroughly religious motive, even if it is not the one to which missionary preaching has been primarily addressed.

The search for a key to conduct perhaps lies behind the apparent legalism that has often followed in the wake of evangelical preaching. People who had turned from the old ways at the preaching of Harris or other African evangelists sometimes asked the newly arrived representative of the mission church whether there was special food that a Christian should eat, or whether it was necessary for Christians to sleep, as Europeans did, above the level of the ground? These were not trivial issues. Having abandoned the rules of one tradition, one must know all the demands of the one that is to replace it.[32]

Apparently Augustine, the Roman missionary in the English kingdom of Kent, faced a parallel situation. The questions that, Bede informs us, burst from the first English Christian converts and inquirers were on topics such as the possibility of two brothers marrying two sisters, or attendance at worship during pregnancy or menstruation or after intercourse.[33] No doubt their pre-Christian rituals were hedged by regulations concerning such things. If the gods who underwrote the sanctions on such prohibitions were being abandoned, it was necessary to know what the new God demanded in such matters. To be without an answer was to leave people confused and in fear of breaking a dangerous taboo. It is worth noticing that many African Independent churches have explicit regulations on these very matters. Like Pope Gregory, to whom Augustine referred his questions, they have noticed that some of them are dealt with in the Holiness Code in Leviticus. Because of this they are able from the sacred book to build up the way of life of a neo-Levitical community. Are they not a kingdom of priests?

Some African Christian Initiatives

A well-known feature of West African life is the prophet-healing churches (in West Africa often called *aladura,* a Yoruba word standing for "praying people.")[34] These are constructed on a model of the church quite different from any Western one, a model that arises from an indigenous reading of the

Scriptures and a lively apprehension of the priorities of many anxious people. Prophecy, healing, divination, and revelation feature regularly in their life. Church order is frequently intricate and precise, the members having differentiated uniforms with symbolic designs and assigned ranks and functions. There may be a charismatic leader; there will certainly be plenty of congregational participation. There may also be a detailed code of regulations, exhortations, and prohibitions, as well as vigorous spiritual exercises involving fasting and prayer. Most will combat witchcraft and sorcery; some will identify witches; still more striking, some will cure witches of their baleful powers.

It is worth remembering that the movement from which many of these spring began among mature lay Christians of evangelical Anglican vintage. It was as a revival prayer group that they first met; as Christians, they were searching for the demonstration of God's power amid human devastation (the influenza epidemic after World War I) and spiritual depression.[35]

Until recently these prophet-healing churches could be held the most significant and the fastest-growing sector of the indigenous churches. This is no longer so certain. Nigeria and Ghana, to name but two countries, are witnessing the rise of another type of independent church.[36] Like many prophet-healing churches, they have often originated as prayer or revival groups inside older churches. Like the prophet-healing churches, they proclaim the divine power of deliverance from disease and demonic affliction, but the style of proclamation is more like that of American adventist and pentecostal preaching. Gone are the African drums and the white uniforms of the aladuras; the visitor is more likely to hear electronic keyboards and amplified guitars, see a preacher in elegant *agbada* or smart business suit and a choir in bow ties. Yet these radical charismatic movements are African in origin, in leadership, and in finance. They are highly entrepreneurial and are active in radio and television and cassette ministries as well as in campaigns and conventions. Another set of churches emerged from radical Christian student groups such as the Scripture Union, seeking a thoroughgoing discipleship amid well-established churches that they see as complacent, compromised, and powerless. A new African Christian asceticism is visible here, an emphasis on prayer and fasting and readiness to suffer. All the new movements share with the prophet-healing churches a quest for the demonstrable presence of the Holy Spirit and a direct address to the problems and frustrations of modern African urban life.

The Evangelical Succession

The fathers of the missionary movement undoubtedly expected that Christianity would assimilate Africans to a European style of life. Their apologetic was directed to those of their contemporaries who argued that this was impossible, that Africans did not possess the mental capacities to participate on equal terms in "civilization," that is, in the European discourse of life. Early missionary effort was thus devoted to proving that given the same opportunities,

Africans could do just as well as Europeans. And by the middle of the nineteenth century they seemed to have made their point. At least one part of Africa, Sierra Leone, had produced a Christian community that had all the features of civilized life. People went to church dressed in European clothes. They sang their hymns and psalms in English. Their children went to school, where the brightest pupils learned Latin. Literacy was higher than in most European countries; there was even a girls' grammar school, which not many English boroughs had by mid-century. It looked as if an African Christian country would be like England in every particular—only better.[37] And when the Reverend Samuel Crowther, later to be bishop, came to London and people heard this grave and gracious black clergyman address public meetings in excellent English, when he visited the palace and answered Prince Albert's intelligent questions about African trade, missionary work appeared to have reached its final justification. Its aim henceforth must be to produce more of the same. An African clergyman and an English clergyman should be identical in everything but color.[38]

But Sierra Leone was a special case. Its core population was descended from people taken from slaveships before they crossed the Atlantic—people of a hundred different languages, people uprooted from their lands with no expectation of seeing them again. They had lost their old identity and were too diverse to reestablish it easily. The alternative was a new identity: a Christian and basically British one. Of course, Krio identity was much more rooted in African soil than people realized; that discovery lay in the future. A quicker discovery was that Africans who had not shared the experience of uprooting did not often want to become black Europeans. They might take selected items from the European package; they might become Christians, but they did not reproduce Sierra Leone, the first model of missionary Christianity.[39]

As the various new models have been constituted, it has been with shared experiences that have not been part of Western Christian experience. African Christians face situations where integrity requires them to find a solution in Christian terms—that is, by the application of the word about Christ and of Scripture—where Western Christianity, the source from which Christian tradition has come, has no answers, because it has no parallel experience. And, by the same word about Christ and the same Scriptures, they face the task of penetrating an accumulated body of wisdom and ways of thought and action that in their way are as coherent as the Greek universe of ideas faced by early Hellenistic Christians.

There is no time for more than the briefest indication of some of the situations where the Christian experience of Africa has been different from that of the West.

God and the African Past

Christians are Gentiles (mostly) who worship the God of the Jews. Early Gentile Christians took over Jewish attitudes to the gods of the nations, and specifically to the popular divinities of Greco-Roman paganism. These were idols, not gods. Zeus or Jupiter was not the God and Father of our Lord Jesus Christ. But an important stream of native Greek thought had also rejected the gods of popular religion, and the Greek philosophical tradition developed the idea of God as highest Good, without name, best described in negatives. It was natural for Greek Christians to fuse this impersonal, nameless being with the God of the Bible, the God of the Jews.

This meant that the God of the Jews no longer had a personal name. He was just *ho Theos,* the God. As Christianity spread to the barbarian peoples of the north and west, they, too, abandoned the deities of their pantheons and substituted for all the gods the neutral term "God," the One for the many.

Generally speaking, however, the experience of African Christians has been different. Right across West Africa the first bearers of the Christian message, even when they assumed they were addressing a polytheistic, idolatrous society, found there the recognition of a creator God who was also the moral governor of the universe. The Mende called him Ngewo, the Akan Nyame, the Yoruba Olorun, the Igbo Chukwu or Chineke. The doctrine of the Fall was adumbrated too, for there were often stories that implied that God was once closer to earth than he is now, that some act of greed or folly on the part of people of old had made him keep his distance. For indeed, Ngewo or Olorun did not play much part in most people's daily devotion. Sacrifices to the Supreme Being might be rare or non-existent, prayer made only in emergencies. Other deities appeared in dreams, possessed mediums—but not Ngewo, Nyame, or Olorun. For these people and others like them there was thus an absolute class difference between the Supreme Being and the lower orders of divinities. There was no possibility of active rivalry between "God" and "the gods," no trace of the knockout competition among divinities that seems to have marked Semitic religious history. The lower orders could readily be accorded separate existence, perhaps limited autonomy; there was no doubt who was "God."[40]

It was natural, therefore, to use the name Ngewo, Nyame, Olorun, for the God of the Bible. (One may add in passing that Muslims have been very reluctant to do this. In Muslim Africa as a whole, only "Allah," no vernacular name, is used.)

In parts of East Africa there was a different situation. When the Arabs sought to bring a nineteenth-century Kabaka of Buganda to the knowledge of Allah, his reply was, "Where is there a God greater than I?" And he was talking in sober earnestness.[41] The Baganda worshiped no deity with more honor than the spirits of the Kabakas. But there was one spirit, Katonda, whose shrine had no fire, who did not appear in dreams, and who rarely received offerings. He was really very much on the fringe of Ganda religion. However, it appeared that Katonda had been the worker of creation, and then he became identified with the God of the Bible. The effect was stunning. The half-forgotten Katonda, whom nobody much had been noticing, was— according to the Christian proclamation—calling everyone to give up the worship of every other *muzimu*—indeed he had sent his son to cause them to do so. The effect was such, in fact, that many people hardly took in the bit about the Son. This was hard for missionaries seeking to show Christ as the perfect sacrifice for sin and to lead on to holy living through the Spirit. But the construction of the Ganda auditorium did not immediately allow these words to be heard. It was the sudden appearance of the neglected Katonda that made the impact.[42]

We must not assume that the impact was therefore superficial. It is worth remembering the earliest proud chapter of Ganda Christian history. Christian profession was still young in Buganda when the Kabaka ("Where is there a God greater than I?") ordered his Christian pages to do acts they saw as forbidden by God. They refused, and numbers of Christian teenagers, Catholic and Protestant, were publicly mutilated and then burned alive.

We have not time to consider the later story, or the difficulty Ganda Christians have sometimes had in filling in the whole void—the pleroma, to use Paul's figure to the Colossians with an analogous problem[43]—between Katonda and themselves. Not everyone is quickly convinced that one brief visit to earth long ago is a sufficient basis on which to take over the whole business of representing the spirit world. The remarkable revival movement that East Africa has known for more than half a century past may represent another stage in the Ganda Christian itinerary. Let me point out only that in Buganda, as in most of Africa, God has a personal name, and that it is a vernacular one. God is thus part of the African past; indeed, as Katonda or Nyame or Olorun, he is part of the Ganda, the Akan, the Yoruba past.

A good deal of current African theological debate is devoted to this question. African Christian scholars are searching the African religious heritage, not, as African Christians were once taught, to denigrate or despise it, but to see the ways of God with their own people. Some anthropologists, both European and African, complain of this as tending to Christianize African religion. A non-Christian African scholar such as Okot p' Bitek complains of being robbed.[44] Some Christian theologians have a different fear—that the process of seeking God in the African past will render the Christian revelation unnecessary.[45]

Once again, we cannot go into the debate. It is worth noting, however, how parallel it is to the debate among second- and third-century Christians about the nature of their own past. Jewish Christians, who could proudly claim to be "circumcised the eighth day, of the tribe of Benjamin," and so forth,[46] knew their whole story from Abraham onward. But what of those Gentile Christians, but lately grafted into the olive tree?[47] Some of them began to point to those in their own tradition who had rejected the false gods and suffered for it, and some started to argue that philosophy was the schoolmaster to lead the Greeks to Christ even as the Lord led the Jews.[48] Second-century Hellenistic Christians who wished to present Christ to those who shared the same cultural heritage had to consider the relationship of Christ to that heritage, to their past as Greeks. No one can have a sense of identity without their past. Kwame Bediako has explored the parallel between the ancient Hellenistic and the modern African identity question.[49] Twentieth-century African Christians have to face the question, Where was God in Africa's past? It is the first question on the African theological agenda. And it is not answerable solely in terms of Western theological experience. Nyame, Ngemo, Olorun is the God of Scripture, the God and Father of our Lord Jesus Christ. Zeus and Odin never were.

The Healing Process

Consider this story from Uganda, as told thirty years ago by a scholarly missionary of great insight, later an English bishop.[50]

> A married woman, a communicant member of the Anglican Church, who was childless, was suddenly seized by the *muzimu* of the prince Luyidde, son of Kabaka Mulondo, whose shrine stands on a hill not far from her village. From her body, which was stiff and numb, two voices spoke, one repeating, "I am Luyidde," and her own saying, "I am a Christian; I cannot go." For days the psychosis continued, no one seemed able to help her, and eventually her brothers and her husband, also a communicant, agreed that nothing could save her but to let her go. She is living now at the shrine on the hill, separated from her husband because she belongs to Luyidde. Once in a while she is possessed [*okusamira*] and speaks with his voice, but otherwise she is quite normal, regularly attends church, and is still a communicant.

Priests, priestesses, mediums, and divines are often called to their life's work through an illness that yields to no treatment. They rapidly recover when they respond to the call and take up their shrine duties or begin the studies of their vocation.

In the case given, the person called was a Christian and did not want to go. Yet nothing in the church's armory availed her in her illness or gave her peace of mind. A recent thesis by Silas Ncozana, from Malawi, reveals how situations like this have now become a major pastoral problem in that country.[51]

In Africa, illness is regularly associated with spiritual powers, and with moral or social offenses and obligations, conscious and unconscious. The chief diagnostic question is not, therefore, What illness is it? but What—or who—caused it? Similarly, the way to recovery is to put right what is wrong (if the diagnosis shows it is one's own responsibility) or try to cope with the attack (if it is revealed to be the result of someone else's malice).

Traditional medicine has certainly used herbal remedies, but a traditional healer needs more than a knowledge of the pharmacopoeia. He must have a deep knowledge of human nature, the ability to ask probing questions, not to speak of his religious or magical expertise. Western medicine, in contrast, belongs firmly to the secular world. We have built our medical practice on the principle of treating the illness. African traditional medicine is based on the principle of treating the person.

But consider the effect of Christian preaching on healing in Africa. Magical practice is forbidden to Christians. Diviners, the heart of the diagnostic system, are equally forbidden. The whole apparatus of traditional healing is thus denied to the sufferer. The answer may be to take pills, and if these come from a pastor or a mission hospital, the pills may be seen as an instrument of God. But there is nothing particularly Christian about taking pills, considered as an act in itself. And in any case, what do you do if there is no medical supply in your area? Prophet Harris's converts, it is said, pressed the Prophet to give a course of action when they were sick—he had already described traditional healing as "nothing" if one believes God. His reply was, in effect, take native medicine if you have to, but while you gather the leaves, pray to God; while you prepare the medicine, pray to God; when you take it, pray to God.[52] The traditional specialist is in this way bypassed.

Harris was making a concession. If traditional medicine is ruled out completely by Christian conviction, the Christian has no defense against illness but prayer and trust in Christ. That stern ethic has carried many Christians through; the more radical Independent churches assert it with vigor, forswearing all medicines. What is the pill bottle but the formal equivalent of the traditional medicine, the white man's fetish substitute for faith? (One of the reasons why the Christ Apostolic Church split from the Apostolic Mission was disillusionment with missionaries who used quinine.)[53] But one can see how it was all too much for many people. So, when illness or trouble comes, a visit to the diviner takes place—but at night, and with a bad conscience, because the sufferers really think they ought not.

It is at this point that the prophet-healing churches speak with special force. They reflect an assurance that Christ is indeed Savior and still saves, that he heals in their congregation; the sympathetic moving of the congregation and the wrestling with evil of the charismatic leader take the illness of the sufferer and its likely causes seriously. The stress on response by the sufferer, in baptism perhaps, and continuing service of God in the church, underlines it further. It provides a framework in which those called as spirit dancers or mediums, like the one in the bishop's story, can be comprehendingly treated, in a battle royal with the spirits before, and with the aid of, the whole congregation.

It is said with truth that the prophet-healers use techniques and styles of interrogation characteristic of traditional diviners and healers. But among the prophet-healing churches are the most implacable foes of the traditional diviner and of those that quietly sneak to his house in the dark. They are insistent as to the source of their healing, locating it firmly with the work of Christ or the Holy Spirit. (They are not always clear about the distinction.) Placing a Bible against the sufferer's head or giving a bottle of water consecrated by prayer may be described as a fetish act, no different from applying a charm; yet when the source of power is so visibly identified with the God of the Bible and with the Spirit of Christ, there is a gap opened up with the old powers of Africa. The traditional African concept of healing the person rather than the sickness is retained, but it is transformed by locating the healing in Christ. It demands a more complete break with "the world" than going to church by day and to the diviner at night.

To tell the suffering woman that Luyidde is dead and cannot hurt her would be useless—she knew differently. Nor would it be Christian, for it would not be applying Christ to her need. Similarly, Western Christianity has effectively been disabled from helping in the desolating situation of witch-craft by the fact that its worldview had no real place for the objective reality of witchcraft. Its principal value has been in saving many people accused or suspected of witchcraft from undeserved suffering. But this does nothing to reduce the fear of witchcraft; indeed, in some circumstances, it increases it. And it does nothing for the tortured soul who goes to the prophet-healer with the confession that she is a witch,[54] insists that she has killed people, names them, and begs to be delivered from this curse of destroying people. That the questioning of suspected witches can be brutal psychological bully-ing goes without saying, but the questions of the skilled healer can also bring to the surface things that are not only therapeutic but edifying. Witchcraft, after all, is hatred objectified. Skilled questioning may reveal the hatred and the jealously that rejoices when a rival's child dies. By this means hatred can be brought to the surface, acknowledged for what it is. Forgiveness, even reconciliation, can then follow. Christ is thus applied to the needs of witch and victim alike and can be acknowledged as Victor, where rationalistic explanation would be futile and a generalized assurance of divine love fall flat.

The Evangelical Legacy

So various, and so luxuriant, has been the fruit of evangelical endeavor in Africa. Many more examples might have been given, some of them—notably the East African revival—closer to the evangelical tradition as it has devel-oped in the West.[55] It has seemed, however, more important to indicate that the results of evangelical preaching have been much more widespread, and much more dynamic, than may be at first apparent. While some of the fea-tures of the evangelical religion that originated the missionary movement— certainly the high place given to Scripture and the recognition of immediacy in personal experience—have been regular features of African Christianity, it is important to note that the fruit of the work of evangelical missionaries has not simply been a replication of Western evangelicalism. The Christian message that they set loose in Africa has its own dynamic, as it comes into creative and critical encounter with African life with its needs and its hurts. Exactly the same thing happened when the Evangelical Revival bridged the culture gap for northern Protestantism to such spectacular effect. Africans have re-sponded to the gospel from where *they* were, not from where the missionaries were; they have responded to the Christian message as they heard it, not to the missionaries' experience of that message.

Nevertheless, the first hearing and the first response is not the whole, nor necessarily the climax, of the story. Perhaps we should give more attention to generational processes in Christian history, carefully observing communal reli-gious itineraries that may take several generations. In many such cases it will be impossible to pass every milestone in one lifetime and dangerous to attempt shortcuts.[56]

As for the missionaries, they achieved—sometimes in spite of themselves—exactly what they believed they had been sent to do. After all, they had not gone to transmit evangelicalism to Africa, but the gospel.

Notes

1. A. Fawcett, *The Cambuslang Revival: The Scottish Evangelical Revival of the Eighteenth Century* (London: Banner of Truth, 1971), 223–35.

2. J. van den Berg, *Constrained by Jesus' Love: An Enquiry into the Motives of the Missionary Awakening in Great Britain in the Period between 1698 and 1815* (Kampen: Kok, 1956), 57–58, 91–92; S. H. Rooy, *The Theology of Missions in the Puritan Tradition: A Study of Representative Puritans* (Grand Rapids: Eerdmans, 1965), 289–93. In 1816 the *Missionary Register,* of Anglican Evangelical provenance, serialized Jonathan Edwards's account of Brainerd.

3. Cf. A. J. Raboteau and D. W. Wills, "Rethinking American Religious History," *Council of Societies for the Study of Religion Bulletin* 20 (1991): 57–61.

4. E. Stock, *History of the Church Missionary Society,* vol. 1 (London: CMS, 1899), 82–83; Charles Hole, *The Early History of the Church Missionary Society to the End of 1814* (London: CMS, 1896), 81–85.

5. The best-known early example was the *Missionary Register,* published in London; a *Scottish Missionary Register* on similar lines appeared in 1820.

6. Some examples appear in van den Berg, *Constrained by Jesus' Love,* 15–28. For the sad story of Justinian Welz, see J. A. Scherer, *Justinian Welz: Essays by an Early Prophet of Mission* (Grand Rapids: Eerdmans 1969). It is significant that the eighteenth-century Tranquebar mission, though supported in the highest circles of state (its formal originator was the king of Denmark) and church (its finances were administered by the Society for Promoting Christian Knowledge), relied on A. H. Francke's pietist establishment at Halle for its staff.

7. Jane Austen, *Mansfield Park* (1814), vol. 3, chap. 16 (= chap. 47 in most modern editions).

8. *Collection of hymns for the use of the People called Methodists* (London, 1780), no. 94.

9. Austen, *Mansfield Park,* vol. 3, chap. 3 (= chap. 34 of modern editions).

10. William Wilberforce, *Practical view of the prevailing religious system of professed Christians in the higher and middle classes of this country contrasted with real Christianity* (London, 1797; many editions).

11. Ibid.

12. *Hymns for the People called Methodists,* preface. The arrangement of the first part of the hymnbook suggests a logical, if not invariably chronological, progression of "real" Christian experience: Part I: Exhorting sinners to return to God—Describing (1) The pleasantness of religion; (2) The goodness of God; (3) Death; (4) Judgment; (5) Heaven; (6) Hell; (7) Praying for a blessing. Part II: Describing formal religion; Describing inward religion. Part III: Praying for repentance; For mourners convinced of sin; For persons convinced of backsliding; For backsliders recovered. Part IV deals with the life and activity of "Believers," and part V with the activities of the Methodist society.

13. W. Carus, *Memoirs of the life of the Rev. Charles Simeon . . . with a selection of his writings and correspondence* (London: Hatchard, 1847), 188.

14. Cf. R. Lovett, *The History of the London Missionary Society, 1795–1895* (London: Henry Frowde, 1899), 194–237. J. Garrett, *To Live among the Stars: Christian Origins in Oceania* (Geneva: World Council of Churches; Suva, University of the South Pacific, 1982), 13–31.

15. Congregationalist missionaries anointed and crowned the king in Tahiti and drafted national law codes in various islands.

16. See the statistical analyses in D. B. Barrett, *World Christian Encyclopedia* (Nairobi: Oxford University Press, 1982); see also earlier pointers in D. B. Barrett, "A.D. 2000: 350 Million Christians in Africa," *International Review of Mission* 59 (1970): 39–54; and Roland Oliver, *How Christian Is Africa?* (London: Highway Press, 1956). Cf. A. F. Walls, "Towards Understanding Africa's Place in Christian History," in *Religion in a Pluralistic Society: Essays presented to Professor C. G. Baeta,* ed. J. S. Pobee (Leiden: Brill, 1976), 180–89.

17. Cf. A. F. Walls, "The Translation Principle in Christian History," in *Bible Translation and the Spread of the Church in the Last Two Hundred Years,* ed. P. C. Stine (Leiden: Brill, 1990), 24–39.

18. On the so-called Nova-Scotian settlers in Sierra Leone, see Christopher Fyfe, *A History of Sierra Leone* (Oxford: Oxford University Press, 1962); and idem, *"Our children free and happy": Letters from Black Settlers in Africa in the 1790s* (Edinburgh: Edinburgh University Press, 1991).

19. A. F. Walls, "A Christian Experiment: The Early Sierra Leone Colony," in *The Mission of the Church and the Propagation of the Faith,* Studies in Church History 6, ed. G. J. Cuming (Cambridge: Cambridge University Press, 1970), 107–30.

20. T. A Beetham, "A Sierra Leone Missionary to Kenya," *Sierra Leone Bulletin of Religion* 1, no. 2 (1959): 56–57.

21. P. E. H. Hair, "The CMS 'Native Clergy' in West Africa to 1900," *Sierra Leone Bulletin of Religion* 4 (1962): 71–72; cf. idem, "Freetown Christianity and Africa," *Sierra Leone Bulletin of Religion* 6 (1964): 13–21.

22. M. L. Pirouet, *Black Evangelists: The Spread of Christianity in Uganda, 1891–1914* (London: Collings, 1978).

23. D. A. Shank, "William Wadé Harris: A Prophet of Modern Times" (Ph.D. diss., University of Aberdeen, 1980; publication expected shortly). See also idem, "The Legacy of William Wadé Harris," *International Bulletin of Missionary Research* 10 (1986): 170–76.

24. G. M. Haliburton, "The Calling of a Prophet: Sampson Oppong," *Bulletin of the Society for African Church History* 2, no. 1 (1965): 84–96.

25. Cf. H. W. Turner, *History of an African Independent Church: The Church of the Lord (Aladura)* (Oxford: Clarendon Press, 1967), 16–32.

26. S. N. Mohlomi, *Kereke ea Moshoeshoe: Lesotho's First New Religious Movement* (M.Litt. diss., Centre for the Study of Christianity in the Non-Western World, Edinburgh, 1977).

27. G. O. M. Tasie, "The Prophetic Calling: Garrick Sokari Braide of Bakana," in *Varieties of Christian Experience in Nigeria,* ed. E. Isichei (London: Macmillan, 1982), 99–115.

28. Among the more important of a legion of works on Kimbangu and the movement and church that emerged from his work, see M. L. Martin, *Kimbangu: An African Prophet and His Church* (Oxford: Blackwell, 1975); and Werner Ustorf, *Afrikanische Initiative: Das aktive Leiden des Propheten Simon Kimbangu* (Bern: Lang, 1975).

29. C. C. Okorocha, *The Meaning of Religious Conversion in Africa: The Case of the Igbo of Nigeria* (Aldershot: Avebury Gower, 1987).

30. Bede, *Ecclesiastical History* 2.13.

31. C. C. Okorocha, "Salvation in Igbo Religious Experience: Its Influence on Igbo Christianity" (Ph.D. diss., University of Aberdeen, 1982).

32. For an example of the concerns, cf. G. M. Haliburton, *The Prophet Harris: A Study of an African Prophet and His Mass Movement in the Ivory Coast and the Gold Coast, 1913–1915* (New York: Oxford University Press, 1973), 222. On the place of the law in the Christian itinerary, see D. A. Shank, "African Christian Religious Itinerary: Toward an Understanding of the Religious Itinerary from the Faith of African Traditional Religion(s) to That of the New Testament," in *Exploring New Religious Movements: Essays in Honour of H. W. Turner,* ed. A. F. Walls and W. R. Shenk (Elkhart, IN: Mission Focus, 1990), 143–62.

33. Bede, *Ecclesiastical History* 1.27.

34. On the origins of the Aladura movement, see Turner, *History;* and J. D. Y. Peel, *Aladura: A Religious Movement among the Yoruba* (London: Oxford University Press for International African Institute, 1968). Turner's companion volume, *African Independent Church: The Life and Faith of the Church of the Lord (Aladura)* (Oxford: Clarendon Press, 1967), gives the fullest account yet available of the life of a prophet-healing church.

35. Turner, *History,* 9–13.

36. The movement is now beginning to attract due attention in the literature. Its importance is signaled by Rosalind Hackett, "Enigma Variations: The New Religious Movements in Nigeria Today," in *Exploring New Religious Movements,* ed. Walls and Shank, 131–42. For a study of a representative movement, cf. Matthews Ojo, "Deeper Christian Life Ministry: A Case Study of the Charismatic Movements in Western Nigeria," *Journal of Religion in Africa* 18 (1988): 141–62.

37. Cf. the picture provided by Henry Venn, Secretary of the Church Missionary Society, in *West African Colonies: Notices of the British Colonies on the West Coast of Africa* (London: Darton and Lacy, 1865).

38. Cf. *An Appeal for a Great Extension of Missions to the Heathens . . .* (London: Christian Book Society, 1873), an anonymous book clearly written by an elderly and scholarly minded Anglican evangelical clergyman: "We have one black Bishop who is at home with his Greek Testament, and administers his diocese of the Niger with zeal and judgment, like any bishop in England. I have a precious photographic picture of him and his son, his chaplain, in the midst of their evangelical work. Perhaps some or many of the African fathers were of the same colour" (32).

39. Cf. J. F. A. Ajayi, *Christian Missions in Nigeria, 1841–1891: The Making of a New Elite* (London: Longmans, 1965).

40. Cf. P. J. Ryan, " 'Arise O God': The Problem of 'Gods' in West Africa," *Journal of Religion in Africa* 11, no. 3 (1980): 161–71.

41. J. V. Taylor, *The Growth of the Church in Buganda* (London: SCM, 1958), 9.

42. Cf. ibid., 252–60.

43. Colossians 1:19, where the *plērōma*—the entire sphere in which the intermediary powers between God and the universe operate—dwells in Christ.

44. Okot p'Bitek, *African Religions and Western Scholarship* (Kampala: East Africa Literature Bureau, 1970).

45. For example, the late Byang Kato, *Theological Pitfalls in Africa* (Kisumu, Kenya: Evangel Publishing House, 1975).

46. Cf. Philippians 3:5.

47. Cf. Romans 16:16–24.

48. On Socrates and others who witnessed to the truth, cf. Justin, *Apology* 1.46; on philosophy as the tutor to Christ, Clement of Alexandria *Stromateis* 1.5.

49. Kwame Bediako, *Theology and Identity: The Impact of Culture on Christian Thought in the Second Century and Modern Africa* (Oxford: Regnum, 1991).

50. Taylor, *Growth of the Church in Buganda,* 211.

51. S. N. Nczana, "Spirit Possession and Tumbuka Christianity, 1875–1950" (Ph.D. diss., University of Aberdeen, 1985).

52. Haliburton, *Prophet Harris,* 54.

53. Turner, *History,* 31–32.

54. Cf. R. W. Wyllie, "Introspective Witchcraft among the Effutu," *Man,* n.s., 8 (1973): 74–79.

55. The East African revival has been mentioned only in passing; in its origins this revival affected both European missionaries and Africans, and its antecedents can be found in both traditions. It has developed as an essentially African movement, though it has had a certain impact on evangelical life in the West, especially in Britain. See J. E. Church, *Quest for the Highest: An Autobiographical Account of the East African Revival* (Exeter: Paternoster, 1981); and P. St. John, *Breath of life* (London: Norfolk Press, 1971); and for the influences, Western and African, R. Anker-Petersen, "A Study of the Spiritual Roots of the East African Revival Movement" (M.Th. diss., Edinburgh Centre for the Study of Christianity in the Non-Western World, Edinburgh, 1988).

56. See Shank, "African Christian Religious Itinerary," esp. 154–57.

THE TWENTIETH CENTURY

16

Fundamentalism and the Varieties of North Atlantic Evangelicalism

IAN S. RENNIE

Twentieth-century American fundamentalism had its roots in nineteenth-century British evangelicalism.[1] In this chapter I attempt to indicate the continuance of the proto-fundamentalist tradition in nineteenth-century Britain and its ongoing existence in the twentieth century, often known as conservative evangelicalism, until the commencement of World War II. The constant links between the two will be noted, with some attention given to Canada in its customary mediating role, where excess Britons could find a fairly congenial home and some become culturally conditioned enough to North America that they could proceed, together with native-born British Canadians, to assume an effective role south of the border.

British proto-fundamentalism began to surface in the 1820s among a section of the Evangelical party in the Church of England, which was actually the United Church of England and Ireland. The primary motive behind this development was fear of liberalism in its theological and social expression. Closely allied was the fear of resurgent Catholicism, in either its Roman or Tractarian form. In addition there was dread of the movement for the disestablishment of the Church of England by politically active evangelical Nonconformists, which was seen as support for the demand for a nonconfessional and even secular state.

A segment of Evangelical Anglicanism was uniquely open to these fears and, under this duress, to putting on the armor of proto-fundamentalism. In the post-Napoleonic world, as Evangelical Anglicanism entered its third generation, it began to penetrate one of the hitherto most resistant classes—the ancient landed families of the gentry and aristocracy of England, Ireland, and even to some extent Scotland. Young converts from this extremely conservative class regularly traveled to the Continent, and there they saw the effect of liberalism on Protestantism. Their hierarchical position was threatened and, if their patrimony was in the south of Ireland, might be swept away altogether. They had no particular commitment to the existing evangelical status quo, and as cultural Romantics, they gravitated to an arsenal characterized by intense supernaturalism, polarity, and apocalyptic.

These young, upper-class evangelicals and their successors were known for much of the nineteenth century as Recordites, after the influential London newspaper managed by one of their leaders. They reemphasized the traditional Calvinism of Evangelical Anglicanism, insisted on the verbal theory of biblical inspiration, popularized premillennialism through books, lectures, and countless sermons, and were committed to maintaining the United Kingdom as a Protestant Christian nation in the form of traditional Christendom. The Recordites also believed that such a day of danger required a strategy of confrontation, and in this approach their newspaper eagerly gave the lead.

By the early 1830s two distinct groups separated from the Recordites, both over the extent of the premillennial concept of the Gentile Apostasy, which was believed to be swiftly approaching its consummation in church and society. The Recordites all believed that Roman Catholicism was apostate, as was rationalistic Continental Protestantism. They thought that Nonconformist attacks upon the state church principle portended the same thing. The question at issue was the place of the Church of England in this apocalyptic stream. The great majority of the Recordites were convinced that at its foundations the Church of England was the most biblical and spiritual of ecclesiastical bodies, and they were committed to its defense.

Those who saw the apostasy choking the life out of the Church of England and who demanded separation from it were the Catholic Apostolics and the Christian, or Plymouth, Brethren. Although the putative head of the Catholic Apostolics was Edward Irving, a Presbyterian Scot ministering to fellow expatriates in London, his most faithful followers were Recordites, who with Irving believed that an effective antiliberal strategy needed a healthy injection of the charismatic.[2] The original Brethren were also almost all Recordites.[3] The problem is that since they have become so well known as the inspirers of American fundamentalism, it is often forgotten that, of those sharing their views, many more stayed in the Church of England than left it. While the Catholic Apostolics went off into splendid apocalyptic isolation, the Recordites within the Church of England, and the Brethren, were the main components of nineteenth-century British proto-fundamentalism, and, for that matter, through their descendants, of twentieth-century British conservative evangelicalism as well.

Although by no means all Evangelicals in the Church of England were in agreement with Recordite distinctives as Queen Victoria ascended the throne, their leadership in the defense of the Church of England as by law established won them grudging appreciation and then wholehearted respect. By mid-century a critical observer estimated that there were five thousand Evangelical clergy in the Church of England—about one-third of the total—with almost half the Evangelicals having discernible Recordite leanings.[4]

The most outstanding clerical figure among the Recordites was Hugh McNeile of Liverpool. A big, handsome Irishman, he was evaluated by a very competent judge as "unquestionably the greatest Evangelical preacher and speaker in the Church of England during this century."[5] He and a number of other eloquent men continually traversed the country speaking interminably to vast gatherings on subjects dear to Recordite hearts. Constantly confrontational, he poured scorn on all who disagreed with him. On one occasion he thundered, "Controversy! People object to controversy, but who can escape it out of Utopia. Controversy! You cannot live without controversy."[6] Liverpool, with its large Irish minority, was made for McNeile, and he became its most powerful citizen. With Irish Catholics as a visible threat and Irish Protestants as his most loyal followers, he helped make Liverpool the most evangelical city in England, and with a definite Recordite hue. When J. C. Ryle became the first Bishop of Liverpool in 1880, he built on the foundations that McNeile had laid.

As the nineteenth century unfolded, increased attack was felt by the evangelicals. *Essays and Reviews* in 1860 indicated that liberal views of theology and the Bible were penetrating the intellectual centers of the Church of England. Catholic forms of ecclesiastical ritual were being introduced to many parish churches. Such developments brought the evangelicals together in a new way. After the publication of *Essays and Reviews,* the *Record* and its more traditional, intellectual, and gentle counterpart the *Christian Observer* continually printed articles attacking what was known as neology.[7] After 1865 many of the evangelicals were united in an anti-Ritualist crusade, seeking "to prove, by court decisions, that ritualistic doctrines and practices within the Church of England were illegal,"[8] which provides an interesting parallel to the use of the courts by later American fundamentalism to protect schools from the teaching of evolutionary theory.

Other influences at work, however, modified, altered, narrowed, and intensified proto-fundamentalism. These included the movement of organized evangelism called revivalism, and also the deeper life of holiness known by its place-name of Keswick. Both came from the United States about 1873. When D. L. Moody, the mass evangelist, first arrived in England, it was under the aegis of a well-known Irish Evangelical Anglican clergyman, William Pennefather, who was also a relative of J. N. Darby of the Brethren. While Moody had phenomenal success in Britain, he had very special links with the Evangelical Anglicans.[9] He helped to break down their Calvinism and bring them out of their relative isolation from Nonconformist evangelicals. On matters of eschatology, he also introduced them to the dispensational premillennialism of their erstwhile Brethren associates, in place of their historicism or simple futurism. The annual Keswick Conference, with its regional satellites, became a center of proto-fundamentalism, always appropriately under firm Evangelical Anglican control. As a result of revivalism and Keswick, British proto-fundamentalism became more similar to American fundamentalism, a process that was encouraged by the mutual transatlantic exchange of evangelists and convention speakers through the late Victorian age.

Under the new American influences, British proto-fundamentalism began to expand. Mission halls appeared in the poorer parts of the large cities and almost invariably came within the proto-fundamentalist orbit.[10] A minority of

English Baptists followed C. H. Spurgeon in his identification with proto-fundamentalism,[11] while more Welsh Baptists, almost all Irish, and some Scottish, including the famous Charlotte Chapel of Edinburgh, espoused his views.

Scottish and Irish Presbyterians had more trouble accepting proto-fundamentalism. Although Calvinism and belief in the verbal inspiration of Scripture had been foundational for the first generation of the Free Church of Scotland after the Disruption of 1843, both were weakening during the late nineteenth century. Premillennialism never commanded widespread support. While many lay Presbyterians and some ministers appreciated the proto-fundamentalist stance, they had to find much of their nourishment from nondenominational evangelistic campaigns, regional Keswicks, and events at mission halls. The presence of Carruber's Close Mission in Edinburgh and the Tent Hall in Glasgow gave remarkable visibility to Scottish proto-fundamentalism, as did the presence of Glasgow's famous Bible Training Institute, the only one of its kind in Britain at the end of the century.

Irish Presbyterianism was only slightly different. The return to orthodoxy under Henry Cooke in 1840, and "the year of Grace" of 1859,[12] left an intense evangelicalism that had affinities with proto-fundamentalism. Whatever may have been the case among the clergy, the Presbyterian Belfast City Mission, with its many congregational mission halls, provided an institutional structure for proto-fundamentalism. Somewhat akin to the prayer huts of Norwegian pietistic Lutheranism, these mission halls held together proto-fundamentalism, loyalty to religious heritage, and national identity for many of the rank-and-file.

At the turn of the century, the Evangelical Anglicans were clearly in the lead of what was then called conservative evangelicalism. Not only were they numerically sizable, but they possessed an institutional infrastructure. This was something the conservative evangelical Baptists did not possess to any significant degree,[13] and that the mission halls did not worry about. For their part, the Brethren pretended to dismiss institutions in principle, although they were busily letting them in through the back door in the shape of peripatetic preachers, periodicals, and family dynasties. The Church of England, perhaps somewhat contrary to initial appearances, provides a remarkable opportunity for certain popular movements to survive. Most denominations, through their infrastructures, are controlled by cultural, intellectual, or bureaucratic elites, regardless of the professions of democratic polity. The Church of England, in contrast, is more like Roman Catholicism and Lutheranism in their heartlands. It constitutes a kind of undemocratic *Volkskirche* in which, within certain guidelines, subcultures are allowed to survive. In various ways the rights of property, group, and ideology are given a chance over against coercive centralized absolutism. Patronage, parson's freehold, voluntary missionary societies, and the provision for nondiocesan theological colleges are all parts of this scheme. What appears like a ramshackle medieval edifice provided the conservative Evangelicals in the Church of England with identity, corporate freedom, and continuity.

Despite some signs of strength, the conservative evangelicals at the turn of the century were falling into difficulty. Liberal evangelicalism was taking a heavy toll, and there was a question—after all the battles of the past, whether among the Baptists over the Downgrade, or the Evangelical Anglicans over ritualism—whether they had really accomplished very much.[14] World War I, when it came, simply added to this feeling of debility. The decline of Irish leadership among conservative Evangelical Anglicans resulted in the expression of more English restraint. Keswick, with its gentle, quasi-mystical concept of holiness, from its very central position, helped to moderate the bellicose. Perhaps Moody had also once again been more successful in Britain than in America. While the leader who deplored controversy often went unheeded by his American fundamentalist descendants, his example was frequently remembered in Britain. So in their attitudes British conservative evangelicals and American fundamentalists may have been passing as ships in the night. But underneath they were never closer.

While the British conservative evangelicals did not usually engage in high-decibel warfare, they were not therefore giving up their convictions. They simply expressed defensiveness instead of anger. This accounts for one historian's referring to the "siege mentality" of conservative evangelicals before World War II, and another, mixing the metaphors of veld and prairie, describing them as having the "appearance of a laager, desperately warding off attacks of theological Red Indians!"[15] In this situation there was no more important icon than Bishop Taylor Smith, beloved by conservative evangelicals of all communions. Chaplain-General to the Forces from 1901 to 1925, and possessed of a great fund of good humor, he was known to be resolutely rigid when faced with chaplains with whom he disagreed.[16] Graham Scroggie, a British preacher well known on both sides of the Atlantic, attempted to describe the British posture. Interestingly enough, he applied it to the United States and Canada as well. While not averse to describing himself as a fundamentalist, he made it very clear that he had no time for fractious organizations. "In Britain, Canada, and the States the vast majority of Fundamentalists are outside the membership of these organizations, and if you ask them why, they will tell you it is because they disapprove of the method and spirit which largely prevail in their defence of the truth."[17]

Before looking at how British conservative evangelicals opposed diverse theological views, it may be wise to remind ourselves of the continuation in their ranks of verbal inspiration and premillennialism, especially that of a dispensational character. It has been suggested, for instance, that the conservative evangelicals in Britain during the first half of this century did not share the same view of biblical inspiration as American fundamentalists—namely, verbal inspiration.[18] While this may be true if one is referring to the refined view of verbal inspiration presented by B. B. Warfield and A. A. Hodge, with such buzzwords as "original autographs" and "inerrancy," it is not correct if one takes into account the British view of verbal inspiration.

This distinctly British approach may be found in C. H. Waller, *The Authoritative Inspiration of Holy Scripture (As Distinct From the Inspiration of Its*

Human Authors) Acknowledged by Our Lord and Saviour Jesus Christ. It was first published as a preface to the *Imperial Bible Dictionary* in 1885, with an introduction by Bishop Ryle, and then separately two years later with an additional foreword by Spurgeon. Waller was an Oxford graduate who as a student was greatly influenced by the redoubtable conservative Dean Burgon. Waller was principal of the Evangelical Anglican theological institution known as the London College of Divinity, originally called St. John's Highbury. Waller was also examining chaplain to Bishop Ryle. His approach was more christocentric, or, as some might say, Cranmerian. It is Jesus' validation of the Bible that is crucial. But once that has been said, there is little or no difference from the Princeton position. The gist of his argument was:

> But when our Lord read the Scripture, He would read it without any imperfection of thought or motive. That which he made his own, must have been fitted to be the vehicle of a sinless mind. . . . The question of the infallibility and perfection of Scripture turns therefore on its relation to our Lord. . . . If the whole word written has been accepted by our Saviour as God's Word and God's law for him . . . then in relation to Him we may, we must, take the whole Scripture to be perfect and infallible. If there can be no spot or stain of sin or error in our blessed Saviour, there can be none in the Scripture regarded as the expression of His mind.[19]

Of particular importance was the fact that Waller worked within the structure of Evangelical Anglicanism. Various writers mentioned by Nigel Cameron in *Biblical Higher Criticism and the Defence of Infallibilism in Nineteenth Century Britain* (1987) did not have such a sustaining context. As a result, their ideas often seemed to die with them and so seemed to signal the end of a theological age. Waller's views, in contrast, were perpetuated for some time through the London College of Divinity, where students were renowned for their strict conservative evangelicalism.[20] W. H. Griffith Thomas, who was at Wycliffe Hall, Oxford, during the first decade of this century, was a key member in the conservative Evangelical network in the Church of England as well as outside, and his view of Scripture was very similar to that of Waller.[21] This position helps to explain how readily Griffith Thomas adapted to North American fundamentalism in both Canada and the United States. The Irish Anglican T. C. Hammond shared a similar standpoint,[22] and his affinity with the view of American fundamentalism was shown by his frequent citation of works from Old Princetonians in his bibliographies. David Bebbington has helpfully listed other Britons who shared some form of verbal inspiration.[23] Thus a common attitude to the Bible was shared by conservative evangelicals in Britain and fundamentalists in America.

Verbal inspiration, premillennialism, and holiness were particularly woven together in Keswick. In fact, Bebbington has noted that dispensationalism was the form of premillennialism generally accepted by Evangelical Anglicans who attended Keswick.[24] The message of E. L. Langston, a very popular conservative Evangelical Anglican clergyman at Keswick in 1933, entitled "The Signs of the Times," gave classic expression to this commitment.[25] If this was true for the dominant conservative Evangelical Anglican contingent, it was likely true for many of the others as well.

The close links between British conservative evangelicalism and American fundamentalism were particularly shown by the presence of Americans on the Keswick Convention platform from year to year. This is especially instructive at a time when it might be assumed that the links would be fraying. American fundamentalism was being significantly changed by a vast influx of continental European adherents, particularly German and Scandinavian.[26] One would imagine that such people would have little interest in things British, in contrast with many Americans of British origin. In fact their reaction against continental state churches should, at least in theory, have alienated them from Evangelical Anglicans, however conservative, who upheld their national church, adhered to an episcopal system of polity, worshiped liturgically with a *Book of Common Prayer,* and dressed in clerical attire. Isolationism both political and spiritual would have seemed to be the order of the day. But in spite of all contrary forces, the British-American links remained strong.

As the twentieth century began, a regular American speaker at Keswick was A. T. Pierson. R. A. Torrey was also welcomed in the early years of the century. Jonathan Goforth, a Canadian Presbyterian fundamentalist missionary, was present in the great missionary year of 1910. A. C. Dixon, another American fundamentalist, was present in 1912. In that year Griffith Thomas was welcomed back on the first of several trips from North America.[27] Lewis Sperry Chafer, fresh from the founding of Dallas Seminary, was present in 1924,[28] and the singularly combative Charles Gallaudet Trumbull of the *Sunday School Times* spoke in 1925.[29]

In the 1930s, as the terrible force of the economic depression began to abate, two leading American fundamentalists were regularly among the speakers. H. A. Ironside, pastor of Moody Memorial Church, Chicago, and unofficially dubbed by many as the Archbishop of American Fundamentalism,[30] participated in 1937 and 1938, giving the honored Bible Readings (that is, informal expositions) in 1939.[31] The historian of Moody Church, with pardonable exuberance, stated that as a result of his summer ministries, Ironside's "acclaim in Great Britain was as wide as in the United States."[32] The other was Donald Grey Barnhouse of Tenth Presbyterian Church, Philadelphia, no shrinking violet among fundamentalists. He spoke in 1935 and 1936 and gave the Bible Readings in 1938.

One other important bond between British conservative evangelicalism and American fundamentalism throughout the years 1900–1939 was the common support of so-called faith missions. This movement was founded in 1865 by Hudson Taylor with the inauguration in England of the China Inland Mission. It contained all the indicators of Conservative evangelicalism fundamentalism[33] and was the model for most of the faith missions, including the Central American Mission, founded by C. I. Scofield of fundamentalist fame.[34]

Another parallel between British conservative evangelicalism and American fundamentalism was the tendency to separation. British conservative evangelicals had strong cultural links to their denominations if they were state churches, such as the Church of England, the Church of Scotland, or the quasi-established Presbyterian Church of Ireland. And in the Church of England they seemed to have the best of all possible worlds, where they could retain both their ecclesiastical identity and their conservative evangelical freedom at the same time. The Brethren and the missions halls were monochromatically conservative evangelical, so the possibility of separation did not arise. The Baptists were most exposed, and they suffered a number of defections.[35] But denominational loyalty was certainly a hallmark of British conservative evangelicalism. If, however, denominational loyalty was largely sacrosanct, the same could not be said of relationships with voluntary societies and organizations. In their own way, amid such associations, conservative evangelicals in Britain were prepared to engage in controversy.

The first twentieth-century British division along modernist–conservative evangelical lines seems to have taken place in connection with R. A. Torrey's evangelistic campaigns from 1903 to 1905. His aggressive theological approach brought strong opposition and the dismissal of his work by many clergy and ministers throughout the United Kingdom.[36] Perhaps this response was intensified, as in Liverpool, because the conservative Evangelical Anglicans and undenominational mission halls received most of the new converts.[37] In spite of this opposition, or perhaps because of it, the overwhelmingly Anglican committee in Liverpool invited Torrey back for a second campaign in 1904. And at the concluding Albert Hall services in London in 1905, it was almost entirely conservative Evangelical Anglicans who stood publicly with Torrey.[38]

The next public division occurred over student work in 1910. In that year the Keswick Convention trustees declined to allow the Student Christian Movement, because of its doctrinal shift, to hold an officially sponsored side-meeting.[39] In the same year the Cambridge Inter-Collegiate Christian Union, almost entirely Anglican, and with the closest of links to Keswick, parted company on doctrinal grounds with the SCM and its vast international network. Just 250 students differing from 152,000 did suggest Athanasius *contra mundum.*[40] To make its more conservative stance clear, the CICCU invited Torrey for a mission to the university in 1911.[41]

The CICCU developed into the Inter-Varsity Fellowship after World War I, which was held unflinchingly to its conservative evangelical position by its first and long-term general secretary, Douglas Johnson, a theologically knowledgeable medical man from a Brethren background who filled the position from 1924 to 1964. "D.J.," as he was widely known, was supported by a large body of conservative evangelicals. Johnson's vision and commitment is shown by the the title of his history of British Inter-Varsity, published in 1979. He gave it the fundamentalistically friendly caption *Contending for the Faith,* because this is what he saw his life work to have been. He was convinced that he stood "in the face of a theological and ecclesiastical landslide, which went far towards carrying away with it the total birthright of the Protestant churches."[42]

A devotee of the Princeton theology long before it was reintroduced to Britain by the Banner of Truth in the 1950s, Johnson continually insisted that there be no involvement between IVF and SCM, led IVF in consistent refusal to participate in inclusive university evangelistic missions, and rejected any co-operation with Frank Buchman and the Oxford Group.[43] When his closest friend, Donald Coggan (who later became Archbishop of Canterbury), refused to affirm the infallibility of Scripture when asked to become a vice-president of IVF, "D.J." had no hesitancy in disqualifying him.[44] While preparing his history of British Inter-varsity, Johnson read Harold Lindsell's *Battle for the Bible* and was happy to acknowledge that his own view and accómpanying strategy were basically identical.[45]

Another disruption took place within the YWCA. In 1917 the Irish YWCA separated from the British National Association. In 1918 a number of English branches formed the Evangelical YWCA, and in 1919 a referendum was circulated, asking "that the teaching given at Conferences, Camps, Training Centers etc., should be clear, definite and sound, untainted with either Sacerdotalism or 'Modernism.' "[46] When there was no satisfactory response to the twelve thousand signatures attached to the referendum, conservative evangelicals in 1920 founded the Christian Alliance of Women and Girls. The key adviser in the referendum process was a clergyman named D. H. C. Bartlett, who had spent nearly twenty-five years in Liverpool before coming to St. Luke's, Hampstead, in London, in 1918, in order to help his fellow conservative evangelicals in conflicts that he saw emerging.

The next schism took place within the greatest of all the Evangelical Anglican organizations—the Church Missionary Society. The first occurred in 1922, when Bartlett presented a resolution to the CMS executive board very much in Waller's terms concerning Scripture, asking that no missionaries, teachers, or officials be appointed "who do not thus wholeheartedly believe and teach."[47] When the majority of the board refused to instigate such a policy, the Bible Churchmen's Missionary Society was formed, as another voluntary society within the Church of England. In addition to its active missionary program, it founded Tyndale Hall in Bristol. While first designed to provide theological training for missionary candidates, it soon became a training college for parish clergy. Famous for the high Calvinism of its second principal, W. Dodgson Sykes, Tyndale sustained in some ways a similar relationship to British conservative evangelicalism as the confessional, Calvinist Westminster Seminary, Philadelphia, did to American fundamentalism.

Concerns with the CMS were not settled, and in 1926 a second schism took place with the formation of the Ruanda General and Medical Mission as a separate auxiliary of the CMS. The officials of the Ruanda Mission expressed satisfaction "that they have received from C.M.S. full guarantee to safeguard the future of the R.G.M.M. in Bible, Protestant and Keswick lines."[48] One of its first missionaries was Dr. Joe Church, who was supported by CICCU and who became one of the fathers of the great East African revival. On his arrival, someone alluding to the tensions in CMS urged Church not to take sides. "His reply," stated Patricia St. John, "was the result of those uncompromising CICCU years: 'There is only one side.' "[49]

In dealing with British controversies, a few lines must be given to the

Prayer Book controversy, a uniquely Anglican disputation. The leadership of the Church of England, and the church in its counsels, had voted for a revised Book of Common Prayer. In response, the conservative evangelicals mounted a powerful campaign in Parliament in 1927 and 1928, supported by many liberal evangelicals and touching the often inarticulate but inherent Protestantism of many English people. In this contest the conservative evangelicals were successful.[50] But it was a Pyrrhic victory, akin to that of the evolution crusade led by William Jennings Bryan in the courts of Tennessee. As in each of their controversies from 1900 to 1939, the British conservative evangelicals received a bad press, being depicted "as mere obstructionists and obscurantists" but consoling themselves that they were upholding basic Christianity.[51]

A final word should be said about conservative evangelicals and movements of revival. The great evangelical awakenings of the eighteenth and nineteenth centuries were now a thing of the past. Revivals in Britain, as in the rest of the Western world, tended to occur in ethnic or regional subcultures where social upheaval existed and where evangelicalism was still the dominant form of Protestantism. Such a movement occurred in Wales during the first decade of this century. It exhibited a conservative evangelical ethos, but the ongoing influence of the Welsh revival declined so rapidly during and immediately after World War I that only small pockets of conservative evangelicalism remained. On a much smaller scale the 1920s saw localized revivals on the Island of Lewis and along the Moray Firth in northern Scotland, as well as in Suffolk in England's rural East Anglia. But the one profoundly important revival occured in Ulster. Amid the troubles that accompanied the dismemberment of Ireland, around 1920 appeared the Irish Presbyterian evangelist W. P. Nicholson.[52]

Few people combined British conservative evangelicalism and American fundamentalism more completely than did Nicholson. In many ways he was an Irish Billy Sunday, a sailor instead of a ballplayer, a man of the people with remarkable histrionic gifts. Trained at the Bible Training Institute in Glasgow, he worked with Chapman and Alexander in evangelism for a couple of years, based himself in Carlisle, Pennsylvania, during World War I, and served at the Bible institute of Los Angeles from 1918 to 1920. Upon returning to Protestant Ulster, "his impassioned oratory . . . swept the Irish working classes into religious revival."[53] And its effect lasted. Whatever might have been the theology presented from the pulpits, a great body of the Irish Presbyterian laity were unswerving in their conservative evangelicalism, and if they migrated to North America, as many of them did, they often took their place in the ranks of fundamentalism.

After examining these British-American connections, we are now in a position to examine Canadian fundamentalism, as it was commonly called, between 1900 and 1939, and its wider relationships with similar movements. Accepted wisdom would simply affirm that Canadian fundamentalism was American fundamentalism transported.[54] The reality, however, was that most of Canada's urban fundamentalist leaders of prominence were British, or had been raised in Christian bodies of singularly British orientation. There is no doubt that these leaders knew American fundamentalism, had contact with it, and welcomed American funadmentalist leaders to Canada; their heritage as Christians, however, was overwhelmingly British. British conservative evangelicalism was so like fundamentalism that when its adherents migrated to Canada, they were almost automatically part of the North American movement. It was the strength of their conservative evangelicalism that targeted them for leadership among Canada's fundamentalists.

The place to begin is Toronto, which had by far the largest English-speaking urban population in Canada and which was viewed as one of the great Protestant cities of the world. Inevitably also we must highlight T. T. Shields of Jarvis Street Baptist Church,[55] superlative biblical and theological preacher, congregational dictator, divider of the Baptist Convention of Ontario and Quebec, leader of the new Union of Regular Baptist Churches, part of the troika with W. B. Riley of Minneapolis and Frank Norris of Texas that ran the North American Baptist Bible Union, and controversialist extraordinary. And in it all a Britisher of the Britishers. It is hard to conceive a greater insult to Shields than to call him an American anything, including an American fundamentalist. His whole ministry was patterned after that of C. H. Spurgeon, including his conflicts, although in this department he far outshone his mentor. But there were other Baptist fundamentalists in Ontario who broke with the convention but did not follow Shields.

This other strain of fundamentalist Baptists did not follow Shields because he was too strict a Baptist and because he had little or no interest in fundamentalist eschatology and interdenominationalism. This group was led by John Linton, a Scot from Edinburgh, who called its thriving work the Fellowship of Independent Baptist Churches.[56]

In Toronto the congregation that was something of a cathedral for funadmentalists was Knox, the oldest Presbyterian congregation in the city.[57] During the heyday of fundamentalism its successive pastors were two Scots. The first was Alexander Brown Winchester from Aberdeen, a great Bible teacher. Upon his retirement he became a regular speaker for some years upon the Bible Conference circuit in the States and Canada, which was an integral component of fundamentalism. A consistent dispensationalist, Winchester opened the doors of the church to an endless series of prophetic Bible conferences and welcomed famous fundamentalist preachers from R. A. Torrey to Christabel Pankhurst.[58] The second minister was John Gibson Inkster, who hailed from Scotland's Orkney Islands and carried on a ministry that deviated little from the lines laid down by his predecessor.

Another famous Toronto fundamentalist during this period was R. V. Bingham, founder of the Sudan Interior Mission.[59] An able fundamentalist entrepreneur, he also edited the *Evangelical Christian,* developed the Evangelical Publishers and its bookstores, started Canadian Keswick, founded the Soldiers' and Airmen's Christian Association, and had a hand in founding the Inter-Varsity Fellowship in Canada.[60] An Englishman from Kent, like many Canadian fundamentalists, Bingham was converted in the Salvation Army, serving with them for a time both in England and Canada. Through his constant missionary travels he retained strong links with the United Kingdom, establishing a Sudan Interior Missions headquarters in Liverpool as well as Toronto, attending Keswick whenever possible, and drawing round him a number of British associates.

Yet another well-known Toronto fundamentalist from Britain was W. H. Griffith Thomas. Although in Canada only from 1910 to 1919 while teaching at the Evangelical Anglican Wycliffe College, he immediately assumed a position of prominence among fundamentalists. He revived the Bible League of Canada in 1913, taught regularly at Toronto Bible College, and became intimately involved with Bingham and his enterprises.[61]

Just to the west of Toronto lies the major steel-producing city of Hamilton, where the outstanding fundamentalist figure was P. W. Philpott.[62] Born in southwestern Ontario, he was converted through the Salvation Army in its early years, when it was an entirely British movement. He founded the Gospel Tabernacle in Hamilton and from 1896 through 1922 pastored a flourishing congregation that was filled with Scottish steelworkers. Out of this congregation grew one of the few indigenous Canadian denominations, the Associated Gospel Churches.[63] From Hamilton, Philpott went to the Moody Memorial Church in Chicago, and from there to the Church of the Open Door in Los Angeles. Contrary, however, to normal expectations in such situations, Philpott returned to Canada, working with Oswald J. Smith, and so demonstrated a strong sense of Canadian or British-Canadian identity.

West of Toronto and Hamilton, the only major urban center on the prairies before World War II was Winnipeg. Here the fundamentalist center was an Independent congregation known as Elim Chapel, founded in 1910. The kindly John Bellingham, from Ballymena in Northern Ireland, was the pastor, but because of the British mission-hall pattern with which the Elim people were familiar, he was called the superintendent. The real power in the congregation, however, was exercised by S. T. Smith, the multimillionaire president of the Reliance Grain Company.[64] He was brought up among the Brethren in London, Ontario, which was as close to being raised in a British atmosphere as it could be. Smith had a meteoric rise in American fundamentalism, being the only Canadian on the board of Moody Bible Institute, the first Canadian on the board of Dallas Seminary, a member of the executive board of the Central American Mission, and almost the only nonlocal director of Pennsylvania's Montrose Bible Conference. He was president of the World's Christian Fundamentalist Association in 1925,[65] and he was responsible for bringing its annual gathering to Toronto in 1926.[66]

On the West Coast the fundamentalist leaders were all British. The Englishman Walter Ellis, a scholarly Old Testament expert with a master's degree in Semitics from the University of Toronto, was first principal of the Vancouver Bible Institute from 1917 until his death in 1944, and for the last eighteen years of his life was also minister of Fairview Presbyterian Church, Vancouver.[67] As a reserved Briton, Ellis had great difficulty with the other leader of Vancouver fundamentalism, the strident and volatile William Robertson. Yet in fact Robertson was as British as Ellis, although from Glasgow.[68] Having developed his platform skills as a socialist open-air speaker, Robertson after his conversion attended the Bible Training Institute. He then became an itinerant evangelist and then pastor of Toxteth Baptist Tabernacle in Liverpool from 1919, which he took out of the Baptist Union. His ministry was obviously appreciated in that unique city, if we are to give any credence to the letter he brought with him to North America in 1926, signed by F. Martyn Cundy, the Anglican secretary of the Fundamentals Fellowship of Liverpool and District.[69] Robertson had at least one prior contact with Canada, when he warned T. T. Shields that L. H. Marshall, who was coming to teach theology for the Baptists at Ontario's McMaster University, was not a conservative evangelical. In order to maintain his British identity, Robertson, like Shields, patterned his ministry after Spurgeon, and so called his Vancouver congregation the Metropolitan Tabernacle. This church was heavily British, having the distinction of a very sizable contingent from the Island of Lewis in Scotland's Outer Hebrides.

In the other West Coast city of Victoria, the most conspicuous fundamentalist was J. B. Rowell, pastor of Central Baptist Church.[70] Raised a Strict Baptist in England, he had been a Wyckliffe preacher for John Kensit's Protestant Truth Society. With a group of British Columbia pastors, he left the Baptist Union of Western Canada in 1927 over the theology taught at Brandon College in Manitoba. While pastoring in Victoria, his ministry was much appreciated in American Bible conferences.[71] Representing probably the most conservative of fundamentalist denominations in British Columbia, Rowell's group, the Regular Baptist Convention of B.C., was also the most British, with over one-third of its pastors from 1927 through 1955 being British; during the same period only 6 percent came from the United States.[72]

In a word, Canadian fundamentalism, though often regarded as an extension of influences from the United States, was thoroughly British in both origin and emphases.

Finally, we conclude by examining briefly the direct contribution from Britain to American fundamentalism, as well as the contributions to American fundamentalism made by Britishers who came via Canada or who were British-oriented Canadians. At the outset it is important to note that clergymen of the Church of England rarely were part of this contribution. The overwhelmingly High Church character of American Episcopalianism did not make it attractive to English conservative Evangelical Anglicans, and there were few points of contact between conservative Anglicans and American Episcopalians. Thus the main body of British conservative evangelicals were largely excluded from American fundamentalism. Despite this fact, the links were strong.

Two representative institutions within American fundamentalism show the strength of this relationship—the Moody complex in Chicago and Dallas Theological Seminary. The Moody establishment had a powerful British connection stretching back into the nineteenth century. What is important to notice, however, is that this contact remained far into the twentieth century, even after World War I and right through to 1939. Each summer, for example, a British guest speaker was on the program of the Bible conferences sponsored by the

Moody Bible Institute in different parts of the United States.[73] In 1917 two Britishers domiciled in North America were on the circuit. One was Joseph W. Kemp, formerly of Charlotte Chapel, Edinburgh, now at Calvary Baptist Church, New York City, and the other was R. V. Bingham of Toronto. In 1918 it was hoped that J. Stuart Holden would be able to be present, but it was not until later in the twenties that he could arrive. Holden was a conservative Evangelical Anglican leader, vicar of Griffith Thomas's former congregation, St. Paul's, Portman Square, London, and chairman of the Keswick Council.[74]

During the 1920s the pattern continued. There was Gordon Watt, a Church of Scotland minister from Aberdeen. Then there was John McNeill, a Scottish minister and evangelist who had been at Cooke's Presbyterian, Toronto, and was now Donald Barnhouse's predecessor at Tenth Presbyterian, Philadelphia. Canon F. E. Howitt of St. George's Anglican, Hamilton, Ontario, was present in 1926, while the famous English Baptist F. B. Meyer was involved in 1927. John MacBeath—Glasgow native, London Baptist pastor, and Keswick speaker—took part in 1928.

The 1930s began with Captain Reginald Wallis of the Dublin, Ireland, YMCA. In 1932 Archibald Wright, an Ulster Presbyterian, was on the platform, and in 1936 it was George Douglas, a Scottish Baptist pastoring in Cardiff, Wales. The year 1937 was the Moody centenary, and in the special services held across North America, the distinguished speakers were Bishop Taylor Smith and Jock Troop, a Scottish evangelist long associated with Glasgow's Tent Hall. In 1939 Moody sponsored the International Prophetic Conference in New York City, where the speakers included George Douglas of Wales, Christie Innis of Knox Presbyterian, Toronto, who had recently arrived from Scotland and within a few years would be pastoring in the United States, and the Scottish R. G. Turnbull, who had been a minster in Blackpool, England, and was on his way to the pastorate of Elim Chapel, Winnipeg, which he would then leave for Presbyterian ministries in Pittsburgh and Mark Matthew's old congregation in Seattle.

During the interwar period, members of the permanent Moody Bible Institute Extension staff, who continually traveled the North American continent, included many Britishers. There was Herbert Lockyer, who had been a pastor in Bradford in Yorkshire. Lockyer was joined by Leonard Sale-Harrison, a leading Baptist pastor from Sydney, Australia, and more English than the English. Alexander Stewart, a former miner from Scotland, came via Canada. John Page was an Englishman, and John Thompson, originally from Australia, had been superintendent of the Scottish Evangelization Society.

The second fundamentalist center with extensive British ties is Dallas Theological Seminary, known in its early days as the Evangelical Theological College. While links between the Moody institutions and Britain might be expected, although perhaps not with such strength, Dallas might seem to an outsider to be quintessentially and imperviously American. But such was not the case. There was a British connection, and a very important one indeed. The three founders were Lewis Sperry Chafer, A. B. Winchester of Knox Presbyterian, Toronto, and Griffith Thomas, who in 1919 had left Toronto and settled in Philadelphia.[75] The original plan was to establish two seminaries, with Griffith Thomas as one of the principals. When a single institution was decided on, it was hoped that he would become professor of theology.[76]

Dallas was based upon the model of Bible exposition as practiced in the Bible conferences. This model had its origin in what was known as the Brethren Bible Reading, itself a reaction against topical preaching, which involved a minute dissection of the words and phrases of the text in sequence, within a strong dispensational theological framework. In this connection many "Bible teachers," as they were called, were invited to Dallas for a period of teaching each year, and among these was A. B. Winchester, who come from Scotland via Toronto. Harold St. John, a well-known English Brethren Bible teacher, was sought as a full-time faculty member in this department in 1928.[77]

On the financial side, it is unlikely that Dallas Seminary would have survived its early years without the munificent interest of William Nairn of Dundee, Scotland. He was a successful businessman who, like so many influenced by Moody, poured his life into mission work among the poor. Within the network of the mission halls he met Chafer, and on the latter's trip to Britain in 1924, he committed himself to pay Chafer's salary for several years. He also purchased Griffith Thomas's library for £5,000 and donated it to Dallas.[78]

Thus the interwar period was not a time, as some have surmised, of the collapse of the transatlantic evangelical alliance. If there was a breakdown, it was in the number who shifted to liberal evangelicalism or modernism. But the remnant in Britain and America, call them what we will—conservative evangelicals or fundamentalists—retained their transoceanic contacts. As a result, this alliance did not have to be rebuilt after World War II. Or at least, it did not need rebuilding on a popular level, whatever gaps may have grown up between Britain and American in academic theology. If Carl Henry did have to do pioneering work after the war in drawing together conservative evangelical intellectuals from Britain and the United States,[79] the story was quite different on the level of evangelism, popular Bible teaching, and missions. Youth for Christ evangelists, especially Billy Graham, were only following well-worn paths when they visited Britain and exerted an influence. The only difficulty such American travelers had to face was an ironic one. In the United States, Episcopalians had little interest in the work of the postwar neo-evangelicals. but in Britain—and so repeating the pattern that we have seen extending back deep into the nineteenth century—many of their most ardent sympathizers were Anglicans. In the person of Billy Graham, Britain's conservative evangelicals were not receiving a fresh import from America so much as they were garnering yet one more dividend from theological investments they had been making in the United States and Canada for over a century.

Notes

1. D. W. Bebbington, *Evangelicalism in Modern Britain: A History from the 1730s to the 1980s* (London: Unwin Hyman, 1989), 75–104, 135–37.

2. A. L. Drummond, *Edward Irving and His Circle* (London: James Clarke, [1937]).

3. H. H. Rowdon, *The Origins of the Brethren, 1825–1850* (London: Pickering and Inglis, 1967).

4. W. J. Conybeare, "Church Parties", in *Essays Ecclesiastical and Social* (London: Longmans, 1859), 50–67.

5. E. Stock, *The History of the Church Missionary Society* (London: CMS, 1899), 1:374.

6. L. Elliott-Binns, *Religion in the Victorian Era* (London: Lutterworth, 1936), 68.

7. K. Hylson-Smith, *Evangelicals in the Church of England, 1734–1984* (Edinburgh: T. and T. Clark, 1987), 137.

8. Ibid., 128–29.

9. P. B. Morgan, "A Study of the Work of Four American Evangelists in Britain from 1873 to 1905, and of the Effect upon Organized Christianity of Their Work There" (B.Litt. thesis, Oxford University, 1958).

10. S. H. Frodsham, *Smith Wigglesworth: Apostle of Faith* (Springfield, Mo.: Gospel Publishing House, 1974). The pilgrimage of the "Bradford Plumber" is almost a mission-hall classic. He traveled out of Methodism into creative contact with the Salvation Army and the Brethren, into mission hall ministry, then into the healing movement, and finally pentecostalism and a worldwide ministry.

11. Bebbington, *Evangelicalism in Modern Britain,* 145–46.

12. J. Carson, *God's River in Spate* (Belfast: Presbyterian Publications, 1959).

13. D. W. Bebbington, "Baptists and Fundamentalism in Inter-War Britain," in *Protestant Evangelicalism,* ed. K. Robbins (Oxford: Blackwell, 1990), 297–325.

14. Hylson-Smith, *Evangelicals in the Church of England,* 232; J. C. Pollock, *The Keswick Story* (London: Hodder and Stoughton, 1964), 152.

15. R. Manwaring, *From Controversy to Co-Existence: Evangelicals in the Church of England, 1914–1980* (Cambridge: Cambridge University Press, 1985), ix; Pollock, *Keswick Story,* 150.

16. Manwaring, *From Controversy to Co-Existence,* 4.

17. *Evangelical Christian* (1924), 446.

18. D. F. Wright, "Soudings in the Doctrine of Scripture in British Evangelicalism in the First Half of the Twentieth Century," *Tyndale Bulletin* 13 (1980): 87–106.

19. Waller, *Inspiration* (Greensboro, NC: Rainbow Publications, 1973), 30.

20. D. Johnson, *Contending for the Faith: A History of the Evangelical Movement in the Universities and Colleges* (Leicester: InterVarsity Press, 1979), 110.

21. W. H. Griffith Thomas, *The Principles of Theology: An Introduction to the Thirty-Nine Articles* (1930; reprint, London: Church Book Room Press, 1945), 118.

22. T. C. Hammond, *In Understanding Be Men* (1936; reprint, Chicago: IVCF, 1948), 36.

23. Bebbington, *Evangelicalism in Modern Britain,* 188, 189.

24. Ibid., 192.

25. W. B. Sloan, *These Sixty Years: The Story of the Keswick Convention* (London: Pickering and Inglis, 1935), 69–70.

26. Moody Bible Institute began Swedish-English courses in 1916, which lasted until 1933 (G. A. Getz, *MBI: The Story of Moody Bible Institute* [Chicago: Moody, 1969], 100–101). The graduates and faculty in the late 1930s indicate that some 40 percent shared this ethnic origin (*The Arch: Year Book of the Moody Bible Institute of Chicago* [1938, 1939]).

27. Sloan, *These Sixty Years,* 69, 71, 83.

28. J. D. Hannah, "The Social and Intellectual History of the Origins of the Evangelical Theological College" (Ph.D. diss., University of Texas at Dallas, 1988), 143.

29. Sloan, *These Sixty Years,* 91.

30. R. G. Flood, *The Story of Moody Church* (Chicago: Moody, 1985), 28.

31. E. Schuyler English, *H. A. Ironside: Ordained of the Lord* (New York: Loizeaux, 1956), 227–28.

32. Flood, *Story of Moody Church,* 31.

33. D. G. Robert, "The Crisis of Missions: Premillennial Mission Theory and the Origin of Independent Evangelical Missions," in *Earthen Vessels: American Evangelicals and Foreign Missions, 1880–1980,* ed. J. A. Carpenter and W. R. Shenk (Grand Rapids: Eerdmans, 1990), 29–46.

34. A. J. Austin, "Blessed Adversity: Henry W. Frost and the China Inland Mission," in *Earthen Vessels,* ed. Carpenter and Shenk, 48.

35. Bebbington, "Baptists and Fundamentalism," 297–325.

36. Morgan, "Work of Four American Evangelists," 661–62.

37. Ibid., 589–90.

38. Ibid., 682.

39. Pollock, *Keswick Story,* 131.

40. F. D. Coggan, *Christ and the Colleges: A History of the InterVarsity Fellowship of Evangelical Unions* (London: IVFEU, 1934), 16.

41. J. C. Pollock, *A Cambridge Movement* (London: John Murray, 1953), 180, 181.

42. Johnson, *Contending for the Faith,* 16.

43. Pollock, *Cambridge Movement,* 233–34.

44. M. Pawley, *Donald Coggan: Servant of Christ* (London: SPCK, 1987), 78.

45. Johnson, *Contending for the Faith,* 344.

46. *Why? A Statement of the Origin of the Christian Alliance of Women and Girls* (London: n.p., 1947).

47. G. W. Bromiley, *Daniel Henry Charles Bartlett, M.A., D.D.* (Burnham-on-Sea: Dr. Bartlett's Executors, 1959), 28.

48. P. St. John, *Breath of Life: The Story of the Ruanda Mission* (London: Norfolk Press, 1971), 55.

49. Ibid., 61.

50. Manwaring, *From Controversy to Co-existence,* 30–38.

51. Hylson-Smith, *Evangelicals in the Church of England,* 235.

52. S. W. Murray, *W. P. Nicholson, Flame for God in Ulster* (Belfast: Presbyterian Fellowship, 1973).

53. Pollock, *Cambridge Movement,* 217–18.

54. R. K. Burkinshaw, "The American Influence upon Canadian Evangelicalism: Greater Vancouver as a Test Case, 1920–1980" (B.A. essay, University of British Columbia, History Department, 1980), 4–12.

55. L. Tarr, *Shields of Canada: T. T. Shields (1873–1955)* (Grand Rapids: Baker, 1967); D. R. Elliott, "Studies of Eight Canadian Fundamentalists" (Ph.D. diss., University of British Columbia, 1989), 138–69.

56. B. A. McKenzie, "Fundamentalism, Christian Unity, and Premillennialism in the Thought of Rowland Victor Bingham (1872–1942): A Study of Anti-Modernism in Canada" (Ph.D. diss., Toronto School of Theology, 1985), 217–18.

57. W. Fitch, *Knox Church, Toronto: Avant Garde, Evangelicial, Advancing* (Toronto: Deyell, 1971).

58. D. Mitchell, *The Fighting Pankhursts: A Study in Tenacity* (London: Jonathan Cape, 1967), 146.

59. McKenzie, "Fundamentalism, Christian Unity, and Premillennialism"; J. H. Hunter, *A Flame of Fire: The Life and Work of R. V. Bingham, D.D.* (Toronto: Sudan Interior Mission, 1961).

60. H. Guinness, *Journey among Students* (Sydney: Anglican Information Office, 1978), 47.

61. McKenzie, "Fundamentalism, Christian Unity, and Premillennialism," 55–56, 111–12.

62. S. D. Clark, *Church and Sect in Canada* (Toronto: University of Toronto Press, 1948), 427, 428.

63. T. Peake, "Fifty Years of Gospel Witness: The Story of the Associated Gospel Churches of Canada, 1920–1970" (Graduate history essay, Bob Jones University, 1970).

64. T. Howison, "Elim Chapel and Sidney T. Smith: A Case Study in Canadian Fundamentalism" (History seminar essay, Regent College, 1979).

65. Hannah, "Origins of the Evangelical Theological College," 131, 222, 234.

66. W. V. Trollinger, Jr., *God's Empire: William Bell Riley and Midwestern Fundamentalism* (Madison: University of Wisconsin Press, 1990), 42.

67. R. K. Burkinshaw, "Strangers and Pilgrims in Lotus Land: Conservative Protestantism in British Columbia, 1917–1981" (Ph.D. diss., University of British Columbia, 1988), 108–9.

68. Ibid., 185–86.

69. 19 June 1926, in possession of the author. The letter speaks of Robertson's "earnest, clear and learned exposition of the Faith and his equally forceful and plain exposure of the attack that is being made today against 'the Faith once for all delivered to the Saints.' "

70. G. Eno, *Courageous for Christ* (Victoria: G. Eno, 1989).

71. Ibid., 133–40.

72. Burkinshaw, "American Influence," 47.

73. "Extension Ministry" Files, Moody Bible Institute Archives.

74. Pollock, *Keswick Story,* 145–49.

75. Hannah, "Origins of the Evangelical Theological College," 8.

76. Ibid., 154.

77. Ibid., 202, 203.

78. Ibid., 163–64, 227.

79. On Henry's transatlantic efforts, see Mark A. Noll, *Between Faith and Criticism: Evangelicals, Scholarship, and the Bible in America,* rev. ed. (Grand Rapids: Baker, 1991), 124, 140.

17

Transatlantic Currents in
North Atlantic Pentecostalism

EDITH L. BLUMHOFER

Like other forms of evangelicalism, pentecostalism has been transatlantic from the start. From 1906, the widely heralded report of the outpouring of the Holy Spirit at Azusa Street in Los Angeles influenced people around the world. But the Azusa Street context had been shaped in part by the Welsh revival and was nurtured through an understanding of "the times" that had been encouraged by popular interpretations of the Welsh revival. Word of the emergence of pentecostalism traveled through well-established transatlantic networks.[1] Through the decades since, pentecostal currents in the American church have deeply influenced the life of Christian communions in Canada and England. But those cultures have also spawned their own variations on the pentecostal theme, influenced the American church, and contributed to the vast array of options that flourish under the umbrella of pentecostalism today.

Contemporary pentecostalism comes in a bewildering variety of packagings: classical, charismatic, non-Trinitarian, Catholic, Protestant, holiness, baptistic, ethnic, denominational, indigenous, to name but a few. By any count, the number of pentecostals in the world is staggering. At the dawn of this century, there were none. By some counts, today nearly four hundred million Christians worldwide—some 25 percent of the total number of Christians counted by the Southern Baptist Convention's statistician, David Barrett—identify with Pentecostalism.[2] In some form—and with varying degrees of success—pentecostalism has engaged every Christian communion. The hundreds of millions of people who have found empowerment, identity, and meaning in this twentieth-century renewal attest both to its remarkable appeal and to its ability to accommodate and adapt to widely different cultural realities.

Twenty years ago, most church historians knew very little about pentecostals. That has changed, and at least the outlines of the story of pentecostalism's humble beginnings are now common knowledge. Historians of pentecostalism have charted the movement's course from Kansas to Texas to California, where between 1906 and 1908 a mission on Azusa Street in a nondescript neighborhood in downtown Los Angeles facilitated pentecostalism's transformation from regional sect to international presence.[3]

That transformation was intentional. As people who regarded themselves as signs of an end-times revival, early pentecostals set out to make their presence known in a burst of intense, focused evangelistic activity.[4] On the masthead of the first issue of the *Apostolic Faith,* a magazine issued from Azusa Street in 1906, stood the injunction: "Earnestly contend for the faith which was once delivered unto the saints." This Bible verse summed it up very well indeed. Pentecostals believed they had recovered "the faith once delivered"; they were intensely earnest about it, and they contended with such zeal that they often became contentious. Although they were counting on Christ's imminent return, they did set out to penetrate the church worldwide and to empower it to accomplish expeditiously its task of evangelizing the world. For them, proclaiming the gospel in every nation was not simply fulfilling the Great Commission; the compulsion to evangelize gained its momentum from their fundamental identity as "end-times people." As one put it, they were "God's little messengers, distributing invitations to the Marriage Supper of the Lamb."[5] They were persuaded of two things: proclaiming the gospel in every nation would facilitate Christ's return, and "Nothing less than the whole Gospel of Jesus Christ will suffice in these last days."[6] They emphasized "whole" in a proprietary sense, and so their parish embraced the world, and their gospel was for both Christians and non-Christians.

Although the convictions about the imminence of the end that sustained early pentecostal fervor have waned, pentecostals—often in spite of themselves—have accomplished a "pentecostalization" of significant parts of the church. Since David Barrett released the first edition of his monumental *World's Christian Encyclopedia* in 1982, pentecostals have pointed with pride to his statistics that chart their rapid rise.[7] Although numbers are always problematic, even casual observers of the world scene must acknowledge the extent and visibility of this twentieth-century phenomenon. In some areas of the world, notably Latin America, parts of Africa, and Korea, pentecostalism today seems virtually uncontainable.[8] It is thriving in places as diverse as Brazil, Nigeria, and Romania, growing in the former Soviet Union, and by some reports, it is the predominant expression of Christianity in China. Some suggest that fully 60 to 75 percent of those swelling the ranks of Latin American Protestantism are pentecostal.[9]

Part of the reason is clearly rooted in pentecostalism's populist character. It both mirrors and responds to the deepest longings of common people. It has been remarkably successful in offering spiritual, social, and economic succor to marginalized people in cultural transition. Another part is certainly the compatibility of pentecostals' emphasis on the Holy Spirit with themes and practices deeply rooted in indigenous religions.

Since it burst into the public consciousness in 1906, then, pentecostalism has relentlessly expanded until its sheer size and its stubborn refusal to go away have made it a force with which others must reckon. It seems to be everywhere, and in some places its presence both transforms other forms of

Christianity and determines the larger Christian agenda. In other places, however, especially in the North Atlantic, classical pentecostalism's story has been strikingly different. In parts of Europe where its history reaches back more than eighty years, pentecostal denominations are perhaps as remarkable for their lack of presence as they are for their visibility elsewhere.

Historians of pentecostalism agree that the movement spread from the United States to other parts of the world through both written reports and the efforts of missionaries and itinerant evangelists. Transatlantic currents both molded the context in which American pentecostalism was born and shaped the channels through which it mediated its influence around the world.

Among the specific events that inclined some turn-of-the-century evangelicals toward pentecostalism, two can serve to illumine the transatlantic connections: R. A. Torrey's world evangelistic tour and the Welsh revival. Torrey's tour helped link those who believed revival was coming. This well-known American evangelist, on whom some thought Moody's mantle had fallen, both fostered and thrived on the notion that the world stood on the threshold of an end-times revival that would defy description. In 1902, with his new song leader Charles Alexander, Torrey presided over revival meetings in Australia that caught the attention of much of the Protestant world. Australia was the first stop on a dramatic, three-year world tour that Torrey was fond of linking to three prior years of Saturday-night prayer meetings at Chicago's Moody Memorial Church. In fact, he was one of a large group of evangelicals on both sides of the North Atlantic who had signed a covenant to pray for revival. Their longings were couched in what later became pentecostal jargon: they prayed for a worldwide "outpouring of the Holy Ghost." When the invitation to Australia came, Torrey opted to regard it as an answer to prayer.[10] From Australia, he and Alexander traveled to India, then on to Britain, where their meetings attracted larger crowds than had Moody's notable services a decade earlier. By 1905, they claimed some 100,000 converts on what they billed as "a revival journey . . . entirely unprecedented in the history of the Christian Church. . . . And it is all the more remarkable when it is considered that it came about suddenly, and entirely in answer to prayer. It is a sheer romance of faith in God. It is a modern addition to those wonders wrought by faith recorded in the eleventh chapter of Hebrews."[11]

At least by the time they reached England, Torrey and Alexander were caught up in the romance. In their own minds, they were no longer ordinary evangelists but agents in an event of enormous and historic import into which the meaning of the past and anticipations for the future would be compacted, promoters of a worldwide revival. It had begun in a prayer meeting in Chicago, had broken out first in Australia, had been kindled gradually in England, and then had burst into flame in Wales. Burning with bright intensity, they were confident, the fire would engulf the world and prepare it for Christ's cataclysmic return. Everywhere they went, they used "the Glory Song" to turn people's longings heavenward. It became perhaps evangelicals' best-loved song of the era:

> When all my labors and trials are o'er,
> And I am safe on that beautiful shore,
> Just to be near the dear Lord I adore
> Will through the ages be glory for me![12]

Evangelicals had no trouble perceiving responsiveness to the Torrey-Alexander campaign as an indicator of vast spiritual hunger. Their meetings relied on the familiar—singing, preaching, praying, and response cards. The Welsh revival was of another character entirely. Despite their recent triumphs, even Torrey and Alexander opted not to interrupt its momentum, engaging only in a brief visit to Cardiff.

Probably no single event quickened expectations for revival worldwide more than did events in Wales during 1904 and 1905.[13] Both the secular and religious press followed the story. The list of journalists and religious leaders who visited Wales was impressive indeed. Evangelicals with well-established reputations in the Bible conference circuit and in those evangelical subcultures long fascinated by language of baptism with the Holy Spirit journeyed to Wales and published their reflections for an eager public. Perhaps the most influential of these for North America came from G. Campbell Morgan and F. B. Meyer. They used the plain language of common people to venture large claims about the revival's true meaning. Both told huge followings on this side of the Atlantic that the Welsh revival was God's indictment of the contemporary church. He had disdained planning and programs and had superseded modern methods with a monumental stirring that was "Pentecost continued, without a single moment's doubt."[14] Morgan noted its apparent disorderliness with the observation that it was, nonetheless, "characterised from the first to the last by the orderliness of the Spirit of God."[15]

The Welsh revival popularized dispensational and experiential language already common in some evangelical circles. It directly challenged people to "obey" the Holy Spirit, and it modeled obedience in unusual ways. Obeying might mean standing in a crowded congregation and confessing a sin; it might mean leading out in a song or making amends for a long-passed offense. In the overwhelming majority of instances, obedience was personal and individualistic rather than communal or social. It dealt with personal behavior and guilt, not with society's inequities.[16]

The Welsh revival gave specific, experiential connotations to language that became common among pentecostals, and its leaders explained it as an end-times Pentecost, the promised "latter rain."[17] None could predict where revival fervor would next erupt; spontaneous testimony, singing, and prayer replaced the promotion, scheduling, preaching, and financial planning that were generally expected when evangelicals thought about revival and about the cost per soul of those who walked the sawdust trail.

This religious tumult, then, kindled deep longings within evangelical hearts around the world. If out-of-the-way Wales could experience dramatic divine visitations, why not New York, Chicago, and Los Angeles? Or why not other, less-well-known communities around the world? Surely few places were less significant to most American minds than the mining towns of Wales. If the end-times Pentecost had come, it would certainly be uncontainable; in short order, it would transform the world if those who understood its true meaning only helped it realize its full potential.

In fact, a prayer circle that focused popular longing for renewal reached around the globe, and it was strengthened by both the religious press and the transatlantic networks that featured the same devotional speakers and authors on both sides of the Atlantic. The language of Keswick, the idiom of the American holiness movement, and the rhetoric of pietism combined with the direct appeals of revivalistic evangelicalism to convince people around the world that prayer for revival was the only tenable solution to the considerable social and political upheaval of the times. In anticipation, they encouraged one another with songs that kindled hope and captured yearning, such as the following:

> Lord, I hear of showers of blessing
> Thou art scattering, full and free;
> Showers, the thirsty hearts refreshing,
> Let some drops now fall on me.[18]

The conspicuous lack of organization, publicity, and control; the predominance of singing, testimony, and spontaneous and emotion-packed prayer rather than of preaching; the conviction among some that an end-times revival was eschatologically due; and the apparently inexplicable course of the Welsh revival—both its ebb and flow—seemed to indicate its dispensational significance. The Welsh revival seemed unique, and to those intent on Christ's physical return, it could readily be construed to indicate the beginning of the end. Such people saw it as the end-times Pentecost, divinely inaugurated to baptize the church with the Holy Spirit and to prepare the world for Christ's return.[19] Reports from Wales greatly heartened prayer groups in Los Angeles whose members hoped to recover New Testament Christianity. And when the Azusa Street mission opened in April 1906, some of them saw this "cradle of American Pentecostalism" as the extension of the Welsh revival.

If events in Wales both sparked and sustained a spiritual hunger among American evangelicals, they also deeply influenced some in Britain who impatiently waited for the revival to move beyond Wales. Among these was Alexander Boddy, the vicar of All Saints' Church, Sunderland, who visited Wales and returned to his parish craving similar fervor. "Fight heaven down," Evan Roberts, a leader in the Welsh revival told him. "Bring it down now and here. Fight it down."[20] Attempting to follow that advice, Boddy inaugurated an ambitious schedule of prayer and evangelism and noted that "good breezes from Wales" seemed to "fan into flame" any who were willing. Two years of united midnight marches, prayer meetings, and "hearts aglow" in his Anglican parish failed to satisfy this determined vicar, however. They verged on an elusive something that had not yet come. They were "preparation for a greater work."[21]

Also prodded by the Welsh revival to anticipate general renewal was

Thomas Barratt, an Englishman transplanted to Norway, where he supervised a Methodist city mission. Barratt spent most of 1906 touring the United States to raise funds for his Norwegian work, but in the course of his travels, he discovered everywhere people who shared his almost overpowering yearning for religious experience. In New York in September, he read in the religious press about revival at the Apostolic Faith Mission at Azusa Street in Los Angeles. He thought he noted a striking resemblance to his own pursuit of personal holiness and spiritual power, so he wrote to the Azusa Street mission, asking for prayer that he would "receive his pentecost." Some six weeks later, still in New York, Barratt had an intense experience, lasting several hours, during which he spoke in tongues.[22] Returning to Norway, he immediately preached about Spirit baptism and invited his congregation to experience it.[23]

"The remarkable thing is how rapidly the Revival spreads over Norway," Barratt wrote in the midst of continuous services in 1907. "Instead of looking up people, they came to us. Crowds thronged the halls we used. They were by far too small to receive the hungry hearts that tried to come in. People came from far and near. Numbers were baptized in the Holy Ghost and took the Fire with them back home."[24] Again, the religious press publicized events, opposition in the secular press provided free advertising, and people came from Sweden, Denmark, Finland, Germany, and England to see the revival for themselves.

On March 4, 1907, Barratt recorded in his journal:

> On Saturday evening, Pastor A. A. Boddy from England spoke. He is a minister of the Established Church, and is come here to pray with us for the fullness of the Holy Spirit. He spoke at all three meetings, and read aloud the names of some of the members of his church who had specially desired the prayers of the assemblies. They were assembled for prayer in England at the same time as us last night.[25]

Boddy wrote home about his impressions: "I stood with Evan Roberts in Tonypandy, but have never witnessed such scenes as those in Norway."[26] He returned home more determined than ever to have his parish experience similar renewal.

By May, Boddy could report progress. He wrote to Barratt that two members of his parish had spoken in tongues. Meetings for those seeking Spirit baptism crowded his busy parish schedule, and he urged Barratt to find time to visit England to help the revival "break through." Meanwhile, that summer Boddy undertook the formidable—and ultimately futile—task of convincing his friends at the Keswick Convention that pentecostalism was the next step in God's dealings with humankind.

In September 1907, Barratt finally arrived in Sunderland. Interested people had gathered from around England. From the day he arrived, people responded to his message by speaking in tongues. In mid-October, after six weeks of daily—and nightly—services, Barratt returned to Norway, leaving behind several hundred people committed to pentecostal teaching and experience. All Saints', Sunderland, had become the center for pentecostalism in Great Britain.

The next year, Boddy began publishing *Confidence,* a monthly magazine that nurtured the growing network of British pentecostals and provided news of the progress of pentecostalism around the world. It drew British pentecostals into a growing family, still based in the United States, but also closely linked to Scandinavia and Germany.[27] He also inaugurated an annual Whitsuntide conference that regularly brought to Sunderland leaders of fledgling pentecostal movements in northern Europe. The indefatigable Barratt was responsible for much of the extension of pentecostalism in Europe, but Boddy—mature and experienced in ministry (he was the son of an Anglican clergyman)—quickly gained prominence as a teacher and organizer. He found a kindred spirit in Cecil Polhill, Squire of Howbury Hall and one of the renowned Cambridge Seven, who had dedicated themselves to missionary service a generation earlier. Polhill had the wealth and leisure to devote to coordinating missions and conferences. Through publications and conferences, the two influenced most of the people who would later lead pentecostal evangelistic efforts and denominations in Great Britain.[28]

In retrospect, the warm personal ties among the early leaders of pentecostal movements in Norway, Sweden, Britain, Holland, and Germany stands in sharp contrast to later animosities that deeply and permanently fragmented pentecostal movements, especially within Germany and Britain. Early leaders shared the experience of Oslo and had a common mentor in Barratt. Like Boddy, for example, Lewi Pethrus, pioneer of pentecostalism in Sweden, was persuaded of the truth of the pentecostal message during a visit to Barratt's meetings in Oslo. Jonathan Paul, pastor in the Established Church in Germany and leader in its pietist subculture, also visited Barratt in Oslo, embraced pentecostalism, and resigned his pastorate to devote his full energies to extending pentecostalism in Germany.

The mobility of these northern European pentecostals, like that of pentecostals in the United States and Canada, is worth noting. Both women and men apparently had the resources to travel widely and frequently to conferences and camp meetings. The movement lacked a single charismatic leader; rather, it had many, and they traveled. Their charisma apparently mattered less than their presence, and having the same people on every conference roster helped unify disparate groups. In the United States and Canada, the expansion and integration of the railroads facilitated a similar cooperation and enabled transregional networking that significantly influenced early pentecostalism. New, faster ships and significantly cheaper fares also made transatlantic travel accessible to many more people. And modern transportation made it possible and acceptable for women to travel alone safely and expeditiously, for the transportation and communications revolutions mitigated danger and cost. Evidence about the extent and frequency of travel as well as about the numbers who traveled suggests that all pentecostals certainly did not fit the underclass stereotypes often assigned to them.

A conference schedule and periodicals informally linked the members of northern Europe's small but growing and tightly knit pentecostal community with one another and with the rest of the world. The new family ties that pentecostalism seemed to forge were strong, reinforced by such common usage as "brother" and "sister." And they readily transcended national barriers. It was not uncommon for Americans to visit the conferences, nor was it unusual for Europeans to attend pentecostal camp meetings in the United States. Direct British ties to the United States were strengthened when in 1909 Boddy made the first of several cross-Atlantic trips to tour pentecostal ministries in the United States and Canada.

Until World War I, Boddy's annual conferences at Sunderland gave a degree of unity to British pentecostalism. Boddy never left the Anglican Church, but a growing number of energetic converts to the pentecostal persuasion from Anglicanism and especially from Nonconforming groups found it impossible to follow his example and remain in their prior affiliations. They established scattered independent missions or affiliated with either the Apostolic Church or the Elim Fellowship, both of which were pentecostal groups rooted directly in the Welsh revival.

During the World War, Boddy followed the Church of England in supporting British military policy. A significant number of non-Anglican pentecostals, however, opposed war on principle and spent the war years in prison or in alternative forms of civil service. After the war, these men did not continue to defer to Boddy. Some of them decided to create yet another organization through which to address their common concerns. Dissatisfied with the Apostolic Church's understanding of the prophetic role and also with the hierarchical polity of the Elim Fellowship, in 1924 they consulted Assemblies of God leaders in the United States about forming a cooperative fellowship modeled on the American Assemblies. Thirty-four congregations that had recently formed the Welsh Assemblies of God joined a handful of English congregations to create the Assemblies of God in Great Britain and Ireland. Although they used the American name, this group had no formal ties to the American Assemblies of God. It did, however, adhere unequivocally to one hallmark of American classical pentecostalism that did not always readily export: the insistence that tongues speech always evidenced an authentic experience of Spirit baptism. Neither the Elim Fellowship nor the Apostolic Church concurred.[29]

In the years that followed, then, English pentecostalism broke free from its Anglican moorings. Fascination for millenarian themes displaced Boddy's Keswickian emphases and did not readily mesh with Anglican traditions. But contacts with the United States did not disappear. Through Smith Wigglesworth, an independent pentecostal evangelist, and Donald Gee, a member of the British Assemblies of God, Britain's pentecostal denominations deeply influenced American classical pentecostalism as well as pentecostalism worldwide. Wigglesworth's radical emphasis on faith—after falling into disuse for a few decades—resurfaced in the 1980s in the faith teaching that swept independent charismatic circles in the United States and spread through their networks around the world. Wigglesworth's books were reprinted, and today he is regarded by some as a modern prophet. Gee influenced classical pentecostals to examine seriously both ecumenism and the charismatic renewal. His thoughful reflections, laced with common sense, gave English-speaking pentecostals some of their most enduring explanations of their movement's meaning and message.

As English pentecostalism coalesced during the postwar years, Canadian pentecostalism was also in the process of finding its own identity, separate from the United States roots that had brought it into being. The two principal centers around which Canadian pentecostal efforts clustered were Toronto and Winnipeg.[30]

James and Ellen Hebden had been active lay evangelicals for many years when they arrived in Toronto from Yorkshire, England, in 1904. In Toronto, they organized a rescue mission and faith home known as the East End Mission. In November 1906, tongues speaking first occurred at the mission, which rapidly became a center of pentecostal teaching and a hub of evangelistic activities. By the time the Hebdens left for Algiers as missionaries in 1910, their mission had spawned numerous others, and pentecostalism had established a permanent presence in Ontario. That presence had links to the remnants of the Canadian network of Scottish-born Australian evangelist John Alexander Dowie and to the emerging pentecostal movement in his erstwhile utopia, Zion City, Illinois.[31]

Reports from Azusa Street and from other early pentecostal missions in the United States directly influenced the course of events in Winnipeg, the other primary center of early Canadian pentecostalism. Various religious publications chronicling pentecostalism's extension across the United States came by mail to the Argue family residence in Winnipeg during the winter of 1906. The Argues had been longtime enthusiastic participants in the Salvation Army and in other holiness networks linking American and Canadian evangelicals of similar interests.[32] Intrigued, Andrew Argue, a farmer turned real estate agent, traveled to Chicago to investigate news of a pentecostal revival in a former Baptist mission. When he returned, he had fully embraced pentecostal teaching and experience.[33] The Argue home hosted the city's first pentecostal services until Andrew Argue found mission premises to lease. He soon traded his sales career for the sawdust trail, where his entrepreneurial instincts contributed to a rapid rise. His family followed his lead, blending their musical and speaking talents to form an evangelistic team that both extended the movement and encouraged the faithful. The Argues traveled widely over the next four decades, and they were well received in the United States as well as in Canada. Radiating from Winnipeg, the pentecostal movement established itself in western Canada.

In eastern Canada in 1919, pentecostals received a federal charter for the Pentecostal Assemblies of Canada (PAOC). The same year, pentecostals in western Canada became a district of the U.S. Assemblies of God. People in western Canada who joined the pentecostal movement were often Americans who had moved north of the border, lured to Canada by the availability of free land. They at first welcomed organic relationship to the American Assemblies of God. The process of separation of Canadians from the United States Assemblies of God was completed in 1925, when the Canadian District of the U.S. Assemblies of God was dissolved and congregations in Canada's western provinces joined the PAOC. Later, other American pentecostal denominations gradually made their way to Canada and to Britain, and pentecostal demography in Canada today mirrors divisions rooted more in the American context than in their own.

By percentage of the population, pentecostalism's most dramatic Canadian success has been in Newfoundland, where the Pentecostal Assemblies of Newfoundland looks back for its origins neither to Toronto nor to Winnipeg but to New England. Alice Garrigus, a middle-aged, single schoolteacher from Connecticut, a graduate of Mount Holyoke, arrived in this Canadian colony in 1910 with the pentecostal version of the full gospel.

Garrigus liked to recount how, at age fifty-two, she had been approached in Rumney, New Hampshire, by a woman she did not know, a woman who claimed to have "a message from God" for her. "I knew God had a message for me," she later reminisced. "There followed a message in tongues and the word, 'Newfoundland,' came forth. At that word, I bounded from my chair and went leaping and dancing and praising God."[34] By the end of the year, she was in St. John's looking for a building to use as a mission. On Easter Sunday, April 16, 1911, she conducted the island's first pentecostal service. For twelve years, she confined her efforts to St. John's, but eventually the movement spread across the island and into Labrador, a dependency of Newfoundland. By the early 1980s, the Pentecostal Assemblies of Newfoundland represented nearly 7 percent of the population of Newfoundland and Labrador. The provincial government provides funding for this pentecostal denomination's parochial schools, as it does for schools of the province's other major denominations.

The histories of Canadian and American pentecostals are intertwined. Adherents recognize a common history through Azusa Street and other early pentecostal centers, and frequent travel between the two countries has been convenient. Pentecostals in both countries subscribed to the same periodicals, heard the same evangelists, and attended the same camp meetings.[35] A steady and influential constituency within the United States Assemblies of God moved permanently to the United States from Canada. Aimee Semple McPherson, arguably the best-known pentecostal evangelist before Oral Roberts and Jimmy Swaggart, was a Canadian transplant in California. Many Canadians and a few British pentecostals settled in the United States and gained positions of considerable influence. Evangelist Charles Price and Assemblies of God missionary statesman Noel Perkin were British born, migrated to Canada, and, as young men, converted to pentecostalism, then spent their careers in ministry in the United States. Alice Luce, daughter of an Anglican priest and formerly Church Missionary Society missionary to India, spent the second half of her life establishing a Bible school for Hispanics in Southern California. Anglican Archdeacon Phair moved among the United States, Canada, and England, as did numerous lesser-known men and women who collectively represent one significant way in which British and Canadian pentecostalism, though considerably smaller than their American counterpart, deeply influenced the American scene. Pentecostals in North America and Britain were also closely linked from the beginning, and the travels of men such as Boddy across Canada, the United States, Great Britain (and Scandinavia, Holland, and Germany) extended the network and strengthened ties rooted in perceptions of common enemies, commitment to common mission, and anticipation of a shared future.

Perhaps perceptions of common identity and purpose were cultivated most assiduously by the editors of the monthly publications that every significant pentecostal center mailed to overlapping mailing lists. It is impossible to overstate the influence of periodicals in blending regional expressions of pentecostalism into a coherent movement. Within a year of the beginning of the Azusa Street revival in April 1906, periodicals were transforming an unlikely event in an out-of-the-way place into a worldwide evangelistic outreach. In a real sense, these publications shaped North Atlantic pentecostalism. They also sustained it as it encountered opposition, and they kept it from becoming mired in a provincial morass. They also mediated influence from one culture to another by reporting and commenting on issues and events in widely scattered pentecostal centers. Their numbers suggest that people widely stereotyped as at worst illiterate and at best little concerned with the printed page in fact invested heavily in print media and were fundamentally shaped as a people by the printed word.

As denominations organized, however, the publications that had forged and sustained common identity either ceased publication or were gradually transformed into denominational organs. These targeted far narrower audiences and promoted restricted agendas, and their changed character minimized their ability to sustain a sense of interdenominational and international network and family. Their role in shaping pentecostalism's general identity and interpreting its broad meaning became significantly limited as their function changed. This both affected and mirrored classical pentecostalism's course. What solidarity existed among North Atlantic pentecostals eroded; similarly, the millenarian urgency that had fueled pentecostalism's early fervor waned. Doctrinal differences, personal rivalries, and deep cleavages splintered pentecostals. Cultural preferences, perhaps minimized in the initial throes of revival, also gradually differentiated among pentecostals in different countries.

In 1948 Canadian pentecostals joined British and U.S. pentecostal denominations to establish the Pentecostal Fellowship of North America. This forum, in which the wider North Atlantic community communicates with each other and with pentecostalism worldwide, meets triennially as the Pentecostal World Conference. Although charismatic movements were better represented at the last (1989) Pentecostal World Conference, the conference remains primarily a gathering place for classical Trinitarian pentecostals.

In Britain, Canada, and the United States, Anglo classical pentecostalism is barely holding its own. Especially in Britain, classical varieties of pentecostalism thrive more among Jamaicans and other large immigrant groups than in the older population. Other movements that claim the pentecostal mantle have arisen, however, and these generally thrive with little sustained contact with classical pentecostalism. John Wimber and the Vineyard is a case in point. Wimber's enormous popularity in Britain, the United States, and Germany forges a commonality among his tens of thousands of followers that eludes contemporary classical pentecostalism and that parallels but rarely intersects with classical pentecostalism.[36] It is more suggestive of an earlier era in pentecostal history. The strength of pentecostal currents in modern Britain cannot be measured by looking at adherents of classical pentecostal denominations. Much of it thrives in house churches, in Baptist congregations, and in other settings that traditional reporting may overlook.

Since its origins in the 1950s, the charismatic renewal in the historic Christian traditions has matured and, to a large extent, has found its place within those traditions. It is less conspicuous to outsiders, though perhaps not uniformly more welcome, than in the past. Among the suggestions of its enduring presence is the inclusion of charismatic choruses in the new hymnals of the historic denominations.

The British story illustrates as well as any how, in this century that encompasses all of the pentecostal movement's history, pentecostalism has come full cycle. Nurtured first in an Anglican parish where they were enjoined to unity, English pentecostals opted instead to follow their separatist instincts. Social class differences and millenarian fervor contributed to the choice. In the end, they formed several competing sects. But shortly after mid-century, pentecostalism came back to the Anglican church, shorn of the divisive millenarian fervor that had overtaken it early in the century.[37] Scenes reminiscent of 1907 occurred in another Anglican parish. These helped launch an extensive and ongoing charismatic renewal that today is estimated to have some 500,000 Anglican participants in England alone. They also coincided with and contributed to the spread of pentecostalism in English Catholicism and evangelicalism. In so-called classical pentecostal denominations, in renewal movements within historic Christian communions, in England's large house-church movement and other independent charismatic settings, English pentecostalism today manifests the ability to adapt its idiom and practice and to speak to the felt longings of people in vastly different circumstances. Around the world, it is doing the same thing. The small memberships of pentecostal denominations sometimes obscure the true extent of pentecostal presence.

The flexible idiom, however, raises a basic question: What is the essence of this twentieth-century impulse we call pentecostalism? The terms are in perpetual flux, but the situation suggests that what unites pentecostalism's disparate adherents in the North Atlantic and around the world is not a formal theology but a persuasion that the divine, the person of the Holy Spirit, longs to overwhelm each of us in a crisis experience that uplifts, enlightens, empowers, and transforms. The history of pentecostalism—especially in the story of its beginnings and development as a transnational North Atlantic movement—suggests that this persuasion stands at the core of pentecostalism's century-long quest to penetrate the church and evangelize the world.

Notes

1. Even a cursory perusal of pentecostal periodicals reveals this pattern of communication. See, for example, *Apostolic Faith; Confidence; Latter Rain Evangel.*

2. David Barrett, "Annual Statistical Table on Global Mission: 1993," *International Bulletin of Missionary Research* 17 (1993): 22–23.

3. For the basic outlines of early American pentecostalism, see Robert Mapes Anderson, *Vision of the Disinherited* (New York: Oxford University Press, 1979); Edith L. Blumhofer, *Restoring the Faith* (Urbana: University of Illinois Press, 1993); Grant Wacker, "Bibliography," in *Dictionary of Pentecostal and Charismatic Movements,* ed. Stanley Burgess et. al. (Grand Rapids: Zondervan, 1988).

4. See Edith L. Blumhofer, "Restoration as Revival: Early American Pentecostalism," in *Modern Christian Revivals,* ed. Edith L. Blumhofer and Randall Balmer (Urbana: University of Illinois Press, forthcoming).

5. D. W. Myland, *The Latter Rain Covenant and Pentecostal Power* (Chicago: Evangel Publishing House, 1910).

6. *Apostolic Faith,* October 1906, 4.

7. David Barrett, ed., *World Christian Encyclopedia* (Nairobi: Oxford University Press, 1982).

8. For analysis, see especially David Stoll, *Is Latin America Turning Protestant?* (Berkeley: University of California Press, 1990); David Martin, *Tongues of Fire: The Explosion of Protestantism in Latin America* (Cambridge, MA: Blackwell, 1990).

9. Tito Paredes opts for the lower figure in "The Many Faces of *los Evangélicos,*" *Christianity Today,* 6 April 1992, 34–35.

10. George T. B. Davis, *Torrey and Alexander: The Story of a World-Wide Revival* (New York: Fleming H. Revell, 1905), 11.

11. Ibid., 10.

12. Charles H. Gabriel, "O That Will Be Glory!" in *Revival Hymns,* ed. Daniel B. Towner and Charles M. Alexander (Chicago: Bible Institute Colportage Association, 1905), no. 1.

13. See Evan Roberts, "A Message to the World," in *The Story of the Welsh Revival,* ed. B. F. Goodrich (New York: Fleming H. Revell, 1905), 5–6. For a discussion of the impact of this revival on pentecostalism, see Edith L. Blumhofer, *The Assemblies of God: A Chapter in the Story of American Pentecostalism* (Springfield, MO: Gospel Publishing House), 1:100–104.

14. G. Campbell Morgan, "The Lessons of the Revival," in *The Story of the Welsh Revival,* ed. Goodrich, 37.

15. Ibid., 38.

16. For details of the revival, see also the *Times* (London), especially January and February 1905.

17. See, for example, Jessie Penn-Lewis, *The Awakening in Wales* (New York: Fleming H. Revell, 1905).

18. Elizabeth Codner, "Even Me," in *Gospel Hymns Nos. 1 to 6 Complete,* ed. Ira Sankey, James McGranahan, and George C. Stebbins (Chicago: Biglow and Main, n.d.), no. 639.

19. Penn-Lewis, *Awakening in Wales.*

20. Alexander Boddy, "Pentecost at Sunderland: A Vicar's Testimony," pamphlet, Assemblies of God Archives, Springfield, MO, 5.

21. Ibid., 5–6.

22. T. B. Barratt, *When the Fire Fell* (London: Elim Publishing, 1928), 129–31. It was said that Barratt was the first to receive Spirit baptism with the evidence of tongues in New York City (136).

23. Barratt summarized his teaching in *In the Days of the Latter Rain* (London: Simpkin, Marshall, Hamilton, Kent, 1909).

24. Barratt, *When the Fire Fell,* 142.

25. Quoted in Donald Gee, *The Pentecostal Movement* (Luton, Eng.: Assemblies of God Publishing House, 1949), 20.

26. Ibid.

27. *Confidence* provides detailed reports of addresses and discussions at annual pentecostal conferences around northern Europe, as well as of Boddy's several trips to the United States and Canada.

28. Alfred F. Missen, *The Sound of a Going* (Nottingham, Eng.: Assemblies of God Publishing House, 1973), 1–4.

29. For overviews of British classical pentecostalism, see Gee, *Pentecostal Movement;* Desmond Cartwright, *The Great Evangelists: The Remarkable Lives of George and Stephen Jeffreys* (Basingstoke, Eng.: Marshall Pickering, 1986); and Colin C. Whittaker, *Seven Pentecostal Pioneers* (Springfield, MO: Gospel Publishing House, 1983).

30. For general historical accounts of classical pentecostalism in Canada, see Gloria Kulbeck, *What God Hath Wrought* (Toronto: Pentecostal Assemblies of Canada, 1958); and Paul Hawkes, "Pentecostalism in Canada: A History with Implications for the Future" (D.Min. thesis, San Francisco Theological Seminary, 1982).

31. Thomas Miller, "The Canadian Jerusalem: The Story of James and Ellen Hebden and Their Toronto Mission," *Assemblies of God Heritage,* Fall 1991, 5–7, 22–23; Winter 1991–92, 22–25, 30–31; Spring 1992, 10–12, 19–20.

32. Zelma Argue, *A Vision and a Vow: The Story of My Mother's Life* (Springfield, MO: Gospel Publishing House, n.d.), 25–35.

33. Zelma Argue, *Contending for the Faith* (Winnipeg: Messenger of God Publishing House, 1928), 20–23. On the rise of pentecostalism in far western Canada, see Robert K. Burkinshaw, "Pentecostalism and Fundamentalism in British Columbia, 1921–1927," *Fides et Historia* 24 (Winter/Spring 1992): 68–80.

34. Alice Garrigus, "Walking," *Good Tidings,* March 1940, 9.

35. Many of the people and periodicals mentioned in the next paragraphs are discussed at greater length in *Dictionary of Pentecostal and Charismatic Movements* and in Blumhofer, *Restoring the Faith.*

36. J. T. A. Gunstone, *Signs and Wonders: The Wimber Phenomenon* (London: Daybreak, 1989).

37. Peter Hocken, *Streams of Renewal: The Origins and Development of the Charismatic Movement in Great Britain* (Exeter, Eng.: Paternoster, 1986).

18

Evangelicalism in Its Settings: The British and American Movements since 1940

DAVID BEBBINGTON

Who are the evangelicals? In the case of Britain there is relatively little doubt that, in the era since the opening of the Second World War, the term has properly been applied to all those Protestants inside and outside the established churches who have been committed to spreading the gospel at home and abroad—the "evangelistic forces" of the land.[1] The case of America is more problematic. One expression of the movement has been the National Association of Evangelicals (NAE), founded in 1942 to coordinate its protean forces, but few have supposed that the label should be restricted to the organization's affiliates. Despite the sniping between the leaders of the association and the avowedly fundamentalist American Council of Christian Churches, established in the previous year, there was no clear line of demarcation between evangelicals and fundamentalists. The two organizations were originally rivals for the support of virtually the same constituency. Nor did the holiness/pentecostal sector of American religion stand apart, for a majority of the early adherents of the NAE was drawn from its ranks.[2] Afro-American churches set up a separate National Black Evangelical Association in 1963, but its very title proclaimed that, though its member bodies were ethnically distinct, they held the same religious position.[3] The charismatics inside nonpentecostal denominations or outside all older denominations, though sometimes more Catholic in churchmanship, were preponderantly evangelical in their emphases.[4] And substantial sections of mainline denominations, together with almost the whole of the vast Southern Baptist empire, fell within the same parameters.[5] Evangelicalism, in America as in Britain, embraced an enormous range of Christians with a common inheritance stemming ultimately from the Evangelical Revival of the eighteenth century.[6]

The constituents of the movement were not necessarily whole denominations or even whole congregations. Groups could gradually move in, as did the Churches of Christ in America during this period, or else move out, as did the liberal Anglicans in England, who gradually faded into the mainstream of the Church of England.[7] In the United States, confessional churches with

Continental roots—both Lutheran and Calvinist—stood on the margins of the movement but could not altogether avoid being swayed by its influence. They shared with their Reformed cousins in Britain—the Free Presbyterians and the Strict Baptists—a pre-evangelical stress on true doctrine and right order.[8] On both sides of the Atlantic the oneness pentecostalists and charismatics whose practice of baptizing in the name of "Jesus only" predisposed them to a modalist theology are hardest to classify; perhaps they should be seen as expressing in an extreme form the lack of Trinitarian finesse common in popular evangelicalism.[9] What is most apparent from this survey is the sheer heterogeneity of the movement. Evangelicals are remarkably diverse.

Yet the variety does not rule out the possibility of defining the movement as a whole. It is true, as Donald Dayton has argued, that evangelicalism in its entirety cannot be located as either Low Church or premillennialist,[10] but it is nevertheless practicable to isolate a number of characteristics displayed by any evangelical group. One common feature is a stress on conversion. In 1944 a broad Evangelical Anglican leader eulogized conversion as "the very heart of the Evangelical approach, the citadel of its doctrine, the key to its pastoralia, the method of its evangelism," and he was quoted with approval by a much more conservative Anglican thirty-four years later.[11] Although the common American equivalent for conversion, "being born again," was far rarer in Britain until recently, the experience—whether sudden or gradual—was looked for in all branches of the movement.

A natural implication is a constant quest for fresh converts, and so a second characteristic of evangelicals is activism. The central task is normally evangelism, though social concern has often been yoked with it. Thus a typical address at the main annual conference of Evangelical Anglicans dealt in 1953 with training the laity to evangelize through regular, systematic house-to-house visitation;[12] and a Californian charismatic congregation thirty-four years later advertised no fewer than fifty-one weekly events.[13]

A third characteristic is the great respect with which all evangelicals treat the Bible. Their most eminent figure on the world stage, Billy Graham, spoke for his coreligionists on both sides of the Atlantic when, in 1956, he argued for "Bible-centered preaching."[14] So insistent was he on the authority of the Bible that he had to guard against criticism by adding that he was not advocating bibliolatry.

A fourth characteristic has been what John Stott, soon to become the leading evangelical in the Church of England, called, again in 1956, "the centrality of the cross."[15] Analyses of the American movement often omit this feature,[16] and even in Britain there was a tendency in the 1970s, partly under the influence of charismatic renewal, for attention to shift away from the atonement toward the resurrection.[17] Yet in 1986 George Carey, subsequently the second evangelical in the period and the first charismatic to be Archbishop of Canterbury, recalled his contemporaries to the priority of the atonement.[18] Likewise Billy Graham would not be shifted from regarding the cross of Jesus Christ as his main theme.[19] The redemptive work of Christ has been the focus of the habitual evangelical preoccupation with soteriology. The cross, rather than the incarnation, the example, or the teaching of Christ, has been the kernel of evangelical proclamation and so should be seen as the fourth element in the cluster of attributes that, together, mark off evangelicalism from broader versions of Protestantism.

No other characteristics have enjoyed comparable prominence across the whole movement, and if further points were to be added, there would be a risk of excluding groups that properly belong. It is not essential that a body should show awareness of the term "evangelical" for it to be included. African-American Bible believers, for instance, do not normally think of themselves as evangelical, and yet few observers would locate them outside the category.[20] All those displaying conversionism, activism, biblicism, and crucicentrism are evangelicals.[21] There can be no doubt that groups with these characteristics on both sides of the Atlantic are outgrowths of a single movement.

This verdict is confirmed by the similarity of the trajectories of evangelicalism in Britain and the United States from the 1940s onward. In both countries the years around 1940 seemed a nadir for the movement. In America, although the Evangelical Alliance survived until 1944,[22] the very word "evangelical" had gone out of fashion, crushed between the upper and nether millstones of modernism and fundamentalism. Those who wished to cooperate in spreading the gospel felt dismayed by the fragmentation of evangelistic bodies, threatened by the growth of government in peace and then in war, and marginalized in a land their forefathers in the faith had once molded. In 1943 the magazines *Time* and *Newsweek* carried fifty-five and thirty-two reports respectively on the mainline churches but only four and five on fundamentalists or evangelicals.[23] In Britain there was a comparable feeling of being relegated to obscurity, especially among evangelicals in the Church of England. Their conservative wing had been given no episcopal appointments during the 1930s.[24] Even Max Warren, the secretary of the Church Missionary Society who professed broader views, wrote in 1944 that "all too commonly to-day, an Evangelical in the Church of England is a person labouring under a sense of frustration and discouragement often so deep as to engender . . . an inferiority complex."[25]

The spirit of dejection, however, masked two great evangelical strengths. The mainline denominations of Britain and America, by and large, were by no means hostile to evangelicalism. The Church of Scotland and British Methodism launched sustained evangelistic thrusts as soon as the Second World War was over, and even the most liberal of the American Presbyterian denominations declared itself in 1946 "a crusading organ for evangelical religion."[26] The other strength was the vitality of evangelistic organizations targeting young people, most notably Youth For Christ and (in Britain) the National Young Life Campaign.[27] From their ranks emerged some of the most dynamic figures in a postwar resurgence of evangelical religion. Billy Graham, the outstanding man among them, did almost as much for advancing the movement in Britain as he did in America. By 1959 there was talk of "a new evangelical revival" in the Church of England, and within less than thirty years, the party possessed a majority of full-time Anglican ordinands.[28] Similarly in America by 1979 ministers who read the evangelical *Christianity Today* were twice as numerous as those who read the more liberal *Christian Century*.[29] Four years later *Time* and *Newsweek* were giving more reports to fundamentalists and evangelicals than to mainline churches.[30] By that time the evangelical sector in both countries had been powerfully reinforced by the impact of charismatic renewal that both rejuvenated congregations of existing denominations and spilled over into fresh groupings outside.[31] Growth and greater visibility were accompanied by an increasing willingness to take up social action as a dimension of Christian mission and to venture deep into the political domain. There was a corresponding decline in the maintenance of such traditional taboos as those against attending the cinema or (in some quarters) drinking alcohol.[32] "Contamination with the world" was less feared; "social involvements" were deliberately fostered.[33] Evangelicalism emerged from its earlier obscurity, undergoing enormous transformation in the process. The whole development was broadly parallel on the two sides of the Atlantic.

There was, furthermore, a great deal of interaction between the two national evangelical communities. Billy Graham was by no means the only American to exert an influence over the British movement. Harold J. Ockenga, a prime mover in the NAE, visited London in 1946, preached in Westminster Chapel, and held consultations with a view to international cooperation.[34] In the same year and three years later Donald G. Barnhouse, a doughty Philadelphia Presbyterian minister, addressed students under the auspices of the Cambridge Inter-Collegiate Christian Union, a post of unusual honor.[35] Only six out of seventeen Keswick conventions between 1946 and 1962 had no American speaker.[36] There were also less formal visits. Carl Henry, for instance, who as editor of *Christianity Today* had kept on his desk an antique inkstand bought in London, spent a year in Cambridge immediately after leaving his job in 1968.[37] The flow continued in the 1980s. John Wimber, the charismatic leader of Vineyard Ministries, began a series of highly publicized conferences in Britain in 1984.[38] The stream of personnel was seconded by the huge output of the evangelical publishing houses in the United States, of which there were over seventy in the early 1980s.[39] The charismatic movement in Britain during the 1960s, for example, drew inspiration from the account of pentecostal missionary work amongst the drug addicts of New York in David Wilkerson's *Cross and the Switchblade*.[40] Novelty in the British evangelical world often turns out, on examination, to have been an American export.

Such evidence of personal and literary influence has led Adrian Hastings to treat the evangelical resurgence in Britain as a mere by-product of postwar American world ascendancy.[41] But that is to neglect the extent to which transatlantic traffic was two-way. A number of prominent British evangelicals settled in the United States. Alan Redpath, for example, moved in 1953 from Richmond upon Thames to become minister of Moody Memorial Church in Chicago, and in 1958 Geoffrey Bromiley was the first of a clutch of British staff to join the faculty of Fuller Theological Seminary.[42] Others were welcome visitors. John Stott first traveled to the New World in 1956 for a four-month program of university evangelism, and seven years later Gilbert Kirby, as general secretary of the World Evangelical Fellowship, addressed the NAE annual convention.[43] Nor were literary influences one-way. Ten of the first fifty-three contributing editors of *Christianity Today* were from Britain (and only five were from any other countries outside the United States); its first five issues each contained an article by a British author.[44] The mushrooming of the pentecostal/charismatic movement in America, as elsewhere, was monitored and in some measure guided by Donald Gee, the editor of *Pentecost* from 1947 to 1966, who lived in Surrey.[45] British evangelical Bible scholarship, initially published by Inter-Varsity Press, was made available in the United States by Eerdmans.[46] Christian methods in Britain also found admirers across the Atlantic. After visiting the Holiday Crusade at Filey in Yorkshire, an observer was impressed by its organizers. "We Americans," he wrote, "could well sit at their feet and learn."[47] Still in the 1990s the March for Jesus, an ebullient walk of witness through city streets, has been imported from Britain to Texas and is likely to spread through urban America.[48] It is clear that even if, as in other spheres, the dominant flow of influence has been outward from the United States, there has nevertheless been a countercurrent of considerable volume. If American ways have helped to mold British evangelicalism, the British movement has also impinged on its counterpart in the United States.

At this point the discussion of evangelicalism needs to be set in a wider context. Historians, political analysts, and others have long been asking whether the United States is fundamentally different from other countries. In what respects, if any, is America unique? One helpful approach to the issue, it has recently been suggested, is to ask how far movements spanning American and other countries are genuinely international, and how far, on the contrary, they reflect American global hegemony.[49] That question can be posed of evangelicalism. How far did those who bore the evangelical characteristics elsewhere reflect the export of American cultural values? Some of the evidence already assembled is useful in framing an answer. The parallel paths of postwar evangelicalism in Britain and the United States imply, according to Hastings, that the British movement drew its strength from its American counterpart. Parallelism, however, does not demonstrate dependence. The extent of British input into the United States shows, on the contrary, that the relationship had elements of interdependence. In that respect evangelicalism turns out to have been a genuinely international movement. But that still leaves open the question of what influences were being transmitted backward and forward across the Atlantic. If they were virtually identical, the exchange could amount to a trade in elements of American culture after all. So the degree of difference between the British and American movements needs to be investigated. Only if there were substantial variations would the autonomy of the British movement become evident. How should the extent of the contrast be examined?

Again a recent contribution to the ongoing debate about American exceptionalism offers useful guidance. It is best, it has been argued, to portray clusters of traits that mark out the United States as different from other countries.[50] That is the approach taken in the remainder of this chapter. Two clusters of evangelical characteristics, each relating to a major issue, are taken for comparison between America and Britain. One issue is the extent of ecclesiastical separatism; the other is the extent of national permeation. Each will be examined to discover how it has been shaped by the different settings of the movements. Although the two issues of internal organization and outward impact have in practice been interwoven, for purposes of exposition the explanatory factors relating primarily to each of them will be treated separately. The resulting analysis should reveal something of why the gospel has related to culture in different ways in Britain and America.

Withdrawal from Christian bodies apparently tainted with error has been much more common in the United States. Two incidents from the premier national organizations linking evangelicals—one from America, the other from Britain—well illustrate the contrast between the countries on this issue. At the preliminary gathering of the NAE in 1942, Harold J. Ockenga set out a challenge that seems to have caused few qualms among his hearers. "Are we willing," he asked, "to dissolve any organizational connection which we may have in order that we, as a group, may adequately represent evangelical Christianity to this nation?"[51] Any such questioning of existing affiliations was normally taboo in the British Evangelical Alliance. When Martyn Lloyd-Jones dared to raise the same subject on its platform in 1966, the effects were catastrophic. His proposal was immediately denounced from the chair by John Stott, there was a fierce outburst of acrimonious controversy, and the following year's National Assembly of Evangelicals had to be canceled.[52] It simply was not done to suggest in public that Christians should leave their existing denominations for the sake of gospel purity.

A corollary of this difference between the national approaches was the contrasting stance of evangelicals on the ecumenical movement. There were widespread suspicions of ecumenical tendencies on both sides of the Atlantic, but whereas over many years in America it was standard for evangelicals to reject altogether the quest for institutional church unity, in Britain there was commonly a willingness to acknowledge its theoretical desirability while maintaining objections to any particular scheme. Thus an early editorial in *Christianity Today* was called "The Perils of Ecumenicity," but when Anglican evangelicals successfully resisted a merger of the Church of England with Methodism, two of their leaders felt duty-bound to put forward alternative proposals for reunion in England.[53] The distinction between the two countries should not be overdrawn, because, for instance, as early as 1954 Billy Graham, when speaking at Union Theological Seminary, was willing to use the word "ecumenical" approvingly.[54] Furthermore, a large number of American evangelicals remained in mainline denominations that were engaging in discussions about unity. In 1968 Carl Henry estimated that at least a third of the members of the constituency of the National Council of Churches were evangelical.[55] Nevertheless it is plain that there was a greater propensity in the

United States for departure from traditional Christian bodies. By 1961 only 38 percent of American Protestants belonged to mainline churches.[56] The bulk of the others were orthodox Christians of conservative theological inclinations. In Britain, by contrast, the chief separatist organization, the Fellowship of Independent Evangelical Churches, was only tiny, and the great majority of evangelicals were in the denominations with long pedigrees. In 1989 self-identified evangelical congregations formed 10 percent of the United Reformed Church (a merger of Congregationalists, Presbyterians, and Churches of Christ), 26 percent of the Church of England, 32 percent of the Methodists, and as many as 80 percent of the Baptists.[57] Ecclesiastical separatism was much more favored in the United States than in Britain.

What accounts for the greater American willingness to go it alone in religion? Part of the explanation lies in the differing patterns of ecclesiastical organizations in the two countries. The plethora of parachurch bodies—societies, missions, ministries, and so on—to which the evangelical public often gave greater loyalty than to their churches was as much a feature of Britain as it was of America, and so the contrast must be located elsewhere. It lay in the balance between sectarian and churchly preferences in the two evangelical movements. Fissiparity was an obvious feature of American religion. By 1980 there were forty-six separate Baptist denominations, not to speak of such robustly independent congregations as the "Rock Solid Baptist Church affiliated to the Lord Jesus Christ" in the village of Tiger, Georgia.[58] Sectarianism was encouraged in part by the huge scale of the holiness/pentecostal sector of evangelicalism in comparison with Britain. The five largest holiness churches had roughly 1.4 million members by the 1980s;[59] in Britain the strongest holiness church (apart from the sui generis Salvation Army, with just over fifty thousand members) had been the International Holiness Mission, which, in 1952 when it united with the Church of the Nazarene, had contained only about one thousand members.[60] Again the quicksilver growth of pentecostalism was among the most striking aspects of postwar American religion. By 1979 an astonishing 19 percent of Americans were willing to identify themselves as pentecostal or charismatic.[61] In Britain a decade later only 12 percent of adult church attenders—about 1.2 percent of the adult population—classed themselves in the same way.[62] The American healing revival of the 1950s and 1960s had carried experience of unusual spiritual gifts outside classical pentecostalism to foster a dynamic new movement that explored the supernatural world with a fresh mixture of reverence and showmanship.[63] There were comparable developments in Britain, such as a healing evangelist visiting an Anglican theological college and encouraging students to be "slain in the Spirit" by pushing them over.[64] Although, paradoxically, a charismatic house church movement with clear sectarian traits emerged in Britain,[65] to a remarkable degree charismatic renewal was contained within existing denominations. In 1989 there were virtually as many charismatic evangelicals in the Church of England alone as there were in all the house churches put together.[66] The fresh currents flowed mainly in traditional channels. The chief English agency of renewal, the Fountain Trust, had taken immense pains to discourage separatism both because it wanted to revitalize the existing churches and because it recognized the strength of denominational attachments.[67] Both Methodism and Scottish Presbyterianism did not wish to endanger the substantial unity they had achieved in the inter-war years, and their forms of church order constantly inhibited divergent tendencies. Even the Baptists spoke in an official document of 1948 of cherishing a place in the one holy Catholic Church.[68] Anglican Evangelicals, who did much to shape the ethos of British evangelicalism as a whole, were used to coexisting with other traditions within their communion. An established church, they realized, was bound to be comprehensive in some degree. Much of the energy of the Evangelical party might go into countering the claims of High Churchmen either in scholarly works[69] or through popular organizations,[70] but they did not expect to expel them from the Church of England. On the one hand, living in a theologically mixed ecclesiastical body came naturally in Britain; on the other, debate with Anglo-Catholics forced Evangelicals to emphasize their own churchly sense. Schism came high on the list of corporate sins.

A second factor explaining the stronger separatist impulse of the United States was its larger share of fundamentalism. Many of the first generation of leaders from the fundamentalist controversies of the years immediately after the First World War were still active in the 1940s. W. B. Riley, for example, did not leave the American Baptist Convention until 1947.[71] Since old wounds remained sore long into the second half of the century, members of the NAE were constantly aware of the need to affirm their orthodoxy in terms acceptable to separatist fundamentalists. George L. Ford, general director of the NAE, was still insisting in 1963 that its supporters disagreed only with the methods, not the theology, of the American Council of Christian Churches.[72] Consequently the center of gravity within American evangelicalism as a whole swung toward positions associated with fundamentalism. Although dispensationalism was never an essential component of their theology, it remained normative among late twentieth-century fundamentalists. Disseminated by the Scofield Bible, Dallas Seminary, and Hal Lindsey, it also became rooted in a much wider evangelical public. During the early 1960s readers of *United Evangelical Action,* the NAE monthly, were being invited to a congress "emphasizing Premillennial and Pretribulation teaching" and to send off for prophetic booklets with such titles as *Satan's Fire Water.*[73] Likewise the principle of the inerrancy of Scripture, which might reasonably be regarded as the theological distinctive of fundamentalism, came to be seen in some quarters as a defining attribute of evangelicalism as a whole.[74] Even though Fuller Seminary formally dropped inerrancy in 1972 and neither holiness nor Afro-American churches had ever contemplated adopting it,[75] Harold Lindsell's *Battle for the Bible* (1976) claimed that inerrancy was the kernel of evangelical belief. It had been used as a test for membership of the Evangelical Theological Society since its foundation in 1949,[76] and even two-thirds of the moderate, anti-fundamentalist section of the Southern Baptists have been willing to endorse it.[77]

In Britain, by contrast with these traits, the label "fundamentalist" was rarely accepted, dispensationalism was weak, and inerrancy was seldom made a touchstone of evangelical orthodoxy. There had been fundamentalist controversies in Britain earlier in the century, giving rise in one case to the Bible Churchmen's Missionary Society as a splinter group from the Church Missionary Society, but they were minor affairs in comparison with their American equivalents.[78] In 1955, when Billy Graham's visit to Britain stirred up criticism of the preacher and his suporters as fundamentalists, evangelicals fell over themselves in their zeal to repudiate the label.[79] Again, dispensationalism, though it was embraced by pentecostalists,[80] was often perceived as an idiosyncrasy of the Brethren movement (the so-called Plymouth Brethren) and so ignored by others. Dispensational teaching had made less headway in Britain than in America before the Second World War, and even among the Brethren it was in decline by the 1960s.[81] Likewise assertions of the inerrancy of Scripture, though occasionally found in obscure journals, were seldom encountered in more representative British writers until the publication in 1958 of *Fundamentalism and the Word of God* by the rising young theologian J. I. Packer.[82] Even a conservative organization such as the Evangelical Movement of Wales preferred to confess only a belief in the "infallible Word of God," and authors such as the Methodist biblical scholar Howard Marshall explicitly rejected inerrancy without losing the confidence of the evangelical community.[83] Both dispensationalism and inerrancy, by positing doctrinal purity as a condition of fellowship, tended to encourage separatist convictions. America therefore not only possessed a much larger and more influential fundamentalist sector committed to separatism but also displayed far more attachment to beliefs that pointed in the same direction.

The ecclesiastical characteristics clustering round separatism can in turn be illuminated by their context in the secular life of the United States. The egalitarianism of the social setting, as a glance at Tocqueville's *Democracy in America* would remind us, was likely to be a major conditioning factor. A mixture of populism, individualism, democratization, and market-making has recently been defined as the essence of the American way, shaping religion, for instance, by creating the expectation that churches should be responsive to their members' wishes.[84] Certainly there is in America a confidence in people power together with a dismissal of tradition and a spirit of "can-do." An English social psychologist has pointed out that whereas in Europe it is general to picture social institutions as trees that grow organically over time, in America it is more usual to think of them as machines that, if they fail to produce results, should be scrapped.[85] In the New World there is a willingness to take fresh initiatives that necessarily affects church life. Thus when, in 1957, a pentecostal woman in St Louis, Missouri, felt that she was receiving too little recognition from her pastor, she set up, with one other female friend, a new church in an old paint store with herself as preacher.[86] A democratic orientation is deeply rooted in the American psyche.

There are a number of consequences of this secular trait. It leads, for instance, to a courting of public opinion and a tendency for the values of the nation at large to impinge particularly deeply on religion.[87] Hence a Dallas-based television station can broadcast a Christian show called simply "Success in Life."[88] Another consequence is a flexing of laypeople's muscles in the cause of truth. There is no British parallel to the Presbyterian Lay Committee, founded in 1964 by seven corporate executives to resist confessional relaxation in the United Presbyterian Church and, after a while, to oppose clerical protests against the Vietnam War.[89] Nor, despite some penetration of Britain, has the Full Gospel Business Men's Fellowship International, devoted from 1951 to spreading a charismatic gospel without the shackles of pentecostal bureaucracy, managed to shed its American image.[90] The offering of a prize to the "Layman of the Year," as was done by the NAE, would be well-nigh unthinkable in Britain, where for long, even in congregations geared for outreach, the laypeople of some denominations were expected to do no more than hand out hymnbooks or organize sales of work.[91] Again, in the United States there were constant fears of religious domineering and attempts to snuff out popular rights. A pastor of the Christian and Missionary Alliance voiced relief that at the organizing meeting of the NAE in 1943 there was "no religious giraffe braying and lording it over the herd."[92] In Britain, by contrast, social inequalities were often regarded as tools to be used in the interests of the gospel. Peers were still sought as figureheads of evangelical organizations, at least in the earlier part of the period, and it was the aim of E. J. H. Nash (always known as Bash) to win key public schoolboys for Christ in the confidence that their intellectual gifts and gentlemanly standing would lead to an extension of Christian influence in the next generation—a confidence that turned out to be entirely justified.[93] Evangelical strategy entailed operating within the existing structures of society. Deference remained almost as powerful a force in Britain as was egalitarianism in America. The contrast in the social settings must loom large in any understanding of why Americans were so often willing to break with the wisdom of the past in creating their own religious organizations.

A related difference between the two countries lay in the field of education. Although both expanded their higher education systems in the postwar era, American participation rates were far greater. By the late 1980s, when about 14 percent of the eligible age cohort went into postschool education in Britain, the American proportion was roughly 50 percent.[94] The British system created an elite; the American equivalent catered for the masses. Within the diversity of American higher education, there were by the 1980s over 450 institutions bearing an evangelical stamp.[95] The Bible colleges, which functioned as the institutional backbone of fundamentalism,[96] had only a handful of counterparts in Britain. Consequently a high proportion of American evangelicals, and especially their intending ministers, inhabited a separate world of experience during their studies. Ministers of all the traditional denominations in Britain trained in or about a select university, the evangelicals among them rubbing shoulders with people of more liberal theological persuasion or of none. Their spiritual nurture was provided by Christian unions affiliated to the Inter-Varsity Fellowship, whose general secretary, Douglas Johnson, was keen to instill solid theological interests.[97] Associated with the Inter-Varsity

Fellowship from 1945 was the Tyndale Fellowship, which, under the guiding hand of F. F. Bruce, cultivated biblical scholarship while explicitly repudiating fundamentalism. Its members, Bruce explained, professed a belief in biblical infallibility, but that principle, far from being identical with biblical inerrancy, meant simply "that the Scriptures themselves, in their proper sense, never lead astray the soul who is sincerely seeking truth."[98] Here was an ethos open to the intellectual world that set the tone for evangelicalism in Britain.

The American movement, by contrast, was often less marked by respect for academic standards. The profile of educational attainment among evangelicals in the United States was lower than for other religious groups, and as late as the 1970s fully 18 percent of Southern Baptist pastors had no education beyond high school.[99] The difference between the movements in the two countries emerged, for instance, in their attitude toward evolution. Whereas a survey of American evangelicals in the 1980s showed that 82 percent opted for special creation in preference to theistic evolution,[100] in Britain the research scientists of the Inter-Varsity Fellowship led the way in endorsing evolution. Another way in which educational patterns impinged on evangelical religion will be noted later, but here it must be concluded that in Britain they tended to discourage attitudes associated with fundamentalism.

A third background factor was geography. The United States is almost half a continent; Britain is merely an offshore island. Consequently land in America, though no longer free for taking, is readily available on a huge scale. Jim Bakker's theme park in North Carolina—Heritage U.S.A.—was carved out of four square miles of "natural wilderness."[101] The creation of sprawling suburbs, perhaps the postwar equivalent of the frontier, was accompanied by the construction of new church buildings on an unprecedented scale. In 1945 there were eight Baptist churches in San Diego, but only fifteen years later, with one having disbanded, there were eighteen.[102] Fresh building operations were rarely impeded by planning controls, by contrast with Britain, where tight restrictions on suburban growth were imposed under the Town and Country Planning Act of 1947.[103] In Britain urban property values scaled new heights, putting sites for places of worship beyond the pocket of most congregations; in the areas zoned for new estates, local authorities frequently made minimal provision for church accommodation. In America the planting of new churches seemed infinitely easier.

The vast land area of the United States also made inevitable the sectionalism that has become ingrained in national life. The East Coast, the Midwest, the Far West, and the South have developed entirely different characters. The southern states, which by one computation in the early 1980s contained about 45 percent of America's evangelicals, were more dominated by Bible-believing religion than any other part of the Western Hemisphere.[104] Although there was a high degree of unanimity over Protestant basics in the South, it was natural for minor points of difference to loom large. Once the seed of dissension was sown, as it was in the postwar period, a harvest of fissiparity would be reaped. Furthermore, at least in the earlier part of the period, local religious cultures were remarkably resilient. In 1950 in half the American counties, one denomination accounted for more than half the church members.[105] Although subsequently, with increasing job mobility, the pattern was eroded, the persistence of local allegiances had permitted the growth of regional religious empires, often predominantly rural, of which W. B. Riley's based on Minneapolis is a good example. As the disintegration of Riley's organizations after his death illustrates, their cement was essentially the personality of the founder.[106] The size of America, at least before the development of cheap internal air travel, discouraged contact between such local potentates. It has been suggested that personal connections go a long way toward explaining the cohesion of the Protestant establishment in America.[107] Although the NAE helped to create similar networks,[108] being left outside its circles was both cause and effect of isolation— and therefore of an inclination toward separation. The small size of Britain, by contrast, encouraged confidence-building contacts between conservative evangelicals and denominational leaders. Thus W. G. Channon, an ardent premillennialist among the Baptists, rose to become chairman of the Ministerial Recognition Committee of the Baptist Union.[109] Likewise the early leaders of the charismatic house churches met regularly and so were able to coordinate their work much more than their equivalents in the United States.[110] Whereas geography promoted centripetal tendencies on one side of the Atlantic, it strengthened centrifugal trends on the other. It joins the social and the educational factors as major underlying explanations of the contrasting ecclesiastical patterns of the two countries.

The second cluster of traits for examination surrounds the issue of participation in public affairs. In 1976, when in Jimmy Carter the American people chose a Southern Baptist as president, it was declared to be "the Year of the Evangelical." Conservative Protestantism was rediscovered by the national media and has rarely been out of the headlines since. In principle, social action had been firmly on the agenda of the NAE ever since the publication of Carl Henry's book *The Uneasy Conscience of Modern Fundamentalism* in 1947, but it was some time before the field became an evangelical priority.[111] Nevertheless a repudiation of any conflict between a personal and a social gospel appeared in the very first issue of Henry's *Christianity Today.*[112] By the later 1960s a social dimension was unblushingly restored to evangelical faith.[113] A second wave of turning toward the world, with Jerry Falwell's Moral Majority in the vanguard, took place in the late 1970s. Fundamentalists who had previously been as chary of social involvement as of religious compromise began to argue that while there must still be biblical separation from modernists in theology, there could be uninhibited cooperation with almost any ally on public questions.[114] The new religious right was forged in time to undergird the presidency of Ronald Reagan.

In Britain, by contrast, evangelicals achieved far less public salience. In 1971, when Maurice Wood was appointed bishop of Norwich, the queen had to have the label for his churchmanship, "conservative evangelical," explained to her. Her Majesty had not previously heard the expression.[115] Although evangelicals did pay increasing attention to social issues, they attracted much less notice. In the same year that the queen asked her question there took place the "Festival of Light," a series of rallies to burn beacons as warnings against the inrush of permissiveness. Instead of pressing on with mass mobilization, however, the festival's organizers chose to turn it into a low-profile body for research and recommendations to government departments.[116] British evangelicals were not normally seen as a force to be reckoned with in national life. The outstanding exception was when, in 1986, an evangelical-led coalition managed to defeat government proposals to allow unrestricted shop opening on Sundays.[117] In general, however, there was far less participation in the public arena. What accounts for the differing degrees of national permeation? Clearly what has already been discussed contributes to the explanation. In Britain, for instance, the weakness of separatist fundamentalism meant that there was too narrow a social base for any counterpart to the Moral Majority. Nevertheless there are several further transatlantic contrasts that shed light on the issue.

The primary reason for the greater impact of evangelicals on national life in America lies in their sheer weight of numbers. In 1976 a Gallup poll found that 34 percent of Americans were willing to identify themselves as "born again," and the proportion rose to 40 percent in 1984. Although there was a tendency in the late 1970s for the media, in the first flush of their discovery, to exaggerate the strength of the movement, the proportion of the population claiming to have been active in personal evangelism and to hold a literal interpretation of the Bible as well as to be born again, at 18 percent in 1976 and 22 percent in 1984, confirmed that evangelicalism was a major force.[118] No British surveys have requested a similar form of self-appraisal, and so the only firm numerical indication of evangelical strength is the finding that in 1989, when 10 percent of the English population attended church, only 28 percent of that proportion worshiped in congregations calling themselves evangelical.[119] The resulting figure of a mere 2.8 percent of the population is not strictly comparable with the American statistics, since on the one hand it includes individuals who might not themselves profess evangelical beliefs and on the other it restricts the label to churchgoers. It is, however, all that is available. It is sufficient to show the enormous difference in size between the evangelical communities on the two sides of the Atlantic.

What is more, conservative Protestantism in the United States was known to be growing, sometimes spectacularly. The Southern Baptists, for instance, organized an evangelistic drive called "A Million More in Fifty-Four," and in the following year there were nearly 29,000 baptisms in the denomination within the single state of Alabama.[120] In the 1950s, however, the evangelical advance was not exceptional, for these were also boom years for the mainline churches. Yet from the 1960s, and even more from the 1970s, it was becoming apparent that, while mainline churches were losing members, distinctly evangelical bodies were gaining them. Between 1973 and 1983, for example, the membership of the United Methodist Church decreased by 8 percent but that of the Assemblies of God increased by 71 percent.[121] Individual congregations attained gargantuan proportions. In 1982 the independent First Baptist Church at Hammond, Indiana, claimed 67,267 members.[122] Likewise evangeli-

cal organizations mushroomed. By the 1970s Navigators had 2,200 staff workers serving in the United States, and by 1988 even the Christian Motorcycle
Association had 28,000 members organized in 300 chapters.[123] In Britain, for
the sake of comparison, the highest Sunday attendance at any church in 1991
was thought to be the just over 3,500 who worshiped at the Kensington
Temple of the Elim Pentecostal Church.[124] It was the United States that could
boast the big battalions.

A second feature of America that conditioned evangelical public activity
was the country's greater prosperity. Throughout the postwar period there
was more wealth per person in the United States than in Britain. By 1988 the
American gross domestic product per captia was over $18,000, while the
British equivalent was under $12,000.[125] Already by 1950 there were striking
symptoms of more widespread affluence in America; in that year, when about
25 percent of British homes were owner occupied, the American proportion
was 55 percent.[126] As Bill Bright, the founder of Campus Crusade for Christ,
expressed it in 1970, God had given the United States not only unlimited
physical and human resources but also unlimited finances.[127] Evangelicals
generally, like many other Americans, nevertheless wished the federal authorities to take away as small a share of the people's money as possible. It was
typical for a Texas evangelist to denounce "the idolatry of excessive government."[128] Facilities in the fields of welfare and health care, which the British
expected as a government service, were left in America to private initiative.
The charitable impulse, favored by the tax regime, was far less quenched in
the United States than in the Britain of the welfare state.

Furthermore, the churches continued to claim the lion's share of the nation's generosity. In 1985 fully 72 percent of all individual giving went to
religious institutions.[129] In the years immediately after the war American
religious organizations, taken together, actually enjoyed a higher annual income than the whole budget of the British government.[130] Although evangelicals included a smaller proportion of the rich than other religious groups,[131]
they shared in the general prosperity and the nation's willingness to give.
Hence their churches commonly employed several ministers, hired full-time
secretaries for church offices, and launched elaborate programs—all rare
phenomena in Britain, at least until the 1980s. Whereas in 1963 the NAE
Stewardship commission organized a session entitled "Should Evangelical
Churches Make Business Investments?"[132] the question would hardly have
been worth asking in Britain. There was an American ethos in which prosperity teaching, with each charismatic evangelist advertising a "master key to
financial success," could take root and flourish.[133] Wealth flowed into organizations that promised to spread the gospel or else to make its values impinge
on national life. In the mid-1970s the reported annual budget of the Oral
Roberts empire reached the dizzy heights of $15 million.[134] Much came in tiny
sums from individuals who, while far from well-to-do, could afford in so rich a
country to part with a portion of their income. Other benefactions came from
a few fabulously wealthy businessmen, among whom J. Howard Pew, head of
the Sun Oil Company, was probably pre-eminent.[135] Successful entrepreneurs

played a much smaller role in Britain. In Methodism, for example, the lay leadership included fewer business leaders in the 1950s than in the 1930s, and though the Brethren housing magnate Sir John Laing was generous to evangelical causes, he was a relatively unusual figure.[136] There was, it is true, an effective organization called Christian Teamwork founded by businessmen in 1957 to carry Christian principles into social and industrial life, but again this body flourished for only half a dozen years.[137] In general it is fair to say that in Britain there were fewer wealthy individuals and there was less inclination to give. The evangelical impact on society at large suffered accordingly.

The contrast between the nations was even sharper in another area—the role played by the media. In more traditional aspects of the communications industry, there was indeed a great deal of similarity. The Christian Booksellers Association of America had a successful British counterpart,[138] and while there was no British equivalent to the Evangelical Press Association,[139] there were many popular evangelical periodicals. But in the making of religious films there was little British competition. At first the whole concept seemed alien and distasteful to some; the weekly newspaper read by many Anglican Evangelicals dismissed a Billy Graham publicity film in 1953 as "crude, garish and unconvincing."[140] In quarters where Christian films were more appreciated, they were often imported from the United States.

The contrast between the two countries was at its most acute in broadcasting. Local radio stations proliferated in postwar America. By 1946 there were some 1,000; by 1963, the number had grown to 5,000; and by 1986, to 10,000.[141] Already in 1944 it was thought essential to add a radio broadcast to any well-conducted evangelistic rally for young people.[142] By 1982 the National Religious Broadcasters, affiliated with the NAE, could list 922 radio stations in its directory.[143] No comparable penetration of broadcasting was possible in Britain because, instead of a plethora of local initiatives, a monopoly of the airwaves was entrusted to the British Broadcasting Corporation. There was a weekly "Radio Mission" over a month in 1954 at the instance of an evangelical bishop, but the experiment caused ruffled debate in the corridors of the BBC. "Austerity," minuted one BBC official in 1952, "should be the watchword in religious broadcasting."[144] It was feared that evangelicals would provoke controversy, and so their contribution was tightly restricted.

The same contrast marked the television systems of the two countries. The so-called electronic church that emerged in the United States after the liberalization of federal regulations in 1960 developed over the next quarter century into a vast array of sixty nationally syndicated programs, five Christian cable networks, and numerous religiously owned television stations.[145] In Britain, however, it was for most of the period impossible to buy television time. In the year 1952–53 only 1 percent of BBC programming was religious,[146] and even after the appearance of commercial television in 1955, its religous content was bound by strict rules that effectively excluded an evangelical presence. As soon as satellite transmission was introduced in the mid-1980s, the largest charismatic grouping screened a thirty-minute program, but its audience ratings were extremely low.[147] There was no evangelical breakthrough into television. Although in America fundraising occupied over a quarter of the broadcast time of religious television,[148] and although the media empire was rocked by the scandals surrounding Jim Bakker and Jimmy Swaggart in 1987–1988, there can be no doubt that the electronic church brought evangelicalism to public notice. It increasingly turned to disseminating conservative values and even, in 1988, acted as the launching pad for Pat Robertson's bid for the presidency. The differing structures of the media in the two countries dictated that British evangelicalism would be denied the advantages—as well as saved from the perils—of involvement in broadcasting.

A further crucial transatlantic difference lay in the structure of politics. Britain has been analyzed as having a centralized government, an administration staffed by selection, and a tight form of party cohesion; the United States, by contrast, possesses a diffuse pattern of government, an administration chosen by election, and a loose style of party organisation.[149] The consequence is that there is far more scope in the American system for the exercise of leverage by minority and regional forces such as sections of evangelicalism. One particular constitutional principle—the separation of powers—has given judicial decisions an importance generally denied them in Britain. Supreme Court rulings against school prayers in 1963 and in favor of abortion ten years later were of first-rate importance in provoking evangelicals to enter the political arena.[150] The former decision, according to Harold J. Ockenga at the time, "leaves America in the same position constitutionally as Communist Russia."[151] The involvement of evangelicals in public affairs, however, was also a product of the higher standards of education many of them achieved in postwar America. With greater awareness of the issues, there came a greater willingness to abandon their earlier quietism and, at least in the earlier stages of the process, to express progressive opinions. In 1968 as high a proportion of evangelicals as of theological liberals favored civil rights and opposed the Vietnam War.[152] The political culture of the United States, however, tended to push evangelical opinion in a more conservative direction. The patriotism of flag and freedom was far more deeply ingrained in America. A poll in the early 1980s showed that whereas 58 percent of the British sample said they were "very proud" of their country, as many as 87 percent said the same in the United States.[153] A civil religion that gave supernatural sanction to America's mission in the world came readily to evangelicals.[154] One of them even wrote in 1975 that the constitution had been "divinely inspired."[155] There was intense hostility to forces that seemed to threaten the liberties of the nation, whether John F. Kennedy, whom the *Arkansas Baptist* saw as a tool of a "ruthless religious totalitarianism controlled from Rome," or international Communism, which led the NAE to resolve in 1953 in favor of a McCarthyite investigation of unsound religious leaders.[156] Long before the mass mobilization of the "New Christian Right" in the late 1970s, there was a tendency for evangelical opinion to gravitate to conservative positions. Despite striking exceptions such as the Sojourners, American evangelicals normally took their stand on the right.

Their counterparts across the Atlantic were at first generally loyal to the twin foci of crown and empire, but tacit monarchism had few practical implications, and the empire was disintegrating. Although allegiance to the Conservative party preponderated, particularly in the established churches, there were also many evangelicals, especially of a younger generation, who voted Liberal or even Labor. There was no possibility of partisan pronouncements, let alone a *levée en masse* for political ends. It was typical that, at the Nottingham Evangelical Anglican Congress in 1977, there was an explosion of protest when two group leaders, one of them a Conservative M.P., the other later ennobled by Margaret Thatcher, tried to steer a discussion group toward reporting that power in a democracy existed primarily to restrain evil rather than to achieve justice.[157] British evangelicals were fundamentally divided on politics and so were incapable of mounting more than discreet campaigns on single issues. The far greater corporate involvement of American evangelicals in the political process goes a long way toward explaining their greater impact on public affairs.

What may be concluded overall? It is clear, in the first place, that evangelicalism on the two sides of the Atlantic was the same diverse phenomenon. That needs to be stressed, since it is sometimes supposed that America (perhaps with Canada thrown in) holds a copyright on the movement. Thus evangelicalism has been described in an academic study, very valuable in itself, as "unique to North America."[158] Yet Bible-believing Christians in Britain have followed approximately the same trajectory as American evangelicals during the era since the opening of the Second World War, and there has been much two-way interaction across the Atlantic during that period. Neither point is surprising, since the four hallmarks of the movement—the emphases on conversion, activism, Bible, and cross—have been equally evident in the two countries. If there have been differences, they have been matters of degree, not of kind.

Yet, for all the common ground, the two national versions of evangelicalism have not been identical. The movement in Britain was not merely an outpost of its counterpart in the United States. There were equally significant contrasts in the two aspects—inward and outward, ecclesiastical life, and public role—that have been subjected to scrutiny. In the first place, the cluster of traits that made the movement in America more prone to ecclesiastical separatism created a rather different religious ethos there. The United States fostered a firmer resistance to the ecumenical movement, a weaker churchly sense, a far more extensive fundamentalism, a stronger leaning to dispensationalist teaching, and a wider attachment to biblical inerrancy. All these tendencies were rooted in the earlier development of American evangelicalism itself, but the ethos was also shaped by the secular context of an egalitarian society with large-scale higher education occupying a vast territory. The expression of the gospel was colored by some of the most typical facets of American civilization.

When we turn to the impact of the movement on national life, the same conclusion must be drawn. As they emerged from the relative obscurity of the 1930s, leading evangelicals in the two countries formulated similar goals. The

Americans aimed, in the words of George L. Ford in 1963, "to penetrate our culture for Christ."[159] The purpose of the graduates' organizations associated with the Inter-Varsity Fellowship in Britain, according to the editor of their magazine in 1948, was "the subjection of all life to the sovereignty of Christ as Lord and Saviour."[160] Despite the same intention, there were different degrees of impact—supremely because of the unequal numerical strength of the two national branches of evangelicalism, but also because of contrasts between the host societies in terms of their wealth, their media, and their political systems. The higher public salience of evangelicals in the United States was the fruit of ampler opportunities as well as larger numbers. The inward and outward differences alike were shaped by the environment in which evangelicals were set. That is not to claim that the pattern of their activity was wholly determined by conditions in the postwar world. On the contrary, the fundamentalist legacy from the interwar years and the high evangelical numbers inherited from a remoter past exerted a powerful influence in distinguishing the American phenomenon from its British counterpart. Yet it is impossible to deny that social, educational, geographic, economic, communications, and political factors each played a part in creating the differences. In both countries the gospel, for good or ill, was interacting with its whole cultural environment. The British and American versions of evangelicalism differed in large measure because of their settings.

Notes

1. J. C. Pollock, "Has England's Glory faded?" *Christianity Today* [hereafter *CT*], 10 December 1956, 9. I am grateful to Jim Douglas for the loan of a set of *Christianity Today.*

2. Joel Carpenter, "The Fundamentalist Leaven and the Rise of an Evangelical United Front," in *The Evangelical Tradition in America,* ed. Leonard I. Sweet (Macon, GA: Macon University Press, 1984).

3. Milton G. Sernett, "Black Religion and the Question of Evangelical Identity," in *The Variety of American Evangelicalism,* ed. Donald W. Dayton and Robert K. Johnston (Knoxville: University of Tennessee Press, 1991), 143.

4. For example, Calvary Chapel, Santa Ana, California. See Randall Balmer, *Mine Eyes Have Seen the Glory: A Journey into the Evangelical Subculture in America* (New York: Oxford University Press, 1989), chap. 1.

5. Despite, in the case of the Southern Baptists, partisan efforts to deny their evangelical identity. See J. L. Garrett, Jr, *Are Southern Baptists "Evangelicals"?* (Macon, GA: Mercer University Press, 1983).

6. A characterization that coincides with Donald Dayton's "classical evangelicalism." See his "Limits of Evangelicalism: The Pentecostal Tradition," in *Variety of American Evangelicalism,* ed. Dayton and Johnston, 48.

7. Richard T. Hughes, "Are Restorationists Evangelicals?," in *Variety of American Evangelicalism,* ed. Dayton and Johnston, 128. See D. W. Bebbington, *Evangelicalism in Modern Britain: A History from the 1730s to the 1980s* (London: Unwin Hyman, 1989), 252–53.

8. Mark Ellingsen, "Lutheranism," in *Variety of American Evangelicalism,* ed. Dayton and Johnston, 238; Mark A. Noll and Cassandra Niemczyk, "Evangelicals as Self-Consciously Reformed," in ibid., 204, 213, 216, 218; Bebbington, *Evangelicalism in Modern Britain,* 56–57.

9. Walter J. Hollenweger, *The Pentecostals* (London: SCM Press, 1972), 311–12.

10. Donald Dayton, "Some Doubts about the Usefulness of the Category 'Evangelical,' " in *Variety of American Evangelicalism,* ed. Dayton and Johnston 248–50.

11. Max Warren, *What Is an Evangelical? An Enquiry* (London: Church Book Room, [1944]), 23; J. I. Packer, *The Evangelical Anglican Identity Problem: An Analysis* (Oxford: Latimer House, 1978), 21.

12. *Church of England Newspaper* [herafter *CEN*], 16 January 1953, 3.

13. Balmer, *Mine Eyes Have Seen the Glory,* 17.

14. Billy Graham, "Biblical Authority in Evangelism," *CT,* 15 October 1956, 6.

15. J. R. W. Stott, *Fundamentalism and Evangelism* (London: For the Evangelical Alliance by Crusade, 1956), 28.

16. Gallup polls identify evangelicals as those professing the other three characteristics (conversion, activism, and biblicism), not this one (*Religion in America: Fifty Years, 1935–1985,* Gallup Report No. 236 [1985], 38). Likewise Timothy L. Smith has listed the evangelical emphases as Scripture, regeneration, and evangelism, while Thomas Askew, agreeing on those three, adds the nurture of spirituality (Robert K. Johnston, "American Evangelicalism: An Extended Family," in *Variety of American Evangelicalism,* ed. Dayton and Johnston, 262, 261).

17. Bill Hopkinson, "Changes in the Emphases of Evangelical Belief, 1970–1980: Evidence from New Hymnody," *Churchman* 95 (1981): 131.

18. George Carey, *The Gate of Glory* (London: Hodder and Stoughton, 1986).

19. *CEN,* 8 July 1966, 1.

20. Sernett, "Black Religion," 137.

21. This evangelical quadrilateral, as it applies to the British movement since the 1730s, is discussed in Bebbington, *Evangelicalism in Modern Britain,* chap. 1.

22. Robert A. Schneider, "Voice of Many Waters: Federation in the Twentieth Century," in *Between the Times: The Travail of the Protestant Establishment in America, 1900–1960,* ed. William R. Hutchison (Cambridge: Cambridge University Press, 1989), 100.

23. Dennis N. Voskuil, "Reaching Out: Mainline Protestantism and the Media," in *Between the Times,* ed. Hutchison, 79.

24. Randle Manwaring, *From Controversy to Co-Existence: Evangelicals in the Church of England, 1914–1980* (Cambridge: Cambridge University Press, 1985), 43.

25. Warren, *What Is an Evangelical?* 7.

26. Robert Wuthnow, *The Restructuring of American Religion: Society and Faith since World War II* (Princeton: Princeton University Press, 1988), 140.

27. Joel A. Carpenter, ed., *The Youth for Christ Movement and Its Pioneers* (New York: Garland Publishing, 1988); Frederick P. Wood and Mary S. Wood, *Youth Advancing* (London: National Young Life Campaign, 1961).

28. *CEN,* 19 January 1959, 6; Michael Saward, *Evangelicals on the Move* (London: Mowbray, 1987), 34.

29. Richard G. Hutcheson, Jr., *Mainline Churches and the Evangelicals: A Challenging Crisis?* (Atlanta: John Knox Press, 1981), 18.

30. Voskuil, "Reaching Out," 79.

31. Peter Hocken, *Streams of Renewal: The Origins and Early Growth of the Charismatic Movement in Great Britain* (Exeter: Paternoster Press, 1986); Andrew

Walker, *Restoring the Kingdom: The Radical Christianity of the House Church Movement* (London: Hodder and Stoughton, 1985); Bebbington, *Evangelicalism in Modern Britain,* chap. 7.

32. James D. Hunter, *Evangelicalism: The Coming Generation* (Chicago: University of Chicago Press, 1987), 58; Bebbington, *Evangelicalism in Modern Britain,* 263–64.

33. *United Evangelical Action* [hereafter *UEA*], September 1963, 9 (Neil Windgarden).

34. Harold Lindsell, *Park Street Prophet: A Life of Harold John Ockenga* (Wheaton, IL: Van Kampen Press, 1951), 121.

35. J. C. Pollock, *A Cambridge Movement* (London: John Murray, 1953), 254–57, 259.

36. J. C. Pollock, *The Keswick Story* (London: Hodder and Stoughton, 1964), 169.

37. *CT,* 29 March 1968, 27; Carl F. H. Henry, *Confessions of a Theologian: An Autobiography* (Waco, TX: World Books, 1986), chap. 16.

38. Walker, *Restorinng the Kingdom,* 193.

39. James D. Hunter, *American Evangelicalism: Conservative Religion and the Quandary of Modernity* (New Brunswick, NJ: Rutgers University Press, 1983), 58.

40. Hocken, *Streams of Renewal,* 148–49.

41. Adrian Hastings, *A History of English Christianity, 1920–1985* (London: Collins, 1986), 453–59.

42. *CT,* 2 September 1957, 3; George M. Marsden, *Reforming Fundamentalism: Fuller Seminary and the New Evangelicalism* (Grand Rapids: Eerdmans, 1987), 188.

43. *CT,* 12 November 1956, p. 31; *UEA,* March 1963, 6.

44. *CT,* 15 October 1956–10 December 1956.

45. John Carter, *Donald Gee: Pentecostal Statesman* (Nottingham: Assemblies of God, 1975), chap. 7; D. Edwin Harrell, Jr, *All Things Are Possible: The Healing and Charismatic Revivals in Modern America* (Bloomington: Indiana University Press, 1975), 109–11, 114–15.

46. Mark A. Noll, *Between Faith and Criticism: Evangelicals, Scholarship, and the Bible in America* (San Francisco: Harper and Row, 1986), 101–5.

47. *UEA,* November 1963, 51.

48. I am grateful to Ian Cotton for this information.

49. Ian Tyrrell, "American Exceptionalism in an Age of International History," *American Historical Review* 96 (1991): 1050.

50. Byron E. Shafer, ed., *Is America Different? A New Look at American Exceptionalism* (Oxford: Clarendon Press, 1991), viii.

51. Joel A. Carpenter, ed., *A New Evangelical Coalition: Early Documents of the National Association of Evangelicals* (New York: Garland Publishing, 1988), 39.

52. *CEN,* 28 October 1966, 3, 5.

53. *CT,* 26 November 1956, 20–22; C. O. Buchanan et al., *Growing into Union: Proposals for Forming a United Church in England* (London: SPCK, 1970).

54. Mark Silk, "The Rise of the 'New Evangelicalism': Shock and Adjustment," in *Between the Times,* ed. Hutchison, 283.

55. *CT,* 5 July 1968, 26. Cf. W. R. Hutchison, "Protestantism as Establishment," in *Between the Times,* ed. Hutchison, 13–16.

56. Voskuil, "Reaching Out," 75.

57. Peter Brierley, ed., *Prospects for the Nineties* (London: Marc Europe, 1991), 30, 42, 26, 28.

58. I am grateful for this example to W. R. Ward.

59. Bassett, "North American Holiness Movement," 73.

60. Peter Brierley, ed., *UK Christian Handbook 1989/90 Edition* (Bromley, Kent: Marc Europe, 1988), 166; Jack Ford, *In the Steps of John Wesley: The Church of the Nazarene in Britain* (Kansas City, MO: Nazarene Publishing House, 1968), 130n.

61. Richard Quebedeaux, *The New Charismatics* II (San Francisco: Harper and Row, 1983), 84.

62. Brierley, *Prospects for the Nineties,* 23.

63. Harrell, *All Things Are Possible,* 145–46, 231–32.

64. *The Charismatic Movement in the Church of England* (London: Church Information Office, 1981), 21.

65. Hocken, *Streams of Renewal;* Walker, *Restoring the Kingdom.*

66. Brierley, *Prospects for the Nineties,* 52.

67. Edward England, *The Spirit of Renewal* (Eastbourne: Kingsway, 1982), chap. 9.

68. "The Baptist Doctrine of the Church," in *Baptist Union Documents, 1948–1977,* ed. Roger Hayden (London: Baptist Historical Society, 1980), 5.

69. For example, A. M. Stibbs, *Sacrament, Sacrifice, and Eucharist* (London: Tyndale Press, 1961).

70. Chiefly the Protestant Truth Society, the National Church League, and the Church Association, the last two of which merged in 1950 as Church Society (*Church Gazette,* July–August 1950, 1).

71. William V. Trollinger, "Riley's Empire: Northwestern Bible School and Fundamentalism in the Upper Midwest," *Church History* 57 (1988): 211.

72. *UEA,* July 1963, 14.

73. *UEA,* March 1963, 31; October 1963, 47.

74. For example, Balmer, *Mine Eyes Have Seen the Glory,* 39 (Norman Geisler of Dallas Seminary); Hunter, *American Evangelicalism,* 7.

75. Marsden, *Reforming Fundamentalism,* 268; Bassett, "North American Holiness Movement," 76–95; Sernett, "Black Religion," 142, 144.

76. Ronald H. Nash, *Evangelicals in America: Who They Are, What They Believe* (Nashville: Abingdon, 1987), 39.

77. I owe this point to Timothy George.

78. D. W. Bebbington, "The Persecution of George Jackson: A British Fundamentalist Controversy," in *Persecution and Toleration,* Studies in Church History 21, ed. W. J. Sheils (Oxford: Blackwell, 1984); idem, "Baptists and Fundamentalism in Inter-War Britain," in *Protestant Evangelicalism: Britain, Ireland, Germany, and America, c. 1750–c. 1950: Essays in Honour of W. R. Ward,* ed. Keith Robbins (Oxford: Blackwell, 1990).

79. *Fundamentalism: A Religious Problem: Letters to the Editor of "The Times" and a Leading Article* (London: Times Publishing, 1955).

80. Bryan R. Wilson, "The Elim Foursquare Gospel Church," in *Sects and Society: A Sociological Study of Three Religious Groups in Britain* (London: William Heinemann, 1961), 25–28.

81. D. W. Bebbington, "The Advent Hope in British Evangelicalism since 1800," *Scottish Journal of Religious Studies* 9 (1988): 107–9; F. R. Coad, *Prophetic Developments, with Particular Reference to the Early Brethren Movement* (Pinner, Middlesex: Christian Brethren Research Fellowship, 1966), 29–30.

82. D. F. Wright, "Soundings in the Doctrine of Scripture in British Evangelicalism in the First Half of the Twentieth Century," *Tyndale Bulletin* 31 (1980): 87–106.

83. J. Elwyn Davies, *Striving Together: A Statement of Principles That Have Governed the Aims and Policy of the Evangelical Movement of Wales* (Bryntirion,

Bridgend, Glamorgan: Evangelical Press of Wales, 1984), 50; I. H. Marshall, *Biblical Inspiration* (London: Hodder and Stoughton, 1982), chap. 3.

84. Byron E. Shafer, "What Is the American Way? Four Themes in Search of Their Next Incarnation," in *Is America Different?*, ed. Shafer, 233–39.

85. Geoffrey Gorer, *The Americans: A Study in National Character* (London: Cresset Press, 1955), 116.

86. Elaine J. Lawless, *Handmaidens of the Lord: Pentecostal Women Preachers and Traditional Religion* (Philadelphia: University of Pennsylvania Press, 1988), 24–25.

87. Nathan O. Hatch, "Evangelicalism as a Democratic Movement," in *Evangelicalism in Modern America,* ed. George Marsden (Grand Rapids: Eerdmans, 1984), esp. 80.

88. Douglas Kennedy, *In God's Country: Travels in the Bible Belt, USA* (London: Unwin Hyman, 1989), 77.

89. Hutcheson, *Mainline Churches and the Evangelicals,* 74.

90. Harrell, *All Things Are Possible,* 146–49.

91. *UEA,* March 1963, 7; Pollock, "Has England's Glory Faded?" 9.

92. *United . . . We Stand* (Boston: National Association of Evangelicals, 1953), 55 (William P. Gilles).

93. John Eddison, ed., *"Bash": A Study in Spiritual Power* (Basingstoke, Hants: Marshall, Morgan and Scott, 1983).

94. Martin Trow, "American Higher Education: 'Exceptional' or Just Different?" in *Is America Different?* ed. Shafer, 141–42.

95. Hunter, *American Evangelicalism,* 58.

96. Joel A. Carpenter, "Fundamentalist Institutions and the Rise of Evangelical Protestantism, 1929–1942," *Church History* 49 (1980): 62–75.

97. "Douglas Johnson," *The Times* (London), 14 December 1991, 16.

98. F. F. Bruce, "The Tyndale Fellowship for Biblical Research," *Evangelical Quarterly* 19 (1947): 56–57.

99. Hunter, *American Evangelicalism,* 54; R. A. Baker, *The Southern Baptist Convention and Its People, 1607–1972* (Nashville: Broadman, 1974), 488.

100. Hunter, *American Evangelicalism,* 63.

101. Kennedy, *In God's Country,* 192.

102. Wuthnow, *Restructuring,* 27.

103. Arthur Marwick, *British Society since 1945* (Harmondsworth, Middlesex: Penguin, 1982), 61.

104. Hunter, *American Evangelicalism,* 52.

105. Edwin S. Gaustad, *Historical Atlas of Religion in America* (New York: Harper and Row, 1962), 159.

106. Trollinger, "Riley's Empire," 211.

107. Hutchison, "Protestantism as Establishment," 6–11.

108. Wuthnow, *Restructuring,* 174–76.

109. *The Baptist Handbook for 1971* (London: Baptist Union, 1971), 378–79.

110. Hocken, *Streams of Renewal,* 190.

111. Marsden, *Reforming Fundamentalism,* 79–82.

112. Addison H. Leitch, "The Primary Task of the Church," *CT,* 15 October 1956, 13.

113. Leonard I. Sweet, "The 1960s: The Crises of Liberal Christianity and the Public Emergence of Evangelicalism," in *Evangelicalism and Modern America,* ed. Marsden, 44.

114. Bill J. Leonard, "Independent Baptists: From Sectarian Minority to 'Moral Majority,' " *Church History* 56 (1987): 514–15.

115. Owen Chadwick, *Michael Ramsey: A Life* (Oxford: Clarendon Press, 1990), 142.

116. Bebbington, *Evangelicalism in Modern Britain,* 265; "Mr Raymond Johnston," *The Times* (London), 25 October 1985, 16.

117. *The Times* (London), 16 April 1986, 1.

118. *Religion in America,* 38.

119. Brierley, *Prospects for the Nineties,* 23.

120. Fred J. Hood, "Kentucky," and J. Wayne Flint, "Alabama," in *Religion in the Southern States: A Historical Study,* ed. Samuel S. Hill (Macon, GA: Mercer University Press, 1983), 121, 23.

121. *Religion in America,* 11.

122. Leonard, "Independent Baptists," 505.

123. Wuthnow, *Restructuring,* 192; Kennedy, *In God's Country,* 218.

124. *Renewal* 184 (1991): 18. I am grateful to Ian Randall for this reference.

125. Richard Rose, "Is American Public Policy Exceptional?" in *Is America Different?* ed. Shafer, 194.

126. Wuthnow, *Restructuring,* 154.

127. Ibid., 248.

128. Ibid., 204 (James Robison).

129. S. M. Lipset, "American Exceptionalism Redefined," in *Is America Different?* ed. Shafer, 28.

130. Robert Wuthnow, *The Struggle for America's Soul: Evangelicals, Liberal, and Secularism* (Grand Rapids: Eerdmans, 1989), 29.

131. Hunter, *American Evangelicalism,* 54.

132. *UEA,* March 1963, 7.

133. Harrell, *All Things Are Possible,* 229.

134. Ibid., 225.

135. Marsden, *Reforming Fundamentalism,* 155.

136. D. J. Jeremy, *Capitalists and Christians: Business Leaders and the Churches in Britain, 1900–1960* (Oxford: Clarendon Press, 1990), 337; F. Roy Coad, *Laing: The Biography of Sir John W. Laing, C.B.E. (1879–1978)* (London: Hodder and Stoughton, 1979).

137. Jeremy, *Capitalists and Christians,* 220–27.

138. Balmer, *Mine Eyes Have Seen the Glory,* chap. 8.

139. Richard N. Ostling, "Evangelical Publishing and Broadcasting," in *Evangelicalism and Modern America,* ed. Marsden, 48.

140. *CEN,* 31 July 1953, 2.

141. *The Times* (London), 23 April 1986, 16.

142. Torrey Johnson and Robert Cook, *Reaching Youth for Christ* (Chicago: Moody Press, 1944), 37.

143. Ostling, "Evangelical Publishing and Broadcasting," 49.

144. Kenneth M. Wolfe, *The Churches and the British Broadcasting Corporation, 1922–1956: The Politics of Broadcast Religion* (London: SCM Press, 1984), 464.

145. Razelle Frankl, *Televangelism: The Marketing of Popular Religion* (Carbondale: Southern Illinois University Press, 1987), 143.

146. *CEN,* 4 June 1954, 1.

147. Steve Bruce, *Pray TV: Televangelism in America* (London: Routledge, 1990), 226.

148. Frankl, *Televangelism,* 133.

149. Steve Bruce, *The Rise and Fall of the New Christian Right: Conservative Protestant Politics in America, 1978–1988* (Oxford: Clarendon Press, 1990), 69–76.

150. Wuthnow, *Struggle for America's Soul,* 55–57.

151. *UEA,* August 1963, 18.

152. Wuthnow, *Restructuring, 187–89.*

153. Lipset, "American Exceptionalism Redefined," 35.

154. Richard V. Pierard, *The Unequal Yoke* (Philadelphia: Lippincott, 1970).

155. Wuthnow, *Restructuring,* 246 (Rus Walton).

156. *Arkansas Baptist,* 8 September 1960, 8, quoted by John L. Eighmy, *Churches in Cultural Captivity: A History of the Social Attitudes of Southern Baptists* (Knoxville: University of Tennessee Press, 1987), 172; Silk, "Rise of the 'New Evangelicalism,' " 281.

157. *CEN,* 22 April 1977, 8. The leaders were Michael Alison, M.P., and Brian Griffiths, from 1991 Lord Griffiths of Fforestfach.

158. Hunter, *American Evangelicalism,* 7.

159. *UEA,* July 1963, 14.

160. *Christian Graduate,* March 1948, 1.

19

On Being Evangelical: Some Theological Differences and Similarities

DAVID WELLS

The attempt to define evangelicalism is growing more difficult because its center—what has provided the unity for people who differ on particulars—has become increasingly elusive and hard to describe. The many attempts to find the ligaments that should properly link center and periphery, unity and diversity, are being frustrated, and the discussion has now turned stale.

So what is happening? Some have argued that this freshly resurgent complexity in the evangelical world is not actually new. It is something that was obscured in the past by some overly facile analysis.[1] Nothing has actually changed in evangelical faith; what is changing is our recognition of its many vagaries and nuances, and this recognition is a good thing.

It is probably true that the older evangelicalism never was the simple, monolithic thing that it was often presented as being, at least in America.[2] Here, the creedal signs of the movement were sometimes read a bit selectively, using only its dominant institutions, organizations, publications, and personalities. The picture that resulted was far narrower and simpler than the reality. After all, in the period after World War II, for example, not all evangelicals were graduates from fundamentalism, not all hankered to send their children to colleges like Gordon, Wheaton, and Westmont, or to seminaries like Dallas and Fuller. Not all belonged to a church represented in the National Association of Evangelicals (NAE). Not all heard in Carl Henry's every utterance their own thoughts and convictions being expressed. Not all revered the mild, generic Calvinism that became more or less synonymous with what evangelicals were thought to believe or thought they ought to believe. Arminians and those self-consciously Reformational, such as the Missouri Synod Lutherans and the Orthodox Presbyterians, typically saw themselves as outsiders to this world. The minimal Calvinism of establishment evangelicalism was too much for Arminians, too little for robust Presbyterians, and too wrongheaded for confessional Lutherans. And though *Christianity Today* was often seen as the flagship of the evangelical armada, its readership among evangelicals has been astonish-

389

ing low, at least until it ceased to be a journal of substance. So who did it really represent during its heyday?

It was not unnatural, therefore, that new images for thinking about the evangelical world began to emerge, especialy when the power to define its nature began to slip from the fingers of its most visible and dominant leaders who had functioned as a kind of informal Curia. Perhaps, Timothy Smith ventured, evangelicalism is really a "mosaic." Or perhaps we should think of it more in terms of an extended family that, despite some strange and eccentric members, remains a single family. Or maybe there are different "types" of evangelicalism much as there are different types of viruses. Gabriel Fackre finds five such types,[3] Robert Webber fourteen.[4] The edges of evangelical practice are telling a story of growing diversity, and whether the types are seen to be few or many, the end result is still the same. Evangelicalism is a complex of theological ideas whose unity now appears in full retreat before the clamor of its many special interests. Its essence, like the morning mist, is disappearing in the bright light of modern pluralism.

A Hypothesis

In this chapter, I wish to propose a hypothesis for explaining why the word "evangelical" is now so ambiguous. This explanation will focus mainly on how the morphology of evangelical faith has changed. The result is an internal transformation that has inclined evangelicalism to settle its external relations to the modern world in new ways. In other words, this essay is attempting to account for the diffuse meanings that evangelicalism has developed on both sides of the Atlantic, not simply in terms of its theological life, but in terms of its psychological location within its respective cultures. And here, what is becoming increasingly important is not the pressure that local culture exerts upon belief—what makes American evangelicalism *American* and what British theology *British*—but what is making both modern. For modernity is a common influence on both sides of the ocean. It is the common dynamic that is lifting belief away from its participation in local culture toward involvement in the universal, cliché culture that is now emerging, one that belongs to everyone who is modern but to no one in particular. Modernity, I shall argue, is what probably accounts for the same rhythms in evangelical life on both sides of the ocean, despite many differences that arise from the respective contexts of that faith in Britain and America. While this reality produces common interests, it is also bringing about a blurring of the meaning of being evangelical. This hypothesis I offer tentatively, for as the events that are being recounted begin to overlap with living memory, they often lose their sharpness, and the spirit in which the analysis is offered must correspondingly be modest.

In sketching out this hypothesis, I will argue that three different centers to evangelical faith have emerged since World War II, three different ways by which evangelicals see themselves as related to one another, despite their differences in denominational loyalty, political outlook, theological tradition, and spiritual practice. These I need to explain briefly before proceeding to see how they have arisen in the evangelical world and with what results.

These three centers I am calling confessional, transconfessional, and charismatic. By the first, I am thinking of the characteristic way of thought that was dominant, on both sides of the Atlantic, from the early 1940s through to the 1970s, and that sought to define evangelical belief in terms of biblical doctrine. It therefore saw its internal bond to be biblical/theological, and during this period much of the evangelical discussion, as measured by both its literature and its controversy,[5] was over how properly to define this central core of belief on which evangelicals could unite. Confession, in this sense, might well include formal confessions of faith, such as Augsburg and Westminster, but it needs to be loose enough to include those who are not self-consciously Reformational but who nevertheless still think that evangelicalism should be defined by what is believed, that what is believed should be biblical, that this cannot involve less than the Reformation's formal and material principles, and that these principles should provide the bond for evangelical belief as well as prescribe its parameters. This kind of evangelicalism found its unity in commonly owned, commonly confessed *truth;* this truth is the thread by which it was tied to the previous expressions of historic Protestant faith.

In the late 1970s, however, a discernible shift began to take place around this organizing center of biblical truth. It was a shift that seems largely to have paralleled the evolution that has often been noted in the way many movements emerge. A transition occurs from the charisma of the founder to the structure, which later seeks to conserve the founding ideas. Here, too, the charisma of the postwar evangelical leaders, a charisma that was undoubtedly personal in many ways but also confessional, has undergone a transformation as evangelicalism has become increasingly organized and bureaucratized. As a result, its outward success, coupled with its growing diversity, has redefined its center or, more precisely, relocated it. The diversity has required a shift from confessional substance to simple, organizational fraternity. This fraternity, almost by virtue of its own diversity, has produced a kind of ecumenical vision in which the older confessional interests have become less important and sometimes have even withered. The ground of relatedness among evangelicals, therefore, has far less to do with living within the definitional parameters of what it meant to be evangelical and far more with belonging somewhere within the entrepreneurial or organizational life of this righteous empire.

As the older confessional lines have been moved to the periphery, new priorities and new habits have emerged in the evangelical world. Thinkers who were important in the flush of Harold John Ockenga's "neo-evangelicalism" and in the early years of *Christianity Today* now paled in comparison with managers, television personalities, and entrepreneurs. The old alliance with the business world, which has marked so many evangelical enterprises since World War II, has, if anything, been cemented even more firmly. The ubiquity of the flow chart has become inescapable as evangelicalism has became more and more bureaucratized. The appearance of the upwardly mobile in evangelical institutions has become a common sight. The pursuit of personal careers is no longer a matter to be concealed, nor yet the pursuit of the loose piles of cash that seem to litter the highway along which American evangelicalism is moving. And everywhere the importance of theological belief is being replaced by the importance of effective strategy, proficient fund-raising, and the bold building of personal bases of power and influence. In many of these developments, American evangelicalism is being quintessentially *American,* yet in Britain some of the same adaptations were also underway at the same time, though in different ways.

In the early 1960s, however, this transition was somewhat aided and somewhat complicated by the emergence of the charismatic movement in both Britain and America. By *charismatic* I am thinking primarily of the renewal movements in both Protestantism and Catholicism that began to gather considerable momentum in this decade. Their relation to the older pentecostalism has, at times, been a complicated one and not fully amicable. Older impulses from pentecostalism do weave through this story that I am attempting to sketch, and so they are also included in my reference to what is charismatic, though it is with the nonpentecostal developments that I am mainly concerned. What pentecostalism and the renewal movements have in common is that both are forms of evangelicalism that are not primarily theologies. Both arise centrally from a spiritual intuition about the presence of the Holy Spirit. Both, therefore, have an entirely different place for biblical confession, as compared with those whom I am calling confessional evangelicals, and both have an entirely different way of relating matters of diversity to that of theological confession. Here, biblical confession arises not as a thing in itself but as an adjunct to the experience of the Holy Spirit; this experience of the Holy Spirit provides the ground on which charismatics desire to meet others, whether Catholic or Protestant.

The almost secondary role that theology has played in the charismatic movement coincided with the habits that have emerged among the transconfessional managers of the evangelical empire, and in this sense they have found themselves on the same wavelength as the charismatics. The charismatics, however, are now busy reestablishing links across the Atlantic and around the world that the earlier confessional evangelicals had sought to forge and that the transconfessional evangelicals had allowed to erode, precisely because of their diminished interest in the confession by which those links had originally been made. In this sense, the charismatic movement is a complication in the organizational fraternity of contemporary evangelicalism.

In developing this story of the changing centers in evangelicalism, however, I am looking back no further than the early 1940s because in both Europe and America, evangelicalism entered an entirely new stage after World War II. The theological impulses of evangelical faith can indeed be seen to have arisen earlier, whether these are located in the eighteenth and nineteenth century revivals, the pietists, the Puritans, or the Protestant Reformers.[6] These impulses, however, have taken on a characteristically evangelical form only in the very recent past. What this means is that much of the fine historical work that has been done in locating the spiritual forebears of today's evangelicals, and in finding theological antecedents upon which today's evangelicals can plant their feet, will not shed much light on how the contemporary evangelical world is thinking about its own theological nature.

The Transatlantic Connection

The Ascendancy of the British Evangelicals

David Martin has developed the interesting suggestion that contemporary evangelicalism has flourished in inverse proportion to its distance from the centers of power in Britain and in North and South America.[7] This "distance" is not always measured in miles, though in the United States it was until relatively recently because the South, which has been so hospitable to evangelical faith, has seen itself as a redoubt, removed from the centers of governmental, educational, and cultural power in the North, or the centers of entertainment on the two coasts. This distance, however, is really a measure of whether or not there is a psychological interlude that divides the believer from the ideas and practices that are considered normative in the nation's various establishments. The stronger the cognitive core of the faith, the more keenly is the dissonance with modern culture felt; the more intense is the dissonance, the more likely will this distance be sought from the nations's centers, from which its governing values are spread. And the greater the distance from those centers, intellectually and psychologically, the more freedom will be experienced in the practice of that faith.

In Britain, this dynamic probably goes a long way to explaining why it is that for most of the last two centuries, evangelical faith has flourished less in England than in Wales, Scotland, and Northern Ireland. In England, working-class associations of religion with the aristocracy are not happy, and the Church of England has rarely shown itself to be sympathetic to evangelical belief. Evangelical movements of dissent have often simply died from suffocation because England is so geographically small that breathing space has proved hard to find. In Wales, Scotland, Northern Ireland, as well as many parts of the British Commonwealth, however, evangelical faith has been able to find a large enough social space to flourish. In England itself, against significant odds, a robust evangelicalism did emerge that, it just so happens, illustrates and embodies many of the important changes that have also taken place in America. England, therefore, serves as an interesting case study while being an important parallel and conversation partner.

For two decades prior to World War II, liberal and conservative evangelicalism was locked in a conflict that paralleled the much fiercer struggle between fundamentalists and modernists in America.[8] The debate between these two wings of English evangelicalism was neither as impolite nor as polarized as in America, and in fact this is one of the more significant differences between

British and American evangelicalism. There was no fundamentalist movement in Britain, though some of the ideas most commonly associated with American fundamentalism such as separatism and premillennialism also had their advocates in Britain.[9]

By the 1950s, the older liberal evangelicalism was but a dying ember, and the first was now carried by the conservative, or "definite," evangelicals. The two main liberal organizations of the time—the Anglican Evangelical Group Movement and the Evangelical Fellowship for Theological Literature—had withered and been replaced in importance by the Theological Student Fellowship, which had been formed in 1938, and the Tyndale Fellowship for Biblical Research, which had begun its annual series of scholarly lectures on the Old and New Testaments in 1942 and had found a home in Cambridge in 1943. To be sure, neither of these organizations was exclusively English or exclusively Anglican, but Anglicans were extremely active in both groups, and the effects of this cooperative work began to be felt far and wide. Perhaps a good measure of the burgeoning effectiveness of this scholarly interest in biblical work can be seen in a comparison of *The New Bible Commentary,* which InterVarsity Press brought out in 1953, with some trepidations about its marketability, and its *New Bible Dictionary,* which came out in 1962, both of which continue to be read and used around the world. The first, as Mark Noll has noted,[10] was written by 43 British authors, only 5 of whom held university appointments; the second had 140 contributors, over 50 of whom held university appointments. It was a telling symbol of the growth of conservative scholarship in the postwar years.

Because British evangelicalism became highly influential in many parts of the world in these years, it is important that we note one of its obvious quirks, namely, that British evangelicals in the twentieth century have thought primarily in terms of Bible doctrine, rather than theology. This has less to do with their evangelicalism and more to do with the way that theology in general has developed in the twentieth century. British theology has not thought much of or about Kant, has been uneasy with all theological systems, has seen as the most prized virtue an ability to be moderate and tempered, and has typically sought to find the middle ground between extremes. It has, as a result, often been anything but theological, most commonly seeking in fine historical work the substitute for dogmatic construction.[11]

Nevertheless, in the early postwar years a powerful alliance was formed with American evangelical leaders, despite the fact that American mental habits were rather different. Although Billy Graham's Harringay Crusade in 1955 ignited a theological storm, it also drew the English evangelicals together and did much to create further bonds between English and American evangelicals. The 1960 Graham Crusade in Berlin did much the same thing in continental Europe. In many ways, the 1950s and 1960s were golden years for the connections that grew across the Atlantic, linking like-minded evangelicals on opposite sides of the ocean and resulting not only in much practical cooperation but also in a commonly defined faith as is evidenced in Carl Henry's

Table 19-1. British authors published by InterVarsity Press

Financial year	Top ten intervarsity titles	
	Number by British author	Percentage of top ten sales by British authors
1950–51	7	67.3
1955–56	6	58.9
1960–61	3	63.3
1965–66	4	63.3
1970–71	2	13.4
1975–76	3	34.6
1980–81	3	32.5
1985–86	3	29.0
1990–91	1	12.0

edited volumes, which both helped define what was being commonly confessed and drew from authors on both sides of the ocean.[12]

There can be no doubt that, along with the Eerdmans Publishing Company, the InterVarsity Press played a major role in linking British and American evangelicalism during this period.[13] Since InterVarsity Press began its production in America in 1946, a total of 27.5 percent of its titles have originated in Britain. This figure, however, hardly tells the whole story because the number of titles published gives no clue to their prominence in the marketplace, a matter that is addressed in Table 19.1.

The figures show the extraordinary prominence that British books had during the first twenty years of the press's life but also the considerable decay in that influence subsequently. Not only have British books captured increasingly fewer sales among the Top Ten books in successive years, but the press has carried increasingly fewer British titles. Beginning with the financial year of 1970–71, and looking at five-year intervals after that, the percentage of British titles carried is as follows: 31.4, 20.4, 20.0, 14.5, and 15.8. The projection for 1991–92 is 4.9 percent. It is possible that other presses have replaced InterVarsity as the favored conduit for British thought, but my preliminary research suggests that this is not the case. The problem seems to lie in the diminished capacity of British evangelical thinking to export itself.

It now seems quite clear, in fact, that what has been transmitted to America has been the British confessional evangelicalism of an earlier period. At first glance the figures cited above appear to contradict this conclusion. The percentage of books sold in the Top Ten list actually jumped in 1975–76 to 34.6 percent, and it was still at about that level ten years later. The explanation for this, however, is the remarkable success of two confessional authors. If the sales of James Packer's *Knowing God,* which began to gather momentum in 1975, and John Stott's *Basic Christianity,* which has been perennially successful, are removed from consideration, the percentage of British books among the 1975–76 best sellers falls to 9.6 percent, in 1980–81 to 10.3 percent, in 1985–86 to 7.0 percent, and in 1990–91 to 0 percent. As far as

InterVarsity Press is concerned, it was the confessional evangelicals who found an audience in America. In contrast, transconfessional authors have not found such an American hearing, despite the fact that the American InterVarsity is not unsympathetic to their outlook. Why, then, has this occurred? It is not possible in this one chapter to examine every development in British evangelicalism that might account for such a change. It is, however, instructive to follow out, in one case, the internal transformation that took place and that, at least in this instance, suggests the kind of wider dynamic that appears to have been at work. The case study selected for consideration here is that of the Evangelical Anglicans.

The Evangelical Anglicans

The seachange in attitude appears to have taken place somewhere between 1967 and 1977, between, that is, the First National Evangelical Anglical Congress held at Keele University and the Second Congress held at Nottingham University. Before the first of these congresses, Evangelical Anglicans thought of themselves primarily as evangelicals; this was what provided the underpinning for their alliance with American evangelicals. After the second, they thought of themselves primarily as Anglicans. With the dissolution of this underpinning, the connection with American evangelicalism increasingly fell away. This decade, then, not only witnessed a profound change within Evangelical Anglicanism, but for that reason, it dealt a devastating blow to the unity of evangelicals in England, with Anglicans and Nonconformists increasingly going their own way, even as Anglican and American evangelicals increasingly went their own ways in the 1980s.

The 1967 Keel Congress, in Randle Manwaring's words, was "perhaps the most significant evangelical landmark in twentieth century Anglicanism."[14] The object of the congress was to engineer the reentry of evangelicalism into the mainstream of the Anglican Church by stressing that evangelicals were worthy and loyal partners. The congress, in fact, focused entirely on the doctrine of the church[15]—its message and mission, structures and activities, unity and place in the world—and the evangelical habit of standing apart from the rest of the Anglican Church was repudiated. John King, the former editor of the *Church of England Newspaper,* observed that from this point onward, Evangelical Anglicans were to think of themselves as being first of all Anglicans who just happened also to be evangelical.[16]

It is important to see that what had changed was not really their view of the church but, rather, how their evangelical theology should accommodate itself to the diversity within the Anglican Church. Evangelical faith is entirely compatible with an understanding of the importance of the church. This was seen at the time of the Reformation, and it has been seen many times subsequently. The Anglican Diocese of Sydney, Australia, is today another good example. To be sure, there are unique aspects to the kind of evangelical faith that has flourished in Sydney for a century and a half, in part reflecting the local culture of Sydney, in part of the region, and in part the strong, entrenched ecclesiastical tradition here.[17] Yet here is a combination of strong evangelical faith of the Reformed kind with an equally strong view of and commitment to the church.

The difference, then, between the situation in Sydney and that which pertains generally in England is in the *nature* of the church culture in which evangelicals are immersed. In England, evangelicals are a minority; in Sydney they are a majority of about 84 percent.[18] In England, the clergy reflect the multiplicity of cultures to be found in England; in Sydney, there is far less diversity, since about 88 percent of the 456 clergy who hold diocesan appointments were born in Sydney, and a full 90 percent received their training at Moore Theological College in Sydney. The whole ethos of Sydney evangelicalism is one in which a strong, cognitively centered evangelicalism is encouraged to find expression n a church-centered form of Anglicanism. The point, then, is that it is not the turn toward the church that, in and of itself, has transformed Evangelical Anglicanism in England but the new *theological* relation that that Anglicanism has now forged within a church culture that is diverse and in which evangelicalism continues to remain a minority viewpoint.

That the leaders at Keele were Packer and Stott no doubt assuaged some of the concern felt by those who wondered whether the euthusiasm for being Anglican might dilute the enthusiasm for being evangelical.[19] Indeed, in October 1966, a year before Keele, Martyn Lloyd-Jones had addressed the National Assembly of Evangelicals on the matter of church unity. He argued for the separation of evangelicals from denominations ruined by theological error, his argument being pointedly applicable to the Anglicans. To the consternation of those present, he was publicly rebuked by Stott, who happened to be chairing the meeting. This was a moment of great symbolic significance. From this time on, as Evangelical Anglicans looked primarily inward, the links to Nonconformist evangelicals in England became increasingly tenuous. By Nottingham, a decade after Keele, talk of this "growing gulf" had escalated. Although non-Anglican evangelicals had their own organizations such as the Baptist Revival Fellowship and the Federation of Independent Evangelical Churches, their most fruitful connection, at least in the interests of a national witness, had now been largely severed, for in England the numerical dominance of the Anglicans is a matter that cannot be ignored.

When the Second Congress got under way at Nottingham, the meaning of the word "evangelical" had become somewhat opaque.[20] Of the various types of evangelical who gathered for the congress, said Neale, "it seemed hardly possible to lump them all together under one label."[21] And it became increasingly unnecessary to do so. Nottingham, John Capon remarks, really marked the "end to the evangelical 'party' " in the Church of England.[22] They would continue to think of themselves as being in the evangelical tradition but no longer as part of a separate, self-conscious group with its own distinctive theology and the strategy to make that theology more audible within the Church of England. The study of evangelicalism that Manwaring has published, covering the period from 1914 to 1980, is therefore particularly aptly titled: *From Controversy to Co-existence.*[23] Although this transition in English Anglicanism was a matter of some complexity, it is difficult to resist the conclusion that at its heart was the change from an essentially confessional movement to one that, on its own terms and through its own ecclesiastical culture, had become transconfessional. About the only resistance to this development has been the stubbornly defiant ministry of Richard Lucas, Rector of St. Helen's, the inspiration behind the annual Evangelical Ministry Assembly, which remains the one certain occasion when the old cognitive convictions will be rehearsed and the old expository preaching will be heard.

It may be no coincidence that among Anglican by 1977 the revival in Puritan spirituality that had been borne aloft on the wings of Banner of Truth's inexpensive paperbacks that first appeared in 1954 had more or less run its course. Perhaps the task of translating Puritan concepts into modern terms in the end proved too daunting, but the thirst for Puritan spirituality had also abated. What had once seemed so invigorating, now looked stilted and disagreeable, and the Calvinism that had lent such substance to the evangelical confession seemed to vanish overnight. "The passing of this era," writes Michael Smout, "has left its leader, Jim Packer, sitting a trifle uneasily amongst the wreckage, as the main course of evangelicalism has gone off in another direction."[24] And so, too, did Packer go off in another direction, as, shortly thereafter, he exchanged his native England for a position at Regent College in Vancouver, Canada.

American Evangelicals

At exactly this same time, America awoke to find itself awash in evangelical believing. Gallup reported that among adults, one in three professed to be born again, and *Newsweek* declared 1976 to be the "Year of the Evangelical."[25] All of this media attention should have been seen as a potent sign of the changed position that evangelicals now occupied in the culture, yet few seemed to anticipate the changes that would soon be following. Evangelicals had been outsiders; now they were insiders, part of the status quo. And with this change came subtle shifts in the way that, in Richard Niebuhr's language, Christ and culture now lined up to one another. Prior to the mid-1970s, when the center of evangelical faith had strong cognitive, theological content, there was always a corresponding stress on Christ standing over against culture. As the cultural position of evangelicals changed in America, and as the influence of British evangelicalism, with its strong insistence on biblical knowledge, began to wane, Christ and culture in America became increasingly indistinguishable from one another.[26]

For this reason, I believe, an entirely different way of thinking about evangelical unity began to gain ascendancy. Evangelicals now sought their unity in being *transconfessional*. This was a time when confessional habits eroded, and the center in which the evangelical essence consisted became diminished. Increasingly, evangelicals found that the growing diversity in their midst could be sustained only if the center around which it turned became minimal, so minimal that it would not collide at all with the growth of diverse

views, practices, and institutions that were springing up all over the evangelical world. As this center thinned out, theologians and biblical scholars became increasingly marginalized in the evangelical world, but so, too, did
anyone who thought that ideas were important. It was not ideas, theological
or otherwise, that were at the center of this evangelicalism but, rather, techniques for marketing, managerial skills, and personal experience.

The emergence of this transconfessionalism was not a self-conscious strategy in most cases. Rather, it seems to have been brought about by the rearranging of evangelicals' internal life by modernity. Martin Marty has asserted that evangelicalism, at least in its more recent expressions, is an inventive adaptation to the forms and values of modernity.[27] Evangelicalism is
flourishing in America, he says, because is so many ways it is an expression of
the modernity that now defines American culture. What therefore has come
to link the far-flung parts of the evangelical kingdom to each other is not so
much common theological understanding but a common encounter with, and
adaptation to, modernity. Whereas for the previous generation in America,
Douglas Jacobsen writes, evangelicalism "represented a *creedal movement,*"
now it is becoming a "*complex theological tradition*"[28]—one, we should add,
with an increasingly invisible center.

Marty does not offer any evidence for his assertions, nor does he offer any
insight into the mechanics of this influence. He is not, however, alone in his
observation. In Britain, Bryan Wilson has argued that the way in which secularization works on religion is not only by way of a frontal assault but also by
disabling it from within. He notes that even those "who count themselves as
believers, who subscribe to the tenets of a Church, and who attend services
regularly, nevertheless operate in social space in which their beliefs about the
supernatural are rendered in large part irrelevant."[29] It is this emptying out of
the social space in which evangelicals live, as well as the emptying out of the
inner life of evangelicalism, that is being described here. Theological ideas,
rather than being rejected, simply lose their power to shape evangelical life.
This, in fact, is the change that James Hunter sought to demonstrate in his
1983 book *Evangelicalism: Conservative Religion and the Quandary of Modernity,*[30] and it is what I have examined at length elsewhere.[31] There were,
nevertheless, many visible symptoms of the changed evangelical mentality.

This changed mood, for example, was nowhere better captured than in the
pages of *Christianity Today.* In the editions of 1959, fully 39 percent of the
space was given to exploring and expounding biblical truth; by 1989, this had
fallen to 8 percent. And whereas the news, which in modern experience is
virtually synonomous with the experience of diversity, had filled only 20 percent of the pages in 1959, three decades later in 1989 it filled 40 percent.

The same changes appeared in the large gatherings where evangelicals
talked to themselves of their world and their strategies for the future. The
World Congress on Evangelism in Berlin in 1966, a meeting of some 1,200
delegates from 100 countries, was the forerunner of these international gatherings. The planning and inspiration for it came from Billy Graham and Carl

Henry. It was both the first such gathering and among the last at which theology was to hold center stage in how evangelical faith was defined as well as how strategies for evangelism would be formulated.[32]

The Anglo-American alliance, nevertheless, was still relatively in tact when 4,000 delegates from 151 countries met at Lausanne in 1974 for the first International Congress on World Evangelization.[33] Out of this gathering emerged, not only the Lausanne Committee for World Evangelization, which, along with the World Evangelical Fellowship, has performed some of the functions that the World Council of Churches has assumed for those of wider theological sympathies, but also the Lausanne Covenant. Stott was its chief craftsman, and in a way, it marked the symbolic public high-water mark of British biblical thinking on the growing world of evangelicalism as well as of the effort to find common ground among evangelicals in a biblical/confessional center. This convenant, which was publicly embraced in the congress and then later signed by evangelical leaders throughout the world, affirmed not only the importance of doing evangelism but the doctrinal framework in which this was to be understood. The latter addressed the nature, character, and triunity of God; his work in creation, revelation, redemption, and judgment; the centrality and uniqueness of Christ in his person and work; the work of the Spirit in inspiring Scripture, illumining its meaning, and regenerating the sinner; human nature as created and fallen; the nature of the gospel; the responsibility of the church to proclaim and model biblical truth until Christ returns; and the Christian responsibility to live with integrity in the midst of a fallen world, to serve those in need, and to seek the reign of Christ in every culture in the world.[34]

In the years that immediately followed, however, confessional evangelicals lost ground. In America in particular they found that their role was being assumed by the growing world of evangelical institutions and corporate managers. In this organizational fraternity, the confessional leaders had no obvious place. As their charisma was transmuted into structure, evangelicalism correspondingly adopted as its hallmark an increasingly slim theological trans-confessionalism. At the same time, however, the influence of American evangelicals was growing in the world. The combination of these twin developments was everywhere evident at Manila, the successor to Lausanne, in 1989.

In Manila, 4,000 delegates gathered from 173 countries—more in fact than were represented in the United Nations at that time—for the second International Congress on World Evangelization. To be sure, those present went on record as establishing their continuity with the past by reaffirming the centrality of the Lausanne Covenant, with its strong doctrinal content. The entire tone, however, was different at Manila. In place of the focus on Christian faith as *truth,* which had marked the earlier congress in Lausanne, was now intruded numerous pragmatic interests from America, such as methods, strategies, church growth techniques, and fascination with bureaucracy. All of this was offered for consumption through a format of entertainment, the master of ceremonies throughout being a television personality.[35] It was a transformation that reflected the dominant mentality in American evangelicalism but that alienated many from the Third World, especially those who worked in contexts of ideological and religious hostility and who had learned that a Christian faith that is not fundamentally about *truth* is a Christian faith without the means of survival.

Also dominant in Manila, however, were not only the transconfessional evangelicals but an increasingly vocal charismatic sector representative of upward of 400 million like-minded worldwide. And in them was to be found the third way in which evangelical unity has been sought. What, for them, is universal is not the theological confession of the earlier evangelical leaders, nor the confessional thinness of their successors, but the experience of the Holy Spirit. The fact that the confessional character of charismatic experience can also be quite thin is evident from the many alliances that have now been forged in North and South America as well as in Europe between Catholics and Protestants, in worship and work, as well as with the ecumenically minded in the World Council of Churches, which suggests that the ground of unity is less what is confessed and more what is experienced. Nevertheless, the charismatic movement has, on its own terms, reestablished links across the Atlantic similar to those of the earlier confessional evangelicals, but which the transconfessional evangelicals have largely been unable to sustain. This, then, is the third way of interpreting the unity at the center of evangelical faith.

The Rise of a New Empire

The antagonism inherent between the earlier type of evangelicalism, which sought to find its unity across denominational lines in a confessional center, and this newer type of charismatic evangelicalism, which first surfaced in England in 1963, became evident almost immediately.[36] Stott was at the height of his influence then, still rector of All Souls Church in London, and among his curates was Michael Harper, who quickly became a leader among the charismatics, later pursuing an independent ministry under the auspices of the Foundation Trust and through the journal *Renewal*. The tension in All Souls Church in the early years of the charismatic intrusion was palpable, and it was not alleviated at all by Stott's rejection of the charismatic theology. In an address given to the Islington Clerical Conference in January 1964, he rejected the notion that the baptism of the Holy Spirit was an experience subsequent to conversion, and this contention was later expanded into his book *The Baptism and Fullness of the Holy Spirit*. It was an especially troublesome matter at this time because Martyn Lloyd-Jones, the leading Nonconformist evangelical, in a series of sermons preached from Westminster Chapel, had come out openly for the view that the baptism of the Holy Spirit was a subsequent experience, though he seemed to associate this more with the coming of revival than with a private, charismatic experience. In time, however, the antagonism among Anglicans subsided, and at Nottingham in 1977, these two sides of evangelical faith made their peace. In America, this kind of tension was somewhat alleviated by the fact that shortly after the NAE was formed in St. Louis in 1942, pentecostals were formally admitted to the household of evangelical faith. The NAE then represented forty denominations;

today it includes seventy-nine denominations and churches. As the NAE's character has changed, moving from being an expression of the kind of evangelicalism that was confessional to what is now transconfessional and extending its embrace ever wider denominationally, it has simply folded the charismatics into its world. Differences in thinking about evangelical unity are regarded in the NAE as of no great importance, but rather as an interesting expression of diversity.

If the most important external linkage among American evangelicals through the 1970s was with the British, by the 1990s the influences were far more eclectic and included, among others, a growing sense that God was bringing about a new order of evangelical believing. This sense was everywhere present in Manila in 1989. The extraordinary transformation of South America seemed like a dramatic case study.

There have, in fact, been two major shifts in the nature of Christian faith in Central and South America. The first was from Catholic to Protestant. Guatemala, for example, is now 30 percent Protestant; Costa Rica is 16 percent, and Brazil is 20 percent, with most of that growth coming since 1980. In some parts of South America, the rate of Christian conversion has been running at 20,000 times the birthrate. The second shift, however, has been from evangelical Protestant to charismatic Protestant. In Central America, for example, charismatics numbered only 2.3 percent of all Protestants in 1936, but now they are over 50 percent. In Chile, they account for 80 percent of the Protestant population.[37] This astonishing growth has provoked numerous church pronouncements throughout South America, but what is notable about them, especially on the Catholic side, is the warmth of the acceptance of what has happened.[38] Insofar as Protestant confession is retained by charismatics, problems may arise, but the charismatic experience itself can easily be accommodated within the framework of Catholic faith, including its view of the sacraments, and it often works to soften what, from a Catholic perspective, is disagreeable about Protestant belief.

The key to this growth, Martin has argued, is that it has been able to find a psychological periphery in which to flourish. Entrenched power in South America has been Catholic or military. Over the last decade, charismatics in particular have been able to find for themselves "a space outside the injuries of class and preponderant power" in which to develop their own view of life and to begin to bind up the wounds festering among those who live in violent, dysfunctional societies.[39] There are regions today where adults have only five hundred calories a day on which to live, where drinkable water is hard to find, and where poverty and violence are hard to avoid. What is happening, however, is that the cultural monopoly is breaking down throughout much of South America, and into the vacuum, charismatic faith is pouring. Interestingly enough, whereas the urban centers of North America have become, through their tacitly secular structures, unfriendly to all expressions of Christian faith, the reverse is increasingly the case in South America. The urban centers are the frequent gathering places for huge churches, most of which are charismatic.

In South America, Africa, parts of Asia, North America, and Europe a form of spirituality is emerging that is able to transcend barriers of literacy and of theology, linking cultures that are still preliterate to those that are now becoming increasingly postliterate, those who are Catholic to those who are Protestant. The kind of evangelicalism that was confessional grew best in the soil of literacy and placed a high value on the kind of logical, clear thinking that a print culture engenders.[40] It is no accident that the missionary movement that has emanated from the West over the last two centuries has always placed a high priority on education.

Charismatic evangelicalism, by contrast, has developed a spirituality that is rooted not so much in ideas as in spiritual encounter. This encounter with the Spirit can be articulated and taught by those who are illiterate, quite as much as by those who are not. This is not to say that the Bible has become irrelevant in charismatic circles or that it is not read. There is, however, a qualitative difference between the kind of spirituality shaped by the habits that literacy and a print culture engender and those arising in cultures that have not been significantly shaped by print or, as is the case in North America, by one in which the habits of the print culture are now being erased by modernity. Strangely enough, it is modernity that has enabled the charismatic movement to be a bridge between spiritualities reflecting both postliterate and preliterate societies, even when some of those societies are premodern.

These three ways of defining the evangelical center—confessionally, trans-confessionally, and experientially—produce very different ways of thinking about the diversity of belief and practice that has now grown up around the evangelical center. They also produce typically different ways of thinking about the relation of Christ to culture. The largest fissure now lies between the first, the biblical/theological confessionalism of the earlier generation, and the second and third. Evangelicals who are transconfessional, precisely because of the thinness at the defining center of their faith, can accommodate the charismatic mentality far more easily than those who have, at the center of their evangelicalism, a strong cognitive element. And whereas the first has built into it a strong antipathy to Western modernity, the latter two do not. Indeed, they typically view culture as neutral and harmless and are ready to adapt it to their purposes.

The Charmed Circle

In Maine, amid the bric-a-brac that is laid out for the unsuspecting tourists, one can often find a rather distinctive manger scene. The inspiration for these carved pieces, it is said, is French. In the Maine version, however, the baby Jesus can be seen wrapped in swaddling bands and lying in—a lobster shack! Nearby are the wise men and women. They come bearing their gifts—gifts of apples, blueberries, lobsters, and a few logs for the fire. This scene is probably to be explained less by the maker's interest in theological contextualization and more by an interest in money. Yet it does illustrate graphically what has, in fact, been a persistent Christian weakness, the flaw of intellectually accommodating Christian faith to cultural circumstances. This inclination has shown itself repeatedly in the life of the church, sometimes in innocent forms like Diego Rivera's mural in the Detroit Institute of Arts, done in 1932, showing the young boy Jesus getting vaccinated, but also in more pernicious forms, such as the perverse and inventive biographies of Jesus written in Europe last century that Albert Schweitzer struck down in his *Quest for the Historical Jesus*.

In the early decades of this century, it was precisely this kind of doctrinal adaptation that was championed by the modernists in Europe and in America. The opposition in Europe was muted on the Protestant side, was strident on the Catholic side, and was loud and vociferous in America. What was unusual about the fundamentalist defense of orthodoxy in America was not primarily the ideas that were defended but the way in which those ideas were defended. In the earlier part of its life, Protestant orthodoxy was affirmed by the main cultural authorities in society. The intrusion of modernization, however, has meant a drastically changed situation. Now the sources of cultural authority are hostile to that orthodoxy. To the extent that orthodoxy retains its cognitive authenticity, it is often driven to seek refuge on the peripheries of modern culture. Fundamentalism thus was distinctive in that it sought not only to defend orthodoxy but also to redress larger issues in the modernizing world that were undercutting orthodoxy. It attacked the cultural centers from which the subversion to faith arose. In this sense, fundamentalism was an ideology and not merely an expression of Protestant orthodoxy.

In 1948, when Harold Ockenga launched the idea of "neo-evangelicalism," he was in effect announcing the end of the fundamentalist ideology.[41] Fundamentalism, E. J. Carnell said, was "orthodoxy gone cultic." It was the cultic aspect, the ideological wrappings, that Ockenga and the neo-evangelicals sought to remove. Theirs was an ambitious program, initially rewarded with spectacular success as Protestant orthodoxy, focused in a biblical/theological center, shed whatever cultural hostility it might have had and began the hard work of building churches and, what was a distinctively American venture, institutions of higher education that would be able to prepare Christians for effective involvement in the nation's various establishments.

In the years immediately after the war, British evangelicals likewise set themselves to work. Not only was there a revival of expository preaching in the churches, but numerous commentaries, dictionaries, and theological treatises and compendia were written. At the Tyndale Fellowship, the scholarly underpinnings began to be laid for the serious work that, in time, launched a significant number of evangelical scholars on teaching careers in the universities. It was precisely the kind of work, in church and academy, that had to be done if evangelicalism was to be defined confessionally. Yet what is striking about this history in retrospect is how meager the intellectual engagement with culture actually was on both sides of the Atlantic. Social issues were addressed, evangelical apathy in regard to these matters was redressed, but the inescapable pressures that modernity exerts on everyone living in a modernized society were overlooked because they were never really understood.

English scholarship, to be sure, has never much cared for this kind of work. One notes, for example, that the sociology of knowledge is virtually unknown in England, though German and North American thinkers have found here a fertile field for understanding the mechanics of modernization. Given widespread access to this kind of analysis, it is quite remarkable that American evangelical scholarship has been nearly as unconcerned about the workings of modern culture as the English have. It would almost appear as if American evangelical leaders assumed that biblical knowledge by itself would be sufficient to ward off the harms that modernity spread. This may partly explain why the issue of biblical inerrancy loomed so large from the 1960s to the 1980s; if this doctrine could be secured, evangelical confession was both defined and secured. Or so it was thought.

Yet modern culture was to visit the evangelical world one more time in revenge, this time subtly rearranging its inner life, despite the fierce palace guard of biblical inerrancy stationed outside. There is little evidence in the evangelical world of massive defections from its former creedal rectitude, but there is growing evidence that those creedal beliefs, and the realm of truth in which they are rooted, have lost their power to shape its spiritual life. It is not, then, that evangelical belief about biblical inspiration, the necessity of regeneration, the divinity and the substitutionary atonement of Christ, or his second coming have been greatly modified. Rather, these beliefs have simply moved from the psychological center to its periphery. Once they were powerful; now they are not. Once it seemed important to defend these ideas; now they may still be the presuppositions of evangelical faith, but they are not the moving forces in the evangelical mind.

During the late 1960s and into the 1970s, postmodernism's impact was felt in art, architecture, literature, and, finally, theology. The term itself has always remained ambiguous, for different people appear to have different things in mind when they use it. There is also a genuine question as to whether it really is *post* modern, or simply the newest chapter in the unfolding story of modernity. Yet it was clear that in these fields a small palace coup was underway. What seems to be held in common by postmodernists is the rejection of overarching interpretive themes or ideologies, coupled with a fascination with what is local, common, and everyday. Postmodernism has therefore become indifferent to consistency, sees no value in continuity, and indeed has sought to elevate the reality of disjunctive experience. The postmodern thinkers therefore have made it their solemn business to assault the fundamental categories of thought and experience by which people read and know their world. Postmodern movies, for example, will pass between opposing emotions as if they were not opposed, such as terror and tenderness, even blending them, or will mix styles of dress and modes of behavior in such a way that the viewer no longer is able to make judgments about their propriety. At a local level, or on a small scale of experience, this blurring of distinctions simply reflects what is now commonplace in the global perspective; namely, what is eclectic and diverse reflects what is multinational and pluralistic. The blend of cuisine, of religion, and of language and ethnicity that are the common ingredients of television and the common experience of modern, urban culture are the disconnected fragments of which life is made. Diversity, in this context, is beyond judgment. Diversity simply *is*.

That confessional evangelicalism began to be superseded by a form of evangelicalism that was transconfessional in the late 1970s, both in England and in the United States, may be a coincidence. Certainly, the diminished influence of the earlier biblically focused English evangelicalism in America in the 1980s was a significant development, yet whether it was, by itself, large enough to account for the internal transformation that has occurred here is doubtful. What does seem to be clear is that, by whatever route and for whatever reasons, America now finds in its midst a form of evangelicalism that is both comfortable in its diversity and quite at home in the undercurrents of postmodernism. The exact connections are, however, hard to pin down precisely. Is this transformation the result of the bureaucratization of evangelicalism, its movement from charisma to structure, or is it the result of a changed relationship to culture? Are both of these contributing factors?

Fundamentalist mentality was a strange blend of orthodoxy and ideology. The contemporary evangelical outlook may be so also if it mimics modernity in its own internal life. In both, evangelical orthodoxy is found. In both are all of its elements: the belief in the Trinity, the divinity of Christ, his atonement, the second coming, the inspiration of the Scriptures, the necessity of regeneration, of sanctification, of the church, of Christian witness and service. Yet it is increasingly hard to find arising from these creedal elements today any *theology,* any fashioning out of what life looks like from the viewpoint of one who stands within that circle of belief.

In the American academy over the past decade a substantial number of theological works have been written, including numerous systematic theologies. There has been a flowering of evangelical works as well. All of this, however, has taken place in the academy and is the fruit of the professionalization of learning that is now so complete in our time. This work cannot be seen as representing the pulse of the wider church, within which theological interest appears to be waning rather then waxing.

Church and academy now appear to be marching to different drummers. Although it is not always easy to see how the intersections occur between private psychology and public assumptions, it is not without significance that this mood in the church does parallel the postmodern mood in society. This mood resents overarching schemes of thought and interpretive schema that are anything but local.

Fundamentalists arrived at their worldview by a process of cultural denial; in contrast, some evangelicals today, however unwittingly, are arriving at theirs by cultural identification. Neither worldview demolishes the evangelical credo, though both significantly affect its function. This creed in fact comes to play two entirely different roles. For fundamentalists, it was used as a weapon to assault the modern world, and the greater the offense caused the better; for some evangelicals, it is used as a means of personal, religious identity within, and often alongside, the modern world. Evangelical faith construed outside the modern world works in one kind of way. Evangelical faith construed inside the modern world works in an entirely different way, for, as a means of self-identity, it can assume almost as many forms as there are personality types and cultural patterns. What, then, is the essence of being evangelical today? Well, that all depends.

Notes

1. See Donald W. Dayton and Robert K. Johnston, "Introduction," in *The Variety of American Evangelicalism,* ed. Dayton and Johnston (Downers Grove, IL: InterVarsity Press, 1991), 1–4.

2. What I am here describing is what George Marsden has called the evangelical denomination. See his sketch in *Fundamentalism and Evangelicalism* (Grand Rapids: Eerdmans, 1991), 62–82.

3. Gabriel Fackre, *The Religious Right and Christian Faith* (Grand Rapids: Eerdmans, 1982), 6–7.

4. Robert E. Webber, *Common Roots: A Call to Evangelical Maturity* (Grand Rapids: Zondervan, 1978), 14.

5. A good illustration of this center is the long, vigorous debate over the inerrancy of Scripture that engaged the evangelical world during the 1960s, 1970s, and into the 1980s. The literature is large, and only a few representative books and essays are cited here: R. T. France, "Evangelical Disagreements about the Bible," *Churchman* 96, no. 3 (1982): 226–40; Harry R. Boer, *Above the Battle? The Bible and Its Critics* (Grand Rapids: Eerdmans, 1975); Donald W. Dayton, "The Church in the World: 'Battle for the Bible' Rages On," *Theology Today* 37 (April 1980): 79–84; Gabriel Fackre, "Evangelical Hermeneutics: Commonality and Diversity," *Interpretation* 43 (April 1989): 117–29; John S. Feinberg, "Truth, Meaning, and Inerrancy in Contemporary Evangelical Thought," *Journal of the Evangelical Theological Society* 26 (March 1983): 17–30; Douglas Jacobsen, "The Rise of Evangelical Hermeneutical Pluralism," *Christian Scholar's Review* 16 (July 1987): 325–35; Mark A. Noll, "A Brief History of Inerrancy, Mostly in America," *Proceedings of the Conference on Biblical Inerrancy, 1987* (Nashville: Broadman Press, 1987), 9–25; Clark H. Pinnock, "Evangelicals and Inerrancy: The Current Debate," *Theology Today* 35 (April 1978): 65–69; Jack B. Rogers and Donald McKim, eds., *The Authority and Interpretation of the Bible: An Historical Approach* (San Francisco: Harper and Row, 1979); John D. Woodbridge, *Biblical Authority: A Critique of the Rogers/McKim Proposal* (Grand Rapids: Zondervan, 1982).

6. See the masterful survey of the historical tributaries to evangelical faith, as well as eddies within it, in Leonard I. Sweet, "The Evangelical Tradition in America," in *The Evangelical Tradition in America,* ed. Sweet (Macon, GA: Mercer University Press, 1984), 1–86.

7. David Martin, *Tongues of Fire: The Explosion of Protestantism in Latin America* (Oxford: Blackwell, 1990).

8. Because of its narrow and unhappy connotations in the United States, the word "fundamentalist" could be used as a term of some opprobrium in Britain. In the aftermath of the Graham crusades of the mid-1950s, a chorus of criticism was heard, not least from Michael Ramsey, who would later become the Archbishop of Canterbury. Echoing his critique was Gabriel Hebert, whose *Fundamentalism and the Church of God* (London, SCM Press, 1957) attempted to saddle evangelicals with these unhappy associations of fundamentalism. He was stiffly attacked by James Packer in his *"Fundamentalism" and the Word of God: Some Evangelical Principles* (Grand Rapids: Eerdmans, 1958). Despite this exchange, which showed that there was a proper and an improper use of the word, James Barr blithely continued the Hebert tradition in his *Fundamentalism* (Philadelphia: Westminster Press, 1978). Unrepentant, he followed this up with *Beyond Fundamentalism* (Philadelphia: Westminster Press, 1983).

9. See George M. Marsden, "Fundamentalism as an American Phenomenon: A Comparison with English Evangelicalism," *Church History* 46 (June 1977): 215–32.

10. Mark A. Noll, *Betwen Faith and Criticism: Evangelicals, Scholarship, and the Bible in America* (Grand Rapids: Baker, 1991), 102.

11. See James I. Packer, "British Theology in the Twentieth Century," in *Christian Faith and Modern Theology*, ed. Carl F. Henry (New York: Channel Press, 1964), 25–31.

12. See, for example, the following works by Henry: *Basic Christian Doctrines* (New York: Holt, Rinehart and Winston, 1962); *Christian Faith and Modern Theology* (New York: Channel Press, 1964); *Contemporary Evangelical Thought* (New York: Channel Press, 1957); *Fundamentals of the Faith* (Grand Rapids: Zondervan, 1969); *Jesus of Nazareth, Saviour and Lord* (Grand Rapids: Eerdmans, 1966); and *Revelation and the Bible: Contemporary Evangelical Thought* (Grand Rapids: Baker, 1958).

13. I am most grateful for the generosity of James Hoover, managing editor of InterVarsity Press, in making available to me the records from which the following statistics have been compiled. I have excluded from consideration the various booklets that InterVarsity produces. On the history and contribution of the press, see Keith Hunt and Gladys Hunt, *For Christ and the University: The Story of InterVarsity Christian Fellowship of the U.S.A., 1940–1990* (Downers Grove, IL: InterVarsity Press, 1992), throughout which there are numerous allusions to or discussions of the press.

14. Randle Manwaring, *From Controversy to Co-existence: Evangelicals in the Church of England, 1914–1980* (Cambridge: Cambridge University Press, 1985), 177.

15. Philip Crowe, ed., *Keele '67: The National Evangelical Anglican Congress Statement* (London: Falcon Books, 1967).

16. John King, *The Evangelicals* (London: Hodder and Stoughton, 1969), 146.

17. See Stephen Judd and Kenneth Cable, *Sydney Anglicans: A History of the Diocese* (Sydney: Anglican Information Office, 1987); Stuart Piggin, "Towards a Bicentennial History of Australian Evangelicalism," *Journal of Religious History* 15 (June 1988): 20–37.

18. I am indebted to John Reid, Bishop of Sydney, for these statistics. Two qualifications need to be made to the figures given in the text. First, there are Sydney clergy who serve in nondiocesan organizations, such as the Church Missionary Society, who are not included in these figures. Second, there are shades of meaning that attach to the word "evangelical." In an Anglican context, it has its fullest meaning when used both of one's theology and of one's churchmanship. There are those in the Sydney diocese who may not meet this full definition but who might think of themselves as being evangelical, or may engage in evangelism, who are not included in these figures.

19. Shortly after Keele, however, Packer alarmed those who were worried by the

evangelical strategy of immersion in the church by cowriting *Growing into Union* with the well-known Anglo-Catholic scholar E. L. Mascall. See Packer's defense of his action in *The Evangelical Anglican Identity Problem: An Analysis* (Oxford: Latimer House, 1978). Along similar lines, though more chaste in his choice of cowriters, was a volume he edited entitled *All in Each Place: Ten Anglican Essays with Some Free Church Comments* (Marcham: Manor Press, 1965). This, too, failed to resolve the nagging questions. It was followed by *A Kind of Noah's Ark? The Anglican Commitment to Comprehension* (Oxford: Latimer House, 1981).

20. An interesting measure of the distance traveled by evangelical Anglicans can be had from comparing two of their best-known authors writing on what the word "evangelical" meant. Philip Hughes gave a classic definition of the theological commitment implied by such a term; Colin Brown argued that since it had become a bone of contention, its use should be sparing. See Philip Edgecumbe Hughes, "What Does It Mean to Be Evangelical?" *New Oxford Review* 47 (June 1980): 13–16; (July–August 1980): 14–16; Colin Brown, "The Concept of Evangelical," *Churchman* 95, no. 2 (1981): 104–9.

21. Eddie Neale, "Nottingham 77," in *77 Notts Untied* (London: Lakeland, 1977), 14. The documents from the congress were published as *The Nottingham Statement* (London: Falcon, 1977). This statement was the result of discussion in the congress, in preparation for which three books had been written: John Stott, *Obeying Christ in a Changing World,* Vol. 1: *The Lord Christ* (London: Fountain Books, 1977); Ian Cundy, ed., *Obeying Christ in a Changing World, vol. 2: The People of God* (London: Fountain Books, 1977); Bruce Kaye, ed., *Obeying Christ in a Changing World,* vol. 3: *The Changing World* (London: Fountain Books, 1977).

22. John Capon, *Evangelicals Tomorrow* (London: Fount Press, 1977), 181.

23. The situation in continental Europe has been rather different. Mark Ellingsen's impressive study *The Evangelical Movement: Growth, Impact, Controversy, Dialog* (Minneapolis: Augsburg, 1988), tells a story of numerous links that have developed between those divided by denomination or nationality. And in the 1990s, after the collapse of the Communist regimes in Eastern Europe and the Soviet Union, these ties are growing stronger and more pronounced. See also Donald Dean Smeeton, "Evangelical Trends in Europe, 1970–1980," *Evangelical Missions Quarterly* 16 (October 1980): 211–16.

24. Michael Smout, "What Is an Evangelical Anglican?" in *77 Notts Untied,* 36.

25. Cf. Alfred C. Krass, "Conversion in the United States Today," *International Review of Mission* 68, no. 270 (April 1979): 148–55.

26. This loss of antithesis between Christ and culture was also evident among those of the religious Right. In the 1970s and 1980s, civil religion reorganized itself, coming into expression in two different forms, one conservative and the other liberal. See Robert Wuthnow, *The Restructuring of American Religion: Society and Faith since World War II* (Princeton: Princeton University Press, 1988), 241–67.

27. Martin E. Marty, "The Revival of Evangelicalism," in *Varieties of Southern Evangelicalism,* ed. David E. Harrell (Macon, GA: Mercer University Press, 1981), 9–11.

28. Douglas Jacobsen, "Re-visioning Evangelical Theology," *Reformed Journal* 35 (October 1985): 18.

29. Bryan Wilson, *Contemporary Transformation of Religion* (Oxford: Oxford University Press, 1976), 6.

30. James D. Hunter, *Evangelicalism: Conservative Religion and the Quandary of Modernity* (New Brunswick, NJ: Rutgers University Press, 1983).

31. See David Wells, *No Place for Truth* (Grand Rapids: Eerdmans, 1992), the first of two volumes.

32. Carl F. Henry and Stanley Mooneyham, eds., *One Race, One Gospel, One Task,* 2 vols, (Minneapolis: World Wide Publications, 1967).

33. J. D. Douglas, ed., *Let the Earth Hear His Voice* (Minneapolis: World Wide Publications, 1975).

34. See John Stott, *The Lausanne Covenant: An Exposition and Commentary* (Minneapolis: World Wide Publications, 1975).

35. In an evaluation of the congress, written in Manila and before the congress was finished, I said: "What had seemed a prayerful program of theological reflection in the program committee [on which I served] in fact turned out to be a relatively insignificant part in a program at Lausanne II, [which was] dominated by music, personalities, the quick movement from interest to interest, and the massive competition from hundreds, if not thousands, of subsidiary interests. So there was much feeling, much good and warm feeling, but it is hard to put one's finger on too much serious engagement with the challenge that now faces us in the modern world. . . . I am inclined to think that the problem lies much more with our age and much less with the Holy Spirit. It is we, rather than the Holy Spirit, who favor impressions over content, experiences over worship, hand-holding over repentance, 'sharing' over biblical exposition. We are becoming the children of the broken and fragmented world whose confusions we have met to understand afresh at Lausanne II, but often we could not think well about them in a sustained way because of ourselves" ("A Theological Response," in *The Whole Gospel for the Whole World: Story of Lausanne II Congress on World Evangelization,* ed. Alan Nichols [Ventura, CA: Regal Books, 1989]).

36. See D. W. Bebbington, *Evangelicalism in Modern Britain: A History From the 1730s to the 1980s* (London: Unwin Hyman, 1989), 229–48.

37. These figures are from Martin, *Tongues of Fire,* 49–55. See also Orlando E. Costas, "Evangelical Theology in the Two-Thirds World," *TSF Bulletin* 8 (September–October 1985): 7–12; Everett A. Wilson, "The Central American Evangelicals: From Protest to Pragmatism," *International Review of Missions* 77 (January 1988): 94–106.

38. See the extensive collection of these documents, which are continental, national, and regional in nature, in Kilian McDonnell, ed., *Presence, Power, Praise,* 3 vols. (Collegeville, MN: Liturgical Press, 1980).

39. Martin, *Tongues of Fire,* 67. There is some useful elaboration of these power structures, which are being shed today, in Irving Louis Horowitz, ed., *Masses in Latin America* (New York: Oxford University Press, 1970); Seymor Martin Lipset, ed., *Elites in Latin America* (New York: Oxford University Press, 1967); and on Rio de Janeiro in particular, see Janice E. Perlman, *The Myth of Marginality: Urban Poverty and Politics in Rio de Janeiro* (Berkeley: University of California Press, 1976).

40. This is a point for which Neil Postman argued in his *Amusing Ourselves to Death: Public Discourse in the Age of Show Business* (New York: Penguin Books, 1985), 44–63.

41. For an account of this transition, see George M. Marsden, *Reforming Fundamentalism: Fuller Seminary and the New Evangelicalism* (Grand Rapids: Eerdmans, 1987).

Afterword: The Generations of Scholarship

This book appears at a key point of transition in historical scholarship dealing with Protestant evangelicals. On the one hand, it is the culmination of a full generation of rapidly maturing historical writing. On the other, it points toward a coming epoch in which new themes, new authors, and new perspectives will almost certainly alter the way in which the history of evangelicalism is recorded.

For more than thirty years, a cadre of professional historians (many of them evangelicals themselves, or at least sympathetic to evangelicalism) have been rescuing evangelical movements of the eighteenth and later centuries from historical neglect. These historians have accepted the standards of the professional guild as the framework for their writing. They have, at least for professional purposes, abandoned the providentialism that characterized most earlier histories of evangelicals (as also of other Christian groups). Yet, while using the standards of academic history-writing, they have presented evangelical movements, personalities, beliefs, behaviors, and interactions with wider culture as matters of integrity and intrinsic interest in their own right. Religiously, these historians have often had some connection with evangelical groups in the older Protestant denominations—in Britain, Canada, and Australia with the establishments (Anglican or Presbyterian) and the hereditary Nonconformist churches; or in the United States with Presbyterian, Reformed, and Methodist churches. For a variety of reasons, evangelical historians who came of age after the Second World War have found more intellectual and even religious satisfaction in their historical study than in the biblical or traditionally theological pursuits that long dominated formal intellectual activity among evangelicals.[1]

However one accounts for the rise of a vigorous history of movements that had been notorious for receiving little interest in academic history, the landmarks of that historiography are now quite clear. Path-breaking studies in the 1950s by Timothy Smith and John Walsh on, respectively, nineteenth-century America and eighteenth-century England, and then shortly thereafter by Haddon Willmer on transformations in nineteenth-century British evangelicalism, opened up new directions in scholarship by placing evangelicals in larger social and cultural settings.[2] Almost as soon as these pioneering studies appeared, the work on evangelical connections in the English-speaking world that paved the way for this volume began to be written as well.[3] In this historiographic resurgence, the publication in 1980 of George Marsden's *Fundamentalism and American Culture* marked a special breakthrough. Although the book dealt only in passing with North Atlantic comparisons, its far-reaching implications for the study of evangelical phenomena throughout the English-speaking world were immediately recognized.[4] Soon *Fundamentalism and American Culture* was serving as an inspiration and model for some in other regions who were also seeking ways of writing about the history of evangelicalism that were both professionally rigorous and yet empathetic with their subjects.[5]

In the years surrounding and after the publication of Marsden's landmark book, a veritable explosion has taken place in historical study of evangelicalism throughout the English-speaking world. A growing shelf of bibliographies and reference works, either treating evangelicalism explicitly or as a major concern of more general study, tracks the course of the explosion.[6] Conferences devoted explicitly to the study of evangelicals have yielded solid books.[7] General studies of evangelicalism in specific regions are proliferating,[8] as are also more general histories of Christianity in which evangelical themes are dominant.[9]

The kind of scholarship represented by this flurry of writing will no doubt continue, and it may very well reach new, unexpected heights. But at the same time, the signs of a new era abound on every side. In an age of intellectual ferment, when older standards of "objectivity" are being challenged from the intellectual Left and Right, the kind of rigorously professional scholarship that a generation of evangelical historians exploited to pursue their interests as both believers and historians now requires a more self-conscious defense than such historians have usually offered.

A further aspect of the more general intellectual climate will certainly have a much more visible effect. Appeals to resurrect the marginalized or forgotten actors in history—especially women and members of racial minorities—will no doubt affect an evangelical historiography that has ventured only episodically beyond the terrain defined by the white men who figure so large in its historiography, as well as its hagiography. In interesting ways, this "worldly" voice recalls evangelicals to cherished values in their own history, since, as several essays in this book have shown, the message of George Whitefield, Jonathan Edwards, John Wesley, Samuel Davies, Henry Alline, and other leaders of eighteenth-century evangelical movements was often studiously unconcerned about rank and station and regularly appealed directly to the social outcasts of their day.

Even more fundamentally, evangelical historiography is on the verge of change because evangelicalism is undergoing significant change. An increasing concern for writing the history of minorities in North Atlantic societies is matched by an increasing awareness of the need to tell the story of dynamic evangelical movements outside the North Atlantic region. Stuart Piggin's chapter on Australia in this book hints at a transfer of evangelical vitality to the Southern Hemisphere, a theme taken up directly by Andrew Walls. As Walls's chapter suggests, Christian developments beyond North America and Western Europe certainly have much to do with evangelical history in the English-speaking regions, but they also possess an innovative character of their own that demands histories written from indigenous, rather than colonial, perspective.

The worldwide growth of pentecostal and charismatic phenomena, as documented in Edith Blumhofer's chapter, is also fraught with implications for evangelical historiography. However much evangelicalism has always been a religion of experience, its story as told by the recent generation of professional historians has conformed as much to modern standards of the professional academy as to the practice of an experiential faith. How the spread of charismatic phenomena will affect the writing of history—not to speak of how it will affect the character of evangelicalism itself—is hardly clear at this point. But it is certain that the spread of charismatic influences will move that history out and beyond the traditional preoccupations of British, Canadian, and American scholars—perhaps back toward providential forms, perhaps to a stress on social liberation, or perhaps in still other directions.

Just as developments within specific regions and religious currents within evangelicalism itself will change the way history is written, so too will changing conditions in the world at large. The shift in the center of evangelical gravity from Britain to America that has taken place over the last two centuries—from, that is, a realm inspired by William Carey, William Wilberforce, and the British and Foreign Bible Society to one taking its cues from Billy Graham, World Vision, and Campus Crusade for Christ International—reveals something about the future as well as the past. When the United States replaced Great Britain as the wealthiest and most influential Western nation, the shift was as momentous for English-speaking evangelicalism as it was for the global balance of power. If, as seems likely, the United States will increasingly give way as an international influence—perhaps to the Pacific Rim, to a unified Europe, or even to rising coalitions from the Third World—the implications for the character of evangelicalism will be as great as was the shift in global power from Britain to America.

In sum, a full generation of disciplined historical inquiry has borne fruit in this book. But since the conditions that shaped that generation—locally, religiously, and globally—are changing, and may change even more rapidly in the decades to come, it is more than likely that the harvest of historical work from the next generation will *differ* from the one just past. To preserve the metaphor in biblical phraseology favored by generations of evangelicals, trees lying further along the river of life will yield different fruit in due season. That fruit will no doubt be as startlingly refreshing as it is now unimagined.

Notes

1. These historians, however, do not all study evangelicalism. For reasons why history may have been more attractive than theology to some recent evangelicals, see

Richard J. Mouw, "Evangelical Historians," *Reformed Journal,* May 1983, 4–5; and Mark A. Noll, *Between Faith and Criticism: Evangelicals, Scholarship, and the Bible in America,* rev. ed (Grand Rapids: Baker, 1991), 32–38, 181–83, 185–87.

2. Timothy L. Smith, *Revivalism and Social Reform in Mid-Nineteenth-Century America* (Nashville: Abingdon, 1957); J. D. Walsh, "The Yorkshire Evangelicals in the Eighteenth Century: With Special Reference to Methodism" (Ph.D. diss., University of Cambridge, 1956); Haddon Willmer, "Evangelicalism, 1785–1835," Hulsean Prize Essay, University of Cambridge, 1962. Only slightly later appeared a work of similar stimulation for Canada: Goldwin French, "The Evangelical Creed in Canada," in *The Shield of Achilles,* ed W. L. Morton (Toronto: McLelland and Stewart, 1968).

3. Many of the specifically comparative works are mentioned in the Introduction as well as at appropriate places in the book's chapters.

4. George M. Marsden, *Fundamentalism and American Culture: The Shaping of Twentieth-Century Evangelicalism, 1870–1925* (New York: Oxford University Press, 1980), with 221–27 on England, and 179–80 among brief references to Canada. On the more general significance of Marsden's work, see David Martin, *Time's Literary Supplement,* 19 December 1981, 1461–62. *Fundamentalism and American Culture* was ranked by other historians of religion in America as one of the two most influential volumes in the decade of its publication; see Martin E. Marty, "The American Religious History Canon," *Social Research* 53 (Autumn 1986): 513–28.

5. See, for example, George A. Rawlyk, *Wrapped Up in God: A Study of Several Canadian Revivals and Revivalists* (Burlington, Ont.: Welch, 1988), 150–52; idem, *Champions of the Truth: Fundamentalism, Modernism, and the Maritime Baptists* (Montreal and Kingston: McGill-Queen's University Press, 1990), vii, xii; Stuart Piggin, "Towards a Bicentennial History of Australian Evangelicalism," *Journal of Religious History* 15 (June 1988): 20 n. 1; and Michael Gauvreau, "Baconianism, Darwinism, Fundamentalism: A Transatlantic Crisis of Faith," *Journal of Religious History* 13 (1985): 434–44.

6. For example, J. D. Douglas, ed., *The New International Dictionary of the Christian Church* (Grand Rapids: Zondervan, 1974; rev. ed., 1978); Samuel S. Hill, ed., *Encyclopedia of Religion in the South* (Macon, GA: Mercer University Press, 1984); Donald W. Dayton, ed., *"The Higher Christian Life": Sources for the Study of the Holiness, Pentecostal, and Keswick Movements,* 48 vols. (New York: Garland, 1984); Stanley M. Burgess and Gary B. McGee, eds., *Dictionary of Pentecostal and Charismatic Movements* (Grand Rapids: Zondervan, 1988); Joel A. Carpenter, ed., *Fundamentalism in American Religion, 1880–1950,* 45 vols. (New York: Garland, 1988); Daniel G. Reid et al., eds., *Dictionary of Christianity in America* (Downers Grove, IL: InterVarsity Press, 1990); Edith L. Blumhofer and Joel A. Carpenter, eds., *Twentieth-Century Evangelicalism: A Guide to the Sources* (New York: Garland, 1990); as well as forthcoming works such as *Dictionary of Scottish Church History and Theology,* edited by Nigel M. de S. Cameron et al.; *Blackwell's Encyclopedia of Evangelical Biography,* edited by Donald Lewis; and a biographical dictionary of Australian evangelicals edited by Stuart Piggin and Brian Dickey.

7. For example, Leonard I. Sweet, ed., *The Evangelical Tradition in America* (Macon, GA: Mercer University Press, 1984); Keith Robbins, ed., *Protestant Evangelicalism: Britain, Ireland, Germany, and America, c. 1750–c. 1950: Essays in Honour of W. R. Ward* (Oxford: Basil Blackwell, 1990); and several volumes sponsored by the Institute for the Study of American Evangelicals at Wheaton College, including George M. Marsden, ed., *Evangelicalism and Modern America* (Grand Rapids: Eerdmans, 1984); Joel A. Carpenter and Wilbert R. Shenk, eds., *Earthen Vessels: Ameri-*

can *Evangelicals and Foreign Missions, 1880–1980* (Grand Rapids: Eerdmans, 1990); and Quentin J. Schultze, ed., *American Evangelicals and the Mass Media* (Grand Rapids: Zondervan, 1990).

8. For example, Ian Bradley, *The Call to Seriousness: The Evangelical Impact on the Victorians* (New York: Macmillan, 1976); John D. Woodbridge, Mark, A. Noll, and Nathan O. Hatch, *The Gospel in America: Themes in the Story of America's Evangelicals* (Grand Rapids: Zondervan, 1979); Doreen Rosman, *Evangelicals and Culture* (London: Croom Helm, 1984); David W. Bebbington, *Evangelicalism in Modern Britain: A History from the 1730s to the 1980s* (London: Unwin Hyman, 1989; reprint, Grand Rapids: Baker, 1992); Michael Gauvreau, *The Evangelical Century: College and Creed in English Canada from the Great Revival to the Great Depression* (Montreal and Kingston: McGill-Queen's University Press, 1991); George M. Marsden, *Understanding Fundamentalism and Evangelicalism* (Grand Rapids: Eerdmans, 1991); Donald W. Dayton and Robert K. Johnston, eds., *The Variety of American Evangelicalism* (Knoxville: University of Tennessee; Downers Grove, IL: InterVarsity Press, 1991); David Hempton and Myrtle Hill, *Evangelical Protestantism in Ulster Society, 1740–1890* (London: Routledge, 1992); and the forthcoming study outlined in Piggin, "Towards a Bicentennial History of Australian Evangelicalism," and Stuart Piggin, Margaret Lamb, and Robert D. Linder, "Work in Progress: Bicentennial History of Australian Evangelicalism: Thesis and Themes," *Lucas* 4 (September 1988): 5–27.

9. For example, George M. Marsden, *Religion and American Culture* (San Diego: Harcourt, Brace, Jovanovich, 1990); George A. Rawlyk, ed., *The Canadian Protestant Experience, 1760–1990* (Burlington, Ont.: Welch, 1990); and Mark A. Noll, *A History of Christianity in the United States and Canada* (Grand Rapids: Eerdmans, 1992).

Index

430

Index

Wesley, John (*continued*)
  involvement, 259; and "real" Christians, 312; and outcasts, 412
Wesley, Samuel, Jr., 24
Wesleyanism in Canada, 257, 267n.8
West Africa, 316, 317, 322
Western Christian Advocate, 208
Westfall, William, 126
Westleyan Methodist Church, Canadian Conference, 257
Westminster Chapel, 368, 401
Westminster Confession, 63, 221, 296, 391
Westminster Theological Seminary (Philadelphia), 309n.64
Westmont College, 389
Wheaton College, 389
White, James R., 91
White, Paul, 306n.14
Whitefield, George, 3–6 passim, 9–11 passim, 35n.16, 122; orphanage, 12n.6; on American Awakening, 19; and Calvinism, 22; as "boy preacher," 23; and moral reformation, 26; on conversion, 27; as "Dissenter preacher," 28; on public preaching, 29; journals, 33, 47, 54n.32; and mass evangelism, 34; as leader, 38, 259; itinerancy, 39–40, 68–69; writings, 41; as entrepreneur, 42; and basic reading list, 44; and correspondence network, 45, 46; and publishing, 47–49; revival career: in England, 25, 58–61; in U.S., 21, 61–63, 71n.16; in Scotland, 63–68, 72n.24; ministry, 53n.12, 61, 79, 104; significance of success, 68–69; preaching style, 70n.7, 119; and Franklin, 78; and hymns, 98; on holidays, 100, 101, 109n.56; as first-generation evangelical, 131; enthusiasm, 156; and social outcasts, 412
Whole Duty of Man, 25
Wigglesworth, Smith, 358
Wilberforce, William, 9, 78, 293–94, 311–12, 413

Wilkerson, David, 368
Williams (Pantycelyn), William, 5, 12n.6, 125
Willis, Sabine, 309n.55
Willison, John, 43, 46
Willmer, Haddon, 411
Wilson, Bryan, 399
Wilson, Charles Reagan, 128
Wilson, John, 85
Wimber, John, 362, 368
Winchester, Alexander Brown, 343, 346, 347
Winnipeg, 344; as center of Canadian Pentecostalism, 359
Witchcraft, 326
Witherspoon, Rev. John, 221–22, 235
Wolffe, John, 10
Women, 67, 145, 156, 200, 264; in Australia, 292, 301, 308n.55; opposition to ordination, 302–3
Wood, Gordon, 145
Wood, Maurice, 376
Woodhouse, John, 302
World Congress on Evangelism (Berlin, 1966), 399
World Council of Churches, 400, 401
World Evangelical Fellowship, 369, 400
World's Christian Fundamentalist Association, 344
Worship, 90, 94–95, 99, 102
Wright, Archibald, 346
Wyatt-Brown, Bertram, 127

Yale, Elisha, 82, 86
YMCA, 257, 261, 270n.50, 298, 346
Young, Rev. George Paxton, 238, 239, 249n.77
Young, Sir George, 293
Young Men's Association, 76, 80
Youth for Christ, 347, 367
YWCA, 341

Zerubavel, Eviatar, 91
Zinzendorf, Count, 28